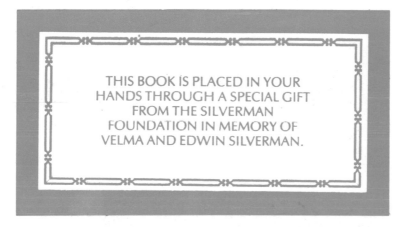

The AMERICAN CANCER SOCIETY® Cancer Book

EDITOR
ARTHUR I. HOLLEB, M.D.
Senior Vice President for Medical Affairs,
American Cancer Society

ASSOCIATE EDITORS
GENELL J. SUBAK-SHARPE
WILLIAM H. WHITE
PHILIP KASOFSKY, M.D.

ILLUSTRATOR
ROBIN LAZARUS

DOUBLEDAY & COMPANY, INC.
GARDEN CITY, NEW YORK
1986

The AMERICAN CANCER SOCIETY® Cancer Book

PREVENTION
DETECTION
DIAGNOSIS
TREATMENT
REHABILITATION
CURE

Library of Congress Cataloging-in-Publication Data
Main entry under title:

The American Cancer Society Cancer Book

  Includes index.
  1. Cancer—Popular works. I. Holleb, Arthur I.,
1921–   . II. Subak-Sharpe, Genell J. III. White,
William (William H.) IV. American Cancer Society.
[DNLM: 1. Medical Oncology—popular works.
QZ 201 C737]
RC 263.C64 1986   616.99′4   85-25318
ISBN 0-385-17847-6

To all people, everywhere, whose lives have been touched by cancer;

> to the two and one-half million volunteers of the American Cancer Society who give unsparingly of their creativity, energies, and skills;

> to the many millions of other men and women across this nation who contribute so generously to the cause of cancer control,

we dedicate this book.

Our hope is that in these pages, readers will find the knowledge and encouragement to help them take an active part in protecting themselves and their families against cancer.

THE AMERICAN CANCER SOCIETY

Acknowledgments

Over the last five years, scores of people have been involved in the creation of this book. While it is impossible to cite all of the many dedicated officials of the American Cancer Society as well as writers, editors, cancer specialists, and patients who have worked with us, there are some whose contributions cannot be overlooked.

Lane W. Adams, Executive Vice President of the American Cancer Society; Theodore Adams; John Mack Carter; Mrs. Alice Fordyce; Mrs. Mary Lasker, Honorary Chairman of the Board; and Adele Paroni all were instrumental in formulating the basic concept for an American Cancer Society book for the general public. Through the years a number of American Cancer Society officials, most notably Irving Rimer, Lawrence Garfinkel, Patricia Greene, R.N., and Diane J. Fink, M.D., all have contributed unstintingly of their time and knowledge. Dr. Philip Kasofsky has been invaluable in working with the various contributors in draft manuscripts. Emily Paulsen, Diane Goetz, Victoria Chesler, Judith Hoffmann, Mary Pat Campbell, and Elaine Green also have helped in the writing and editing. Our editors at Doubleday—Loretta Barrett and Cynthia Barrett, Chaucy Bennetts, and Glenn Rounds—are due special thanks for their patience and thoughtful editing of the final manuscript.

Finally, a special tribute is extended to the many people with cancer who have shared with us their experiences. Their openness and special insight have provided the basic framework for this book.

Contents

Contributors

HARVEY W. BAKER, M.D., Medical Director, Comprehensive Cancer Program, Good Samaritan Hospital, Portland, Ore.

LEAH O. CULLEN, M.D., Director of Psychiatric Oncology, Rhode Island Hospital, and Assistant Professor of Psychiatry and Human Behavior, Brown University, Providence, R.I.

K. MICHAEL CUMMINGS, Ph.D., M.P.H., Research Scientist, Department of Cancer Control and Epidemiology, Roswell Park Memorial Institute, New York State Department of Health, Buffalo, N.Y.

JEROME J. DECOSSE, M.D., Ph.D., Associate Chairman, Department of Surgery, Cornell University Medical College, New York, N.Y.

VINCENT T. DEVITA, JR., M.D., Director, National Cancer Institute, National Institutes of Health, Bethesda, Md.

THOMAS B. FITZPATRICK, M.D., Professor and Chairman, Department of Dermatology, Massachusetts General Hospital, Boston, Mass.

KATHLEEN M. FOLEY, M.D., Chief, Pain Service, Memorial Sloan-Kettering Cancer Center, New York, N.Y.; Associate Professor of Neurology and Pharmacology, Cornell University Medical College, New York, N.Y.

EMIL J FREIREICH, M.D., D.Sc. (Hon.), Head, Department of Developmental Therapeutics, University of Texas System Cancer Center; M.D. Anderson Hospital and Tumor Institute, Houston, Tex.

MARC B. GARNICK, M.D., Associate Professor of Medicine, Harvard Medical School, Dana-Farber Cancer Institute, Boston, Mass.

PATRICIA GREENE, R.N., Associate Vice President/Medical Affairs, American Cancer Society, New York, N.Y.

S. B. GUSBERG, M.D., D.Sc., Distinguished Service Professor, Chairman Emeritus, Department of Obstetrics and Gynecology, Mount Sinai School of Medicine, City University of New York, New York, N.Y.

VICTOR HERBERT, M.D., J.D., Chief, Hematology and Nutrition Laboratory, Bronx Veterans Administration Medical Center, Bronx, N.Y.; Professor of Medicine, Downstate Medical Center, State University of New York, Brooklyn, N.Y.

KAY HERMES, B.S., Senior Research Assistant, Department of Thoracic Surgery, University of Texas System Cancer Center; M.D. Anderson Hospital and Tumor Institute, Houston, Tex.

C. STRATTON HILL, JR., M.D., Associate Professor of Medicine, University of Texas System Cancer Center; M.D. Anderson Hospital and Tumor Institute, Houston, Tex.

JIMMIE C. HOLLAND, M.D., Chief, Psychiatry Service, Memorial Sloan-Kettering Cancer Center, New York, N.Y.

ARTHUR I. HOLLEB, M.D., Senior Vice President for Medical Affairs, American Cancer Society, New York, N.Y.

SUSAN M. HUBBARD, Director, International Cancer Information Office, Office of International Affairs, National Cancer Institute, National Institutes of Health, Bethesda, Md.

NORMAN JAFFE, M.D., Professor of Pediatrics, Chief, Division of Solid Tumors, Department of Pediatrics, University of Texas System Cancer Center; M.D. Anderson Hospital and Tumor Institute, Houston, Tex.

FREDERICK A. JAKOBIEC, M.D., Chairman, Department of Ophthalmology, Director of Laboratories, Manhattan Eye, Ear and Throat Hospital, New York, N.Y.; Lecturer in Pathology, Columbia University School of Physicians and Surgeons, New York, N.Y.

GEORGE W. JONES, M.D., Professor of Surgery and Urology, Howard University College of Medicine and Hospital, Washington, D.C.

PHILIP KASOFSKY, M.D., Clinical Instructor of Medicine, Columbia University College of Physicians and Surgeons; Medical Director, Time Inc., New York, N.Y.

MORTIMER J. LACHER, M.D., Associate Attending Physician, Memorial

Sloan-Kettering Cancer Center; Clinical Associate Professor of Medicine, Cornell University Medical College, New York, N.Y.

WALTER LAWRENCE, JR., M.D., Professor and Chairman, Division of Surgical Oncology, Director, Massey Cancer Center, Medical College of Virginia, Richmond, Va.

MARGARET LEWIN, M.D., Hematologist/Oncologist, Lenox Hill Hospital, New York, N.Y.

HENRY T. LYNCH, M.D., Professor and Chairman, Department of Preventive Medicine, Creighton University School of Medicine, Omaha, Neb.

ROBERT J. MAYER, M.D., Associate Professor of Medicine, Harvard Medical School, Dana-Farber Cancer Institute, Boston, Mass.

ROBERT J. MCKENNA, M.D., President, American Cancer Society; President, Wilshire Oncology Medical Group, Los Angeles, Calif.

CURTIS J. METTLIN, Ph.D., Director of Cancer Control and Epidemiology, Roswell Park Memorial Institute, New York State Department of Health, Buffalo, N.Y.

DANIEL G. MILLER, M.D., Director, Strang Clinic, New York, N.Y.

CLIFTON F. MOUNTAIN, M.D., Professor and Head, Department of Thoracic Surgery, University of Texas System Cancer Center; M.D. Anderson Hospital and Tumor Institute, Houston, Tex.

GERALD P. MURPHY, M.D., D.Sc., Institute Director, Roswell Park Memorial Institute, New York State Department of Health, Buffalo, N.Y.

ELLIOTT F. OSSERMAN, M.D., Professor of Medicine, Columbia University College of Physicians and Surgeons, New York, N.Y.

R. BEVERLY RANEY, JR., M.D., Professor of Pediatrics, Chief, Division of Pediatric Oncology and Hematology, University of Virginia School of Medicine, Charlottesville, Va.

ELEANOR M. RICE, Editorial Assistant, Office of the Director, National Cancer Institute, National Institutes of Health, Bethesda, Md.

EDWARD F. SCANLON, M.D., Stanton and Margaret Rogers Palmer Professor and Chairman of Surgery, Evanston Hospital, Evanston, Ill.

WILLIAM R. SHAPIRO, M.D., Head, Laboratory of Neuro-Oncology, Memorial Sloan-Kettering Cancer Center, New York, N.Y.; Professor of Neurology, Cornell University Medical College, New York, N.Y.

JESSE L. STEINFELD, M.D., President, Medical College of Georgia, Augusta, Ga.

PHILIP STRAX, M.D., Medical Director, Guttman Breast Diagnostic Institute, New York, N.Y.; Medical Director, Strax Breast Cancer Detection Institute, Fort Lauderdale, Fla.; Clinical Professor of Oncology, University of Miami School of Medicine, Miami, Fla.; Associate Clinical Professor of Community and Preventive Medicine, New York Medical College, New York, N.Y.

ROBERT N. TAUB, M.D., Ph.D., Professor of Clinical Medicine, Columbia University College of Physicians and Surgeons, Deputy Director for

Cancer Control, Columbia University Comprehensive Cancer Center, New York, N.Y.

WILLIS J. TAYLOR, M.D., Radiation Oncologist, Virginia Mason Clinic, Seattle, Wash.

MARILEE WILLIAMS, R.N., Research Assistant, Head Nurse, Department of Community and Family Medicine, University of Missouri Cancer Society, Kansas City, Mo.

PAUL A. WILLIAMS, M.D., Professor and Vice Chairman, Department of Community and Family Medicine, Family Practice Residency Program Director, University of Missouri Cancer Society, Kansas City, Mo.

JOYCE M. YASKO, R.N., Ph.D., Director of Oncology Nursing, University of Pittsburgh, Pittsburgh, Pa.

INTRODUCTION

An Overview of Cancer Today

Arthur I. Holleb, M.D.

In recent decades remarkable progress has been made in the diagnosis and treatment of cancer. More than five million living Americans have a history of cancer. Three million of them developed the disease more than five years ago, and many are now considered cured, meaning there is no longer any sign of cancer and the person can expect to live as long as someone who has never had cancer.

Of the 910,000 Americans diagnosed with cancer in 1985, 340,000 will be alive and well in 1990. Contrast this with the outlook in the 1930s: then only one out of five cancer patients survived five ·or more years. By the 1940s the figure had risen to one out of four; in the 1960s it was one out of three. Today it is three out of eight, or about 50,000 more people a year than were saved only two decades ago. The statistics are even more encouraging when they are adjusted to take into consideration other factors affecting life expectancy—for example, dying of heart disease, accidents and other causes. Then the relative survival rate rises to 49 percent, a figure considered to be a more accurate indicator of the real progress in the war against cancer.

The statistics could be even better. Of the 462,000 Americans who succumbed to cancer in 1985, it is estimated that 160,000 could have been saved by earlier diagnosis and treatment. In addition, most lung cancers could be prevented by not smoking. This is particularly significant because lung cancer now claims 125,600 victims a year—87,000 men and 38,600 women, making it the number one cancer killer of both sexes. (Until 1985, breast cancer was the leading cause of cancer death among women, but in that year lung cancer is taking over this dubious distinction. This change can be directly attributed to the increase in cigarette smoking among women.)

Although most of us think of cancer as a single disease, it is actually a family of more than 100 different types, all characterized by uncontrolled growth and spread of abnormal cells. The disease occurs among all ages and social classes, although it becomes more common with advancing age. Of today's total population in the United States, about 71 million, or about 30 percent, will eventually develop cancer if present trends continue.

Each year significant gains are being made both in our understanding of cancer and in its diagnosis and treatment. We still do not know what causes most cancers. Normally all body cells grow and reproduce in an orderly fashion. In cancer, certain cells undergo abnormal changes that result in uncontrolled growth and spread. At first the cancer cells usually grow in their original site; in this stage the disease is still localized and, if detected, can often be cured. If unchecked, however, most cancers will spread, either by invading adjacent tissue and organs or by having some of the cells travel through the blood or lymph to other parts of the body, a process called metastasis.

Recent research has pointed to factors that may set in motion the complex process of uncontrolled malignant cell growth. One of the most promising lines of research involves oncogenes. Each cell contains 30,000 to 50,000 genes. These genes have myriad biochemical functions: some control the product of enzymes that are instrumental in biochemical responses throughout the body; others determine the structure of proteins that make up various body parts; still others control growth. Oncogenes stem from normal growth-controlling genes. When oncogenes are somehow "turned on," they produce a protein that causes the cell to begin growing in an abnormal fashion.

Although much remains to be learned about the exact role oncogenes play in cancer, many research scientists think they represent one of the biggest gains to date in understanding cancer. Since all cells contain oncogenes and there may be many thousands of factors that can activate them, many research scientists theorize that we have cancer cells forming in our bodies throughout life, and that our immune system is on a constant alert to detect and eliminate these abnormal cells. Only when the immune system is incapable of destroying these malignant cells will cancer develop. This theory has been bolstered by what happens when the immune system breaks down as it does in patients with AIDS (acquired immune deficiency syndrome). Several rare types of cancer, such as Kaposi's sarcoma, Burkitt's lymphoma, and chronic myeloid leukemia, are common among AIDS victims. More recently other cancers as well have been noted.

Current research is centered on identifying factors that "switch on" the oncogenes. This is tremendously complex. For example, research has found that one particular oncogene has some 6,000 critical chemical bases, and an alteration in any one of these bases can convert it from a normal gene into a cancer-causing one. Viruses, certain carcinogens, and genetics are among the many possible factors now being studied.

In addition to providing important clues about the basic mechanisms of cancer development and growth, oncogene research is also directed at finding better tests to detect cancer in its earliest stages. Some scientists believe that oncogenes also may provide a basis for developing a vaccine against cancer. Or it may be possible to develop agents that block the action of oncogenes or their proteins in the cells.

Viruses have long been suspected as a cause of certain cancers, but concrete evidence of a cancer-causing virus in humans has been lacking. Researchers now think they have identified a virus, HTLV (for human T-cell leukemia virus), that is thought to cause a rare type of adult leukemia. A number of other viruses, such as hepatitis B, which causes liver disease; the Epstein-Barr virus, which causes infectious mononucleosis; the strain of papilloma virus that causes venereal warts, and some types of herpes viruses, all have been linked with an increased risk of certain cancers. Again, the development of an anticancer vaccine against specific viruses represents an exciting possibility in the ultimate prevention of cancer.

Closely tied to oncogene research are studies using monoclonal antibodies. Using genetic engineering and cloning techniques, these laboratory-developed antibodies are designed to seek out specific cancer cells. Their use in both the diagnosis and treatment of cancer represents another new frontier in research. (See section on monoclonal antibodies in Chapter 9, "Experimental Treatments and Research.")

Oncogenes and other areas of molecular biology are only one of the many facets of ongoing cancer research. Improved diagnostic tests, using computerized tomography (CT scanning), biological markers, and other techniques, now make it possible to detect cancer while it is in its earliest, most successfully treatable stages. Research directed at further refining these techniques and developing other, even better methods is being carried out at dozens of institutions across the United States. One of the most promising is magnetic resonance imaging (MRI—formerly called NMR, or nuclear magnetic resonance), a technique that uses a huge electromagnet to detect tumors by sensing the vibrations of the different molecules in the body and then using a computer to translate these vibrations into an image. This technique may eventually provide better insight into what is happening in the body than CT scanning, with the distinct advantage of not exposing the patient to radiation. Other diagnostic techniques that are being studied as potentially improving early detection of cancer include ultrasonography, the use of high-frequency sound waves to "map" internal structures; thermography, a technique that detects minute differences in body heat to locate "hot spots;" and diaphanoscopy, the use of a beam of light to detect abnormalities. However, ultrasonography, thermography and diaphanoscopy have yet to prove their value in finding very early cancers in controlled clinical trials.

Cancer prevention is still another area of intensive research. Identifying environmental and other factors that may cause cancer is an important part of this effort. Many cancers are thought to be caused by a two-stage process involving exposure to initiators, substances that may "pave the way" for cancer provided there is subsequent exposure to promoters, substances that actually cause the cancer. Asbestos is an example of an initiator. If someone exposed to asbestos is also exposed to a promoter— for instance, cigarette smoke—the risk of developing lung cancer is markedly increased. Identifying cancer initiators and promoters can be an important part of cancer prevention. Sometimes exposure to an initiator is unavoidable, but if a person knows that subsequent exposure to a promoter means an extra risk of cancer, preventive action can be taken.

Whatever the ultimate cause, most cancers take many years to develop. In many instances twenty or thirty years or more may elapse between the initiating event and the development of the disease. For example, until relatively recently lung cancer was rare among women. After World War II it became socially acceptable for women to smoke, and millions took up the habit. Now, about four decades later, lung cancer has become the number one cause of cancer death in women. Similar time lapses have been observed between exposure to radiation or certain chemical carcinogens and the subsequent development of cancer. Studies have found that removing the cancer-causing agent reduces the risk of future cancer; specifically, smokers who give up tobacco have a lower risk of lung cancer than those who continue to smoke, and the longer they go without cigarettes, the lower the risk. At this time no one knows whether there is a "safe dose" of a cancer-causing agent. Therefore it is important to identify as many cancer-causing agents as possible. Some, such as certain food dyes or other unnecessary additives, can be and have been eliminated. Others can either be avoided or used with special caution.

Another important area of cancer prevention is the identification of substances that protect against the disease. Recent research suggests that vitamin C, vitamin A and closely related substances may protect against some forms of cancer. Studies also are under way to determine whether low-fat diets may help prevent breast or colon cancers. The possible preventive role of dietary fiber in colon cancer is another area of ongoing study.

Of course, finding increasingly effective treatments remains a major objective of cancer research. So far some fifty chemotherapeutic drugs have been developed which are known to produce regression of human tumors, and others are being tested. In the last thirty years, cancer chemotherapy has emerged as one of the three major cancer treatments, along with surgery and radiation therapy. Thanks to chemotherapy, large numbers of people with leukemia and other once-hopeless cancers are now being cured. The use of chemotherapy in conjunction with surgery and/or radiation therapy has also improved the survival of patients with Hodgkin's disease, and cancer of the breast, bone, and testicle. Advances also have been made in radiation therapy, with more precise protocols, improved equipment, and better means of administering it.

Research is going forward on new, still experimental therapies that show great promise. Immunotherapy—stimulating the body's immune system to fight cancer—remains a promising potential form of treatment. Interferon, a natural body substance that stimulates the immune response, is being studied as a potential treatment in a number of different cancers, including those associated with AIDS. The use of monoclonal antibodies to improve cancer chemotherapy and also to detect, and perhaps ultimately block oncogenes, may someday develop into a useful tool. Better, more exact ways of delivering radiation therapy, including the administration of X-ray treatments at the time of cancer surgery, are under study. Hyperthermia, which uses heat to kill cancer cells, also is being studied. The use of bone marrow transplantation is providing new hope for patients with leukemia and aplastic anemia that cannot be cured by other therapies.

Improved survival has been paralleled by increased attention to the quality of life after cancer treatment. Rehabilitation of the cancer patient is now a major part of many treatment programs. Physicians are increasingly aware of the psychological effects of cancer on both the patient and family members, and caring for emotional and social needs is now a recognized aspect of overall cancer treatment. The American Cancer Society has been instrumental in developing effective rehabilitation programs; it also supports numerous organizations to foster emotional support to patients and their families. (See Directory of Resources in the Appendix.)

These are but a few of the areas covered in this book. Recognized experts in all aspects of cancer research, prevention, detection, diagnosis, treatment, and rehabilitation are among the many contributors. Every effort has been made to present the most up-to-date information, but since our understanding of cancer is advancing at a rapid pace, there are some areas that become outdated even as they are being written.

Despite the many gains of the last few decades, much remains to be done. All aspects of cancer research and treatment are costly; continued funding and public support are vital if the gains of recent years are to be continued. There is little doubt that the millions of dollars from private contributions and taxes earmarked for the "war on cancer" in the 1970s are now paying rich dividends. Bright young scientists who became cancer researchers, thanks to grants made then, are now in their most productive years. Granted, we have not yet found a "magic bullet" for all cancers—indeed, most investigators now agree that there probably never will be a single cure for the hundred or more forms of cancer. But as we learn more about the basic mechanisms of cancer, further inroads against the disease will undoubtedly be made.

The American Cancer Society, founded in 1913 as the American Society for the Control of Cancer, has remained dedicated to the fight against cancer through its three-pronged approach of research, education, and service. As the largest voluntary health agency in the world, it relies on the efforts of more than two million devoted volunteers who serve nationwide in the Society's fifty-eight divisions. Funding is derived solely from the contributions of the public—the ACS accepts no monies from city, state, or federal governments.

In this book we have brought together experts in the various areas of cancer research and treatment to bring you up-to-date and comprehensive information about the subject. Many of these experts are also volunteers who give their time unstintingly to the American Cancer Society.

It is our hope that this book will provide readers with the knowledge they need to participate actively in the early detection of cancer, and to join with their physicians in decisions about diagnosis, treatment, and aftercare.

A well-informed public is essential to the ultimate defeat of cancer.

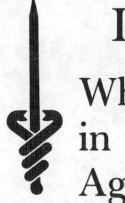

I

Where We Stand in the Battle Against Cancer

1

New Insights and Attitudes

JIMMIE C. HOLLAND, M.D.,
AND LEAH O. CULLEN, M.D.

INTRODUCTION

Why read a book about cancer? You may well be approached by others and asked why you are reading about such a distasteful subject. Their displeasure with the topic is unlikely to be concealed, and you find yourself defending your curiosity about cancer. Such an exchange demonstrates society's general attitude about cancer—"I don't want to think about it." Even use of terms like "the Big C" avoids uttering the word "cancer," thus maintaining the negative, fearful attitude our society has toward the disease. This attitude must be overcome to permit a rational approach to an illness that statistically is far less lethal than heart disease.

Try, however, to get the many doubters you are likely to encounter to believe that!

Fortunately, attitudes do change when information replaces ignorance and appropriate action can then replace paralysis and fear. In this book, we will present many facts about cancer and some new insights into the disease which we hope will destroy the myths that surround it and encourage a more rational attitude toward it.

A HISTORICAL VIEW OF CANCER AND ATTITUDES

There are several reasons cancer has always been associated with fear and stigma. First, in the early part of this century cancer, along with tuberculosis, was the major killer. The causes and methods of transmitting these diseases were unknown. Little effective treatment was available for either disease until the cure for TB was discovered. After that, only cancer remained clouded by mystique and fear of the unknown.

"Cancer equals death" was the equation widely accepted among lay people and physicians alike in the early part of this century. When people developed symptoms even slightly resembling those of cancer, they frequently delayed going to a doctor, thinking that "nothing can be done anyway." Surgery was the only known treatment for cancer at that time, and it was effective only when the cancer was detected early and could be totally removed. Since cure hinged on removal of the tumor, it was important that individuals knew and were able to recognize the early warning signs of cancer.

The American Cancer Society, formed in 1945 from the American Society for the Control of Cancer, which was founded in 1913, pioneered public education to reduce irrational fear of the disease and encourage consultation with a physician when a suspicious symptom appeared. The organization's mandate was to "disseminate knowledge concerning the symptoms, treatment and prevention of cancer." A special division, the Women's Field Army, was developed as a separate unit and charged with the responsibility of teaching women the signs of early breast and gynecological cancer. But modesty combined with fear prevented many women from seeking treatment for these cancers until it was too late.

The first article about cancer to appear in the popular press was published in May 1913 in the *Ladies' Home Journal.* It contained the admonition not to procrastinate when a cancer symptom appeared, and it underscored the need for truthfulness:

> Be careful of persistent sores and irritations, external and internal. Be watchful of yourself, without undue worry. At the first suspicious symptoms, go to a physician and demand the truth . . . The risk is not in surgery, but in *delayed* surgery.

The first slogan popularized by concerned lay people was "Fight cancer with knowledge." This followed the popular slogan against TB, "Tuberculosis should be seen, not heard," which referred to the fact that considerable education was needed to convince people that it was better to diagnose a visible "spot on the lung" in a chest X ray than to wait until more advanced symptoms of TB could be heard through the doctor's stethoscope. Emphasis was placed on teaching the public to overcome this fear of disease and to seek consultation at an earlier and potentially more treatable stage.

The social stigma attached to cancer during the first decades of this century was also a considerable problem. People felt they could never reveal the terrible "secret" that a family member had cancer. The irrational myths about cancer contagion caused shame and social ostracism. Often the "secret" was kept from the person's own children as if it reflected a family "taint" which would bring disgrace to future generations. Obituaries reflected this view by stating that cancer patients died of "a lingering illness." Not until twenty years ago was cancer ever mentioned as the cause of death in newspaper obituaries, and even today many newspapers will avoid labeling cancer as the cause of death.

Skin and other cancers produced unsightly sores that often mimicked the lesions of syphilis, an equally common, untreatable, and stigmatizing disease of that period. Because of this similarity, people with these cancers suffered the additional burden of guilt and embarrassment of having a sexual meaning added to their disease. Even today cancer is used as a metaphor for social problems that are evil, insidious, and destructive. Susan Sontag, in her book *Illness as Metaphor,* describes how these social attitudes cruelly and needlessly add to the emotional burden of the cancer patient.

Given the attitudes of the early 1900s and the almost certain fatal outcome of cancer at that time, it was not surprising that most physicians chose not to tell their patients the truth when the diagnosis was cancer. Only a close family member was told in hushed tones, out of the patient's earshot. The sense of conspiracy between physician and family added to the patient's sense of isolation and ostracism. The custom was the same in Europe. In *The Death of Ivan Ilyich,* Tolstoy describes Ivan's loneliness and frustration with his family, who pretend cheerfully that he is not seriously ill. Only his servant acknowledges his plight and talks with him about it.

Some doctors and family members were actually concerned that the patient would commit suicide if the diagnosis of cancer was revealed. While the custom has gradually changed in the United States to the point where most doctors now use the word "cancer" and reveal the nature of the disease, it has not changed in many other countries. The older custom of not using the word "cancer" continues. Clearly, a society's attitudes and customs are strong determinants in this matter. However, experience has shown that at least in the United States, most patients prefer (and currently even demand) to know their diagnoses, prognoses, and treatment options. Cooperation with needed treatment is far easier when the patient understands what needs to be done and why. This position even has legal backing today.

Actually, the debate of telling or not has long hinged on using or not using the word "cancer." Those working in the psychological aspects of cancer have changed the emphasis to how, when, and by whom the illness should be discussed with the patient. Whether one uses the term "cancer" or replaces it with "tumor" or "blood disease," the important issue is that the patient be told kindly, even slowly over more than one session. But whatever word is used, the treatment and the expected benefits and problems associated with treatment must be outlined. The bottom line is that one should not tell a lie that an illness isn't cancer when it is, since lying breeds mistrust at a later time when trust is one of the most important aspects of the doctor-patient relationship. Some persons simply do not choose to hear the word "cancer," even when spoken. All of us are psychologically different and respond to stress in different ways. That innate difference must be respected and the doctor must know the person well enough to judge the level and amount of details the person may want to know. Some persons feel secure only with all the facts; others are secure hearing as few of the facts as possible. Both must be respected.

NEW INITIATIVES AND TREATMENTS

In the 1930s, the International Union Against Cancer was formed, consolidating the effort against the disease which crossed all national boundaries. At the same time radium was recognized as an effective treatment for cancer, while surgical procedures, with better anesthesia and technological support, became more extensive and more radical, but also more curative. These advances increased the probability that a surgeon could entirely remove the cancer. The Halsted radical mastectomy and the Whipple procedure for pancreatic cancer became increasingly popular, since radical surgery offered the best hope for cure.

Patients for whom cure was impossible were often sent for radiation therapy, which was viewed by the public as a palliative treatment only, rather than a cure. (Unfortunately these views persist to this day, despite radiation therapy's curative role in several tumors.) Biochemical data began to provide a sounder basis for diagnosis and treatment, and by 1940 there was a more sophisticated level of scientific inquiry in the new field of oncology and abnormal cell growth.

The passage of the National Cancer Act in 1937 assured federally supported biomedical research into the disease and provided for the establishment of the National Cancer Institute (NCI). Its research efforts have been of seminal importance in the United States, serving as a model for cancer research throughout the world. Research and training of young investigators were its initial major goals. These early efforts were later broadened to include an initiative for cancer control which permitted the rapid transfer of new information from the research laboratory to the practicing physician and thus to the patient's bedside.

In 1944 the ACS began an important new initiative through its field and service programs, training lay volunteers to provide information and counseling to cancer patients and their families and to provide sickroom supplies and transportation for cancer patients. These activities, developed by local communities, were focused on the individual needs of cancer patients to help reduce feelings of isolation that accompanied their illnesses.

Significant use of patients themselves as volunteers for support of other cancer patients began in the 1950s in a similar manner to that of Alcoholics Anonymous, whose model had already proven effective. The need for advice and mutual understanding from a veteran cancer patient, someone who had been through the experience and had faced the same obstacles of returning to normal life, emerged as a positive support for other cancer patients and their families.

An example of this was the Cured Cancer Club, a self-help group formed in 1956 to help cured patients cope with the problems of jobs and insurance and to provide emotional support for one another. Patients who had undergone surgery for cancer were also sought by surgeons to help counsel new patients who were reluctant to undergo radical but curative surgical procedure. Some people felt that using a bag to collect body waste following a colostomy for colon cancer, for example, was "worse than death." But talking with somebody who had recovered from such an experience and had adjusted to it, gave courage to the prospective surgical patients. Similarly, patients who had had laryngectomies and had learned to speak without a voice box were tangible evidence that life could go on after surgery. This need for patient-to-patient communication led to the development of ostomy clubs for colostomy patients, and the Lost Chord Society for laryngectomy patients.

Reach to Recovery was started in 1952 by Terese Lasser, a New York woman who had undergone a mastectomy. Based on her own experience, she knew that very little emotional support was available to women who had gone through this traumatic experience. This woman-to-woman support group, now one of the ACS programs, has been invaluable to thousands of women who have successfully rehabilitated and regained a healthy self-image following treatment of breast cancer.

NEW CURES AND INSIGHTS

The addition of chemotherapy to surgery and radiation extended the physician's armamentarium against cancer. The first cure of cancer by drugs alone was obtained in choriocarcinoma, a gynecological cancer, in the 1950s. Treatment became increasingly more effective against several tumors when chemotherapy, surgery, and radiation therapy were combined. Hodgkin's disease and osteogenic sarcoma, a bone tumor, proved to be increasingly curable by drugs, and prolonged survival became possible for patients with many other cancers. Immunology, an important new concept in cancer treatment based on enhancing the body's own defenses against disease, was added to the treatment modalities in 1970 and continues to advance to this day. For example, current research in immunology includes the study of interferon, a protein released by infected cells in the body, which may play a role in fighting viral infections.

During the 1960s, evidence increased that the practice of not revealing the diagnosis of cancer was more detrimental than helpful to the patient. Research surveys of cancer patients revealed that most preferred to know their diagnosis and participate in treatment decisions. The earlier attitudes of letting the doctor take care of everything were no longer acceptable in a society that placed increasing value on informed self-determination. Federal guidelines were established to legally define the information required for a patient to give informed consent for experimental and investigational procedures. These guidelines explicitly require a full explanation of the diagnosis, proposed treatment, expected benefits, side effects, and the alternative treatments available.

PSYCHOLOGICAL SUPPORT

Psychiatrists who traditionally dealt with the mentally ill and physically healthy for years had little opportunity to study the problems of medically ill patients. Cancer patients, because their situation was assumed to be hopeless, received even less psychological attention than patients on general medical wards. The placement of psychiatry units in general hospitals in the 1960s, however, facilitated psychiatric consultation with patients who were having serious emotional problems. It also encouraged the development of a new branch of psychiatry called "consultation-liaison," which deals exclusively with medically ill patients. Initial efforts directed toward studying problems of intensive care units, coronary care units, and surgical recovery rooms and their impact on patients were soon directed toward cancer wards and outpatient cancer clinics as well.

The National Cancer Plan of 1972, a major national effort aimed at the control of cancer, attempted to combine education, physical restoration, and psychosocial readjustment with the full array of new technology in detection, prevention, diagnosis, treatment, rehabilitation and continuing care. This broad mandate provided the first opportunity for federal support to investigate public attitudes about cancer and to study psychosocial and rehabilitative aspects of cancer care. However, the initial studies got off to a slow start because potential researchers either had extensive knowledge of cancer and little knowledge of social science research methods, or were knowledgeable investigators who had little experience working with cancer patients. In addition, the lack of research tools to measure psychological and social phenomena and the lack of experience in designing such studies for cancer patients limited proper scientific investigation. But the door had been opened, and by 1980 over 400 articles had been published in this area of cancer care.

In retrospect it becomes clear that a certain level of effective medical treatment, resulting in improved survival and cure rates, was necessary before the field could turn its efforts toward the psychological aspects of patient care and comfort. Pain management, nausea and vomiting control, anxiety and depression, anorexia, insomnia, rehabilitation, home versus hospital care, sexual problems, quality of life—all issues that had previously been largely untouched—became potential areas of study directed toward improved care of the cancer patient once it was established that patients had a good chance of surviving the disease.

CANCER RISK AND BEHAVIOR

An equally important factor in understanding popular attitudes and behavior toward cancer is the recognition that some substances in the environment are cancer-causing. The first observation of an association between a tumor and environmental exposure dates to 1775 when Percival Pott recognized that cancer of the scrotum appeared frequently among the young chimney sweeps of London. Despite Pott's astute observation, two hundred years elapsed before any precaution was taken to protect chimney sweeps from acquiring the disease, a testament to the slow change in attitude and practice, even when information is available.

Other cancer-causing occupational exposures were later recognized, including radiation, uranium, arsenic, benzene, aniline dyes, asbestos, and polyvinyl chloride. The recognition of the relationship between tobacco and cancer was the first association of a personal habit linked with the risk of cancer. The epidemic of lung cancer in American men and its association with cigarette smoking was first brought to widespread public attention in 1956. Cigarette smoking first became popular in this country in the late 1800s, and usage increased tremendously between 1890 and 1910. After a time lag of twenty to thirty years, lung cancer reached epidemic proportions by the 1940s and 1950s. The past twenty-five years have proved disappointing in changing this dangerous habit, even when the facts of cancer risk are known. Tragically, the same thing is now happening to women, who began to smoke in large numbers in the 1940s, and lung cancer has now exceeded breast cancer as the most common cause of cancer death in women. Techniques to stop smoking have proved only partially effective; few are more effective than simply putting out the last cigarette and quitting "cold turkey."

Alcohol, diet, sun exposure, and other lifestyle factors have also emerged as cancer risks. The component of personal behavior and responsibility has clearly been added to the unknown, environmental, and hereditary factors of cancer risk and prevention.

CANCER RISK, PERSONALITY, AND EMOTIONS

Human beings have a particular need to know why something is happening, and this is especially true in the case of cancer. Some people look for a simple cause such as a blow or trauma that may have caused the disease, while others see God's will in the event. Still others merely accept their bad luck. Recently the old view that emotions, personality, or stress may cause cancer has resurfaced, leading people to blame the afflicted for bringing the disease on themselves. The patient may be someone who readily accepts blame and responds by believing the accusation. Others speculate that stress, often from a loss or divorce, caused the cancer to develop, and out of anger, a cancer patient may blame another person for the illness. Furthermore, our society has a strong need to look to the belief of "mind over matter." It is an attractive thought that if emotions are a factor, then logically, by managing them correctly one should be able to avoid getting cancer.

Is there any scientific evidence to support these claims? There is certainly little hard data to support the concept of a specific vulnerable personality type for cancer. The concept has been explored extensively in women with breast cancer, and no specific personality type has been associated with greater risk for the development of this disease, which randomly strikes one out of eleven women.

Little is known about the relationship between personality and the "fighting spirit" and how this affects survival, although patients who cooperate and struggle to maintain as normal a life as possible appear to cope better in battling cancer. Whether those patients who give up the fight alter the natural course of their disease is not clear, although the use of all mental resources should be encouraged. Norman Cousins and others have written highly readable and graphic descriptions of the importance of laughter, humor, and optimism in dealing with human crises such as disease.

The Simonton method utilizes relaxation and mental imagery techniques. While the Simonton technique may serve to encourage a sense of reestablishing control and mastery over disease, it offers a potential for excessive guilt in those patients who are prone to self-blame and who already worry that "they waited too long to go to the doctor," by suggesting that the person *did* have a role psychologically in getting cancer. Patients can become more depressed by this type of reaction to the treatment; they should be aware that there is no proof that a particular personality type causes cancer.

Grief and depression are the two emotional states that appear to have the most potential for possibly affecting the body's physiological mechanisms, and this could affect one's cancer risk. Research studies on the subject have shown that the immune system may be controlled in part by the central nervous system, meaning that emotions may have an effect on immune states. Less is known about how the immune state might control the vulnerability of cells to abnormal division and development of malignancy. Until more is known, it would be premature to associate the development of cancer in humans with depression, grief, or other emotional states.

NEW ATTITUDES TOWARD CANCER

Increased knowledge about prevention, detection, and treatment of cancer has remarkably altered attitudes and dispelled many myths about the disease. Optimism has replaced pessimism as data from the National Cancer Institute shows that cancer mortality has dropped markedly in people under age twenty-five. This drop is largely due to improved survival in Wilms' tumor, acute lymphocytic leukemia, testicular tumors, osteogenic sarcoma, and Hodgkin's disease. Those under age forty-five also have a lower mortality from cancer today, and among those under age sixty, mortality rates have leveled off. Old attitudes are beginning to fade, permitting society to recognize cancer as just one of *several* serious diseases facing modern society, one that is sometimes cured, sometimes chronic, and sometimes fatal.

With improving cure and survival rates, there has been an increased interest in the "human" side of cancer. Greater attention is being paid to the emotional, physical, and behavioral consequences of the rigorous treatment regimens and the quality of life for long-term survivors is being addressed. Full rehabilitation can be expected more often and patients are taking a more active role in treatment decisions. This encourages better communication with physicians, who are now sharing more medical information about the illness, outlook, and available therapies.

COMMON CANCER FEARS IN THE 1980s

The major fears that accompany cancer have been termed the "five D's": death, disfigurement, disability, dependence, and disruption of key relationships. They constitute the meaning cancer has for each individual, and are tempered by that person's age and how the diagnosis of cancer threatens personal life goals and activities. While it is normal to have concerns, sometimes concerns are increased by misinformation and even myths about cancer. For example, cancer is often associated with fears of uncontrollable pain. In a study done at Memorial Sloan-Kettering Cancer Center, only 40 percent of cancer patients were found to experience pain, and it was almost always controllable by current means.

As diagnosis and treatment methods have improved, the likelihood of being struck by any or all of the "five D's" has diminished. Death is a far less certain outcome than it was even a decade ago, and knowledge continues to grow. Advances in surgery permit far more opportunity for plastic cosmetic repair, and better prostheses have been designed for use after extensive surgery. Furthermore, radical surgery is required less frequently today than in the past. Disability and increased dependence on others are appropriate concerns, but they are often exaggerated in people's minds. Major efforts are now being made to attain full rehabilitation of the cancer patient. Patients often assume that friends and family will have negative reactions to their illness, but those too can be overcome with appropriate information. For example, concerns about cancer's being contagious have been widely dispelled. These fears are the psychological concerns of cancer, and the way in which patients, families, and health professionals deal with them constitutes the humanistic side of cancer care. Openness and understanding can go a long way toward reducing the sense of burden.

Sometimes, however, these fears can be so great that they prevent individuals from going to their physicians with a symptom suspicious of cancer, or, conversely, lead to pathological preoccupation with the idea of having cancer. This excessive fear is called cancerophobia, and the people become so anxious about cancer that they cannot function. The mildest and most transient form of this phobia develops following the illness or the loss of a close friend or relative with cancer. The person becomes anxious about a minor physical symptom, often one that the deceased suffered from in the course of the illness. Many times the person recognizes a symptom he or she would have ignored in the past. A thorough medical checkup is the best reassurance that no cancer is present, and should be sufficient to allay anxiety. Some people with cancerophobia cannot accept this assurance, however, and despite repeated negative examinations and tests, they persist in the belief that they have cancer. This reaction may indicate a serious underlying psychological problem, and a physician should be consulted. Once it is firmly established that no cancer exists, psychological consultation may be advisable.

DELAY

"An ounce of prevention is worth a pound of cure" is an old adage worth remembering when it comes to cancer. The most important thing a person can do when confronted with even a remote possibility of cancer is to seek an early consultation with a trusted or recommended physician. There has long been a tendency for individuals to delay seeing a doctor despite a symptom suspicious for cancer. Delaying diagnosis and treatment out of fear is the most dangerous thing one can do. Earlier in this century ignorance was the most common cause for delay. Yet today, despite better patient education, delay continues. Fears can immobilize the person who feels alternately, "It couldn't be cancer, so I don't need to go," and "Nothing can be done anyway, if I do have cancer, so I don't need to go." Some people are at greater risk for delay and they include those who have had a diagnosis of cancer in the family, the elderly, people with a language barrier or less education, those who have no personal physician, and those with either serious psychological problems or attitudes about cancer that evoke guilt, shame, and excessive fears. Early diagnosis very often can lead to a complete cure, while a delay may lead to spread of the disease and significantly lower the chances of cure.

It is safe to say that altered attitudes have led to new insights for managing the stresses of cancer in oneself or a family member. Since attitudes are derived from society, family and associates, and one's own personality and beliefs, it is helpful to review guidelines in these areas:

1. Remember that "old ideas die hard" and that many persistent attitudes in our society about cancer are no longer appropriate. These relate particularly to excessive pessimism about cancer and the stigma which used to be attached. Open communication of diagnosis and treatment with close relatives and trusted friends promotes emotional support and reduces stress.

2. Attitudes of your family and close friends about cancer have a strong impact on your own views. Be sure that the ideas you acquire are valid and are based on facts, not misinformation. Remember there are hundreds of different kinds of cancer; family views may be based on an experience with one kind of cancer that may have little relevance to another cancer type.

3. The data for the existence of a specific cancer-prone personality are unsupported. A link between emotions and vulnerability to cancer remains scientifically unproven. Control of tumor growth by psychological means should also be regarded with skepticism.

4. Attention to *proven* cancer risks such as cigarette smoking should be observed. Try to get more information when early news of a cancer hazard is first reported by the media. Don't become phobic about cancer; check with your local American Cancer Society for more information.

The more attitudes change toward the acceptance of cancer as a potentially curable disease, the more research can be done and the more lives can be saved, until one day, perhaps cancer will go the way of tuberculosis and other diseases of the past.

SUGGESTED READING

Cousins, Norman. *The Anatomy of an Illness.* New York: Bantam, 1981.

Graham, Jory. *In the Company of Others: Understanding the Human Needs of Cancer Patients.* New York: Harcourt Brace Jovanovich, 1981.

Sontag, Susan. *Illness as Metaphor.* New York: Random House, 1979.

Springarn, Natalie. *Hanging in There: Living Well on Borrowed Time.* New York: Stein & Day, 1982.

Tolstoy, Leo. *The Death of Ivan Ilyich.* New York: Bantam, 1981.

2

Cancer Prevention: Steps You Can Take

DANIEL G. MILLER, M.D.

INTRODUCTION

Every age in the evolution of humankind is associated with a little-understood and greatly feared disease of one kind or another. In the biblical age, leprosy played this role; in the Middle Ages, it was the plague; in the industrial age there was tuberculosis; and today there is no question that cancer is the disease that is considered its greatest scourge. While prevention has played a major role in the control of each of the earlier diseases, the prevention of cancer remains an elusive goal.

Prevention has proven most successful when it could be accomplished by vaccination or other public health measures. When left to the free choice of an open society, however, prevention becomes a much more difficult task, whether we are dealing with automobile accidents, cardiovascular disease, or cancer. The task is complicated by the fact that cancer is not one, but many diseases, with many causes. Some cancers, especially those with industrial or occupational causes, are amenable to control by public health measures. But if recommendations for individual action are to be made and followed, there must be a reasonable consensus of medical opinion supporting and explaining the steps to be taken. Otherwise controversy will cloud the public's perception of the advice being given, and the result will be far less beneficial than it could be with widespread support and compliance.

EARLY DETECTION AND CANCER SCREENING

Early detection of cancer refers to the diagnosis and cure of the disease before it has spread to other parts of the body. In the case of premalignant conditions, treatment must be administered before the tumor transforms into a malignancy. Sometimes the terms "early detection" and "cancer screening" are used interchangeably, since both have the same goal—finding cancer while it is still localized and curable. However, there is an important distinction between these two expressions: early detection refers to an attempt to diagnose cancer in a curable stage, while cancer screening is just one of the strategies used to achieve this goal.

Ideally, early detection should be a continuous day-by-day process of self-observation and heightened awareness. It implies a degree of individual responsibility for self-care together with ready access to medical facilities for diagnosis and treatment. It means paying attention to symptoms and seeking prompt help should anything unusual be detected. Cancer screening, on the other hand, must be done intermittently or periodically by a health professional. Screening is aimed at detecting symptomless curable cancer at a stage before the individual would be able to detect its presence. Early detection includes every individual continually monitoring for early signs and symptoms of cancer.

EARLY WARNING SIGNS

For many years the American Cancer Society has publicized seven warning signs of cancer, the appearance of which could indicate the presence of cancer and so deserve medical evaluation. These warning signs should be closely watched for: a change in bowel or bladder habits; a sore that does not heal; unusual bleeding or discharge from genital, urinary, or digestive tract; a thickening or lump in a breast or elsewhere;

indigestion or difficulty swallowing; an obvious change in a wart or mole; a persistent cough or hoarseness.

Awareness of such signals is undoubtedly useful, but it is generally agreed that these symptoms do not always reflect early curable cancer. Furthermore, many people, afraid of what might be found, deny the existence of symptoms until it is too late. While the fear of cancer is present in greater or lesser degree in everyone, the courage to admit that a problem exists may result not only in an early diagnosis of cancer but in a complete cure of the disease and a normal, healthy life until old age. On the other hand, the denial of the presence of symptoms may give the disease a chance to spread, reducing the possibility of a complete and relatively painless cure and increasing the chances of serious, prolonged illness and even death.

In any individual there may be past medical events, family history, personal habits or occupations that influence the frequency of cancer. Of all these risk factors, the greatest is age. In Table 1 it can be seen that for every decade over twenty-five, there is roughly a doubling of the incidence rates of cancer. Figure 1 emphasizes the remarkably high rates of cancer for those over sixty years of age, pointing out the importance of cancer awareness among people in that age group. Rectal bleeding in a sixty-year-old will be much more suspicious than in a twenty-year-old. Table 2 lists some of the prominent risk factors influencing susceptibility to cancer. The presence of any of them should heighten awareness of the possibility of cancer, and serve as a source of motivation for good preventive practices.

Table 1: Incidence Rates* (All Sites, Total and Age Specific)

Age 15	15–24	25–34	35–44	45–54	55–64	65–74	Total
Incidence 12.4	36.3	118.9	200.9	407.9	789.6	1,344.0	306.7

* Crude rates, both sexes, per 100,000.

Table 2

RISK FACTORS	PREVENTIVE ACTION

Cancer of the Skin

• Extremely fair skin.
• Prolonged exposure to the sun (more than 4 hours a day for 4 months out of the year.
• A history of skin cancer or malignant moles.
• Moles on the soles of the feet or in areas irritated by tight clothing or shaving.
• Scars from severe burns.
• A nonhealing scaling sore on the skin.

Wear protective clothing, such as sun hats; lightly cover overexposed parts of body when out in the sun for long periods.
Avoid excess sunbathing if you are fair-skinned; apply sunscreening ointment (different from regular suntan lotion) to filter out harmful rays.
Avoid contact with arsenic (found in some insecticides) and coal-tar derivatives, since these agents play a role in the development of skin cancer.

Cancer of the Larynx

• Heavy smoking.
• Heavy drinking.
• Cancer of the oral cavity or lung.

WHEN DETECTED EARLY, CANCER OF THE LARYNX CAN BE CURED. Cut down on drinking and smoking. Alcohol and smoke are irritants to the lining of the mouth and throat. Any reduction of this kind of irritation decreases the risk.

Cancer of the Mouth and Throat

• A broken tooth that irritates the inside of the mouth.
• Broken or ill-fitting dentures.
• Heavy smoking or drinking.
• A nonhealing sore or white patch in the mouth.

Any sores of the mouth, throat, or gums that do not heal properly should be brought to the attention of a physician or dentist.
Minimizing alcohol consumption and eliminating smoking are important preventive measures and can reduce risk.

Cancer of the Lung

• Cigarette smoking: the smoker's risk of developing lung cancer is proportional to the number of cigarettes smoked, number of years

Risk for lung cancer can be reduced by avoiding cigarette smoking. Cigarette smoking cannot only lead to death from lung cancer, but

RISK FACTORS	PREVENTIVE ACTION

smoking, age at which smoking started, and how deeply smoke is inhaled.
• Occupations that bring the worker into contact with asbestos, nickel, chromates, or radioactive material.
• A history of tuberculosis.
• A chronic cough.

can also increase the chances of dying from other lung diseases (asthma, emphysema, pneumonia) or heart disease.
Occupational exposure to the cancer-causing agents mentioned should be avoided or carefully controlled. Be aware of the materials you work with.

Cancer of the Kidney and Bladder

• Congenital abnormalities of the kidney or bladder (your physician should have informed you if these conditions exist).
• Exposure to certain chemicals such as naphthalines, aniline dyes, or benzidines (be sure to read labels).
• Blood in urine.
• Frequent urinary tract infections, especially after age fifty.
• A history of schistosomiasis (a tropical disease).
• Heavy cigarette smoking: smoking leads to the presence of chemicals in the urine that may contribute to the development of cancer of the urinary tract.

Avoid occupational exposure to cancer-causing chemicals and seek medical attention when any symptoms exist.
Blood in the urine is always an important sign and requires immediate medical evaluation.
These symptoms are not specific for cancer; more commonly, they are found with bladder infection.
However, a physician should be consulted. Frequent urinary tract infections may be due to underlying cancer.

Cancer of the Prostate

• A history of venereal disease.
• A history of prostate infections (more than two).
• Risk increases after the age of fifty.

The occurrence of cancer of the prostate cannot be controlled, since the causes are not known. However, the death rate can be greatly lowered if men, especially those over age fifty, are familiar with the symptoms of the disease and if the prostate is examined regularly.

Cancer of the Testes

• Undescended testicle not corrected before age six.

There is a high incidence of cancer of the testicle in males born with an undescended testicle, so this condition should be corrected early.

Cancer of the testicle is most common in men under forty. Perform testicular self-examination once a month after a warm bath or shower, when the scrotal skin is most relaxed.

Examine each testicle gently by rolling it between the thumb and fingers. Feel for a firm lump about the size of a pea. Most lumps are noncancerous.

Cancer of the Stomach

• A lack of normal stomach acid.
• Pernicious anemia.
• Chronic gastritis or stomach polyps.

Ulcers and ulcer symptoms may be mistaken for stomach cancer and vice versa. If any symptoms last more than one month, consult a physician.

Cancer of the Colon

• Polyps in the colon.
• A family history of cancer of the colon or rectum.

Any changes in your regular bowel habits should be reported to your physician promptly.

Cancer of the colon is infrequent in countries where the diet is high in fruits, vegetables, and fish and low in meat.

Cancer of the Cervix

• Completed pregnancies (more than five).
• Intercourse before age eighteen.
• A history of syphilis or gonorrhea.
• Multiple sexual partners.

Cancer of the cervix is usually slow-growing and can be detected by the Pap smear and cured. Examination of any adult female should include a Pap smear and pelvic examination as well as an examination of the breasts.

Cancer of the Endometrium

• Having completed the meno-
pause.
• Never having been pregnant.
• A family history of cancer of the
endometrium (lining of the uterus).
• Diabetes.
• Hypertension.
• Obesity.

Cancer of the Ovary

In most cases, a woman is unaware of the presence of tumors in
the ovaries. There are seldom
early symptoms. The ovaries are
examined at the time of a Pap and
pelvic examination. These examinations should be done on a regular basis.

Cancer of the Breast

• A family history of breast cancer.
• Never having had a baby or hav-
ing a first baby after age thirty.
• A high-fat diet.
• Previous breast cancer.

Breast cancer is curable if detected early. Breast examinations
should be performed regularly, at
least annually, and in conjunction
with a pelvic examination. Ask the
doctor or nurse to teach you to do
breast self-examination. Practice
this self-examination once a month
two or three days after end of menstrual period. Many women have
cystic breast disease. When cysts
are present it is advisable to have
breast examinations more frequently. This is not a premalignant
condition; it just makes the breasts
more difficult to examine. Most
lumps are found by women themselves; therefore regular self-examination is necessary. If you find
any of the symptoms of breast can-

RISK FACTORS

PREVENTIVE ACTION

cer, take immediate action. Remember, breast cancer is curable if identified at an early stage.

FORTUITOUS DETECTION

Early detection often results from a fortuitous finding in the course of an examination for another reason. For example, a physician examining a patient for respiratory infection may notice a suspicious lesion on the skin of the face. Or an early testicular cancer may be found while checking a patient for a hernia. These are findings by chance and depend on the serendipity of the examining physician. The concerned, competent physician is therefore always alert to the possibility of incidentally finding cancer in the course of an examination for any other purpose. Early cancer is commonly detected under such circumstances, but this random method is not reliable enough to act as the basis for an early detection

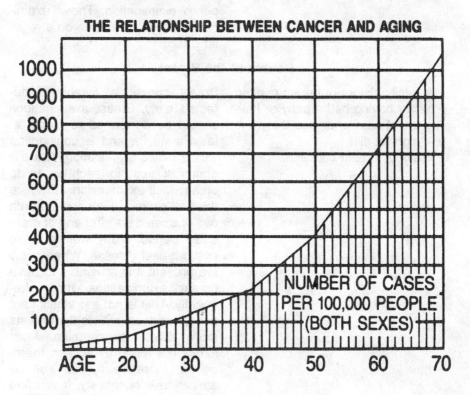

THE RELATIONSHIP BETWEEN CANCER AND AGING

NUMBER OF CASES PER 100,000 PEOPLE (BOTH SEXES)

Figure 1

program. Many physicians carefully incorporate a schedule of cancer detection procedures into their contact with each patient. This type of designed program should be an important part of your self-surveillance procedures.

SCREENING

Professional cancer screening should also be part of your personal detection program. Screening is a prediagnostic procedure to determine the probability of the presence of cancer, while diagnosis is to determine whether or not a disease is present and if so, what it is and how far it has progressed. Screening is customarily directed at apparently healthy individuals, the vast majority of whom will be found to be free of cancer. Thus certain basic screening principles have evolved.

First, the screening test employed should be acceptable to the patient, cause a minimum of discomfort and inconvenience, pose no significant risk, and should not be excessively costly. Second, the test should be reasonably accurate, with only a minimum number of missed cases (false negative results) and cancers incorrectly suspected (false positives). Third, the results of treatment of cancer detected in an early stage through screening must be better than if the screening had not been performed and the disease had been detected at a later, symptomatic stage.

"Reasonable accuracy" must be defined for each screening procedure. A higher number of false positive findings would be more acceptable if it indicated the need only for a simple low-risk diagnostic procedure rather than major surgery or surgical biopsy. On the other hand, too many false negatives would give patients a false sense of security and increase the danger of cancer spread as well as discrediting the screening program.

The third principle of screening, that the treatment should produce better results than if the screening had not been performed, is complicated by two issues. First, if a disease is diagnosed early as a result of screening, the patient will at first appear to live longer with the disease regardless of the outcome of treatment, merely because it was detected sooner. This early diagnosis factor, often called "lead-time bias," must be considered in evaluating the outcome of any screening program. Therefore the best way to evaluate the effectiveness of screening is not by comparing the length of survival but rather by determining whether the screening procedure resulted in a lowered death rate. However, long-term survival rates may also be considered a reasonable index of cure. The best evidence for the value of early diagnosis comes from the observation of long-term survival rates of patients with localized cancer compared to those with non-localized disease (Figure 2). When a special effort is made to detect cancer early, as in targeted screening programs, early cancer will be detected more frequently than ordinarily occurs, as shown in Figure 3.

A second complicating issue in determining the outcome of treatment after screening is the biological activity of the disease. Is it slow- or fast-

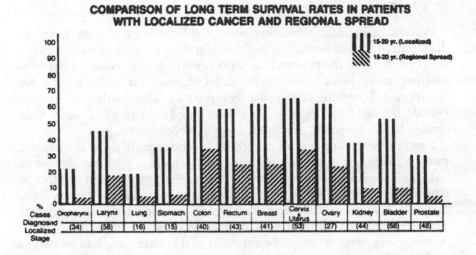

Figure 2

growing? Years ago, doctors believed that the results of treatment were biologically predetermined: if the disease was slow-growing, it was likely to grow to a detectable size while still localized, causing symptoms that would lead to surgery and a favorable outcome; the opposite was assumed with a fast-growing cancer.

Today, this is recognized as an oversimplification that contains a measure of truth. The rate of tumor growth does affect the efficiency of any screening program because fast-growing tumors are more likely to arise and grow large enough to cause symptoms in the interval between screening and examinations. These "interval" or missed cases are likely to be the more malignant tumors. Conversely, the slower-growing tumors, in which there is a significant length of time between the appearance of detectable disease and the time it begins to spread, are then more likely to be picked up in a screening program.

A recent study of tumors of the head and neck region showed that those fast-growing cancers with a short symptomatic period had a particularly poor prognosis and were more likely to be missed by screening programs. The growth rate factor does not diminish the value of screening for early detection. Rather, it poses a separate problem and carries with it the

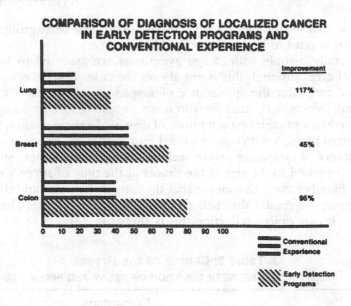

**COMPARISON OF DIAGNOSIS OF LOCALIZED CANCER
IN EARLY DETECTION PROGRAMS AND
CONVENTIONAL EXPERIENCE**

Figure 3

implication that some part of the early detection program must, in order to achieve a real effect, be continuing and ongoing. Access to medical care must not be limited to the periodic screening examination, but must be an all-year-round process to which patients and doctors are committed. Patients who develop suspicious symptoms shortly after an annual examination must be educated not to wait until their next checkup to have them evaluated, and should seek immediate evaluation of any unusual prolonged symptoms.

Considering that screening programs are directed primarily towards asymptomatic individuals, most of whom will not have the disease, it follows that screening should be carried out at two levels. The first should be primary screening to determine patterns of risk factors that may increase the probability of developing cancer. This can be accomplished through simple, inexpensive testing which can be carried out by allied health professionals rather than physicians. The second level of screening is carried out selectively, with additional tests individually ordered on the basis of an analysis of risk factors. This method is called "prescriptive screening," and several cancer screening programs have been organized in this way.

The screening process, in addition to providing a set of examinations and tests, should also be an opportunity for health education in such areas as breast self-examination, stop-smoking programs, personal and occupational health hazards, and to help determine what groups of the population tend to be most susceptible to cancer.

Generally, people with cancer symptoms are assumed to be under medical care, although this is not always the case. The delay in seeking medical care after the appearance of suspicious symptoms is a serious problem in cancer control. Far too many people ignore or do not know what to do about their first symptoms of disease. In some studies, up to 40 percent of patients with cancer waited four months to one year after the appearance of symptoms before seeking medical care. Patient survival is strongly related to the size of the cancer at the time of surgery or treatment. Simply stated, this means that the longer the delay and the larger the tumor, the greater the chance of dying from the disease. The experience in breast cancer reflecting this is shown in Table 3.

Table 3: Cancer of the Breast
RELATIONSHIP BETWEEN DURATION OF DELAY AND PROGNOSIS

DURATION OF DELAY IN MONTHS	SURVIVED 4 YEARS	Percentage DEVELOPED POSTOPERATIVE RECURRENCES	MORTALITY RATE
Less than 1	31	14	5
1–3	29	14	17
3–6	24	27	16
6–12	24	27	26
More than 12	16	35	37

Screening examinations for the detection of cancer have been studied for effectiveness by the American Cancer Society (ACS), the Canadian Task Force on the Periodic Health Examination, and the International Union Against Cancer. The ACS stresses that the recommendations shown in Table 4 are interim guidelines, subject to revision as the results of ongoing screening programs are obtained.

Table 4: Cancer-Related Checkups

The following guidelines for the early detection of cancer in people without symptoms are recommended by the American Cancer Society:

AGE 20–40	AGE 40 & OVER
Cancer-Related Checkup Every 3 Years	**Cancer-Related Checkup Every Year**

Should include the procedures listed below plus health counseling (such as tips on quitting cigarettes) and examinations for cancers of the thyroid, testes, prostate, mouth, ovaries, skin, and lymph nodes. Some people are at higher risk for certain cancers and may need to have tests more frequently.

Breast
- Exam by doctor every 3 years
- Self-exam every month
- One baseline breast X ray between ages 35 and 40
Higher Risk for Breast Cancer: Personal or family history of breast cancer, never had children, first child after 30

Breast
- Exam by doctor every year
- Self-exam every month
- Breast X ray every year after 50. Between ages 40 and 49, breast X ray every 1-2 years
Higher Risk for Breast Cancer: Personal or family history of breast cancer, never had children, first child after 30

Uterus
- Pelvic exam every 3 years

Uterus
- Pelvic exam every year

Cervix
- Pap test—after 2 initial negative tests 1 year apart—*at least* every 3 years, includes women under 20 if sexually active
Higher Risk for Cervical Cancer: Early age at first intercourse, multiple sex partners

Cervix
- Pap test—after 2 initial negative tests 1 year apart—*at least* every 3 years
Higher Risk for Cervical Cancer: Early age at first intercourse, multiple sex partners

Endometrium
- Endometrial tissue sample at menopause if at risk
Higher Risk for Endometrial Cancer: Infertility, obesity, failure of ovulation, abnormal uterine bleeding, estrogen therapy

AGE 20–40	AGE 40 & OVER
	Colon & Rectum • Digital rectal exam every year • Stool blood test every year after 50 • Proctosigmoidoscopy exam—after 2 initial negative tests 1 year apart—every 3 to 5 years after age 50 *Higher Risk for Colorectal Cancer:* *Personal or family history of colon or rectal cancer, personal or family history of polyps in the colon or rectum, ulcerative colitis*

Remember, these guidelines are not rules and only apply to people without symptoms. Talk with your doctor. Ask how these guidelines relate to you.

These recommendations for screening in these diseases are conservatively made and must be carefully interpreted in light of each individual's medical history. These recommendations and limitations notwithstanding, there is one other serious problem in cancer screening—the cost of the examinations. Screening examinations, especially if they include mammography and proctosigmoidoscopy, are expensive and often they are not reimbursed by insurance. When it is possible to obtain insurance riders for these examinations it should be done. Each individual must determine the value of these examinations, and arrive at a decision whereby he or she is willing to pay for protection against a perceived threat. This comes under the heading of doing the best you can to protect yourself against cancer.

DETECTION THROUGH CHECKUPS

Early detection can also be the result of a standard medical checkup. Reassurance is unequivocally the main reason most individuals have regular medical checkups. Under these circumstances, an individual applies to a physician for a diagnostic evaluation, not a screening examination, and in most instances expects to pay for this service as a private patient. The individual wants reassurance that he does not have any form of cancer and can walk away with a clean bill of health. The cigarette smoker who applies for an examination will not forgo the chest X ray, but he wants to be told that he does not have cancer of the lung. The woman over forty applying for an annual pelvic examination will not forgo a Pap smear because she wants to know that there is no evidence of cancer. Many people see this type of testing as the most cost-effective, since they are not looking only for cancer but are having their overall health status checked. The wise physician will exercise his best judgment to minimize risk and expense to the patient while providing his best efforts for early diagnosis.

REDUCING EXPOSURE TO CARCINOGENS

Reducing exposure to cancer-causing agents is one of the major recommendations for cancer prevention. By avoiding known carcinogens in food, alcohol, tobacco, and drugs as well as radiation and occupational hazards, cancer risk can be considerably reduced. These recommendations are based on observed differences in cancer incidence among those exposed to some degree to these substances as compared with those not exposed. Animal and laboratory studies also provide evidence of cancer-causing action in certain substances, although it is often difficult to extrapolate from animal studies to man. Furthermore, population differences, especially those in different geographic areas, may be complicated by many factors other than the condition under study, raising valid questions about the accuracy of such data. Still, given the immediacy of the cancer problem, it is necessary to make reasonable recommendations with the information on hand.

DIET AND CANCER RISK

Diet and nutrition may well have a major impact on the occurrence of cancer in the United States. They appear to be particularly relevant in breast and colon cancer, and possibly in cancer of the prostate and uterus as well. The most significant dietary element implicated in the origin of cancer is dietary fat. Studies of the occurrence of breast and colon cancer in different countries have revealed a direct relationship between the number of deaths due to these diseases and the amount of fat in the diet. Argentina, for example, which exceeds the U.S. in consumption of beef, also exceeds the U.S. in breast and colon cancer mortality rates. In Asian countries where intake of beef and other fatty foods is low, these forms of cancer are much less frequent. Furthermore, when a population moves from a low-fat-consumption country such as Japan to a country such as the United States, where the consumption of dietary fat is considerably higher, the pattern of cancer changes. Studies have shown that Japanese immigrants to the U.S. have higher colon, breast, and prostate rates than people of the same age in Japan. In addition, second-generation Japanese-Americans have cancer patterns that are practically the same as those of other Americans.

Additional evidence of the influence of dietary fat comes from studies of vegetarians, who also have a lower incidence of these diseases than do other segments of the population. Increasing the fat intake increases cancer development in animals as well, especially breast and colon cancer. There is insufficient evidence to distinguish between different types of fat as promoters of cancer, and it is not clear what the mechanism is regarding the effect of fat on the development of cancer. It is known that fat stimulates the secretion of bile acids, some of which are cancer-causing and may play a role in the development of intestinal cancer. Fats may also increase hormone production, a possible factor in the development of breast and prostate cancer. Some researchers believe that because fats are able to retain water-insoluble, cancer-causing chemicals, they may be responsible for prolonged exposure of tissues to these toxic materials.

Dietary fiber is believed by many researchers to have a protective effect against colon and rectal cancer. There are different types of dietary fiber, and the evidence is insufficient to indicate which is responsible for the beneficial effects. Although a recent study by the National Academy of Sciences found the evidence supporting the protective effects of dietary fiber to be inconclusive, the prudent no-risk, no-cost advice would be to increase consumption of high-fiber foods such as whole-grain cereals and breads, fresh fruits, and vegetables.

There has recently been great interest among both researchers and the general public in the possible cancer protective actions of vitamins. Particular attention has been paid to vitamin A, since several human and animal studies have shown increased susceptibility to several chemically induced cancers in the presence of a vitamin A deficiency. Because high doses of vitamin A are toxic, however, it is recommended that adequate vitamin A intake be accomplished through a balanced diet rather than with vitamin supplements. Vitamin A is present in liver, green and yellow vegetables, and carrots. An increase in these foods in the diet should provide adequate vitamin A.

Evidence for the cancer-preventing effects of vitamins C and E are derived mainly from laboratory studies in which these substances inhibited the formation of some natural cancer-causing agents. This may be important in lowering the risk of cancers of the stomach and esophagus. There is as yet no strong evidence for a protective effect of vitamin E and the B vitamins.

Population studies show that people residing in areas where the selenium levels in soil and water are low have a somewhat increased cancer risk. Several animal studies have shown selenium to have a protective effect, but there is still insufficient evidence to recommend selenium supplements in the diet. Cancer of the esophagus has been associated with a long-standing iron deficiency, but normal dietary ingestion of iron affords adequate protection, and iron supplements are not recommended. Other mineral and trace elements are under study, but no conclusions are expected for many years.

After examining population, animal, and laboratory studies, both the American Cancer Society and the National Academy of Sciences made recommendations for cancer prevention through diet. The ACS nutrition statement, which incorporates most of the earlier recommendations from the Academy of Sciences, specifies:

1. *Avoid obesity.* The twelve-year Cancer Prevention Study I conducted by the ACS found markedly increased incidences of cancers of the uterus, gallbladder, kidney, stomach, colon, and breast associated with obesity. When data for people 40 percent or more overweight were reviewed, the risk of cancer was 55 percent greater for women and 33 percent greater for men, compared to the risk of normal-weight persons. Thus for people who are obese, weight reduction may be one way to lower cancer risk.

2. *Cut down on total fat intake.* Accumulating evidence from both human and animal studies implies that excessive fat intake increases the risk of cancers of the breast, colon, and prostate. Both saturated and unsaturated fats have been found to enhance human cancer growth in some studies. Americans now consume about 40 percent of their total calories as fat. A decrease to 30 percent of total calories from fat has been suggested by the National Academy of Sciences. For most people, this should mean a simple change in food habits, readily achieved by moderation in the consumption of fats, oils, and foods rich in fats. This is also an effective way to reduce total calories.

3. *Eat more high-fiber foods, such as whole-grain cereals, fruits, and vegetables.* Agreement on fiber's role in cancer prevention is not universal. But even if fiber itself may not prove to have a protective effect against cancer, consumption of fruits, vegetables, and cereals that are high in fiber can be recommended as a wholesome substitute for fatty foods.

4. *Include foods rich in vitamins A, C, and E in the daily diet.* Dark green and deep yellow vegetables and certain fruits are rich in carotene, a form of vitamin A. Many laboratory and population studies indicate that vitamin A (and certain synthetic chemicals related to it) may lower the incidence of certain cancers, including those of the larynx, esophagus, and lung. Examples of foods rich in carotene are carrots, tomatoes, spinach, apricots, peaches, and cantaloupes. Excessive vitamins A and E in the form of tablets or capsules are not recommended, however, because of the possibility of toxic overdoses. In addition to the leafy vegetables, whole-grain cereals, nuts, and beans are good sources of vitamin E.

As for vitamin C (ascorbic acid), epidemiologic studies indicate that people whose diets are high in fruits and vegetables rich in this vitamin are less likely to get cancer, particularly of the stomach and esophagus. It is uncertain whether it is vitamin C itself or other constituents of the fruits and vegetables that have the protective effect. It is known that vitamin C inhibits the formation of cancer-causing nitrosamines in the stomach, but whether this does indeed lower the incidence of stomach or esophageal cancer has not been proved.

5. *Include cruciferous vegetables, such as cabbage, broccoli, brussels sprouts, kohlrabi, and cauliflower in the diet.* These vegetables belong to the mustard family; they derive their name "cruciferous" from the fact that their flowers have four leaves in the pattern of a cross. Laboratory and population studies both suggest that these vegetables may reduce the risk of cancers of the gastrointestinal and respiratory tracts. Other studies are underway to determine what components of these foods protect against cancer.

6. *Be moderate in consumption of alcoholic beverages.* Heavy users of alcohol, especially those who are also cigarette smokers, are at unusually high risk for cancers of the mouth, larynx, and esophagus. Alcohol abuse also can cause cirrhosis, which sometimes leads to liver cancer.

7. *Be moderate in consumption of salt-cured, smoked, and nitrate-cured foods.* Hams, some types of sausage, smoked fish and other conventionally smoked foods absorb some of the tars that result from incomplete burning, or combustion. These tars contain numerous cancer-causing substances that are chemically similar to the carcinogenic tars in tobacco smoke.

Salt-cured or pickled foods have been linked to an increased risk of stomach and esophageal cancers. These cancers are common in parts of the world where nitrate and nitrite are in food and water, such as in Colombia, or where cured and pickled foods are eaten in large quantities, such as in Japan and China.

Nitrite has been used in meat preservation because it helps prevent botulism (food poisoning), and it also improves color and flavor. The Department of Agriculture and the meat industry already have lowered the amount of nitrite in prepared meats and are searching for improved methods of meat preservation. Also, although it is known that charcoal broiling deposits cancer-causing compounds such as benzopyrene on the surface of foods, it has no harmful effects if used in moderation.

In its dietary statement, the ACS also noted that there are several areas in which there is not enough evidence to make specific recommendations, even though they have received considerable public attention. These include the roles of food additives, vitamin E, selenium, artificial sweeteners, coffee, cholesterol, and meat and fish cooked at high temperatures.

"An optimal diet cannot yet be defined," the ACS notes. But "there is abundant evidence that the usual American diet is not optimal and this is adequate reason to recommend modification."

TOBACCO

There are nearly 144,000 cases of lung cancer in the United States each year. At least 100,000 of them could have been avoided by abstinence from tobacco. Tobacco has been strongly implicated in the cause of cancer of the mouth, throat, larynx, esophagus, pancreas, and bladder. While cigarette smoking plays the chief role in the origin of lung cancer, the use of tobacco in all forms—cigar, pipe, chewing tobacco, and snuff—contributes to the development of these cancers.

It is unlikely that anyone in this country today is unaware of the dangers of cigarette smoking. Yet the annual consumption of cigarettes continues to rise. Cigarette smoking is high among American youth, especially teenage girls. And although there has been a decline in the proportion of male adults smoking, the average smoker now consumes more cigarettes. We may well question the effectiveness of government admonitions and public education methods. Nevertheless, even though there are still about 54 million active cigarette smokers in the U.S., there are over 30 million ex-smokers. In the final analysis, while it is an individual decision whether or not to adopt self-destructive lifestyles, social and governmental organizations can assist in determining the outcome of that decision. Education regarding the dangers and undesirable effects of cigarette smoking (yellow teeth and fingers, hampered athletic and intellectual performance, etc.) should begin in early school years. Parents can serve as nonsmoking role models, and peer pressure should be oriented against smoking.

Stop-smoking programs for adults generally show a 60 to 70 percent success rate at the completion of the program, but at the end of a year only about 25 percent remain nonsmokers. Nevertheless, if these results could be extended to the smoking public at large, they would have a positive impact on decreasing the incidence of tobacco-related cancers.

Cigarette smoking is particularly hazardous in conjunction with exposure to gases, fumes, or dust of other potentially cancer-causing agents. Exposure to asbestos, for example, increases the risk of developing one form of lung cancer but when combined with cigarette smoking sharply increases the risk. The same effect has been seen in occupational settings such as rubber or chemical plants and in jobs that expose workers to the dusts of coal, iron ore, nickel, and chromates.

The use of cigarettes and alcohol together markedly increases the cancer-causing effects of the tobacco, particularly in the mouth, throat, and esophagus, although not in the lung. It is believed that the use of alcohol facilitates contact between the cancer-causing agents in tobacco and the lining of the upper digestive tract. Cigars, pipes, and chewing tobacco also generate carcinogenic substances, especially when combined with alcohol. (For a more detailed discussion, see Chapter 3, "Smoking and Cancer.")

OCCUPATIONAL FACTORS

It has been known for hundreds of years that cancer may be associated with certain occupations. One of the earliest successes of preventive medicine occurred in eighteenth-century England when it was found that cancer of the scrotum in chimney sweeps could be eliminated if they washed after work. There are many occupations in our highly industrialized twentieth-century society in which workers come into contact with toxic fumes, gases, vapors, dust and airborne particles, as well as potentially dangerous liquids and solids. In addition to the immediate danger to the worker, there is considerable evidence that occupational cancer hazards may reach beyond the workplace to the family. Workers may unknowingly take home dust particles of cancer-causing material on their bodies, clothes, or personal belongings and expose family and friends to possible hazards. In the case of the airborne cancer-causing substances, members of a community adjacent to the source of such material may be at increased risk. A study of three communities where vinyl chloride plants were located found higher than normal rates of cancer of the nervous system among the entire population. Carcinogens are passed in other discrete ways as well: Any automobile brake repairman in the U.S. would be exposed to asbestos dust from the brake drum linings, as would millions of construction workers who handle asbestos products. Thus the hazards of occupational cancer are more pervasive than would at first appear.

To protect workers and those incidentally exposed from dangers in the workplace, Congress passed the Occupational Safety and Health Act in 1970. This legislation established two government agencies—the Occupational Safety and Health Administration (OSHA) and the National Institute for Occupational Safety and Health (NIOSH). OSHA issues and enforces workplace standards, conducts work-site inspections, and responds to worker complaints, while NIOSH performs research in occupational safety and health.

OSHA safety standards require employers to:

Inform workers of the provisions of the standards that apply to them; provide regulated work areas restricted to authorized personnel; monitor workers' exposure to the hazardous substances; assure that workers' exposure does not exceed permissible limits; provide medical surveillance for emergencies, maintenance or decontamination; keep up-to-date records of workers' medical conditions and amount of exposure to hazardous substances; allow workers access to their medical records; inform workers of the special hazards of the regulated substances; train workers in safe work practices that will keep their exposure within permissible limits.

Workers also have certain guidelines to follow. They must read the OSHA poster the employer must display in the workplace; comply with all applicable OSHA standards as well as health and safety rules of the employer; report any apparent health hazards immediately to a supervisor; report to the supervisor any job-related illness; cooperate full with the OSHA compliance officer who inspects the workplace; practice good personal hygiene; encourage and support the formation of such groups as safety and health committees.

Table 5 outlines some occupational groups associated with high cancer risks. A more complete list and additional information can be obtained from the Occupational Safety and Health Administration in Washington, D.C.

RADIATION EXPOSURE

Radiation is of great concern because of its potential for causing cancer and/or genetic damage. This effect is proportional to both the dose and duration of exposure. Ionizing radiation, the form of radiation used for most medical purposes, is capable of displacing an electron from an atom in a cell (ionizing the atom). The ionized atom can cause damage to the molecule and the cell, although the body has the ability to repair radiation-induced damage so that ionizing radiation is not always harmful. Other non-ionizing forms of radiation, such as infrared and ultraviolet, can also be harmful if not properly used.

The most common sources of exposure to ionizing radiation for medical reasons are diagnostic radiology, nuclear medicine, and radiation therapy. It is almost impossible today for anyone to reach adult life without having some form of diagnostic X rays. In most cases these X rays can lead to life-saving or limb-saving medical efforts, and are responsible for significant improvements in medical care. Great strides have been made in medical diagnosis in the last two decades as a result of advances in radiation technology. For example, the early diagnosis of breast cancer by mammography has resulted in a higher cure rate in the treatment of this disease. Computerized tomography (CT scan) has been of immense diagnostic assistance, particularly in the identification of brain tumors. The ability to introduce small catheters into the heart and other organs and inject radiopaque material to detect abnormalities is a powerful tool for physicians and surgeons. Yet there is always concern about the potential hazards of radiation.

Because of this concern and the overall increase in the use of diagnostic

Table 5
OCCUPATIONAL GROUPS ASSOCIATED WITH HIGH RISKS FOR CANCER

OCCUPATIONAL GROUP	SITE(S)
Benzoyl chloride manufacture	Lung
Chemists	Brain Lymphatic and hematopoietic (blood-forming) tissues Pancreas
Coal miners	Stomach
Coke by-product plant workers	Colon Pancreas
Foundry workers	Lung
Leatherworkers	Bladder Larynx Mouth Pharynx
Metal miners	Lung
Oil refinery/petrochemical workers	Brain Blood (leukemia) Multiple myeloma Stomach Esophagus Lung
Painters	Blood (leukemia)
Printing workers	Lung Mouth Pharynx
Rubber industry workers	Bladder Blood (leukemia) Brain Lung Prostate Stomach
Textile workers	Nasal cavity and sinuses
Woodworkers	Lymphatic tissue Nasal cavity and sinuses

radiology, new guidelines for safety have evolved. These include the following:

1. Pregnant women should receive no elective X rays at all, unless there is an absolute medical indication. The physician should be informed of the pregnancy and adequate shielding used to ensure that there is no damage to the fetus. If possible, any elective X rays should be taken within ten to fifteen days from the onset of the menstrual cycle to avoid exposure to as yet undetected pregnancies.

2. Patients receiving intestinal or abdominal X rays should have their sexual organs shielded whenever possible. Patients in the reproductive years or younger should ask for a lead apron over these areas when being examined and should ask if the area of exposure exceeds the area of diagnostic concern. Patients deserve a straightforward response and should not be intimidated by office personnel. It is particularly important for parents to speak up for the protection of their children. There are still radiologists who will do barium enema examinations in males and include the unprotected genitalia in the film. Risks like these are both unwarranted and unnecessary.

3. The size of the X-ray film taken should not exceed the area of diagnostic concern. The technique of limiting the X ray to the target alone and not including other portions of the body is called "collimation." X-ray films are held in cassettes and the X-ray beam is directed to the cassette. The size of the cassette should be approximately the size of the area to be X-rayed. Appropriately sized cassettes should be used for children. Great emphasis has been placed on teaching X-ray technicians to direct the X-ray beam so that it does not hit an area larger than the cassette.

4. Dental X rays should be done only as needed. Some people request dentists to X-ray their teeth, but the American Dental Association has stated that X rays should not be a routine part of the dental examination, but left up to the judgment of the dentist.

5. Similarly, people often ask their physicians for X rays of a portion of the body in which they have symptoms, and in other cases physicians may take X rays to protect themselves from malpractice suits. If a patient has a medical problem he or she should seek a diagnosis, not an X ray, first.

6. Patients should keep a record of when and where they have had X rays. This may eliminate the need to do repeat X rays.

7. Charts and X-ray records are frequently destroyed after seven years, although this varies from state to state according to legal requirements. If this is the case in your state, ask the physician or hospital to send the X rays or at least the reports regarding them to your home address. This may save unnecessary X rays in the future.

8. Fluoroscopy delivers a larger dose of X ray than the taking of X-ray films, and therefore if there is an alternate means of making the diagnosis, fluoroscopy should be avoided. This test is, however, a necessary part of a GI series, barium enema, and other special procedures.

The conditions under which X rays are carried out are important, since the regulation of their use differs according to state laws. The degree of care with which the safety of X-ray equipment is monitored and the reliability and training of personnel using the machines vary from state to state and hospital to hospital. Although diagnostic X rays must be ordered by a physician, the taking of X rays is not always supervised by a radiologist. In fact, in one survey only 60 percent of diagnostic studies were supervised by radiologists. In 1978, 11,700 X-ray systems were installed, but only 3,152 safety tests were carried out. In seven states there was no safety-compliance testing at all.

In 1978, 161 million diagnostic X rays were performed for medical purposes and 86 million for dental reasons. The Public Health Service estimates that as many as 30 percent of these tests were unnecessary. In addition, there is no adequate estimate of the degree of unnecessary exposure in the course of X-ray examinations that were medically indicated, but not properly performed.

To ensure a maximum level of safety during diagnostic radiology, the patient should inquire if the individual taking the X rays has been accredited as an X-ray technician. An office that takes a lot of X rays is more likely to have a certified X-ray technician than the practitioner who takes only an occasional X ray in his office. Since 90 percent of the exposure of the average citizen comes from man-made, low-level radiation from medical and dental sources, adequate surveillance of the quality and quantity of diagnostic X rays remains an important aspect of environmental protection that has not yet been achieved.

NUCLEAR MEDICINE

Nuclear medicine is an entirely new diagnostic specialty that has developed since World War II. In this new specialty, radioactive isotopes—chemicals that give off radiation—are taken into the body, and their location in organs and tissues can be used to diagnose abnormalities. Very sensitive radiation-measuring devices are placed over the area of accumulation of the isotope, and impulses are transmitted to a cathode ray tube (CRT) for visualization.

Since these isotopes give off a form of ionizing radiation called gamma rays, the goal in nuclear medicine is to use the shortest-lived isotope possible. Most importantly, the physician who refers a patient for a nuclear medicine examination for cancer detection must exercise the best judgment in selecting such a test, since the entire body will be exposed to radioactive material for a short period of time. The same advice applies here as to diagnostic X rays: the procedure should be employed only when a medical decision depends on the outcome, not merely as an extra test.

Nuclear medicine is one of the fastest-growing medical specialties, and is estimated to be increasing at the rate of 15 to 20 percent each year. Its use is much more strictly controlled and supervised than diagnostic radiology, although the risks are similar in nature.

RADIATION THERAPY

The only indication for radiation therapy is a confirmed diagnosis of cancer. In earlier years, radiation therapy was used for treatment of such benign conditions as fungus infection of the scalp, enlarged tonsil, acne, enlarged thymus gland, and osteomyelitis. These practices have been completely discontinued as the risks involved in radiation have become more clearly defined. Radiation therapy should be administered by board-certified physicians who specialize in the administration of this form of treatment for cancer. Furthermore, the decision regarding whether to use surgery, radiation therapy, or chemotherapy should be made in consultation with the radiation therapist and the physician who diagnosed the cancer and will follow the patient after treatment.

The dose of X ray delivered by radiation therapy is many thousand times greater than that of standard diagnostic X rays. The trend is toward the use of higher-voltage X-ray equipment for greater penetration, less scattering of radiation within the body, and less damaging effects on nearby normal tissues. Through "treatment planning," the radiation field can be carefully targeted so that the X-ray beam touches as little normal tissue as possible. This is accomplished through mathematical calculation to locate the malignancy within the body. Fewer side effects and long-term complications will occur with careful treatment planning. (For a more detailed discussion, see Chapter 8 "Radiation Therapy.")

SUMMARY

While there remain numerous mysteries yet to be solved in the search for cancer cures, there are already known precautions that everyone can and should take. Self-examination and awareness of cancer symptoms can help detect an early-stage disease. The fear of having cancer must be far outweighed by the knowledge that it is likely to be curable if treated at the earliest possible time. Routine checkups and periodic cancer screening as well as monthly self-examinations should be part of your ongoing cancer detection program.

Even before considering detection and early treatment, consider prevention. There are several known cancer-causing agents which many people take into their bodies on a daily—sometimes hourly—basis. The importance of avoiding these substances cannot possibly be stressed enough in the individual pursuit of cancer prevention. Fatty foods should be avoided, while high-fiber foods and those containing vitamins A, C, and E should be incorporated into the diet. Tobacco in any form should be avoided, especially when combined with alcohol consumption.

Those who work in high-risk occupations and are regularly exposed to carcinogenic substances should follow the guidelines set up by OSHA, and be sure that employers do too. Good personal hygiene should be practiced to avoid taking toxic substances home and exposing family and friends to risk.

Radiation of any kind should be used for medical purposes only when absolutely necessary, and precautions should be taken to protect the genitals and unaffected tissues from the X-ray beam.

In general, everyone should be aware of the elements in our society and our environment that actively contribute to cancer. Whenever possible, they should be avoided. By following these guidelines, everyone can personally decrease cancer risk.

3

Smoking and Cancer

JESSE L. STEINFELD, M.D.

INTRODUCTION

WARNING: The Surgeon General has determined that cigarette smoking is danger-ous to your health.

Emphatically, unequivocally, this alarm—no matter how low-key it may appear at first blush—should serve notice to us all that cigarette smoking is the single largest unnecessary and preventable cause of illness and early death in the United States. At present, over 32 percent of all American adults smoke, and the frequency of life-threatening diseases—cancer, heart attacks, and emphysema in adults, and birth defects and crib death in the babies of women who smoke—caused by tobacco, tar, nicotine and other substances in cigarettes remains alarming. For the 53 million American smokers, teenagers and adults, men and women, the single most effective step they can take to prolong their lives and improve their health is to stop smoking completely.

HISTORY OF SMOKING

Smoking is a profoundly American habit, invented by the Indians and made known to European civilization by the explorers and settlers of the New World. Smoking and the other uses of tobacco—snuff and chewing—became increasingly fashionable and popular in the seventeenth and eighteenth centuries, both in Europe and America. According to one medical historian, the first observation of an association between the use of tobacco and cancer was made in 1761 by Dr. John Hill of England in his work "Cautions Against the Immoderate Use of Snuff," which reported on tumors of the nose in people who sniffed tobacco. Thirty years later, Dr. Soemmerring in Germany noted a relationship between the use of tobacco and cancer of the lip. It was not, however, until the early decades of this century that many doctors in several countries independently reported in medical journals that there appeared to be a consistently higher percentage of lung cancer in smokers than in nonsmokers.

These findings pointed to the need for more definitive studies, which were then undertaken in the 1950s. It was in that decade that four larger, careful surveys were completed in the United States, looking back at the smoking habits of lung cancer patients and comparing them with an otherwise equivalent group of nonsmokers, a group known in medical research as a control group. Since all four of these surveys uncovered a strong, valid, statistical relationship between smoking and lung cancer, the logical next step was to apply prospective epidemiological principles (epidemiology is the study of disease patterns in population groups) to the problem. In the early 1950s, three such prospective studies on smoking were started. In contrast to the previous studies, which had concentrated on the past history of a population group (a retrospective study), prospective studies follow many thousands of initially healthy people over time and compare causes of death with their smoking habits. The forward-looking, or prospective, studies confirmed that smokers had a significantly increased death rate. This excess mortality—increase in the number of deaths attributable to smoking—was made up of a higher risk of lung cancer and other cancers, coronary artery disease, emphysema, bronchitis and other lung disorders, ulcers and stroke. By 1962 enough evidence had been accumulated, from both American and European studies, that the advisory committee to the Surgeon General of the United States was able to examine it and, in 1964, issue to Congress and the American people the landmark Surgeon General's report, "The Health Consequences of Smoking."

The Office of the Surgeon General and the American Cancer Society, among others, have since then sought and obtained corroborative evidence from many other medical sources, including autopsy data and experimental research. The consistent strength, specificity, time relationship, and general logical coherence of the evidence all reinforce the fact that cigarette smoking leads to early death. No scientifically-designed study has been able to suggest any other conclusion. The only organization that claims that the effect of smoking on health is merely statistical and unproved is the Tobacco Institute, an organization created and funded by the tobacco industry to serve as its public relations and information vehicle. In short, stopping smoking remains the single most effective action that smokers can take to improve their health and prolong their lives.

CANCER AND SMOKING

Epidemiological studies indicate that cigarette smoking is related to about 30 to 40 percent of all cancer deaths and that these deaths are therefore potentially avoidable. The overall cancer death rate in men who smoke cigarettes, for example, is more than double that of nonsmokers.

Smokers who consume two or more packs of cigarettes a day—not an unusual amount in a country in which the average per-person consumption is about two hundred packs a year—die from lung cancer at a rate of 15 to 25 times that of nonsmokers. The range is due to the variation in population groups and in their smoking habits, including the number of cigarettes smoked, the age at which smoking began, the amount of tar in the cigarettes, the depth of inhalation, and other factors.

SMOKING AND LUNG CANCER

Clearly, smoking is the single most powerful cause of lung cancer. The increase in risk has been observed not only in men, but more recently also in women, for smoking has come to symbolize their liberation to engage in activities formerly considered the domain of men. Women as a group started smoking in the 1940s, about twenty years later than men, and lung cancer—long the leading cause of cancer death among American men—is now also the number one cause of cancer death among women.

The increased risk for lung cancer rises with the number of years one has smoked, as well as the number of cigarettes smoked each day. The tar and nicotine content is the third major determining factor. Other factors, such as the degree of inhalation and whether the cigarette is smoked down to the end, also modify the degree of exposure and risk. These measurable aspects of smoking behavior make it clear that there is a direct and definite dose-response relationship between the smoking dose and the development of cancer. Furthermore, no safe lower threshold exists below which the dose, or the number of cigarettes smoked, is without risk. Smoking one half pack of cigarettes a day will increase the risk of cancer. Even being in the frequent presence of cigarette smoke may increase the risk to a nonsmoker—for example, the situation that exists when a nonsmoker is married to a heavy smoker. This dose-response rule can, in general, be applied to all cancers.

Lung cancer occurs more frequently in cities than in rural areas, but then, smoking is also more common in cities. Although air pollution has been cited as a possible factor in causing lung cancer, there is not enough evidence to permit any scientific conclusion about a statistically significant increase in lung cancer. But smoking in the presence of certain environmental pollutants has been shown to increase the risk of lung cancer. Specific cancer-causing agents found in particular industrial settings, such as asbestos, are known to interact synergistically with cigarette smoking to produce an even higher risk of lung cancer.

The frequency of lung cancer in the United States has increased six times over since 1940, and the upward trend is continuing. Overall, cigarette smoking is now related to more than 75 percent of all lung cancers. The survival rate for lung cancer is low—only 9 percent of patients with lung cancer are alive five years after the first appearance of symptoms. Even with improved diagnosis and combinations of surgery, radiation therapy, and chemotherapy, lung cancer remains one of the most deadly of all cancers. Even recent extensive studies of various diagnostic screening methods for the earlier detection of lung cancer show little improvement in survival. These studies have included frequent, regular chest X rays and periodic cellular (cytologic) examination of the sputum for abnormal or premalignant cells. Yet by the time the cancer is detected, using these screening methods, it has already advanced to an incurable stage in more than 90 percent of patients. Therefore a chest X ray taken for a yearly examination and reported as normal should not be considered a sign of reassurance to a smoker. Lung cancer can develop slowly and insidiously, too small to be noticed this year but growing large enough to be both diagnosable and incurable the next. All too often an unremarkable, virtually unnoticeable little spot on a chest X ray, not different in any apparent or predictable way from the other spots and shadows normally observed, is recognized only too late and in futile retrospect as having been the site or origin of a cancer that shows up in subsequent X rays. (For a more detailed discussion, see Chapter 23, "Lung Cancer.")

SMOKING AND CANCER OF THE LARYNX

About one percent of all American cancer deaths are caused by cancer of the larynx (voice box). The incidence is five times greater in men than in women, a difference that has been steadily narrowing, as in lung cancer, because of increased cigarette smoking among women. Approximately one third of the 11,000 Americans who get this type of cancer each year will die of it. Epidemiologic studies based on thousands of patients indicate that smoking is the single most important factor in developing this cancer. Smokers have twenty to thirty times the chance of contracting cancer of the larynx than do nonsmokers, an increase in the relative odds that is even greater than in lung cancer.

CANCER OF THE ORAL CAVITY

Twenty-seven thousand cancers of the oral cavity—the mouth, lip, tongue, and pharynx—occur in the United States each year and nine thousand Americans die of these cancers. Cigarette smoking is, once again, the strongest causative factor that emerges from any epidemiologic study.

In the development of both oral and laryngeal cancers, people who smoke pipes and cigars suffer the same increased risk as do cigarette smokers. The hazard increases with the number of years one smokes and also with the number of cigarettes, cigars, or pipes smoked daily. Cigarette smoking in conjunction with excessive alcohol use may increase the risk even more. Individuals who drink alcohol immoderately smoke more often than teetotalers or occasional drinkers, and the use of alcohol in combination with smoking results in an even greater chance of oral and laryngeal cancer. The risk for those who both smoke and drink is much greater than for those individuals who adopt only one of those habits. Alcohol consumed in immoderate amounts is itself associated with some degree of increased oral cancers, and the carcinogenic (cancer-causing) potential of both smoke and alcohol evidently adds up to more than the sum of its parts. This is called synergy, a well-known biological phenomenon—in this case, a highly destructive one.

Some smokers develop areas of precancerous tissue in their mouths that can be identified on sight by a doctor or dentist. These areas are whitish discolorations, called leukoplakia, or reddish discolorations, called erythroplasia, that can revert to relatively normal tissue if the individual stops smoking. The same precancerous tissue occurs in the larynx, but since this organ is not easily or routinely viewed, it usually is not detected. (For a more detailed discussion, see Chapter 25, "Cancers of the Mouth, Pharynx, and Larynx.")

CANCER OF THE ESOPHAGUS

Cancer of the esophagus (food pipe) is one of the most rapidly fatal and least curable of human cancers. More than 8,500 Americans die from esophageal cancers each year. Cancer of the esophagus rarely produces symptoms until the disease has spread beyond the curative capabilities of modern medicine. Again, smoking is the major cause of this type of cancer. People who smoke two packs of cigarettes a day have a greatly increased risk—ranging up to a factor of twelve—of getting this disease as compared to nonsmokers. The more one smokes, the greater the risk. People who smoke a half-pack a day, for example, have an incidence of esophageal cancer that is four times that of nonsmokers. Cigar and pipe smoking increase the risk of this kind of cancer, and alcohol consumption in more than moderate amounts also raises the risk. (See Chapter 19, "Cancer of the Esophagus.")

SMOKING AND CANCER OF THE URINARY BLADDER

Cancer of the urinary bladder occurs about four times more often in men than in women, with about 38,500 new cases diagnosed in 1983 in the United States. It is estimated that cigarette smoking increases the risk of this disease 50 percent in men and about 10 percent in women. Cigarette smoking is the most potent of the tobacco-related risk factors. People who both smoke and are exposed to other environmental risk factors, such as dyes and some other chemicals that may cause bladder tumors, are especially predisposed because of the dual cancer-causing influences. (For a more complete discussion, see Chapter 33, "Urinary Tract Cancer.")

SMOKING AND OTHER CANCERS

In addition to cancers discussed so far in this chapter, tobacco smoking has been identified as the single major cause of cancers of the kidney and pancreas.

SMOKING AND OTHER CAUSES OF DEATH

Eventually everyone dies; however, premature death, especially from an avoidable cause, is a tragedy. The illness, suffering, financial cost, and premature death caused by tobacco use is immeasurable. The chance of a smoker's dying from cancer is at least double that of nonsmokers. Men who smoke more than one pack a day increase their relative odds from two to three times that for nonsmokers. Women smokers, who generally smoke less than men, have about a 20 percent increase in their chance of dying of cancer, and their mortality from tobacco-related cancer is steadily increasing as they smoke more and longer.

While the association between cancer and smoking is the best known to the general public and the best documented by epidemiologic and other studies, cancer is by no means the only disease linked to tobacco use. Coronary artery disease, stroke, emphysema, chronic bronchitis all are more common among smokers than nonsmokers. Pregnant women who smoke are more likely to suffer miscarriage and stillbirths; sudden infant death syndrome (SIDS or crib death) is also more common in babies born to mothers who smoke.

Coronary artery disease, the buildup of fatty plaques in the blood vessels that nourish the heart itself, is the major cause of heart attacks— the leading cause of death in the United States and most other industrialized countries of the world. It is estimated that smoking is related to nearly 25 percent of all deaths from cardiovascular disease, or about 225,000 of the nearly one million deaths from this disease each year. Smokers who have high blood pressure or elevated levels of blood cholesterol—two other leading risk factors in heart disease—are in even greater jeopardy.

There are several ways in which smoking affects the cardiovascular system. It causes constriction or narrowing of the coronary arteries, which may lead to a spasm in one of those vessels. This is now known to be a relatively common cause of chest pain (angina pectoris), and some researchers also believe that coronary spasm is one of the causes of sudden death from a heart attack. Smoking also increases the "stickiness" of blood platelets, a basic component in the body's clotting mechanism— another factor that researchers think is instrumental in atherosclerosis, the development of the fatty plaques that clog the coronary arteries. Smoking increases the blood level of carbon monoxide, leading to a reduction of oxygen supplied to the heart muscle and microscopic changes in the heart muscle cells themselves. Smoking also is closely linked to changes in the peripheral blood vessels, leading to sharply reduced circulation of blood to the lower legs, feet, and hands, a condition known as peripheral vascular disease. This commonly results in intermittent claudication, a disorder more common in men than women and one that causes pain when walking or during exposure to cold weather. Many victims of peripheral vascular disease develop leg ulcers and, in advanced cases, gangrene of the feet, toes, and fingers, which requires amputation of the affected digits or limbs, resulting in increased disability. Still another peripheral circulatory problem linked to smoking is Raynaud's syndrome, which affects the hands and fingers. In all these peripheral vascular disorders, the most successful treatment is cessation of smoking.

The destructive effect of smoking on the lungs is found in 80 percent of all cases of emphysema and 75 percent of chronic bronchitis in the United States. Smokers also experience more colds, pneumonia, and other respiratory illnesses, as well as slower recovery from such illnesses, than nonsmokers. Some studies have found that smokers lose three to five times more days from work per year than do nonsmokers, with costs of absenteeism that run into the billions of dollars annually.

In many instances, smokers suffer from chronic symptoms so firmly entrenched that they consider them almost normal. The so-called smoker's cough is one example; many smokers have had it for so long that they consider it to be normal when, in fact, it is not. Indeed, many smokers eventually become respiratory cripples, with such extensive damage to lungs that they can barely walk one block, climb a flight of stairs, or go to the bathroom without needing an oxygen respirator.

SMOKING AND PREGNANCY

Not only does cigarette smoking affect the health of the living, but smoking by a pregnant woman also has a profound effect on the unborn. Pregnant women who smoke suffer a marked increase in miscarriages and stillbirths, and are more likely to have a premature or low-birth-weight baby than women who don't smoke. *Placenta previa,* an abnormal development of the membrane or sac holding the developing fetus in the lowermost portion of the womb, is also more common in pregnant women who smoke. And the adverse effects do not stop at birth; as noted earlier, crib death, or SIDS, is more common among infants of women who smoke. Babies born to smoking mothers also are more likely to have birth defects, including poorly developed lungs. Their birth weight is often lower than normal even though they may be full-term babies, and they also are of shorter stature. Low-birth-weight babies are more likely to have respiratory infections, lowered intelligence, retarded emotional development and other problems such as dyslexia, abnormal behavior patterns, hyperactivity and maladaptation.

How smoking may cause these adverse effects on the offspring of women who smoke during pregnancy is unknown, but it appears to be related to the lowered oxygen content (anoxia) in both fetal and maternal blood that is caused by cigarette smoke. Researchers have shown that laboratory animals exposed to cigarette smoke during pregnancy produce offspring with cardiovascular and other abnormalities, but whether the mechanisms responsible for these defects also apply to human beings is as yet unknown. However, one can say with certainty that not smoking during pregnancy is one of the most important things a woman can do to help ensure having a healthy, normal baby.

In addition to the hazards of smoking during pregnancy, research has also shown that women who smoke and use birth control pills have a significantly increased incidence of heart attacks, stroke, and other cardiovascular problems, such as high blood pressure and development of blood clots. In fact, smoking is now a contraindication for prescribing oral contraceptives for women over the age of thirty-five, and many gynecologists discourage their use by women of any age who also smoke.

HOW SMOKING CAUSES CANCER

Many private and public institutions, including the American Cancer Society, the National Cancer Institute, and the World Health Organization, among others, are trying to persuade tobacco manufacturers to identify the toxic and cancer-causing ingredients in their tobacco products. Cigarette smoke contains a number of known carcinogenic substances, such as polyaromatic hydrocarbons, as well as poisonous chemicals such as carbon monoxide, nitrogen oxide, ammonia, and cyanide. A number of the substances have been shown to cause cancer in laboratory animals, but isolating a particular substance and then proving that it causes cancer in human beings is a difficult and highly complex procedure. Add to this the fact that there are more than six thousand different chemicals in the gaseous and particulate phases of burning tobacco, a factor that makes it even more difficult to identify the specific carcinogens for human cancers. There have been some indications that nicotine itself —perhaps the strongest single addictive element in cigarette smoking— or one of its metabolic by-products also may be a carcinogen, or a co-carcinogen, but this has not yet been proved.

It has been suggested that some unusual elements or contaminants in tobacco, such as arsenic and cadmium, or even polonium in its radioactive form, may be instrumental in causing lung cancer in smokers. This theory is backed by the observation that radioactive polonium remains almost permanently in the lung tissues of smokers in three times the concentration found in nonsmokers.

The combined use of tobacco and alcohol also has been the subject of scientific investigations, and several explanations have been proposed for the synergistic cancer-causing effect of the two. For example, alcohol may serve as a solvent for the carcinogens in tobacco smoke or it may alter their metabolism in the body, making them even more potent carcinogens. Alcohol, when consumed in large amounts, may also lead to deficiencies of trace minerals and other micronutrients—naturally occurring substances that are needed in very small amounts by normal cells—thus rendering the cells more susceptible to cancer. Similarly, explanations have been advanced for the increased rate of cancer of the kidney, pancreas, and urinary bladder of smokers, since these organs are not directly exposed to the tobacco smoke. The smoke may contain organ-specific chemicals that cause cancer in their target organ after absorption into the circulation through the lungs. Carcinogenic substances such as nitrosamines may develop in the stomach, esophagus, and pancreas following the natural clearing mechanism of the lungs that brings up mucus and the chemicals dissolved in it. Some of the mucus may then be swallowed, either consciously or subconsciously, bringing it into the digestive system. It is also reasonable to suggest that the kidneys, which collect and concentrate wastes, and the bladder, which stores them, may be affected by the presence of concentrated carcinogens in the urine.

RISKS IN PASSIVE SMOKING

There is currently a good deal of debate over the rights of smokers vs. those of nonsmokers. At first the social pressure to limit smoking, especially in public places or in situations where one cannot escape from the smoke, such as trains or airplanes, was related mostly to the distaste, odor, and annoyance caused by smoking. Recent studies, however, indicate that there may be important health reasons to restrict smoking in public places. These studies have found that tobacco smoke can affect the health of involuntary (passive) smokers—those who breathe in the smoke without actually smoking themselves—as well as actual smokers. The effects may not be as profound, except in people who are hypersensitive to tobacco smoke, but they exist nonetheless. Sidestream smoke, which is produced by the cigarette when it is not being puffed, is in some ways different from mainstream smoke, which is deliberately drawn into the smoker's lungs. The differences are related to temperature, dilution and other factors. On the whole, however, both contain the same components, some in higher and some in lower concentrations.

There are indications that passive or involuntary smoking also results in deposits of substances from the tobacco in the lungs and leads to precancerous changes in the bronchi, just as they do in smokers, albeit in lesser amounts. Nonsmokers in a smoke-filled room with poor ventilation have higher blood levels of nicotine and carbon monoxide than when in rooms without smoke. Since no safe level of exposure has been established, any exposure must be considered a health hazard. Epidemiologic studies tend to confirm this thesis. Two surveys concluded that nonsmoking wives of husbands who smoked heavily had twice the risk of lung cancer of women who were married to nonsmokers. Another study found little or no increased risk. Although this evidence is not complete, there is enough to warrant further research on this public health problem. Additional evidence is all the more important at the present time because the tobacco lobby and others are using political and economic power to weaken restrictions on smoking in public places under the guise of "smokers' rights" legislation. The major goal is to weaken the restrictions on smoking in such places as elevators, airplanes, buses, classrooms, and places of public assembly. In this respect, the major consideration must be for the health and rights of the nonsmoking majority; if a person wants to jeopardize his or her own health in the privacy of the home, this is a personal matter. But no one should have the right to knowingly jeopardize the health of others through a voluntary act, such as smoking.

TRENDS IN SMOKING

In 1950, more than 53 percent of American adults smoked some form of tobacco. This figure has now dropped to 32 percent. Despite this encouraging decline in smoking among adults, there are still highly disturbing trends. Large numbers of women, especially young ones, have taken up the habit; the number of youngsters who start smoking remains alarmingly high; and despite the recent decline in the percentage of smokers, the incidence of cancers related to smoking continues to rise. Why? For one thing, we are now seeing the result of the tremendous increase in smoking among Americans from the 1920s to the 1950s. Many cancers take ten to thirty years to develop; men who were heavy smokers for many years and then quit still are not completely safe, although their risk is lower than that of people who do not stop smoking. And the fact remains that nearly a third of all adults continue to smoke—indeed, many have smoked for decades and are now major candidates to become grim cancer or heart disease statistics.

Men have stopped smoking in greater numbers than women; since the first Surgeon General's report on smoking in 1964, the percentage of men who smoke has decreased by 25 percent, compared to a 3.5 percent decline for women. Even so, people who continue to smoke buy more cigarettes than ever before. The yearly per capita consumption of cigarettes has doubled since 1940, going from about 2,000 per person in that year to 3,800 in 1982. These increasing figures, together with the declining percentage of Americans who smoke, imply that those who do smoke are consuming more cigarettes than ever before.

There have been other changes in smoking over the last few decades. Since the tobacco industry introduced filter-tip cigarettes, their popularity has grown to the point where more than 90 percent of all cigarettes now have filters. In addition, the tar and nicotine content of most cigarettes has been markedly reduced. Part of any benefit that might come from these so-called less hazardous cigarettes has been offset by a gradual but steady increase in the number of cigarettes that the average smoker consumes; in fact, some researchers have suggested that confirmed smokers, consciously or unconsciously, increase the number of cigarettes to try to adjust for the accustomed nicotine level that was derived from smoking the older, stronger types. In addition, smokers of low-tar cigarettes seem to inhale more deeply and to take more puffs per cigarette. For the cigarette companies, which have reduced the weight of tobacco in each cigarette by fifteen percent over the last fifteen years, the profit margins for low-tar cigarettes appear to be even greater than for the regular cigarettes. The tobacco industry has recognized this and now budgets most of its advertising dollars for the low-tar brands.

When we look at smoking habits around the world, we find that the United States still leads all other countries in cigarette consumption. Japan is a close second. Thus while real gains have been made in reducing the percentage of Americans who smoke, we still have a long way to go.

TEENAGE SMOKING

Adolescent and teenage smoking is a continuing problem in the United States. Those teenagers who smoke consume more cigarettes than ever before. In addition, youngsters are beginning to smoke at an ever younger age. Some studies, such as those conducted by the University of Minnesota School of Public Health, have found that by the end of the seventh grade nearly a third of all youngsters are at least experimental or occasional smokers. (Remember, only 32 percent of all adult Americans smoke.) The Minnesota researchers also have found that the younger the age at which one begins to smoke, the harder it is to quit. Those who start smoking at a very early age also tend to be heavier smokers than those who start when they are older.

Over the last two decades the percentage of boys who become regular smokers has declined, but the percentage of girls who smoke has actually risen; in fact, 13 percent of all teenage girls are now regular smokers, compared to 10 percent of the boys. Since they are beginning to smoke regularly at a younger age than in the past, we can expect to see the resulting cancers develop in an ever-younger age group.

In the last few years, increasing attention has been given to developing more effective methods of discouraging young people from starting to smoke. Most public health officials and others who have studied the smoking habits of teenagers find that there are several influencing factors, but the most potent one is peer acceptance and pressure. When asked why they smoke, many youngsters respond that "all the kids do it," or that "it gives me confidence and makes me feel like an adult." Of course not all of the kids do it, but when the University of Minnesota researchers asked seventh-graders to estimate the percentage of their peers who smoked, virtually all put the figure much higher than it actually was. These researchers, who have since developed a model "Smoking Prevention Program" that has now been tested for more than five years in the Minneapolis public schools, also found that the most effective way to discourage youngsters from beginning to smoke was to engage admired peer leaders in each classroom to work with the teacher in the smoking prevention sessions. Distant health consequences such as cancer and heart disease are mentioned, but the real focus is on the more immediate social consequences that are likely to be of real concern to young adolescents: things like impaired athletic performance, bad breath, stained hands and teeth, the smell of stale tobacco on hair and clothes. The Minnesota project compared the results in terms of the number of teenage smokers in schools where the program was offered against control schools where it was not, and found that it was highly effective in reducing the number of youngsters who started smoking. The adoption of similar programs on a broader, nationwide scale might be one way of reducing the number of young smokers and, at the same time, embarking on a major preventive medicine program that could potentially save millions of Americans from premature death and untold billions of dollars in health care and other costs.

IS THERE A LESS HAZARDOUS CIGARETTE?

Over the last fifteen or twenty years, the tobacco industry has reduced not only the average tar and nicotine content of cigarettes, but also the actual tobacco by weight per cigarette, leading to speculation that this has made cigarettes less hazardous. Indeed, some studies have shown that people who smoke low-tar, low-nicotine cigarettes do have a somewhat reduced incidence of cancer. But are these cigarettes truly less hazardous? This is not a term one should ever apply to cigarettes. In dealing with carcinogens, we assume that there is no safe level. When it comes to cigarettes, there is no evidence of a threshold below which it is safe to smoke. The more one smokes, the greater the chances of developing cancer. The higher the tar and nicotine content, the greater the risks. Reducing the number of cigarettes smoked and lowering tar and nicotine seem to lower the risk, but these measures do not remove it. Even moderate smokers are found to have an increase in premalignant cell changes in the bronchi and lungs. Moreover, filter tip, low-tar, and low-nicotine cigarettes pose the same risks as the 1930s cigarettes for heart and lung diseases and complications to the pregnant woman and her fetus or newborn infant.

Research has been conducted in many institutions in an attempt to satisfy the aspects of smoking that are judged pleasurable (but which represent addiction) without producing the harmful effects. Unfortunately, the key ingredients in tobacco that cause illness and death—the nicotine and as-yet unknown compounds in the tar—are what make smoking addicting. Smoking delivers these drugs to the brain within eight seconds; substitute methods of using nicotine, for example, have failed to satisfy the response sought in the same way as smoking. Similar observations have been made about the dose of tar, which closely parallels the dose of nicotine. All attempts so far to remove all tar and nicotine and to add flavorings to satisfy the smoker's desire for nicotine and other trace chemicals have not produced a satisfactory substitute.

Still, for people who cannot quit smoking—and they seem to number in the millions—using a filter-tip cigarette with the lowest possible tar and nicotine content helps. But it is folly to think that these are truly less hazardous cigarettes: the chance of developing lung cancer is still about eight times higher than that of nonsmokers. Use of these cigarettes appears to lower the risk of coronary artery disease by modest amounts—10 percent in men and 19 percent in women. But no beneficial effects have been reported in lowering the rates of chronic bronchitis, emphysema, miscarriage, low-birth-weight babies, or allergic response.

SMOKELESS TOBACCO

Smokeless tobacco, whether loose-leaf chewing tobacco, moist "dip," or snuff, has become increasingly popular over the last decade, particularly among young athletes. Professional baseball and football players often can be seen with cheeks bulging from a wad of tobacco; a growing number of high school and college athletes are taking up the habit, often thinking that it is a safe alternative to smoking. It is now estimated that more than seven million Americans use smokeless tobacco, and there is mounting evidence that it is as addictive as cigarette smoking and may have an even greater risk of causing mouth and throat cancers. For example, a study conducted among 752 North Carolina white women who used snuff showed an almost fifty-fold increase in the risk of mouth cancer.

Smokeless tobacco has been exempted from many of the rules and taxes placed on cigarettes. Congress canceled the federal excise taxes on smokeless tobacco in 1965, on the grounds that it is a "poor man's product." Unlike cigarettes, smokeless tobaccos can be advertised on television, and many of the commercials feature popular sports figures. The products also carry no health warnings. The U.S. Tobacco Company, manufacturer of Skoal and Copenhagen moist snuffs, spent $30 million in 1984 to promote its smokeless tobaccos; the company also reported that its earnings had increased from $12 million in 1974 to $83.7 million in 1984. Recently there has been a concerted effort by the American Cancer Society and others to require warnings on smokeless tobacco and also to limit television advertising of these products. In the meantime, it is important that people realize that smokeless tobacco is addictive and greatly increases the risk of highly lethal mouth and throat cancers.

BENEFITS OF QUITTING

Given the fact that any smoking can produce precancerous changes and that no cigarette can be considered truly less hazardous, many people take the negative attitude that their fate is sealed, so why bother quitting?

This attitude is quite wrong. A number of scientific studies have found that there are distinct benefits to be gained from quitting. Since all diseases caused by smoking are dose-related, any reduction in the total number of cigarettes consumed will help—provided, of course, that permanent tissue damage and changes have not occurred. The reduced risk is not necessarily in proportion to the reduction in the actual number of cigarettes smoked or in the daily dose of tar and nicotine; living biological systems do not appear to work this way.

Once the process of premalignant changes has started, only complete abstinence has any chance of totally ending or reversing it. In other words, if abnormal lung cells have developed, simply halving the number of cigarettes smoked probably will not remove the threat, although it may be slowed. But studies have found that completely stopping smoking will enable the body to repair some damage, and some of the damaged cells may eventually be replaced by normal ones.

Stopping smoking produces other measurable benefits. Within a half day there is a speedy reduction in the level of blood carbon monoxide, a factor related to heart disease. Endurance improves and the senses of taste and smell, which are markedly impaired by smoking, begin to return to normal. At a far slower rate—a testimony to the pervasive injury inflicted by the toxic elements in cigarette smoke—actual cellular recovery begins to take place, provided, of course, the damage has not progressed to cancer. As time goes by, the mortality rates slowly begin to drop and again approach that of nonsmokers. But this recovery process takes at least ten to fifteen years of abstinence. After fifteen years, the rate of lung cancer in former smokers is still about twice that of people who have never smoked—a marked improvement in the odds for continual smokers, but still higher than normal. The period of recovery for the cardiovascular system seems to be seven to ten years. The rate of progressive emphysema also slows with quitting, but once emphysema develops, total recovery cannot be expected. The smoker's cough, bronchitis, and excessive phlegm production all generally improve over six to eighteen months after quitting. Women who stop smoking completely before becoming pregnant can avoid the increased risk of tobacco-related complications of pregnancy.

In sum, there are distinct benefits from stopping smoking. While they may not be as great as never having started, they still make the effort worthwhile in terms of improved health and life expectancy.

HOW TO QUIT

The difficulties in quitting smoking are well known. Addiction to nicotine and the other chemical products of tobacco smoke seems to be one of the strongest habituations known. Surveys of smokers who have tried to quit demonstrate that the number of cigarettes smoked daily is often closely related to the difficulty of quitting. The more one smokes, the harder it is to quit. The length of time smoked and the age at which one starts also are factors; long-time smokers who started at an early age have more difficulty quitting than individuals who took up the habit relatively recently and at a later age.

Many studies have been made in an attempt to correlate smoking with various personality types. While the scientific validity of these studies can be questioned, they do tend to show that smokers often consider themselves to be directed more by fate, luck, and events beyond their control than do nonsmokers, who, in contrast, feel they are more firmly in control of their lives. Other studies have found that smokers tend to be greater risk-takers, more impulsive, more likely to divorce and change jobs, more extroverted, and more aggressive than nonsmokers. Smokers are also more likely to use drugs, marijuana, and more alcohol than nonsmokers.

Smokers who have succeeded in quitting permanently have been described as having a strong need for achievement, increased lifestyle stability, and an increased tendency toward outgoing social behavior. No correlation between success in quitting and educational level has been identified.

Over 70 percent of those who have successfully quit admit to having tried to give up the habit at least once before. It is estimated, however, that fully 90 or 95 percent of the more than 33 million American smokers who have quit smoking have done so on the basis of their own efforts without outside help. Permanent abstinence from smoking is difficult to maintain on the first try; relapse rates have been placed as high as 90 percent in some studies. More encouraging is the fact that the odds for permanent success improve with each successive attempt to quit, so if one fails the first time, this is no indication that success won't follow on a second or third try.

The most effective way to quit seems to be "cold turkey"—to give up smoking all at once rather than to cut down gradually. The withdrawal syndrome usually lasts from seven to fifteen days, although it may be longer in some people, and then subsides. Thus if one can get through the first couple of weeks, the chances of success improve.

Smokers who participate in formal stop-smoking programs—and no single program has been identified as being measurably and reliably more successful than any other—have a better record for long-term abstinence than those who quit on their own. Their favorable termination rates range from 20 to 40 percent, but while American smokers willing to quit express verbally an interest in these activities, only a small number actually follow through. Furthermore, the cost per smoker who quits in an organized program is relatively high, but even so, much lower than the medical costs of continued smoking.

Techniques used at these formal programs vary greatly. Some groups establish a set goal of gradually reducing the number of cigarettes smoked each day until all smoking is eliminated, while others may emphasize smoke-aversion therapy, in which the smoker is required to smoke cigarette after cigarette in a closed room until he or she no longer has any desire to smoke. Behavior modification techniques, hypnosis, a system of rewards for not smoking, and penalties for smoking are among other techniques offered in various stop-smoking programs. A number of nonprofit organizations, most notably the Seventh-Day Adventist Church, the American Cancer Society, and the American Heart Association, also offer programs and help in stopping smoking. Indeed, the "self-help" information hot-lines and kits supplied by the American Cancer Society have proved nearly as successful as the more formal programs that require fees, meetings, and attendance.

Studies have shown that doctors, too, can play an important role in helping patients quit smoking. A two-minute discussion during which the doctor encourages the patient to give up smoking and suggests methods that might be especially effective for that particular individual results in an average of a 3 percent cessation rate. When compounded over a number of years, this would result in a considerable nationwide reduction in the number of smokers. The yearly rate can be improved to 5 or 6 percent if the doctor provides a four-minute discussion on stopping smoking, and also gives the patient literature about the benefits of stopping. Doctors all too often feel that it is futile to speak to their patients about smoking, but the facts show that on the whole they are a powerful influence, and could become even more so, in reducing the total number of smokers in the United States.

As noted earlier, smoking prevention programs directed at young people also are an important and highly effective means of reducing the total number of smokers. Since the most effective of these are directed to youngsters at the time when most are beginning to experiment with cigarettes—usually in the seventh or eighth grade—and are carried on in school, making funds for these programs available to all schools is an important factor. It is difficult to think of a health-education program that is more important or ultimately more cost-effective than one directed at preventing youngsters from smoking. Yet a surprising number of schools fail to offer smoking prevention programs, on the grounds that funds for new health education programs simply are not available. This is one area in which parents should investigate what is offered at their children's schools, and if no smoking prevention programs are included in the curriculum they should request that they be added. Programs like the University of Minnesota Smoking Prevention Program mentioned earlier are available to other school systems. (Information about the Minnesota program may be obtained by contacting the University of Minnesota

Smoking Prevention Program, School of Public Health, Stadium Station, University of Minnesota School of Medicine, Minneapolis, Minn. 55455.)

THE ECONOMICS OF SMOKING

The American Medical Association has estimated that up to 25 percent of the total medical bill for health care of Americans, which now stands at a staggering $350 billion a year and is rising, is directly related to cigarette smoking. This translates to as much as $75 billion a year in added health care costs. Add to this the indirect costs of disability, work days lost due to illness, reduced family earnings because of early death and other less easily quantifiable costs of human suffering. There also are the costs of cigarette-related property damage and injury. For example, fire investigators report that about 56 percent of all fatal fires are related to cigarette smoking.

Much of these added costs are borne by the government, meaning that as taxpayers, they fall on all of us. For example, in 1976—a year for which good figures are available—the tobacco industry, through crop sales, fertilizer purchases, worker payrolls, tax revenues and advertising and other expenses, contributed $12 billion to the national economy, $6.7 billion of which was in direct taxes to national, state, and local governments. Health care costs (which have risen sharply since then) directly associated with smoking cost $18 billion. This leaves an obvious imbalance of $6 billion. In addition, in 1976 the average American smoker used about 5 percent of his or her personal income directly for smoking.

Despite this imbalance, the federal government continues to maintain a complicated and extensive system of subsidies and price supports for tobacco growers. Since 1933, more than $6 billion has been lent, interest-free, to tobacco farmers by the U.S. Department of Agriculture, even though that department paid over $500 million in interest to the U.S. Treasury to borrow the money, thus effectively passing the burden on to the taxpayer. Tobacco exports from the U.S. were valued at over $2 billion in 1978. (Incidentally, the warning label mandatory on all cigarette packs marketed in the U.S. and to American servicemen stationed abroad is eliminated from products destined for a foreign market.)

The question of jobs made available by the tobacco industry is a sensitive one, especially in times of high unemployment and economic hardship. The Tobacco Institute, a nonprofit organization supported by twelve tobacco-producing companies, has published considerable data to demonstrate the importance of the industry to the American economy. The industry claims to have 400,000 full-time workers and another 1,600,000 in related industries—packagers, distributors, matchbook makers, and so forth—amounting to 2.5 percent of the private labor force. In Kentucky, 7.4 percent of all employment is tobacco-related; in North Carolina it is 6.8 percent.

Although taxes paid by the industry are sizable, when one considers the tremendous health costs and other factors such as illness, suffering, and the burden of disability and premature death, the balance sheet is still heavily weighted against the tobacco industry.

GOALS OF THE AMERICAN CANCER SOCIETY

Smoking is one area in which the American Cancer Society would like to see the American public drastically change its habits to the point where all tobacco use is eliminated. Unlike the use of alcohol, which in moderate amounts at the appropriate time generally is not harmful, any amount of smoking is harmful. The Society offers its own self-help programs for quitting smoking and also maintains referral lists of programs that are available to the general public.

Smoking control goals and recommendations are reviewed yearly and revised as needed, based on recent medical and scientific evidence. The recommendations are both specific and general and relate to educating health-care professions, public information, legislation, and government affairs. The major points of the most recent ACS task force program include limiting advertising; listing of tar, nicotine, and carbon monoxide levels; banning sales of cigarettes to minors; phasing out the Department of Agriculture's price supports for tobacco; encouraging doctors, dentists, and nurses not to smoke themselves and to educate their patients to follow suit; encouraging the increased taxation of cigarettes, perhaps on a scale related to the tar, nicotine, and carbon monoxide content; seeking federal, state, and local legislation to establish nonsmoking areas in all public places; increasing educational efforts on the hazards of smoking and benefits of quitting or not starting; and underwriting research on methods of stopping smoking. Other goals include encouraging efforts to make the workplace a smoke-free environment; encouraging the government to sponsor a national advertising campaign against smoking, and regulating cigarette content by the Food and Drug Administration. This agency, as the government body that regulates the sale of both prescription and nonprescription drugs, has yet to take any action on one of our most widely used drugs—namely, cigarettes.

How realistic are these goals? The considerable progress that has been made since the release of the first Surgeon General's Report on Smoking in 1964 in making the public aware of the dangers of smoking fosters the hope that even more progress can be made. We fully recognize that the issues are complex and that there are no easy answers. But with so many lives at stake and with such a staggering cost in both human suffering and money, the campaign against smoking must remain a top priority until these goals are achieved.

4

Living with Cancer

JIMMIE C. HOLLAND, M.D.,
AND LEAH O. CULLEN, M.D.

INTRODUCTION

What is it like to have a family member receive a diagnosis of cancer?
Whether it be a spouse, parent, child, or even oneself, this question faces
one in every five families annually in the United States. What should be
expected about the illness and its treatment? And what response should
be expected of the physician, family, friends, and particularly oneself in
this situation? Answers to these legitimate questions lie on the one hand
with the medical facts, and on the other hand with the emotional reactions of all those involved. The medical and psychological aspects are
intimately intertwined in any discussion of what it is like to live with
cancer, and both must be taken into account.

FEARS ABOUT CANCER

The diagnosis of cancer elicits an emotional response that results from fears of the future in the face of a potentially life-threatening disease. This psychological aspect of cancer, as outlined in Chapter 1, "New Insights and Attitudes," is characterized by fear of the "five D's": death, disfigurement, disability, dependence, and disruption of key relationships. The fears center first around the threat to life itself, and then around the threat to the quality of that life, represented by fears of dependent relationships with other people, the disruption of close ties, the possible loss of a vital function through therapy or the disease itself, which might lead to the inability to work or the possible loss of attractiveness.

These fears are normal, expected, and appropriate when facing any serious illness. Both patient and family *should* show concern, and those who do not are avoiding and denying a potential danger. A tolerable level of worry and distress is a helpful reminder that this situation is serious and warrants both physical treatment and psychological support. Abnormally few or abnormally excessive worries bordering on panic, however, inhibit proper action.

The patient and family must learn to cope with the emotional, as well as the medical, consequences of cancer. Coping with the stresses of cancer helps to keep the emotional burden at a tolerable level, and permits the individuals involved to use rational judgment in facing illness and treatment. Maintaining a comfortable quality of life despite a serious illness is significantly influenced by this psychological element.

FACTORS AFFECTING PSYCHOLOGICAL ADJUSTMENT

The factors that affect the ability to cope with cancer and the ensuing change in a person's quality of life are both psychological and medical. The psychological factors stem from several sources: the cultural context and societal views of the disease; the patient's ability to handle stress; availability of emotional and social supports through family, friends, work associates, and community groups, as well as financial support for the necessary treatment. The time of life at which cancer strikes and how the disease and its treatment affect the person's ability to meet life goals are also important. Finally, psychological and emotional support from the physician and the health care team plays an important role.

ABILITY TO HANDLE STRESSES

As a general rule, those who have been able to cope well with major personal loss or illness in the past, and face crises with courage and resolution, will probably deal with cancer in the same way. Those of us who work with cancer patients are often impressed by their strength and courage. Clinical research has suggested that the kind of person who best manages the stresses of cancer is one who feels responsible for maintaining his or her own good health and can be expected to respond to a suspicious symptom of cancer by seeing a doctor and following through with diagnostic tests. The cancer diagnosis causes distress which serves as an impetus to obtain more information about the disease and its treatment by talking with doctors, sometimes seeking a second opinion, reading and talking to others who have had the same disease. This type of patient will have an optimistic outlook and will fight the disease with no tendency toward giving up. He or she also will maintain close contact with family and friends, talking about the illness with them, expressing and sharing both positive and negative feelings.

Patients who cope well will develop a sense of humor, particularly about things that cannot be changed. This psychologically strong individual will have used the same methods of coping with crises in the past. Perhaps reliance on religion and prayer was an important factor in past crises, or maintaining a physically compatible workload, or indulging more often in a favorite but less taxing recreation such as reading, improving a chess game, or visiting with friends and family.

It is important that each day provide pleasure, however limited, to counter the hours consumed by illness and treatment. Although it is not known what positive effect affection, hope, love, joy, and laughter have on the body's function and disease, we do know that they are tied to a far better psychological outlook that could possibly contribute to a better medical outlook.

In contrast, denying the seriousness of the illness, rejecting recommended treatment, and relying on alcohol or smoking to reduce tensions are not constructive ways of coping with a serious illness. Such attitudes complicate the picture and signal the need for professional psychological counseling.

EMOTIONAL SUPPORT: IMPORTANCE OF FAMILY AND FRIENDS

Most individuals who develop cancer are part of a family who must also learn to cope with the disease because of their love and concern for the patient. In this way, cancer is a "family disease," meaning it affects every member of the group. Someone with no family or close friends who must face the stress alone is far more vulnerable to psychological deterioration. At times, close friends can fill the gap of an absent or lost family. The ability of those immediately around the cancer patient to offer support is a critical factor in adaptation. Furthermore, some studies have shown that when the "significant other" person has his or her own help in coping, this may also help the patient to cope better.

The family unit is the nuclear structure in which we begin our lives and which most of us continue to live in or near throughout adulthood. Families have life and stress management styles just as do individuals. These interpersonal relationships range from warm, helpful, supportive and empathetic families, to those that exist in the best of times in chronic conflict, which will probably grow worse in the face of cancer.

Part of the psychological evaluation of the patient includes identifying how the family can help or hinder. The helpful, supportive family encourages and maintains close communication about the illness and treatment with the patient and the physician. Many physicians aid this process by insisting that all conversations about the patient's condition take place with the patient and a family member present. This encourages discussion of the facts when the physician leaves and eliminates the creation of secrets and the growth of misconceptions.

The supportive family understands the low-spirited moments which are a necessary part of adaptation to a life-threatening situation, at the same time enabling an overall outlook of hope and optimism to dominate. Even if the patient is poor at managing stress, a strong, close family can promote a higher level of adaptation to illness-related problems. The inclusion of grandparents or other relatives who can perform some functions for the ill person is even more helpful. The burdens of child care, home maintenance, hospitalization and insurance forms and, more importantly, providing the financial support needed for continued treatment, can be greatly reduced when loved ones share the load.

Friends from work, social groups, and church or community groups may want to help, and their emotional response is also very important if it provides the patient with support. The patient's first contacts with close friends following diagnosis constitutes the earliest reentry into normal activities. The ill person is apt to be self-conscious and a little uneasy about the possible reception, since others know about the cancer diagnosis. It is even harder when the patient is not sure and must begin to decide who and what he or she wants to tell. Healthy individuals must be aware of the significance of their behavior in the presence of a cancer patient, and there are some basic guidelines to follow.

Those who are visiting or dealing with a cancer patient should act naturally and unselfconsciously, behaving just as they would have before the illness. If a kiss or handshake was part of the greeting before, be sure to carry it out in the same way, for the patient will be sensitive to possible signs of rejection. A warm, friendly smile is important, but not a jocular approach that pretends the person has not been ill. Allow the patient to lead the conversation, and be available to follow the discussion even when it leads to painful thoughts. Patients generally choose friends carefully for this kind of discussion of normal worries. One should not be fearful and turn away from such discussions but should feel privileged to be permitted to share these inner thoughts. All evidence suggests that sharing and exploring worries and depressed feelings with a trusted friend helps lessen the pain. It is not necessary for the listener to feel that he or she should be responsible for solving the problems or cheering up the patient. Just being there, listening and understanding, is the most important thing.

If the patient is in the hospital, always knock before entering to ensure his or her right to privacy. The ability to maintain personal integrity and dignity in the unnatural hospital environment is an important aspect of control with which friends can help. This is a world that otherwise can make patients feel powerless. The visitor should sit in a chair, relax, and listen, rather than stand over the patient or sit on the bed. Time may go slowly after "how are you?" and twenty minutes may be a long visit for a fatigued patient. Talking about the illness is part of opening the conversation, but don't forget to mention who won the ball game, what concerts you've attended, mutual friends, the office, and other news of the outside world to provide food for thought after you leave.

AGE AND TIME OF CANCER DIAGNOSIS: HOW IT AFFECTS ACTIVITIES

Cancer patients are often heard to say that the disease couldn't have occurred at a worse time in life. The fact is that there is never a good time to be struck with a serious illness. Life is filled with milestone tasks that are part of normal development from infancy to old age, and cancer and its treatment may interfere and disrupt these anticipated activities, forcing the patient to adapt and often to alter life goals as a part of rehabilitation.

The infant and very young child who has cancer will experience the interruption of developmental steps such as sitting, crawling, beginning to say words, or interacting with the familiar faces of parents. The cancer causes a slowing of growth or regression to an earlier stage of development. The new, strange faces of physicians and nurses accentuate anxiety and increase insecurity. Observing as normal a relationship with parents as possible, maintaining continuity of staff, and instituting play to stimulate developmental achievements can help reduce the psychological impact. Happily, small children who are cured of cancer often have no later memory of the illness and few emotional scars, and go on to become normal, healthy adults.

The adolescent and young adult attempting to achieve independence from family and find peer acceptance will have a different reaction to cancer. This is the time of life when personal identity is being developed and school or early career goals are sought. Dating and interaction with potential mates is also of key importance at this age. Cancer treatment, which can cause hair loss, thinness, and school or work absence, is difficult to endure at an age when one's body is already changing due to puberty and when simply being "different" is so painful. The threat to sexual attractiveness and interruption of school or work are serious blows to the young adult which require attention, and at times counseling, to help prepare for potentially permanent losses such as infertility.

Middle-aged and elderly adults who have reached their career peak and now face the rewards of retirement will find cancer very unwelcome, although it is more apt to occur in later years. Concerns at this age center around financial and job security and avoiding dependence on offspring. Very often the older cancer patient has lost a spouse or friends to cancer or other tragedy, and may lack the important and necessary support network for facing this illness. Counseling on the living situation and finances, and help in obtaining treatment are important in fostering positive adaptation. Counseling can also offer emotional reassurance and aid the patient in constructing new sources of support.

PSYCHOLOGICAL SUPPORT FROM PHYSICIANS AND STAFF

The last variable in psychosocial adjustment, and certainly not the least important, is how comfortable the patient feels asking questions of the doctor, and how willing the doctor is to explain what is happening. Several studies show that the more patients feel they know and trust their doctors, the more apt they are to take prescribed medication. Trust in the doctor, belief that what is prescribed is likely to help, and recognition that not taking the medication may lead to worsening of the disease are important in the acceptance and continuation of treatment, as found in a collaborative study by the Psychosocial Collaborative Oncology Group.

The side effects of cancer treatment, particularly nausea and vomiting from chemotherapy, vary from minor to quite severe. Patients are appreciative when they sense that the nurse who administers the treatment is doing her best to minimize side effects, even if the effort is not completely effective. They are also willing to endure the sometimes arduous treatment if they feel that the staff is concerned about them as individuals. The sense of disappointment with staff members who appear uninterested is real and should be made known, when possible, for they can sometimes forget how keenly sensitive patients are. Hospitals and doctors that attend to these aspects of care and encourage patients to provide observations as a way to improve services recognize that medical attention involves more than just technology. Machines and medicines represent the science of medicine, but effective human interaction represents the art of medicine.

MEDICAL FACTORS

Although cancer is thought of as a single disease, it is actually more than a hundred diseases varying in cause, treatment, and body location. Certain tumors are more common at different ages. Testicular tumors, for example, may occur in young men around the years when sexual fertility, marriage, and childbearing are critical concerns. Any discussion with the physician before surgery or chemotherapy at this age must therefore include information about the effects of treatment on sexual performance and fertility. Often sperm-banking can assure the potential for parenthood if desired at a later time, and should be offered if risk of sterility exists.

For many people the most frightening aspect of cancer is the prospect of intolerable and uncontrollable pain. Pain is not nearly so common a symptom of cancer as is popularly believed. One study at Memorial Sloan-Kettering Hospital in New York City found that 40 percent of patients had some degree of pain but that in none was it uncontrollable. One major problem in pain management is the patient's fear of addiction. This worry is exaggerated in people's minds, perhaps because they know many of the painkillers are narcotics that are frequently described in the news as dangerous drugs. Experience has shown that true addiction in cancer patients is quite rare, and patients generally reduce or discontinue pain medications without difficulty when the pain subsides.

As physicians become better educated in pain control, they are able to use the same range of drugs with increasing skill. Doctors have recognized that patients with cancer are very responsible in use of painkillers. Giving the patient enough medication on a regular schedule rather than waiting until pain returns and requiring that the patient ask for it as needed (or "prn") helps prevent anxiety and promote better pain control. (See Chapter 12, "Cancer and Pain.") With the patient's participation in noting effectiveness and timing, the proper drug can be prescribed and regulated with excellent results.

Like many other diseases that threaten life, cancer varies in outcome. This constitutes one of the most troublesome psychological problems of the disease—living with uncertainty. Against this shifting background are the day-to-day changes that the illness may bring, causing emotional ups and downs. Psychological adaptation requires a flexible day-to-day readjustment to each individual illness as it follows its natural course. However, these uncertainties can be reduced by making sure that the best course of evaluation, diagnosis, and treatment is being followed.

CONSULTATION WITH A PHYSICIAN

Despite the importance of prompt consultation with a physician when a possible symptom or sign of cancer develops, the first visit is delayed for an average of nine months. Patients who have a personal physician whom they feel comfortable calling generally delay less than those who have no family doctor. Even if the word cancer is not used when testing a suspicious lump or lesion, most people can sense what is being done, and sometimes patients are driven away by fear before the workup is finished. A sensitive assessment of the patient by family and physician should be made as quickly as possible to avoid such a possibility. The physician should avoid delay in reporting the diagnosis to the patient and family, since waiting can be agonizing.

TELLING AND HEARING THE DIAGNOSIS

What should the patient expect when the diagnosis is, in fact, cancer? Having the diagnosis explained by a consultant whom the patient has not known long may be difficult. The doctor who knows the patient personally can take into account how he or she will react and will be the best judge of how to present the diagnosis (see Chapter 6, "The Treatment Team"). It is helpful to have a spouse or a close friend or relative present to hear the discussion, as sometimes patients get nervous or confused when faced with such information and forget what was said. Some doctors tape-record the discussion and give a cassette to the patient to play at home and discuss with family members at a calmer moment. Patients should not be embarrassed by a display of emotions that might include tears upon hearing a diagnosis of cancer. The patient and relatives should request clarification of the medical findings in simple, lay terms and, if necessary, ask for a diagram to be drawn for clarity. No question is too simple, obvious, or trivial. One session may not be enough to absorb the information, and a second meeting for further discussion may be necessary.

Few patients today continue to deny the facts; this was more typical in earlier days when both doctors and patients were less direct in talking about cancer. However, there are still patients who need to diminish the emotional impact of the diagnosis, temporarily or permanently, by not accepting what the doctor says. This, too, should be respected and the denial should not be punctured initially by pushing the facts. Once the information is given, those patients who choose to deal obliquely with the facts may do so. It is equally unwise for a physician to lie about a cancer, saying it is not present when it is. The doctor would run the risk of destroying the trust in his or her relationship with the patient. This trust is essential to maintain the maximum participation and cooperation from the patient that is necessary for the treatment of a lengthy illness.

Doctors have an obligation to be honest, but that does not carry with it the right to be cruel. Many patients given a limited life sentence like "six months to live" have long outlived the life expectancy for that type of cancer. No one can reliably predict how long a patient will live. Factors that control cancer growth are poorly understood, and new treatments are being developed with over fifty effective chemotherapy drugs now in existence. These points support a realistic but optimistic outlook that can help the patient through a difficult time of uncertainty and illness.

Once a patient has accepted the diagnosis of cancer, a period of emotional turmoil characterized by anxiety, depression, poor sleeping, little appetite, poor concentration, and perhaps the inability to carry out daily activities often follows. Deep anger may be a part of the picture, with questions of "Why me?" This turmoil diminishes as treatment plans evolve and confidence increases that something can be done. Most patients alter their response to the crisis within a couple of weeks. If the emotional response is severe or prolonged, however, a psychiatric consultation should be requested. Mild tranquilizers and counseling may be needed for anxiety or depression related to the crisis, and unless the person has had a previous psychiatric disorder it is unusual to see any serious psychological deterioration. If the patient has had prior psychiatric disturbance, however, it may be triggered again by the illness and should be watched for. It is important to remember that some degree of distress aids in adapting to the information. Knowing that such a reaction may occur helps a relative to know what to expect. And it is reassuring to the individual going through it to know that "I'm not losing my mind; other people feel this way too." It is also reassuring to know that the distress will pass.

TREATMENT

Once the diagnosis has been discussed, the proposed treatment plan and all of the possible alternatives should be explored with the patient, the family, and the physician. The fears associated with cancer should be addressed at this time as should the risks and benefits of each type of treatment. Questions of cost, pain, appearance, sex life, hair loss, social participation, and professional activity should be discussed as well.

The first treatment for cancer is often surgery, which is still seen by most specialists as the surest cure for many forms of the disease. The surgeon can be expected to describe the procedure, the probable postoperative course, and the risks and benefits of the surgery. Questions about anesthesia, postoperative pain, recovery, and any long-term limitations are important. A good outlook is best attained by a frank discussion that establishes a patient-surgeon relationship that is satisfactory and based on trust and optimism. Distrust only adds to the psychological burden.

Surgery is often followed by chemotherapy, radiation therapy, or other treatments to be sure that any remaining malignant tissue is destroyed. The same principles apply in finding a radiation therapist or medical oncologist as in finding a surgeon. Generally this specialist will be recommended by your physician. The radiation therapist or medical oncologist —internists who have special training in the medical treatments of cancer —will outline the therapy, including possible side effects. The more the patient knows about what is being planned, the less anxiety will be generated. The planned treatment is outlined in a special hospital permission form that is to be signed by the patient, physician, and a witness.

Chemotherapy and radiation therapy, in contrast to surgery, are treatments that must be taken over weeks to months, requiring regular visits to the clinic or doctor's office which interrupt the normal daily routine. Both treatments produce fatigue which, in the case of some chemotherapies, can be severe. Close contact with the physician and nurse can help to control these undesirable side effects. It is important to have a nurse or doctor to contact outside office hours, since side effects can be frightening. Knowing how to monitor for signs of infection or obtaining a wig before hair loss starts are ways of being prepared and having a solution to the problem before it occurs.

PROTOCOL TREATMENT

Over the past twenty years, advances in cancer treatment have been made by treating the same tumors with the same prescribed regimen. This has allowed careful assessment of the results and evaluation of the treatment against a particular cancer. Treatment through an investigative protocol is a method of developing newer and better cancer treatments by comparing the best-known treatment for cancer in a clinical trial to a newer regimen with the potential to be even more effective. The cures for acute lymphocytic leukemia, Hodgkin's disease, and testicular cancers were obtained by this technique. These investigational therapies are closely supervised by the Food and Drug Administration (FDA) and the National Cancer Institute (NCI) and can only be performed on patients who have signed a lengthy consent form. (See Chapter 9, "Experimental Treatments and Research.")

These studies are usually performed in university hospitals, although efforts by the NCI are now under way to make these new investigational treatments, largely anticancer drugs, available in community hospitals so that more of the population can benefit from new findings. Studies suggest that most patients decide to accept an investigational treatment because they trust the doctor, believe it will help, and recognize that their illness may get worse if they don't follow this course.

UNPROVEN REMEDIES

One needless tragedy for some cancer patients is that fear of cancer and its known treatments can be so great that they fall prey to quack cancer "cures" that promise no undesirable side effects. These unproven cures fit the present national trend toward holistic health and most claim a "naturalistic" or "self-healing" approach. Known remedies are often described as "poisons" and "worse than the disease." Sadly, this view may be believed at the very time when proper treatment could be curative, and when delay has a dangerous effect. Quack cures are usually supported by devoted cults who do not insist on evidence of efficacy but instead depend on anecdotal and unsubstantiated stories of cures. Patients and their families who grasp at straws in the face of crises are easy prey for those who exploit these fears for sometimes enormous financial gain.

There seems to be a new unproven cure every ten years. Krebiozen, popular in the 1960s, was replaced by laetrile in the 1970s. Laetrile, a substance derived from apricot pits, also became the vehicle for promoting the individual's right to whatever treatment he or she desired. The FDA currently will not permit the sale of any drug that has no proven efficacy. The popular outcry forced a national clinical trial, run by the NCI, in which patients with advanced cancer were given laetrile and closely monitored. There was no prolongation of life as a result of this substance. The argument that organized medicine fears competition and suppresses potential cures that originate as home remedies is untrue. The NCI has long maintained a division that experiments with roots, herbs, salves, plants, and animal tissues and tests them systematically in mice for activity in fighting cancer. Some active anticancer agents have originated from this source, and any proposed treatment can and should be put through this testing procedure.

Other unauthorized cancer treatments that are more difficult to assess are those based on "mind over cancer," such as the Simonton technique. This is a series of exercises that combine relaxation, group counseling, and visual imagery to attain a sense of mastery by "doing something to help." The activities are said to help patients control cancer by mental imagery and by correcting personality patterns that caused the cancer in the first place. Since biofeedback is known to be capable of altering blood pressure and brain waves, and since emotional distress affects hormone levels, the suggestion is made that immune states, and thus cancer growth, can be controlled in this manner.

Patients are exultant at the outset when they begin the exercises. Fortunately, most do not accept the idea that their personality helped to cause the disease, but rather concentrate on the possible efficacy of activities in controlling cancer growth. Some patients who are already feeling guilty about not going to the doctor sooner or who tend to blame themselves for anything that goes wrong are vulnerable to being made worse by the Simonton technique. They should be identified and aided in avoiding depression and guilt. Another hazard is that patients may become so convinced that the "mind over cancer" method will work that they will forgo traditional medical treatment and jeopardize their chances of cure.

The American Cancer Society maintains a committee on Unproven Methods of Cancer Treatment. They reported no proven efficacy, by the research data provided, for the Simonton approach in controlling tumor growth. The possibility that emotions can affect the central nervous system hormones and the immune system is intriguing and currently under active study. However, the area requires much research and until more is known, patients and families should be aware that no scientific data exist to support visual imagery as a treatment for cancer. It can, however, be a useful form of intervention to treat accompanying psychological distress. (See also Chapter 13, "Questionable Cancer Remedies.")

ENDING TREATMENT

Rehabilitation is the important stage which comes after the treatment, whether it be surgery, chemotherapy, radiation, or a combination of therapies. A positive mental outlook with early return to normal activities is critical to returning to the stage of life and lifestyle enjoyed before the illness. Physical rehabilitation must be accompanied by psychological rehabilitation. The time following head and neck surgery or amputation of a limb or breast can be particularly stressful. It is normal to go through a few weeks of feeling depressed, crying easily, being irritable, and avoiding contact with friends and family. Psychiatrists recognize this as a stage of normal "grieving" for something that has been lost. Sometimes families get frightened and insist on a "stiff upper lip" attitude, which does not allow the normal emotional healing to occur.

It is both acceptable and necessary to mourn a loss. Psychiatrists do begin to be concerned, however, when the mourning continues beyond a few weeks with no sign of improvement or a return to normal activities and family role. Counseling can help at this stage, and it should not be viewed as a weakness to seek it out. A small amount of psychological help can go a long way toward better mental health. When a crisis such as cancer surgery is handled well, one often feels stronger mentally, and family members sometimes become closer, appreciating one another more.

Another psychological reaction patients may experience is a second period of depression at the completion of an extended chemotherapy or radiotherapy program. While one would expect patients to be pleased that the treatment is over, the fear about cancer and the feeling of being left on one's own when no longer coming regularly for treatments may generate a transitory return of anxiety or depression. This is a normal and common reaction which will go away as the patient gains confidence and feels less worried about the recurrence of the disease. Patients often require more frequent contact with the doctor or nurse by telephone or office to allay these fears or concerns. (For a more detailed discussion, see Chapter 11, "Rehabilitation of the Cancer Patient.")

WHAT IS IT LIKE TO BE CURED?

When a person has pneumonia it is generally treated, recovery is complete, and the experience can be forgotten. Cancer is different, however, for although it can be treated and recovery can be complete, one can never forget the experience. The fear of recurrence can be so great as to be psychologically debilitating. Cure is assumed for most cancers after five years. However, it is normal for anyone who has had cancer to have fear or temporary panic when an ache or pain, otherwise ignored, occurs. Confidence grows as time goes by, but finding ways of coping with the fear of recurrence is an important part of rehabilitation.

Cancer is a "family illness." When one member has cancer everyone in the family feels the stresses. A family may try to overprotect the patient when he or she has been cured and is trying to forget about it. Families must be encouraged to "let go" after treatment and allow the patient, especially a teenager, to live as normally as possible.

It is also normal for the cured patient to maintain a close bond to the hospital staff and fellow patients who went through the treatment with him or her. These ties are helpful, not harmful, and should be encouraged. A painful side for the cured patient is the memory of those who did not do well during treatment. Often families discourage these contacts to protect the patient from the loss of patient-friends. It is normal to mourn these friends and even at times feel guilty about having survived when others did not. These feelings can be channeled into life goals and a keener appreciation of self, others, and pleasures of everyday life.

RECURRENCE

The hope of a successful cancer cure is at times dashed by evidence of recurrence. This event requires significant psychological adaptation to the idea of more treatment and the fact that the cancer is still present. It is wise to remember that new treatment methods are now far better able to control cancer for many years, even after recurrence. The psychological reaction of anxiety and depression, even the inability to function normally for a week or two, are all evidence that the mind is adjusting to unpleasant and painful news. Medical oncologists are generally the proper physicians for patients with recurrent cancer, and will work closely with the patient's primary physician.

PROGRESSIVE ILLNESS

Much of the publicity associated with cancer has been about those patients who do not survive, rather than those who do, and this has led to more pessimism than necessary. Still, maximal support must be given to the patient with progressive cancer. Today much more effort is being made to treat these patients at home. Nurses who can provide support services are available, and mobile vans have become part of some hospitals' services. When this help is provided to the family, including psychological support and the security of a telephone number for advice and aid around the clock, many families and patients prefer the home-care approach to remaining in the hospital.

There is a strong human tendency to protect children and not let them know that a grandparent, parent, or sibling is seriously ill. This is never wise, since children are often aware of the illness without being told, and keeping it a secret makes it all the more frightening to the child who may think, "It is so bad nobody will talk about it." Children fare better when they know the facts, however grim, since this allows for adaptation and psychological preparation.

Children can be forgotten members in a family caught up in a serious illness of one of its members. Watching them for nightmares, bed-wetting, or fear of going to school is important. Sudden truancy, stealing, or refusal to visit the sick person should be treated not punitively but with compassion, while recognizing that it is important to understand the child's reaction to the illness of someone close.

Hospice units similar to those in Europe can be operated either independently or in association with a hospital. They offer both home care and in-hospice beds that provide care aimed at maximal comfort, control of pain and symptoms, plus psychological support for those with chronic disease. Facilities for the care of chronic cancer patients are continuing to evolve and improve. This alternative type of care can be explored by referral through local chapters of the American Cancer Society.

Available financial support for families and patients to explore alternatives to hospital care has been inadequate. A recent evaluation of hospice units has resulted in the establishment of reimbursement for this service through Medicare for patients over sixty-five. Better insurance plans and home-related care would encourage more families to attempt it. A change in emphasis in oncology centers toward the development of active home care programs would also be helpful. Oncology nurses are particularly adept in management of pain through home visits, with telephone consultation from the responsible physician who has managed the patient through his or her illness, and can offer most appropriate medical and emotional support.

PSYCHOLOGICAL SUPPORT

Psychological support for cancer patients has been increasingly recognized as an important aspect of care. Research in this area is beginning to take its place alongside biomedical research in cancer. Counseling is offered by a range of staff members associated with patient care: physicians, nurses, social workers, clergymen, and rehabilitation specialists. Support from the doctor providing the medical care is central. The nurse or radiation therapist technician who gives treatments can also observe the patient closely and offer counseling. Social workers are an excellent source of help, as can be a clergyman, if the patient wishes. A supportive, empathetic approach should be taken by all staff members, including the receptionist and secretary and anyone who comes in contact with the patient.

Self-help groups have become an increasingly important source of support. They are focused in one of two ways: either providing help for all patients at the same stage of cancer, such as Make Today Count and The Cured Cancer Club, or offering support for patients with specific disabilities or physical losses as a result of treatment, such as Reach to Recovery for breast cancer patients, Lost Chord societies for laryngectomees and their families, and Ostomy clubs for those who have had a colostomy or ileostomy. Some groups have been organized according to the patients' ages, such as teenage cancer groups. Others offer mutual support for relatives or surviving spouses of cancer victims. All of these groups share the common goal of bringing together people who have similar problems in order to seek solutions to the psychological and physical difficulties they encounter as a result of cancer. The consensus is that, far from being detrimental as some psychologists feared in the past, groups for cancer patients provide important support which can only be appreciated by those who have shared the same experience.

A new program has evolved at Memorial Sloan-Kettering Cancer Center in New York in which veteran cancer patients donate their time as volunteer counselors to patients suffering from the same type of cancer. Administered through the Psychiatry Service, which assumes responsibility for their work, this program is jointly supported by the Social Work and Volunteer departments. The program provides the opportunity for the counselor to gain emotional strength while giving needed psychological support to others.

In certain cases, psychotherapeutic intervention by mental health professionals is necessary. This type of care, usually based on a crisis-intervention model, is aimed at helping the patient retain a sense of self-esteem and worth, while offering emotional support with insight into the problems. Counseling increasingly includes a friend or relative who is key to the emotional well-being of the patient.

Cancer and its treatment often produce effects on the nervous system such as an unexpected personality change, marked mood changes, or confusion. Such reactions cannot be attributed solely to the stresses of illness, and the patient should be examined by a physician. If a psychological consultation is required, an examination by a neurologist or psychiatrist may be recommended by the primary physician in order to provide adequate evaluation of medical versus emotional causes. It is better to obtain an evaluation when symptoms first appear and when treatment can be instituted most effectively, than to wait in the hope that the condition will correct itself.

PSYCHOTROPIC DRUGS

When psychological problems are severe, treatment may include crisis-intervention psychotherapy combined with minor or major tranquilizers. These medications are effective against anxiety, some depressed states, and recurrences of prior psychiatric disturbances. Experience with cancer patients has shown that many feel that taking a tranquilizer is a sign of weakness or that they may become addicted. This is similar to fear of painkillers, and is equally unfounded. Marked anxiety tends to occur in the face of crises, and a tranquilizer may reduce the distress. Taken at regular intervals over two to three days, the symptoms of jitteriness, fear, and loss of appetite or sleep may disappear and the drug can be reduced or discontinued. A new generation of short-acting antianxiety medications are safe when taken as directed by the doctor and can appreciably reduce fears in patients waiting to have a biopsy, starting a new treatment, or anticipating adverse reactions to chemotherapy.

Sleep, which is often difficult for cancer patients due to fear and depression, can be restored through the use of antidepressant drugs or bedtime hypnotic medication. The result will be sound sleep and an increased sense of well-being during the day. Drugs for relief of both pain and psychological distress are underused in cancer patients. Abuse is a rarity and, with proper management, is less of a concern than are those patients who insist on "being a hero."

BEHAVIORAL APPROACHES

Behavior modification is gaining in use and acceptance and appears to be effective in controlling anxiety, tension, pain, nausea and vomiting. Relaxation exercises, hypnosis and mental imagery aimed at reducing tension and distress are part of this technique. Relaxation exercises coupled with positive suggestions are adjunct to pain management by drugs, and most pain clinics at major hospitals offer these treatments.

About one in four patients shows a conditioned response of nausea and vomiting in which the symptoms occur before receiving chemotherapy. Behavior modification techniques have successfully reduced this response and are currently under continued investigation. Conditioned nausea and vomiting occur after several chemotherapy treatments (usually not under four) and especially in patients receiving drugs with a propensity for producing vomiting. Many patients fear "I'm losing my mind," without recognizing that this conditioned response of nausea and vomiting is the same as the condition Pavlov noted in his dogs who salivated at the sound of a bell. It is a common, normal response, currently being widely studied both to control it and, finally, to prevent it.

SUMMING UP

In summarizing the major points of this chapter, we can offer the following rules for living with cancer:

1. There are normal fears associated with cancer, namely the five D's: fear of death, disfigurement, disability, dependence, and disruption of key relationships. These normal concerns can be successfully managed by the patient and family by recognizing them and using techniques that promote the best psychological adjustment.

2. It is normal for the patient to be upset, especially when cancer is first diagnosed. The distress abates as the person develops coping techniques to confront the problems and attempts to solve them. This is facilitated by open communication, the enlisting of support from significant others, the minimization of loss of activity and function threatened by illness or treatment through careful planning, rehabilitation, and compassionate care.

3. Unproven remedies and quack cures are tempting snares that can lead to delay at a time when early treatment is most efficacious, thus reducing chances of cure.

4. Finishing treatment carries with it much the same increase in fears, and even depressed feelings, as beginning it does. This normal increase in concern that the cancer may return should be recognized and may require more frequent visits or phone calls to the doctor for a few weeks.

5. Like other serious diseases, cancer can be cured, it can recur and become chronic, or it can become progressive. Cured cancer patients have their own psychological concerns and fears, which should be recognized: fear of recurrence, of aches and pains, and concerns with special meaning for survival.

6. Recurrence of cancer requires a new adaptation to disease and treatment. Treatment by a physician who is trusted and who can combine psychological support with medical care is important.

7. Serious illness in a family member is reflected by stresses in all members. Children are particularly vulnerable and may manifest their distress in ways that are not immediately recognized as related to the illness. All family members should be monitored, especially those with previous psychological disturbance.

8. Psychological support is increasingly available and is now more often recognized as an important part of total treatment. It is important that all members of the treatment team provide counseling and support. Professional help should be available for any cancer patient or family member. Self-help groups using fellow or veteran patients who have had the same illness or treatment are valuable sources of support.

9. Psychotropic drugs and behavioral medicine techniques are both useful in overcoming psychological stress. The use of a tranquilizer during a crisis period should not be considered a sign of weakness. Hypnosis, relaxation, and mental imagery are all techniques that aid in reducing pain, anxiety, and anticipatory nausea and vomiting associated with chemotherapy.

10. Psychological distress during cancer may be compared to a roller coaster ride, with brief periods of distress that usually abates as the person returns to more normal situations. Psychological support from family and community resources should be enlisted.

Above all, it is important to recognize that people can and do live with cancer. Good coping strategies, support from close relatives and friends, and competent, compassionate medical help all are vital elements. An optimistic outlook, coupled with prompt and appropriate treatment, offers the best recipe for successfully living with cancer.

ADDITIONAL READING

Alsop, Stewart. *Stay of Execution.* New York: Harper & Row, 1973.

Cassell, Eric. *The Healer's Art.* New York and Philadelphia: J. B. Lippincott Co., 1979.

Chemotherapy and You—A Guide to Self-help During Treatment. Bethesda, Md.: National Cancer Institute (NIH Publication No. 81-1136), 1980.

Coping with Cancer: A Resource for the Health Professional. Bethesda, Md.: National Cancer Institute, 1980.

Proceedings of the American Cancer Society's Third National Conference on Human Values and Cancer. Washington, D.C., April 23–25, 1981.

Radiation Therapy and You—A Guide to Self-help During Treatment. Bethesda, Md.: National Cancer Institute (NIH Publication No. 80-2227), 1980.

Springarn, Natalie. *Hanging in There: Living Well on Borrowed Time.* New York: Stein & Day, 1982.

Taking Time: Support for People with Cancer and the People Who Care About Them. Bethesda, Md.: National Cancer Institute, 1980.

The Psychological Impact of Cancer. New York: American Cancer Society, Professional Education Publication, 1954.

Weisman, Avery. *Coping with Cancer.* New York: McGraw-Hill Book Co., 1979.

5

Modern Cancer Therapy

Vincent T. DeVita, Jr., M.D.,
Susan M. Hubbard, and Eleanor M. Rice

INTRODUCTION

We often hear that cancer is the disease people fear most. It has been used in our society as a metaphor for death, but in a way this is a strange paradox because cancer, although often fatal, is today one of the more curable chronic diseases. Fully 58 percent of more than the 1.2 million Americans who will develop any kind of malignant growth this year can expect to be cured using existing forms of treatment. Although they are excluded from the survival data, virtually all of the 400,000 patients with cancer of the skin and *in situ* cancer of the cervix can be cured, and approximately 50 percent of the remaining 800,000 patients with the more serious forms of cancer are fully curable using surgery, radiation therapy, and chemotherapy alone or in combination. When we use the term "cure" we mean that cancer patients who have been treated can expect to be alive and free of evidence of disease for five or more years and have the same life expectancy as other individuals of the same age and sex in the same time period who have never had cancer.

Although tumors were described as early as 1600 B.C., the ability to cure cancer is a relatively recent achievement (Table 6). Before 1900, few patients with serious cancers survived for long periods following the development of their disease. Around the turn of the century, ether became available for general anesthesia and antiseptic methods were introduced, making the development of cancer surgery possible. During the same period X rays were discovered and identified as a potential means of treating localized cancers. The development of anticancer drugs following World War II enabled physicians to treat patients with advanced cancer that, because it had spread throughout the body, could not be completely removed surgically or treated by the administration of X rays.

Prospects for complete cure and prolonged survival are steadily improving because of significant advances in our knowledge about the biology of cancer. Our ability to develop therapies that selectively kill cancer cells has increased dramatically. Researchers have been particularly successful in treating the cancers that occur most often in children and young adults and there has been a marked increase in cures of at least twelve types of cancers, many of which strike this age group (see Table 7). It is also encouraging that since 1970, the rate of death from cancer for older individuals with some of the more common malignancies also has begun to fall and is now on the decline for all patients under the age of fifty-five.

HISTORICAL OVERVIEW OF CANCER THERAPY

Surgery has always been the mainstay of cancer treatment. Surgical removal of a tumor is performed for three reasons: to determine whether or not the tumor is malignant, since some tumors are not; to assure the best chance for cure by removing all or most of the cancer cells if the tumor is malignant; or to determine whether malignant cells have spread to other parts of the body. This information helps the physician decide whether radiation or drugs should be given to kill malignant cells that remain in the body after surgery. The first commonly used surgical procedure based on a firm set of principles was developed in the early 1900s by Dr. William Halsted. He based this surgery on the belief that cancer spreads by first directly invading tissues in the area surrounding the tumor. Because he believed that such extension was the way cancer eventually killed patients, he designed an extensive surgical procedure for women with breast cancer—the radical mastectomy, which removed the entire breast and all of the tissues surrounding it. For women whose cancer was confined to these tissues, this operation did produce cures. As the elements of modern anesthesia, antibiotics, and blood transfusion were incorporated into cancer surgery and as surgical techniques were refined, the cure rate began to climb steadily until 1950, when it leveled off.

Since the lethal effects of X rays on tumors were also discovered just after the turn of the century, the use of radiation was also investigated as a way to kill cancer cells. As with surgery, early techniques were unsophisticated and produced many unpleasant and dangerous side effects. By the 1920s, radiation therapists had discovered that by giving small doses of radiation over a period of time, rather than one large dose, the treatment could be made more tolerable, and could destroy tumor cells without causing irreparable damage to normal surrounding tissues. As scientists developed the ability to generate powerful X rays that penetrated deep into the body and reached deep-seated tumors, cure rates with radiation alone or in combination with surgery began to increase. The impact of radiation therapy on national mortality statistics, however, become apparent only after the 1950s.

By the mid-1920s, with surgery and radiation therapy to treat localized forms of cancer, physicians were able to cure between 20 and 25 percent of cancer patients (see Table 6). With further refinements of surgical and X-ray techniques, this rose to 33 percent by 1950.

During the 1950s, however, the rate of improvement began to plateau and it became clear that new approaches were needed if cure rates were to continue to improve. About this time scientists studying the biology of cancer began to realize that even tiny tumors often shed viable cancer cells into the bloodstream and lymphatic system. They also recognized that these circulating cancer cells were capable of growing in other organs that were distant from the site of the primary tumor, a process known as metastasis, or the development of secondary deposits of tumors in organs distant from their original site. These secondary deposits of cells as they grow and form secondary tumors are the usual cause of death of most cancer patients. The existence of these microscopic metastases, which are often present at the time the cancer is diagnosed and are the source of later secondary deposits, gave researchers the critical piece of information to understand why treatments were not always effective in patients who appeared to have truly localized cancer. Another approach was needed to develop a therapy capable of reaching small amounts of undetectable metastatic tumor cells that had spread to other parts of the body.

By the early 1950s scientists had discovered antibiotic drugs, which could selectively kill organisms that caused previously fatal infectious diseases like malaria and tuberculosis. These breakthroughs stimulated cancer researchers to search for chemicals that would selectively kill cancer in a similar manner.

It is essential to know a few facts about cell biology in order to understand how anticancer treatments, especially drugs, work. We have three types of cells in our bodies: static, expanding, and renewing. In normal individuals, static cells, such as muscle and nerve tissue, lose their ability to divide and grow after they have reached a specific size, determined by hereditary and environmental factors. If damaged or lost, these cells are irreplaceable, because the cells have lost their capacity to reproduce.

The expanding cells of the body stop growing when the organ or tissue reaches its normal adult size, but if the tissue is damaged or removed, the cells are able to "switch on" and grow again. The liver is a good example of an organ formed by expanding cells. If a part of it is removed or damaged through illness, the remaining liver cells can begin to divide and grow until the liver once again reaches normal size. Cells of the kidney and certain glands that produce hormones also have this ability to expand in size.

Renewing cells are those that have a short life span and are continually lost and replaced at regular intervals. Cells forming the skin, hair, the lining of the intestinal tract, and blood are all constantly replenished as they become old and die normally, or are injured or killed by trauma or disease. Tissues made up of renewing cells seem to have an internal feedback mechanism that maintains a balance between cells that are dying and new cells that are developing to replace them. While the rapid turnover of these cells resembles cancer growth, the ability to obey signals to stop growing distinguishes them from cancer.

Unlike any of these three cell types, cancer cells appear to lack the control mechanism that switches off the growth of normal cells. Because cancers are composed of cells that continue to grow without restraint, they impair the ability of adjacent normal-tissue cells to function by crowding and compressing them and by competing for nutrients. Although cancer cells do not grow faster than normal cells, they do divide more often. Thus at any given moment there is a higher proportion of cancer cells in the growth process, which increases the total cell population and causes the tumor to grow in size.

The discovery of the anticancer effects of two chemicals, nitrogen mustard and, later, methotrexate, helped stimulate the development of cancer drugs. The anticancer effects of nitrogen mustard were discovered during World War II under unusual circumstances. An explosion of mustard gases occurred in Naples, Italy, and physicians observed that, as an aftermath of this explosion, many of the soldiers exposed to those gases developed fatal atrophy or wasting away of the lymph glands, and the blood cells normally formed in the bone marrow disappeared. These observations prompted researchers to test a similar chemical, nitrogen

Table 6. Survival Statistics: Then and Now

1894: Roentgen discovers X rays. Halsted describes the radical mastectomy for breast cancer.

1900: Few cancer patients are curable by any means.

1925: Surgery improves but is "disfiguring." Because of dosing problems, X rays prove "toxic." About 20 percent of cancer patients are curable.

1955: With surgery, blood transfusion, antibiotics, and the development of 250 Kv X-ray units, survival curves for all cancers plateau at about 33 percent. The National Cancer Institute's drug development program is started.

1957: Cobalt 60 units become available. The first linear accelerator is installed at Stanford University.

1960–68: With better X-ray machines, radiation proves less toxic. Survival statistics rise to about 37 percent, including some patients cured by chemotherapy.

1976: The percentage of cured patients rises to 41 percent; this increase reflects continued improvement in radiation therapy and additional numbers of patients curable by chemotherapy alone. Surgery becomes less disfiguring as sophisticated radiation therapy decreases the need for radical surgery.

1980: The National Cancer Institute estimates that 45 percent of all "serious" cancers are curable.

- 1,230,000 new cases of cancer are diagnosed in 1980. (445,000 of these cases were easily curable skin cancer and *in situ* cervical cancer)
- 785,000 new cases of "serious" cancers are diagnosed in 1980.
- Estimates of the number of cancers curable by different modalities in 1981:

Localized disease curable by surgery alone	219,850
Localized disease curable by radiation therapy alone or in addition to surgery	90,000
Locally invasive disease (micrometastases likely to be present) curable by chemotherapy with surgery, radiation therapy, or both	32,000
Curable by chemotherapy alone when visible metastases are present	14,400
Total curable	356,250

Of the 785,000 "serious" cancers, 356,250 or 45 percent curable.

Since 1982: All cancer therapy is less toxic *in toto* because combined
modality therapy (integration of surgery, radiation and/or chemotherapy as primary treatment at diagnosis) allows:

> • *Limb preservation* (in some cases of osteogenic sarcoma)
> • *Less radical surgery for:*

>> Breast cancer
>> Testicular cancer
>> Prostate cancer
>> Rectal cancer
>> Bladder cancer
>> Cervical cancer

> • *Life preservation:*

>> Fifty percent of children with cancer are now curable.
>> National mortality from cancers that occur below age forty-five is
>> decreasing.
>> Disease-specific national mortality for successfully treated can-
>> cers is falling for all age groups in:

>>> Childhood cancers
>>> Testicular cancer
>>> Hodgkin's disease
>>> Diffuse lymphomas
>>> Rectal cancer

> Survival statistics show improvements nationwide during the
> 1970s in:

>> Seven out of ten major cancers in white patients, and
>> Six out of ten major cancers in black patients.

mustard, in the treatment of patients with advanced lymphomas, malignant tumors of the lymphatic system. This was first tried in 1943 in patients at Yale University.

In 1947 research on folic acid, one of the forms of vitamin B, led to the discovery by Dr. Sidney Farber that the administration of folic acid to patients with acute leukemia appeared to accelerate the production of abnormal white blood cells by the bone marrow. He decided, therefore, to administer a folic acid antagonist, a drug that inhibits the effects of folic acid, to a child with acute leukemia, to see if this drug would suppress the production of leukemic cells. The experiment proved effective, and methotrexate was identified as the most useful of the various compounds tried. In the mid-1950s methotrexate was also tested in women with choriocarcinoma, a rare but at that time inevitably fatal cancer of the placenta. Administration of methotrexate produced complete regression of the tumor and cured a significant fraction of women, even some with advanced cases that had spread to the lungs. Today virtually all women who develop this tumor can be cured, using chemotherapy.

Such dramatic results led Congress to appropriate five million dollars in 1955 to establish a cancer drug development program at the National Cancer Institute. Another important advance was the discovery of cancers that could be transplanted into animals, enabling scientists to test potential anticancer drugs in mice before administering them to human beings. The NCI research effort continues today and has played a large part in the development of the more than sixty drugs now available to treat cancer.

Much of the clinical research conducted between 1955 and 1970 was devoted to determining whether chemotherapy, when used alone, could cure patients with advanced cancer that was not curable with surgery or radiation therapy or both. At first only a single anticancer drug was administered at a time. Then studies in animals indicated that combinations of drugs, given in rotation repeatedly in a cyclical fashion, could cure mice with leukemia and would be more likely than single drugs to cure human cancers. This led to the use of drug combinations for leukemia and advanced Hodgkin's disease in the early 1960s. Both diseases, which had been invariably fatal, were now curable in more than half of cases. By 1970, combinations of chemotherapeutic drugs were being used to cure certain patients with advanced forms of cancer that had previously been considered incurable.

WHAT TO EXPECT WHEN A DIAGNOSIS IS MADE

In order for patients and their families to understand how and why one form of treatment has been chosen over another, it is important to understand the general course of events that take place when the diagnosis is

Table 7
TWELVE CANCERS IN WHICH A PERCENTAGE OF PATIENTS
WITH ADVANCED DISEASE CAN BE CURED WITH CHEMOTHERAPY

Choriocarcinoma
Acute lymphocytic leukemia in children
Hodgkin's disease
Diffuse histiocytic lymphoma
Nodular mixed lymphoma
Testicular carcinoma
Ovarian carcinoma
Acute myelogenous leukemia
Wilms' tumor
Burkitt's lymphoma
Embryonal rhabdomyosarcoma
Ewing's sarcoma

cancer. Therefore a brief description of the diagnostic evaluation precedes the discussion of currently available forms of treatment.

A diagnosis made by examining a biopsy of the tumor, called the pathologic diagnosis, and a thorough evaluation of the patient are extremely important in determining the type of treatment that should be prescribed and in making a prognosis, or medical forecast, about the probable course of the disease. For example, research has now shown that breast cancer that is confined to the original primary lump and does not involve the adjacent lymph glands or nodes in the underarm requires surgery less extensive than radical mastectomy. In some cases it can be treated with just a biopsy and radiation therapy to the breast, sometimes followed by chemotherapy, instead of extensive surgery.

STAGING

The extent to which a cancer has spread is described by its stage. Staging is a diagnostic process that provides a concise summary of which tissues and organs the tumor has invaded—in other words, of which stage the disease was reached. Staging assists the physician in determining a prognosis, and knowing the stage helps in planning treatment and evaluating its results. Most staging systems use initials and are based on an assessment of the size of the primary tumor (T), regional lymph node involvement (N), and metastases (M), as shown in Table 8. Roman numerals or their alphabetic counterparts describe the extent to which the cancer has spread to neighboring tissues, lymph nodes, and distant sites.

Staging is important because it tells the physician whether localized

Table 8
CRITERIA FOR STAGING

NUMERICAL SYSTEM	TUMOR, NODE, METASTASIS CLASSIFICATION	ALPHABETIC SYSTEM
I	T = the size and/or degree of local extension by the primary TUMOR	A
II	N = the condition of the regional lymph NODES that provide primary lymphatic drainage from the primary tumor	B
III	M = the presence or absence of distant METASTASES	C

treatment such as surgery or radiation therapy alone is appropriate, or whether a systemic form of treatment is necessary to kill cancer cells that have spread to involve distant organs. By studying the course of disease in past patients, physicians can predict with some degree of accuracy what course the disease is likely to follow. If no metastases, or secondary tumors, are found but the probability of undetectable metastases is known to be high in patients with the stage of disease, another form of therapy may be prescribed in an effort to kill circulating residual cancer cells before they have an opportunity to grow in other organs.

It should not alarm patients if several days to two weeks are devoted to determining the correct diagnosis and stage of disease. An accurate diagnosis and staging evaluation requires a biopsy as well as many laboratory tests, X rays and other procedures. While time-consuming and sometimes uncomfortable, these procedures are essential to determining what, if any, additional treatment is needed after removal of the primary tumor.

Following the staging evaluation, the status of a patient with a small, truly localized tumor would be described in the following way using the TNM system described in Table 8. If a numerical staging system is used, the tumor would be Stage I. If an alphabetical system is used, the tumor would be classified as Stage A—T1N0. A patient with a large primary tumor, no involvement of the regional lymphatics, but evidence of involvement of an organ at a distant site would be described as T3N0M1 (Stage C or Stage III). With some tumors, the presence of widespread involvement of visceral organs is specified in the staging system as Stage IV or Stage D disease.

In situ cervical cancer is a very localized cancer described as $(T_1N_0M_0)$. (*In situ* means that it has remained where it originated and not spread to other sites.) It can be treated with either surgery or radiation therapy, since the cure rate is greater than 98 percent with either treatment. The staging system for cancer of the colon or rectum (colorectal) uses an alphabetical system. Stage A cancer of the colon or large bowel is a term that means that the cancer is very superficial, involves only the lining of the gut and the mucosa, and has not invaded the muscular wall of the bowel. When tumors are found at this stage, there is little risk that cancer has spread to other sites. Approximately 80 percent of patients with Stage A cancer can be cured with surgery alone because the tumor is truly local. In Stage B colorectal cancer the tumor has begun to erode into the bowel wall and the risk that secondary, but undetectable, metastasis has already occurred is significantly higher. The cure rate with surgery alone drops to about 40 percent because such microscopic involvement of other sites, such as the regional lymph glands, cannot be detected, so further treatment with X rays or drugs is not often recommended. In Stage C disease, the bowel wall has eroded and the cancer has gone through it and obviously involved the lymph nodes within the abdomen. The cure rate with surgery alone for Stage C colorectal cancer is normally lower than 20 percent, so chemotherapy is generally recommended in addition to surgery. Stage D colorectal cancer indicates that the tumor has already spread widely and involves the liver and other organs. Systemic treatment with drugs that can kill cancer cells in distant sites offers the only hope for improved survival. The differences in cure rates with different stages at diagnosis emphasize the value of regular examination, such as proctoscopy, to pick up localized tumors, especially in individuals who are forty years of age or older, since the risk increases with age.

Once the cancer has been diagnosed and staged, a decision about treatment is made. There are many factors which both the patient and physician must consider in developing this plan. Besides the type of cancer and its stage, the patient's age, sex, general health, menopausal status if female, and other factors influence the selection of treatment. If the patient's general health is good, the most rigorous course of treatment is wisest if it offers the patient the possibility of a prolonged remission or total cure with a normal life expectancy. If, on the other hand, the patient's condition is weakened by other serious health problems, rigorous treatment may not be advisable. If it is not, the chosen treatment should be aimed at palliation of troublesome symptoms to improve the quality of remaining life.

The patient should expect to continually undergo some of the staging procedures, such as chest and abdominal X rays and CT scans, during and after therapy, because these procedures yield information vital to monitoring the effects of therapy on the cancer. Some of these tests will be used to determine the extent of tumor regression with treatment, while others will be used to measure the severity of toxic effects of the treatment, such as suppression of blood cell production by the bone marrow. While inconvenient or uncomfortable, these tests are essential to determine whether disease has disappeared following treatment, and whether normal tissues have recovered from any untoward effects of treatment. When tests that were positive for the presence of cancer become negative, the physician has proof that tumor regression has occurred, which further influences the overall treatment plan.

If the treatment plan calls for surgery or radiation therapy, or both, followed by chemotherapy, the patient can expect to be cared for during treatment by a variety of specialists in surgery, radiology, and medical oncology. Throughout the course of treatment, the patient should have a primary physician who coordinates the overall treatment plan. (See Chapter 6, "The Treatment Team.") This physician is usually the one who cares for the patient after the treatment is completed and the patient has returned home to resume a normal life. Any physician taking care of a cancer patient should be knowledgeable about the principles of surgery, radiation, and chemotherapy as well as type of tumor and when and how it spreads, in order to increase the patient's chances of cure or long-term survival, as well as to ensure the best quality of life.

MODERN SURGERY IN THE TREATMENT OF CANCER

Approximately 220,000 cases of cancer diagnosed each year are curable by surgery alone. Surgical procedures play a major role in the diagnosis and staging of cancer, so surgeons play a major role in the planning of successful cancer therapy. Increasingly, surgery is being used to reduce the size of a tumor to make it more vulnerable to radiation and chemotherapy. In addition, developments in surgical technique have made it possible for surgeons to graft skin and bone successfully, to rejoin portions of the bowel after a section has been removed, to relieve pain and other distressing symptoms, and to perform reconstructive procedures in patients who once would have been permanently disabled or disfigured by radical cancer surgery.

TREATMENT OF CANCERS WITH RADIATION

The field of radiation therapy has made similar advances, as knowledge of radiation physics and cell biology has increased. More than 90,000 cases of cancer diagnosed each year are curable by radiation alone or in conjunction with surgery. The development of cobalt and then linear accelerator X-ray machines, and the concept of dividing the total dose of radiation into multiple daily doses (known as fractionation of dosing), have enabled radiation therapists to minimize damage to normal tissues while maximizing the lethal effects of radiation on the tumor. Advances in radiation therapy, some of which grew out of the government's support for research in atomic physics, have also lead to tremendous improvements in the field of diagnostic radiology which, in turn, has led to much better understanding of how and where tumors spread. Our ability to diagnose and localize very small tumors deep within the body using ultrasound and computer-assisted tomography (CT or CAT scan), a highly sophisticated computer-enhanced X ray, has in turn led to the development of new strategies in cancer treatment. (See Chapter 8, "Radiation Therapy.")

HOW ANTICANCER DRUGS WORK

DNA is the part of each cell that contains all the genetic information, the blueprint, to reproduce it. Each strand of DNA is made up of building blocks called purines and pyrimidines, which are bound together in such a way that a double-stranded helical structure, shown in Figure 4, is formed. Several effective drugs interfere with the formation of purines and pyrimidines and by causing the formation of incorrect building blocks, these drugs cause false genetic instructions to be incorporated into the cell's DNA, preventing normal cell division. These anticancer drugs are called antimetabolites because they actively interfere with the formation of metabolic substances that are essential to building DNA. One of the antimetabolites, called arabinosyl-cytosine, a naturally occurring substance found in ocean sponges, is one of the most effective drugs against leukemia.

Another class of anticancer drugs, called alkylating agents, kills the cancer cells by causing a tangle of the strands of DNA rather than by interfering with its formation. When the affected cell tries to divide, it cannot because the DNA strands cannot separate and duplicate the genetic information. Procarbazine, a drug that is highly active against Hodgkin's disease, is another type of alkylating agent which nicks and breaks the DNA, instead of cross-linking it.

Adriamycin (doxorubican), Blenoxane (bleomycin), Cerubidine (daunorubicin), and Mutamycin (mitomycin) represent yet another class of anticancer drugs, the antitumor antibiotics. Antibiotics are substances produced by bacteria to prevent the growth of other organisms in the surrounding environment. In the body, these agents slip between the two strands of DNA and interfere with the duplication of DNA needed for cell division.

Two other naturally occurring anticancer drugs, vincristine and vinblastine, are derived from a type of periwinkle plant. These two natural products do not affect the formation or duplication of DNA directly. Instead they interfere with the separation of the cell's essential genetic information into two distinct daughter cells.

There are a number of reasons to use drugs in combination rather than as single agents. The development of resistance to cancer drugs is a problem. Cancers are not made up of homogeneous collections of cells, like eggs in a carton, but rather are a mixture of heterogeneous cells that are genetically unstable and prone to mutation. A mutation is a permanent, inheritable change in characteristics that daughter cells inherit from the parent cell. Because millions of cells already exist in a small tumor mass, there may well be cancer cells that have already further mutated and are already resistant to some cancer drugs at diagnosis, and others that mutate within a relatively short period, developing genetic characteristics that make them resistant to drugs they have not been exposed to

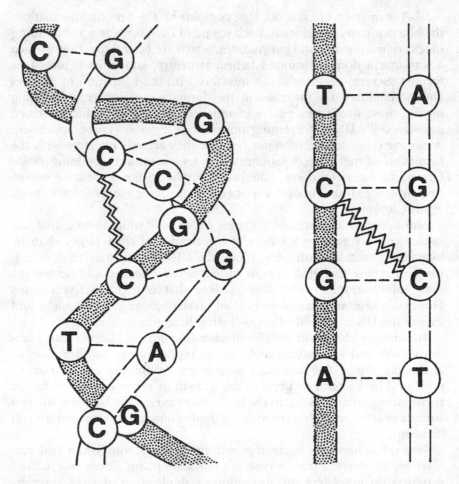

Figure 4   A diagrammatic representation of the double-stranded helical structure of DNA.

before. Using a combination of drugs increases the chances that the mutant will not survive. In addition, active combinations decrease the cancer cells' ability to repair damage and delay or prevent the development of resistance. Effective drug combinations also cause multiple lesions in cancer cells and produce a greater antitumor effect than would be achieved by giving each of the drugs in sequence.

Use of drugs in combination with surgery and radiation therapy increases the anticancer effects of each while minimizing the toxic side effects. For this reason the major thrust of current cancer research is on the use of a combination of treatments against a number of common cancers such as breast, colon, and lung. Because drugs are given systemically, either by mouth or injection, they are distributed throughout the entire body and can kill cancer cells that have implanted at secondary or distant sites. Since it is likely that undetectable metastases exist in patients with cancers that recur often after surgery or radiation therapy, even when the tumor appeared to have been completely local, chemotherapy is often used to destroy these undetectable residual cancer cells. This approach to the treatment of cancer has been increasingly powerful as more and more effective programs of combination chemotherapy have been developed and improvements in surgery and radiation therapy have occurred. The use of chemotherapy in patients who have a high risk of recurrence after surgery or radiation therapy is called adjuvant chemotherapy. Successful results with adjuvant chemotherapy have led to the use of less extensive and less debilitating surgery.

It has been demonstrated quite recently that tumors occurring in the soft tissues of the arms and legs can now be treated effectively with limited surgery, radiation therapy, and adjuvant chemotherapy, thereby sparing the patient the loss of the limb. The use of a combination of treatments for breast cancer has also increased. Extensive surgery, once thought to be necessary to cure breast cancer, may not be needed if effective drug treatment is given to kill any metastatic cancer cells following removal of the breast lump. Studies designed to test this proposition are in progress.

WHERE TO GO FOR CANCER TREATMENT

Finding the best available treatment for a cancer patient is not always simple and can require determination and perseverance. The first step is finding a physician who has qualifications and experience in the treatment of cancer. The physician who diagnoses the cancer can help by providing a referral to a cancer specialist for a second opinion. Most physicians do not feel slighted if a patient requests a second opinion and would, in fact, encourage patients to seek a second opinion for advice about treatment when the disease is as serious as cancer. To use a nonmedical example, the best choice of lawyers for a criminal problem is not one who specializes in real estate law. Likewise, a physician who specializes in the treatment of arthritis is probably not the best-qualified physician to treat a patient with cancer. It cannot be overemphasized that patients and families should seek the best possible treatment at the time the cancer is diagnosed in order to increase chances of cure.

Excellent cancer treatment is available at the cancer centers located throughout the United States. Some of these centers are funded by the NCI and are designated as Clinical Cancer Centers and Comprehensive Cancer Centers (see Directory of Resources in the Appendix). In addition, there are many cancer specialists, known as medical or surgical oncologists, in private practice with formal training and experience in the treatment of cancer. The NCI has also established a computerized database on cancer treatment capability called PDQ, an acronym for Physicians' Data Query. Using a home or office computer, doctors and patients alike can obtain information about cancer treatment and where, within a region, it is given. The computer file provides up-to-the-minute information on the best available treatments for a particular cancer, the latest survival statistics, and the names of institutions and individuals performing NCI-sponsored research.

Cancer centers are not the only places that offer expertise in the care of the cancer patient. Many of the cancer centers maintain active outreach programs which connect them to community hospitals. The NCI will continue to ensure that excellent cancer care is readily available at community hospitals and clinics throughout the country with programs such as the National Cooperative Groups, the regional groups, the National Surgical Adjuvant Breast Project (NSABP), and the new Community Clinical Oncology Program (CCOP).

The NCI has also funded three medical centers (UCLA, Fox Chase Cancer Center, and University of Washington—Seattle) to construct sophisticated high-energy radiation therapy equipment called neutron generators together with funding for clinical trials. The goal of this program is to test this newly developed radiation therapeutic treatment for cancer patients and to stimulate further basic and clinical research in the field of radiology and radiation biology.

The term "clinical trials" is an important one for patients to understand if they are going to consider participating in the evaluation of a new treatment for cancer. The purpose of clinical trials is to evaluate a new treatment and to determine its value in the overall treatment of patients with the disease. In some clinical trials, patients receive the same drug but at different dosages in an attempt to define the right dose for future studies. In other kinds of clinical trials the optimal dose and schedule are known, and all patients receive the same dose and schedule in an attempt to determine the overall rate of tumor regression with the new treatment.

In still other kinds of clinical trials, patients are randomly assigned to one course of treatment as opposed to another in order to avoid any bias in the selection process. This type of selection, known as randomization, is performed when the full value of a new version of a proven approach has not yet been determined. Clinical trials may also compare one combination of drugs against another combination or compare combination chemotherapy with surgery or radiation therapy, or an approach that includes all three. Randomized clinical trials are not performed when it is known that one of the treatments offers a patient a better chance of cure or prolonged survival. (See Chapter 9, "Experimental Treatments and Research.")

COMPLICATIONS OF CANCER TREATMENT

Surgery, radiation therapy, chemotherapy—each has particular side effects. The side effects of surgery relate to the loss of an organ or a body part, the formation of scars, and the development of postoperative complications such as bleeding and infection. The side effects of radiation therapy are related to the damaging effects of X rays on normal tissue that lies within the treatment field. Patients may have to cope with various gradations of skin irritation, nausea, diarrhea, hair loss, and loss of energy. The constellation of side effects is generally determined by where and how much radiation is administered. However, technologic developments in radiation therapy have made it possible to minimize damage to healthy tissue and avoid many of the toxic side effects that complicated its early use.

The side effects of chemotherapy also include damage to normal tissues of the body. The cells most often affected are those that have a high rate of growth because of their short life span, meaning they must be replenished constantly.

Important strides have been made in lessening reactions caused by cancer therapy. For example, nausea, a side effect of radiation and many anticancer drugs, can be relieved with a variety of drugs, including tetrahydrocannabinol (THC), the active ingredient of marijuana. A concerted effort is being made to develop other, more effective drugs to alleviate this distressing side effect of treatment. Loss of hair, another side effect associated with radiation and certain chemotherapy drugs, is due to toxic effects on the cells of the hair follicle. Hair loss is generally a transient, reversible problem that can sometimes be prevented or minimized by the application of cold packs that constrict peripheral circulation and prevent diffusion of the drug to the scalp during the drug treatment. The availability of comfortable hairpieces at low cost has made hair loss tolerable for those patients for whom cold packs are not appropriate.

Anemia, fatigue, and general malaise are other common side effects of anticancer drugs and radiation therapy. They are caused by the toxic effects of treatment on blood cell production in the bone marrow and can be moderated somewhat by careful drug scheduling. Specific measures, such as increasing fluid intake to dilute the concentration of drugs that are toxic to the kidney, can be taken to prevent damage to normal cells during treatment.

While the side effects of cancer treatment are generally reversible and disappear when drug therapy is completed, some long-term side effects have been seen in patients who have successfully completed therapy. These include adverse effects on the heart, loss of fertility, and an increased risk of developing a second cancer. However, it is essential to remember that these effects have been evident only because cancers that were previously fatal in patients are now curable, and prolonged cancer-free survival has been observed. Concerted efforts are being made to avert or minimize these toxic side effects by administering radiation therapy in new ways, by developing better methods of shielding normal tissues, and by developing effective drugs that do not have undesirable effects. The National Cancer Institute and private pharmaceutical firms are constantly working to develop such second-generation drugs from chemicals known to be effective against cancer. In the final analysis, however, all the risks and side effects of cancer therapy must be balanced against the potential effects of the treatment in terms of cure, as well as improvement of overall survival rates.

INITIATIVES IN CANCER PREVENTION

The National Cancer Institute (NCI) has made a major commitment in the area of cancer prevention. Research activities in the area of environmental causes of cancer have increased 43 percent between 1978 and 1980. NCI epidemiologists have compiled cancer mortality statistics for the period from 1950 to 1969 for all counties in the United States and assembled maps that show "hot spots" for various cancer sites. More than forty subsequent epidemiologic studies have been performed to identify whether exposure to a specific environmental agent can account for the increase in cancers in those areas.

Fundamental research into the causes of cancer has provided data on the development of cancer, indicating that certain types may be preventable. Studies have indicated that cancers affected by the environment may develop in two stages, initiation and promotion. While the first, initiation, produces a permanent heritable change in the cell, it is not sufficient in itself to cause cancer until the second event, promotion, causes expression of the malignant transformation. By removing the promoter from the environment, we may be able to reduce the incidence of cancer. For example, the increased incidence of endometrial cancer among American women, associated with widespread use of replacement estrogen at menopause, has been quickly reversed by the more judicious prescribing of these agents.

Likewise the addition of certain dietary substances may prevent malignant transformation from occurring when premalignant tumors exist or when the risk of cancer from exposure to a carcinogen, such as cigarette smoke, is known to be high. Studies of beta-carotene (a precursor of vitamin A) and several retinoid compounds (relatives of vitamin A) have suggested that the incidence of cancer may be decreased in high-risk populations. A division of NCI was created to conduct studies in applied prevention in the areas of smoking and health, diet and nutrition, asbestos, exposure to low-level radiation, and occupational cancer. This division is coordinating and supervising the development and establishment of Community Clinical Oncology Programs and their activities so that research in prevention and treatment will flow quickly and effectively into the community.

WHERE WE STAND

There is no single, simple cure-all for the more than one hundred diseases encompassed by the fearful word cancer—and probably never will be. We have learned over the past ten years that cancer is, in actuality, many different diseases, and each cancer must be approached as a unique entity. We have made great strides in curing many cancers now that we understand that drug therapy can be used to eradicate undetected cancer cells left behind after surgery or radiation therapy. There is great reason for continued optimism, given the research that is under way to improve effective therapies currently available and to prevent or mitigate untoward side effects of treatment. Some of the major advances of the recent past are listed below:

• The overall five-year survival rate for all patients with cancer has risen to 50 percent with treatments that existed in 1980, and is expected to be higher when the effects of currently available treatment can be documented statistically.

• Half of all children with cancer can now be cured.

• Testicular cancer, the leading cause of cancer death in young men, is now curable in 98 percent of patients with localized tumors and in more than 70 percent of patients with widespread disease. These dramatic improvements in cure rates have occurred within the past five years. They are directly related to use of the drug cisplatin in combination with other effective agents, and to the development of new techniques that can accurately determine the presence of residual tumor cells. Now, treatment can be continued until the cancer has been totally eradicated.

• In Hodgkin's disease, a cancer of the lymphatic system, significant improvement in cure rate has been achieved with the widespread use of combination chemotherapy alone or with radiation therapy. More than 80 percent of patients with localized disease are curable by radiation therapy and more than 50 percent of those with advanced disease involving the liver, bone marrow, lung or other organs can be cured with combination chemotherapy.

• Other lymph gland cancers, called the non-Hodgkin's lymphomas, are curable with radiation and drug combinations. In the case of diffuse large-cell lymphoma, one of the most lethal forms of lymphoma, about half of the patients can be cured with effective drug combinations.

• In soft-tissue sarcoma, a highly malignant cancer arising in soft tissues, cure rates higher than 80 percent have been achieved through the use of surgery and chemotherapy. This is notable since during the 1960s five-year survival with surgery was less than 40 percent.

• In osteogenic sarcoma, a highly malignant cancer of the bone, cure rates have improved from 20 percent in the 1960s to 70 percent at the present time because of new diagnostic equipment, improved surgical techniques, and the use of chemotherapy after surgery.

• In rectal cancer, recent clinical trials funded by NCI suggest that following surgery with radiation and chemotherapy prolongs disease-free survival in patients, and the national mortality in all age groups for rectal cancers is falling.

• In lung cancer, especially the small-cell variety for which no effective treatment existed prior to the 1970s, the use of radiation and chemotherapy has produced dramatic, often complete regressions of tumors, and many patients now live two years after diagnosis.

• In breast cancer, data from two clinical trials sponsored by the NCI—one conducted in Italy, the other in the United States—have demonstrated a 57 percent increase in survival in premenopausal women with breast cancer who received chemotherapy following surgery. In these women, the cancer had spread to the lymph nodes in the axilla (underarm) and they were therefore at high risk for recurrence. In addition, current data from studies that are evaluating less radical breast surgery in conjunction with primary radiation therapy to treat early breast cancer indicate that radical surgery may not be needed in many instances.

6

The Treatment Team

PAUL A. WILLIAMS, M.D.,
AND MARILEE WILLIAMS, R.N.

INTRODUCTION

People who have, or suspect they have, cancer are afraid. This fear is
often accompanied by loneliness, confusion, anger, and even feelings of
guilt, arising from a sense of imagined failure. In addition, cancer patients
often feel that they are being punished, perhaps for some past wrongdo-
ing. These feelings may be compounded by the insecurity of friends and
relatives in dealing with cancer, causing the patient to further withhold
sharing emotional and physical burdens with those who could offer valuable support and understanding. This sense of isolation and rejection can
sometimes intensify the problem of how to deal with cancer to the point
that patients actually fail to receive the best possible care.

Despite their understandable feelings of isolation, the fact remains that cancer patients are not alone. Indeed, if patients look for assistance, they may even become confused by the multiplicity of people, organizations, and institutions that offer help. Many willing and eager hands reach out to cancer patients who are ready to be met halfway during this very difficult time of need. These sources of help vary greatly in style, intent, and quality. The goal of this chapter is to help the cancer patient, family, and friends make informed, intelligent choices among the many sources of assistance that are available.

THE TEAM APPROACH

The present complexity involved in cancer diagnosis, treatment, and rehabilitation has resulted in the evolution of a team approach to dealing with the disease. The members of this team and their functions are many and varied. Not every patient requires every service that each member of the cancer team offers. The number and complexity of the team members will be confusing, even frightening, to the uninitiated patient who is trying to sort out where to go, whom to see, how to begin the process of dealing with cancer. In fact, the most important responsibility facing the patient and family involves making several early decisions regarding the consultants who will oversee the diagnosis and treatment. While it is important to avoid delay, it is also important to take enough time to study the various alternatives and to select the most suitable course at the outset. Once embarked on a particular course, the patient may find it is at times very difficult to change direction. It is certainly easier to choose the best road first than to be forced to make changes later in the process of dealing with this disease. This is not to say that changes in institutions, locations, or doctors cannot be made during the course of treatment, but there are some actions that cannot be easily undone if a different treatment option is later desired.

How does one make the proper decisions? The most basic aspect of early decision-making in dealing with cancer may be philosophical rather than medical. This involves the recognition that when a person has cancer it is not the time for him or her to be a rugged individualist who tries to make decisions alone. Many times a cancer patient wants to spare loved ones the agony—real or imagined—that is so closely identified with this disease. While this may seem noble on the surface, it can be self-defeating. It is far better for all concerned if patients learn early on to share their concerns, to seek support and help from those with whom they have a trusting relationship, and to avoid false folklore and those erroneous bits of advice that can be both alarming and untrue.

First and foremost, a person with cancer should be as honest and straightforward as possible with family members and other loved ones.

Often they will be as confused and frightened as the patient, but they at least should be given every opportunity to share these feelings and concerns. Bringing the worries and other facets of the problem into the open where they can be faced squarely is the right thing to do. This sharing, of course, is by no means limited to blood relatives; in this age of highly mobile populations and changing family relationships, those people in whom we might elect to confide might not necessarily be family members. An unmarried individual, for example, may have his or her closest ties in a city far from the original home and family. Close friends or other members of this extended family certainly qualify as people with whom to share the problem—and the responsibility—of making critical treatment and other decisions. Even so, a balance must be struck. Many patients find that well-meaning friends, relatives, and colleagues exert enormous pressure to "leave no stone unturned," to explore all of the methods of cancer therapy, including those of unproved or dubious merit. Many of these treatments are of unquestioned value, but unfortunately cancer patients are often urged to turn to therapies grounded in pseudoscience, mysticism, or cultism. Above all, the patient should seek advice about the very best established treatments available and shun the unproved or questionable.

The treatment team will vary, depending on the site of the cancer, its nature and extent, and the presence of additional diseases, such as diabetes, high blood pressure, or heart disease, that might influence the course of treatment. The extent of available financial resources is another obvious factor that must be considered.

At the very outset, the cancer patient should recognize that the ultimate decisions about diagnosis and treatment are, above all, his or hers to make—that in essence, the patient is also the treatment team leader (Figure 5). All too often, the cancer patient and family feel that "things are beyond their control," that they are powerless to say yes or no, or even to ask questions regarding diagnosis and treatment. But for the patient to be fully involved, he or she must have a professional advisor with whom a close relationship based on implicit trust can be established. This person will function as team advisor or coordinator. No patient should be treated by a collection of professionals without the selection of a qualified person—referred to in this chapter as the physician advisor—to orchestrate the various doctors, therapists, and other cancer-care resources. This team advisor is responsible as well for coordinating all diagnostic and therapeutic efforts directed toward the patient.

Who should assume this role as physician advisor? In some instances, the best choice may be the personal family physician. In others, the physician advisor will be the specialist—for example, a medical or surgical oncologist, who is overseeing treatment of the cancer. There are instances in which the personal family physician is not suited to the role of treatment team advisor. If the doctor seems uncomfortable or distant—remember, many doctors are also fearful of and uncomfortable when dealing with cancer—ask for a referral or seek a second opinion from another doctor. Many patients hesitate to ask for a referral or another opinion, fearing that this will somehow offend their doctor. This should not be the case; a physician who is secure in his or her own ability will not be threatened or offended by a second opinion. But this should be done as early as possible; once a doctor starts a case, most people find it difficult to change.

In any event, patients should not feel that they are limited to their present doctors. If the present physician is in any way inadequate, or if the patient does not have a personal doctor to act as a close team advisor, a search for one to fill this function should be undertaken with several basic questions in mind: What kind of doctor? Should he or she be a specialist or a generalist? Since the physician advisor must coordinate the entire diagnostic, treatment, and rehabilitation processes, which in some instances may be quite prolonged, he or she should be equipped to render long-term, continuing care.

Once a physician advisor has been tentatively selected, the patient or family should go one step further to ensure that the doctor is both suitable for the role and has the right qualifications. It is relatively easy to

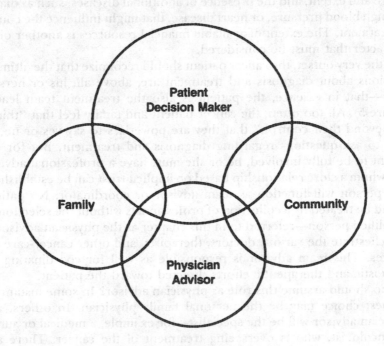

Figure 5 Supporting spheres of influence.

check a doctor's professional credentials. Although some patients argue that they are hesitant or are not qualified to check on a doctor, it seems folly not to make every effort to do so, especially when one considers the money that will be spent for the physician's expertise and the fact, also, that one's physical and psychological well-being is going to be entrusted to this person.

How does one go about checking out a physician, especially one who is going to coordinate a cancer treatment program? The most common method is to ask a trusted friend or relative about their experience with a particular physician. Perhaps a more reliable starting point, however, is a visit to the local library to look up the doctor(s) in question in the Directory of Medical Specialists and the American Medical Association Directory. The first reference lists only those doctors who are board-certified, meaning that they have passed comprehensive tests in their particular specialty and are judged competent by their fellow physicians in that medical discipline. If this approach is not practical or if the library does not have these books, call the state or local Department of Health, County Medical Society, or state chapter of the American Academy of Family Physicians, or the American College of Physicians. These organizations will be listed in the telephone directory by state—for example, the Indiana Academy of Family Physicians—county, or city.

Still another approach involves calling the office of one of the department chairmen, such as the head of oncology, internal medicine, surgery, or family practice, at the nearest medical school or teaching hospital. These people usually have lists of doctors in communities throughout the area and will be able to provide useful information. Other sources of information are the American Cancer Society or the National Cancer Institute. (See the Directory of Resources in the Appendix for addresses and telephone numbers.)

Location is a prime consideration in dealing with any prolonged illness, which includes many forms of cancer. The convenience of transportation to and from the office, the ease or difficulty of reaching the doctor by telephone, familiarity with local hospital and emergency medical services, availability to family members and close friends—these are but a few of the factors that should be considered in selecting a physician advisor to coordinate the cancer treatment process.

The type of practice in which a physician is engaged is still another consideration. If the doctor is associated with a multispecialty group, he or she will have more access to the varied opinions regarding a particular problem. Doctors associated with a specialty group housed in a single building or clinic with a common record system offer the advantage of providing greater accessibility to reports, X rays, laboratory and consultant opinions and other records when a colleague is called upon as a substitute. In contrast, solo practitioners may have less stimulation and input from their colleagues, and their records may not always be available to covering physicians unless care has been taken to communicate this information beforehand. These should not be overriding considerations, however, since a solo practitioner who is skillful and knowledgeable can render superb care and can easily make provisions to have the records and other data available when needed.

After the initial checking has been done and the choice of a doctor has been narrowed to a few—two or three at the most—the patient should telephone each physician's office for an appointment. It is a good idea to be accompanied by a trusted friend or close family member on the first visit. The receptionist should be informed of the purpose of the visit— namely, the possibility of becoming a new patient, and that a serious health problem may be involved if, in fact, a diagnosis of cancer has been confirmed. In this instance, the objective will be to discuss the situation with another physician who may be called upon to coordinate the treatment. Knowing this, the receptionist can schedule extra time or can relay important information that could save time and fees. For example, the receptionist would know if the doctor would be unlikely to take the case, perhaps because the current patient load is too heavy or because this particular physician is reluctant to assume a case started by others. One should not feel discouraged or rejected if this happens; a doctor has a professional and ethical right to choose patients initially, just as a patient has a right to choose a doctor. Extra sensitivities enter the picture when cancer is involved; it is important that the patient be aware of the two-sided selection process and not feel that "even the doctors are reluctant to step in."

The patient should expect to pay for the doctor's time and advice on this initial interview-visit. By the same token, the patient should make use of the opportunity to develop some idea of the doctor's style, because personality and rapport are, in many respects, as important as scientific competence in dealing with worried and ill human beings. In a real sense the office environment that the doctor has created, as indicated by location, decoration, and the personalities of nurse, receptionist, and other supporting personnel, offer clues as to the doctor's attitude in dealing with patients. Does the doctor adhere to scheduled visits? Is the office attractive, neat, and comfortable? Is the office run in a pleasant yet efficient fashion? These may seem like minor points unrelated to medical expertise, but they are valid factors in evaluating a doctor's compatibility and attitudes. Outward appearances are not everything, to be sure, but they are often a good reflection of inner realities. This is not to say that an excellent, concerned, very humane physician cannot practice in a dingy, inefficiently run office with grumpy office help, but one would have to ask what price is being paid to function in an environment marked by inconvenience, stress, inefficiency, and emotional unrest.

Even more important than the office environment is the manner of the physician. The first thing a prospective patient should observe in interviewing any doctor—for, in a sense, that is what is taking place during this initial visit—is the ease of communication between them. Is it open and free? Is it understandable? Is it willing? Does the doctor seem to be kindly and interested in the problem? Does he or she appear knowledgeable about the particular cancer problem? Does the doctor's overall attitude seem to be supportive and is it one that inspires confidence? This visit should be used as an opportunity to ask questions. What hospital staff does the doctor belong to? What position does he or she hold? Has the doctor treated similar cases in the past? While the doctor should not be expected to know all the answers to every question, there should be a willingness to seek the answers. Ask, too, whether he or she holds a teaching appointment at a medical school, teaching hospital, or local residency program. Ordinarily such appointments are given to doctors who are up-to-date and respected by peers, and they provide the opportunity to have a broader referral base and to know more consulting physicians.

The doctor also should be questioned about substitute coverage during an absence. Will he or she make house calls? What is the doctor's attitude toward using consultations out of the immediate referral area, such as to a cancer center or a medical center affiliated with a medical school? A candid discussion about second opinions should be undertaken to determine the willingness to involve other physicians in his or her private cases. Usually the responses to these questions will be gratifying, frank, reassuring, and kindly; if they are not, one should look elsewhere. Any doubts or hesitations should either be faced and resolved or taken as a strong indication that this particular doctor is not the right person for the case. Of course there are instances in which a physician advisor will not be able to fulfill all of the outlined requirements; some of these may be relegated to other members of the team. But there is no member of the decision-making team (other than the patient himself) who will be more important, and the time and effort invested in the selection process is well spent.

After the physician advisor has been chosen, the patient should work to develop an open line of communication and make sure that it stays open. Don't hesitate to ask questions. Many patients are reluctant to "take up the doctor's time" or to ask questions that might sound "dumb." In this situation, there are no dumb questions; if something is worrisome or not fully understood, questions should be asked. In turn, the doctor should strive to answer questions fully in an understandable manner. Family members or close friends also should feel free to talk with the doctor. These various individuals constitute a personal support system for the patient and should come to depend upon the physician advisor rather than well-meaning friends, colleagues or others who are likely to be uninformed, or at least not as familiar with the circumstances involved as is the doctor. It is hard to overemphasize the importance of following the counsel of a skilled health professional. Doctors and patients both should remember that most warning signs of cancer are not cancer, and that more and more patients who do develop the disease are cured when they are afforded the benefits of a wisely led team effort.

ROLE OF NURSES

Nurses play an important role in the care of patients with cancer in a variety of settings. During the diagnostic and staging phase of the illness, nurses will explain the procedures to the patient and family so that they will know what to expect and be able to assist the physician or technician in performing the procedure. If the patient is hospitalized, nurses will provide day-to-day care. In many hospitals a primary nurse is assigned to coordinate and evaluate the patient's care. In the hospital, the nurse will provide information to patients and their families about the treatment and anticipated side effects. With the patient and his family, the nurse will plan care that will minimize and manage the problems that occur as a result of therapy. The nurse will provide physical care that may involve dressing changes, management of surgical wounds, administering chemotherapy, or apply treatments to the skin or mouth to prevent or minimize side effects of treatments.

In many treatment centers there are oncology nurses or clinical nurse specialists with special educational preparation in cancer nursing at the master's degree level. These nurses work with patients in all settings and provide care at different phases in their illness. They often give most of the chemotherapy treatments and teach patients how to manage the effects of treatment.

STAGES IN THE TREATMENT PROCESS

In most cases, cancer treatment involves at least three distinct phases: diagnosis, treatment, and rehabilitation and follow-up. The nature and course of treatment will, of course, depend upon the type of cancer involved. The physician advisor will undoubtedly perform several initial diagnostic studies. Questions that need to be answered at this point include: What type of cancer is involved? What stage is it in? Has it spread to other organs or parts of the body? What is the patient's general physical condition? After some or all of these questions have been answered, the doctor, patient, and family should decide jointly where and by whom the treatment will be administered.

Very often a number of different specialists or consultants will be rec-

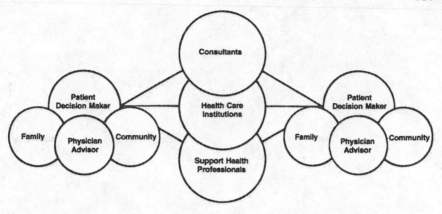

Figure 6 Diagnostic decisions.

ommended (Figure 6). The diagnosis may very well be made at one institution under one medical team, and then the patient will be referred to another institution and another medical team for treatment (Figure 7). This is the typical course when treatment methods are complex—one particular institution may gain expertise and experience in a specific group of diseases. In most instances, however, the treatment is well established and fairly straightforward and can be administered by local institutions. In addition, many of the Comprehensive Cancer Centers, as designated by the National Cancer Institute, have special linkups with local community hospitals, enabling the specialized center to work directly with the local hospital in administering the treatment.

The third major area of decision-making involves the post-treatment or rehabilitation phase (Figure 8). In many types of cancer, the rehabilitation should be planned even before the treatment begins. Who will be available for continuing care, follow-up, and support? Most cancer patients want to know when they can go home, often before they enter the hospital. This of course depends upon the type of cancer and follow-up treatment, the distances involved, and the circumstances at home. Does the patient live alone? Is the home nearby or in another city? Are there support members of the team available to help? What is the patient's general physical condition? What sort of community resources are available? Many people tend to overlook community resources, but they are very important elements of the treatment team. These include voluntary health agencies, especially the local American Cancer Society (see Directory of Resources in the Appendix). The clergy and church groups are skilled in rendering spiritual support, even if religion does not hold an important place in the patient's life. The workplace also represents a

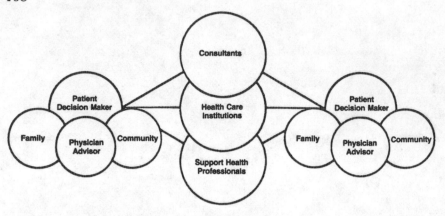

Figure 7 Treatment decisions.

source of support and concern. Still other community resources include fraternal and social service organizations and government agencies. For example, the National Cancer Institute, an arm of the federal government, was founded to coordinate efforts in cancer care and research. Its cancer information services include a toll-free telephone inquiry system to supply information about cancer and resources to the general public, cancer patients, their families, and health professionals.

City and county health departments are yet another available resource. Many run screening and educational programs as well as informational services for the general public. The hospital, of course, is the hub of health activity in most communities, offering not only treatment services,

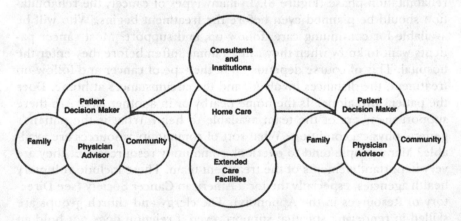

Figure 8 Continuing care decisions.

but also literature, counseling, and a variety of educational programs. Hospitals with cancer units generally employ postdischarge program planners and social workers who are important support members of the treatment team.

Self-help groups, sometimes formed as local constituents of national organizations, are particularly important in any treatment and rehabilitation effort. Even during the active treatment phase, it is very helpful to patients and family members to meet their counterparts who have had similar experiences. Examples include ostomy clubs, Reach to Recovery of the American Cancer Society and other breast-cancer rehabilitation groups, the International Association of Laryngectomees, and a number of other such organizations. (These are described more fully in Chapter 11, "Cancer Rehabilitation.")

THE QUESTION OF FINANCES

A vital question that must be faced at the beginning involves financial considerations (Figure 9). Modern cancer therapy can be very costly; therefore financial support looms as one of the most important factors that should be considered in the background of all other decisions that have to be made. Very few of us can afford to carry the cost of cancer treatment ourselves; hence the team must include a financial advisor. The patient should not hesitate to share financial concerns openly. The physicians and other medical personnel often can do little to alter the cost faced by cancer patients and their families, but financial guidance can, and should, be offered.

Assessing the family's financial situation and exploring resources soon after cancer has been diagnosed may eliminate the accumulation of large and frequently unexpected debt arising in the course of the disease. A conference involving the physician, patient or family member, social worker, and a hospital financial or medical insurance administrator should be held before or soon after admission to the hospital. The patient's insurance policy should be examined to determine the extent of coverage. Explanations of hospital and physician policies on payment of expenses beyond those covered by insurance are important elements in financial planning.

In American society today, medical care is not based solely on the ability to pay for it, although financial aid and medical insurance programs may vary in benefits and eligibility requirements from area to area. Hospital departments of social services, the American Cancer Society, and offices of the Cancer Information Service (see Directory of Resources in the Appendix for addresses and telephone numbers) all can supply information and counsel about federal and other governmental aid programs, such as Medicare, Medicaid, Veterans' Administration benefits,

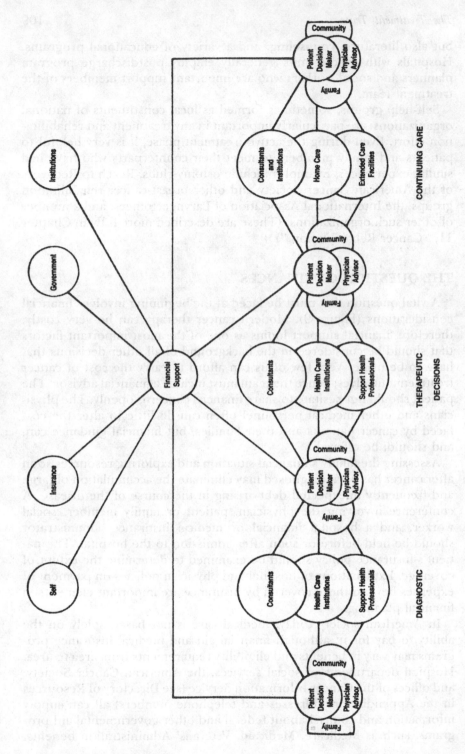

Figure 9 The total picture.

Social Security, Disability and Supplemental Security Income, among others.

The kind and amount of financial aid available depend upon many factors, including such variables as local eligibility requirements and the nature of the treatment to be given. For example, research programs supported by government agencies through a grant system may be available to the patient at little or no cost for certain kinds of cancer. Private insurance will usually pay for covered expenses, but the exact extent of policy coverage varies widely. Some policies provide extra benefits for cancer patients, such as disability or income maintenance payments during the treatment and rehabilitation periods, while others have a ceiling on total payment. Many health plans, especially those made available by employers, unions, and other groups, often have a major medical provision that insures against catastrophic illness. This policy will pay medical costs beyond ordinary insurance policy coverage.

Other sources of aid include diagnostic and treatment programs sponsored by hospitals that have received federal aid for construction through the Hill-Burton Act and by law are required to treat needy patients. The hospital's department of social services can provide information on this possibility.

A number of organizations provide useful adjunct services at little or no cost. The American Cancer Society, for example, provides a number of services, including transportation, the loan of equipment to be used at home, and even such help as baby-sitting. Churches, civic clubs and associations, and fraternal and service clubs often offer health care services. Armed Services personnel, including retired veterans and their dependents, are eligible for benefits through the Armed Services Insurance Program.

Financial planning should include knowledge about the patient's expected physical capabilities after treatment to help the family realistically gauge future work capacity. Cancer patients who wish to return to work are now protected by the Rehabilitation Act of 1973, a federal statute that prohibits discrimination against handicapped persons. It mandates affirmative action in some circumstances and requires states to include cancer patients in vocational rehabilitation programs. These vary from state to state, however, and the treatment team's financial advisor should provide information on what is available.

Finally, it should be emphasized that despite the high cost of cancer treatment today, ways can be found to pay for it in most instances. It is important to confide financial worries to the appropriate members of the treatment team so that resources can be provided. Although financial concerns are a legitimate worry, they should not loom so large that they overshadow the patient's ability to concentrate on the more immediate decision-making involved in overcoming the disease itself.

SUMMING UP THE INITIAL PLANNING PHASE

All of the steps described so far are concerned with the initial decision-making. To review: the patient has confided his or her worries and concerns over the possibility of cancer to family members or close and trusted friends. After careful research and personal contact, a physician advisor who will coordinate the entire treatment and follow-up effort has been selected. Treatment facilities and programs have been researched, as have community and other resources. The patient and family members have learned more about the specific type of cancer and what will be involved in treatment and rehabilitation. At this point, the patient is now ready to make informed decisions concerning the disease. But before moving to the next step, it is well to reevaluate the situation. If the patient is not comfortable with members of the treatment team, particularly the physician advisor, it is not too late to look further. Before starting all over, however, the patient should ask: "Am I really unhappy with the level of communication, concern, competence, or am I really looking for someone who will simply tell me what I want to hear?" A well-informed patient who has complete confidence in his or her medical advisors is in the best position to make sound decisions. The ultimate goal is to utilize the advisors to formulate the best and most comfortable plan that will lead to the highest quality and greatest length of life.

As emphasized earlier, emotional issues also must be recognized and dealt with in this initial evaluation period. The diagnosis of cancer should be met with the same attitude that we assume in viewing other diseases. All disease is a misfortune; cancer is one misfortune among many, but it does not warrant the singular horror and hopelessness with which it was once regarded. Times have changed greatly, as have attitudes, but even so, cancer evokes a fear that is not manifest in other diseases. Patients and health care personnel emotionally and intellectually accept the continuing care of heart disease, high blood pressure, diabetes, and other chronic illnesses, and every effort is made to assist an individual in living as normal and productive a life as possible within the limits imposed by the disease in question. Cancer should be considered in the same way and not be regarded as a special dread gnawing away in painful silence. Attitudes of loneliness, uselessness, and despair are no more appropriate to cancer than to any other disease. Many cancers are totally cured; others are controlled for years, and patients with the disease in many of its forms live longer and better lives than many people with heart disease, lung disorders, kidney failure, and chronic degenerative diseases. Knowing this and acting accordingly greatly enhance the chance for a favorable outcome.

Finally, realistic assessment of financial considerations rounds out this initial phase of planning and decision-making. At this juncture the patient and family should be over the initial shock, anger, and bitterness, thereby freeing the energy and confidence of all those closely involved for future decison-making and concerted efforts to overcome the disease, or at least to assist the patient in living as long and as good a life as possible.

DESIGNING THE THERAPEUTIC COURSE

In the preceding section we presented an overview of the planning phase of cancer treatment and the roles of members of the decision team; we now turn to the specific steps and personnel involved.

As would be expected, the treatment begins with an accurate diagnosis. In many instances, the patient is the first to suspect the disease. Again it should be stressed that most symptoms that raise a suspicion of cancer are not confirmed. For example, only one out of every seven or eight lumps in the breast actually turns out to be cancer. Rectal bleeding is more often due to hemorrhoids than to cancer. The vast majority of moles and other skin growths are benign. But this does not mean that symptoms should be ignored—all should be checked against the possibility of cancer. Even though the odds of cancer may be small, the importance of early diagnosis cannot be overemphasized, and this far outweighs the cost and time involved in checking out any suspicious symptom.

Of course, early cancer very often produces no symptoms. Even so, cancers that are detected in this early asymptomatic stage are the most curable. Therefore people who fall into certain high-risk categories—cigarette smokers, people with a strong family history of certain cancers, people who are exposed to known cancer-causing agents such as chemical or asbestos workers, those in certain age groups, among others—should undergo periodic cancer screening tests.

The initial diagnostic studies are often done by the family physician, who will determine whether further testing is necessary. Before cancer can be confirmed, a "tissue diagnosis" must be obtained. This entails taking all or part of a suspected lesion—a biopsy—and sending it to a pathologist, a doctor who specializes in examining tissues microscopically. Another example is the Pap smear, in which a sampling of cells shed from the cervix, bronchial tubes, or other body parts is collected and examined under a microscope for any changes that may indicate cancer. In most cases the Pap smear itself does not confirm a diagnosis of cancer; instead it points to changes that indicate that a biopsy or further testing is advisable. (Exceptions are Class IV Pap smears of the cervix or pleural fluid, which are diagnostic of cancer.)

Even when a biopsy is positive, meaning that cancer is present, there are instances in which a second opinion is advised. Occasionally a patient may doubt or have a hard time accepting the diagnosis. Sometimes the primary physician may be of a similar opinion. Many cancers have several specific subcategories, and treatment and prognosis may depend heavily on specific information about the type involved. All of these issues are valid reasons for seeking a second expert opinion. The physician advisor has the responsibility for ensuring that the diagnosis has been determined as precisely as possible, a responsibility that should never be taken lightly and one that requires up-to-date knowledge about the suspected cancer. For example, a breast biopsy usually entails removal of the suspicious lump and examination of tissue from it for signs of cancer. In recent years it has been learned that this tissue also should be tested for estrogen and progesterone receptors to determine whether it is dependent upon these hormones—a factor that is important in treating this specific type of breast cancer if recurrence develops later. If the test is not done at the time of the biopsy, the opportunity to determine this important fact may be lost.

The physician will also want to know what stage the cancer is in. "Staging" is a diagnostic process that doctors perform to learn the extent of the cancer, where it is located, and other important facts. Staging is absolutely essential to treatment planning. Again we can cite breast cancer as an example; treatment of early, localized breast cancer is very different from the treatment usually prescribed for advanced disease that has spread to other parts of the body. The same is true of Hodgkin's disease and many other cancers.

Staging may take several forms. As much information as possible is first obtained by "clinical staging," meaning what the doctor can see, feel, and detect by X rays and other laboratory tests. "Surgical staging" is used to evaluate the extent of the disease by biopsy or surgical exploration. "Pathological staging" is the determination of the disease stage by examining the tumor directly under a microscope.

Although staging has great prognostic value, its major value is in designing the course of treatment rather than in advising the patient as to the overall outlook. Even if the statistical chances are slim, treatment should not be based on statistics; what happens to each individual is 100 percent, regardless of the statistics. Therefore it is up to the physician advisor to urge optimum care for all patients regardless of the length of time the individual is likely to live. Even more importantly, the patient must achieve the best possible quality of life for the time remaining, whether it is six weeks, six months, or a normal life span. Patients invariably want to know how much time is left, but such statistical prognostications are meaningless. Doctors are rarely asked to forecast a patient's chance for survival in other chronic diseases, many of which have a poorer prognosis than cancer. The important thing is to focus on the type and stage of cancer and to determine the optimum treatment that will provide the longest, and best quality of life.

THE CANCER CONSULTANTS

The first major group of medical consultants who may be brought in by the physician advisor overseeing the treatment team are surgeons, because in many instances they will be called upon to obtain the tissue necessary for the biopsy and staging studies. General surgeons usually perform most of these procedures, because of their availability at hospitals of all sizes and their skills in handling a wide variety of problems. Surgical exploration of lymph nodes, muscle, skin and underlying tissue and, particularly, of the abdominal cavity is the field of endeavor for general surgeons. Exploration of the chest cavity is usually undertaken by thoracic surgeons, who have special training in that area. In other specialized fields, such as the brain or reproductive organs, surgical exploration is usually left to specialists in the particular part of the body under question—for example, neurosurgeons or gynecologic oncologists.

The second group of specialists who play a prominent role in the diagnostic phase is the endoscopists. These are physicians who specialize in examining internal organs using instruments made of tubes equipped with a light, lens, and a system of fiberoptic bundles that conduct pictorial images (very much as electricity is conducted) to the doctor's eye. Endoscopic examinations may be performed by a family physician, surgeon, or internist with special training and experience in the procedure. Gynecologists use similar instruments and techniques to examine a woman's reproductive organs, while chest specialists are able to examine the lungs through flexible instruments called bronchoscopes. Indeed, fiberoptic technology has revolutionized the diagnostic process by enabling direct visualization and biopsy by special accessory devices attached to the scopes, thereby reducing the need for exploratory surgery of internal organs.

Diagnostic radiologists are still another group of physicians usually added to the diagnostic team. These are X-ray specialists who interpret X-ray films, ultrasonic tracings, computerized tomographic (CT) scans, and various other radiographic studies.

Other specialists who may be called in, depending upon the type of cancer, include medical oncologists, hematologists (blood specialists, who would be consulted in cases of cancers of the blood, bone marrow, and lymph system), neurologists (for cancers of the brain and central nervous system), and pediatric oncologists (specialists in childhood cancers). Most cases, however, will not require a long list of specialists, and helping find the right consultant for an individual problem falls in the province of the physician advisor who is acting as the team coordinator.

WHERE TO GO FOR DIAGNOSIS AND TREATMENT

The first diagnostic location from which the entire process is initiated is usually the physician advisor's office. In many instances the initial diagnostic tests—Pap smear, biopsy of accessible organs, etc.—will be performed here. If the diagnostic needs cannot be handled in the doctor's office, the second most likely medical resource will be either a hospital or the office of a consultant recommended by the physician advisor. Of course most of the subsequent diagnostic studies and treatment will be performed in a hospital or medical center. The question is: What kind of hospital?

Evaluating a hospital involves much the same process as evaluating a physician. In many instances the questions can be answered by the physician advisor. In any case, questions should be asked before settling on a particular hospital or treatment center. A call to the hospital to speak with an administrator is probably the most efficient way to evaluate a community hospital if its qualifications are unknown. The first question to ask is: "Is it an accredited hospital?" Accreditation is provided by the Joint Commission on Accreditation of Hospitals and indicates that the hospital has achieved a minimum standard of adequate care. It carries no implication of any special expertise in dealing with cancer, however. There are about 7,000 hospitals in the United States and approximately 1,600 of these lack accreditation. Some organizations, such as the American College of Surgeons, maintain directories of hospitals with cancer programs, an effort supported by the American Cancer Society.

The second important piece of informaton is: "How many beds are in the hospital?" Usually hospitals with more than five hundred beds offer more services and have more experience in treating cancer patients than smaller hospitals. There are about three thousand hospitals in the United States with fewer than one hundred beds, and these usually treat very few cancer patients, although there are a few outstanding exceptions to this rule.

Location is also important. If the local hospital does not seem to provide the needed services, the physician advisor should refer the patient to the proper specialist affiliated with a hospital that is better suited to handle the problem. It should be noted, however, that many common types of cancer can be adequately treated at a local or community hospital. Referral to a specialized center may be preferable when a complicated or experimental treatment is indicated, or when physicians at a community hospital have limited experience in treating the specific type of cancer. In selecting a hospital, one should also keep in mind the need for emotional support gained from frequent visits from friends and relatives, as well as the added expense of traveling long distances to get care that could be rendered just as well locally.

Clinical cancer centers have been established in many medical centers that receive support from the National Cancer Institute. These specialized centers offer many of the same services as found in the Comprehensive Cancer Centers, which are institutions designated by the National Cancer Institute to undertake experimental treatments. These centers offer the most extensive range of cancer treatment available in the United States. It would be helpful to know if the hospital under consideration has one of the centers and also whether it has an approved cancer program sponsored by the American College of Surgeons. Hospitals in the latter category have been voluntarily surveyed by an interdisciplinary cancer committee and have fulfilled additional requirements for the treatment of malignant diseases.

Hospitals that are directly connected to or controlled by medical schools generally provide a wider range and higher quality of care because they can attract leading clinicians, researchers, and medical educators for their faculties and staffs. Teaching hospitals have internship and residency programs to train new doctors and are usually affiliated with but not directly controlled by a medical school. Their facilities are often excellent, but in many instances not as extensive as those in hospitals directly connected with a medical school. Again, the range of treatment required depends upon the disease to be treated.

In recent years, an increasing proportion of medical care, including cancer treatment, has been rendered in outpatient services or ambulatory care departments that are associated with a hospital, clinic, or medical center. Outpatient surgical centers may be competent to biopsy and stage a breast cancer or suspected uterine cancer, for example. Cancer chemotherapy, radiation therapy, and other treatments may be administered on an outpatient basis.

OTHER MEMBERS OF THE TREATMENT TEAM

Once the diagnostic/treatment site has been selected, other members of the treatment team will begin to fall into place. These members and their respective roles are described briefly here.

Nurses

Nurses generally administer the day-to-day care of cancer patients. Many larger hospitals have oncology nurses who have special education and training in caring for cancer patients. They work with the patient and family to help minimize the problems that arise from the cancer and its treatment as well as to provide direct care, such as administering chemotherapeutic drugs, changing dressings, or giving other treatments prescribed by the doctor. (See Chapter 10, "Coping with Problems Related to Cancer and Cancer Treatment.")

The Social Worker

Cancer, in addition to its medical problems, entails many practical and emotional difficulties, and often the medical social worker at a hospital or medical center is the expert best qualified to help a patient and family cope with these problems. The medical social worker, for example, knows the various support resources of the community and also knows how to coordinate the many services and organizations that are available to help, both in the hospital and at home. The social worker is particularly important at the time of the initial diagnosis to help in planning the logistics of treatment, and again at the time of hospital discharge to plan follow-up and rehabilitation efforts. Many people are overwhelmed and unable to assimilate the great amount of information involved in the diagnosis, treatment choices, financial details, and aftercare. All of these important matters lie within the province of the medical social worker, who can help clarify and sort out details so that appropriate decisions can be made.

Supporting Medical Specialists

As noted earlier, a surgeon is very often the principal medical consultant, since operations remain a leading form of cancer treatment. The surgery team will of course include various supporting specialists, such as an anesthesiologist who is responsible for the patient's well-being during the operation. A plastic, or reconstructive, surgeon may also be consulted, either before or after the actual cancer surgery. In some instances the cancer surgery is planned to both remove the cancer and facilitate later reconstruction. This is increasingly the case in breast cancer surgery, in which reconstruction is often planned to follow a mastectomy. Facial surgery or other operations that are disfiguring or disabling are also planned with eventual reconstruction in mind. Increasingly satisfactory reconstructive procedures make a major difference in the quality of life following disfiguring surgery. Patients should know beforehand what options are available, as well as the risk of the operation and the likely results of appearance and ability to function. What the patient will look like and be able to do are important issues; if the doctor does not volunteer such information, the patient or family member should not hesitate to ask.

Increasingly, medical or surgical oncologists are assuming a central role in planning and directing treatment and, often, rehabilitation of patients with cancer. These oncologists are usually medical specialists—

internists, general surgeons, or surgery specialists—with additional training in the treatment of cancer.

Physiatrists and Physiotherapists

Patients who have been in bed or immobilized for long periods become weakened by both the treatment process and their immobility. Physiatrists and/or physical therapists are therefore important members of the treatment team. These specialists help exercise and stimulate muscles to regain strength and independence. Treatment by the physiotherapist may include occupational therapy, or this may be the domain of another team member. These therapists help disabled patients learn to perform tasks in new ways, ranging from simple everyday activities such as brushing teeth, dressing, and doing household chores to walking with an artificial limb or adjusting to an ostomy.

Dietitian

The nutrition of a cancer patient is an essential part of the overall treatment, therefore the dietitian is yet another very important member of the treatment team. Many cancer patients have difficulty with their appetite, either because of altered taste, cancer chemotherapy, the type of surgery involved, or some other facet of the disease and its treatment. The dietitian may be asked to plan an adequate nutritious and palatable diet. In some cases maintaining nutritional status is so important that intravenous feeding with concentrated nutrients may be added. (See Chapter 10, "Coping with Problems Related to Cancer and Cancer Treatment.")

Radiation Oncologists

Increasingly, cancer is treated by a combination of therapies, and many of these include radiation in the form of X rays, cobalt, or radium therapy. There are two basic methods of administering radiation therapy: externally, in which large machines generate the rays that are beamed into the patient's body to destroy the rapidly dividing cancer cells while, as much as possible, sparing the slower-growing normal cells; and internally, in which radioactive materials in the form of rods or needles are implanted within the cancerous tissue. (See Chapter 8, "Radiation Therapy.") In either instance the treatments are administered by a radiation therapist, also known as a radiation oncologist. These specialists differ from the radiologist, whose primary role is one of diagnostician. The radiation therapy team also may include technicians or other support personnel who operate the machines and help patients cope with or minimize side effects of radiation, such as skin changes, nausea and other adverse reactions. Very often, radiation treatments are administered on an outpatient basis, although the first few may be given while the patient is still hospitalized.

Cancer Chemotherapists

Over the last decade many powerful anticancer drugs have been developed that have vastly changed the outlook for certain types of cancer, particularly those of the blood and lymph system, as well as many solid tumors. These are potent drugs that must be given with great care to make certain that the dosage is sufficient to counteract the cancer but within limits that the body as a whole can tolerate. Chemotherapy is usually directed by a medical oncologist, a specially trained internist or cancer specialist, or hematologists, physicians who specialize in blood disorders. In any instance, the patient should know who will be overseeing this important aspect of treatment. This member of the treatment team should be available to discuss the various options of treatment, side effects, expected results, and complications. The chemotherapy may be administered in a doctor's office, hospital outpatient department, or during hospitalization, depending upon the type of cancer and individual circumstances. In many instances, oncology nurses who have special training in administering chemotherapy will give the drugs and also evaluate the patients for side effects. These nurses also are responsible for teaching the patients about the treatments and how to manage possible side effects.

In some instances an experimental protocol may be recommended that will require going to a specialized Comprehensive Cancer Center or one of the hospitals affiliated with these centers. However, as the use of anticancer drugs becomes increasingly common, more hospitals and physicians are acquiring the necessary experience in their use. The growing tendency to administer cancer chemotherapy in a local community hospital or physician's office is a direct result of this increased experience. And in a growing number of cases the patients themselves take the drugs at home, with periodic checkups by the doctor who is overseeing the chemotherapy. Even so, the patient should ask about the chemotherapist's experience and whether the drugs are being given under the supervision of, or in consultation with, a cancer center. The center may be miles away but linked to the local physician by computer or phone. This association enables the cancer center to monitor the effects of chemotherapy at appropriate intervals which may be weekly, monthly, or longer, depending upon the disease and regimen. (Cancer chemotherapy and experimental treatments are discussed more fully in Chapters 7 and 9.)

Other Rehabilitation Therapists

Rehabilitation of the patient with cancer is playing a greater role in the team approach to cancer and represents still another important area of decision-making. As noted earlier, the rehabilitation is often planned even before treatment begins. In any instance, the patient and family should be told of the types of rehabilitative efforts that will be required to resume as normal a lifestyle as possible. These efforts may involve a speech therapist or speech pathologist to help with speech retraining following surgery of the larynx (voice box) and mouth. An enterostomal therapist—most often a nurse who is trained to teach patients how to use the artificial openings made following either rectal or bladder surgery for eliminating body wastes—will be an important member of the rehabilitation team for these patients. Physical or occupational therapists may be enlisted to help in relearning tasks with artificial limbs or other physical changes. Patients and family members should ask the physician advisor to enlist the services of these and other trained rehabilitation therapists. In some instances the rehabilitation will be started in the hospital during the treatment phase; in others it may be offered at home or at an outpatient center. (For more details, see both Chapter 11, "Rehabilitation of the Cancer Patient," and the Directory of Resources in the Appendix.)

Volunteer Support Groups

Former cancer patients and other concerned volunteers have formed a number of volunteer support groups whose primary purpose is to help the new cancer patient through the difficult periods of adjustment during and after treatment. One of the oldest and best-known of these groups is the Reach to Recovery program of the American Cancer Society, made up of women who have been treated for breast cancer and then received training to help other women who have recently had similar treatment. The Reach to Recovery volunteers will call on a woman while she is still in the hospital, but the visit must be requested by the woman's physician. Women who have breast cancer should let their doctors know they would welcome a visit from a Reach to Recovery volunteer. Newer aspects of the Reach to Recovery program include reconstruction information and visits by volunteers who have had reconstruction or surgical procedures other than total mastectomy.

Other volunteer support groups include ostomy clubs organized by the United Ostomy Association; the Leukemia Society of America, a group made up of leukemia patients and family members; the International Association of Laryngectomees of the American Cancer Society, made up of patients who have had their larynxes removed, among others. Many organizations are under the auspices of the American Cancer Society, and information about them can be obtained from the local American Cancer Society (or the Directory of Resources in the Appendix).

In recent years there has also been a proliferation of volunteer organizations intended to help people deal with the broad issue of coping with cancer. Such groups include CanSurMount, a national program designated by the American Cancer Society as a therapeutic community made up of the patient, family members, CanSurMount volunteers, and health professionals. I Can Cope is another American Cancer Society program that is intended to help patients and families understand the problems of cancer through education. Make Today Count is still another nationwide program of people who have experienced cancer, either personally or through loved ones. Candlelighters, a nationally sponsored program of the American Cancer Society, is a support organization of parents whose children have had cancer. These parents provide emotional support through educational programs, meetings, hospital visits, and a toll-free telephone number. The Salvation Army, the YMCA and YWCA, American Red Cross, and numerous other voluntary organizations also offer a variety of support programs for cancer patients and family members. (For more complete listings, addresses, and telephone numbers, see the Directory of Resources in the Appendix.)

Although most of these support groups offer invaluable comfort and help that comes only from personal insight, experience, and sharing, one word of caution should be sounded: Make sure the volunteer is indeed recognized and trained by an official organization, such as the American Cancer Society. The vast majority are concerned, responsible groups performing a valuable service, but there are those few that are made up of unscrupulous individuals who prey upon the misfortunes of others. Some are cultists who try to persuade the cancer patient or family to seek an unproved type of treatment. If there are any doubts about the purpose or legitimacy of the volunteer or group, the physician advisor or hospital social worker should be consulted.

Hospice Services

The hospice, a special facility for patients with advanced disease, including cancer, is relatively new in the United States, but it is a growing movement spurred by the increasing willingness of people to control the circumstances of death. A hospice may be a separate facility or it may be located within a hospital. In addition, some hospitals have established hospices without walls—a range of services for dying patients in the home or in the hospital. Their concept is to provide a cheerful, open environment for both the patient and family members, whose purpose is to make the patient as comfortable and as happy as possible when death is inevitable and no further treatment to prolong life is planned. Hospice services are not available in many communities, but more information may be obtained by writing the National Hospice Organization, 765 Prospect Street, New Haven, Connecticut 06511, or Hospice Action, P.O. Box 32331, Washington, D.C. 20007, or the local American Cancer Society.

Going Home

Patients with cancer are now sent home from the hospital as early as possible after surgery and initiation of radiation therapy and chemotherapy. Radiation treatments may continue for a month or two after discharge; in contrast, chemotherapy—with a few exceptions—is often given over a prolonged period, and may stretch on for years. While these patients will continue to be closely monitored by their physician advisors and selected consultants, once the diagnosis and early treatment have been completed they usually are able to continue their care at home in reasonable comfort and function quite well.

The advantages of home care are numerous. Foremost is the return to a normal and familiar environment. This helps ease fear, anger, loss of personal and family identity, and the discomfort associated with prolonged hospitalization. It permits patients to carry on normal activities as much as possible while still undergoing treatment. Also, in this time of rapidly rising health care costs, the more treatment that can be given at home, the lower the overall cost to the family and the nation as a whole. In the coming years the United States will see an increase in home care for a number of chronic illnesses that now require hospitalization, including a larger portion of cancer treatment. Will this result in a lower quality of care? Evidence to date points in the opposite direction; as more and better home care health services are offered, we can expect increased quality of care. But this means that more members of the treatment team will be involved in the at-home aftercare phases than at present. Even today, however, many members of treatment teams are involved in the at-home period.

During the aftercare period, the physician advisor remains the main source of contact for the patient, family, and various consultants. When home care becomes an option, it is critical that the original decision-making team of patient, family, physician advisor, and principal consultants gather to discuss the homecoming arrangements for continuing care. This moment may be one of mixed emotions for the patient and family—joy at the prospect of going home, but also reluctance, hesitation, and fear over leaving the security of the hospital. In reality, going home should be viewed as a welcome return to familiar surroundings, with the secure knowledge that continuing care will be provided by the same treatment team.

The hospital social worker should be involved in planning the discharge and details of home care. If the patient and family have not already been in touch with the various organizations and agencies that will provide continuing medical, emotional, and financial support, this should be done by the social worker before discharge.

In a typical situation, the home care team may include a home health nurse, nursing aide, and homemaker for household chores. These services may not be covered by insurance, but many agencies offer them on the basis of the family's ability to pay. For example, in many communities there are public health or county nurses who provide nursing services at home. Physical and occupational therapists will frequently make home visits, as do speech and other therapists. Most communities have a visiting nurse association which offers professional care and relays information to the physician. Also, can the doctor be counted on to make house calls if needed? (This question, as noted earlier, should be resolved in the initial physician selection process.) Although there has been a decline in physician house calls in recent years, we can expect to see a return of this service as home care becomes more common throughout the country. In fact, many doctors feel that they can learn more on one home visit about a patient's needs and life situation than in the course of dozens of visits made in the hospital or office.

Special equipment may be required during this stage of home care; if so, it often can be obtained as a loan from the American Cancer Society. The ACS and other community organizations also stand ready to provide transportation and numerous other services. Rehabilitation programs that may have been discussed or even started in the hospital obviously should be continued and even accelerated after the patient goes home.

Even under the best of circumstances, one should anticipate that there will be emotional problems affecting patient and family alike. A psychiatric social worker, family or marriage counselor, clergyman or other professional trained to give counseling should be consulted if the need arises. In many instances, however, recognizing fears and other feelings and discussing them openly and honestly with each other and the physician advisor will help resolve the problem.

It also should be noted that not all patients will be able to go home directly from the hospital; instead, the next move may be to an extended care facility where the needs of patients who are still too sick for home care, but not ill enough to require full hospital care, can be met. Many hospitals, medical centers, and cancer care centers have affiliated extended care facilities. For still other patients, a hospice or hospice service may be required. Each situation must be viewed individually by the patient and other decision-makers. The important factor is to remember that a number of options are available, and that with proper guidance and investigation the combination can be found that will provide the best care and at the same time ease the burden of the disease for all those involved.

SUMMING UP

In this chapter we have attempted to outline the processes involved in the team approach to diagnosis, treatment, and aftercare of the cancer patient. Although a diagnosis of cancer understandably leaves the patient and loved ones fearful and with a feeling of hopelessness, it is important to know that there are many sources of help, treatment, and comfort. By seeking out these resources and learning as much as possible about the disease and what is involved in overcoming it, the patient is in the best position to make the right decisions. Members of the health-care team should provide a basis for evaluating and recommending additional support services. The choice of a physician advisor who will coordinate the various activities of the treatment team is among the most important decisions that the cancer patient must make. It is this physician advisor who should provide the continuity essential to avoid the fragmentation of care and information.

The patient should never lose sight of the fact that he or she is the most important member of the cancer treatment team; it is the patient who should be in full control. By retaining control, the patient is spared the dehumanization of an artificial division between mind and body, with the body further subdivided according to ailments. A well-organized program coordinated by a health care team of the patient's choice can be tremendously effective, and can make the difference between continued good health and recovery on the one hand or illness and chronic disability on the other. The fact of having cancer cannot be changed, but facing the disease with hope and a sense of control gives a person the greatest opportunity to find the most appropriate care, which in turn affords the best chance for the best quality of life for the longest possible time.

7
Principles of Cancer Chemotherapy

Margaret Lewin, M.D.

INTRODUCTION

Cancer chemotherapy involves the use of powerful medications to kill cancer cells. Whereas surgery and radiation therapy are used to treat cancer localized to a small part of the body, chemotherapy—which is carried by the bloodstream—can reach and destroy cancer cells that have traveled (metastasized) to parts distant from the original location.

Depending on the circumstances and the type of cancer, chemotherapy can be used as the sole means of treatment (as in the leukemias) or it can be used in conjunction with surgery and/or radiation therapy (as in breast and testicular cancers). The objectives of chemotherapy, again depending on circumstances and the type of cancer, are either to cure the cancer or to provide palliation to prolong survival, or to relieve the discomforts and disability caused by the cancer.

The first chemotherapeutic drug active against cancer was discovered during World War II, when American seamen were accidentally exposed to a chemical designed for use in gas warfare. Because the lymph glands of these seamen were affected, the chemical was tested in patients with cancer of the lymph glands (lymphoma) and produced the first chemotherapy-induced cancer remissions. Since that time, many new drugs that are effective against many different types of cancers have been developed.

To design new anticancer medications, researchers must understand the functions of cancer cells. Early studies involved the injection of leukemia cells into mice. It was found that one leukemia cell divided to become two, which, in turn, divided to become four. Subsequent divisions eventually produced a "tumor burden" sufficiently large to kill the mouse. This suggested that if cancer cells are allowed to grow and divide, even one cancer cell can eventually overwhelm the host and cause its death. Thus anticancer drugs must interfere with cell growth and reproduction, and must lead to the destruction of the last viable cancer cell before cure can be achieved.

Further studies over the years have resulted in a basic understanding of how cells function and in the development of chemicals that interfere with these functions in order to destroy the cells. Briefly reviewing the life cycle of cells will lead to some insight into how chemotherapy works.

THE CELL CYCLE

Both normal and cancer cells go through phases of the "cell cycle," as shown in Figure 10.

1. Cells in the G_0-phase usually perform functions specific to their cell type, but are "resting" in the sense that they are not actively involved in cell division. In this phase, they are minimally vulnerable to chemotherapy.
2. Cells in the G_1-phase manufacture RNA, enzymes, and other proteins necessary for reproduction. When they are actively making such products, they are vulnerable to those drugs that interfere with these processes.
3. Cells in the S-phase synthesize new DNA, duplicating these molecules in preparation for cell division. Cells in this phase are vulnerable to drugs that interfere with accurate duplication of the DNA.
4. Cells in the G_2-phase produce RNA, proteins, and the structures necessary for the physical process of dividing into two cells; they are vulnerable to drugs that interfere with this production.

5. During the M-phase, the cell's contents segregate into equal halves, and "daughter" cells are formed when these halves are fully separated from each other. Certain drugs interfere with the structures allowing this separation.

Thereafter, the daughter cells reenter the cell cycle at G_1 (in preparation for further division), or they leave the cell cycle, resting in G_0 where they are invulnerable to most chemotherapy.

Vigorous research efforts are aimed at developing new drugs which interrupt cell function in new ways, and at developing new methods of administering drugs with proven efficacy against cancer cells. For example, chemotherapy is toxic to cells actively proceeding through the cell cycle at the time the medication is given. Continuous administration of the drug over hours, days, or weeks exposes the cancer cells to the drug for longer periods of time and increases the likelihood that the drug will find the cell outside of the resting G_0-phase. Another approach would be to develop a new drug which can "bump" cancer cells from the resting G_0-phase back into the cell cycle, where it can be destroyed by other medications.

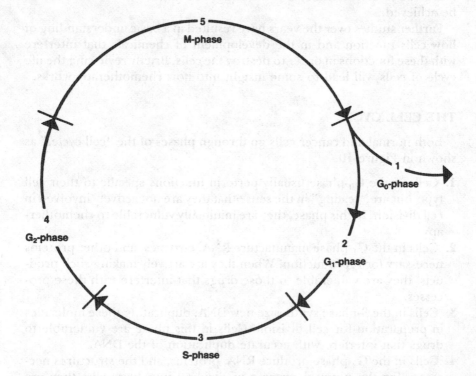

Figure 10 The cell cycle.

PRINCIPLES FOR USE OF CHEMOTHERAPY

Many years of cancer research by scientists from many disciplines have led to certain principles which guide the chemotherapist in tailoring treatment of a specific cancer in a specific patient.

1. Chemotherapeutic drugs do not distinguish between normal cells and cancer cells, both of which go through the cell cycle. Therefore a balance must be found between tumor destruction and the side effects caused by harming normal tissues.
2. Most chemotherapy drugs act best against rapidly dividing cells that spend little or no time in the resting G_0-phase of the cell cycle. This accounts for many of the side effects of these drugs, such as the loss of hair, bone marrow suppression, and the development of sores in the mouth and along the intestinal tract because hair, bone marrow cells, and the cells lining the mouth and other parts of the intestinal tract all divide rapidly.
3. As tumor masses grow larger, more cells enter the resting G_0-phase; the rate of division (and vulnerability to chemotherapy) therefore decreases. Thus chemotherapy is most effective against small tumors.
4. Most of the chemotherapy now being used works by a mechanism known as "first-order cell kill." This means that a given dose of drug will kill a given percentage (rather than a given number) of cancer cells. Take, for example, a drug with a kill rate of 90 percent and a tumor mass of one billion cells (a little smaller than your little fingernail). One course (administration) of the drug will kill 90 percent of the cancer cells, leaving 100 million cells. The second course will kill another 90 percent, leaving 10 million cells. Each successive course of chemotherapy will leave behind a viable 10 percent. Since even one remaining cell can multiply until the tumor mass reaches the critical size, cure of the cancer requires that therapy continue until that last cancer cell is destroyed.
5. The greater the number of cancer cells, the more likely that some of those cells will become "resistant" (immune) to a given type of chemotherapy drug.

Using the general principles above, chemotherapists frequently employ several different classes of drugs in high doses. This is done in order to attack cells in different parts of the cell cycle, to circumvent cancer cell resistance to one class of drug, and to balance the drugs' different toxicities. Enough time is scheduled between treatments to allow adequate recovery of normal cells, but not full recovery and renewed growth of the cancer cells.

TOXIC EFFECTS OF CHEMOTHERAPY

Anticancer drugs are potent, highly toxic chemicals which require skill-ful use. The chemotherapist (usually an oncologist or hematologist) must carefully balance benefits against risks for the individual patient, and adjust doses and timing accordingly. High levels of toxicity may be ac-ceptable when the therapeutic objective is cure of the cancer. However, when the objective is palliation, the side effects of the chemotherapy must be less distressing than the effects of the cancer itself.

Regardless of whether the goal is cure of the cancer or relief of symp-toms, chemotherapy may need to be stopped or the drugs changed if severe adverse reactions (such as kidney damage, weakening of the heart muscle, or lack of adequate bone marrow recovery) occur. Other adverse effects, such as nausea and vomiting, hair loss, mouth sores, and fatigue, can usually be managed at acceptable levels. Specific side effects and advice on how to minimize them are discussed in Chapter 10, "Coping with Problems Related to Cancer and Cancer Treatment."

ADMINISTRATION OF CANCER CHEMOTHERAPY

Chemotherapy is usually given by mouth (in pill or liquid form) or intravenously (directly into the vein). Administered in these ways the medications enter the bloodstream, which carries them to nearly all parts of the body that might contain cancer cells. Under special circumstances it might be advantageous to aim the medications more directly; this can be done by administering them directly into the artery that feeds a spe-cific part of the body, into abnormal fluid accumulations in the chest or abdominal cavities, or into the spinal fluid that bathes the brain and spinal cord.

Anticancer drugs can be separated into classes according to their ori-gin, chemical nature, and method of action. The most commonly used drug classes include the alkylating agents, antimetabolites, antitumor antibiotics, plant alkaloids, and hormones.

A major side effect of the first three drug classes is "bone marrow suppression," and is usually the limiting factor in the frequency and dosage with which these drugs can be given safely. The bone marrow is contained in the center of bones (similar to the marrow in animal bones used to make soups) and produces the white blood cells that fight infec-tions, the red blood cells (corpuscles) that carry life-sustaining oxygen to the body's organs, and the platelets, which help the blood to clot. When the bone marrow is suppressed, fewer blood cells are produced and the patient becomes more vulnerable to infections, anemic and at risk for serious bleeding.

Before chemotherapy is given, a blood test is done to determine how many white blood cells, red blood cells, and platelets are circulating in the blood. The dosage of chemotherapy is calculated on the basis of the results of this blood count. After chemotherapy is administered, it is expected that the blood count will decrease over days to weeks (depending on the drugs used), reflecting the bone marrow's suppression. After the marrow has recovered, the blood count will return to normal and the next course of chemotherapy can be given.

CLASSES OF ANTICANCER DRUGS

A brief description of the anticancer drug categories (and of the most frequently used drugs in those categories) follows.

Alkylating Agents

These are the oldest and most numerous of the chemotherapeutic agents. They work by damaging the internal chemistry of the DNA, RNA, and other protein molecules of cells by releasing an unstable chemical entity (the "alkyl group"), which links the molecules in abnormal ways. Since the function of these molecules depends upon their biological structure and physical shape, the abnormal linkages interfere with the cells' production of the enzymes RNA and DNA, necessary for survival and reproduction.

Alkylating agents cause their greatest damage to cells in any active phase of the cell cycle; in high doses they can also kill cells in the resting G_0-phase.

Resistance to the alkylating agents appears to result from the cancer's development of cells that can repair the molecular damage faster than the drugs can inflict it. Since all alkylating agents work in similar ways, development of resistance to one alkylating agent usually implies resistance to the others. This phenomenon is known as cross-resistance.

The alkylating agents are effective against many types of cancers, including breast and lung cancers, and certain leukemias and lymphomas. Although similar in their mechanisms of action, specific alkylating agents tend to be used against specific types of cancer (see Table 9).

Antimetabolites

The antimetabolites are usually drugs that resemble normal molecules essential for the synthesis of DNA. The substitution of these counterfeit molecules leads to the production of incompetent DNA and cell activity. Since the antimetabolites act by interfering with DNA synthesis, they are active only against cells in the S-phase of the cycle. Since cells are in the

Table 9: Alkylating Agents

CHEMICAL NAME OF MEDICATION (BRAND NAME)	EXAMPLES OF RESPONSIVE CANCERS	COMMON ROUTES	MOST COMMON SIDE EFFECTS
busulfan (Myleran)	Chronic myelogenous leukemia	By mouth	Bone marrow suppression
chlorambucil (Leukeran)	Chronic lymphocytic leukemia, breast, lymphoma	By mouth	Bone marrow suppression, mild nausea
cyclophosphamide (Cytoxan)	Breast, lung, ovarian, prostatic; lymphoma, some childhood cancers	By mouth or vein	Bone marrow suppression, bladder irritation and bleeding, hair loss
melphalan, L-PAM, L-phenyl-alanine mustard (Alkeran)	Multiple myeloma, breast, ovarian	By mouth	Bone marrow suppression, hair loss, mouth sores
nitrogen mustard, mechlorethamine (Mustargen)	Hodgkin's disease	By vein	Bone marrow suppression, nausea, vomiting; burns if it leaks out of vein
Nitrosoureas: carmustine, BCNU (BiCNU) lomustine, CCNU (CeeNU) semustine (methyl CCNU)	Brain, colon, gastric, lung, melanoma, pancreatic, Hodgkin's disease	By vein By mouth By mouth	Prolonged bone marrow suppression, nausea, vomiting
triethylenethio-phosphoramide (Thiotepa)	Breast, ovarian; bladder	By vein by direct infusion	Bone marrow suppression

S-phase for only a small percentage of their reproduction cycle, the longer the cells are exposed to the antimetabolites, or the more frequently these drugs are administered, the more likely that a specific cell will be exposed during its vulnerable period. Some of these drugs are therefore administered continuously over hours, days, or even weeks.

Cancer cells can become resistant (immune) to antimetabolites by producing more normal molecules with which to compete with the counterfeit antimetabolite molecules, by increasing their ability to repair the damage inflicted on the DNA by these drugs, or by finding ways to block entrance of these drugs into the cell or speeding their expulsion from the cell. The most commonly used antimetabolites, their side effects, and the cancers they are used against are listed in Table 10.

Anticancer Antibiotics

Chemotherapeutic drugs in this category are termed anticancer "antibiotics" because they are produced by bacteria and have some activity against bacterial infections. Because of their toxicity they are not, however, used to treat infections. The anticancer antibiotics insert themselves into the DNA molecule (thereby interfering with its function); or they interfere with the synthesis of or normal repair mechanisms of DNA. Drugs in this category are summarized in Table 11.

Plant Alkaloids

Two major subclasses of chemotherapy drugs are derived from plants. These are the "vinca alkaloids" (derived from the periwinkle family of plants), which include vincristine and vinblastine; and the epipodophyllotoxins (derived from the mandrake plant), which include VP-16.

The vinca alkaloids work on cells in the M-phase of the cell cycle by interfering with the structures necessary for division. The mechanism of the epipodophyllotoxins is still under investigation, but these drugs appear to exert their major anticancer effect on cells in the S and G_2 phases of the cell cycle and can cause breaks in the DNA molecule. Plant alkaloids are summarized in Table 12.

Hormones

Hormones are molecules produced by a body organ and released into the bloodstream to produce their natural effects at multiple locations remote from their source. They have profound effects on the growth and metabolism of their target cells and organs.

Hormones used in the treatment of some cancers include corticoste-

Table 10: Antimetabolites

CHEMICAL NAME OF MEDICATION (BRAND NAME)	EXAMPLES OF RESPONSIVE CANCERS	COMMON ROUTES	MOST COMMON SIDE EFFECTS
cytosine arabino-side, Ara-C (Cytosar-U)	Leukemias	By vein, under skin, into spinal fluid	Bone marrow suppression, mouth and intestinal ulcers, nausea, vomiting, diarrhea
5-Fluorouracil, 5-FU (Fluorouracil)	Breast, colon, gastric, pancreatic, prostatic, skin	By vein	Bone marrow suppression, skin darkening, diarrhea, watering of eyes, nausea, vomiting, mouth sores
mercaptopurine, 6-mercaptopurine, 6-MP (Purinethol)	Leukemias	By mouth	Bone marrow suppression, liver inflammation
methotrexate	Breast, cervical, head and neck; choriocarcinoma; leukemias, lymphomas	By vein, into spinal fluid	Bone marrow suppression, nausea, vomiting, mouth sores
thioguanine	Leukemias	By mouth or vein	Bone marrow suppression, nausea, vomiting, mouth and esophagus ulcers

Table 11: Anticancer Antibiotics

CHEMICAL NAME OF MEDICATION (BRAND NAME)	EXAMPLES OF RESPONSIVE CANCERS	COMMON ROUTES	MOST COMMON SIDE EFFECTS
bleomycin (Blenoxane) (Cytosar-U)	Cervical, head and neck, testicular, Hodgkin's disease, lymphomas	By vein, under skin	Skin darkening, mouth and intestinal ulcers, lung scarring, fever, allergic reactions
dactinomycin, actinomycin-D (Cosmegen)	Testicular, choriocarcinoma, sarcomas, some childhood cancers	By vein	Nausea, vomiting, mouth and intestinal ulcers; burns if it leaks out of vein
daunorubicin (Cerubidine); doxorubicin (Adriamycin)	Breast, bladder, cervical, ovarian, testicular, thyroid; Hodgkin's disease, leukemias, lymphomas, sarcomas	By vein	Bone marrow suppression, weakening of heart muscle, nausea, vomiting, mouth sores, hair loss, red urine (on day of therapy); burns if it leaks out of vein
mitomycin (Mutamycin)	Breast, colon, gastric, pancreatic	By vein	Bone marrow suppression, nausea, vomiting; burns if it leaks out of vein

Table 12: Plant Alkaloids

CHEMICAL NAME OF MEDICATION (BRAND NAME)	EXAMPLES OF RESPONSIVE CANCERS	COMMON ROUTES	MOST COMMON SIDE EFFECTS
etoposide, VP-16 (VePesid)	Lung, genital, Kaposi's sarcoma, lymphomas, leukemias	By vein	Bone marrow suppression
vincristine (Oncovin)	Breast, lung, Hodgkin's disease, Kaposi's sarcoma, leukemias	By vein	Numbness and weakness of hands and feet, constipation
vinblastine (Velban)	Breast, testicular, Hodgkin's disease, Kaposi's sarcoma	By vein	Bone marrow suppression, nausea, vomiting, constipation; burns if it leaks out of vein

roids, such as cortisone, and the hormones responsible for male and female sexual function, such as testosterone and estrogen respectively.

Other cancers can be treated with a drug that blocks the hormone necessary for their growth or by destroying the organ that produces the hormone.

Corticosteroids are produced by the adrenal gland. When used in cancer therapy, they are given in doses much higher than the body usually produces. Many synthetic and natural forms of these steroids are available for clinical use; examples are cortisone, hydrocortisone, prednisone, methylprednisolone, and dexamethasone. Their actions are very similar.

These steroids have multiple uses in the treatment of cancers. They have a direct effect against such malignancies as lymphomas, some leukemias, and some breast cancers. In other malignancies they simply alleviate symptoms—for example, by decreasing the swelling around brain tumors they might decrease headache or paralysis temporarily.

Used in high doses for prolonged periods of time, these steroids can produce increased susceptibility to infection, ulcers, high blood pressure, elevated blood sugars, muscle weakness, personality changes, thinning of the bones (osteoporosis), fluid retention, skin fragility, and dependence on continued use of the drugs (since the adrenal gland stops making its own). Some of these adverse effects can be avoided by giving the steroids in short courses over several days, with a few weeks between courses. Hormones used in cancer chemotherapy are summarized in Table 13.

OTHER CHEMOTHERAPY DRUGS

A number of chemotherapeutic drugs do not fit neatly into the earlier categories, either because they have a unique mode of action or because they work in several of the ways described above. These drugs are summarized in Table 14.

Table 13: Hormones

CHEMICAL NAME OF MEDICATION	EXAMPLES OF RESPONSIVE CANCERS	MOST COMMON SIDE EFFECTS
Adrenocorticoids (for example, prednisone, cortisone, dexamethasone)	Breast; multiple myeloma, Hodgkin's disease, leukemias, lymphomas	Increased appetite, mood changes, fluid retention, acne, increased blood pressure, elevated blood sugar, intestinal ulcers, lowered resistance to infection
Estrogens (female hormones)	Breast, prostatic	Nausea, fluid retention, breast enlargement, increased propensity to blood clots
Antiestrogens	Breast	Nausea, hot flashes
Androgens (male hormones)	Breast	Deepening of voice, increased body and facial hair, fluid retention, enlargement of the clitoris
Progestational agents	Breast, uterine	Side effects are rare

138

Table 14: Other Agents

CHEMICAL NAME OF MEDICATION (BRAND NAME)	EXAMPLES OF RESPONSIVE CANCERS	COMMON ROUTES	MOST COMMON SIDE EFFECTS
asparaginase, L-asparaginase (Elspar)	Leukemias	By vein or into muscle	Fever, allergic reaction, confusion, inflammation of liver or pancreas, bleeding
cisplatin, cisplatinum, DDP (Platinol)	Bladder, head and neck, lung, ovarian, prostatic, testicular	By vein	Nausea, vomiting, kidney damage, hearing loss
dacarbazine (DTIC-Dome)	Hodgkin's disease, lymphomas, melanoma, sarcomas	By vein	Bone marrow suppression, nausea, vomiting, irritation at site of injection
hydroxyurea	Chronic myelogenous leukemia	By mouth	Bone marrow suppression
procarbazine hydrochloride	Hodgkin's disease, lymphomas	By mouth	Bone marrow suppression, nausea, vomiting, lethargy
streptozocin (Streptozotocin)	Pancreatic, Hodgkin's disease, malignant carcinoid	By vein	Kidney damage, nausea, vomiting

SUMMARY

Chemotherapeutic drugs are used to treat cancers either alone or in conjunction with surgery and/or radiation. They work by interfering with the function of both normal and cancer cells. The types of drugs used and their doses, frequency, and routes of administration must be carefully tailored to the type of cancer and its extent, the objectives of therapy, and the medical condition of the patient.

Future chemical strategies against cancer are likely to take advantage of the growing body of knowledge about cellular function and about antibodies that can selectively target cancer cells for destruction while sparing normal cells.

8

Radiation Therapy

WILLIS J. TAYLOR, M.D.

Radiation therapy, the use of X rays and other forms of radiation to treat cancer, is truly a twentieth-century medical specialty. About half of the more than 900,000 patients who are diagnosed as having cancer each year in the United States will undergo radiation therapy. Very often the radiation treatments will be combined with surgery and chemotherapy. But more than 100,000 cancer patients are rendered free of the disease each year by radiation therapy alone. These advances are due to a number of factors, including the use of different kinds of radiation in cancer treatment, a greater understanding of how cancers grow and react to radiation therapy, and the development of more precise diagnostic tools and computer-designed treatment plans to meet the needs of individual patients.

HISTORY OF RADIATION THERAPY

Radiation therapy can be traced to the discovery of uranium by the French physicist Henri Becquerel in 1896 and to Marie and Pierre Curie, who identified the even more radioactive substances polonium and radium in 1898. For these discoveries, the three shared the Nobel prize in physics in 1903. Parallel to these discoveries was the pioneering use of diagnostic X rays by the German researcher Wilhelm Conrad Roentgen, who discovered that these rays could be used to visualize the bones and other internal structures. Experiments using the new phenomenon to treat skin cancers followed soon after, with some striking successes. It was also discovered that X rays could be used to treat some cancers of the cervix. But the early X-ray machines were relatively weak and could not penetrate into the body to reach deep tumors. Instead these conventional "orthovoltage" machines, with a range of 250 to 400 kilovolts (a kilovolt is one thousand volts), deposited much of their radiation close to the skin surface. This often caused burns and other skin problems, including later cancers (as was discovered years after the use of X rays to treat such conditions as acne and tonsillitis). But a series of rapid technologic advances have completely changed the nature of modern radiation therapy. By the 1950s radioactive cobalt, an artificial radioisotope that delivers higher energy rays with deeper penetration into the body and fewer skin problems than orthovoltage X-ray machines, came into use to treat a variety of cancers.

A decade later, in the 1960s, higher-energy supervoltage machines appeared. These could deliver rays of 4 to 40 megavolts (a megavolt is one million volts) with even deeper penetration but with still less skin damage. Today most radiation therapy units are equipped with several types of machines: a high-voltage beam, a cobalt machine, and a low-energy machine for skin cancers. A computerized system, often monitored by a major cancer treatment center, usually is employed to control the course of treatment. There are also instances in which radioactive materials are implanted directly into the tumor or close to it. The purpose is the same—namely, to employ radiation to destroy the fast-growing cancer cells with a minimum of damage to healthy tissue.

THE EFFECT OF RADIATION ON CANCERS

X rays are similar in nature to light rays, but they travel at vastly higher energy levels and are invisible to the human eye. The cosmic rays that are detectable on a Geiger counter are natural forms of X rays from space and make up part of the background radiation to which all of us are exposed without identifiable ill effects. An ordinary chest X ray exposes the patient to about 120 times the usual background radiation, but this is still considerably less than the typical dosage given to treat a cancer patient.

In anticancer radiation therapy, the ultimate target for the radiation is the deoxyribonucleic acid (DNA) in the malignant cell. DNA is the genetic material controlling a cell's reproduction. The DNA of a malignant cell is more susceptible to radiation damage than that of a normal cell. The radiation disrupts the structure of several of the chemical elements in the DNA portion of the cell nucleus, leading to cell death. This destruction of the cancer cell is not immediate; instead, it occurs over a period of hours or even days. Sometimes several exposures of the rapidly dividing cancer cells to the high-energy radiation are required, and even then enough tumor cells may survive to permit regrowth of the cancer. To prevent this, the radiation therapist calculates the total amount of radiation that will probably be required to destroy the cancer, and then spreads that amount over a number of treatments. This increases the probability of killing all the tumor cells without excessive damage to normal tissues. In this way the cancer will be destroyed over a period of time, by killing the individual cancer cells at a faster rate than they can repair themselves and reproduce. To minimize further the radiation damage to the skin and other normal tissue, the radiation dosage will be directed at the tumor through several different "ports" or sites on the skin surface. In other words, the target is always the cancer, but the radiation may be beamed to it via different pathways.

In theory, no cancer exists that cannot be destroyed by radiation. The problem is delivering the required amount of radiation to the cancer without causing excessive harm to the patient. For example, if a radiation therapist knows that 6,500 rads will be required to destroy a certain type of cancer, a regimen course of treatment must be devised that will permit the delivery of this dosage to the cancer itself with only minimal exposure to the rest of the body. A single dose of only 700 rads administered to the entire body would prove fatal to more than half of the people receiving such exposure. Thus the task is to deliver the required amount of radiation to the cancer itself while sparing the healthy part of the body. This is not always possible for a variety of reasons. As a result, part of the tumor may be destroyed, but enough cells will remain that can repair their X-ray injuries and then reproduce to form new tumors. Or some of the cancer may escape exposure to the radiation—a situation referred to as a "geographic miss." This sometimes occurs when there are multiple sites of cancer or when some cells on the outer reaches are not exposed to the full dose and are able to reproduce and spread.

Still another important factor in the outcome of radiation therapy is the nearness of the tumor to sensitive normal tissues or organs that cannot withstand exposure to high doses of radiation. A tumor along the spinal cord, for example, may be very difficult or impossible to treat with radiation because the X-ray dosage needed to destroy the tumor might also destroy the spinal cord. A weakened general physical condition caused by the cancer or other diseases such as diabetes, alcoholism, or kidney failure also may reduce a patient's tolerance to radiation therapy. But even with these potentials for failure, large numbers of cancer patients can be effectively treated and even cured with radiation therapy.

DEVELOPING THE TREATMENT PLAN

For cancer patients undergoing radiation therapy, developing a treatment plan that takes into account not only the nature and stage of the disease but also individual factors such as age and overall health is the primary consideration. Computers and a host of highly accurate diagnostic tests are very often used in developing the treatment plan that will be followed. For example, pinpointing the exact location of the tumor is essential if the radiation therapist is to deliver the correct dosage to the right spot. New diagnostic tests, such as computerized tomographic (CT) scanning and ultrasound examination, enable the therapist to tell exactly where the tumor is located.

Computers now play a vital role in individualizing radiation therapy. Complex computer programs also have been developed that calculate precisely how much radiation should be delivered. A computer can simulate a treatment plan that will deliver the right amount of radiation to kill the cancer without endangering nearby vital organs. The computer also can allow for dosage adjustments to prevent undertreating cancer cells in the tumor margins and can take other measures to minimize the possibility of failure. These careful calculations are essential because it is the last 10 or 15 percent of the total radiation dose that guarantees the destruction of the last few surviving cancer cells, thus preventing recurrence. Data processors, video display terminals, and computer graphics—all space-age devices that are commonplace in today's radiation therapy department—give the radiation therapist the accuracy needed to assure successful treatment. Experiments have shown that even a few remaining cells can, in some varieties of cancer, result in total regrowth of the cancer. Indeed, without computers radiation therapy would not be the exact science it is today.

As in all cancer therapy, designing an appropriate plan for radiation therapy is a team effort involving a number of people. In this instance the treatment team is directed by a radiologist or radiation oncologist (a radiologist who specializes in treating cancer) who usually works with an oncology nurse, medical physicist, technicians, and others involved in this specific type of cancer therapy. Very often radiation therapy will be combined with other forms of treatment, particularly surgery. Theoretically surgery and radiation therapy are synergistic—that is, they work together to produce a more positive result than can be obtained by either treatment alone. X ray eradicates the individual cancer cells or microscopic disease, but is not as effective in treating large cancers. In contrast, surgery is the most effective way of removing the cancer mass, but it often misses the very small or microscopic disease. Indeed, it still is not known whether surgery increases the likelihood of cancer cells' entering the bloodstream to form new cancers in other parts of the body (metastases). If this is the case, then it would appear that the radiation therapy should precede the surgery. On the other hand, preoperative radiation may increase surgical complications such as infection, slower healing, weakened suture lines and other problems. These can be minimized by careful timing of the two procedures, planning the surgical incision lines with respect to radiation ports, and paying particular attention to the overall condition of the patient.

Chemotherapy is also combined with radiation therapy to treat many cancers. For example, radiation therapy is often combined with chemotherapy in the treatment of Hodgkin's disease and certain breast cancers. When the two therapies are combined, special care must be taken to avoid possible adverse interactions. For example, the lungs are especially sensitive to radiation, and treatment involving the chest often results in radiation-caused lung disorders. These are usually relatively minor and heal in time. However, if the anticancer drug also affects the lungs, as is the case with bleomycin—an agent used to treat cancers of the mouth, oral cavity, and testes—then particular care must be taken in combining the two therapies to avoid serious, even fatal, lung complications. Similarly, combining radiation therapy with the use of methotrexate, a drug used to treat leukemia, may result in severe nerve damage.

WHAT TO EXPECT DURING RADIATION THERAPY

Patients receiving radiation therapy are understandably apprehensive, especially if they do not know what to expect. The precise course of treatment varies from patient to patient and depends upon many factors, including the type of cancer, its site and stage, the general condition of patient and other considerations. The total radiation dose and timing of the treatments are carefully calculated and, as stressed earlier, the radiation must be accurately beamed to the cancer with as little exposure as possible to healthy tissues. Modern X-ray and other radiation therapy machines are designed to achieve this goal. In addition, special restraints and other mechanical devices are used to keep the patient absolutely still during a treatment session. These gentle but firm restraining devices are made of lucite, plaster, lead and other materials. They may be fashioned for each patient individually, or adjusted as needed in the mold shop that is an integral part of every radiation therapy department.

Lead shields are particularly important in protecting healthy tissue because they act as a barrier to X rays. Lead does not completely block the radiation, but—depending upon the thickness of the lead and energy of the X-ray beam—the dosage can be reduced to less than one percent of its original level, resulting in a negligible exposure to normal tissues. Thus radiation therapy can be given to the lymph nodes in the middle of the chest to treat Hodgkin's disease, for example, while the sensitive surrounding lung tissue is protected from the high-dose radiation by precise lead forms made to match the patient's lungs. In general, muscle and nerve tissues are the most resistant to radiation injury, followed by the skin. The intestines, kidneys, and bone marrow are particularly sensitive; in fact, the sensitivity of the kidneys and gastrointestinal tract greatly restricts the use of generalized radiation therapy for abdominal cancer.

Although external beam radiation is most commonly used, a number of relatively new alternative means of delivering radiation have been developed. Increasing use is being made of materials made radioactive by cyclotron radiation that are then implanted directly into the tumor or very close to it. This technique, called brachytherapy, is constantly being refined. It is now used either alone or in addition to the external beam. Typically, the radiation is administered through implanted "seeds" and wires, which may be made of gold or an even rarer element, iridium. The radiation from these seeds does not penetrate for more than a third of an inch of tissue, meaning that the implants must be carefully and closely spaced to expose all of the tumor to intense curative doses. In this way the cancer is exposed to continuous radiation, albeit at lower levels of intensity usually amounting to only about 30 to 50 rads per hour. These radioactive seeds may be implanted directly into the cancer, as in treating prostate cancer in men, or may be implanted in a hollow organ space (intracavitary), as in the treatment of cancer of the uterus. CT scans and ultrasonography make it possible to place these seeds and wires with accuracy. Special molds to hold the radioactive seeds in place may be required for those inserted into hollow spaces, particularly when the spaces are irregularly shaped, such as the nose or ear canals. Some implants are permanent—for example, those used to treat some kinds of prostatic cancer. Others may be left in place for a few days or weeks, and still others deliver precise dosages that require the patient to wear the mold for specific time periods. A nasal mold holding radioactive seeds, for example, may be worn for three hours and seventeen minutes on eight consecutive days. Accuracy in determining the amount of radiation needed to destroy all cancer cells is vital, because it is the last 10 or 15 percent of the radiation that kills the last remaining cancer cells, thereby preventing recurrence.

COMMON SIDE EFFECTS AND HOW TO PREVENT THEM

Many patients fear undergoing radiation therapy because they have heard stories of complications and adverse effects that make the cure sound almost worse than the disease. While adverse effects do occur, constantly improved techniques and machines have done much to minimize complications. In addition, thoughtful preplanning can eliminate or minimize many of the common complications. For example, mouth sores, radiation-induced dental cavities, and tooth loss are relatively common adverse effects of radiation therapy of the head and neck region. Poor dental hygiene worsens the problem. By receiving needed dental care before radiation therapy, having needed preparatory tooth extractions and using fluoride during the course of treatment, many radiation-related dental problems can be avoided.

During radiation therapy, sores or ulcers (mucositis) often develop in the mouth, throat, intestines, genital areas and other parts of the body that are covered by delicate mucous membranes. Mucositis often develops among patients undergoing radiation therapy for cancers of the head and neck, lung, esophagus, and abdominal organs. This can be a serious problem when patients have difficulty eating because of mouth sores. If a cancer patient is unable to eat, he or she is likely to become malnourished and further weakened. Mouthwashes, lozenges, frequent examination for thrush or other fungal infections, good oral hygiene, and soft diets all are measures that minimize this potential side effect of radiation therapy.

Women undergoing radiation of the pelvic cavity to treat cancers of the cervix, body of the uterus, vagina or other pelvic organs may develop rectal ulcers, fistulas, bladder ulcers, diarrhea, and colitis. Simple measures such as douches with vinegar diluted with warm water, stool softeners, good hygiene, and, when indicated, dilation of the vagina to prevent the development of adhesions, will help prevent or minimize complications. Antibiotics also may be recommended to prevent abscesses in cases where infection might be a problem.

Nausea and vomiting, side effects that have often been exaggerated in the media, can be minimized by timing of treatments and the use of antinausea drugs. When nausea and vomiting do occur, they tend to be short-lived.

Postirradiation cataracts can be prevented by proper screening of the eye when cancers of nearby structures are being treated. As noted earlier, the lungs are particularly vulnerable to complications from radiation. Radiation pneumonitis, an inflammation of the lung tissue, may result in reduced lung function—but this is more common in patients who have preexisting lung problems such as bronchitis. Most radiation pneumonitis subsides in time, except in very weakened patients, and it is not always an indication to avoid further radiation therapy.

Since radiation passes through the skin to reach its ultimate target, it is understandable that the more obvious effects of radiation therapy appear in the skin. At first no reaction is seen, but as the radiation therapy continues, redness (erythema) and darkening caused by increased pigmentation appears in the exposed skin areas. The redness itself is a relatively minor problem and can be minimized by using vitamin A and D ointment or a mild (1 percent) hydrocortisone cream for more intense cases. (Before applying any cream or ointment, be sure to consult your doctor or radiation therapist; lotions or alcohol should never be used for any radiation skin reaction.) The radiation burns that sometimes occurred in the past are now rarely seen. Following radiation treatment, however, the skin may be unusually sensitive to the sun, therefore it is a good idea to avoid exposure to the sun or to apply a sunblocking lotion or cream if the sun cannot be avoided.

After about four weeks of therapy, a second skin reaction may appear; namely, peeling of the exposed skin. If the hair follicles are not swollen, the peeling will be dry; if the hair follicles are swollen, moist peeling and crusting of the skin can be expected. Both these reactions can be treated by following basic dermatologic principles. If the outer skin is dry and intact, it should be kept that way with cornstarch—do not use talcum powder. If the outer skin is moist and peeling, the surface should be treated with mild saline soaks and gentle soap and water to remove crusts and dead skin. Severe moist peeling may, in some cases, necessitate halting the radiation therapy until healing occurs. Skin ulcers caused by destruction of small areas of skin should be treated by a physician; however, they are almost always self-limited and not a cause for undue alarm.

Some skin problems do not show up for many years. For example, several years after the radiation therapy, the tissues just beneath the skin may become hard and fibrous, making the area feel somewhat thickened. This is particularly true if a shallow tumor has been treated, or if a large radiation dosage was administered just below the skin surface. Sometimes the skin slowly becomes white, scarred, and thin. This is the result of destruction of the small capillaries that run through the skin. Later, occasional small visible surface blood vessels may form, a condition called telangiectasis. If these are cosmetically troublesome, they can easily be removed by plastic surgery.

In treating cancers of the skin itself, remarkably fine cosmetic results can be obtained by using electron beam radiation. This type of radiation employs subatomic particles, which penetrate only shallow depths of human tissue. By using appropriate shields and protective molds, cancers of the skin, lips, eyelids and nose can be effectively treated without the scarring that may occur from surgical removal. Very low dosage conventional X rays also may be used to treat skin cancers with good cosmetic and medical results. (For more discussion see Chapter 10, "Coping with Problems Related to Cancer and Cancer Treatment.")

GENETIC CONSIDERATIONS

The genetic effects of radiation are a major consideration in planning X-ray treatments, especially for younger patients. Pregnant women or women of childbearing age should not be exposed to X rays unless absolutely necessary. When X rays of any kind are administered during pregnancy, precautions are always taken to protect the fetus.

Exposure of the gonads—the testes or ovaries—to X rays also raises the question of possible genetic damage to future offspring. The problem is more acute for women, who have a limited number of eggs that come to maturity, than for men, who constantly produce new sperm. If exposure occurs in men, the defective sperm are likely to be cleared from the system in a couple of months, although a low sperm count may persist for six months or longer. In women the long-term effects are unknown, but it is probably wise to wait at least six months or longer after exposure before attempting conception. In that time, the defective ova may have died and the viable ones may have repaired their genetic injury. In any instance, the gonads should be protected from radiation exposure by lead shielding. If abdominal radiation is necessary, the ovaries can sometimes be temporarily moved surgically from the radiation target area, and then returned to their original position following treatment.

CANCER-CAUSING POTENTIAL

When dealing with radiation, the question of causing or promoting new cancers always arises. Sufficient doses of radiation can produce cancer in time. In using radiation therapy or any other treatment, one must always weigh the risks against the benefits. The potential benefit of using radiation therapy to cure a cancer obviously outweighs any risk of possibly causing another cancer at some future date. For example, Hodgkin's disease patients who receive radiation therapy do have a slightly higher incidence of leukemia, but many more live longer because of the treatment, and the benefits derived vastly outweigh the potential risks.

Of course, the fear of X rays' causing cancer is not limited to high-dose radiation therapy; even diagnostic procedures such as mammograms to detect breast cancer or chest X rays have been questioned because of their cancer-causing potential. Although no X-ray procedure should be performed routinely unless there is definite benefit to be gained, one should remember that the risk involved in these procedures is negligible when very low doses are used, as is the case in mammography using modern X-ray equipment.

THE FUTURE

As in all rapidly advancing scientific endeavors, we can say without exaggeration that part of the future of radiation therapy is already here. Radiation therapy has been greatly advanced into a much more precise discipline by the introduction of computer technology. In fact, most radiation therapy departments are now being equipped with treatment computers that get information directly from diagnostic computers. The improvement in diagnosis and locating a tumor has also made radiation therapy more precise and effective. We can now construct treatment plans with a precision that was unknown just a decade ago, and even more precise and effective machines and techniques appear on the horizon. Now, forms of heavy-ion radiation—alpha particles, neutrons, pi mesons, protons and other subatomic particles—can be aimed at several kinds of tumors and can achieve high cure rates. These exotic forms of radiation are being explored in university medical centers, often in collaboration with physics departments, using their subatomic particle accelerators.

Drugs and chemicals that sensitize cancer cells to the destructive effects of radiation, thereby making it possible to destroy the cancer cells at lower doses, are also being developed. Still another experimental technique involves the use of hyperthermia—higher than normal body temperature that can be induced by computer-directed microwave radiation. By using this complicated-sounding but relatively simple method of raising the temperature of a particular part of the body, the cancer cells can be made even more vulnerable to radiation. Cancer cells that are subjected to higher-than-normal temperature are particularly sensitive to damage from radiation, possibly because of the compound effects of altered metabolism, radiation damage, and changes caused by the heat itself. Furthermore, the cancer cells deep inside a tumor do not have as much oxygen as those located nearer the surface. It seems that these oxygen-poor cells are more sensitive to heat than those that have a more oxygen-rich environment. Again, the effect is to make the combination of heat and radiation even more effective in reaching the core cancer cells.

SUMMING UP

Radiation therapy is an integral weapon in the fight against cancer, and one that is certain to become even more so as today's technology develops ever more precise and effective treatments. Many patients are alive and well today with no evidence of cancer who just a few years ago would have died of cancer. Over the coming years we can expect to see even more and safer cancer cures, thanks to the rapidly expanding use of expert and sophisticated radiation therapy.

9

Experimental Treatments and Research

EMIL J FREIREICH, M.D., D.SC. (HON.)

INTRODUCTION

We have the good fortune to live during what is almost certainly the golden age of medicine. Over the last century our potential as individuals to live happy, successful lives has increased enormously. No one needs to be reminded about the miracles of antibiotics, vaccination, surgery, radiation therapy and the host of other advances in medicine which relieve suffering and prolong life. All of these changes in medicine have resulted from experimental therapies and research. It is clear, therefore, that the development of new knowledge has contributed in the past, as it almost certainly will in the future, to an improving prospect for the control of cancer and other major illnesses.

RESEARCH PHOBIA

Despite the advances made by laboratory and clinical research, such investigations evoke strong emotions in some members of the public. The word "experiment" often conjures up the image of a guinea pig. Many people assume that clinical investigation using patients or healthy volunteers means that the subjects will undergo procedures and treatments which are potentially harmful. There are many stories in the media which support the notion that human beings can be "experimented" upon. In our culture, whether clinical investigative procedures are legally, ethically, and morally permissible has been significantly influenced by events that occurred during World War II, when humans were experimented upon in the same sense that experimental animals would be. The reaction to those events has been the development of a formal and legalistic approach to clinical investigations, and in virtually all of the Western world participation in any type of scientific investigation is totally voluntary. Using humans as guinea pigs in research is legally impossible in the United States and most other developed countries.

"Research" is another word frequently encountered by cancer patients. To many lay people, research conjures up a laboratory, some type of white uniform, and an environment which is not totally therapeutic—that is, one that does not have the patient's interest as the first concern. This is unfortunate because research explicitly means the careful, systematic observation of events, using elaborate methods of inductive reasoning to draw conclusions which then form the bases for hypotheses to help make predictions about the future. These predictions are subsequently tested by observations. The discrepancies between predictions and observations allow scientists to sharpen their own knowledge and to improve the quality of all knowledge which we can draw upon to improve our perspectives for living.

The air of suspicion, secrecy, and negativism that has been associated with the words "experiment" and "research" in the minds of some people detracts from the enormous importance of the scientific method, which has made modern medicine possible, has more than doubled the human life expectancy, and has improved the quality of life in all areas of human activity.

RESEARCH SAFEGUARDS

In order to investigate any new procedure involving humans, a researcher must carefully consider the proposal in elaborate detail and prepare a research protocol. An important part of this protocol is a written informed consent form which contains a clear statement of the purpose of the investigation and a presentation in lay language of its potential benefits and risks. These informed consent documents are used to ensure that people who participate in such studies will receive the necessary information to decide on voluntary participation. The protocol is invariably reviewed by each of the authors and contributors to the investigation, who represent a variety of disciplines, and must be approved by the department head responsible for the study in the institution where it will be conducted. After that the protocol will be reviewed by the institution's research committee, usually made up of the administrative chiefs of its various departments, who examine the protocol's scientific objectives in light of potential risks and benefits. All such proposals must now have an additional level of review for human safety. Institutions that conduct clinical investigations are required by the federal government to have such a committee, whose only purpose is to review from the patients' perspective any potential risks which are not far outweighed by the potential for benefit. Such committees usually include an attorney or a judge and a theologian, and sometimes members of the local community, as well as a number of other lay individuals whose perspective may be different from that of the academic medical community.

WHO SHOULD PARTICIPATE IN CLINICAL RESEARCH?

It is common to consider clinical investigative therapy as suitable only for patients who are hopeless, for whom there is no present treatment of proven value. Certainly such patients are candidates for clinical investigation, for one of the major missions of this research is to discover treatments where none exist. However, many major advances in therapeutics have been made in patients where excellent treatment is already available. One major example is the primary treatment of breast cancer, in which the overall cure rate approaches 50 percent and is even 90 percent in certain stages.

The two major goals for improving the treatment of early disease are finding absolutely reliable treatment—that is, treatment which is effective in virtually 100 percent of individuals—and improving the quality of the treatment by developing procedures that are less mutilating, less expensive, less painful, and require less time to apply. In breast cancer, for example, there are now a number of studies that have investigated a more limited surgical removal of the primary tumor; when used with local radiation therapy, this can preserve the main structures of the breast, and such treatments can be conducted without increasing the risk of later metastatic disease. Treatments that work for 50 percent or more of all individuals with a certain malignancy are still subjects of clinical investigation for almost every form of cancer, and patients with early and newly diagnosed disease are potential candidates for such research. These studies have similar objectives: testing a new treatment that either has potential for being better than the currently effective treatment for a great number of patients, or that will result in a reduction in side effects or a decrease in the disabling effects of a treatment.

There are many opportunities for people who are completely normal and have no evidence of malignancy to participate in clinical investigations, such as early detection and prevention projects. For example, there are studies using mammography (X rays of the breast) to detect malignancies before they can be detected by physical examination or other tests, thus increasing the number of individuals who can be diagnosed while the cancer can be cured by currently available methods. Cancer prevention trials include investigations of a number of new chemicals which have been shown to prevent the occurrence of cancer in experimental animals after exposure to cancer-inducing chemicals. Such prevention studies do, however, have the potential for harm since some of these drugs, if given over long periods of time, may create harmful side effects.

CONSIDERATIONS IN THE DECISION
TO PARTICIPATE IN RESEARCH

Anyone involved in a clinical investigation must understand that participation is totally voluntary. A potential participant has the privilege—in fact, the right—to know about all aspects of the clinical investigation, so that consent truly is informed consent.

Many other factors enter into the patient's decision to participate. One of the most important is the relationship between the individual and the attending physician. Relationships with family members and the community, the financial situation, and the availability of support from social agencies are a few of the other factors that will enter into the decision. Regardless of these factors, the greatest need of the patient in making the decision to participate is thorough information about his or her condition, and the best source of information is the physician. Most physicians in this country now keep their patients fully informed about any knowledge that they have. In the past, and even now in many other countries, physicians have often withheld the diagnosis, or even the suspicion of malignancy, from the patient in an effort to shield him or her from undue emotional trauma. This practice has fallen into disrepute in this country largely because of the increasing number and quality of treatment options.

A major source of additional information is a second opinion. Over the last quarter of a century the subspecialty of oncology, which deals with the diagnosis and treatment of malignant disease, has developed. There are oncologists in all of the medical specialties and subspecialties, including surgery, medicine, gynecology, otolaryngology, urology, cardiology, and gastroenterology. These physicians have received postgraduate training in all aspects of malignant disease. Whenever a diagnosis of malignancy is being considered, it is wise to have a consultation with a specialist in malignant disease who can work together with the primary physician in constructing the best possible treatment plan.

In addition to professional sources of information, a number of resources are available in the community, among them the American Cancer Society, the National Cancer Institute (NCI) in Washington, D.C., and many comprehensive cancer centers throughout the country. The NCI provides information to the public about a variety of malignancies and their treatment and maintains a register of all of the clinical investigative studies funded through the National Institutes of Health. This register is helpful to the patient's physician or the consulting physician in determining the scope of treatment options available to the patient.

The Comprehensive Cancer Centers are so called because they provide patient care, conduct research, run education programs (at both the undergraduate and postgraduate levels), and are responsible for continuing education in cancer matters for professionals and the public. Their services include programs in cancer prevention, early detection, and rehabilitation. Many of them maintain telephone information services for lay people and consulting services so that patients and physicians can discuss specific questions of cancer care with members of their faculties.

In addition to these resources, virtually all academic medical institutions, particularly medical schools, have significant programs in cancer research and treatment and provide additional sources of support. Many of the academic institutions are combined together in "cooperative groups," funded by NCI, which meet together on a regular basis to design and adopt specific studies to recommend to their patients. The cooperative groups have formal connections with oncologists in private practice throughout the community. Regional oncology groups have also been formed so that physicians in private practice can work together with a comprehensive cancer center or with a cooperative group to develop patient care protocols and make new treatments available to patients.

HOW NEW TREATMENTS ARE TESTED

Each year thousands of chemical compounds are screened for their possible anticancer effects. Some of these substances are synthesized in laboratories because a scientist has an idea about how to interfere selectively with cancer cell growth. In other instances scientists take chemical

compounds known to interfere with the growth of cancer and add, sub-
tract, or rearrange certain molecules in an attempt to improve their
activity against cancer cells while decreasing their toxic side effects. Many
of these chemical compounds tested are donated by private industries
while others are developed at the NCI or by NCI-supported scientists.
Some are tested because clues in the scientific literature lead scientists to
think that the chemical may have an inhibitory effect on cancer cells.

The process of drug identification and evaluation for potential usefulness as a cancer treatment is known as screening. In order to identify
compounds with antitumor activity, the drugs are given to mice or other
laboratory animals that have a variety of cancers. Researchers study the
compounds' ability to retard the growth of tumors, prolong survival, or
produce objective signs of tumor regression. A second, control group of
animals with the same type of cancer receives a placebo, which is a
biologically inactive substance. If the animals given the test substance live
significantly longer or have smaller tumors than those in the control
group, the substance is considered biologically active.

In its original form the substance may be crude, since it may be a plant
extract or come from bacteria or marine animals. Once its effectiveness
against cancer cells has been established, the test compound is examined
and purified. During this formulation process the compound is refined
and its exact chemical structure identified so that it can be formulated
into pills or solutions for injection. The refined material is then tested in
other groups of mice, and in some cases in dogs, to determine a starting
dose that has antitumor activity without prohibitive toxic effects on normal tissue. Once a safe starting dose has been established and acute side
effects are known, an application for use in humans is made to the Food
and Drug Administration. The drug then undergoes testing in humans
who have serious, otherwise untreatable forms of advanced cancer. The
risk of any unpredicted harmful side effects must be balanced against the
risk of the progression of their cancer and the urgent need for some
treatment where none is known. Even then, the first treatments are usually given at less than one third of the dosage that has been demonstrated
to have no serious harmful effects in the experimental animal. The one
third figure is a standard guide for the clinical scientist, since at that level
the initial treatments will very probably not have harmful side effects.

Phase I

There are four phases of clinical trials, or clinical evaluation in humans.
The same kind of four-phase testing is done for new treatment procedures, such as hyperthermia (the therapeutic use of elevated body temperature), and new surgical techniques as for drugs. The first phase is the
initial clinical evaluation, which attempts to find a safe and tolerable dose

and schedule for administration while watching for effects against tumors. The initial dose can be safely estimated from the earlier studies performed in animals. Only those drugs that have been shown to have activity against cancer in these animals are given in Phase I trials. During this initial phase of clinical evaluation, the new drugs are given only to patients with widespread cancers which are not responsive to other forms of therapy.

A significant portion of patients who have received drugs in Phase I studies have shown improvement. The clinical trial is usually conducted in such a way that a small number of individuals, three to five, are treated at the initial dose level. If no extraordinary side effects are observed, this dosage level is progressively increased in subsequent patients until the schedule, dose, and route of administration that can be tolerated by the majority of people are identified.

Still, the primary purpose of the Phase I trial is to benefit the patient. It is hoped that beneficial effects will be observed for some, and possibly all, of the individuals who participate in this phase of clinical testing. The evaluation of the degree and frequency of effectiveness cannot be done very well during this phase of drug testing because most of these individuals will receive a dosage which is almost certainly safe but unlikely to be optimally effective. However, the clinical scientist does advance the dosage and schedule for the individual patient with an eye to detecting a beneficial effect on the disease.

Phase II

When a consistently safe and tolerable dose of a drug has been determined for patients, the new drug is then ready for Phase II evaluation, generally called a "detection-of-activity" study. The goal of a Phase II study is to determine whether the compound retards the growth of tumors and extends survival of patients with various other common forms of cancer, or only works for patients with the specific type of cancer tested in Phase I. It is important to understand that cancer treatments are quite different for the various kinds of cancer originating from different organs. There are hundreds of different malignancies that are grouped under the diagnosis of cancer. Treatments work differently in cancers of the breast than they do in cancers of the bowel. During Phase II, a sufficient number of individuals with similar cancers must be studied to determine whether this treatment is sufficiently effective for regular use in patients with that specific diagnosis. Patients with a somewhat less advanced condition are generally investigated because many of the treatments require weeks of observation before positive effects can be observed. During Phase II the clear objective is therapeutic; its purpose is to detect significant activity against a specific form of cancer. It is important for lay people to understand that treatment of a small number of individuals can frequently result in overlooking treatments which are highly effective for a significant number of others.

A drug that is found to be inactive against many types of cancer may still be highly effective against a small group of tumors or a single cancer. For example, cisplatin, a relatively new anticancer drug, appeared to be ineffective against most types of cancer. Fortunately, before it was discarded it was tested in patients with widely disseminated, drug-resistant ovarian and testicular cancers and found to produce dramatic tumor regression. Cisplatin is now used in combination with other active drugs and can produce cures in patients who had previously been incurable. In fact, cisplatin in conjunction with other drugs has made testicular cancer an almost totally curable disease.

Phase III

When a new agent like cisplatin is found to be effective as a single agent in Phase II trials, the drug is then evaluated in Phase III trials. Here the new drug is compared with conventional forms of cancer therapy to determine whether the new agent is as good as or better than therapies that are currently available. Studies are frequently conducted in a "prospective randomized concurrent controlled" format. This technique has generated the most concern among patients and their doctors because the treatment is assigned by the process of random allocation. But random allocation is necessary when even a thoughtful and methodical evaluation of benefits and risks of the two choices do not clearly show that one treatment or the other is recommended. Random assignment assures that the patients who receive the two different treatments will be comparable. Since humans are so varied and their cancers are also varied, it is important to be sure that the comparisons between treatments are made in large enough groups of patients to assure that any differences are due to the drugs themselves and not to differences in the patients being studied. The outcome of such a trial is that physicians in the future will be confident in selecting and prescribing one or the other treatment because this comparison has proved objective, providing a quantitative basis for comparison and choice. Regardless of the experimental plan used in the Phase III study, it is important for the patient to recognize that the physician recommending participation in the clinical trial does so honestly believing that participation will offer the patient the best choice of treatment at that moment.

If the new agent is effective or is better than existing therapies it is advanced to Phase IV trials, where it is used with other drugs or treatments in the primary treatment of patients with newly diagnosed cancer in an attempt to improve the rate of cure.

Phase IV

During Phase IV clinical trials, scientists refine the integration of the new drug (or surgical technique or radiation therapy), and determine its value in the primary treatment plan. The new agent is often combined with other effective drugs for the primary therapy of patients with advanced cancer, or used in programs of adjuvant chemotherapy along with surgery and radiation therapy. In these types of clinical trials, drug combinations, surgery, or radiation therapy are often compared with other forms of treatment known to be active against cancer. An example of this kind of clinical trial is the National Surgical Adjuvant Breast Project (NSABP), which is trying to determine the best treatment of breast cancer at various stages of the disease. In these studies, some patients have a mastectomy while others have only a biopsy of the lump followed by treatment with radiation therapy and several different types of adjuvant chemotherapy. Data from these large studies increasingly indicate that it is unnecessary for women with certain types of cancer to undergo extensive surgery to improve their chances of cure.

Besides developing new drugs effective against cancer, one of the biggest challenges for researchers is to choose the right drugs and determine the best sequence in which to administer them. This is one of the major priorities of cooperative clinical trials now being carried out throughout the country for many different cancers. Many of these studies are designed by cancer experts and supported by the National Cancer Institute. Physicians from all over the country participate in these clinical trials and may enroll many hundreds of patients. A protocol, or treatment plan, is distributed to all participating physicians so that all patients are treated in a consistent fashion. Patients are carefully chosen according to age, type and stage of cancer, as well as to other factors that affect prognosis, so that the results obtained in different studies will be comparable. This type of study is the most certain way for a patient to get the best available state-of-the-art cancer treatment, since all protocols must start from this point.

IMPORTANT NEW APPROACHES TO CANCER TREATMENT

The goal of cancer research is constantly to seek ways to decrease cancer deaths by developing new methods for prevention, detection, and treatment of cancer or improving currently available ones. Experiments are under way with high-energy subatomic particles that generate a radiation beam that is more deeply penetrating and less dependent upon the presence of oxygen than traditional sources of radiation energy.

Compounds that may sensitize cancer cells to the lethal effects of radiation—radiosensitizers—are being developed in an attempt to render the cancer cells more sensitive to radiation. Furthermore, substances that selectively protect normal cells from radiation damage, called radioprotectors, are also under development. At some centers radiation therapy is being administered directly to an organ during surgery in an attempt at better tumor control with fewer side effects. Finally, researchers are testing the implantation of various radioactive substances near the tumor that emit radiation for short, well-defined periods.

Over the past fifteen to twenty years, scientists studying tumor immunology and other host-tumor biological interactions have accumulated an enormous amount of information. We now know that at least some human tumors are recognized by the host as foreign or antigenic. A new program has been created to explore whether biological substances can be used to modify immune responses to cancer. These biologic response modifiers control the growth and development of various components of the immune system. Their anticancer activity is mediated through changes in the immune system, rather than by direct toxic effects on cancer cells. These substances, often made by the body, may strengthen the body's own ability to fight cancer and may produce fewer undesirable side effects.

Major advances in cancer biology may lead to better methods of detection and treatment in the very near future. Technological developments have permitted scientists to fuse cells in hybridomas, entities which produce pure monoclonal antibodies that seek out unique proteins on cancer cells. The diagnostic and therapeutic potential of this development is enormous. (See the following section on monoclonal antibodies.)

Better ways to target the delivery of drugs to the site of the cancer are also being explored. In ovarian cancer, researchers are looking at direct exposure of all organs in the abdominal cavity to a prolonged "bath" of effective drugs, since this tumor spreads throughout the abdominal cavity but usually does not spread outside the abdomen. In these patients, semipermanent catheters are being implanted so that drugs can be introduced safely and easily into the abdominal cavity to treat microscopic metastases. Normal tissue, such as the bone marrow and tissue of the gastrointestinal tract, can to some extent be spared the toxic effects of the drugs when they are administered in this fashion.

Researchers are working with fatty sacs called temperature-sensitive liposomes, which melt in the presence of warm, tumor-bearing tissue, to determine whether these sacs can be filled with specific anticancer drugs directed to the tumor, where the drugs would be released to act on the cancer cells. Hyperthermia, the use of heat to kill cancer cells selectively or make them more sensitive to chemotherapy, is also an area of active research.

These and many other new approaches are being examined in laboratories and clinical research centers in many parts of the country. Unlike quack remedies, all of these new approaches must undergo rigorous examination and comparison in large, carefully planned studies before their real value in the treatment of cancer can be estimated.

Interferon

Interferon has appealed to the public and professional imagination perhaps more than any new cancer treatment approach in recent history, despite the fact that it has not proved to be effective in the treatment for the common malignancies. The reason for this interest is that in the history of cancer therapy, the treatments used have been destructive to at least a portion of the patient's body. Interferon, however, is a major component of what has been termed "immunotherapy" a new, possibly nondestructive way of curing cancer. It has been demonstrated in almost every type of cancer that other normal cells in the person are attempting to control the malignant process. Immunotherapy involves the strengthening of the body's ability to control, reject, and ultimately kill the malignant cells without affecting the normal ones. This very appealing approach to the control of malignancy has led to the development of a number of "vaccines" which have been studied as potential anticancer compounds.

To understand how interferon works, it is helpful to know something about the biology of cells. It is difficult for a person to imagine how small a cell is, but it takes one billion cells to make up approximately one gram of tissue—the size of the tip of the smallest finger on a person's hand. A person weighing approximately 155 pounds is made up of 70,000 billion cells, and every one of them is an identical twin, an exact copy of the original cell from which a person begins, the fertilized egg. This cell is repeatedly copied, and this continuous multiplying results in enough cells to make an adult person. Although the cells are genetically identical, they each specialize. Cancer is a disease of individual cells that can begin in a single cell or in a very small number of cells, perhaps ten or one hundred. It always begins as a microscopic change that is virtually impossible to detect, and by the time our current methods can detect a malignancy it is already a fairly extensive tumor with several billions of cells. By the time a malignancy has developed, the body's defenses have been literally overwhelmed. All of the extrinsic agents that have been used to stimulate the body's defenses have proved to be relatively feeble; they have not been able to control or cure an established malignancy. To a much less serious degree, the same thing happens when a person has an infection and the bacteria spread to the point where they overwhelm the body's defenses and he or she becomes critically ill.

Interferon is a protein product of human cells that enables the cells to resist infection by a virus; thus the name "interferon," for interference with viral infection. Interferon is manufactured by cells that are stimulated either by a viral infection or by several other agents. Scientists noted that the interferon secreted by an affected cell has the ability to confer the resistance on unaffected cells. They also noted that interferon affects the growth of cells, an activity known as its antiproliferative effect. Evidently interferon plays a normal physiological role in regulating the growth of cells. For example, in defending itself against a foreign protein or infection, the body manufactures antibodies and stimulates the proliferation of the cells that make the specific antibody protein to neutralize the bacterial toxins. But the body also needs some way to control this proliferative process, otherwise these cells would themselves become a tumor. The cells that are stimulated to make antibodies also manufacture interferon, which suppresses further proliferation and eventually shuts off the proliferative response. The process works something like the thermostat in a house, which is sensitive to a deficiency of heat and turns on the furnace, then recognizes when there is sufficient heat and turns the furnace off.

The observation that interferon can suppress the proliferation of certain tumors in humans and in experimental animals rekindles the hope that the body's defenses can prove sufficiently effective for the control of malignancy. Interferon therefore becomes the leading edge of what we hope will be a long list of "biological response modifiers." These substances would be manufactured by the body's own cells for the specific purpose of controlling the growth of other cells, and would be responsible for the orderly development of organs in a person's body. Such substances both stimulate proliferation and suppress it. The technology for growing human cells in test tubes has advanced to the point where many different types of cells can be grown in tissue culture and can be induced by a variety of stimuli to manufacture biological response modifiers like interferon. If the activity of these materials is identified and the specific proteins isolated, it is possible, with the technology of monoclonal antibodies and genetic engineering, to manufacture these human proteins in test tubes. Thus we have the potential for making a whole new generation of drugs that operate just like insulin for diabetes or like cortisone for replacing the function of the adrenal glands. This is one of the most active and most significant approaches to cancer control and perhaps the one that has the greatest potential for the future.

Hyperthermia

The word "hyperthermia" refers to an increase in temperature, literally making things hotter than normal. It has been consistently observed that tumors, either in test tubes in cell cultures or in experimental animals, have much greater difficulty adapting to any change in temperature than do normal cells. Therefore if, as a result of infection or other causes of fever, the temperature of tumor cells is increased above the temperature that the body could normally achieve by itself, the tumor cells are damaged more than normal cells. Studies conducted in the laboratory either with cancer cells or with animals bearing tumors indicate that the heating of tumors may be an important approach to cancer treatment. One way to heat tumors is to heat the entire person, and there are two methods for doing this. The first is to put the patient in a thermal covering, a form of space suit, and provide external heat that is absorbed through the skin's surface. To prevent the loss of heat from the surface and to add heat energy, many methods have been devised, including hot-air space suits or boxes and immersion in hot liquids such as water or wax. With these methods it is possible to reach temperatures at which significant regressions of cancers have occurred. The problem with this form of treatment is that the heat is also injurious to normal cells, particularly those of the brain and heart. The degree and duration of heating are limited by the side effects to these normal organs. Total body heating is also extremely unpleasant and patients generally have to be anesthetized to endure it.

Another major method for heating the whole body is to create a circuit of blood outside the body—that is, to put a tube in an artery and divert the blood through a heating device, usually a water bath or hot air, and then to reinject the heated blood into a major vein. This heats the body from within by heating the blood, rather than heating the surface. This method, like the external method, has similar limitations based on its deleterious effects on normal organs, but both methods are being actively investigated in a number of centers.

Although the effects of heat alone are not curative, significant responses have been seen in some tumors. This has encouraged further clinical investigation to include the studies of heat in combination with other forms of treatment, such as radiation or chemotherapy. At present, hyperthermia given to the whole body must still be considered an investigational treatment, but the indications of its antitumor activity encourage its use for advanced tumors where other forms of treatment are not effective.

A third major method of hyperthermia is localized hyperthermia. With modern physical methods such as diathermy, ultrasound, and microwaves, it is possible to induce rapid local heating. All of us are familiar with the microwave oven, in which, although the oven itself is not hot, energy can be transferred to food surfaces which absorb it. In a similar fashion, it is possible to aim energy at tumors so that the temperature increase will be confined to the tumor. This avoids many of the side effects of hyperthermia on the other organs. Localized hyperthermia alone has found significant application and is also effective in combination with forms of radiation therapy delivered by cobalt or by linear accelerator. The combination of localized hyperthermia and chemotherapy is also being investigated in a number of centers. As with systemic hyperthermia, although localized hyperthermia has clearly been shown to be effective, its role in the overall treatment of cancer remains experimental at present.

Diet

Diet has always been a matter of great concern to individuals and, strictly from an intellectual point of view, it seems obvious that what we eat should be a major factor in what we are. The chemicals that make up our body and replace the parts of the body which have been injured must come from the foods we ingest. For this reason, both sick and healthy individuals must have an adequate diet. A patient with cancer differs from a healthy individual in that the malignancy itself adds a burden to the body, which requires additional nutrition to sustain the normal cells. In fact, the cancer actually competes with the other normal body cells for nutrients. Unfortunately, the patient with cancer frequently has a serious loss of appetite which, in combination with an increased nutritional requirement, frequently results in major weight loss. Thus attention to diet is an important component in treatment. Calorie intake must be significantly increased to avoid weight loss. In addition, there is a specific increase in the need for certain vitamins, beyond what can be supplied by a normal diet, making vitamin supplementation an important part of cancer treatment.

There have been a number of popular claims that extraordinarily large doses of vitamin C or vitamin A, as well as of imaginary vitamins such as laetrile (vitamin B_{17}) or pangamic acid (B_{15}), can actually result in the regression of cancer. Evidence has been obtained in experimental animals and in test tubes that large concentrations of chemicals that resemble vitamins may have some effect on the progression of cancer. However, in the clinical situation there is no evidence that megadoses of vitamins, far above those required for adequate nutrition, play any role in combating cancer.

If the progression of the tumor does result in severe weight loss, "parenteral nutrition"—providing nutrients by injection into the blood or into the tissues—has been developed to deliver needed calories and overcome the profound loss of appetite that can afflict cancer patients. As a result of these advances in nutrition replacement, a patient with cancer no longer needs to experience weight loss. Maintenance of normal healthy body tissues and weight can be regularly accomplished and is an important component of all the effective cancer treatments available today.

AVAILABILITY OF CANCER "BREAKTHROUGHS"

We are constantly being informed by the media about "major cancer breakthroughs." For those who have cancer or who have loved ones who have cancer, such announcements raise hope that the latest breakthrough will, indeed, solve their cancer problem.

How can a person decide how to act when he or she learns of great cures? The best source of information is the patient's physician. Through the physician, the patient can frequently contact the cancer specialist as well as the usual sources of community information. Federal and local agencies, universities, and cancer centers can provide additional information. The important thing is to recognize that such breakthroughs are announced in the media primarily to keep the public informed about continuing progress in the understanding of cancer and its treatment. This communication is vital because it encourages continuing support for cancer research and assures continuing progress toward the eventual goal of cancer control. Unfortunately, the information that stimulates the interest of healthy individuals may create false hope in the mind of those already affected with cancer. It is important to recognize that many of these breakthroughs provide leads for potential application in the clinic, but the time between such discoveries and the establishment of effective treatment may be decades. The prolonged period of development from the laboratory to the very earliest clinical testing to final, general availability is due to two important considerations. The first is that cancer is always a chronic disease and requires years of follow-up before confidence about the long-term benefits of such treatments can be obtained. Second, concern for the safety of the patients participating in the studies mandate that such studies proceed deliberately, cautiously, and systematically in order to avoid unpredictable harmful effects. Cancer treatments improve progressively, in small increments, over many years. Breakthroughs announced are findings that have come with years of effort and evaluation, not sudden increments in knowledge that have just occurred and are ready for general use.

MONOCLONAL ANTIBODIES

Philip Kasofsky, M.D.

Monoclonal antibodies were invented in 1978 in a laboratory in Cambridge, England. The immense importance of that accomplishment was not comprehended at the time for, like many revolutionary scientific events, it was considered to be largely a curious achievement of interest only to specialized scientists. At present the potential for monoclonal antibodies in many fields of human endeavor, not only in medicine but also in a wide range of industrial and academic pursuits, has made them one of the most active areas of research. The commercial prospects alone may reach billions of dollars. In fact, one British observer has noted that the general concept of a monoclonal antibody was not patented by its discoverers, yet the potential value may exceed that of North Sea oil. The benefit to mankind from medical uses could be extraordinary, and early results have done nothing to restrain this enthusiasm.

A monoclonal antibody is a highly specific antibody produced by a special kind of man-made hybrid cell called a hybridoma, which makes the antibody in greatly increased quantity. In contrast, the antibodies with which most of us are familiar in their role of defending us against allergens and other disease-causing organisms are manufactured by a family of several antibody-producing cells in relatively minuscule amounts and are not truly specific or uniform in their biological properties.

Normally when a human being is exposed to a substance the body recognizes as "foreign" or different from its own tissues and chemicals, several protective systems attempt to neutralize, weaken, and dispose of the invading substance. For example, the body may react through its various metabolic processes to alter the chemical structure of the foreign substance. Both the kidney and liver contain a wide range of enzymes that react with foreign substances, including drugs, metabolizing them into substances that are either used by the body or excreted. The immune system also deals with foreign substances, particularly bacteria and viruses.

The human immune system operates in several ways. Cellular immunity works through specialized cells that directly attack foreign invaders. Humoral immunity works through cells that make compounds to attack and neutralize foreign proteins. The complex molecules we know as antibodies were the first of these substances to be recognized. Antibodies are produced by plasma cells, a line of cells found principally in the bone marrow, lymph nodes, and spleen. The answers to the crucial questions of how these cells "know" when a foreign substance is present and which antibody to make in order to neutralize it are complex and just becoming clear to researchers in immunology.

In a sense, however, there are certain pivotal steps to the process that are not very precise. In fact, the plasma cells respond by making many different kinds of antibodies to a foreign protein, some of which may work well in neutralizing it while others work poorly or not at all. This range of effect or lack of it occurs because foreign proteins are generally very large molecules, and while some antibodies may be highly effective because they are strongly directed against a vital part of the foreign protein's molecular structure, others may be ineffective because they are weak or directed against an unimportant part. The creation of monoclonal antibodies was a significant achievement because it created a method for the continuous production in the laboratory of a single antibody selected specifically for its unique properties.

This is the way it works: Normal animals, usually a purebred strain of mice, are exposed to the foreign protein to which antibodies are desired. The plasma cells in the mouse's spleen are stimulated to react, producing a wide range of antibodies, both effective and ineffective. The mouse's spleen is removed and its plasma cells are separated out. They are then fused by a variety of processes with a cancerous plasma cell, called a plasmacytoma, producing the hybridoma. The cancerous plasma cells are taken from a mouse with multiple myeloma, a malignancy of plasma cells that is similar to the human disease with the same name. These cells have many of the general properties of cancer cells, including uncontrolled rapid growth and disordered metabolic processes. They also produce a single antibody in greatly increased amounts, hundreds or thousands of times more than is required by a normal system. With luck, the hybridoma that results from fusing a single "immortal" plasmacytoma cell with a normal cell will have the desired properties of each parent cell. It will produce a single highly specific antibody in great amounts and be stable, meaning the cell line will not die out or gradually reduce its level of antibody production. In practice, many thousands of hybrids are produced and are then screened to select the ones with the desired properties.

Present laboratory methods permit the selection and culturing of animal cells that are descended from a single cell by a consecutive series of cell divisions—a process known as cloning. A monoclonal antibody is the unique molecule derived from a single clone. Conventional antibodies, in contrast, are generally a collection of several types of antibody molecules and are called polyclonal.

Medical researchers and clinicians are now using monoclonal antibodies to improve the diagnostic accuracy of many laboratory tests that previously were based on conventional antibodies. More importantly, monoclonal antibodies are being used for new diagnostic tests, with a goal of finding new ways to diagnose and treat cancer.

Cancer researchers have long searched for markers—substances found in the blood or urine that are secreted by a cancer and indicate its presence or degree of activity. Such markers, if they exist, could be used to evaluate the effectiveness of treatment and also in follow-up monitoring after treatment. An increasing concentration of the markers might indicate a relapse or regrowth of cancer cells, possibly long before the onset of new symptoms. In addition, tests for markers might be used to screen otherwise apparently healthy people for cancer.

At present only the monitoring function can be performed by using antibodies against carcinoembryonic antigen (CEA) and alphafetoprotein (AFP), two substances that are secreted into the blood stream by tumors of the colon and liver respectively. Tests for these substances, based on conventional polyclonal antibodies, use indicators to show whether the

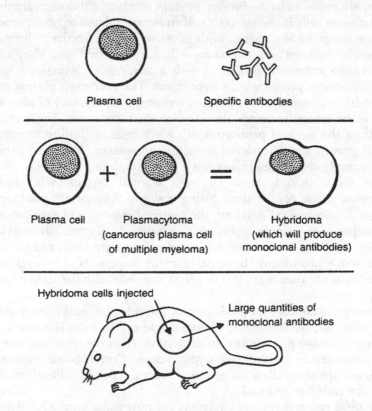

Figure 11 Monoclonal antibody production.

antibodies have reacted with the substance in question. Monoclonal antibodies can and are being used to improve the accuracy of these and other tests.

The discovery of oncogenes, the atypical genes that are being found in association with several common types of human cancer (breast, lung, bladder and others), may increase our basic understanding of the processes that lead to the malignant transformation in normal cells. The mechanism by which oncogenes control the transformation process is being intensively studied. Evidence to date indicates that the abnormal oncogene is formed by mutation or by transfer from a virus. The abnormal gene, which may differ from a normal one in only a very small part of its structure, results in the synthesis of either an abnormal protein or enzyme. This substance, which may actually occur under normal conditions but is now produced in inappropriately high or low amounts, influences the control of cellular metabolism and reproduction, giving the cell the characteristics of a malignant growth. The final result, which may in fact require the combined effects of two different oncogenes, is a cancer cell capable of growing abnormally and invading other tissue.

Researchers have identified approximately twenty human oncogenes, which fall into three main groups. The abnormal protein manufactured under the direction of the oncogene can be identified and synthesized in a laboratory, and monoclonal antibodies can then be made against these substances or used to search for them in blood and urine. Researchers hope that the sensitivity and accuracy of monoclonal reaction may make them a promising tool in finding cancer markers.

Monoclonal antibodies that react with several known products produced by cancer cells are being used in laboratories to identify cell types in tissue undergoing biopsy. This application is especially important when pathologists are faced, as often they are, with an obvious cancer whose particular organ of origin is not readily apparent. More importantly, these antibodies can form the basis for a new imaging technology to locate cancers and determine their extent. Monoclonal antibodies to a particular type of cancer cells can be made with radioactive iodine and then injected into the patient's bloodstream. The monoclonals should then attach themselves to those cancer cells anywhere in the body and then be detected by special sensing devises. This method has been used experimentally in animals and in a few human subjects without ill effect. Monoclonal scanning is expected, within a few years, to become a valuable method to assess the extent of cancer and to follow the results of treatment.

Monoclonal antibodies offer their greatest potential, however, in the actual treatment of cancer. For example, theoretically monoclonals can be used to selectively destroy or damage cancer cells. Monoclonal antibodies that bind to cancer cells also may be used to deliver anticancer drugs to their specific targets and thereby increase their destructive action without causing so much damage to healthy tissue.

Still another potential use of monoclonal antibodies takes advantage of the fact that cancer cells secrete substances that inhibit or encourage the growth of other cancer cells of the same type. These substances, called "tumor growth factors" (TGFs) or "tumor inhibitory factors" (TIFs), can be inactivated by monoclonal antibodies that bind specifically to them.

Before these and other potential benefits can be achieved, however, some serious problems remain to be resolved. For example, most monoclonal antibodies are now derived from mice. Administering mouse antibodies to humans could result in serious side effects or even death from immune-system responses to these foreign molecules from a different species. Work on human monoclonals is under way, but many problems remain. Instability is another problem in human hybridomas, which are more difficult to manufacture than those made from mice. Third, cancers of one organ, not only in different patients but in the same patient, may not be all of the same cell type. It may be necessary to develop several lines of monoclonal antibodies, each directed against one particular cancerous cell line, to treat an individual patient.

This requirement obviously increases the expense, lengthens the time from diagnosis to treatment, and creates manufacturing and other problems. Even so, customized monoclonals have been used in a few patients with leukemia under experimental protocols with encouraging results. Carefully controlled clinical trials in several research centers must be performed to show efficacy, safety, and superiority over present treatments before the Food and Drug Administration will approve monoclonal antibodies for general use in treating cancer. Thus monoclonal antibody therapy is probably still several years away from becoming a standard component of cancer treatment—provided, of course, the various problems discussed earlier are solved.

10

Coping with Problems Related to Cancer and Cancer Treatment

JOYCE M. YASKO, R.N., PH.D.,
AND PATRICIA GREENE, R.N., M.S.N.

INTRODUCTION

People with cancer encounter many difficulties, not only from the progress of the disease itself, but also as a result of the treatment, be it chemotherapy, radiation therapy, or surgery. These difficulties are made

This chapter has been adapted from J. Yasko *Guidelines for Cancer Care: Symptom Management* Reston, VA: Reston Publishing Co., 1984 worse by worries about the future, finances, and the problems of coping with everyday life complicated by a chronic disease, and by all of the emotions—anger, fear, resentment, and depression—that go with it. All these are normal responses that need to be coped with.

Patients with cancer are discouraged to find that in many forms of the disease the treatment actually makes them feel worse, at least for a while. Surgery, radiation therapy, and chemotherapy all involve a degree of disability, albeit temporary in most instances. In the following sections we outline methods for coping with and living with different aspects of cancer therapy. Some are well known and may be included in the patient's instructions from the physician. Others have been developed by nurses who care for people with cancer and their families. Not all of these methods will work for all patients. Very often ingenuity and trial and error are required to find the best way of overcoming problems. Of course, the patient should always inform his or her physician before embarking on any course of action. What may seem like a trivial change might have damaging effects on the treatment regimen.

The following symptoms or problems may be due to cancer itself, to its treatment with surgery, radiation therapy, or chemotherapy, or to psychological reactions to the diagnosis of cancer or cancer treatment. These signs and symptoms do not affect everyone to the same degree, nor do they occur with the same frequency or duration.

ANEMIA

Anemia is a decrease in the number of red blood cells (erythrocytes) in the circulating blood. Without sufficient red blood cells, the circulatory system's oxygen-carrying capacity is impaired. The patient will usually experience pale skin, muscle weakness, and fatigue. If the amount of oxygen reaching the brain is insufficient, dizziness, depression, irritability, and headache can result; if the amount of oxygen reaching the tissue surrounding the heart is insufficient, angina-like chest pain may result.

The most pervasive symptom is fatigue, and the patient may find that he or she is unable to regain energy and strength even after rest. The section on fatigue gives methods of reducing or coping with this troublesome symptom.

BLEEDING DUE TO THROMBOCYTOPENIA

Thrombocytopenia is the decrease in the number of platelets—cells essential to clotting—that circulate in the blood, which may result in bleeding from the skin and mucous membranes, or internally. The decrease may be caused by a failure of the bone marrow to produce megakaryocyte cells (the precursors of platelets) as a result of radiation therapy or chemotherapy, or for unknown reasons. It may also be caused by abnormal destruction of platelets in the circulating blood by certain forms of cancer, by allergic reaction to specific medications such as quinidine, quinine, digitoxin, sulfonamides, or thiazides, or by physical and emotional stresses that increase the pulse rate and blood pressure, decreasing clot formation and increasing the potential for hemorrhage.

Since protein is essential for megakaryocyte proliferation, the patient should eat protein-rich, high-calorie foods and beverages. Alcohol, which decreases platelet function, should be avoided in all forms (wine, beer, and other types of liquor).

It is most important that patients with thrombocytopenia do everything possible to prevent bleeding. They should:

· Avoid activities with the greatest potential for physical injury.
· Use an electric razor when shaving.
· Use an emery board or fine mesh file for nail care to prevent or repair rough edges.
· Avoid tight-fitting clothing and harsh fabrics, which may irritate the skin.
· Avoid the use of tourniquets.
· Use acetaminophen (e.g., Tylenol or Datril) in place of aspirin, which can exacerbate bleeding problems.

If external bleeding does occur, the patient or a helper should apply pressure to the site for five to ten minutes. If an arm or leg is involved, elevate it above the level of the heart and apply pressure to the bleeding point for a few minutes. If bleeding continues for more than five minutes, the patient should notify his or her physician.

People suffering from thrombocytopenia should not put any excessive pressure on the body. They should avoid strenuous activity, lifting heavy objects, and bending over from the waist. They should also avoid holding the breath while bearing down (known as the Valsalva maneuver) when having a bowel movement, moving up in bed, or in daily activities.

The mucous membranes that line the mouth and the gastrointestinal, upper respiratory, and genitourinary tracts are especially vulnerable to bleeding. Drinking an adequate amount of liquid—at least eight to ten glasses a day—is important to keep skin and mucous membranes from becoming overly dry and to help prevent constipation.

To prevent bleeding of the gums or mouth, the patient should:

· Eat a soft, bland diet and avoid foods that are very hot in flavor or temperature and foods like popcorn or hard pretzels that may irritate the mouth.
· Lubricate the lips with cocoa butter or petroleum jelly.
· Use a soft-bristle toothbrush and a mouthwash with a low alcohol con-

tent to cleanse the teeth, gums, and inside of the mouth gently. Avoid using dental floss. If the platelet count is severely depressed, it may be necessary to clean the teeth with sponge-tipped applicators, gauze moistened with salt water and wrapped around a finger, or an irrigating syringe.
• Check with the treating physician before having any dental work done.
• Drink an adequate amount of liquid—at least eight to ten glasses a day—unless otherwise instructed.

To protect the mucous membranes of the gastrointestinal tract, the patient should:
• Avoid constipation by drinking adequate liquids and getting regular exercise.
• Use stool softeners on a regular basis—daily or as needed.
• Avoid enemas, suppositories, harsh laxatives, and the use of rectal thermometers.
• If on steroids, take them with an antacid or milk to help prevent irritation of the stomach lining. Also, the treating physician's instructions regarding steroid use should be carefully followed.

To protect the mucous membranes of the upper respiratory tract, the patient should:
• Avoid forcefully blowing the nose. If it is necessary, the patient should blow gently through both nostrils simultaneously.
• Humidify the room air with a cold-water vaporizer.
• In case of a nosebleed, the patient should apply firm pressure to the nostrils below the bridge of the nose and tilt the head forward. (Tilting the head backward is sometimes advised, but care should be taken to make sure that the bleeding is not in the back of the nostril.) If bleeding does not subside in a few minutes, place ice bags on the bridge of the nose and at the nape of the neck. If bleeding continues for longer than five minutes, the patient should notify a physician.

To protect the mucous membranes of the genitourinary tract, the patient should use a water-based lubricant such as K-Y Jelly prior to sexual intercourse to avoid excessive friction, and should avoid the use of douches and vaginal suppositories.

CONSTIPATION

Constipation may be caused by the progress of the cancer itself, as when tumors invade the gastrointestinal tract, or by other related factors such as prolonged periods of confinement to bed without exercise. Certain chemotherapeutic drugs, notably vincristine (Oncovin) and vinblastine (Velban), can slow down or temporarily immobilize the peristaltic action of the bowel, which moves waste through the intestines. Narcotics, anticonvulsants, antidepressants, tranquilizers, and muscle relaxants are other agents that can cause decreased peristalsis.

Constipation can also result from inadequate intake of food, dehydration, inadequate roughage in the diet, or the psychological impact of cancer—anxiety and depression.

To prevent constipation, the person should:

• Respond immediately to the urge to defecate, preferably in a private environment that reduces distraction.
• Increase the amount of high-fiber foods in the diet. Fiber increases the volume of the stool, makes it softer by increasing the amount of water retained in it, and causes it to pass through the bowel more rapidly, decreasing the occurrence of an impacted bowel. High-fiber foods include whole-grain products, bran, fresh raw fruits with skins and seeds, fresh raw vegetables, nuts, coconut, corn, popcorn, raisins, dates, prunes, and prune juice.
• Avoid cheese products and refined grain products.
• Drink at least eight to ten glasses of fluid a day. Fresh fruit juices and warm or hot liquid upon arising are especially helpful.
• Try to get as much physical activity as can be tolerated. This facilitates the passage of feces through the intestine.
• Use a stool softener such as Colace or Metamucil daily. This is especially important for patients receiving vincristine (Oncovin), vinblastine (Velban), or opiate narcotic analgesics. With a cellulose, bulk-producing drug such as Metamucil, fluid intake of ten glasses a day is especially important.

DIARRHEA

Diarrhea, like constipation, can be caused by tumors located in the gastrointestinal tract or by methods of cancer treatment. About 75 percent of persons being treated with chemotherapy or radiation therapy to the abdominal region experience this symptom. The degree and duration depend on the dose and the duration of therapy. Diarrhea usually continues for two to three weeks after treatment.

Anxiety and increased stress tend to increase the secretion of gastric juices and gastrointestinal motility, contributing to diarrhea. Other causes include lactose intolerance (the inability to digest regular milk and milk products), fecal impaction, and dietary supplements that have a high osmolarity, meaning they tend to draw water into the intestines.

To prevent or minimize diarrhea, a low-residue diet that is high in calories and protein but low in fat and fiber is recommended. Foods to emphasize include:

- Cottage cheese and low-fat cheeses (if the patient can tolerate milk products).
- Eggs (not fried).
- Boiled low-fat milk, natural yogurt, buttermilk.
- Broth, bouillon, consommé.
- Fish, poultry, and ground beef that is baked, broiled, or roasted until tender.
- Rice pudding, custard, and tapioca (made with low-fat milk), and gelatin.
- Cooked cereals such as cream of wheat or rice.
- Bananas, applesauce, peeled apples (apples contain pectin, a natural antidiarrheal agent), apple juice, grape juice.
- White bread, toast, crackers made with refined flour.
- Macaroni, noodles, white rice.
- Baked, boiled, or mashed potatoes.
- Cooked, mild vegetables such as asparagus tips, beets, green and wax beans, carrots, peas, spinach, squash; also cream soups from these vegetables.
- Nutmeg, which may decrease the motility of the gastrointestinal tract and should be added to foods wherever appropriate.

Foods and beverages that should be avoided are any that might irritate or stimulate the gastrointestinal tract. These include:

- Whole-grain bread and cereal such as bran and granola.
- Nuts, seeds, coconut.
- Fried and greasy or fatty foods such as pork.
- Fresh and dried fruits, fruit juices except those mentioned above.
- Raw vegetables.
- Rich pastries.
- Popcorn, potato chips, pretzels, nuts.
- Strong spices and herbs such as chili powder, licorice, pepper, curry, garlic, horseradish.
- Olives, pickles, and relishes.
- Flatus-forming foods such as broccoli, onions, and cabbage.
- Foods and beverages containing caffeine, such as chocolate, coffee, tea, caffeine-containing soft drinks.
- Alcoholic beverages, including liquor, beer, and wine.
- Tobacco products.

If diarrhea is present, the patient should report it to the physician or nurse and keep a record of the number, amount, and character of the bowel movements. Kaopectate or Pepto-Bismol may be effective for mild diarrhea, but for diarrhea lasting longer than a couple of days the physician may want to prescribe something stronger, such as Lomotil or paregoric.

If weakness or fatigue accompanies the diarrhea, potassium levels may be depleted and the patient should include high-potassium foods such as baked potatoes, bananas, green beans, halibut, and asparagus tips in the diet. Potassium supplements may be necessary if diarrhea persists, although these supplements often cause gastrointestinal discomfort.

To help prevent dehydration, at least eight to ten glasses of liquid should be consumed daily. Especially good are the following, which help restore sodium, potassium, and other important ions to the body: bouillon, fruit ade, apple juice, grape juice, Gatorade, weak tepid tea, and gelatin. Caffeine-free carbonated beverages that are allowed to go flat before drinking are also acceptable (carbonation may aggravate diarrhea). If the diarrhea is severe, eliminate solid foods and limit the diet to these liquids, then gradually add low-residue foods to the daily diet.

People experiencing diarrhea should eat small, frequent meals and avoid extremely hot or cold foods. Since extremes in temperature may aggravate diarrhea, foods should be served warm or at room temperature.

If the diarrhea is caused by lactose intolerance, the person should avoid all regular milk and milk products used alone or in cooking and baking, as well as cheese, ice cream, and sour cream. Cocoa and chocolate should also be avoided, since these foods contain lactose. The following dairy products are usually tolerated:

• Buttermilk and yogurt. Lactose is altered by the lactobacillus contained in these foods.
• Processed cheese.
• Lactose-free dairy substitutes (brands include Non-Dairy Creamer, Dairy Rich, Cool Whip and Party Whip).
• Milk with Lact-aid, a tablet containing lactase, which digests the milk within twenty-four hours, rendering it lactose-free.
• Lactose-free nutritional supplements such as Ensure or Citrotein.

If the anal area becomes irritated by frequent bowel movements, the person can:

• Cleanse the anal area after each bowel movement with warm water and a mild soap such as Dove or Ivory, rinse well, and pat dry with a soft towel.
• Apply a perianal cream such as Desitin or Proctodon.
• Apply a local anesthetic in ointment or spray form. Corticosteroid sprays or creams may be prescribed by the physician to reduce inflammation.

- Take frequent sitz baths or sit in a tub of warm water.
- Wear loose-fitting clothing and allow the area to be exposed to the air.
- Wear a sanitary napkin or a product such as Assure if incontinent of liquid stool, to avoid embarrassment and the need for frequent changes of clothing.

DIFFICULTY IN SWALLOWING

As a side effect of chemotherapy or radiation therapy, the mucous membrane lining the esophagus can become inflamed, causing a condition known as esophagitis. This condition is often first noted because of difficulty or pain in swallowing, and can sometimes progress to include painful ulceration, hemorrhage, and secondary infection. To prevent or minimize the effects of esophagitis, avoid the use of tobacco and alcohol, as well as foods that are too hot or too cold, spicy or acidic, or hard, crunchy, or coarse.

If inflammation does develop, the person can promote healing and make eating more comfortable if he or she will:

- Eat a well-balanced diet high in protein (necessary to renew the damaged tissue cells).
- Coat the mucous membrane by drinking milk and eating milk products such as sour cream, yogurt, or cottage cheese.
- Add liquids, gravy, sauces, mayonnaise, or mild salad dressings to solid foods to make swallowing easier.
- Cut food into bite-sized pieces or put it in a blender if necessary.

If pain is a problem, liquid aspirin or acetaminophen and topical anesthetics may be used. Narcotics may be prescribed for more severe pain.

DRY MOUTH

Dry mouth, or xerostomia, is a dryness of mucous membranes of the mouth that occurs when saliva production is inadequate or absent. This symptom is often accompanied by taste alterations or loss of appetite.

The major cause of inadequate saliva production is exposure of the salivary glands to radiation. The dose of radiation, the duration of treatment, and the size of the treatment field determine the degree and duration of xerostomia. Decreased saliva begins seven to ten days after the start of therapy, reaches its peak within two to three weeks, and continues for a period after therapy. The absence or inadequate production of saliva may be a permanent side effect of radiation therapy. Even if the disruption is temporary, production may not reach a normal level for six months to a year.

Other causes of inadequate saliva production include the presence of a tumor in the salivary region, dehydration, administration of antihistamines, narcotics, or drugs containing atropine, infections inside the mouth, and the use of tobacco and alcohol.

Inadequate saliva results in inadequate digestion of starches, risk of irritation or damage to the mucous membranes, acceleration of the development of mouth sores, decreased taste acuity (since food must be in solution to be tasted), difficulty in chewing solid food, increased potential for the development of dental caries and oral infections, and difficulty in speaking, since dryness of the membranes hampers the usual speech patterns.

If saliva production is severely impaired or ceases permanently, artificial saliva, available by prescription, may be necessary. For temporary or moderate reduction of saliva, simpler measures may be sufficient. The person should:

- Drink water and other nonirritating liquids such as apple juice, grape juice, or fruit ades several times each hour.
- Use a thermos with a special spout for sipping if a convenient water source is not available.
- Lubricate the lips with K-Y Jelly, cocoa butter, or a lip balm (such as Chap Stick).
- Suck on smooth, flat, sugarless candy or lozenges. Sour substances usually stimulate saliva production.
- Humidify the air with a pan of water near the source of heat, a cold-water vaporizer, or a humidifier installed as part of the central heating system.

Since saliva digests starch and helps prevent dental caries, people with inadequate saliva should avoid starchy foods and take special precautions to avoid caries. The oncologist can prescribe a fluoride gel and special apparatus for using it which is very effective in preventing dental caries. In addition, the person should take the special precautions for brushing the teeth and rinsing the mouth that are listed in the section on mouth sores.

To summarize, tobacco and alcohol should be avoided, as well as foods that are highly spiced, carbonated, very hot or very cold, difficult to chew, or acidic (such as citrus fruits and juices). If the person has difficulty in swallowing, liquids and semiliquids such as gravies, sauces, or mayonnaise can be added to food. Food should be thoroughly cooked and cut into small pieces, or pureed if necessary.

FATIGUE

Fatigue is a very common problem for persons with cancer. It can be caused by anemia, accumulation of waste products from the cell destruction caused by radiation or chemotherapy treatments, protein-calorie malnutrition, disruption of sleep patterns, chronic pain, anxiety, depression, and the stress of coping with the disease.

Although most patients find they can do everything they did before the cancer developed, some must give up certain activities. People with cancer should realize that fatigue is an expected, temporary side effect of chemotherapy and radiation therapy. It is not necessarily an indication that the cancer is increasing in size or that metastasis is occurring. When the treatment plan is complete, fatigue will gradually diminish.

Persons with fatigue may find it easier if they:

• Rest more often. A rest period prior to or after cancer therapy and sleeping later in the morning or going to bed earlier at night are usually beneficial. Minimizing noise and other distractions and using relaxation techniques may also be helpful.
• Maintain as closely as possible their usual lifestyle, but pace their activities according to their energy level. They should avoid doing too much too soon, but gradually increase their activity level as they begin to feel better. Slowing down to maintain a normal range of activities can keep patients from becoming depressed about giving up things they enjoy, which can lead to more fatigue.
• Plan consistent periods of active exercise if they are able to tolerate it.
• Drink adequate fluids, at least eight to ten glasses a day, to keep cellular waste products from accumulating.
• Work part-time if a full schedule is no longer feasible. Some employers will encourage this to avoid losing a valued employee.
• Have their physician or nurse telephone the employer to explain the necessity for rest periods or absences for medical treatment during the day.
• Delegate household tasks such as child care, meal preparation, housework, and home maintenance to other family members or friends, or hire services if possible.

HAIR LOSS (ALOPECIA)

Sudden loss of hair, or alopecia, is a side effect of chemotherapy and radiation therapy that is usually temporary, except with very high doses of radiation. It occurs at different rates and to different degrees in individuals.

Chemotherapy and radiation therapy result in atrophy of the hair follicle; the hair produced is weak and brittle and either breaks off at the surface of the scalp or is spontaneously released from the follicle. Loss of scalp hair associated with chemotherapy varies in degree from slight thinning to complete baldness, depending on the dose and length of therapy. Some patients find that their hair is only slightly thinner after weeks of chemotherapy; others lose all hair immediately. Changes in hair color or texture may occur during regrowth. Often the new hair is softer and thicker than before; gray hair sometimes grows back in its original color.

Loss of other body hair is less frequent and less severe, because the hair has a shorter period of active growth and thus receives less exposure. Nevertheless, hair loss can occur on the eyebrows and other parts of the face, the chest, underarms and groin, and arms and legs.

Alopecia can also be the result of chronic stress, protein malnutrition (since hair, like protein, is composed of amino acids), medications, or other medical conditions unrelated to cancer.

Compared to the life-threatening nature of cancer, temporary loss of hair may seem minor or insignificant, but many patients, both men and women, have said that it was the most stressful event they experienced during their illness. Because hair is often an important part of body image, patients experiencing even a temporary loss may feel anger, sadness, embarrassment, and fear of rejection.

Fortunately, new techniques can minimize the extent of hair loss. Recent research indicates that use of a cold compress or "ice turban" on the head during the chemotherapy restricts circulation to the head, preventing the drugs from reaching the scalp hair follicles. Scalp tourniquets have also been used for the same effect. Although studies are not yet conclusive and these techniques are not applicable in all types of cancer or with all types of chemotherapeutic drugs, they may prevent or minimize hair loss.

Patients with cancer can do much to minimize the amount of hair loss and to protect the hair when regrowth begins by minimizing unnecessary manipulation of the hair. They should:

- Have it cut in an easy-to-manage style before treatment begins.
- Use a mild, protein-base shampoo, cream rinse, and hair conditioner every four to seven days. Avoid excessive shampooing, rinse the hair thoroughly, and gently pat it dry.
- Avoid using an electric hair dryer, or use it only at the lowest setting. Ideally, the hair should be air-dried.
- Avoid electric curlers and curling irons, hair clips, elastic bands, barrettes, and bobby pins. Hair spray, hair dye, and permanent solutions may increase the fragility of the hair and should also be avoided.
- Avoid excessive brushing and combing of the hair. Combing with a wide-tooth comb is best.
- Use a satin pillowcase to decrease hair tangles.

Persons receiving chemotherapy should ask their doctors whether to expect hair loss and if so, how much. Persons expecting total hair loss should:

• Select a wig in advance. A wig as close as possible to the color and style of the hair can be more easily selected before the hair loss occurs. If the hair loss has already occurred, the patient should take an earlier photograph to the wig shop to assist in selection.
• Do comparative shopping for a wig. Wigs should be stylish, lightweight, and reasonably priced. Synthetic wigs are usually more comfortable, easier to care for, and less expensive than human-hair wigs. The approach of the sales person is important: one who offers privacy and empathy can do a great deal to minimize a potentially traumatic event.
• Investigate resources for obtaining a wig. Many American Cancer Society units and some hospitals maintain wig banks to supply wigs at no charge. Wigs and hairpieces are tax-deductible for persons with cancer and some health insurance policies will reimburse the patient whose doctor has written a prescription for a wig.
• Begin to wear the wig before treatment begins. Adjusting to wearing a wig is easier if it becomes part of the lifestyle before hair loss begins.
• Wear a hat, nightcap, scarf, or turban to conceal hair loss. Such accessories are attractive as well as stylish.
• At home, use a hairnet to minimize shedding of hair in bed or on clothes.
• Use eyebrow pencil or false eyelashes if necessary.
• Keep the head covered in summer to prevent a severe sunburn and in winter to prevent heat loss.

INFECTION

Infection—the invasion of the body by bacteria, viruses, and fungi that multiply under favorable conditions and cause injury to or destruction of the cells—is the most frequent cause of illness in the patient with cancer. The most common infection sites are the respiratory and genitourinary tracts, the skin and mucous membranes, and the blood (septicemia).

Cancer itself and cancer treatment both impair the body's defense mechanisms in various ways and leave patients very susceptible to infection. Those receiving chemotherapy are especially vulnerable eight to fourteen days after administration of the drug or drugs when the white blood cell count falls to its lowest point.

Surgery, diagnostic measures, the use of supportive treatment measures (injections, catheters, suction tubes, drainage tubes), and even the mere fact of being in the hospital all increase the chance of exposure or susceptibility to infection.

The patient should do everything possible to decrease the risk of infection, eating a balanced and adequate diet (see Loss of Appetite) and conserving energy with adequate and uninterrupted periods of rest and sleep (see Fatigue). In addition, the patient can avoid exposure to potential sources of infection by avoiding:

• People with transmissible illnesses (bacterial infections, cold sores, shingles, colds, flu, chicken pox, measles).
• People recently vaccinated with live or attenuated vaccines.
• Bird, cat, and dog feces. Since feces contain high levels of fungi and bacteria, patients with cancer should not clean birdcages and cat litter boxes and should avoid areas where dogs are frequently walked.
• All sources of stagnant water, such as that in flower vases, denture cups, irrigating containers, respiratory equipment, soap dishes, and liquid soap. To decrease the growth of microbes, a teaspoon of chlorine bleach should be added to each quart of water used in flower vases and a teaspoon of vinegar to each quart of water or saline solution used for respiratory equipment.
• Contaminated equipment. Equipment should be cleaned by vigorous rubbing with a 70 percent alcohol solution, a solution of one part Clorox to thirty parts water, or a 1 to 2 percent iodine solution.
• When the white blood count is exceedingly low, patients should avoid all possible sources of harmful microorganisms. These include unpared fresh fruits, raw vegetables, flowers, house plants, raw eggs, raw milk and products made from raw milk, and cold cuts and deli items that may have been handled by others. Foods prepared in a blender that cannot be adequately cleaned also should be avoided.

Patients should wash their hands frequently with powdered soap or dehydrated soap flakes (such as Ivory) before preparing or eating food and after using the toilet. They should also cleanse the perianal area after each bowel movement with a mild soap such as Dove and a soft towel, washing, rinsing, and patting dry from front to back. Women should be especially careful to keep the vaginal area clean, and should avoid douches and bubble baths. Finally, precautions should be taken to avoid injuring the mucous membranes, where infectious agents can easily enter the body (see section on bleeding).

Annual vaccination against pneumococcal and pseudomonas bacteria is a wise idea. In addition, patients should be vigilant for signs of infection and report them to the doctor at once. These include:

• Any fever over 100 degrees Fahrenheit (38 degrees Centigrade)
• Sore throat, coughing, or other cold symptoms
• Chills or sweating
• Frequent or painful urination

• Cuts, boils, pimples, or sties that do not heal, or become red or swollen
• Vaginal discharge or itching

ITCHY SKIN (PRURITIS)

Dehydration, the release of specific enzymes by certain kinds of tumors, as well as the effects of the progress of cancer and its treatment can cause intense itching of the skin known as pruritis. Stimuli that can initiate the itching sensation include heat, inflammation, constriction due to tight clothing, and the presence of chemical irritants.

Patients can do a number of things to alleviate the itching and they can learn how to react to it. They should:

• Lubricate the skin with a water-based, rather than oil-based, moisturizer.
• Drink large amounts of fluids, at least eight to ten glasses a day.
• Protect the skin from wind and temperature extremes.
• Keep indoor temperatures cool and stay out of the sun on very hot days, remaining indoors if there is a fan or air conditioner.
• Use only cool or lukewarm water in showers and baths. Cornstarch, baking soda, oatmeal (Aveeno), or soybean powder added to the bath may be soothing.
• Apply cool wet packs every twenty minutes, remove, and allow the skin to air-dry. Reapply as necessary.
• Avoid excessive exercise.
• Wear loose-fitting, lightweight cotton and avoid wool, corduroy, or other scratchy fabrics. Lightweight cotton nightclothes and a cotton thermal blanket are also helpful.

The doctor may prescribe antihistamines for generalized itching, or corticosteroid creams for small areas of itching. Local anesthetics may also be used.

A large part of controlling itching is learning not to scratch, since the itch-scratch-itch syndrome can actually become a conditioned response that makes itching worse. The following methods may help the patient suffering from intense itching:

• Applying cool, wet packs, an ice bag, or stroking with a piece of ice.
• Distraction, relaxation techniques, and positive imagery (see Chapter 12 "Cancer and Pain").
• Using a vibrator or putting pressure on the itchy spot with the thumb, fingertips, or heel of the hand.

LOSS OF APPETITE

Proper nutrition is crucial for the patient with cancer in fighting off the many effects of the disease. But, unfortunately, loss of appetite, or anorexia, is common among people with cancer. This should not be confused with anorexia nervosa, which is a loss of appetite due to psychological problems. While anorexia in patients with cancer can have some origin in the psychological, social, and cultural impact of the diagnosis of cancer, it is also due to the cancer itself and its treatment.

Loss of appetite and taste alterations are two of the major causes of malnutrition, particularly inadequate intake of protein and calories, among people with cancer. Protein-calorie malnutrition is the most life-threatening form of malnutrition because it involves depletion of the body's stores of fat and of the protein stored in the muscles and organs. It is also characterized by a weight loss of 10 percent or more within several months.

A balanced diet with adequate calories and protein improves the well-being of the person with cancer by providing the nutrients needed to repair normal cells and thus reduce the side effects of cancer therapy and keep the immune system functioning at an optimal level. The well-nourished person also has more energy.

To maintain an adequate protein and total calorie intake, persons with cancer should eat:

- A minimum of three servings daily of a variety of protein-rich foods such as meat, fish, poultry, eggs, milk, and milk products.
- A minimum of six servings daily of fruits and vegetables high in vitamins A and C. These include cantaloupe, watermelon, apricots, mango, papaya, strawberries, citrus fruits, tomatoes, green peppers, cabbage, broccoli, spinach, kale, escarole, white potatoes, yams, carrots, and acorn squash.
- A minimum of five servings daily (if diarrhea is not present) of whole-grain bread and cereal. For example, whole-wheat bread, brown rice, wheat germ, barley, oatmeal, and bran.

To minimize weight loss and increase energy, patients should incorporate high-calorie foods into the daily diet. Unless a high-fat diet is contraindicated, strategies include:

- Mayonnaise on sandwiches and in casseroles and desserts.
- Margarine on sandwiches and toast and in all cooked foods when feasible.
- Peanut butter on crackers, toast, bananas, and chocolate bars.
- Sour cream in potatoes, cakes, cookies, sauces, and gravies.

- Whipped cream in coffee and tea and on puddings, gelatins, and desserts.
- Cream cheese in casseroles and cheesecake and on meat sandwiches and bagels.
- Milk or fruit juice instead of water in cooking. If an incompatibility does not exist, medications should be given with a high-calorie beverage rather than water.

Adequate protein is essential to the repair and regeneration of cells. Patients can increase their protein intake by:

- Using double-strength milk—mixing dry skim milk with liquid milk instead of water.
- Mixing breakfast drinks or snacks (such as Carnation Instant Breakfast) with double-strength milk.
- Using evaporated, condensed, or double-strength milk to make casseroles, hot cereals, sauces, puddings, milkshakes, and soups.
- Eating cheese and crackers as a snack between meals; adding cheese to casseroles, baked potatoes, vegetables, sauces, and sandwiches; sprinkling shredded cheese on salads; layering cheese between vegetables and noodles in lasagna; serving cheesecake as a dessert or a snack between meals or at bedtime.
- Drinking eggnog made with instant breakfast drink, one cup of milk, and custard or a parboiled egg. (For patients with cancer, the egg should be parboiled for one minute to reduce the risk of salmonella infection.)
- Adding eggs to salads, casseroles, and sauces; making omelets with double-strength milk, cheese, butter, mayonnaise, and thinly sliced meats; using desserts containing eggs, such as angel food cake, sponge cake, custard, and cheesecake.
- Adding meat, poultry, and fish to salads, casseroles, and sandwiches; strained and junior baby meats to soups and casseroles.
- Snacking on cocktail wieners, deviled eggs, deviled ham and crackers, cream cheese on crackers topped with caviar.
- Adding beans and peas to casseroles; wheat germ to casseroles, cereals, yogurt, and meat loaf.

When their appetites are poor, some people find they are able to eat better if they:

- Exercise before meals. A five-to-ten-minute walk, or even range-of-motion exercises in bed (the physical therapist has specifics), can perk up the appetite.
- Make mealtime an event; wash the hands and face, rinse the mouth with half-strength mouthwash to freshen it before eating.
- Serve all foods attractively and in a pleasant environment. Company, soft music, and a glass of wine (if allowed) may stimulate the appetite.

- Eat smaller, more frequent meals—six or eight small meals rather than three full meals a day. Many hors d'oeuvres provide high-protein food in small amounts.
- Avoid foods that are filling or gas-forming, such as salads, the gas-forming vegetables (e.g., cabbage or broccoli), fruits, and beer.
- Enhance the food with bacon bits, toasted almonds, lemon slices, slivers of ham; or by using marinades, herbs, spices, wine sauces, or butter in cooking.
- Avoid liquids with meals or in the hour before, since they can be filling enough to spoil the appetite. In any case, liquids should be nutritious—milk, juice, or soup rather than soft drinks or water.
- Make sure there is a varied selection of food on hand.
- Experiment with herbs, spices, and sauces. Try adding fresh or dried gingerroot to soups, sauces, and gravies for a pleasant flavor.
- Take advantage of the fact that breakfast is usually the meal when the appetite is at the highest level and make it one of the day's larger meals.
- If pain is present, take an analgesic thirty to sixty minutes prior to mealtime.
- Eat more slowly to allow the stomach to empty while eating, thereby reducing nausea and vomiting. Chew everything thoroughly.
- Counteract a strange taste in the mouth with fresh fruit, juice, or sour hard candy. (See section on taste alterations.)

Even with all of these suggestions, the patient may not receive enough protein to keep the body functioning properly and to maintain adequate weight. If adequate nutrition cannot be accomplished with ordinary foods, a nutrient supplement may be necessary. There are a number of brands and flavors on the market and the person should check with his or her doctor or dietitian to see what might be most appropriate. The supplement also may be added to other foods, such as fruit to make a milkshake; substituted for milk in various dishes such as cereals, soups, puddings and other desserts; or frozen to eat like a popsicle.

A major barrier to adequate nutrition is the task of cooking itself. Many people with cancer simply feel too tired at the end of the day to cook a complete meal. If they have enough energy in the morning, they may want to do the day's cooking then, and reheat as necessary. If not, they should not be shy about accepting friends' invitations to dinner or offers of help with cooking. They should learn to rely on convenience foods—nutritious frozen dinners or take-out food from a delicatessen or local restaurant. They can also cook double batches on good days to freeze and eat on bad days. Finally, they may want to investigate a Meals on Wheels program through their hospital social worker or local American Cancer Society chapter.

MOUTH AND THROAT SORES

Chemotherapy and radiation therapy, as well as dehydration, protein malnutrition, and infection, can cause sores and inflammation of the soft tissues within the mouth (stomatitis) and the mucous membranes (mucositis). They can progress to include painful ulceration, hemorrhage, and secondary infection, causing sufficient pain to make eating very difficult and sometimes leading to discontinuation of cancer treatment. Fortunately these conditions can sometimes be prevented, or at least minimized, by a careful daily regimen of oral care.

Careful daily mouth care is the key to minimizing the development of sores in the mouth and esophagus. Patients should check the mouth daily and report changes in sensation, appearance, or taste. During and after each course of chemotherapy, they should practice oral hygiene every four hours while awake and within a half hour after eating. This means:

• Brushing the teeth, using a soft nylon bristle toothbrush. Soaking the brush in hot water before brushing and rinsing it with hot water during brushing increases the softness of the bristles. The toothbrush should be rinsed well after use and stored in a cool, dry place. To brush, the patient should place the brush at a 45-degree angle between the gums and the teeth and move it in short, circular strokes.

• Using a nonirritating dentifrice such as a baking soda solution. Lemon and glycerin should never be used. Although in the past this combination was frequently used in hospitals for mouth care, it has been found to irritate the oral tissues.

• Flossing between the teeth twice daily with unwaxed dental floss unless advised otherwise. (In cases where the platelet count is low or there are bleeding problems, flossing should be avoided.)

• Rinsing the mouth thoroughly with half-strength hydrogen peroxide (never full-strength) or baking soda and water solution. Commercial mouthwash containing alcohol may be irritating or drying and should be avoided. A mouthwash can be made with one part 3 percent hydrogen peroxide and one or two parts water, plus a pinch of salt.

• Cleaning dentures, if they are worn, in the same way and according to the same schedule.

Among other steps to minimize mouth sores are:

• Lubricate the lips with a water-based lubricant such as K-Y Jelly, or with cocoa butter or a lip balm such as Chap Stick.

• If possible, include in each meal some food that needs to be chewed, since chewing will promote circulation in the gum tissues. Gently mas-

saging the gums with a finger or the rubber tip on a toothbrush is also helpful.
• Avoid irritating foods: those that are very hot, either in temperature or in flavor, very acidic, such as vinegar, or crunchy or rough, such as toast, pretzels, crackers, or popcorn.
• Refrain from smoking or chewing tobacco or drinking alcoholic beverages.
• Make sure that if dentures are worn, they fit properly, since they can be a major source of irritation if they are too loose. If it is not possible to improve their fit, dentures should be worn only for eating.

If a mild irritation develops, rinse between brushings with one of the solutions suggested above. Flossing should be discontinued if it causes pain. A child's soft toothbrush may be less irritating. If the pain makes eating a problem, the doctor may prescribe a topical analgesic, as well as a topical protective agent to promote healing.

Sipping lukewarm tea may help healing, as may a substrate of antacid, which can be made by allowing an antacid such as Maalox or Gelusil to settle, pouring off the liquid and applying the remaining paste to the sore with a cotton-tipped applicator. After fifteen to twenty minutes the mouth can be rinsed with a saline solution or water.

A high-protein diet with vitamin supplements is important to promote cell repair and replacement. People with cancer may find room temperature foods and beverages more soothing than warm or cold foods. Some persons may find it easier to eat if they have their favorite foods. They can have friends or family bring fruits, ethnic treats, or desserts to the hospital and ask the nurses whether there is a refrigerator to store snacks and a stove or oven to warm up food.

If the inflammation becomes severe, the oral hygiene routine should be increased to every two hours while awake and twice during the night. Topical protective agents and analgesics can also be used more frequently, and antifungal agents and antibiotics may also be ordered. The person should discontinue using a toothbrush, floss, and dentures. The teeth can be cleaned instead with a sponge-tipped applicator, a Water Pik set on the lowest setting, or even sterile gauze wrapped around a finger.

NAUSEA AND VOMITING

Inability to enjoy or retain food because of nausea and vomiting is one of the most upsetting problems faced by people with cancer. It is a common side effect of both chemotherapy and radiation therapy, but it is by no means universal. Many people never experience nausea or vomiting.

Fortunately, most people can be helped by medications called antiemetics, which combat nausea and vomiting. For maximum benefit these drugs should be given before the first chemotherapy session, for the following reason: people tend to associate nausea with specific situations. A person who develops nausea and vomiting after eating a particular food in a restaurant may avoid that food—and the restaurant—for years or a lifetime. Similarly, after experiencing nausea or vomiting after one or more chemotherapy treatments, some people develop nausea or vomiting or both immediately before the therapy is given. This is called anticipatory or conditioned nausea and vomiting.

Antiemetics are usually prescribed six to twelve hours prior to chemotherapy. They are continued every four to six hours for at least twelve to twenty-four hours, or as long as the nausea persists. To maintain enough drug concentration in the body to prevent the onset of nausea and vomiting, the medication often must be taken every few hours around the clock during chemotherapy treatment. Sometimes the most effective antiemetic, dose, and frequency must be established by trial and error.

There are many other means besides drugs to prevent or alleviate nausea and vomiting. Finding the best ones may also require experimentation. Methods that have worked for many patients include:

- Recalling strategies that were successful during pregnancy, illness or other times of stress. For example, some people find that eating a few bland crackers or sipping on a flat cola drink before getting out of bed in the morning helps.
- Eating foods that are cold or served at room temperature, such as sandwiches, cottage cheese, cereals, and desserts. These foods are usually better tolerated than warm or hot foods, since the odors of hot foods often aggravate the feeling of nausea.
- Using a clear liquid diet that includes apple juice, cranberry juice, lemonade, broth, ginger ale, cola or lemon-lime drinks, popsicles, gelatin, tea, or Gatorade.
- Experimenting with sour foods such as lemons, sour pickles, sour hard candy, or lemon sherbet. Rinsing the mouth with water mixed with a little lemon juice may also help, if there are no mouth sores.
- Avoiding sweet, fatty, highly salted, and spicy foods, as well as food with strong odors, such as cheese or salami. Bland foods like mashed potatoes, applesauce, sherbet, crackers, toast, and cottage cheese are usually better tolerated.
- Avoiding sights, sounds, and smells that can stimulate nausea—cooking odors, strong perfume, or other people vomiting.
- Eating various kinds of candy during chemotherapy administration. Some that have helped decrease the unpleasant metallic taste are hard or soft mints and sour candy.
- Experimenting with various eating patterns. For example, some patients

avoid eating or drinking for one to two hours before and after chemotherapy administration, while others have a large meal three or four
hours before, and then light meals for the rest of the day. Some patients
do better with a liquid diet up to twelve hours before and twenty-four
hours after chemotherapy. Others are able to eat solid food if they have
frequent but small meals every five to six hours.

- Getting fresh air from an open window or by taking a walk outside.
- Using relaxation techniques or positive imagery, or self-hypnosis, which
  can be learned from a qualified therapist or a specially trained nurse.
- Using distraction, such as music, television, or movies, video games,
  crafts, games, and conversation.
- Sleeping during episodes of nausea or when it is anticipated. If nausea is
  present when the patient awakes, it may help to take the prescribed
  antiemetic and rest in bed for another thirty minutes to an hour.

If vomiting occurs, the patient should note the amount and character to
report to the nurse or doctor. If the episodes are frequent, he or she
should refrain from eating or drinking for four to eight hours, or twenty-
four if necessary, but rinse the mouth with a mixture of water and lemon
juice after each episode. When the vomiting has subsided, the patient can
suck on ice cubes or sip small quantities of liquid slowly. Broth, Gatorade,
ginger ale, cola, lemonade, tea, and gelatin are usually easily tolerated.

In the past, marijuana as a preventive for nausea and vomiting has
gained a good deal of media attention. Some physicians have recommended marijuana for this purpose, but this is seldom done today since
the antiemetic drugs are more effective and predictable.

PAIN

Most people mistakenly think of cancer as a very painful disease. If
cancer caused pain earlier, there would be fewer problems with detection.
Pain is not an inevitable part of cancer. In fact, most people with cancer
suffer little or no pain, especially if the disease is detected early. Often,
the only pain is that associated with surgery or other treatments, and it is
manageable with medication. Advanced cancer can be painful, but many
patients even with advanced disease feel only discomfort or slight pain,
which can be treated with mild painkilling drugs.

Many factors affect pain perception, including physiological, psychological, cultural, and social factors. Pain causes anxiety and stress, which
can exacerbate any pain. People vary in their tolerance to pain, and in
how they express their discomfort. The number and arrangement of
nerve cells in the painful area also has a great effect on how much pain
sensation is transmitted to the brain.

The pain generally associated with cancer is chronic, as opposed to acute, and usually persists longer than six months. It may be caused by a number of factors, including infiltration of nerves by tumor cells, disruption or destruction of a nerve, blockage of a body organ or duct, pressure on a nerve, reduction in blood supply, or destruction of the bone from invading cancer cells. Fear, guilt, anxiety, and other difficult emotions also play a part in pain.

There are many methods of controlling or eliminating pain. The ones most often used for patients with cancer are: drugs (usually oral), nerve blocks, transcutaneous electrical nerve stimulation (a painless electrical pulse that blocks the pain message), and a variety of self-treatment techniques including relaxation, imagery, and distraction. Each of these is discussed in detail in Chapter 12, "Cancer and Pain."

RESPIRATORY PROBLEMS

Shortness of breath is a serious problem for patients with lung cancer or metastases to the lung, but other patients may also suffer decrease in respiratory function, especially in the lung's ability to defend itself against infection. Chemotherapy, anemia, and malnutrition are but a few of the factors that affect the proper functioning of the lungs, but there are several things patients can do to make breathing easier, to promote adequate blood circulation, and to ensure that the maximum amount of oxygen possible gets into the blood from the lungs. They should:

• Learn to breathe properly, inhaling through the nose and exhaling slowly through the mouth with the lips pursed, as if blowing out a candle. Exhaling should take about twice as long as inhaling. In breathing, use the abdominal muscles rather than the chest muscles. The abdominal muscles should be relaxed and pushed out while inhaling, contracted while exhaling. In other words, while the air comes in, the abdomen goes out and while the air goes out, the abdomen comes in.

• Assume a comfortable position when experiencing shortness of breath. In bed, the patient should use one or more pillows or a back support to elevate the upper body at least 45 degrees, and tilt the shoulders forward while supporting the body with the arms spread away from the sides and resting the feet on a footboard or other support. To keep the lungs as clear as possible, the patient should alternate positions, lying first on one side and then the other, with the upper body elevated. If the person is sitting up, he or she should lean forward and rest the elbows and forearms on a desk or table.

• Move around or stand at the bedside to help circulation, even though this may seem difficult to those chronically short of breath.

• Avoid sitting in one position too long and avoid crossing the legs, since this inhibits circulation to the feet. Special antiembolism stockings should be worn by both men and women, especially those taking steroids.

- Do simple arm and leg exercises, even if confined to bed. Range-of-motion and isometric exercises will maintain mobility and improve muscle tone. A physical therapist, doctor, or nurse can recommend specific exercises.
- Drink sufficient quantities of liquid—as much as eight to ten glasses a day—to help keep the mucous membranes functioning properly so that they are able to clear the lungs of secretions.
- Cough effectively to help clear the lungs. Practice "staged coughing":
  1. Breathe deeply two times.
  2. On the third breath, inhale and hold for two or three seconds.
  3. Brace the feet on the floor or against the foot of the bed and cough three times. The coughs should come from deep in the chest.
- Humidify the air with a cold-water vaporizer, a pan of water on a source of heat, or a humidifier as part of the central heating system.

If shortness of breath becomes a chronic problem, the patient may get a doctor's prescription for oxygen therapy at home. One big tank or several smaller ones with extension tubing can serve various rooms, and a portable tank can be attached to a wheelchair, permitting the patient to go out. Safety precautions must be taken with oxygen use. The patient, visitors, and family should beware of flames of any type: cigarettes, pilot lights, and so on can cause an explosion. Care should be taken not to get kinks in the tubing that will obstruct the flow. The flow rate should not be increased beyond the physician's instructions.

SEXUAL AND REPRODUCTION PROBLEMS

Virtually every person with cancer is concerned about the ability to continue to have a satisfying sexual relationship with his or her partner, yet this important concern often goes unmentioned. Health-care professionals are sometimes as uncomfortable about discussing sex as patients are in bringing it up. Yet the continuation of as normal a relationship as possible is, for many people, a key factor in the recovery process.

The progress of the disease itself, the side effects of treatment (such as nausea and fatigue), the lack of privacy for hospitalized patients, and the anxiety, fear, and anger that go with the diagnosis of cancer can all contribute to loss of sexual desire or the inability to function sexually. If the patient's oncologist, primary care physician, or an oncology nurse does not volunteer information about what the person can expect of his or her particular type of cancer and treatment, then the patient should request it. Being prepared and knowing which symptoms will be temporary and which will last longer or be permanent will relieve much of the anxiety and allow the patient to begin to make adjustments.

The other important person to share this information with is the patient's partner, who may be feeling some of the same anxiety and frustrations, who may feel very left out, and who may be afraid to initiate sexual contact. Neither the patient nor the partner can assume that the other will be aware of needs, fears, and frustrations unless they are openly expressed. The importance of communication seems so obvious that we are hesitant to mention it, yet lack of it may be at the root of sexual problems.

Unless their family is complete or they are not planning on having children, the couple must also share their feelings regarding parenthood. They should seek information about the immediate and long-term effects of treatment on the reproductive organs, so that decisions regarding parenthood can be made. For example, it may be possible for a male patient to deposit sperm in a sperm bank prior to treatment. If permanent sterility is anticipated, they should feel free to seek counseling to help them deal with its consequences.

Couples who wish to have children should seek genetic counseling. To avoid stillbirths and birth defects due to chromosomal damage to the ova of a female patient, or to allow the male patient's sperm count to return to usual levels, the couple must wait up to two years following completion of treatment before attempting to conceive. During treatment and during the waiting period, they should use an effective means of birth control, such as one of the following:

- Condoms, used with a vaginal lubricant if the female partner is the patient.
- Diaphragms used with spermicidal jelly or foam, and checked for size by a gynecologist if there has been a weight loss of ten pounds or more.
- Oral contraceptives, other than those containing a high progesterone level, which present an increased risk of *Candida albicans,* a common vaginal infection. Oral contraceptives should be avoided by female patients who have estrogen- or progesterone-dependent tumors.
- Intrauterine devices (IUD). These are not advised if the female partner is the patient, since they present a risk of bleeding and infection.

Continuation of sexual relationships during and after treatment will take understanding and adjustment. The couple should realize that sexual interest and drive may be diminished or absent during this time and that the male patient may suffer temporary impotence. The patient should avoid alcoholic beverages, narcotics, or sedatives for an hour or so prior to intercourse in order not to further decrease sexual interest or fulfillment. The couple should not forget, as some people tend to, that intercourse is only one part of a fulfilling sexual relationship. Kissing, caressing, just holding each other can be very satisfying. Sometimes it is more satisfying, because there is no urgency and no pressure to perform.

The patient and his or her partner may find sexual relations easier if they change the time or the position. If fatigue increases in the early evening, having intercourse in the midmorning or early afternoon may help. If a man finds it too strenuous to be on top, or if a woman finds her partner's weight too much for her, they might try having intercourse with the man lying on his back and the woman kneeling astride him. Or they might try lying on their sides, the man behind.

If the female partner is the patient, she should use a water-based lubricant such as K-Y Jelly to compensate for any loss of vaginal lubrication and to protect against injury to the mucous membranes. She should report any suspected vaginal infection, noticeable by the presence of redness, swelling, foul-smelling discharge, or itching, to her doctor and should avoid intercourse if the mucous membrane lining the vagina becomes irritated.

A woman with cancer should also tell her doctor when her menstrual period is expected. The doctor may prescribe oral contraceptives to be taken throughout chemotherapy treatment to prevent menstruation when there is a risk of thrombocytopenia (see section on bleeding). She should also inform the doctor if she suspects she is pregnant.

Women with cancer of the uterus, cervix, or vagina may suffer additional sexual problems as a result of the cancer itself or radiation treatment to this area. These include vaginal discharge, which may be bloody and foul-smelling; decreased vaginal lubrication; bleeding and discomfort or pain during sexual intercourse; and the growth of adhesions from fibrous tissue in the vagina, called vaginal fibrosis. A sanitary napkin—not a tampon should be worn while the drainage continues and the woman should cleanse the vaginal and rectal area following each pad change. Many physicians recommend a douche at least once a day with a tablespoon of white vinegar in a quart of warm water.

Vaginal fibrosis can usually be prevented by having regular intercourse. If a woman does not have a regular partner or anticipates a prolonged disruption in her sexual relationship, she should speak to her radiation therapist or gynecologist about using an obturator—a cylindrical device used to dilate the vagina. In the absence of intercourse, the obturator should be inserted at least three times a week for a year following radiation therapy. The physician or nurse can explain its proper use.

SKIN REACTIONS

Both chemotherapy and radiation therapy can cause skin changes or problems when the cells in the upper layer of the skin are damaged or destroyed. With radiation, these changes are usually confined to the site of radiation treatment; with chemotherapy, they may be local or generalized. Many of them are temporary and will disappear on their own soon after treatment is finished.

Chemotherapy reactions include:

• Red patches (erythema) or hives (urticaria) at the site of the chemotherapy injections or on other parts of the body. Depending on the drug used, the red patches may appear over pressure points such as the elbows, knees, fingertips, and shoulder blades, or on the face, or in a general, overall pattern. The hives may develop along the vein used for administering the chemotherapeutic drug or may be generalized. These two reactions generally disappear within several hours.
• Darkening of the skin. This may occur in the nail beds (sometimes in bands), inside the mouth, on the gums or teeth, as lines along the trunk, or along the veins used for chemotherapy administration, or it may be generalized. It usually occurs two to three weeks after chemotherapy and continues for ten to twelve weeks after completion of treatment.
• Sensitivity to sun and light. Photosensitivity is a common reaction that causes some people to suffer an acute sunburn after just a short exposure to the sun. They should be careful to avoid exposure as much as possible, to wear protective clothing such as a wide-brimmed hat and a long-sleeved cotton shirt, and to use an effective sun screening agent (one that has a sun protection factor of 15 or more). Effective sun screens include Coppertone Super Shade Sunblocking Lotion, Total Eclipse Sunscreen Lotion, Elizabeth Arden Suncare Sun Blocking Cream, Clinique 19SPF Sun Block, and Estée Lauder Sun Cover Cream. (See Chapter 30 "Skin Cancer," for other specific measures.) The hypersensitivity will disappear once treatment has stopped.

These are the most common skin reactions to chemotherapy. There are others, including a thickening of the skin known as hyperkeratosis, an acne-like reaction, and skin ulcerations, that may occur with only one drug or a group of related drugs. In any case, patients should check with the oncologist before treatment begins so that they will know what to expect.

"Radiation recall" is a reaction that can occur when chemotherapy is given after radiation therapy. It may occur several weeks or even months after radiation therapy has ended, and involves only the skin that has been previously irradiated. The usual symptoms of radiation recall are patches of redness and shedding or peeling of the skin, but there may also be blisters and wet, oozing areas of skin that peel. After the skin reaction heals, the skin will be permanently darkened. While it is present, the patient should:

- Gently cleanse the skin at the site of the reaction. The skin should be washed by patting it gently with a soft cloth, using a mild soap like Dove or Aveeno and tepid water; rinsing and then gently patting it dry with a soft towel.
- Gently apply creams or lotions containing Vitamins A, D, and E to the site to alleviate the dry skin if inflammation and peeling are present. Use a cream or aerosol spray containing cortisone, prescribed by the physician, if necessary for itching, but refrain from rubbing, scratching, or massaging the skin.
- If the reaction is more intense, cleanse the area with half-strength hydrogen peroxide and saline solution. Mix the solution immediately before use for maximum effectiveness and apply with an irrigating syringe to avoid friction. Rinse the area with saline solution or water, gently pat dry, and expose the area to air as often as possible. If the drainage is copious, use a nonadhesive absorbent dressing (gauze) and change it as soon as it becomes damp.
- Follow the same precautions necessary for irradiated skin (see below).

Radiation therapy also causes changes in the skin that are generally confined to the area under the focus of the radiation beam. The degree or intensity of the skin reaction will be greater in persons receiving a large daily dose of radiation, in those with fair, thin skin, and in those who are not receiving adequate protein in their diet. Because of the texture or location, certain areas of skin are more sensitive to the effects of radiation therapy. These include:

- Skin surfaces subject to friction and moisture: the skin under the breasts, between the buttocks, under the arms, and the groin and vulva.
- Smooth, thin skin such as that on the face and perineum.
- Skin with a poor blood supply: back of the hand, top and sole of the foot, midline of the back.
- Skin that has been injured by surgery or accidents, or that is inflamed or infected.

The effect of radiation therapy on the skin begins seven to ten days after it is initiated and is progressive in nature. The four stages of reaction are:

- Inflammation of the skin in the treatment field, the color ranging from pink to red, and slight swelling. The reaction is similar to a first-degree sunburn and damage to the cells is minimal. With this and the next stage, there may be some pigmentation resembling a suntan. It may be patchy and interspersed with patches of thin, silvery white skin.
- Inflammation and dry desquamation (peeling), like that after a sunburn. The skin becomes dry and scaly due to the destruction of the oil glands in the treatment field.

• Inflammation, swelling, and oozing. Blisters form and the skin resembles a second-degree sunburn. Although the damage is reversible, radiation therapy is usually discontinued until the skin heals. Other reactions may include patches of thin, white or silvery skin that heal poorly, leathery skin with little elasticity, and fibrosis or atrophy of the lymph nodes.
• Telangiectasis. These small, reddish areas of the skin are caused by enlargement of blood capillaries. Although the condition is permanent, it may become less noticeable over time.
• Loss of hair in the treatment field. With high doses of radiation, the loss may be permanent and the activity of the oil and sweat glands in the area may be suppressed.

Because the skin in the treatment field is especially vulnerable to injury and infection, patients should take special precautions during and for a month or so after radiation therapy treatment. These precautions include:

• With mild reactions, gently cleanse the skin with water or, if necessary, with a mild soap such as Dove or Aveeno and a soft cloth. Skin should be gently patted dry with a soft towel.
• If more serious reactions are present, follow the precautions previously listed under radiation recall.
• Avoid wearing rough fabrics such as wool or corduroy, or tight-fitting clothes. Nothing should leave a mark when removed—no elastic on underwear or tight straps or belts. Cotton is the most comfortable fabric; nylon and other synthetics do not permit perspiration to evaporate. If possible, expose the skin in the treatment field to air.
• Wash underclothes or any clothes that will come in contact with the treatment area with a mild detergent, such as Ivory Snow.
• Avoid shaving or using cosmetics, perfumes, or deodorants on the skin in the treatment field.
• Avoid exposing the skin to wind or any source of heat (including hot water bottles, heating pads, and sun lamps) or cold (ice bags, cold weather).
• Refrain from swimming in salt water or chlorinated pools.
• Be especially careful to protect the skin from exposure to the sun, even after radiation therapy is completed. The affected area can be covered with sun-blocking lotions—those with a sun protection factor (SPF) rating of 15 or more. Scarves and broad-brimmed hats provide fashionable shade on sunny days. Lightweight cover-ups should be used at the beach.
• Shave only with an electric razor and, if possible, avoid shaving the affected site.
• Do not use medications, deodorants, perfumes, powders, and cosmetics

on the skin in the treatment area. Tape, dressings, and adhesive bandages should also be avoided.

TASTE ALTERATIONS

A taste alteration is a change in the usual patterns of taste perception that is unique to the person experiencing it. Because of the disease or its treatment, patients with cancer may experience alterations ranging from a decrease in taste sensitivity, making most foods seem bland and difficult to distinguish, to alterations that give certain foods peculiar or unpleasant tastes, to total loss of taste. These alterations may manifest themselves in an aversion to sweet foods or an increased threshold for them, an aversion to bitter tastes and foods high in amino acids, such as beef and pork, or a constant metallic or medicinal taste sensation. Taste alterations make it difficult to enjoy meals, and some patients may have to force themselves to eat in order not to endanger their health further (see section on Loss of Appetite).

In addition to maintaining adequate nutrition, persons experiencing taste alterations should take measures to prevent or minimize sores and dryness of the mouth (see sections on Mouth and Throat Sores and Dry Mouth). The latter is important because foods must be in solution to be tasted. To help make food more appealing, they can experiment with the following:

- If nausea is not a problem, taking in the aroma of food cooking may help stimulate the appetite.
- Using flavor enhancers such as lemon, salt, vanilla, and cinnamon, while avoiding stronger spices.
- Eating sugar-free mints, chewing sugar-free gum, or eating other foods that have a pleasant taste to mask a metallic or bitter taste sensation.
- Eliminating foods that stimulate an unpleasant taste sensation. Other high-protein foods (fish, poultry, eggs, beans, cheese) can be substituted for beef or pork if these are a problem.

URINARY TRACT PROBLEMS

Problems of the urinary tract, especially the bladder and kidneys, can result from the physiological and metabolic effects of tumor growth, from side effects of chemotherapy and radiation therapy, and from infection, to which persons with cancer are particularly susceptible.

To protect the mucous membranes of the genitourinary tract, the patient should use a water-based lubricant such as K-Y Jelly prior to sexual intercourse to avoid excessive friction, and should avoid the use of douches and vaginal suppositories. Patients should be alert to the signs of urinary tract infections and report them to the doctor. These include:

• Frequency or urgency of urination.
• Burning on urination.
• Urine that is cloudy, dark, reddish or brownish in color, or contains blood.
• Fever, chills, or weakness.
• Low back or flank pain.

It is important to have the doctor determine the nature of the problem, since treatment will differ depending on the type of infection.

If the diagnosis is cystitis, or inflammation of the bladder, the patient should:

• Increase fluid intake to a minimum of three quarts a day, distributed evenly over the twenty-four hours.
• Avoid foods and beverages that may be irritating to the lining of the bladder, such as coffee and tea, alcoholic beverages, foods containing spices such as pepper or curry, and avoid tobacco products.
• Acidify the urine to prevent infection by taking ascorbic acid (vitamin C) daily as prescribed by the physician. Cranberry juice, a popular folk remedy, is only effective in acidifying the urine if it is taken in quantities of three quarts a day.
• Void frequently, as soon as there is an urge, but try at least every two hours.

If there is excessive uric acid in the blood (hyperuricemia), the person should:

• Increase fluid intake to at least three quarts a day to help the kidney clear the uric acid from the blood.
• Avoid consuming legumes (lentils, dried peas, or beans), organ meats, sardines, anchovies, tea, and wine, which are high in purines and thereby increase uric acid production.

11

Rehabilitation of the Cancer Patient

ROBERT J. MCKENNA, M.D.

INTRODUCTION

Until about ten years ago, most rehabilitation services were prescribed almost exclusively for persons with physical handicaps due to accidents, stroke, polio, and other such problems that limited normal activities both at home and at work. Recently, however, rehabilitation efforts have been extended to other areas, most notably to patients with heart disease or cancer—a most welcome advent.

Nearly all patients who have been treated for cancer need some rehabilitation. There are many reasons for this, including the increased longevity for cancer patients. Today nearly half of all cancer patients can expect to live for at least five years; many of them are cured and can expect to live out their normal life-spans. Even for those who are not cured, rehabilitation is still an integral part of their comprehensive care. In a study comparing the mortality statistics of cancer, stroke, and heart disease, researchers found that at least half of the stroke patients died within the first year and 30 percent of the heart attack patients did not survive their initial convalescent period. In contrast, most cancer patients could expect to live longer than either the stroke or heart attack victims, making a strong argument for the suggestion that cancer patients are more in need of rehabilitation than those with these other major illnesses.

Ideally, rehabilitation should begin as soon as the diagnosis of cancer is made and should be continued throughout the entire treatment and follow-up effort. Rehabilitation may be defined as the team effort to enable the cancer patient to achieve a lifestyle that is as close to normal as possible. To attain this goal, cancer rehabilitation should attend to the patient's physical, social, psychological, and vocational needs and should never be delayed until after treatment has been completed. The focus of cancer rehabilitation should be on the whole person and not on the particular type of cancer, although this is a factor and the organs involved will direct the emphasis of the rehabilitation plan.

HISTORICAL PERSPECTIVE

The first meaningful cancer rehabilitation effort started in 1952 with the founding of the International Association of Laryngectomees (IAL). The organization was dedicated to promote and support total rehabilitation of patients who had undergone a laryngectomy (removal of the larynx or voice box) through the exchange of ideas and information among its members and the public. The American Cancer Society has been the sole sponsor of the national IAL office since its formation. In 1985 there were 325 affiliated chapters, representing forty-seven states and sixteen foreign countries registered with the national IAL. Its major activities include the development of educational materials, assistance with speech therapy, and counseling, both before and after the operation. Public and professional educational programs in first aid and artificial respiration, seminars for prospective speech teachers, and publicizing new surgical methods and new electronic or pneumatic devices for communications are among the important activities arranged by the IAL. In addition, the organization leads a national effort to overcome the reluctance of companies to hire people who have undergone laryngectomies.

A second major cancer rehabilitation program is Reach to Recovery, which started for women who had had a mastectomy, but now covers all aspects of breast cancer treatment. Since the formation of these two pioneering cancer rehabilitation programs, a number of other organizations, such as the United Ostomy Association, CanSurMount, I Can Cope, Candlelighters, and the Amputee Visitor Program have been developed. (All of these will be reviewed in later sections of this chapter and in chapters devoted to the specific types of cancer.)

Federal legislation in 1954 provided some limited funding to states for demonstrations, research, training, and service to disabled patients, but this program was almost never used by the cancer patient. Severe restrictions imposed by rules prevented state rehabilitation agencies from accepting the patient unless he or she was free of cancer for at least eighteen months after therapy was completed—obviously a counterproductive policy, since rehabilitation should be an integral part of the overall treatment of the disease. Fortunately this limitation was changed in 1966 through the efforts of Mary Switzer, who not only made government agencies aware of the problem but also was able to get some degree of federal funding for cancer rehabilitation demonstration projects.

Cancer rehabilitation efforts received a major boost in 1971 with the passage of the National Cancer Plan, which listed cancer rehabilitation among its seven objectives. In December 1972 a National Cancer Rehabilitation Planning Conference was sponsored by the National Cancer Institute to explore ways to improve the quality of life of the cancer patient, and four objectives of cancer rehabilitation were identified:

1. Psychological support once cancer has been diagnosed;
2. Optimal physical functioning following cancer treatment;
3. Vocational counseling when indicated, as early as possible; and
4. Optimal social functioning as the ultimate goal of all cancer control and treatment.

Over the next decade, in addition to the continuing rehabilitation programs of the American Cancer Society, nearly all cancer rehabilitation demonstration and research projects were funded by the government through the National Cancer Institute. Nevertheless, federal and state cancer rehabilitation programs have developed very slowly and have had minimal usage, for a variety of reasons. All too many people still consider cancer a hopeless disease, and either are unaware of rehabilitation programs or are reluctant to avail themselves of them. In the past decade, however, major organizations, principally the American Cancer Society, have greatly expanded service activities to include rehabilitation and have addressed many of the social, economic, psychological, vocational, and insurance needs of cancer patients.

GOALS OF CANCER REHABILITATION

The goal of cancer rehabilitation is to return patients to the point where they can function at their best possible level. Cancer rehabilitation is now seen as a major component of the spectrum of cancer therapy, along with diagnosis, treatment, and follow-up care. There are two reasons for this. First, patients with many kinds of cancer are surviving much longer than in the past, which allows attention to be turned from survival alone to the quality of the survival. Second, throughout medicine there now appears to be a growing awareness, perhaps promoted by the patients themselves, of the need to view them not as isolated diagnostic problems but as human beings with a whole spectrum of psychological, as well as physical, needs. In cancer therapy this has led to an awareness on the part of all members of the cancer care team that patients need to be prepared for what will follow diagnosis, to be supported through that period, and to be helped to return to a life as similar as possible to their existence before the diagnosis of cancer.

In its broadest sense, cancer rehabilitation provides for the readaptation to everyday life in light of the effects of the cancer and its treatment. It consists of an accommodation and adjustment of the patient's personal needs and habits to achieve and improve physical, psychological, financial, and vocational well-being. The rehabilitation effort should be extended to include supportive care, involving such services as hospice programs, referral for ongoing counseling, and other long- or short-term supportive care.

In general there are four categories of cancer rehabilitation: preventive, restorative, supportive, and palliative. Preventive interventions occur when certain disabilities can be predicted and education and training can be used to lessen their impact. An example of a preventive intervention would be a preoperative visit to explain physical and other therapy to a woman about to undergo mastectomy. At this time the woman would learn the exercises she should use after surgery to help prevent loss of arm function and ameliorate other problems. Restorative efforts allow the patient to return to a state as close as possible to that which existed before the cancer diagnosis and treatment. Reconstructive breast surgery for a woman who has had a mastectomy is an example of a restorative procedure that is coming into wider use.

The third type of rehabilitation program consists of supportive interventions for patients who will have permanent or disabling conditions as the result of cancer treatment, but can still gain considerable control of the ordinary activities of daily life and can learn to cope with the condition. An example would be a patient undergoing a total laryngectomy, in which the larynx or voice box is removed, resulting in a permanent speech disability. Supportive interventions include teaching alternative ways of speaking. Palliative interventions—the fourth category of rehabilitative efforts—are efforts undertaken when the cancer is so advanced and disabling that recovery is unlikely, but comfort, emotional support, and assistance in day-to-day functioning can be provided.

The goals for realistic rehabilitation may be set for each patient, depending upon what is appropriate. This will allow for prevention of anticipated disability, whenever possible, through education and training, while those conditions that cannot be prevented are dealt with according to the stage of the disease and the functional capabilities of the individual patient. Unfortunately, even though the feasibility of effective rehabilitation has improved greatly in recent years, for many cancer patients there still are barriers to securing adequate rehabilitation. Many community hospitals, for example, do not have all of the personnel resources necessary to build a complete rehabilitation team. Many physicians are more familiar with diagnostic and therapeutic issues than they are with rehabilitation, and there is a relative lack of awareness of the readaptation needs of cancer patients. A nurse, for instance, who may have a basic understanding of cancer cannot be expected to provide the personal one-to-one teaching that a mastectomy patient needs in arm care, chemotherapy, or concerns about sexuality and self-image. Social workers are generally aware of many of the services of the American Cancer Society and some of the major programs offered by other organizations dedicated to helping the cancer patient and family. But without an organized cancer rehabilitation program to act as a conduit for cancer resources and information, some social workers may lack the awareness of specific resources that are the most appropriate in a given situation. Similarly, the other professionals who should be involved in the cancer rehabilitation team will not function effectively if services are not coordinated. In this regard, federal and state agencies are often of little help because they traditionally have assigned cancer patients their lowest priority, largely because of the stigma that was once attached to the disease and a continuing failure to recognize the vastly improved outlook for most cancer patients.

PSYCHOLOGICAL NEEDS OF THE CANCER PATIENT

It has been repeatedly observed that about 40 percent of all cancer patients have psychological problems associated with their disease. While this does not mean that in all instances direct psychological or psychiatric care is indicated, it does imply that the emotional aspects should be kept in mind during all other rehabilitative activities. The problems that give rise to emotional concerns are many and varied. For example, about 30 percent of patients need assistance with activities involved in daily living and in coping with pain. Another 15 to 20 percent have problems with either housing, neurological function, family support, finances, or nutrition. About 15 percent are deeply concerned about their physical appearance. About 10 percent suffer arm or leg swelling or breathing problems, and about 7 percent have needs in communication or transportation, as well as a variety of other perceived or actual needs. Many, of course, have multiple difficulties, making the need for counseling even more acute.

Even though aid in many of these areas is available, too many cancer patients are unaware of its existence or how to get it. This was brought out recently in a study by the California Division of the American Cancer Society, which surveyed the needs of 800 patients and more than 100 family members. Participants were questioned about needs for support, information, and services to help deal with stress, family problems, and the financial impact of the disease. The study found that about three fourths of the group were unaware of many of the social, medical and governmental resources available to them. Furthermore, when informed of these important services, most made use of them.

This study showed that for the largest proportion (30.5 percent) the key stress period was just after the diagnosis of cancer, and for 16.7 percent it was the period of hospitalization and initial treatment. For 11.1 percent it was the time of release from the hospital. Many patients found it very difficult to share their feelings about their illness with either family or friends. Some coped very well with stress during the initial diagnosis and treatment stages, but experienced delayed reactions six or more months later. Depression and embarrassment often persisted for prolonged periods, even after successful treatment.

The impact of cancer on the family was significant in more than a third of those surveyed. Problems included altered behavior of children, fear of dying, anger caused by the diagnosis of cancer, financial burdens, sexual difficulties, neglect by the spouse, drinking, gambling, and frequent absences of the spouse, and even the completely ungrounded fear of "catching the cancer." Not unexpectedly, the greatest period of stress for the family of dying patients comes with the realization that death is inevitable.

The financial burden of the disease was extreme for 15 percent of those surveyed. Major changes in lifestyle were necessary for 13 percent; nonwhites were affected more than whites. The inability to work was the major reason for financial hardship, and patients with family incomes of less than $7,500 were twice as likely as those in higher income groups to have employment-, disability- and pension-related problems. Health insurance proved to be a highly significant factor in lessening the financial impact of cancer. Only 40 percent of the patients reported that all hospitalization and medical costs were covered by their insurance. Almost 20 percent of the patients employed at the time of the study worried about whether their cancer would affect their fringe benefits at work, and some others reported that the net effect of having had cancer was to lock them into their present jobs.

About 25 percent of the people surveyed reported changes in their living arrangements related to their illness. The vast majority of the patients and families said that no social services had been offered or made available to them. The need for such services, as would be expected, was greatest for those with advanced cancer or for the families of dying patients. Individuals who were living alone also experienced greater need.

As a result of this study, the California Division of the American Cancer Society proposed the following:

1. Each cancer patient's psychological needs should be assessed at the time of the diagnosis.

2. Social services and psychological counseling should continue through the treatment phase and after hospital discharge to help combat stress and to ease the changes in roles, attitudes, and lifestyle made necessary by the disease.

3. Communication between health-care providers and patients must be improved.

4. Counseling and emotional support should be made available in hospitals.

5. Continuing contact with the patient should be maintained, when necessary, by trained counselors, and in the case of the dying patient this service should be continued with family members for an appropriate period following death.

THE REHABILITATION CARE TEAM

Cancer care should be directed by the primary physician and rehabilitation of the cancer patient must result from an agreement between the patient and the doctor that such care is necessary and desirable. (See Chapter 6, "The Treatment Team.") The physician overseeing the rehabilitation should be the one closest to the patient and directing the treatment team. This usually will be the family physician, but it may well be a cancer specialist, surgeon, or other physician who has assumed this responsibility.

Not every patient will necessarily require the services of the rehabilitation team, because personal needs, desires, and resources vary, but the physician should nonetheless be alert to the potential need for services, especially if a cure has not been achieved. It is important to recognize that the need for rehabilitative care does not cease when the patient leaves the hospital; indeed, rehabilitation must continue after discharge and be effectively coordinated to have its full impact. Any cancer rehabilitation program must recognize the goal that every patient with cancer has a basic right to readapt and to live as normal and full a life as possible. It is the responsibility of the physician and the rehabilitation team to facilitate this readaptation.

Members of the rehabilitation team, in addition to the primary physician, will vary. In some instances a physiatrist—a doctor who specializes in rehabilitation techniques, including the strengthening of muscles, the use of artificial limbs, and retraining in the day-to-day activities of normal life—may be required. This specialist is able to help define the expected disabilities and outline rehabilitation goals, institute an appropriate program, and establish a system to supervise treatment and follow-up. While a physiatrist is available in many large hospitals and medical centers, smaller hospitals may not have one. In that case, the family physician and other trained therapists should be prepared to fill the need. If the problems are extensive and beyond the capabilities of local health professionals, referral to a rehabilitation center may be considered. It should be noted, however, that this would be an unusual situation; most hospitals, including small ones, have the capabilities to meet the rehabilitation needs of most cancer patients if their resources are fully utilized.

Another important member of the rehabilitation team for many patients is the physical therapist. These professionals are trained by physiatrists and perform important functions, such as teaching patients exercises and other physical techniques to overcome disabilities, or how to use artificial limbs or braces. Occupational therapists, sometimes working with the physical therapist, teach patients the skills needed to perform job functions. For example, these two therapists may work with a mastectomy patient to teach her the arm exercises that will help overcome swelling, weakness and other problems that interfere with both personal and work-related tasks.

The oncology or cancer nurse is still another important member of the rehabilitation team. These nurses are specially trained in caring for cancer patients, and also in providing a variety of educational programs for patients before, during, and after treatment. Examples include preparing the patient for surgery, radiation therapy, or chemotherapy. Oncology nurses also provide the specialized care for patients undergoing operations that alter lifestyle or body function, such as an ostomy for bowel or bladder cancer. In such cases they will also assist the family in helping the patient become more independent. Very often it is the oncology nurse who is called upon to plan at-home care and rehabilitation. They also help patients and family members deal with the many psychosocial issues involved in cancer.

Social workers, as indicated earlier, are important in the overall rehabilitative effort. They help the patient in planning personal and family activities, the use of available community resources, and, together with the physiatrist or physical therapist, in finding appropriate vocational or other counselors. The social worker also may be called upon to provide emotional support and psychological guidance. In this regard, a member of the clergy or a lay volunteer also may be helpful in providing assistance and advice in both religious and personal matters.

Psychologists and other mental health professionals may be called in for help in dealing with the stress and emotional problems that are so common among cancer patients and family members. Many people are reluctant to discuss personal fears or problems—changes in sexual or body functioning or in appearance are common examples. A professional trained in helping people adjust to emotional difficulties is most important in successful rehabilitation. Lay volunteers who have faced similar problems—a woman who has undergone a mastectomy or a patient who has mastered living with a colostomy, for example—also are of tremendous aid in helping others overcome similar difficulties. These lay volunteers can give advice and demonstrate a positive attitude and behavior based on their own personal experiences with cancer. The patient sees that others have experienced the same fears and difficulties and have managed to adapt.

Other people who are frequently called upon in the rehabilitative process include specially trained therapists, such as speech pathologists who assist people who have undergone laryngectomies to learn new ways of speaking; for example, esophageal speech. Dietitians are helpful in identifying special nutritional needs and problems of cancer patients, during hospitalization and for nutritional planning at home. A pharmacist can assist patients receiving chemotherapy, artificial (parenteral) feeding, or pain medication by providing advice and patient education materials about anticancer drugs and pain control.

Home health care agencies and services, such as those provided by the American Cancer Society, visiting nurses, public health departments, and others should also be utilized in the ongoing rehabilitative efforts following hospital discharge. Vocational rehabilitation counselors may be needed over a period of time to assist in the return to productive work.

For patients with advanced cancer that cannot be cured, hospices provide invaluable services. These include continuing care in an institutional setting or at home, pain management, family counseling, and other supportive care aimed at easing the burden of the disease.

This is but a general overview of the many types of rehabilitative services available to cancer patients and their families. The physician responsible for the patient's overall care is the one who should help select those services that are most appropriate for the individual's particular needs.

SPECIFIC CANCER REHABILITATION PROGRAMS

As stressed earlier, rehabilitation is an integral part of treatment of all cancer patients, and the specific type of rehabilitation service depends upon a number of factors, including cancer site, stage of disease, attitudes of the patient and family, treatment method, financial status and so on.

Following are specific types of rehabilitative services that are widely available; other approaches to rehabilitation are outlined in more detail in the chapters dealing with the individual types of cancer.

Breast Cancer

In recent years there has been considerable change in the approach to breast cancer. In the past, surgeons would biopsy the breast in the operating room and use rapid diagnostic techniques to determine whether the suspicious area was indeed cancer. If cancer was present, a mastectomy would be performed immediately. As a result, a woman undergoing a breast biopsy never knew in advance whether she would wake up missing a breast. Today women may elect a two-step procedure in which the biopsy is performed at one time, and the mastectomy or other therapy is performed after the woman has had an opportunity to discuss the situation with her doctor. It is during this holding phase between diagnosis and treatment that good patient-physician communication should be established, with a thorough exploration of treatment alternatives and a clear understanding of what is to take place and why. At this time, rehabilitation also should be discussed and planned.

Many women about to undergo treatment for breast cancer find that a visit with a person who has undergone similar treatment is particularly encouraging. It is never easy for a woman to accept the loss of a breast, and talking to others who have gone through this experience helps considerably. The emotional needs of other family members, particularly the husband, also should be tended to. A strong husband-wife relationship can be of great psychological support to the woman, but all too often the emotional struggles of the husband are overlooked in the effort to make the experience more bearable for the woman. In this regard, counseling both the husband and wife can prove beneficial. The fear and anxiety concerning possible death as a result of breast cancer can be overwhelming, but on the other hand the more immediate expected loss of physical attractiveness and sexuality may require a period of psychological adjustment. Deformity of any kind is hard to take; the loss of a breast in a society in which breasts are so closely linked with beauty and sexuality is even more difficult. The patient should be encouraged to explore and express feelings, fears, and concerns about the possible breast loss. The awareness that cosmetic rehabilitation can restore the physical appearance— temporarily with an external prosthesis (a specially designed artificial breast pad that is worn inside a brassiere) or permanently with plastic surgery to reconstruct a natural-looking breast—often makes the prospect of mastectomy more bearable.

Women about to undergo a mastectomy also should know that the swelling and possible limitations in arm use that were common in the past can be prevented or at least minimized by early physical therapy of the upper arms. Preventive care of the skin of the arms and fingernails also are important in reducing the number of problems.

Physical rehabilitation for mastectomy patients should begin as soon as possible after the operation and be practiced on a continuing basis. Assuming, for example, that it is decided that a modified radical mastectomy, which involves removal of the breast and the lymph nodes in the armpit should be performed, special catheters will be used to drain off the fluid that collects under the skin flap. Physical therapy of the arm should begin as soon as possible, preferably on the first day or so after surgery, to help prevent swelling caused by the accumulation of fluid. The woman should be encouraged to perform the regular activities of daily living, including exercises and motions like combing or brushing the hair that are very beneficial in restoring proper arm function.

Volunteers from the Reach to Recovery program of the American Cancer Society—all women who themselves have had treatment for breast cancer—are available to visit patients while still in the hospital or following their discharge to give practical advice on resuming normal life. These volunteers have had special training. They will provide a kit containing a booklet of exercises for the affected shoulder and arm, a temporary breast prosthesis for those who have had a mastectomy, and information about clothing. The visit by a Reach to Recovery volunteer must be approved by the patient's physician, however; if the doctor has not suggested it and the woman would like such a visit, it would be well to ask the doctor to request it. No physician, nurse, or physical therapist who has not personally been treated for breast cancer can provide the same added degree of psychological reassurance and practical advice as a woman who has experienced the same illness and discovered ways of reducing the effect of the difficulties that arise in its course.

Still other helpful sources of information available for breast cancer patients include sets of records and audiotapes. One such set, "Conversations After Mastectomy," is distributed nationally by the National Cancer Institute and Stuart Pharmaceuticals. It presents a patient group discussion about breast cancer surgery, the psychological problems involved, physical reactions encountered by patients, family, and friends, and practical advice on coping with the disease and its treatment.

As would be expected, worries over appearance and what kind of clothes can be worn following a mastectomy are uppermost in the minds of many women undergoing this operation. In general, most women find that they can wear all of their regular clothes, although some may not be comfortable in low-cut, revealing styles. As soon as the site of the operation has healed adequately, a patient should seek a referral to have a breast prosthesis fitted to replace the temporary one provided by the Reach to Recovery visitor. Many of the places that provide these prostheses also can give advice about swimming suits and other clothes. It should be emphasized, however, that most women can continue to wear their regular clothes, including tennis dresses and other sports clothes.

An increasing number of women are undergoing breast reconstruction surgery following a mastectomy. In some cases this can be done at the time of the mastectomy, but many surgeons prefer to wait until healing is complete and other treatments such as radiation therapy or chemotherapy have been completed.

For all mastectomy patients, exercises that preserve the range of motion of the shoulder and arm and help prevent the swelling (lymphedema) caused by removal of the lymph nodes are crucial to successful rehabilitative efforts. A number of factors such as radiation therapy, infection, or formation of blood clots (thrombophlebitis) can contribute to the problem. Depending upon the factors involved, antibiotics, diuretics, and compression bandages may be prescribed in addition to the exercises. These complications are the exception rather than the rule, however; exercise alone will be all that is required for most women.

During follow-up examinations, attention should be given to evaluating the emotional as well as the physical health of the woman. The return to work and resumption of normal activities occur at an earlier time and with a more complete recovery in those patients to whom full rehabilitation efforts have been provided. Of course, this does not happen overnight, but most mastectomy patients can expect to resume their normal activities within six to eight weeks. (For further discussion, see Chapter 17, "Breast Cancer.")

Colon-Rectal Cancer

Cancer of the colon or rectum is very common in the United States, with 138,000 new cases diagnosed in 1985. Most patients mistakenly fear that the diagnosis inevitably means a colostomy—surgery to make an opening in the abdominal wall to allow emptying of the large intestine. In fact, very few patients need a colostomy, either temporarily or permanently. A permanent colostomy is required only when a rectal cancer is located near the anus and the rectum needs to be removed to ensure a greater chance of eradicating all the cancer. A colostomy also may be needed when a rectal cancer cannot be totally removed and has obstructed the bowel, preventing normal bowel movements. In these instances, a colostomy allows the patient to eat normally and also relieves the blockage of the lower bowel. A temporary colostomy may be needed to protect the rejoining of the intestines to encourage the healing process. In such a case, the temporary colostomy is closed when the intestines have healed, usually within two or three weeks.

In any instance, a patient who will have a colostomy—either temporary or permanent—should be carefully briefed on what to expect. Some people can accept the need for a colostomy when it is lifesaving or will make remaining life more comfortable. Others will deny the need and have intense fear, confusion, and despair about the prospects of living with a colostomy. In either instance, counseling by the primary physician, surgeon, and enterstomal therapist (a nurse who is trained in the care of stomas, the artificial openings created in the treatment of some cases of bowel and urinary bladder cancers) should help ease these fears. Also, the patient should be made aware of the ostomy rehabilitation program of the American Cancer Society and the United Ostomy Association, which provides volunteers who have undergone similar surgery and have been trained to provide a one-to-one psychological and social reassurance that is so important in the rehabilitative process. Ideally, visits by both the enterstomal therapist and the volunteer should begin before the surgery and be continued after the operation. The family also can benefit by taking part in some aspects of the pre- and post-operative rehabilitation program.

All ostomy patients, or ostomates, should recognize that at some point they will have difficulties. It takes time to learn how to accommodate to altered body function, to control odor, to prevent skin irritation and other problems. This is why it is important to return to the hospital stomal clinic at some point following discharge, and to request a home visit by a volunteer from the United Ostomy Association. While one or two setbacks can be expected, the majority of patients with a colostomy or ileostomy soon learn to manage the stoma and are able to return to work, to travel away from home, to live a normal life without fear or embarrassment. (For further discussion, see Chapter 18, "Cancer of the Colon and Rectum.")

Lung Cancer

Cancer of the lung is one of the most common and also most lethal of all cancers seen in this country. It is well established that smoking is the leading cause of lung cancer. Smoking cessation, by the person with lung cancer and by other family members, should be the highest rehabilitation priority. Continued smoking predisposes the patient to a second lung cancer or a second cancer in another site, such as the oral cavity, esophagus, pancreas, or urinary bladder.

Treatment of lung cancer almost always involves removal of part of the lung. Obviously, if other lung diseases such as emphysema or chronic bronchitis are present, rehabilitation will be even more difficult. In all patients with lung cancer, respiratory physical therapy that will maximize the remaining lung function should begin before surgery and continue afterward. Breathing exercises and training in voluntary coughing strengthen the respiratory muscles and improve posture, movement of air in the lungs, and the effectiveness of coughing. Patients should be taught postural drainage, which involves using different head-down positions, gravity, and even some back-pounding to encourage the removal of secretions from the bronchial tree.

The rehabilitative techniques used following chest surgery are designed to reduce the effects of impaired lung function, prevent the blockage of lung passages and pneumonia, and minimize pain. Vaporizers are often recommended to moisten the air, which helps decrease the stickiness of lung secretions and clears the bronchial tree. Exercises designed to promote lung expansion will help in using remaining lung capacity. Getting out of bed as soon as possible following the surgery and moving around also will help. Even so, a respirator may be needed for some time following the operation to assure adequate ventilation, especially for patients with additional lung disorders.

Even patients who are treated by irradiation or chemotherapy without surgery can benefit from respiratory rehabilitation, because these treatments decrease lung function by scar formation. Once again, the rehabilitation should start before the treatment and continue for as long as needed following treatment. (See also Chapter 23, "Lung Cancer.")

Uterine Cancer

Cancers of the cervix are the most curable of all major cancers afflicting women and also require the least rehabilitative effort. But this does not mean that no rehabilitation is necessary. Much misunderstanding exists about the function of the uterus, its role in sex and childbearing. The small localized, noninvasive *(in situ)* cancers of the cervix very often can be treated without a hysterectomy or other methods that would preclude future childbearing. This is not the case for cancers involving the lining (endometrium) or body of the uterus, for which a hysterectomy—removal of the uterus—is usually the treatment of choice, ending a woman's ability to bear children.

Even though a hysterectomy does not necessarily diminish a woman's ability to enjoy sex, many women feel that they are no longer "complete" —a feeling that often translates itself into sexual dysfunction. If this occurs, frank discussion with a doctor or sex therapist—counseling that may include the sexual partner—should help allay fears and improve this important aspect of normal life. (See also Chapter 28, "Cancer of the Female Reproductive Tract.")

Other Cancer Sites

Each cancer site can pose special rehabilitation problems. For example, cancer of the head and neck areas may require special rehabilitation efforts for maintenance of breathing and nutrition. Small cancers in the oral cavity or larynx may be treated relatively easily with surgery and radiation; more advanced cancers may involve extensive surgery such as removal of the jaw, larynx, and other parts of the head or neck. In these cases reconstructive surgery to restore function and improve appearance may be required. Physical or speech therapy also may be needed.

Tumors occurring in the bones or soft tissues of the body are relatively rare, accounting for less than 2 percent of all cancers. The newer treatments involving combinations of radiation and chemotherapy, along with more conservative surgery, have decreased the number of amputations required. But when amputation is needed, physical, psychosocial, and vocational rehabilitation are very important aspects of the total treatment plan. Since many of these bone cancers occur in teenagers and young adults, the rehabilitation often requires a concerted family effort. As in other types of cancer rehabilitation, the sooner the effort can begin, the better. Early ambulation and prosthesis fitting, along with proper training, are essential to the resumption of a normal, productive lifestyle.

Patients with brain tumors have many neurological problems that vary with the location of the tumor; they may require extensive physical therapy and often vocational rehabilitation. The use of multiple methods of cancer therapy requires extensive education for both the patient and family, and a coordinated team approach aimed toward readaptation.

The child with cancer has all of the problems involved in adult disease plus the psychological and economic impact on other members of the family, including, very often, young siblings. Recent advances in treating cancer in children have doubled the survival rate, and the outlook for the future should continue to improve. Greater efforts in rehabilitation of children are needed; fortunately, increased attention is being given to this aspect of cancer treatment at many centers.

SPECIAL PROBLEMS IN CANCER REHABILITATION

Nutrition

Good nutrition improves the healing and well-being of cancer patients. Very often, severe protein loss (cachexia) develops in the debilitated and malnourished cancer patient. This is characterized by weakness, loss of weight, and increased loss of appetite so often associated with cancer.

When this happens the patient often becomes apathetic, anxious, restless, and appears to have lost all will to live. Although many people regard this as an inevitable part of the disease, it usually can be prevented by making sure that good nutritional status is maintained.

All too often, the cancer patient will complain of extreme loss of appetite (anorexia). Why this occurs is poorly understood, and no doubt a number of factors contribute to it. In addition, some types of cancer may actually interfere with eating—for example, cancers of the mouth, esophagus, or stomach. Infection, which is frequently associated with many types of cancer, also interferes with adequate nutrition. Pain, as might be expected, decreases a person's desire to eat. Treatment itself also may account for loss of appetite or inability to eat. This is particularly true during the postsurgery period and during radiation and chemotherapy, which may cause nausea and vomiting, alter taste, or decrease production of saliva.

A number of steps can be taken to help protect the cancer patient from malnutrition. These include such obvious but often neglected steps as making sure that meals are planned to provide adequate nutrition and served in an attractive and appealing manner. In some instances special artificial feeding may be required. Food may be provided temporarily through a tube that is placed either in the nose or directly into the stomach. This may sound frightening, but in reality it is a surprisingly simple and effective way of making sure that patients who are unable to eat still receive adequate nutrition. Sometimes special intravenous feedings called hyperalimentation or TPN (total parenteral nutrition) may be used. These consist of concentrated solutions of sugar, amino acids, and fats along with vitamins and minerals. Blood transfusions will benefit the anemic patient because a poorly nourished person will not make blood as well as one who is healthy and receiving adequate nutrition. Dehydration can be avoided or corrected by giving intravenous fluids.

MANAGING CANCER PAIN

All too often, cancer is mistakenly thought to be an invariably fatal disease accompanied by considerable pain. As has been repeatedly emphasized in this book, advances in cancer treatment in recent decades have greatly improved chances of survival. In addition, adequate methods of pain control are now available to physicians treating cancer. Pain is a highly subjective sensation, varying from person to person. It may be magnified when a patient is convinced that pain is inevitable and its control is impossible. Some types of cancer involve little or no pain; others can be quite painful unless steps are taken to control the pain. Very often, simply treating the cancer will lessen or eliminate the pain. For example, the pain due to cancer that has spread to the bones might be relieved by radiation therapy or chemotherapy. Surgery to remove or bypass a bowel obstruction caused by colon or rectal cancer will, in addition to treating the cancer, relieve the pain. And, of course, there are a number of drugs now available to relieve cancer pain. (For a more complete discussion, see Chapter 12, "Cancer and Pain.")

INFORMATION AND GUIDANCE

At one time physicians and others involved in treating cancer patients assumed that the person with cancer was better off knowing as little as possible about the disease. While it is doubtful that this attitude ever worked in the best interest of the cancer patient, it certainly has no place in today's world. The uninformed patient is at a severe disadvantage in the treatment of his or her disease. Today's patient wants—and deserves —to share in decisions about his or her care. Unfortunately some families still try to protect the cancer patient from the truth, not realizing that uninformed fantasies can be worse than the truth. In short, withholding the truth from a patient of sound mind is a great disservice, rather than a kindness.

The physician is the one who can and should tell the truth to the cancer patient. This should be done as hopefully and realistically as possible with the correct sense of judgment and proportion. All questions should be answered directly, truthfully, and convincingly. Most patients do not grasp the total picture of their illness at the time of the first discussion with the physician. Repeated question-and-answer sessions will be needed throughout the illness, and indeed should be considered an integral part of both the treatment and rehabilitation. The aware physician will ask the patient at appropriate intervals whether he or she understands what is going on and whether there are any questions regarding the illness and its treatment. At this time the counseling should be realistic and nonescapist. Sufficient information must be given to enable the patient to understand and accept the illness.

The patient also needs encouragement and positive thinking. Such communication allows the patient with advanced or incurable cancer to understand and to plan appropriately. By the same token, patients whose cancers are treatable and who have a good chance of cure also need to understand to be able to plan and participate in their treatment. Chances and probabilities should be discussed. Even in advanced cases it is important to retain hope; the removal of hope implies abandonment and provides a frequent impetus to search for unproved methods of cancer treatment. Misguided information, or advice from the uninformed or from publicists of persons offering unproved methods of cancer treatment all too often lead the patient or family to seek out such treatment with the hope of a cure rather than endure the side effects of scientifically valid cancer treatment. Cancer is one disease in which it is essential for the patient and family to understand that in order to get better, it may be necessary for the patient to undergo a treatment that may make him or her feel worse for a period of time before improvement or a cure can be expected. Sadly, countless lives are lost each year by attempting to avoid the established and proved treatments in favor of less toxic but usually totally ineffective unproved treatments. (See Chapter 13, "Questionable Cancer Remedies.")

Communication is a two-way process that requires time, ability, and interest. The complexity of communication among all members of the rehabilitation team makes it difficult to keep everyone informed about the patient's condition, prognosis, complications, and concerns. Coordination is the solution to this communication problem and is the responsibility of the physician overseeing the entire process. Some patients need a great deal more help than others. Each follow-up visit to the physician should allow sufficient time for the patient to ask appropriate questions. All too frequently, patients complain that their doctor either was too busy, or they thought he was too busy, to answer their questions. If a patient feels that the information is inadequate or beyond comprehension, this should be made known to the doctor. Many people hesitate to ask about the things that may be bothering them the most. But remember that the doctor is not likely to anticipate all questions or areas of concern and unasked questions are likely to go unanswered.

COPING WITH CANCER

No two people with cancer react in exactly the same way. Considerable research is under way into the psychosocial and behavioral aspects of cancer care, but there are no pat answers that can be applied to all patients. Everyone has different emotions, fears, and concerns, including those involving treatment, finances and death. We often tend to forget that the person who becomes ill with cancer is the same person as before the illness struck, with the same likes, dislikes, needs, and responsibilities. A diagnosis of cancer may seem to change a person, but this is largely a matter of circumstances and appearances. Some people cope well; others manage poorly or not at all. The inability to cope may be related to denial of the diagnosis or prognosis, concealment of the diagnosis from the patient, inappropriate behavior within the family, a failure to cooperate or comply with treatment, or the concealment of true feelings and emotions. Difficulty in coping generates further denial, avoidance of reality, and isolation. Distrust may eventually evolve into depression. In contrast, honest discussion of the diagnosis and prognosis can improve patient care and can also reassure the family. Direct, consistent advice and emotional support of the patient by the cancer team will prevent confusion, distrust, and lack of compliance that follow misinformation and unrealistic goals. Social rehabilitation should focus on the patient's ability to adjust to his or her environment, which includes the home and work settings.

EMPLOYMENT

Return to work represents an important milestone in cancer treatment and it is the obvious evidence to the cancer patient and loved ones that he or she is again on the way to financial independence. Most patients, when they first hear the diagnosis of cancer, equate it with the inability to return to work followed by eventual death. Such attitudes and expectations do not reflect current knowledge about successful cancer treatment. A study by the Bell Telephone Company in 1972 involving 1,350 employees who had been diagnosed as having cancer found that 77 percent of them returned to work. A Metropolitan Life Insurance Company study found that 55 percent of its workers who had had cancer were still working five or more years following the initial diagnosis. Today's results are even more encouraging and will continue to improve.

Attitudes of employers and fellow employees, however, still reflect many totally groundless fears, including the belief that the cancer might be contagious or that the patient will have obvious physical and cosmetic handicaps that will affect other employees. Employers often assume that cancer patients will continue to require time away from the job. In reality, studies have found that recovered cancer patients often have better work records than those who have not had the disease, and that they are more anxious to perform and succeed following a bout with cancer. A study carried out among white-collar workers who had had cancer found that 54 percent identified one or more problems at work as being due to their having had the disease. Nearly a fourth reported overt hostility by fellow workers. Other problems included no salary advances, reduced health benefits, and exclusion from life or disability insurance. Some recovered patients were afraid to use their sick leave, even when it was justified. Many employees would have benefited from counseling before returning to work, regarding what they should tell their employers and colleagues about their sickness and what, if any, limitation should be placed on their job duties and security. Many found it difficult or impossible to get a new job; twenty-two percent had at least one job application rejected because they had had cancer. They cited such problems as increased insurance premiums, ineligibility for pension or disability plans, anticipated absenteeism, inadequate physical strength, and not being perceived as a "whole" person. Some job applicants felt that the clerk or receptionist at the personnel office acted as a screener and turned away job applicants with a past history of cancer even though this may not have been the company policy. Obviously, much more public education is required to make it easier for the cancer patient to return to work without having to overcome misconceptions about the effects the disease might have upon ability to perform a job. It should be noted, however, that these adverse reactions were not universal.

Indeed, most employers were fair and welcomed the recovered cancer patient back to work. Even so, certain company policies often make it difficult for the returning cancer patient. The health examination required by many companies is a case in point. Some companies employ physicians as medical directors who may be uninformed about the potential of recovered cancer patients to work, and consequently they may recommend early retirement or disability leave. While such medical directors may be in the minority, it still should be recognized that the recovered cancer patient may face problems on returning to work.

Other studies have found that blue-collar workers fared no better than their white-collar counterparts. For example, a 1978 study noted that thirty-five percent of the cancer patients surveyed were discriminated against at work, in addition to the twenty-three percent who either left their previous place of employment or were rejected for at least one other job because of their illness. In all, thirteen percent were denied new jobs because they had a history of cancer. Eleven percent were either excluded from health benefits or suffered a reduction in them. On a more positive side, forty-four percent of the workers had no absences from their jobs after the initial treatment period, and the average absence for cancer treatment was only nine weeks.

The American Cancer Society is well aware of the employment problems faced by many cancer patients and is acting as a patient advocate or ombudsman to counsel both employer and employee. There is a need for further public education regarding the hopeful side of cancer and the prospects of patients resuming responsible positions following treatment. Significant progress has occurred in the past decade, especially in the governmental sector where previous personnel policies prevented the employment of a person who had had cancer in the preceding five years. Many states have instituted strong legislation to protect the rights of a recovered cancer patient and to prevent discrimination. Often, however, there is a problem in the legal and practical interpretation of terms like "disability" and "recovered cancer patient."

CANCER REHABILITATION IN THE YOUNG

Adult workers are not the only ones who suffer from discrimination because of a diagnosis of cancer; young people experience similar difficulties in returning to school following treatment for cancer. A 1980 study of young people ages thirteen to twenty-three who had undergone cancer treatment found that fifty-one percent experienced problems related to their disease upon their return to school. These problems stemmed either from the illness itself or from the attitudes and behavior of others. Those who had jobs experienced work problems, such as exclusion from health insurance or other benefits, changes in work assignment, negative attitudes of colleagues, wage reduction, denial of job advancement, or dismissal without due cause. Among the younger patients, particularly those returning to high school, a large number experienced loss of friends, isolation, and taunting because of lack of coordination, speech impairment, or other difficulties. Many of the youths felt frightened and humiliated because no one had explained to them what cancer meant or what to expect from the treatment. Many physicians believe that parents are the ones who should tell their children about the cancer and its treatment, but the patients in this study felt differently; they saw this as the physician's duty. Indeed, this particular study pointed up the important role that the family physician plays in the quality of the youngster's ability to cope with cancer.

The study also pointed out the need for teachers and counselors to be better equipped to help young cancer patients return to school or work. For these young patients, the problems did not end when they finished school; many also found that their history of cancer worked against them when they applied for jobs following graduation. Still, these negatives were, for the majority, balanced by at least some positive experiences; 62 percent reported positive events. Most agreed, however, that their lot would have been made much easier by more preparation of what to expect and how to handle certain situations and also by more knowledge and understanding from their peers, teachers, or employers.

VOCATIONAL REHABILITATION

Although cancer is often a life-threatening disease, once it is treated its victims are usually still able to work. Vocational counselors frequently find, however, that both the patient and employers harbor considerable confusion and misunderstanding about the employment and performance potential of cancer patients. Discriminatory industrial hiring practices are but a reflection of outdated public and medical attitudes regarding cancer. These practices present a particularly difficult problem for young people who have not yet established careers. The worker who has been away from the job for some time is often hard pressed to meet basic living expenses, especially when disability income or unemployment insurance fails to meet his or her needs. These financial pressures create resistance to consideration of anything but getting any job as soon as possible, no matter what its long-term potential.

Some patients who have recovered from cancer require vocational rehabilitation. The laryngectomee and the amputee, as mentioned earlier, are good examples. In contrast, patients who have had a mastectomy or ostomy seldom need vocational rehabilitation. Still, these patients often are subjected to the same job discrimination as those who may be more severely limited in their ability to perform certain tasks. Obviously, requiring a recovered cancer patient to wait for a prolonged period which may be several years to determine whether he or she will survive free of cancer is inhuman, illegal, and uneconomical. Depending on the handicap, vocational training could focus on getting a job in a competitive market, self-employment, working in a sheltered situation, or homemaking. Above all it should be emphasized that people with any disability, including blindness, can be served.

INSURANCE

The California study on the social, economic, and psychological needs of cancer patients, referred to earlier in this discussion, revealed some interesting interrelationships between insurance and employment. Continued employment and the securing of new jobs for people with a history of cancer often involve insurance discrimination. These insurance barriers include cancellation of existing coverage, reduction of health insurance benefits, increase in premiums, refusal of new insurance applications, extended waiting periods for coverage, exclusions for any coverage related to cancer, loss of insurance due to loss of employment, and the experience of being locked into a job for fear of losing insurance coverage.

In contrast to employment discrimination in which various advocates and legal forces are available, there is no support system that can effectively assist individuals, groups, or agencies wishing to engage in effective intervention regarding insurance coverage of recovered cancer patients. Generally speaking, there is no legal requirement that an insurer grant coverage to anyone. In addition, insurance companies have the legal right to set premiums at any level provided they are based on sound actuarial practices. Group insurance is thus generally one of the best options available to the person with a past history of cancer.

Still, there are some avenues open to the recovered cancer patient. The Rehabilitation Act of 1973 specifically lists patients with a history of cancer under the federal definition of the disabled, and as such, employers who receive federal funds must provide equal fringe benefits, including insurance, to disabled individuals as they do to other employees. These same employers are prohibited from discriminating against the disabled person in terms of hiring or promotion, and cannot ask questions about an employee's health unless the questions are specifically job-related. By the same token, noninsurability cannot be used as a reason to deny employment. Certain employers receiving federal funds also must take affirmative action to ensure that disabled persons receive equal employment.

Prepaid health plans and health maintenance organizations that meet federal requirements are forbidden by federal law from canceling the coverage of any individual because of frequent utilization of its services; in addition, they must provide an annual period of open enrollment during which time coverage is offered on the same basis as it is to all other members. It also is illegal to charge higher premiums to those deemed more likely to require increased usage.

For the individual who is not covered by group health insurance that is protected by the federal Rehabilitation Act of 1973, or by a prepaid health plan of a health maintenance organization, insurance discrimination can have a profound effect. Most state laws do not protect the recovered cancer patient in insurance matters. Patients must be aware of the fine print in health insurance policies, especially those with provisions for preexisting conditions. Where discrimination exists, it should not be ignored if positive changes are to be made. Toward this end, one may complain about discriminatory insurance practices to the appropriate authorities and also lobby employers to negotiate insurance contracts that are in the interest of recovered cancer patients.

ECONOMIC BENEFITS OF REHABILITATION

The direct cost of cancer in the United States was recently estimated at about $20 billion a year. This figure includes hospital and outpatient expenses, physician fees, nursing services, home care, and drugs. About 72 percent of patients under the age of sixty-five are covered by private insurance, and for those over this age, 85 percent of the costs are covered by Medicare or supplemental insurance. The indirect costs of cancer, such as lost wages, liquidation of assets, home nursing, and transportation are estimated to total about $31 billion. No figure can be estimated for the physical disability, suffering, pain, grief, or altered lifestyle.

Many of these costs can be reduced through effective rehabilitation. Examples include reduced length of hospital stays, minimized disability, and improved quality of life permitting an earlier return to work.

SUMMING UP

Rehabilitation, or readaptation, is an essential part of comprehensive cancer care. The goals of rehabilitation, whether preventive, restorative, supportive or palliative, should be defined before treatment begins. Rehabilitation can best be carried out when the primary physician and the cancer care team consider rehabilitation as an integral part of the overall treatment. This allows for early recognition of an actual or potential disability and appropriate referrals to accomplish realistic goals. (See Directory of Resources in the Appendix for specific referral services and centers.)

Total rehabilitation includes physical, psychological, social, vocational, legal, and economic issues. In any instance, the overall goal of rehabilitation is to return the cancer patient to as near a normal life as possible.

12

Cancer and Pain

KATHLEEN M. FOLEY, M.D.

INTRODUCTION

Although many people harbor the mistaken notion that cancer inevitably involves pain, the fact is that the majority of people with the disease do *not* experience unusual pain. Physicians who specialize in treating cancer report that only about 30 percent of cancer patients undergoing therapy will experience pain—mild or severe—as a result of their disease. Among those with terminal illness the rate is higher, perhaps 60 percent. For those cancer patients who are in pain, most can obtain relief through advances in pain research and treatment. In fact, almost all patients with cancer pain can be helped through a combination of pain-relieving drugs, nondrug methods and symptomatic relief, permitting them to function as well as the other manifestations of the disease permit. The shared goal of physician and patient alike is to achieve this result with as few side effects as possible and allow that patient to function at the level he or she chooses.

THE NATURE OF PAIN

Pain is often a highly informative symptom. It serves to keep our consciousness alert to things that are going wrong with our bodies, so that we can react appropriately. At times a new pain of unknown origin may be the first sign of a cancer, prompting diagnostic procedures to identify the problem. It is, however, unusual for that first sign of cancer to be severe pain.

Pain can have different characteristics. It can be dull, sharp, aching, constant, intermittent, mild, or severe. The inherent physical character of the pain is, however, only one of its two determinants. The other is the individual patient, who contributes his or her personality, attitudes, behavioral patterns, and reactions. Age, sex, religion, cultural background, environment, and level of anxiety all influence the perceived intensity and severity of pain.

Researchers do not truly understand the many physical processes that result in pain. They do know that several types of specific nerve fibers carry pain signals to different regions of the brain from almost everywhere in the body. When these signals reach the brainstem and hypothalamus, they are processed in much the same way a computer processes information, and the information that something is not right is reported to our consciousness. These reports are not always accurate, because our consciousness and nervous systems are not equipped to precisely report and localize every type of pain. Exactly what stimulates the nerve endings is not always clear. In the case of the intestines or gallbladder, distension and pressure are the physical causes that stimulate the nerve pain fibers. Local biochemical factors also play a role.

The prostaglandins, a group of natural substances that seem to be found almost everywhere in the human body, are known to be important factors in causing inflammation and pain. Aspirin and many of the newer kinds of pain relievers—particularly the nonsteroidal anti-inflammatory drugs that are often prescribed to treat arthritis—reduce pain and inflammation, apparently by inhibiting several key prostaglandins. The brain has at higher levels reacted, through an evolutionary process, to the presence of pain by creating its own form of painkillers. These substances, the endorphins and enkephalins, can be described as "natural opiates," our own body's morphine. They reduce the patient's perception of pain by exerting an effect similar to narcotic drugs. They bind to the same locations in the brain, specifically at the "opiate receptors" on the surface of brain cells. Curiously, these natural substances made by the brain reduce the distressing effect of chronic or acute, severe pain. Exactly how the endorphins and enkephalins work is not fully understood, but many researchers in university centers and pharmaceutical companies are looking into them carefully in the hope of developing a new family of potent painkilling drugs.

SOURCES OF PAIN

How cancer causes pain is generally understood, although in individual cases the reason is not always fully known. Pain may result from something as common as stiffness in the muscles and joints as a result of forced inactivity, or it may be as complex as bone pain that comes from a host of factors which together result in microscopic fractures.

More serious discomfort can result from inflammation and infection surrounding a solid cancer. Pressure on nerves from adjacent tumor masses and microscopic infiltration of nerves by tumor cells are major causes of pain and discomfort. The invading cells affect the conduction of impulses by the nervous system, sometimes resulting in constant, dull, poorly localized pain and altered sensation. Blockage of the blood in arteries and veins, again both by pressure from nearby tumor masses and by infiltration can decrease oxygen and nutrient supply to tissues. This deficiency can be perceived as pain similar in origin and character to cardiac pain, or angina pectoris, which is chest pain from an insufficient supply of oxygen to the heart.

Perhaps the most unpleasant pain experienced by cancer patients originates in bone. The rich supply of nerves, limited space for relief of pressure, altered local metabolism, weakening of the bone structure, and fractures ranging from large to microscopic all contribute to the intense discomfort. Fortunately, analgesic medication and high-dose radiation therapy almost always result in prompt relief if the problem is localized.

Blockage of a hollow organ and its ducts is another source of pain. This effect of tumor masses can be seen in gastrointestinal obstruction by stomach or colon cancer. Obstruction of the ducts leading from the gallbladder and pancreas is common in cancer of these organs, although jaundice is a more frequent early symptom than pain. Cancer of the throat or esophagus can obstruct these organs, leading to difficulties in eating or speaking. There is, however, a wide variety of surgical procedures to relieve obstruction and to bypass blocked ducts and engorged hollow organs. Cancer treatment can also cause pain. Surgery for cancer is an obvious source of pain, as are the mouth sores that can arise in the course of chemotherapy. Radiation therapy can also cause mouth discomfort and dryness. Stiffness from inactivity results in dull muscle ache.

The frequency of pain as a symptom varies with the type of cancer. The malignancy that has one of the worst reputations for generating pain is pancreatic cancer, eventually causing symptoms in up to 70 percent of patients. The more common cancers of the lung and breast cause pain in about 50 percent of cases, in large part because of their metastasis to bone. Cancer that itself originates from bone is probably the malignancy that causes pain most frequently, perhaps in as many as 85 percent of cases. Blood cancers and cancers of the lymph system give rise to pain in only 5 percent of cases. Overall, about 30 percent of cancer patients undergoing cancer treatment will experience pain, and for the vast majority the discomfort is readily managed.

ANALGESIC DRUGS

The mainstay of treatment for cancer pain is analgesic (pain-relieving) drugs. These drugs fall into three major categories: nonprescription painkillers, such as aspirin, acetominophen, and ibuprofen; the relatively new group of nonsteroidal anti-inflammatory drugs (NSAIDs); and the narcotics, such as codeine or morphine.

Nonprescription Painkillers

Aspirin was invented over 100 years ago and has long been the mainstay for patients with mild to moderate pain. The mechanism by which aspirin relieves pain is not completely known, but it appears to reduce inflammation and inhibit the action of prostaglandins, both important factors in countering pain.

Aspirin can be purchased almost anywhere, but that accessibility is no reason to reject it as low in effectiveness. On the contrary, aspirin alone or in combination is highly effective and equal in pain relief to many of the more powerful painkillers. For most people with mild to moderate pain, two aspirin tablets (650 milligrams) provides as much relief as a half grain of codeine, 65 mg. of propoxyphene (Darvon) or 50 mg. of meperidine (Demerol). Aspirin when combined with these drugs provides additive analgesia and these combinations are often useful to control mild to moderate pain.

Aspirin is also available in combination with such additives as caffeine, buffers to decrease stomach acid, or antihistamines. These combinations have been developed to minimize side effects. Only caffeine can sometimes provide additive analgesia.

Many patients discount aspirin as a useful drug, not only because of familiarity but also because they do not take enough of it on a regular schedule. Eight to twelve aspirin tablets a day in three or four divided doses is safe for most adults. Higher doses should not be taken without regular medical supervision because of potential bleeding problems and other side effects.

Side Effects

The side effects of aspirin increase with higher doses and at these levels, after several days or weeks of regular administration, a few people will feel mild headache, ringing in the ears, excessive sweating, nausea, vomiting, or diarrhea. Patients with these problems should reduce the dosage from one fourth to half the original dose. If the problem does not subside within forty-eight hours, the patient should see a doctor. The more significant complications from aspirin are bleeding problems and ulcers, but the frequency of these complications is relatively low. Of patients who can tolerate aspirin, the vast majority should have no problem. Obviously, patients with preexisting ulcers, bleeding problems, or known intolerance or allergy to aspirin should not take the drug. The cancer patient who is receiving chemotherapy should not use aspirin without the approval of his or her physician.

Acetaminophen, popularly known by its most common brand name, Tylenol, is the second most common nonprescription drug for the relief of mild to moderate pain. Equal doses of aspirin and acetaminophen afford equal degrees of pain control and fever reduction, but there are important differences between the two compounds. Acetaminophen does not reduce the swelling caused by inflammation, nor is it the drug of choice for joint pain. On the other hand, acetaminophen does not cause clotting problems or gastric irritation as aspirin may, and can be taken by patients with these tendencies. Although large doses of acetaminophen, or moderate doses taken over many years, may induce kidney and liver damage, the drug rarely causes side effects. Its usual dose is eight to twelve tablets a day in three or four equal doses. For extra-strength tablets, eight is the recommended maximum daily dose. Acetaminophen's mechanism of action is not precisely known.

Nonsteroidal Anti-inflammatory Drugs

Nonsteroidal anti-inflammatory drugs were first introduced about fifteen years ago, and have been used mainly in the treatment of arthritis. Until recently they were available only by prescription. Now, however, ibuprofen (sold under the brand names of Advil and Nupren) can be bought without a prescription. Ibuprofen, in a stronger dosage, is still sold as a prescription drug under the brand names of Motrin or Rufen. Ibuprofen and other NSAIDs act in a way similar to aspirin—by inhibiting prostaglandin function. This makes them effective for reducing inflammation as well as pain, particularly in joints. In its nonprescription forms, ibuprofen comes in 300 mg. and 400 mg. tablets to be taken three or four times a day. Although this drug is generally safe and effective, it is not without potential side effects (indeed, no drug is). It can cause stomach irritation and water retention, factors to consider in patients with a history of ulcers or high blood pressure.

There are a large number of other nonsteroidal anti-inflammatory drugs available on the U.S. market for pain relief and reduction of inflammation, but as yet they are sold only by prescription. These drugs are very similar in action and in the side effects they produce; they vary more in how frequently they must be taken and how much they cost. Nevertheless most physicians prefer one or two of them and generally prescribe them over the others when appropriate. It is useful to have several alternatives because different patients may get better results from one drug than from another. Most doctors feel the prescription nonsteroidal anti-inflammatory agents may be somewhat more potent and more convenient to take than aspirin, requiring fewer pills per day. There also may be less potential for bleeding problems.

Narcotics

The narcotic drugs, a group for which a doctor's prescription is always required, are used for the relief of moderate to severe pain. Until the advent of the nonsteroidal anti-inflammatory drugs, narcotics were the most common prescription analgesics. Narcotic drugs as a group have a bad reputation, since they are associated with dependence, addiction, overdose, and drug abuse, as well as side effects like drowsiness and mental dullness. These problems should not be used to distort the real truths about the narcotic analgesics—they are the strongest painkillers available and their actual side effects are usually manageable or easily tolerated. Their real probability for addiction is minimal—less than 1 percent—and quite arguably irrelevant in the face of severe chronic pain.

The widespread belief that narcotics result in addiction is false. "Street addicts" take narcotics illegally for a variety of emotional, psychological, and physical needs unrelated to pain relief and appropriate medical therapy. Patients on narcotics are not addicts, no matter how much or how long they take the drugs. Narcotics should be considered an important method of pain control, and their use to relieve pain should not be confused with the street addict's desire to feel good.

Occasionally patients on narcotics experience physical dependence, characterized by signs of withdrawal when the drug is stopped suddenly. Gradual withdrawal usually prevents this. Most patients, even those who are physically dependent, can readily stop or reduce the narcotics if their pain can be controlled by other drugs or methods. Once medications are tapered, patients do not continue to have the psychological need for narcotics, the craving for them for reasons other than pain control, or the preoccupation with obtaining them that characterize street addicts.

Many doctors confuse street addiction (psychological dependence) with physical dependence and have a regrettable tendency to underprescribe narcotic analgesics, leaving the patient in pain. And many patients choose to have pain rather than take a narcotic drug. In fact, the best way to give narcotic drugs is to find the right dose to relieve the patient's discomfort and then give it on a regular basis to keep the patient free of pain. Some doctors feel that the patient should be awakened from sleep to receive the medication so as not to let the blood level of the narcotic drop. Newer medications that are slow-release tablets are now available to avoid that inconvenience. Patients who are on self-medication programs of narcotics rarely take more than is needed.

Tolerance

Patients taking narcotics may, over a period of days or weeks, require increasing doses to achieve the same degree of pain control. This phenomenon is called "tolerance." The first sign of tolerance is the patient's complaint that the medication works for only three hours instead of four. It does not necessarily occur in every patient. This reaction is not addiction. When the pain has been effectively healed by surgery, radiation therapy, or chemotherapy, the medication can be withdrawn. Tolerance can be treated by increasing the drug's dosage and frequency, by switching to another narcotic drug, or by adding another nonnarcotic to the regimen. If a switch is made to another narcotic, it is usually given at about one half its presumed equivalent analgesic strength because "cross-tolerance" is not usually 100 percent complete. Withdrawal from medication can be easily done by gradually reducing the drug dose. This withdrawal method is not uncomfortable and does not resemble the false and exaggerated concept played up by the media.

Commonly Used Narcotic Drugs

Codeine, alone or in combination with aspirin or acetaminophen, is one of the most frequently used narcotics for mild to moderate pain. It is structurally similar to morphine, but not as potent. It is an excellent analgesic drug for mild to moderate pain. Its usual dosage is one-fourth to one-half grain (15 to 30 mg.) every four to six hours and it is usually given by mouth. Its side effects are also moderate in comparison with the stronger narcotics, although constipation is a significant problem.

Oxycodone is another congener of morphine and is available alone in liquid form or in tablet form in combination with aspirin (Percodan) and acetaminophen (Percocet, Tylox). It is a useful first-line narcotic for mild to moderate pain in patients who do not tolerate codeine.

Other frequently used major narcotic drugs include oral morphine, hydromorphone, methadone, and meperidine. These drugs are only available by prescription and are called "controlled substances" under supervision of both federal and state authorities. All are opiates and bind to specific receptors in the brain. They all possess approximately the same degree of potency. It is useful to have a choice of analgesics because of the wide and unpredictable variations in individual patient response. This gives the doctor the opportunity to optimize the degree of pain control and minimize the undesirable reactions, guaranteeing that almost any patient will be comfortable without paying an unacceptable price in sedation, confusion, or gastrointestinal problems. Nausea and vomiting are sometimes a problem with these drugs because they stimulate the areas in the brain that control those reactions. Antinausea drugs can be given to counteract these problems.

Heroin

Heroin belongs to the same family as morphine and the other narcotics. It used to have the reputation for superior relief but with a greater chance of addiction. These beliefs are both part of the mythology of heroin, which is, in fact, simply another major narcotic. Experience in England, where heroin has been widely prescribed by physicians for pain control, has not shown it to possess any unique property or advantage over morphine, which is widely available throughout the world.

Side Effects of Narcotics

Sedation, nausea and vomiting, constipation, and depressed respiration are common side effects of narcotics. These reactions often are the limiting factors to the use of narcotics, and doctors must be careful to recognize them early and take appropriate action. Narcotics are contraindicated, or at least must be very carefully administered, for patients with lung disease, head injuries, serious abdominal problems, mental clouding, changing neurological symptoms, and confusion. None should be taken with alcohol, which compounds these side effects.

Sedation or drowsiness varies from narcotic to narcotic and is affected by the dosing schedule. It occurs most often with the drugs such as methadone that are slowly metabolized by the body. Switching to lower doses at more frequent intervals can eliminate the problem. Stimulants such as amphetamines have also been used to counteract the sedative effect. Most patients stabilized on narcotics on a proper timing and dosing schedule are able to function without sedation.

When sedation occurs, it is often caused by the medical deterioration of the patient. Other medications such as barbiturates or tranquilizers may interact with the narcotics and greatly increase their sedative effects.

Seriously depressed breathing occurs rarely, but when it does it is usually preceded by drowsiness and mild confusion. It can be promptly reversed by the intravenous injection of Naloxone, a rapidly acting drug that prevents the narcotic from exerting its effect on the nerve cells.

However, reversal of respiratory depression occurs along with reversal of pain relief, and this drug should be used cautiously.

Constipation is another side effect of the narcotic drugs. Narcotic drugs react with the opiate receptors in the gastrointestinal tract, diminishing the frequency and strength of its contractions. This in turn slows the passage of the stool through the intestinal tract. The stool becomes hard as more water is absorbed from it by the intestinal wall, and constipation, often severe, practically inevitably results. Constipation can be minimized by using stool softeners, drinking plenty of fluids, and increasing intake of dietary fiber. Laxatives or enemas also may be needed. Prevention of constipation is particularly important for elderly and bedridden patients.

Dry mouth is one of the minor but irksome narcotic side effects. Its unpleasantness can be diminished by drinking a lot of fluids, brushing the teeth regularly, sucking on candies or ice, and avoiding antihistamines or other drying agents that can aggravate the problem.

ADMINISTRATION OF ANALGESICS

Knowledgeable doctors generally observe a set of practical rules when they administer analgesic drugs to patients. They start with a specific drug for each category of pain, taking into consideration the patient's diagnosis, the location of the pain, its character, severity, and likelihood of improving or getting worse. Although there are many analgesic drugs on the market, most doctors choose to become familiar with several, but not all, in each category. By concentrating on a few they are able to know more thoroughly the mechanisms, interval of onset of action after administration, peak and duration of effect, side effects, and possible interaction with other drugs. This is different from other diseases where doctors choose agents they prefer in each category and use them often, resorting to others only if necessary.

The doctor will adjust each drug's dosage and schedule as required. Individual differences in the reaction to any drugs must be respected, but this is especially important with narcotics. People metabolize narcotics in such a variety of ways that individual differences in pain control and side effects should be presumed to result from patients' chemical processes and not their psychological states.

Generally doctors administer analgesics on a regular basis in order to at least keep the patient's pain at a tolerable level. Regular dosing may actually result in the reduction of the total amount of the drug taken during each twenty-four-hour period. In other words, more but smaller doses may be more effective than fewer, larger doses in keeping the pain at a lower level.

Before a particular narcotic analgesic is judged ineffective in an individual patient, the drug should be given on a dosing schedule that takes into account the drugs' known duration of effect. Otherwise the conclusion that it is ineffective may well be incorrect.

The route as well as the schedule of administration should be suited to the needs of the patient. Orally administered drugs have a slower onset of action than drugs given by injection intramuscularly (faster) or intravenously (fastest). Rectal administration should be considered for patients who cannot take drugs by mouth or who have clotting disorders that make injections likely to result in painful intramuscular bleeding. There is a trade-off between route of administration, speed to onset of action, and duration of action. Intravenous narcotics, for example, act within fifteen minutes or less but must be repeated every one to two hours to maintain their effect. Intramuscular narcotics may take thirty minutes to work but need only be given every three to four hours.

Similarly, the dosage must be adjusted for each route of administration. In general, the slower the onset of action, the greater the dose required. The dose of a drug given orally may have to be two to six times that of the same drug given by injection.

In some instances patients in intractable pain are treated by continuous subcutaneous and intravenous infusion of narcotic drugs. A number of small portable pumps have been designed for this purpose, and their use can provide pain relief to patients who require repeated intramuscular injections or continuous intravenous drugs.

SELF-MEDICATION

Patients in pain should feel free to take what they need without hesitation or guilt. Indeed, one reason to treat round-the-clock and regularly, rather than in response to patients' requests for medication, is to relieve the patient's feelings of responsibility and awkwardness in repeatedly requesting painkillers. Stoicism may be admirable, but it is not at all necessary.

Studies suggest that when patients are given control of their analgesic regimen, they manage their own pain better after a period of regular round-the-clock administration.

Patients taking narcotics on their own, by mouth or injection, should carefully adhere to their doctor's suggested range of dosing. If inadequate relief is obtained, the patient should consult with the doctor before increasing the dose above the suggested limit.

DRUG COMBINATIONS

If a major narcotic is unable to control pain, the doctor may decide to use it in combination with a nonnarcotic analgesic agent, thus producing an additive effect. Narcotics can also be combined with several drugs for enhanced pain relief. The combination method enables the doctor to increase the patient's comfort level without increasing the narcotic regimen. Three general categories of drugs have proven useful as adjuvants to narcotics. Tricyclic antidepressant agents such as amitriptyline (Elavil) increase pain control, regardless of whether the patient shows any significant changes in mood or behavior, specifically depression. The antihistamine hydroxyzine (Vistaril) also produces added relief when given with morphine, with only a mild increase in sedative effect. Simple aspirin or acetaminophen in combination with a narcotic will very often improve the degree of pain control.

Drugs that do not enhance analgesia when used in conjunction with narcotics are the tranquilizers, including diazepam (Valium) and antipsychotic drugs, such as chlorpromazine (Thorazine). These tranquilizers will, however, result in increased sedation, a problem which can effectively limit the amount of narcotic that can be used, a clear disservice to an oversedated patient still in pain. Cortisone, other steroids and some anti-convulsant drugs have sometimes served as adjuvant drugs to enhance the relief obtained.

Analgesic drugs may interact with not only other pain control drugs, but with other types of medications given for other reasons. Obviously the doctor should be aware of such possible problems as reduced efficacy or unexpectedly exaggerated efficacy, with attendant side effects and complications. Drug interactions cannot always be logically deduced. Still, painkilling drugs can be safely used in judicious combination with other analgesic agents and with drugs of their categories, if the doctor is familiar with their uses and manages them wisely.

OTHER PAIN CONTROL METHODS

Pain control methods that achieve their effect without the use of drugs have long been of interest to doctors and patients. They involve a range of mental and physical techniques with the assistance of trained instructors, family, or friends. The most frequently used psychological methods are relaxation, meditation, imagery, and distraction and hypnosis. How effective they are depends on the individual patient, but they do at times produce highly satisfactory results without the side effects of drugs. Far too often, physicians neglect to counsel patients to try these mental techniques.

Two physical nondrug ways to improve pain control are physical therapy and local stimulation of the skin. Exercise is particularly useful but the patient's physician should be consulted before beginning even a mild exercise program to make sure no harm can come of the exertion. In selected patients, transcutaneous electrical stimulation can provide some reduction of pain in localized areas. This approach is commonly used as part of a physical therapy program to rehabilitate the cancer patient.

It is important to recognize that each of these nondrug approaches can be used alone or in combination with analgesic drug therapy providing the patient with sufficient pain relief and function at a higher level than previously. They also work to provide the patient with a sense of control over their pain which is a crucial aspect in helping to minimize the psychological impact of pain.

ANESTHETIC AND NEUROSURGICAL METHODS OF PAIN CONTROL

There is a series of anesthetic and neurosurgical methods of pain control that can be performed to manage certain cancer pain states. Nerve blocks with a local anesthetic can temporarily relieve pain and, if effective, permanent interruption of the nerve with pain relief is possible using alcohol or phenol injected into the nerve or nerve root. This is a common method used to relieve abdominal pain in patients with pancreatic cancer, by injection of nerves in the area with alcohol. These techniques require the expertise of an anesthesiologist with experience in the approaches, and the patient should understand in advance the complications of the treatments because they are not without risks.

There are also several very useful neurosurgical approaches to pain control in the cancer patient. They include either interruption of a pain pathway by surgically cutting it or by stimulation of pain pathways to inhibit pain. The most common procedure done for cancer pain is a cordotomy, in which the surgeon makes a cut in the spinal cord and in a pain pathway, interrupting transmission from the site of pain to the patient's conscious level. More recently, neurosurgeons and anesthesiologists have placed catheters directly in the cerebrospinal fluid, which is in direct contact with the brain and spinal cord, in an attempt to provide patients with more selective pain relief. This method is reserved for patients who cannot tolerate pain medication by any other method because of side effects. It is considered an experimental approach.

SUMMING UP

The techniques of pain control now available are sufficient to guarantee that almost every cancer patient can be assured of comfort and dignity without unacceptable side effects. There are no specific formulas or predetermined doses, but there are well established guidelines for success in pain control. Many major hospitals, especially those that treat a large number of patients, have teams of consultants that specialize in pain relief and operate pain clinics. However, the physician overseeing the patient's treatment should be the patient's ombudsman, providing supportive care and sympathetic pain relief. Drug therapy, specifically the use of the narcotic analgesics, should be considered the mainstay of treatment to maximize the patient's comfort. However, both the patient and physician must recognize that these approaches to pain control work only in part to relieve the suffering of a patient with pain, particularly the dying patient, and the psychological needs also must be addressed and managed.

13

Questionable Cancer Remedies

VICTOR HERBERT, M.D., J.D.

INTRODUCTION

Cancer is an area in which questionable, often worthless, and frequently harmful remedies abound. Each decade seems to bring a new generation of faddist "cures." And each year the American public spends billions of dollars on these remedies, often in lieu of effective therapies that could be lifesaving. While it is regrettable that anyone would knowingly prey upon the victims of a disease, the unfortunate fact is that cancer faddism has always existed and undoubtedly will continue to thrive until the disease is finally eradicated.

The majority of these questionable therapies involve diet—everything from the extract of apricot pits (laetrile) to macrobiotics. Others involve drugs, sometimes made from plant and animal products or byproducts. A small number involve mechanical or electrical devices. These remedies may be sold outright (often by mail order or in health food stores), promulgated in books, or may be available only from their developers, some of whom are licensed medical doctors who have set up clinics and facilities outside the consumer protection canons of medicine to offer treatment that may involve a combination of methods, such as vitamins, drugs, special diets, extracts of animal parts, herb teas, and enemas. One recent such clinic was offering "immune-system augmentation" without any acceptable proof that such immune enhancement was produced. This clinic was closed after it was discovered that some of the serum being used contained the deadly AIDS virus, which actually destroys the immune system, as well as hepatitis B virus and other harmful organisms.

In the United States alone, more than 50,000 cancer patients annually have their health harmed, often have their lives shortened, and their money wasted by unscrupulous promoters of cancer "cures." Why does this go on? Patients are most susceptible to unproved remedies when they feel helpless, not in control of their therapy, or without hope. The practice thrives on specious slogans and beliefs—such as the simplistic concept that "natural" is good and "synthetic" is bad—that appeal to people's need to control their destiny and their environment.

CHARACTERISTICS OF FAKE CANCER REMEDIES

Specious logic is characteristic of cancer charlatans. The patient's need for control is often accompanied by a lack of respect for knowledge, a repudiation of knowledge, the perception of genuine experts as untrustworthy parental authority figures, and the perception of the charlatans as courageous, independent persons with the foresight to penetrate the fakery of the establishment. Those most vulnerable to unscrupulous individuals are the many desperate patients who are unable to distinguish genuine experts from charismatic purveyors of worthless remedies, or one "doctor" from another.

Promoters of questionable remedies frequently use legitimate scientific words or phrases, distort their dictionary meanings while retaining their emotional impact, and then use them as misleading and deceptive code phrases in pseudoscientific jargon that lends legitimacy to their ineffective remedies. Common phrases include "nutritional therapy," "metabolic therapy," "holistic therapy," "alternative therapy," and "nontoxic therapy." Each of these phrases strikes a responsive chord because of its dictionary meaning, but the regimens used by cancer charlatans disguised by these innocuous cloaks are almost uniformly nutritionally and metabolically destructive rather than helpful.

These phrases imply that there is such a thing as "alternative" therapy versus "orthodox" therapy. In fact, there is only competent therapy versus incompetent therapy. Competent therapy means using the optimal treatment for the specific circumstances of the patient, as compared to using other responsible methods—or even doing nothing. There are three fundamental ethical questions with respect to any proposed therapy: 1) Is it more effective than doing nothing? 2) Is it as safe as doing nothing? 3) If there is any question about safety, is the balance between effectiveness and safety weighted for or against the patient? Any proposed therapy that has not successfully answered two of these three questions should never be sold for money because it is either experimental (that is, new and as yet not adequately tested) or quackery (that is, tried but never objectively demonstrated to be effective).

Promoters of faddism in cancer treatment ignore these three basic ethical questions. The laetrile fad is a good example of this. In 1980, a cancer researcher named Koeffler and colleagues designed a study to determine whether laetrile, which contains the poison cyanide, was effective against cancer. They put human cancer cells in one test tube and normal human cells in another and dripped laetrile into both. They demonstrated that the dose of laetrile that killed the cancer cells always killed the normal cells. That is not effective chemotherapy. Effective chemotherapy requires a drug that can kill the cancer without killing the patient. Laetrile proponents ignore this reality.

Some promoters of diet "cures" in cancer therapy also use starvation in the treatment of cancer, such as extreme macrobiotic diets, and ignore the fact that starvation, like laetrile, will kill the patient before it kills the tumor.

Recently, Professor James Harvey Young of Emory University provided a ten-point profile of health quackery, paraphrased below. It applies with full force to all forms of questionable cancer therapy.

1. Exploitation of fear.
2. Promise of painless treatment and good results.
3. Claims of a miraculous scientific breakthrough.
4. Simpleton science: Disease has but one cause, and one treatment is all that is needed to fight it. Bad nutrition causes all disease; good nutrition cures it.
5. The Galileo ploy: "Like Galileo, we cult gurus are misunderstood by blind scientists but are destined to be heroes to future generations." They often feign bitterness about being outcasts and upholding unpopular views and will cite "pioneer" scientists of the past who were forced to fight against the scientific establishment of their day.
6. The conspiracy theory, also known as "the establishment is out to get us." Another clue to whether a cancer therapist is responsible is his or

her willingness to consult with other doctors. Most charlatans are not interested in having their diagnosis or treatment evaluated by another, and will reject the result if it is.

7. The moving target: Shifts in theory to adjust to circumstances. Laetrile went from drug to "vitamin," from cure to palliative, from palliative to preventive; from low to high dosage, from working alone to never working alone; from one chemical formula to another, and so forth. "B_{15}" ("pangamate") is another classic example. According to the F.D.A., it has "no standard of identity," which is legalese for "there is no such substance," and purveyors of pangamate put in the bottle any chemical they choose. Our laboratory has published evidence suggesting the two most used chemicals actually may promote the development of cancer rather than retard it.

8. Reliance on testimonials. Since they eschew responsible research and reporting, these practitioners rely heavily on testimonials from patients they have "cured" and from others who have been influenced by them. These testimonials do not separate cause and effect from coincidence, or from suggestibility, or from the natural history of cancer, which rarely includes spontaneous remission. They proclaim the one spontaneous remission as a cure, but ignore the hundred patients who died, including those that proper treatment would have cured. Unfortunately, many of their supporters are those with a public following but no solid scientific background in oncology—writers, actors, lawyers, and statesmen.

9. Distortion of the idea of freedom: By distorting "freedom of informed choice" to mean "freedom of misinformed choice." There is obviously no freedom in a choice based on false information.

10. Most significantly, large sums of money are involved. Many cancer charlatans accuse the medical community of withholding information about "the real cure" for cancer because it would jeopardize their incomes. Yet they sell secret substances that are only available from their companies or espouse costly treatments that only they (or those who have been personally "trained" by them—for a fee) can provide. Anyone who alleges they have a cancer cure whose nature they will not publish is by definition a charlatan.

Nutrition cultism is a more than $7-billion-a-year industry in the United States today. According to a report in the New York *Times*, sales of vitamins and "health food" alone came to $5.75 billion in 1980, not counting the many millions spent for books and magazines promoting nutrition faddism. Laetrile was still a billion-dollar-a-year industry in the United States as of 1983, despite a multi-institution study demonstrating once again that it is worthless, and the 1983 arrest of Ernst Krebs, Jr., creator of the laetrile industry, for some of his laetrile-connected activities.

FALSE CREDENTIALS

Lack of public education in logic and lack of discrimination between quality and incompetence also contribute to the public's readiness to accept as an authority anybody who uses the title "doctor." The public does not realize that the appearance of legitimate scientific credentials is no guarantee that they are solid or that what the individual says is sound. In April 1983 the Senate Committee on Aging noted that health and medical "quackery" was the most frequent and most lucrative fraud perpetrated on the elderly, and that there were "schools for scoundrels run by cons to teach other cons how to make a 'sting.' " In 1983 an FBI investigation resulted in bringing thirty-nine diploma mills, some of them health credential mills, before a grand jury.

To test two "mills," I have obtained certificates as professional members of the American Association of Nutrition and Dietary Consultants and International Academy of Nutrition Consultants, respectively, for my dog Sassafras and my cat Charlie. They were acquired simply by filling in their names and addresses and nothing else on their applications and sending fifty dollars on their behalf. At least ten thousand people also have obtained these certificates, and it is safe to assume that many, if not most, are now practicing "nutrition therapists." One of them, Gary Pace of New York, in 1985 was restrained by a court order from calling himself a doctor and from performing physical examinations, and in a related action, the State of New York also filed a civil suit against Kurt Donsbach, a leading California promoter of questionable health practices, including a computerized "nutrient deficiency questionnaire" programmed to report that the client needs supplements.

Many mills also offer mail order Ph.D.s in nutrition. Of course, these are not accredited by the Council on Postsecondary Accreditation (One Dupont Circle N.W., Washington, D.C. 20036). Any meaningful American Ph.D. in nutrition must come from an institution listed in the annual registry of the Council on Postsecondary Accreditation. Among other "degrees" available from unaccredited correspondence schools are N.D. (Doctor of Naturopathy) and Ph.N. (Philosopher of Naturopathy) and Ms.D. (Doctor of Metaphysics).

We should ask our state legislators to pass laws prohibiting persons with mail order or diploma-mill Ph.D.s from calling themselves "doctor" or using "Ph.D." after their names. A New Jersey appellate court recently forbade a psychologist whose doctorate was granted from an unaccredited institution from using the title "doctor" or the designation "Ph.D." The New York State Attorney General stated in a 1985 consumer fraud court action against a Donsbach Ph.D., Donsbach, and Donsbach University that it is illegal for anyone to call themselves "doctor" or "Ph.D." in New York based on a Ph.D. in nutrition from the unaccredited Donsbach University in California, and illegal for Donsbach to advertise or sell his correspondence course Ph.D.s in New York. Donsbach sells more Ph.D.s in nutrition through the mails than are given by all the accredited universities in New York and California put together.

HOW TO EVALUATE CLAIMS

The most obvious thing all promoters of questionable therapies have in common is the failure to prove that their methods work. Because they eschew biopsy, often on the grounds that it spreads the cancer, there is no way of knowing whether the patients they treat actually had cancer in the first place. Some of their patients may never have had cancer; others may have had their cancer confirmed by biopsy and cured by conventional means (although they fear they have not). Sometimes the fake "cure" will be given in addition to responsible methods. Any of these circumstances make it easy for proponents of questionable methods to claim success.

All the claims for questionable cancer remedies are based on deception by omission. The promoters omit the fact that their remedies have never been demonstrated to be better or safer than doing nothing. Instead, they provide anecdotes and testimonials that do not separate fact from fiction. Cause and effect are confused with coincidence, suggestion, or the natural history of the disease under study.

How does one evaluate claims of therapy? There are four basic canons that health scientists recognize as binding in evaluating any claim of therapy:

1. Does it go beyond personal observation to stand the test of scrutiny and criticism by other scientists? Is it a study or a story? Is it science or anecdote?

2. Was it tested in placebo studies that controlled for patient suggestibility? That compared it to other treatments or to doing nothing? What is the "natural history" of the disorder, the course it will pursue in the absence of any therapy at all? Was the observed result cause and effect, or coincidence due to the natural history of the disorder?

3. Has it been proved safe? Safe compared to what? Is the risk justified? What is the risk-to-benefit ratio? Is there a net benefit?

4. The burden of proof is on those who propose the treatment, especially if it involves a remedy or procedure not well established in responsible medical practice. The best evidence that their proof is solid and accepted by their peers is publication of their research in established, reputable scientific journals, the kind acceptable for the shelves of the

National Library of Medicine. This means that their research has been reviewed by a committee of their peers and that it is open to scrutiny and replication by other scientists. If the methods can't be replicated, or if the results of small-scale studies don't hold up when demonstrated on a larger population, their work will ultimately prove worthless.

Before accepting a claim of cure as valid, it is necessary to ascertain that:

1. the patient had the disease;
2. the claimed cure resulted from the therapy, and was not merely coincidental with the therapy;
3. the disease is in fact cured, and not progressing silently;
4. the patient has survived the treatment.

Every claim of cancer cure with laetrile or other "nutritional and metabolic" therapy that has been investigated by responsible health professionals has fallen into one of the following categories:

1. The patient never had cancer: A woman with hormone-dependent cystic breast disease, which waxes prior to menses, wanes after, and often goes away with no treatment, is told by a charlatan that the lump in her breast is cancer and that she can be cured with laetrile. When the lump disappears, the "doctor" takes the credit, and the woman will swear in court that she was cured of cancer. Experienced attorneys will not let these patients testify, because they have no biopsy to demonstrate that they ever had cancer.

2. The cancer was cured by responsible therapy, but laetrile or other "nutritional and metabolic" therapy was given as well and erroneously credited with the cure. Promoters of questionable practices also take credit for the occasional spontaneous remission.

3. The cancer is progressing silently to eventual death, but is being represented as cured. For example, the *National Health Federation* (NHF) *Bulletin,* a publication known for promoting questionable remedies, reported that Chad Green, a boy with leukemia, was doing well on laetrile therapy. In fact, the article appeared in the November 1979 NHF *Bulletin* —a month after he died while on laetrile given by the Contreras clinic in Tijuana, Mexico. An autopsy showed leukemia and cyanide in his tissues. He had had a type of leukemia that is 50 to 80 percent curable with established therapy.

NUTRITION FADDISM AND CANCER

Nutrition is an area that is especially susceptible to faddism, particularly when cancer is involved. Of course, fiction can be destroyed by cold facts, but only when those facts are easily available. Several recent books have helped to provide accurate information: *Nutrition Cultism: Facts and Fiction, Vitamins and "Health" Foods: The Great American Hustle,* and *Health Quackery* are three examples. However, books promoting cancer fads far outnumber the reliable ones. Health food stores are a major source of literature promoting faddism in cancer nutrition and they rarely carry any of the responsible books on nutrition and cancer for either lay people or health professionals.

The American Cancer Society, the U.S. Department of Agriculture, the National Research Council, the American Heart Association and similar responsible groups have made recommendations for daily consumption of fruits and vegetables, grains, milk products and meat products that meet the three basic rules of moderation, variety, and balance (see Chapter 2, "Cancer Prevention: Steps You Can Take"). It is folly to say "natural is good and more is better" and then take a single substance out of food and concentrate it into a pill, powder, or potion, claiming it will prevent or cure cancer without demonstrating that the concentrated substance is either effective or safe.

Listed below are some of the more destructive cancer "treatment" regimens that are represented as nutrition science:

1. *No meat, fish, or fowl.* These are the major sources of absorbable iron in the American diet. Lack of these foods results in a much higher frequency of iron deficiency and iron-deficiency anemia, thereby weakening rather than helping patients with cancer.

2. *No dairy products.* These are the major source of calcium in the American diet. Lack of adequate calcium results in damaged bone maintenance, thereby weakening rather than helping patients with cancer.

3. *No animal protein.* This is the entire source of vitamin B_{12} in the American diet. Lack of this vitamin interferes with basic biochemical processes in normal tissue, again weakening rather than helping patients with cancer. Some promoters of macrobiotic cancer "cures" recommend spirulina, a substance derived from algae skimmed from ponds in Mexico, to supply vitamin B_{12}, but there is published evidence that the majority of the substance purported to be "vitamin B_{12}" in spirulina is not, and some of it may actually interfere with vitamin B_{12} metabolism.

4. *Increased ingestion of fruits and vegetables.* Such a diet is high in bulk and low in calories, exactly opposite to the nutritional needs of many cancer patients. This diet may be too low in needed animal protein and may also be marginal in vitamin D, calcium, and phosphorus. Deficiencies of zinc and other trace minerals may be found in people who eat no meat (a major source of trace minerals) and who consume large amounts of bran, cereals, and other plant products loaded with fiber or phytate, which may decrease the absorption of minerals.

Furthermore, fruit stones, apple seeds, and many nuts—almonds, for example—and vegetables, such as green peppers, mushrooms, lettuce, carrots, celery, or bean sprouts, contain various quantities of the enzyme beta-glucosidase. Since beta-glucosidase releases the cyanide from laetrile into the digestive tract, patients on diets high in these foods who are also given oral laetrile can develop cyanide poisoning. Contrary to the popular belief that cyanide either kills or does nothing, chronic low doses of cyanide produce headache, dizziness, fever, malaise, nausea, vomiting, diarrhea, abdominal tenderness and cramps, rash, enlarged liver, spleen and lymph nodes, slowly progressive fatigue, weakness of arms and legs, progressive loss of vision and hearing and other nerve damage.

5. *Megadoses of vitamin C.* Our laboratory has published data showing that megadoses of vitamin C release some cyanide from laetrile, thereby further promoting cyanide poisoning in all patients on a combined vitamin C-laetrile regimen. Other possible side effects of megadoses of vitamin C range from kidney stones to death (from a large intravenous dose). An objective scientific study of megadoses of vitamin C as therapy for advanced cancer coordinated by the National Cancer Institute showed it to be worthless. In fact, in experimental situations, megadoses promote some cancers and retard others. The National Academy of Science report "Diet, Nutrition and Cancer" specifically rejects vitamin C supplementation as being of any known value in preventing cancer. The same report similarly rejects supplements of vitamin A and of selenium. Megadoses of each of these nutrients are highly toxic.

6. *Megadoses of vitamin E.* These are of no clear value in the treatment of cancer and may have a variety of undesirable side effects. Charles Marshall's book, *Vitamins and Minerals: Help or Harm?* provides information on many of these effects.

7. *Oral pancreatic enzymes.* These have no value except as a replacement in pancreatic disease for the missing pancreatic secretion into the intestine. When given to patients with esophageal or stomach lesions, oral pancreatic enzymes may erode the lining adjacent to the tumor and hasten the patient's death. A similar phenomenon may occur when such enzymes are given by enema. Injecting these enzymes can produce a fatal allergic reaction, anaphylactic shock.

8. *"Pangamic acid," or "vitamin B_{15}."* This is a "vitamin" by trade name only. It has no standard of identity, and therefore does not exist except as a label. It is illegal to sell B_{15} in the United States as either a food supplement or a drug, according to the Food and Drug Administration.

9. *Laetrile.* Also trade-named "vitamin B_{17}," laetrile is listed under its chemical name, amygdalin, in the *Merck Index.* It is a cyanogenetic glycoside and has been known as a poison since the pharaoh's priests in ancient Egypt used it in the form of a water extract of peach kernels to execute their enemies. Laetrile has been a cancer "remedy" since 1840, ten years after its isolation in pure form by two French chemists, when a French country doctor reported that he had cured six cancer patients with it. He based his conclusions on the fact that he gave laetrile to them for two months and all six were still alive after the two months. The quality of subsequent evidence is equally unconvincing.

OUTLOOK

Will sound scientific research and proven methods of therapy capture the public imagination as have faddism and charlatans? One would hope so, but this is not likely to happen until there is adequate enforcement of laws and a change in the attitudes of the media and the public. Deceptive and misleading promotions for various "remedies" can legally appear everywhere but on the label of the product—hence the separate shelves for products and literature in health food stores and the separation of the millions spent in advertising from the promotional articles in many irresponsible publications. The U.S. Postal Service, Food and Drug Administration, and Federal Trade Commission are prevented by inadequate funding from enforcing the laws against deceptive and misleading advertising of worthless nostrums. And each year thousands of desperate cancer patients willingly place themselves in the hands of unscrupulous charlatans who prey upon their misfortune.

In 1984 Representative Claude Pepper held a hearing into "Quackery: A $10-Billion-Dollar Scandal." At that hearing I testified on the need for the Justice Department to strike off a portion of the organized crime task force to go after health charlatans under the RICO conspiracy law (Racketeer Influenced and Corrupt Organizations Act), which allows the government to confiscate the assets acquired as a result of a proved conspiracy. The proceedings of the hearing are available by writing to Congressman Claude Pepper, U.S. House of Representatives, Washington, D.C. The 230-page document provides considerable information about the different forms of questionable remedies for cancer and other health-care frauds. So far, one conspiracy indictment has been brought, involving a large health food chain, by a federal grand jury in Buffalo.

14

Genetics and Cancer

HENRY T. LYNCH, M.D.

INTRODUCTION

Although there is still much to learn about why cancer develops in some individuals and not in others, hereditary makeup appears to play a major role in certain forms of this disease. For this reason, the family history—a record of diseases, and cause and age of death of family members—is particularly important. It may contain a wealth of information relevant to the patient and the disease at hand. In fact, it may have the potential to predict cancer in certain families, with more accuracy than even that offered by much of advanced technology.

Several key questions should be raised by patients and physicians when they consider heredity as one of the causes of cancer. How extensive a family history is generally required before one should suspect the presence of hereditary cancer within a family? What clinical evidence might lead the physician to suspect that something is out of the ordinary? How does this lead to the identification of hereditary cancer? What differences exist between families that justify some being identified with specific hereditary cancers? What promise does research hold for improving the early recognition and treatment of patients who are at high risk for hereditary cancer? What lifestyle changes in high-risk patients could aid in the prevention of cancer? What are the prospects for genetic engineering in repressing or reversing cancer-causing genes? By trying to answer these questions, we may be able to resolve some of the vexing dilemmas about cancer as a major public health problem and thereby benefit many patients at high risk for hereditary cancer.

MAGNITUDE OF THE PROBLEM AND GENETIC MECHANISMS

Precise information about the importance of genetics as a cause of cancer is difficult to obtain. This problem is compounded by the fact that there are more than 100 distinct varieties of cancer, and the cause of each form may be different. Nevertheless, cancer researchers estimate that between 5 and 7 percent of patients show clear-cut evidence of the existence of hereditary factors. Most hereditary (single-gene determined) forms of cancer fit what is called the "autosomal dominant" inheritance pattern. This means that, on the average, 50 percent of the children of a cancer-affected parent will ultimately develop the same cancer. The type of cancer inheritance will often be very specific. In some diseases, the cancer itself is not necessarily inherited. What is inherited is a disease that predisposes the patient to a specific cancer. For example, colon cancer will be the predominant malignancy in a hereditary disorder known as familial multiple polyposis of the colon (FPC). These cancers are determined by a single gene.

Various distinct hereditary patterns involving several genes and many different factors account for about 20 to 25 percent of all cancer. This means that in high-risk families multiple genes, in interaction with environmental factors, play a direct role in the production of cancer. Although cancer may be more frequent in these particular families, the findings do not fit any known patterns of inheritance. Geneticists therefore refer to this type of cancer clustering as "familial" as opposed to strictly "hereditary."

Genes do not operate in a vacuum. Internal and external environmental factors are known to interact in the production of cancer. In some forms of hereditary cancer, environmental influences may be less apparent than in others. For example, in a disease known as hereditary retinoblastoma, a form of eye cancer, the condition may appear at birth or shortly thereafter, with most cases appearing when the child is two to three years old. Both eyes are usually affected. The nonhereditary form, on the other hand, develops slightly later and is restricted to one eye. If environmental factors are also involved in the hereditary variety, they cannot be very significant, given the very young age of the child when the disease appears and the likelihood of having both eyes affected.

Not all cancer-causing genes necessarily result in cancer. In some cases the influence of the gene is not apparent, or not apparent enough to cause the cancer. Then, in the terminology of geneticists, the gene has not been "expressed" and its influence has not "penetrated" to the person involved. Failure to develop hereditary retinoblastoma when it would otherwise be expected may be due to effects of other genes. For example, certain genes may prevent the action of the harmful cancer gene.

Environmental factors, which are minimal in the hereditary form, may be important in influencing the "expression" of the cancer-causing gene. Alfred Knudsen, has developed a "two hit" theory that attempts to explain the relationship of hereditary and environmental forms of cancer. His theory is that the first "hit" or injury to patients with the hereditary form is a genetic susceptibility to a particular cancer. In the case of hereditary retinoblastoma, all of the cells of the retina of the eye are primed by their genetic makeup for a second "hit," which comes from some factor in the environment. This may explain the earlier onset and the tendency to affect both eyes. The nonhereditary form, on the other hand, lacks the first "hit" and requires two environmental "hits." This may explain the later onset and the involvement of only one eye.

The odds of developing a hereditary cancer in predisposed families is significantly greater than, for example, the cancer risk to atomic bomb survivors, vinyl chloride or asbestos workers, or heavy cigarette smokers. This is why it is very important to pay careful attention to genetic factors. Once a family is clearly identified as being prone to cancer, screening programs—for example, periodic lung X rays or Pap smears—could be targeted to specific areas or organs of the body and could be lifesaving.

The Family History

The family tree or pedigree is very useful to the geneticist. It shows very clearly the degree of distribution and the pattern of spread of any disease, including cancer, within a group of blood relatives. More than 3,000 human traits and diseases, both common and uncommon, are controlled by heredity to varying degrees. While people have no control over the genes they have inherited, they can be aware of them and act prudently. The first step is to make this information available to the family physician, and this is easily done by constructing a family tree that shows the entire relevant family history, including age and causes of death.

Clinical Factors of Hereditary Cancer

There are several clinical factors, or disease characteristics, which occur more frequently in hereditary forms of cancer. When one or more of these characteristics is found in a patient or his family, the doctor should consider the possibility of hereditary cancer. These factors include an unusually early age of onset of a particular cancer as compared to the age when it affects the general population. For example, in hereditary breast cancer, the average age of onset is forty-four years, while that for the general population is around sixty.

Another factor is the occurrence of several different primary cancers in the same patient. This does not mean that a given cancer is spreading to other parts of the body, but rather that a separate process is occurring within the same or other organs, resulting in successive, distinct cancers of the same or of differing types. Multiple primary cancer may occur in as many as half of hereditary cases. In the general population, on the other hand, the susceptibility to a second primary cancer after a first one has been cured is substantially less—only about 3 to 5 percent.

Hereditary forms of cancer often occur in several generations of a family in accord with the "autosomal dominant" rule of genetic transmission—that is, approximately half the children in each generation. But there are at least thirty types of cancer that are inherited in other patterns. The important point is that patterns of cancer distribution in the hereditary variety are often very predictable and the parts of the body where the cancers are found fit into specific patterns that depend upon the specific genetic disease. Recent evidence has shown improved survival for certain forms of hereditary cancer of the breast and colon and, possibly, for malignant melanoma. Knowledge about what is responsible for this improved survival could apply to cancer in general.

What Is the Evidence for Genetics in the Cause of Cancer?

The evidence for genetics in the cause of cancer in animals is overwhelming, and has been extremely helpful to scientists studying cancer genetics in humans. Most of the evidence linking genetics to certain forms of cancer in man is derived from several solid observations. One observation is that certain precancerous disorders may have clear-cut physical signs that occur in several members of the family. For example, in familial polyposis of the colon (FPC), a disease already mentioned, the characteristic feature is the occurrence of multiple polyps covering the surface of the colon. These polyps precede development of colon cancer and provide telltale evidence that the affected individual is the carrier of the cancer-causing gene.

Another observation is that there are various biochemical signs (called markers) or chromosomal changes which may be correlated with a strong susceptibility to cancer (see section at end of chapter). Disorders with these types of markers may not necessarily be associated with visible physical signs. The high predictability of family members developing certain types of cancer even without associated physical signs provides powerful evidence for the role of genetics in the cause of cancer. The ultimate proof of a hereditary cause would be the isolation of an actual cancer-causing gene. But this must await future developments in genetic engineering. Conceivably such research could lead to the prevention of specific hereditary forms of cancer.

Privacy and Confidentiality

The main objective in collecting medical information about the family tree is to benefit patients and their high-risk relatives. For maximum benefit, this information should be shared with all physicians caring for members of the family. This takes close cooperation among the patient, key informed relatives, and the physician, and it should be made clear that all information is strictly confidential.

National Registry of Cancer-Prone Families

A national registry of families prone to cancer would provide important information to all physicians caring for members of such families. It would also offer unique genetic research opportunities to investigators with a particular interest in hereditary cancerous and precancerous diseases. Such a registry could be coordinated through sophisticated computer systems at the national level, and the use of computers would provide confidentiality for the families involved. Regional service units located throughout the country could effectively serve the needs of practicing physicians and their patients, providing pedigree interpretation and genetic counseling. These service units could be coordinated effectively within existing organizations such as Creighton University's recently developed Hereditary Cancer Institute (HCI). This is a nonprofit organization whose primary mission is education, early detection, better management, and research into all forms of hereditary cancer. For more information, write to: Hereditary Cancer Institute, Creighton University, Omaha, Neb. 68178. Phone 402-422-6237.

This concept has already been put into practice elsewhere. St. Mark's Hospital in London, for example, has compiled a directory of families with familial polyposis of the colon which has functioned successfully for several decades. The benefit to high risk patients has been early detection of this disease with appropriate early preventive surgery.

GENETICS AND COMMONLY OCCURRING CANCERS

The fraction of cancer occurrences which are genetic for any one given category may be relatively small, but one must realize that the actual total number may be large when all occurrences of the particular disease are considered. In addition, once a single family is encountered, the risk to first-degree relatives of a patient with hereditary cancer may approach 50 percent. Hereditary patterns of cancer can be seen in several of the most frequently occurring cancers in the United States, including breast, colon, lung, and ovary.

Breast Cancer

Cancer of the breast is the most common cancer affecting women. The American Cancer Society estimates about 115,000 new cases in 1985, and the number is rising each year. According to the medical literature of ancient Roman times, cases of familial breast cancer were first recognized as early as 100 A.D. Data now indicate that approximately 20 percent of patients with breast cancer will have the familial form, wherein one or more of their first-degree relatives will also have the disease. Further study of these familial cases can lead to the identification of sisters or daughters who will have a 50-50 chance of developing breast cancer. The problem is, however, not that simple, because hereditary breast cancer can also occur in association with other forms of cancer. This is known as "genetic heterogencity." For example, there are hereditary varieties of breast cancer which show a high association with cancer of the ovary in the same family.

Some of these patients will develop both breast and ovarian cancer. Still other families show an association between breast cancer and cancer of the gastrointestinal tract, particularly the colon and stomach. In each of these cancer groups, 50 percent of all first-degree female relatives will get the disease. Patients with all forms of hereditary breast cancer will be affected at an earlier age and have a higher incidence of primary cancer appearing first in one breast and then in the other.

While a woman might realize, because of her family tree, that she has a high risk of developing hereditary breast cancer, she should also understand that this knowledge allows her and her doctor a better chance of detecting it early, significantly raising her chances for a cure. The American Cancer Society recommends that a woman begin breast self-examination at about age twenty and do it faithfully each month following her menstrual period. All women should have a mammogram (a specialized breast X ray) between the ages of thirty-five and forty to give a base line against which to judge any changes in her breasts. A woman at a high risk for hereditary breast cancer should have a mammogram between the ages of twenty-five and thirty and mammography should be repeated every one to two years until the age of forty and then annually thereafter. She should also have her breasts examined by a physician twice a year. These recommendations take into consideration the marked early age of onset of hereditary breast cancer.

Patients who develop cancer in one breast, and who fit the hereditary category, must become extremely vigilant about examining the other breast because of the increased risk of developing a new primary cancer in the opposite breast. Some doctors recommend that patients with early breast cancer consider removal of the other breast as a preventive measure, with later reconstruction of both breasts by plastic surgery. However, only very strong clinical or pathological indications or both warrant this preventive operation.

Colon Cancer

Cancer of the colon is, after lung cancer, the second most frequent serious malignancy in the United States. Several different disorders of the colon, including some such as familial polyps of the colon, which begin with multiple benign polyps, are known to have a strong hereditary pattern. In addition, patients with familial polyps and its variants may be at risk for other forms of cancer, including those of the small bowel, stomach, thyroid, and adrenal cortex. Because of the high probability that those with FPC will develop colon cancer—virtually 100 percent by age fifty and even, on rare occasions, in childhood—doctors recommend that cancer screening procedures be initiated early (Figure 12). Tests for hidden microscopic blood in the stool should be started at age ten and done routinely three times a year, and a full evaluation should be done if blood is detected. Because sigmoidoscopy (examination of the rectum and colon with a long hollow tube called a sigmoidoscope) is especially difficult in young children, this exam should not be started until age fifteen, provided there are no symptoms before then, and it should be done twice a year thereafter. A colonoscopy or barium enema should be performed at age twenty to provide a base line against which to measure changes, and it should be repeated at three-year intervals or more often if necessary. The polyps in FPC generally first appear in the rectum and lower colon, the areas that are the most common sites of the colon cancer.

A patient with FPC is strongly urged to undergo removal of the colon as a preventive measure when the problem is first diagnosed. If the rectum does not have a great number of polyps, it may be saved. The lower section of the small intestine is then connected to the rectum and any recurring polyps are surgically removed from the rectum. The patient must then be meticulously examined periodically for possible develop-

255

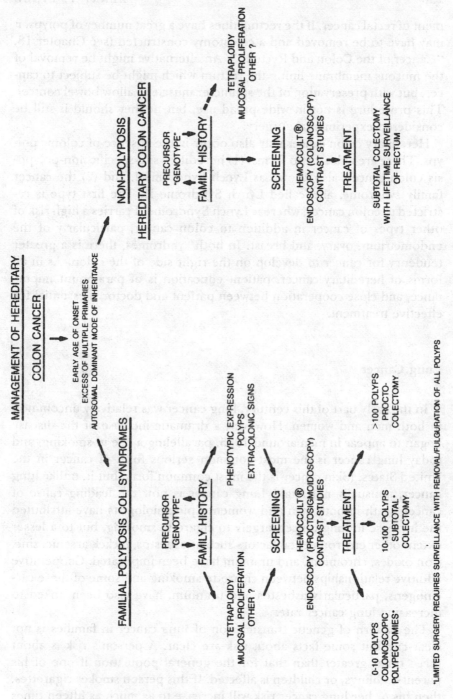

Figure 12 Management of hereditary colon cancer.

ment of rectal cancer. If the rectum does have a great number of polyps, it may have to be removed and a colostomy constructed (see Chapter 18, "Cancer of the Colon and Rectum"). An alternative might be removal of the mucous membrane lining the rectum which might be subject to cancer, but with preservation of the sphincter muscle to allow bowel control. This procedure is not in widespread use, but neither should it still be considered experimental surgery.

Hereditary colon cancer may also occur in the absence of colonic polyps. There are at least two forms: (1) hereditary site-specific non-polyposis colon cancer, also known as Lynch Syndrome I, and (2) the cancer family syndrome, also called Lynch Syndrome II. The first type is restricted to colon cancer, whereas Lynch Syndrome II carries a high risk of other types of cancer in addition to colon cancer, particularly of the endometrium, ovary, and breast. In both syndromes, there is a greater tendency for cancer to develop on the right side of the colon. As in all forms of hereditary cancer, patient education is of paramount importance, and close cooperation between patient and doctor is essential for effective treatment.

Lung Cancer

In the early part of this century, lung cancer was relatively uncommon in both men and women. However, a dramatic increase of the disease began to appear in men around 1935, paralleling a rise in smoking, and today lung cancer is the most common serious form of cancer in the United States. (Skin cancer is the most common form, but it, unlike lung cancer, is usually not fatal.) Lung cancer is now the leading cause of cancer death in both men and women. Epidemiologists have attributed the increase in lung cancer largely to cigarette smoking, but to a lesser extent other environmental factors such as asbestos, nickel, arsenic, zinc, iron oxides, chromium, and uranium have been implicated. Cooperative additive relationships between cigarette smoking and some of these carcinogens, particularly asbestos and uranium, have also been linked to increasing lung cancer rates.

The pattern of genetic transmission of lung cancer in families is not clear-cut, but some facts about risk are clear. A person's risk is about three times greater than that for the general population if one of his parents, siblings, or children is affected. If this person smokes cigarettes, then his or her lung cancer risk will increase to as much as fifteen times the risk of the general population.

Cancer of the Ovary

Cancer of the ovary has been increasing in frequency during the past thirty years, particularly in Western industrialized nations. It is now the most lethal form of cancer of the female genital tract. The study of genetics has led to the recognition of an increasing number of hereditary disorders which involve cancer of the ovary. Women who are sisters (especially the identical twin of a sister with ovarian cancer) or daughters of women with ovarian cancer, and who are members of families showing hereditary ovarian cancer, should be watched very carefully, and once they have had their children they may be considered candidates for preventive surgical removal of the ovaries.

GENETICS AND CHILDHOOD CANCER

Cancer is now, after accidents, the number two killer of children. All forms of cancer, nevertheless, remain relatively rare during the first two decades of life. As with cancer in adults, scientists do not know what proportion of childhood cancer is caused by hereditary factors. Undeniable evidence exists, however, for the role of genetics in the cause of several varieties of childhood cancer. Furthermore, it is reasonable to assume that genetics may play a larger role in certain cancers in children than it does in adults because of the short development time needed for cancer to appear in children. Environmental agents would have had only a relatively brief time for their cancer-causing effect to operate. Also, a genetic predisposition to cancer may be brought out more rapidly by environmental influences.

Population surveys and family studies as well as case reports have provided much of our existing knowledge about the role of genetics in the cause of childhood cancer. One of these surveys, done in Great Britain, revealed that children who had brothers and sisters with cancer were more likely to develop cancer. In fact, more than 100 families were found where two or more children had cancer. Even when cancers with a known genetic component were excluded, the risk to a brother or sister of a child with malignant disease was still about twice that seen in the general population. The largest single type of childhood familial cancer was retinoblastoma, a cancer of the eye. The second-largest group of familial cancers was leukemia, and brain tumors were third.

It was concluded that if a child was diagnosed as having one of several cancers showing familial tendencies, there was a small increase in the risk that a brother or sister would also develop one of those diseases, most likely the same one. Other childhood tumors with some component of hereditary patterns include neuroblastoma of the abdomen and Wilms' tumor of the kidney. Early diagnosis, possibly based on the available family history, will improve the chances of recovery. Because of its potential for producing cancer, therapeutic or diagnostic radiation should be used carefully in all young patients.

SKIN CANCER GENETICS

Cancer of the skin is the most common form of malignancy in the United States. The two major types are squamous and basal cell carcinoma. Malignant melanoma, a third variety, is the most lethal form (see Chapter 30, "Skin Cancer"). Sunlight is the most important cause of skin cancer and, as might be expected, the incidence of this disease is highest in the Southwest, where sunlight exposure is most prominent.

The darker a person's skin, the more protection there is from sunlight and consequently the lesser the risk of developing skin cancer. Thus, skin cancer is relatively rare in blacks, and more common in people of northern European and Scandinavian background, who typically have fair skin, blond or red hair, and blue eyes.

Malignant melanoma was first described by Hippocrates, who recognized its serious potential. Hereditary malignant melanoma may have been first described by an English surgeon in 1820 when he detected this disease in his patient, the patient's father, and in some of his children, all of whom had multiple moles scattered over their bodies. This family may have been the first recorded example of a hereditary melanoma disease called Familial Atypical Multiple Mole Melanoma (FAMMM) syndrome.

One of the most important factors in the successful treatment of this disorder, as in all forms of cancer, is early diagnosis. In the case of hereditary melanoma, intensive education is required for the patient and close relatives, especially the patient's spouse, who should inspect areas of the patient's body that the patient cannot see. Physicians must also become knowledgeable about this recently described genetic disease. All concerned parties must be aware of how it progresses and especially of the significance of changing patterns of moles. Any mole that changes in color or size should become suspect, requiring an evaluation by a physician, and probably removal.

Von Recklinghausen's Neurofibromatosis

Von Recklinghausen's neurofibromatosis is the best known and most common example of a skin disorder strongly associated with cancer. It follows the autosomal dominant inheritance pattern, meaning that an average of 50 percent of all an affected patient's children, brothers, and sisters will also get the disease. The "Elephant Man" of the Broadway play of the same name had this disorder, which is characterized by neurofibromas, or lumpy growths of nerve endings underneath the skin, and is rarely fatal. Cancers of the nervous system, primarily brain, spinal cord, auditory and optic nerve tumors, occur in 10 to 25 percent of affected patients. Rapid strides have been made in the diagnosis of these tumors, providing for their earlier recognition. It is very important for patients who may have findings suspicious of neurofibromatosis to advise their physician about any cases of this disease in the family, and family members at risk should be carefully watched.

Ataxia Telangiectasia

This is an inherited disease characterized by a disorder in the body's ability to repair damaged chromosomes. Patients with this disease have nerve damage leading to gait and balance problems. Other symptoms include the presence of telangiectasia (small blood vessel-like formations) in the conjunctiva membrane which covers the eye, the mucous membranes of the nose, and skin of the ears. People with this disease are also at high risk for leukemia, Hodgkin's disease, medulloblastoma (a type of brain cancer), and stomach cancer, as well as other forms of cancer.

GENETIC MARKERS

Genetic markers are signs that are not symptoms of a disease or condition itself, but are an indication of an inherited predisposition to that condition. There are two types of genetic markers. The first is physical signs, such as the distinguishing skin conditions in cancer-associated skin disease, or multiple polyps of the colon. The second consists of biochemical, physiological, or chromosomal signs which must be tested for in the laboratory. Physical signs that are clearly visible or can be seen with the use of simple diagnostic tools, such as a proctoscope or barium enema for detection of colonic polyps, are important for early cancer diagnosis. In the case of biochemical and cytogenetic (chromosomal) markers, new knowledge is rapidly emerging.

Only a few types of hereditary cancer are consistently associated with genetic markers. One of them is known as multiple endocrine neoplasia, and patients who have it or are at high risk for it may have an elevated level of a chemical known as calcitonin in their blood. This disorder is also associated with a serious form of thyroid cancer, known as medullary thyroid cancer, and with adrenal cancers called pheochromocytomas.

A study of young individuals who had an elevated calcitonin level, and whose thyroids were removed as a preventive measure, showed that a high percentage had precancerous changes which, had they been allowed to run their usual course, would have developed into cancer and resulted in much poorer chances of recovery and survival. Instead, many of these individuals have been virtually assured of a cure.

GENETIC ENGINEERING

Remarkable advances have been made in genetic engineering, particularly during the past decade. For example, the technology is now available to take from chick embryos the genetic material necessary for production of a specific enzyme and insert it into cultures of mouse cells that are low in the same enzyme. The deficiency in the mice can then be actively overcome. There is also evidence that bacteria can be programmed to produce human insulin and interferon, a substance released by cells that may inhibit the growth of cancers. Undoubtedly many other important biological products will be produced in the same way through genetic engineering technology. This knowledge will probably one day be applied to benefit patients at high risk for hereditary cancer. For example, if we could isolate cancer-resistant genes and transplant them into human cells that are deficient in them, we could conceivably prevent the influence of the cancer-prone genes and produce a higher degree of resistance to cancer-causing agents. In fact, plans to do just that are on the drawing boards of a number of genetic engineering laboratories throughout the world. Finally, new breakthroughs in understanding so-called oncogenes may lead to better methods for turning these possible cancer-causing genes off by employing "anti-oncogenes."

SUMMING UP

Knowledge gained in the discipline of human cancer genetics reflects a growing consensus about how particular cancer-causing genes contribute to the overall frequency of cancer in the general population. Cancer risk can be viewed as a combination of genetic susceptibility and environmental forces. While some genes are of themselves cancer-causing, most hereditary patterns of cancer seem to be based on a combination of environmental and inherited factors. Early recognition of these genetic disorders can lead to appropriate screening, prevention, and treatment.

II

Specific Cancers and Their Treatment

15

Cancer of the Bone and Connective Tissue

Although people tend to regard the skeleton as a static collection of bones that, once full growth is achieved, changes very little, it is in reality one of the most active organ systems in the body. In addition to the obvious function of providing support and protection for internal organs, the skeletal system also performs a number of important chemical functions. For example, it acts as a storage and distribution center for a number of essential minerals, most notably calcium, and plays an instrumental role in the manufacture of red blood cells.

The skeleton is made up of more than 200 bones, held together by cartilage and ligaments or connective tissue. All bones are composed of the same basic elements—calcium and phosphorus (mineral salts), water, and protein. The mineral salts and protein combine to form the basic structure of bone cells; the minerals are calcified to give bones their hardness. The outer sheath of the bone (the periosteum) contains blood vessels; the interior contains the spongy marrow tissue in which blood is manufactured (Figure 13). Not all bones perform the same function. Some, such as the skull bones, contain very little marrow and are basically protective structures. Long bones—those of the arms and legs, for example—act as levers to facilitate movement. Still others, such as the flat bones of the hips and ribs, produce large quantities of red blood cells in their marrow. Like all other body tissue and organs, the bones and connective tissue may be afflicted with cancer. Most bone cancers are actually secondary tumors, meaning they arise from cancers that have metastasized or spread from other parts of the body, usually the breast, kidney, prostate, or thyroid. Cancers that actually arise in the bones and connective tissue, known medically as sarcomas, are relatively uncommon and occur mostly in young people. Each year about 2,000 primary cancers of the bone and 4,500 cancers of the connective tissue are diagnosed in the United States. This is somewhat less than one percent of all newly diagnosed cancers (excluding cancers of the skin and carcinoma *in situ*, such as localized cancerous changes of the cervix).

In the past, the treatment of most sarcomas involved surgery to remove or eradicate the cancerous tissue, usually with rather poor results. More

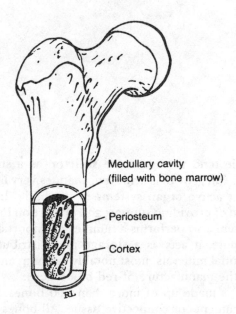

Figure 13 Normal bone.

recently, however, combinations of treatments have been adopted with a greatly improved survival rate. This interdisciplinary approach usually includes conservative surgery (as opposed to the more extensive operations), radiation therapy, and anticancer chemotherapy. The use of chemotherapy, a relatively recent innovation, is probably responsible for the marked improvement in survival. Its goal is the destruction of microscopic cancers that have spread to other parts of the body from the sarcoma. These distant cancers may or may not be detected at the time of the initial diagnosis, but because of the nature of this particular type of cancer they are generally presumed to be present in most patients at the time of diagnosis of sarcoma. In addition, new chemotherapy strategies have been developed that are designed to eradicate the sarcoma itself, and these are being used with increasing frequency.

BONE SARCOMAS

There are two major types of bone sarcoma: osteosarcoma, which mostly affects the fast-growing portions of the bones in children; and Ewing's sarcoma, which develops in the bone marrow. Other, less common forms of bone cancer include fibrosarcoma, chondrosarcoma, malignant giant cell tumor, and reticulum cell sarcoma. (There are also other kinds of cancer such as certain lymphomas or multiple myeloma that affect the bones; these are discussed in the chapters dealing with those specific diseases. (See Chapter 24, "Hodgkin's Disease and Other Lymphomas," and Chapter 26, "Multiple Myeloma.")

Osteosarcoma and Ewing's sarcoma are most common in patients under the age of twenty, and most frequently in ten- to twenty-year-olds. In contrast, reticulum cell sarcoma, fibrosarcoma, and chondrosarcoma usually occur in older patients, with a peak incidence in the forty-through-sixty age range. Osteosarcoma sometimes seems to be associated with other disorders, particularly Paget's disease, a form of bone degeneration, or the formation of multiple bone spurs (exostoses). It also may occur in bones that have been exposed to previous radiation therapy.

Symptoms

The first signs and symptoms of bone tumors vary considerably from patient to patient. Osteosarcoma starts in the cells that form the bone cells and frequently afflicts the legs, beginning in or near the knee. The most common early symptoms are pain and swelling that limit everyday activities. The pain is often described as dull and aching and is usually limited to the area of the swelling. However, tumors of the hip and spine may cause pain throughout the leg and thigh. At first the pain may be eased by aspirin or other painkillers and rest, but as the disease progresses, the pain becomes more difficult to control and often keeps the patient awake at night. Osteosarcoma softens the bones, causing them to break easily, seemingly for no apparent reason. In many instances there may be a history of minor bone injury that is sometimes incriminated as causing the cancer; in reality, however, the cause of most bone cancers is unknown.

In some instances the early symptoms may be so subtle and intermittent that the patient does not see a doctor until the disease has spread to other parts of the body. When this happens, the symptoms include generalized aches, swellings, and, if the lungs are involved, a cough with blood-stained sputum. Patients with Ewing's sarcoma, which most commonly occurs in the shafts of long bones, may also have fever, malaise, fatigue, poor appetite, weight loss and other signs of general, widespread (systemic) illness. This spectrum of symptoms is less frequent in osteosarcoma.

Diagnosis of Bone Cancer

The diagnosis of bone tumors begins, as in all medical problems, with a complete medical history and a thorough physical examination. X rays will be taken of any bones that seem to be causing pain. Since many bone cancers spread to the lungs, even in very early stages, the X rays are often followed by tests to determine whether there is any evidence of lung involvement. These may include conventional chest X rays as well as cross-sectional X rays (pulmonary tomograms) and the newer computed tomography (CT scans), and occasionally fluoroscopy, the use of a special fluorescent screen to view internal organs via X rays. To determine the extent of local bone destruction, CT scans also will be taken of the bone or bones harboring the tumor. In addition, the entire skeleton may be studied by radionuclide scans to detect any early spread to other bones.

While all of these tests provide important information, the single most important diagnostic examination is the bone biopsy, in which a small portion of the bone is removed and then studied under the microscope. The purpose of the biopsy is to firmly establish the diagnosis of cancer and to determine exactly what kind of cancer is present. The biopsy may be open, meaning that a surgical incision will be made to obtain the bone sample, or it may be made by inserting a hollow needle into the bone to withdraw a small amount of tissue. If an open biopsy is performed, special care should be taken in the placement of the incision and to make it as small as possible so as not to interfere with future surgery or radiation therapy. A misplaced, overly large biopsy may result in poor healing and spread of the cancer. If it appears that surgery will be included in the subsequent treatment, it is advisable to have the surgeon who will perform this operation also do the biopsy to ensure that it will not jeopardize the success of the subsequent surgery. In any instance, no attempt should be made to remove the entire tumor during the biopsy, as is sometimes the case in dealing with other types of cancer, nor should there be any attempt to obtain unnecessary bone samples, for fear of spreading the tumor cells.

If Ewing's sarcoma or any other cancer involving the bone marrow is suspected, bone marrow aspiration will be performed. This is done under local anesthesia and is not painful, although there may be some discomfort when the anesthesia is injected. A small, hollow needle is used to remove bone marrow cells (Figure 14), which are then examined under a microscope to see whether the blood-forming cells are normal or abnormal or have been replaced by cancerous cells.

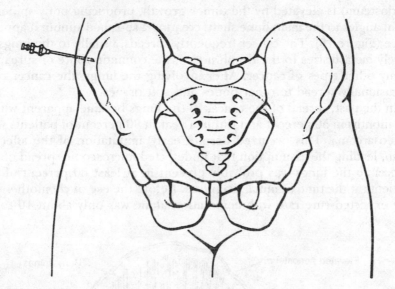

Figure 14 Bone biopsy using a marrow aspiration needle.

As our knowledge of cancer increases, the biochemical and blood tests that are performed during the diagnostic process are becoming even more important. These tests usually include a battery of liver function studies, a complete blood count, measurements of serum sodium and potassium, and kidney function tests. Still other tests, such as an evaluation of serum protein, may be performed in patients with suspected multiple myeloma (see Chapter 26, "Multiple Myeloma") or other cancers that weaken the bones and produce abnormal images of bones in X-ray studies.

Osteosarcoma

About 300 new cases of osteosarcoma are diagnosed each year in the United States. This disease occurs more often in boys than in girls, usually arising in areas of rapid bone growth. Therefore it is most likely to occur during the growth spurt of puberty and at the sites of especially rapid growth, such as the ends of the leg bones, upper arms, and hips.

Typically, the disease may be brought to a parent's attention by a child's complaints of persistent pain after a relatively minor injury, such as a fall or bad bruising. X rays show an enlargement near the growing end of the bone, with areas of excessive new bone formation and destruction. The layer of tissue that surrounds and protects normal bone (the periosteum) is elevated by the tumor growth, producing bony spines at right angles to the main bone shaft, creating a so-called sunburst appearance (Figure 15). The cancer frequently spreads, usually to the lungs. It rarely metastasizes to the lymph nodes, the common route of spread in many other types of cancer. After involving the lungs, the cancer cells occasionally spread to other bones and soft tissues.

In the past, spread of the cancer to the lungs became apparent within six months in 50 percent and within a year in 80 percent of patients with osteosarcoma. This occurred despite early amputation of the affected limb, leading the assumption that undetected microscopic spread of the cancer to the lungs was probably present in at least 80 percent of the patients at the time of initial diagnosis. Before the use of chemotherapy, the expected cure rate with amputation alone was only about 10 to 20

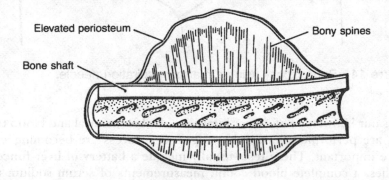

Figure 15 Schematic radiographic pattern in osteosarcoma with excessive new bone growth, elevated periosteum, and bony spines formed at right angles to bone shaft.
(Modified from Huvos, Andrew G. *Bone Tumors: Diagnosis, Treatment and Prognosis.* Philadelphia: W. B. Saunders Co., 1979.)

percent. Because of this bleak outlook, radiation therapy was at one time used as the initial means of treatment, with the intent to avoid amputation in patients who were probably going to die from their lung metastases. Following this logic, the primary bone tumor was irradiated and amputation was performed only if the patient did not appear to have lung metastases within four to six months.

As a result of this treatment strategy, some patients could occasionally avoid amputation if local irradiation of the bone tumor produced good results. Very often, however, cancer spread occurred during (or before) the radiation therapy and amputation had to be performed later to relieve suffering and prolong life as much as possible. Thus, amputation remained a standard form of treatment.

Recent advances have markedly improved the overall survival rate and changed the approach to treatment, again demonstrating the giant steps forward that have been made in cancer therapy in recent years. Today's typical treatment involves surgical removal of the primary tumor, followed by chemotherapy to destroy the microscopic lung metastases that remain despite surgical treatment in more than 80 percent of osteosarcoma patients.

The dramatic change in the outlook for osteosarcoma began in the 1970s with the discovery that several chemotherapeutic agents were effective. (These include such potent anticancer drugs as methotrexate with citrovorum factor, adriamycin, cisplatin and cyclophosphamide.) Chemotherapy has now been used for about a decade and has produced survival rates of about 70 to 90 percent.

There is some dispute, however, over whether this improved survival can be totally credited to the addition of chemotherapy to the treatment regimen. Researchers at the Mayo Clinic, for example, contend that there has been a "natural" increase in survival that cannot be attributed entirely to chemotherapy. Be that as it may, the fact that a number of anticancer drugs are effective in treating osteosarcoma is not disputed, and this has prompted studies to determine whether chemotherapy alone can be used to treat the primary tumor as well as the lung metastases, thereby avoiding amputation. This treatment plan, known as "limb salvage," is being investigated at several leading cancer centers in the United States. It involves the administration of anticancer drugs before surgery. In the subsequent operation, only the tumor itself (rather than the entire limb) is removed, and a metal bone prosthesis is inserted.

In some instances in which the tumor is extremely small, the preoperative chemotherapy may be eliminated. Following the removal of the tumor, most patients continue to receive chemotherapy for varying periods of time. This approach is still experimental and is being tried on only a small number of patients. Selection is based on age, the potential for surgical removal of the tumor without resorting to amputation, and the attainment of maximum growth in patients with cancers of the lower limbs. This method of experimental treatment follows the guideline that any new therapy must be expected to be at least as effective as present therapies, if not more so, and should be tried in only a small group of closely monitored patients in order to produce a clear conclusion as to its efficacy and possible advantages.

In addition, at several cancer centers the use of preoperative chemotherapy is being studied in patients about to undergo amputation. These studies are intended to determine, by actually observing the effects of preoperative drugs on tissues that are later removed, whether a chemotherapeutic regimen designed to treat the primary tumor also works against microscopic disease. This effort is being further enhanced by the recent development of cell culture techniques that permit the testing of various anticancer drugs to measure their effectiveness in a laboratory setting. The technique is similar to that used in laboratory tests to determine which antibiotics should be used to treat a particular bacterial infection.

Although spread of the cancer to distant organs is still very common in osteosarcoma, it should be emphasized that the outlook for patients with this disease has improved dramatically in recent years. With the current highly effective multidrug regimen, cures are being achieved in patients who would have been considered hopeless just a few years ago. Therefore a diagnosis of metastatic disease is no longer a death warrant. Metastases are usually treated with a combination of surgery, drugs and, occasionally, radiation therapy. Overall, a 40 percent cure rate can be expected in patients who even at the initial diagnosis are found to have lung metastases. The cure rate for those patients who later develop metastases to the lung also is steadily improving.

In dealing with osteosarcoma, it should be noted that there are at least three types of the disease, and determining the particular type is important in designing the approach to treatment and judging the probable prognosis. The least malignant type is called parosteal or juxtacortical osteosarcoma. Another closely allied type is designated the periosteal variety. These occur most commonly in the midshafts of the long bones rather than at the growing ends. These particular types are very slow-growing, and any metastases usually occur later in the course of the disease. Treatment generally consists only in the removal of the tumor, although in some cases amputation may be required. The cure rate is about 80 percent, even without adjuvant chemotherapy. In fact, use of chemotherapy in these types of osteosarcoma is debatable because the drugs themselves involve risks that may outweigh any increased benefit from them. However, this is a situation that varies, and any such judgment should be based on the circumstances of the individual patient.

The second type is known as multifocal osteosarcoma, and, as its name suggests, it occurs in several bones simultaneously, or it may arise in one bone and metastasize to other parts of the skeleton without first involving the lungs. This particular form of osteosarcoma is highly malignant and has a poor prognosis. Treatment is usually the surgical removal of the major tumors and chemotherapy. Radiation therapy also may be used as a palliative measure.

A third type is called soft-tissue osteosarcoma because it occurs mostly in the soft tissues. It is treated like conventional osteosarcoma, although its prognosis is not as good. Fortunately this variation of osteosarcoma is extremely rare.

Chondrosarcoma

Chondrosarcoma is a cancer that arises in the cartilage cells and occurs most often in older people. It is extremely rare in children; only 2 to 3 percent of this type of cancer occurs in people under the age of twenty. The most common sites are the hips; the most frequent early symptom is the appearance of a lump or mass in the pelvic area, followed by pain.

The prognosis is difficult to assess. In adults, the cancer does not seem to be as malignant as osteosarcoma, while in children the disease is more difficult to control. Late spread to the lungs is common, as is spread of the primary tumor to surrounding tissue.

Surgical removal of the tumor or amputation is the usual treatment. If the chondrosarcoma is judged to be of the low-grade, slow-growing type, adjuvant chemotherapy usually is not given. Drugs may be used in the faster-growing high-grade variation.

Ewing's Sarcoma

Ewing's sarcoma is a rare cancer that develops within the bone marrow. It may arise in almost any bone; typically, however, half of all Ewing's sarcomas are in the thighbone (femur), the shinbone (tibia) or the upper arm (humerus). The disease most commonly strikes children ten to twenty years old, but also may occur in both older and younger patients, with a slight predilection for boys.

Pain and then swelling are usually the first symptoms. Fever and other signs of infection such as a high white blood cell count may lead to an initial incorrect diagnosis of osteomyelitis, an inflammation of the bones caused by a bacterial or fungal infection. X rays tend to show extensive involvement of the solid outer part of the bone (the cortex), with new bone formation in the protective lining of the bone's outer surface, resulting in an onionskin appearance (Figure 16). Often a large soft-tissue mass can also be seen. Occasionally other bones may be affected simulta-

272

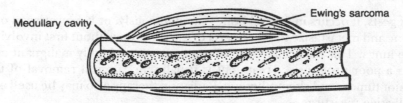

Figure 16 Schematic radiographic pattern in Ewing's sarcoma with on-ionskin appearance.
(Modified from Huvos, Andrew G. *Bone Tumors: Diagnosis, Treatment and Prognosis.* Philadelphia: W. B. Saunders Co., 1979.)

neously, giving the impression that the disease originates in more than one site. Metastasis to the lungs is common.

Radiation therapy is the most common treatment for Ewing's sarcoma, although surgical removal is performed in some cases, depending upon location of the tumor. Chemotherapy usually is given along with the radiation therapy. More recently, however, an experimental treatment has been developed to study the usefulness of chemotherapy alone as the initial therapy, followed in two or three months by surgery or radiation therapy or both.

Radiation therapy in any type of bone cancer must be given with extreme care and precision to avoid destruction of healthy tissue. The bone marrow, in particular, is very sensitive to irradiation. Once started, however, treatment should be continued for the full predetermined course despite any quick disappearance of the tumor and symptoms—something that occurs frequently. The total required radiation dose is about 6,000 to 6,500 rads delivered over six to seven and a half weeks in combination with several anticancer drugs. The initial 4,000 rads is delivered to the primary tumor, surrounding soft tissue, and the entire inner (medullary) portion of the affected bone. The final 2,000 to 2,500 rads are directed intensively to the tumor itself. The treatments are generally given daily. Antinausea drugs may be given to help prevent nausea and vomiting, which may occur as side effects of the radiation therapy and/or anticancer drugs.

During the actual radiation treatments, the patient is usually placed in special restraining devices. Many patients find this a frightening aspect of undergoing radiation therapy, but the devices are important to prevent any movement and to ensure that the radiation is correctly beamed. (See Chapter 8, "Radiation Therapy," for a more detailed overview of this form of cancer treatment.) In addition, a program of active exercise for all treated joints should be instituted at the start of therapy. The degree of damage to the solid outer (cortical) bone by the tumor growing from the inner (medullary) area determines the type of exercises that should be undertaken and also whether or not the bones should bear any weight during the course of treatment. If proper precautions are followed during radiation therapy, satisfactory use of the bone usually will be regained.

Recent studies have been undertaken to determine whether the total radiation dose can be reduced if chemotherapy is used as the main treatment. This is important because large radiation doses may cause later complications, even though the disease is cured. These studies show that in most patients, three months of chemotherapy destroys a large portion of the tumor. What remains is then removed by surgery, and the site is treated by radiation therapy. This approach allows the total radiation dose to be reduced to about 4,000 rads. It should be noted, however, that this approach is still considered experimental and is available in only a few centers. Furthermore, it is suitable for only selected sites, such as the pelvis or ribs.

When Ewing's sarcoma occurs in children under the age of seven years and affects the arms or legs, the best treatment is immediate amputation. Radiation will inevitably retard the growth of the limb, while the healthy limb will continue to develop normally. Eventually there would be a tremendous discrepancy in limb length, requiring amputation. Rehabilitation is more effective if the amputation is performed early rather than later, even though most parents find it difficult initially to accept this concept. In addition, this approach has an added advantage in that it usually avoids radiation therapy, which may have even more pronounced later complications when administered to young children.

Chemotherapy of Ewing's sarcoma may entail giving drugs, such as dactinomycin or doxorubicin, which worsen the adverse effects of radiation therapy. Therefore in any combined approach using these drugs, considerable skill on the part of the treating physicians is required to ensure that the chemotherapy and radiation are properly integrated. (Other drugs, such as vincristine or cyclophosphamide, which do not compound the adverse effects of radiation, may also be used.) In addition to the combined therapy, anticancer drugs are usually administered for another one to two years to destroy any metastases to other parts of the body.

Although the treatment for Ewing's sarcoma may be complicated and difficult for the patient, the results justify the effort. Following these combined approaches to treatment, 60 to 70 percent of patients with Ewing's sarcoma can expect to be cured, defined as being well and free of disease five years later. Although late metastases may still occur, this is a dramatic improvement over the past. Before the advent of chemotherapy, only about 5 percent of the patients could expect to be cured.

Unfortunately, the outlook is not as optimistic when Ewing's sarcoma has metastasized. In such instances, a combination of treatments will be used and may include experimental protocols. Radiation therapy may be administered to the tumor sites. Chemotherapy usually follows for one to two years, and regular physical and X-ray examinations are important in the follow-up.

Studies involving patients treated with this intensive regimen have yielded a 30 to 40 percent symptom-free survival at a median time of thirty-four months—a marked improvement over the past, but one that will require more time to determine whether or not the patients are indeed cured. Following treatment, patients should undergo X rays of the chest as well as the cancer site at regular intervals of one to six months for five years, and annually thereafter. Any unusual symptoms, particularly at the site of the radiation treatments, should be reported promptly to a doctor.

SOFT-TISSUE SARCOMAS

Soft-tissue sarcomas are a family of cancers that arise from supportive (connective) tissue other than the bones. Specifically, soft-tissue sarcomas may afflict the muscles (rhabdomyosarcoma and leiomyosarcoma), fibrous tissue (fibrosarcoma and malignant fibrous histiocytoma), fat cells (liposarcoma); the blood vessels (angiosarcoma), and the joints (synovial cell sarcoma). Children are the most common victims of these soft-tissue sarcomas; adults are rarely affected.

Soft-tissue sarcoma usually starts as a painless mass or lump, although in some cases pain occurs before the lump, but only for a short time since these cancers grow rapidly. Any unexplained lump should be investigated promptly, particularly if it is in the thigh since many soft-tissue sarcomas originate in that region. Similarly, a lump in the groin may indicate a sarcoma of the bladder, vagina, or uterus, although other disorders such as a hernia or lymphoma are more frequent causes. Recurrent earache or facial paralysis may be an early symptom of rhabdomyosarcoma of the middle ear. This type of sarcoma also may originate in the supporting structure of the eye.

Diagnosis

In addition to a thorough physical examination, specific diagnostic studies used when soft-tissue sarcoma is suspected include (depending upon the affected part), X rays, CT scans, ultrasonic (echo) examinations, kidney studies and others. A biopsy is an essential diagnostic step, and precautions such as those followed for bone biopsies should be taken. Tissue for biopsy may be obtained either through a surgical incision or with a hollow needle. In any instance, care should be taken to minimize the damage and to make sure that the wound is closed without drains to reduce as much as possible the risk of spread and infection.

Before developing a treatment plan, staging to determine the extent of disease and specific type of cancer is usually recommended. Microscopic examination of the sarcoma cells also is recommended by many authorities to determine the cell grade. Grade One sarcomas have cells that are fairly well differentiated and have few reproducing or dividing cells. In contrast, Grade Three sarcomas are relatively undifferentiated and have many reproducing cells. Grade Two sarcoma lies between these two. In general, the lower the grade, the better the prognosis.

The treatment of soft-tissue sarcoma has traditionally involved extensive surgery aimed at removing the cancer and surrounding tissue. Often this meant limb amputation and removal of muscles. More recently, however, a combination of treatments—less radical surgery, radiation therapy, and chemotherapy—has been used with good results. The timing and administration of the treatments depends upon staging, grade and other circumstances. In most cases limbs and muscles can be saved without lowering the rate of cure. Surgical treatment, however, may entail removal of the lymph nodes from the area of the tumor to help prevent the cancer's spread to other parts of the body. Postsurgery radiation therapy may be given to the tumor site and regional lymph nodes.

The prognosis for soft-tissue sarcoma appears to be improving with the increased use of combination treatment. This is especially true for children. The success rate is clearly related to the stage of the disease and possibly to the grade of tumor cell. For example, Stage I and II rhabdomyosarcoma in children has a 60 to 80 percent cure rate, compared to cure rates of 40 and 15 percent respectively for Stages III and IV. The prognosis is also related to the site of origin. Rhabdomyosarcoma of the eye and of the genitourinary tract are generally associated with a good prognosis (approximately 60 to 80 percent survival) compared with a 20 percent survival among patients with rhabdomyosarcoma affecting the arms and legs. As for cell grades, Grade One sarcoma is associated with a survival in the 80 percent range; Grade Two, a 40 percent survival; and Grade Three, a 20 percent survival. It should be emphasized that these are only survival rates for large numbers of patients. One cannot predict the outcome in any individual patient.

Complications of Treatment

As noted throughout this book, all cancer therapy involves certain short-term adverse reactions and possible long-term consequences. Nausea, vomiting, loss of hair, depressed production of white blood cells and resulting increased susceptibility to infection are among the short-term complications of cancer therapy. Although these can be very troubling and uncomfortable at the time, they are self-limiting and end when the therapy is completed. Some anticancer drugs may produce sterility, either temporary or permanent. Others affect the heart and other vital organs. Although these are serious problems, the potential benefits generally outweigh the adverse effects.

Radiation therapy also produces adverse effects, including an increased potential for developing cancer in the area exposed to the radiation. Thus radiation therapy is limited to the minimum effective dosage and is carefully administered to protect surrounding tissue as much as possible. The effects of surgery, particularly amputation, are immediate and generally permanent. The development of effective combinations of treatments that minimize the radical surgery have spared the limbs and muscle tissue of many victims of bone and soft-tissue sarcomas. Improved prosthetic devices and increased attention to rehabilitation, particularly of young patients, have added greatly to the quality of life following surgery.

SUMMING UP

Our knowledge about sarcomas is constantly increasing; this improved understanding of a relatively rare but important group of cancers has resulted in marked improvement in survival. Since sarcomas so often strike the young, these advances have made it possible for many young people, who only a few years ago would have been doomed to an early death, now to look forward to a normal life-span.

16

Tumors of the Brain

WILLIAM R. SHAPIRO, M.D.

INTRODUCTION

About 20 percent of all cancers affect the brain and central nervous system, but only a relatively small number—about 13,700 cases a year—actually arise in those vital areas. The majority of brain tumors are the result of metastases of other cancers, particularly from the lung and breast. The cause of primary brain cancer is unknown but heredity and cancer-causing genes (oncogenes) may play a part, especially in children.

Brain tumors present several difficult problems that set them apart from other cancers. Perhaps most important is the fact that the brain is the seat of our intelligence and emotions. The idea that intelligence and consciousness are threatened is hard for both patient and family to accept. On the positive side, considerable progress has been made in widening our understanding of the effects of brain tumors and their treatment on the patient's mind and ability to function. Still, even though many brain tumors are either curable or potentially curable, on the whole, cancers of this organ remain an unsolved medical challenge.

THE MASS EFFECT

The contained physical environment within the skull and spinal column leads to problems not usually encountered with cancers of other organs (Figure 17). Although cancer can destroy vital brain tissue, the major problem encountered in all brain tumors, benign or malignant, is related to their crowding, or "mass effect." Because they are enclosed within the skull and vertebral column, the tumors have a very limited area in which to grow. Pressure from the expanding tumor can displace adjacent structures, with repercussions to numerous other organs and body functions. Not very much tumor is required to produce a mass effect. A mass as small as 100 grams (3.5 ounces) within the confines of the brain can prove fatal, perhaps a tenth of what the body can tolerate elsewhere. The mass effect is much the same for benign tumors as for malignant; the only difference may be that malignant tumors tend to grow much faster than benign ones.

The fibrous structures that divide the brain cavity into several major compartments (Figure 18) present additional barriers to tumor movement and consequently cause other impairments in function. Shifts, or herniations as they are often called, can develop in these compartments, leading to impaired function that often is undetected in the early stages because the signs may be very subtle. Displacement of the lower part of the brain that joins the upper part of the spinal cord disrupts the control of the basic physiologic processes of respiration, blood pressure, and heart rate. Pressure on these structures can become a medical emergency requiring rapid intervention by medical and, if necessary, surgical means.

The mass effect causes other problems besides displacement. As the tumor grows, it causes swelling and a buildup of fluid (hydrocephalus). This results in decreased blood circulation, first in small vessels near the tumor and, as pressure increases, to the entire brain. The heart attempts to maintain adequate flow to the brain by increasing blood pressure, but this is usually not enough. The flow of cerebrospinal fluid, which bathes and cushions the central nervous system, is also impeded (Figure 19 A and B). Evidence of high cerebral pressure can be seen when a doctor looks into the back of the eye with a simple hand-held ophthalmoscope. The optic nerve, which is actually an extension of the brain rather than being a true nerve, will often be visibly engorged and swollen—a condition called papilledema—because of the high pressure behind it.

Partial obstruction of the flow can result in increasing hydrocephalus,

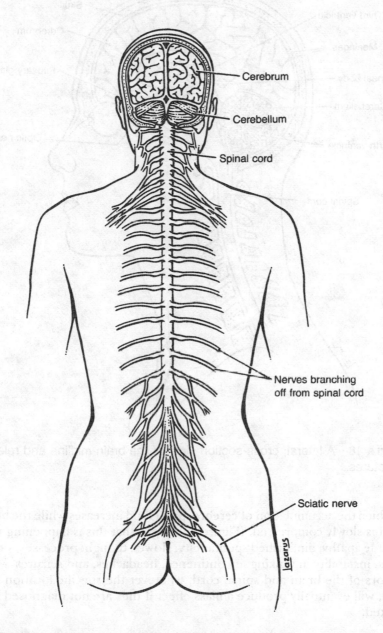

Figure 17 Relation of brain and spinal cord.

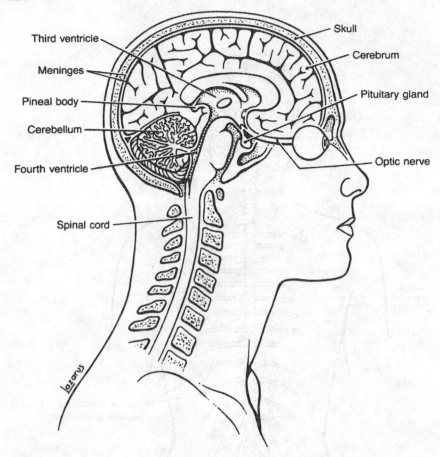

Figure 18 A lateral, cross-section view of the brain midline and related structures.

in which the accumulation of cerebrospinal fluid increases while the brain itself is slowly compressed. (Figure 20). Signs that this is happening may include apathy, diminished spontaneity, slowed thought processes, sleepiness, instability in walking, incontinence, headaches, and seizures. Most tumors of the brain and spinal cord, whatever the specific location and type, will eventually produce a mass effect if they are not diagnosed and treated.

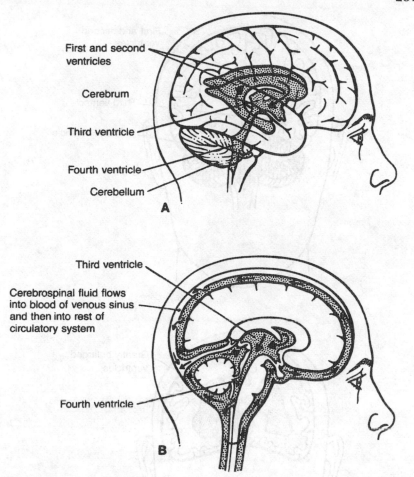

First and second ventricles

Cerebrum

Third ventricle

Fourth ventricle

Cerebellum

A

Third ventricle

Cerebrospinal fluid flows into blood of venous sinus and then into rest of circulatory system

Fourth ventricle

B

Figure 19 Circulation of cerebrospinal fluid.

DIAGNOSIS

The diagnosis of brain tumor is not always easy or evident because the onset of symptoms may be gradual, vague, and only recognized in retrospect. Headache is a common symptom but, contrary to popular belief, it is not always severe or persistent. Instead, the pain may be vague and variable in pattern. Often, the pain can be relieved by aspirin, acetaminophen, or other moderate painkillers. If the tumor invades or stretches the meninges—the nerve-rich membranes covering the brain and spinal cord —the headaches will be more severe. Some are similar to migraines. If

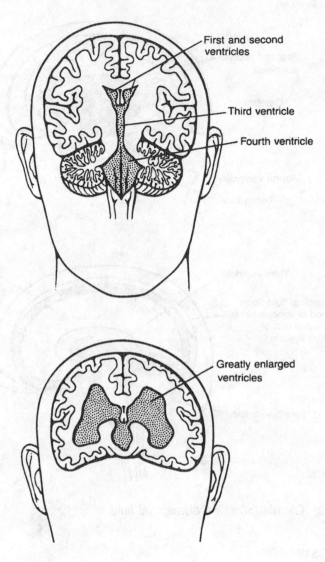

Figure 20 Hydrocephalus.

there are general characteristics associated with the headache of brain tumors, they are that the pain is perceived as being deep and it is often worse at night or early in the morning. The apparent location of the headache is not truly a good indicator of the tumor site. Nausea and vomiting unrelated to food occur in about 25 to 30 percent of brain tumor patients, frequently in association with headache.

Sometimes a seizure in a person over forty years of age who never has had one before is a warning sign of a possible brain tumor or metastases to that organ. The seizure is caused by increased pressure, which "irritates" nerve tissue near the tumor.

The effects of a brain tumor on other parts of the body are strongly correlated with the site of the tumor and its pattern of growth. A tumor of the cerebellum, the part of the brain that helps control coordination of movement, will result in progressive movement difficulties, such as an unsteady gait. Analogously, a tumor originating in the centers that control speech or vision will first produce symptoms involving those functions: blurred or double vision, slurred or difficult speech. Figure 21 shows the parts of the brain where various functions are controlled.

Even before CT scans and other sophisticated imaging methods were available, neurologists often were able to pinpoint the location of a tumor simply on the basis of the patient's symptoms and a thorough neurological examination—a rather strange medical drill using things like pins, tuning forks, colored charts, memory and other simple mental tests, and the familiar reflex hammers.

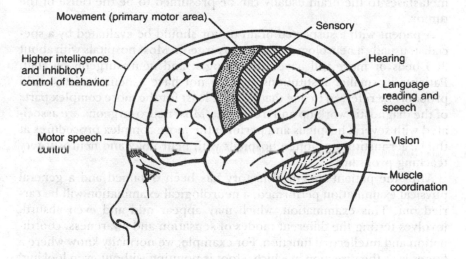

Figure 21 Control centers of brain.

Probably the most frequent signs of a brain tumor, however, are subtle changes in personality, memory, and intellectual performance. These changes are variable and puzzling to the patient, who may be aware of them and make attempts to hide them or compensate for the problems they cause. The changes are often dismissed by friends and family members as trivial or growing idiosyncrasies until they can no longer be ignored. Unexplained changes in personality and mental function always should be investigated. Of course, not all such changes are due to a brain tumor, but the possibility should be ruled out at an early stage.

Accurate diagnosis is particularly important because many brain tumors are benign and potentially curable. Even in instances of cancerous or metastatic tumors, treatment can relieve the symptoms and extend life and improve its quality, even if a cure is not achieved. Sometimes it is difficult to differentiate a stroke from a cancer. Not all strokes come on suddenly; some may evolve slowly, mimicking the gradual development of a tumor. Conversely, hemorrhage into a small, symptomless tumor may enlarge it, suddenly causing it to mimic a stroke.

The diagnostic work-up of a suspected brain tumor usually will include CT scans of the brain as well as conventional X rays. Even with CT scans and other new imaging techniques, surgery may be required for an accurate diagnosis. Although neurosurgery is not always necessary to diagnose a tumor nor is it clearly expected to help the patient, the fear of missing a curable problem is a compelling reason to undergo it. This does not apply when there is proven cancer in other organs; in such instances metastases to the brain usually can be presumed to be the cause of the tumor.

A patient with a suspected brain tumor should be evaluated by a specialist, usually a neurologist or a neurosurgeon. Most hospitals with about 300 beds or more will have a neurologist and neurosurgeon on staff. Patients in smaller institutions that do not have a neurologist should probably be referred to one that does, at least for the more complex parts of the diagnostic work-up and treatment. Most neurosurgeons are associated with several hospitals and perform the more complex procedures at the larger institutions, often hospitals with neurology and neurosurgery teaching programs.

After the patient's medical history has been obtained and a general physical examination performed, a neurological examination will be carried out. This examination, which may appear odd and even absurd, involves testing the different modes of sensation and awareness, coordination and intellectual function. For example, we normally know where a finger is or the direction in which a foot is pointing without even looking. During the test, a patient may be asked to bring the two index fingers together without looking or to walk forward or backward with eyes closed. The actual actions requested of the patient—walking heel-to-toe, rotating the hands as quickly as possible, looking up and down, responding to pinpricks, feeling tuning forks vibrate, and answering simple questions—are all calculated to give the examining physician an idea of the state of the entire nervous system. This examination, when performed by an experienced neurologist, can pick up very small abnormalities or defects that the patient and family may not yet be aware of.

Sometimes metastasis to the brain is the first sign of an undetected cancer elsewhere in the body. The general physical and laboratory examination should pay special attention to determining whether there is a hidden cancer elsewhere in the body, especially one that has a high probability of early metastases to the brain. The breasts in women, testicles in men, kidneys in both, and lungs in smokers deserve special attention. Much more common, however, is the development of metastatic brain cancer in the patient who has earlier undergone treatment for cancer in another organ. In fact, 80 percent of all cases of metastatic brain cancer fall into this category; only 20 percent involve previously undiagnosed cancers.

New imaging techniques that enable a doctor to "see" inner structures of the brain without resorting to surgery have revolutioned diagnostic neurology. The neuroradiologist, a specialist in imaging the brain, is now a key member of the diagnostic team. CT scans are almost routine in diagnosing brain tumors, but many older tests, such as electroencephalograms (EEGs), cerebral arteriograms, and pneumoencephalograms still may be valuable. Eventually magnetic resonance imaging (MRI), a still-experimental technique that produces images without ionizing radiation, may be even more useful than CT scanning in giving physicians enough information about the location, size, and number of masses within the head.

Cerebral angiography, which entails injecting a dye into the carotid artery and then taking X rays to define the extent of the mass by outlining abnormal blood vessels feeding it, is generally reserved for patients for whom precise surgical planning is required. There is some risk involved in injecting the dye into the cerebral circulation.

Pneumoencephalography, the injection of air into the ventricles, the cavities of the brain normally occupied by spinal fluid, is now rarely performed, and is reserved for small tumors of the pituitary and pineal glands as well as investigating obstruction in the flow of spinal fluid. This examination can be highly uncomfortable and often produces severe nausea and vomiting, and has largely been replaced by CT scanning.

Radionuclide scanning is useful to distinguish a stroke from tumor, but is not a substitute for a CT scan if definite information is required. EEGs, which are generally interpreted by the neurologists, show abnormal electrical waves and can demonstrate a tendency toward seizures.

Another test that is frequently required in diagnosing a neurological problem is a spinal tap or lumbar puncture. Many people needlessly fear this test because they have heard it is dangerous or painful. Both are exaggerations: there is little or no discomfort. The test takes about fifteen minutes from start to finish, can be performed on an outpatient basis or at the patient's bedside, and it involves very little risk except in unusual circumstances. To do a spinal tap, a thin, hollow needle is inserted between two vertebrae in the lower back (Figure 22). A small amount of spinal fluid is withdrawn and sent to the laboratory for analysis. Increased protein, evidence of blood, or abnormal cells suggests the presence of a tumor. Sometimes a headache may occur after a spinal tap, but this usually can be avoided by lying in bed for a few hours after the procedure.

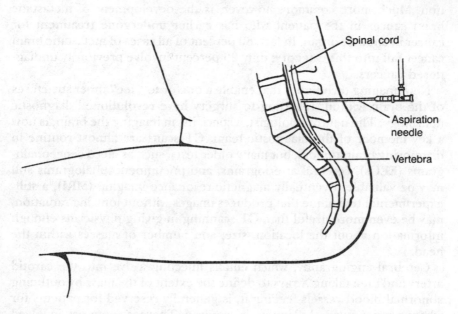

Figure 22 Spinal tap/lumbar puncture.

A spinal tap can be hazardous if there is increased intracranial pressure because of tumor mass. In this instance, a sudden reduction of pressure because of a spinal tap can cause a rapid shift of brain structures with serious, even fatal, consequences. But most brain tumors give evidence of their presence long before they are large enough to make a spinal tap unsafe. In any event, CT scanning has reduced the need for many spinal taps, and like any invasive procedure, the test should be performed only if the information to be gained will significantly alter the treatment plan.

A biopsy is not usually performed, even though there may be neurological symptoms and an identifiable mass. (An exception might be to diagnose diffuse or degenerative neurological disorders, such as multiple sclerosis or Alzheimer's disease.) Instead, neurosurgery may be planned, at which time a definitive diagnosis of whether the tumor is benign or cancerous is made and treatment is carried out. This might range from complete removal of the mass and a cure, to reduction in tumor mass and relief of the intracranial pressure. Neurosurgery probably will not be advised for metastatic disease or for patients whose general medical condition does not indicate a good outcome.

TREATMENT

Surgery, radiation therapy, and chemotherapy all may be employed in the treatment of a brain tumor. Surgery is almost always needed to establish the particular cell type of the tumor and to achieve a cure or as much relief of symptoms as possible. This may be followed by radiation therapy or chemotherapy.

Surgery

To gain access to and operate on the brain, it is necessary to remove a portion of the skull. Since the scar is usually placed under the hairline or in an unobtrusive place and the bone flap is returned to its original site and wired firmly to the adjacent bone, the final appearance of most patients after surgery is unaffected.

The total length of time required for the operation is four to eight hours, depending on the complexity of the procedure. Although CT scans and other tests reveal a good deal about the brain, the neurosurgeon does not know exactly what to expect before the actual operation. In about 15 percent of patients, the tumor will be a metastasis from elsewhere in the body. How much of the growth can be removed without unacceptable damage to nearby structures can be determined only at the time of the operation. Areas of the brain that control speech, vision, and movement are more important for a satisfactory postoperative quality of life than the "silent" areas of the frontal lobes. There is still a degree of unpredictability in some tumors as to what the postoperative result will be. If total removal is impossible, the neurosurgeon will still remove as much of the tumor as possible. Removal of even a small amount of tumor can greatly improve a patient's quality and length of life because of relief of the mass effect. Reduction of pressure within the skull also gives the treatment team valuable time in which to plan additional approaches to treatment.

Some benign tumors, such as meningiomas, can be cured only by total surgical removal. If this is impossible, partial removal is nonetheless greatly beneficial and a repeat procedure can be attempted later to reduce the bulk of the tumor again.

Surgeons also perform shunting procedures to divert the flow of cerebrospinal fluid from blocked pathways. The goal of shunting and decompression may be short-term relief of pressure or long-term control of symptoms. Sometimes the coverings of the brain are simply left open beneath the skull and scalp to let the fluid travel elsewhere in the body. If long-term survival is expected, tubes may be implanted to shunt the fluid from the cerebral ventricles to locations such as the abdominal or chest cavities. Shunting by tiny pumps placed near the body surface and activated by finger pressure is also performed. The technique of shunting has been of great benefit especially in children born with congenital defects that cause hydrocephalus. There are potential complications, such as blockage and infection, but neurosurgeons have become adept at dealing with them. Shunt replacement is a common procedure in any large neurosurgical unit.

Radiation Therapy

Radiation therapy is effective in many cases of primary brain tumors as well as in patients with metastatic tumors originating in the lung and breast. From 4,500 to 8,000 rads are delivered from "ports" on opposite sides of the skull directed at the tumor and suspicious areas by computerized methods. In most institutions this radiation dose is administered over a fifteen-to-thirty-day period, on an outpatient basis when possible. The benefits from radiation therapy are concentrated in the first year with about 70 percent achieving relief of symptoms and an improved quality of life, even though survival may not be prolonged.

During radiation therapy there may be loss of hair, fatigue, and other relatively minor although personally distressing complications. (See Chapter 8, "Radiation Therapy," and Chapter 10, "Coping with Problems Related to Cancer and Cancer Treatment.")

The major complications of radiation therapy to the brain usually appear eighteen to twenty-four months after a total dosage of 6,000 rads or more. The radiation may damage brain cells and arteries, causing the formation of diffuse scar tissue. The consequences depend upon the areas of the brain irradiated. Paralysis or movement problems may develop if the spinal cord or the movement centers in the brain are irradiated. Intellectual decline may occur if the cerebral hemispheres are diffusely exposed. The prolonged survival of brain tumor patients has increased the incidence of radiation complications. Nevertheless, the benefit far outweighs the risk. There is little in the way of alternatives. Slow neutron and alpha particle rays, which have little effect on most brain tumors, have been used with considerable success in benign pituitary tumors without producing diffuse radiation damage, perhaps because of precise targeting.

Chemotherapy

Chemotherapy has been of small benefit to brain tumor patients. Many of the anticancer drugs do not cross the blood-brain barrier in sufficient amounts to destroy cancer cells. Injection of anticancer drugs directly into the spinal fluid, occasionally by utilizing an implanted reservoir mechanism, may be used in academic institutions.

Chemotherapy following surgery and radiation therapy has prolonged survival in some studies, but the true benefit does not seem to be substantial. Chemotherapy is largely ineffective against most metastatic brain tumors, with the possible exception of those arising from testicular cancer. Spread of a metastatic tumor over the surface of the brain and its linings, meningeal carcinomatosis, has been treated with some success by a combination of radiation therapy and chemotherapy. The anticancer drugs used most often in brain cancer are BCNU (carmustine), methotrexate, hydroxyurea, and procarbazine.

There are, however, a number of other drugs that are important in the overall treatment of brain cancer. Both corticosteroids and anticonvulsant drugs play a central role. Steroids may be given to rapidly reduce the swelling and buildup of fluid surrounding both primary and metastatic brain tumors. The benefit from the reduction of the mass effect generally, as well as the improvement in function, can be striking. It is often seen within twelve to twenty-four hours and may return speech, thought processes, and movement to normal, at least temporarily. Since tumor growth is not slowed by steroids, the symptoms may reappear as the growth increases. But even partial relief can be significant. Care should be taken to avoid sudden withdrawal of the steroids, since this can cause a rapid return of edema. Intracranial pressure mounts and symptoms quickly return, often with evidence of dangerous shifts.

Steroids also may be given to suppress brain swelling after surgery and radiation. They are also effective in giving the neurologist and neurosurgeon time to plan therapy without the immediate need to surgically reduce the pressure within the cranial cavity. Although steroids have a number of serious side effects, such as thinning of the bones, increased susceptibility to infections, mental changes and others, the benefits outweigh the complications when dealing with brain cancer.

Depending on the tumor's specific type and location, between 20 and 70 percent of brain tumor patients will have seizures at some point. The seizures are usually the grand mal type, which begin in one place and spread quickly to involve the entire body. Even if a patient has not had a seizure, Dilantin or phenobarbital, the two most commonly used anticonvulsant drugs, are given routinely on a preventive basis. They control the seizure problem almost without side effects. Stopping or reducing the dosage of anticonvulsant medication is not advised, since this can precipitate the very problem the drugs prevent.

TYPES OF BRAIN CANCERS

Until now, we have concentrated on giving an overview of brain tumors, both benign and cancerous, because they have many common characteristics and problems. If the tumor turns out to be cancerous, it will be further classified by its specific cell type (Table 15). These include:

Table 15
TYPES OF BRAIN TUMORS

I PRIMARY TUMORS	II METASTATIC TUMORS
Gliomas	Metastatic carcinomas
Glioblastoma multiforme	Meningeal carcinomatosis
Astrocytoma	
Ependymoma	
Medulloblastoma	
Oligodendrocytoma	
Acoustic neuroma	
Meningiomas	
Benign pituitary adenomas	
Craniopharyngiomas	

Gliomas. This is the largest group of primary brain cancers, accounting for about 45 percent of all cancers arising from brain cells. They have been subdivided into several major categories, according to cell type and clinical behavior.

Glioblastoma multiforme accounts for approximately 25 percent of all primary brain tumors and so constitutes more than half of all gliomas. It is considered the most malignant of all brain cancers and steadily infiltrates surrounding tissue. Cancers of this group are graded according to their microscopic appearance from I (least aggressive) to IV (most aggressive). Typical patients with this cancer are middle-aged. Over 30 percent have convulsions which, together with early signs of widespread brain disturbance, are the major symptoms when the patient is first seen by a physician. Surgery is performed as soon as possible, both to relieve symptoms and to make certain that the problem is not potentially curable. Only extremely high-risk patients with evident incurable disease will be advised to forgo surgery.

The cancer cannot be removed entirely, but decompression of the intracranial pressure and reduction of tumor bulk relieve symptoms and increase survival. Postsurgery radiation and chemotherapy, principally with BCNU, have proved useful in some patients. Advances in surgical technique have improved the results for glioblastoma patients, although 5 percent will die within the postoperative period. About 50 percent of patients will live for six to twelve months after surgery. A small number are still functioning at an acceptable level after two years. Bleeding, tumor growth, and increasing intracranial pressure complicate the later stages of disease.

Astrocytoma, ependymoma, medulloblastoma, and oligodendrocytoma. All of these cancers are members of the glioma group and are named for the type of cells or parts of the brain from which they originate. They generally are not as aggressive as glioblastomas and long-term survival is not uncommon. Astrocytomas account for 10 percent of all primary brain tumors; each of the others accounts for 4 to 5 percent.

Astrocytomas have a relatively low degree of malignancy, although after many years some undergo transformation into a more aggressive form. Astrocytomas often produce movement disorders in children, which often can be cured by total removal of the tumor. Children recover surprisingly well from brain surgery, since another part of the brain seems to compensate for the portion that had to be removed. Most astrocytoma patients are adults who first notice minor vague symptoms that may remain undiagnosed for years. Unexplained headaches, thought disorders, and seizures may occur, but eventually symptoms progress to the point where the cancer becomes more evident. An uncommon site of origin of this cancer is the optic nerve. CT scanning is crucial, especially since the results of all other neurological testing may appear normal in the early stages of the disease.

Astrocytoma is treated by surgery followed by radiation. Chemotherapy is of no benefit. Survival depends on the location of the cancer and its degree of malignancy. Survivals of up to ten years after the onset of symptoms are common, with the average at five to six years. Repeated surgery to remove slowly enlarging tumors has extended survival in some patients.

Oligodendrocytomas are similar to astrocytomas, although seizures are unusual with this soft, slow-growing cancer. Survival averages four to five years. Surgery is the definitive method of both diagnosis and treatment. Transformation into a more malignant grade of cell type can occur with this cancer.

Medulloblastoma commonly occurs in children and only rarely in adults. The tumor is fast-growing, and since it begins in the lower brain near vital structures and cerebrospinal fluid channels, symptoms are evident early in the course of disease. The initial symptoms are apathy, headache, unexplained vomiting; these are soon followed by evident neurologic signs, particularly difficulty in walking. Papilledema—a swelling of the optic nerve—is easily seen in most children with medulloblastoma. Treatment entails surgery followed by radiation—a course that achieves five-year survival in most patients. Chemotherapy may be a useful adjunctive measure. Shunting procedures to relieve the pressure buildup caused by blockage to the flow of cerebrospinal fluid are often required.

Ependymomas originate in the linings of the ventricles, the spaces in the brain that produce and contain the cerebrospinal fluid. These cancers are most common in children and young adults. The initial symptoms are related to increased intracranial pressure and hydrocephalus. A typical location for ependymoma is the fourth ventricle, one of the narrowest and most easily blocked channels. Surgery is the major treatment. Ependymomas vary in their degree of malignancy, but the average survival after surgery is ten years for low-grade cancers. Postoperative radiation appears to be of some benefit, and shunting procedures relieve intracranial pressure. The tumor can later recur in a more invasive form, but most patients do well for a long period of time.

Metastatic carcinomas. These cancers arise elsewhere in the body and behave very much like glioblastoma except that 80 percent of patients are known to have a cancer elsewhere. The clinical picture depends upon whether the widespread manifestations of the disease are more evident than the neurological problem. In most patients the discovery of a brain metastasis does not meaningfully affect the treatment or outcome of the primary malignancy. Meningeal carcinomatosis, the spread of a metastatic cancer over the surfaces of the brain, results in confusion and a variety of neurological symptoms. It is not easily diagnosed unless abnormal cells are found during analysis of spinal fluid.

A few anomalous neurological syndromes can occur in the presence of carcinomas without actual invasion of the nervous system. These distant manifestations of cancer, thought to operate on a chemical basis, can appear as brain degeneration leading to dementia, diffuse damage to the cerebellum with movement disorders, and problems in muscular strength that vaguely resemble multiple sclerosis or myasthenia gravis. The incidence of spread to the central nervous system is highest in melanoma, occurring in 75 percent of all patients with this skin cancer. Cancers of the lung, breast, kidney, mouth, thyroid, intestines, and gynecologic system metastasize to the brain, in order of declining frequency, in 25 to 50 percent of patients. Surgical removal of single metastases may be best in a few patients. For most, however, radiation and corticosteroids remain the best course.

Acoustic neuroma. These are by far the most common of several tumors that originate in the specialized cells that form the protective sheaths of nerve fibers. Acoustic neuroma is benign, but its steady growth puts pressure on and deforms adjacent brain structures, affecting walking, movement, and balance. Because it involves the nerve leading from the inner part to the brain, deafness, ringing in the ear, dizziness, and vertigo occur, if only to a mild degree, in almost every case.

Typically, acoustic neuroma is seen most often in middle-aged women. Testing of hearing and CT scanning confirm the diagnosis, although sometimes an acoustic neuroma is strongly suspected but cannot be proved. Repeated testing and close observation are in order for such patients. A spinal tap may be safely performed if there are no signs of increased intracranial pressure. Increased protein in the fluid may help confirm the diagnosis. Surgery is the sole method of treatment and may be performed by a specialist in ear surgery if studies indicate that growth has not extended beyond the acoustic nerve. A neurosurgeon may be more appropriate for larger tumors. The operative incision and areas of bone removed are quite small. Over 75 percent of patients are cured, especially those with tumors under one inch in diameter with no evidence of neurological damage to nearby brain tissue. Recurrence can be treated by repeat surgery in some patients.

Meningiomas. These tumors arise from the meninges, the fibrous tissues that cover the brain's surface on the spinal cord. These tissues form a protective covering and make up part of the envelope containing the cerebrospinal fluid. Meningioma accounts for 15 percent of all primary brain tumors. It is benign except for a few unusual instances that undergo late malignant transformation. Meningiomas are more common in women than men and their incidence rises steadily with age, beginning in middle adulthood. Some neurologists have suggested a possible connection between head injury and meningioma, but most experts disagree with this. Meningioma can develop from the meningeal layers anywhere, but the most common locations are over the surface of the brain and near the bone structures at its base.

The tumors, which are grayish and firm, cause displacement of normal brain structures. Seizures are common. Skull X rays may show evidence of erosion of bone, presumably because of pressure from the growth beneath. Meningiomas enlarge slowly and can cause a confusing array of symptoms. Evaluation by spinal tap is generally safe and usually shows elevated protein. Angiography and CT scanning produce characteristic images that aid in diagnosis. Surgery is the mainstay of therapy, and the neurosurgeon's skill is often crucial because cure depends on total removal. Preoperative radiation may be used to reduce the rich blood supply typical of meningiomas and to reduce the problem of bleeding during surgery. Radiation or repeat surgery are indicated for recurrent growth. Chemotherapy is ineffective.

Benign pituitary adenomas. These tumors, which are benign, make up 7 to 10 percent of primary brain tumors. They appear in middle age, more often in women than men. Problems caused by these growths are related to endocrine abnormalities caused by either reduced or excessive levels of hormones controlled by the pituitary gland. This gland, which is located near the base of the brain, secretes a number of hormones that have an effect upon other endocrine glands. It is often referred to as the master endocrine gland, because its hormones are instrumental both in growth and metabolism and in controlling other endocrine glands.

The tumor's encroachment on adjacent structures, particularly the optic nerve, is common. Slow enlargement of these tumors erodes the delicate bony structures that surround the normal gland. X rays of the skull, with particular attention to the pituitary area, and precise examination of the patient's field of vision are the key diagnostic tests for tumors that have attained moderate size. CT scans are also useful, as are blood hormonal studies. Hormonal changes are often present and can occur before any other manifestation of abnormality in the size of the pituitary gland. Spinal puncture is not done because it usually does not contribute any relevant findings.

Symptoms are related to hormonal imbalances caused by the tumor, and they point to the tumor's particular cell type. Acromegaly (or gigantism) indicates high levels of growth hormones, Cushing's disease points to excessive steroid hormones, and inappropriate production of breast milk indicates high prolactin levels. Enlargement of the gland by a tumor of one cell type can result in oversecretion of its hormone and undersecretion of others.

Pituitary tumors can extend outside its protective cavity (the sella) and sometimes enlarge rapidly because of bleeding within the body of the tumor. On the other hand, many small pituitary growths that produce little or no abnormality in hormonal function are never diagnosed, remaining silent forever.

Treatment of pituitary adenomas is complex. The oversecretion of some hormones must be controlled while appropriate replacement therapy of undersecreted hormones must be instituted. For example, suppression of ACTH (adrenocortico-stimulating hormone) and TSH (thyroid-stimulating hormone) will result in dangerously low levels of steroids and thyroid hormone respectively. Accurate laboratory testing is widely available and replacement programs have been well defined. Surgical treatment, either via the side of the skull or through the back of the nose, may be performed to stop oversecretion of certain hormones and to prevent blindness from fast-growing tumors. Lifelong replacement therapy of thyroid, corticosteroid, and perhaps gonadal hormones is almost always needed after surgery. Radiation therapy is an alternative to surgery; it produces a slower result with some chance of treatment failure, but avoids the risk of surgery. Radiation therapy may be the treatment of choice for small, nonsecreting tumors but is not advisable for tumors that have grown outside the normal confines of the pituitary.

Craniopharyngiomas. These are benign tumors that occur in the area of the pituitary but they do not have the ability to secrete hormones. These tumors, which account for about 5 percent of primary brain tumors, commonly appear during childhood and are thought to be remnants of structures that inappropriately remained in place after embryonic development. It causes symptoms by putting pressure on the pituitary gland and by extending into adjacent areas.

Most craniopharyngiomas can be cured by neurosurgery. Blockage of flow of the cerebrospinal fluid may require shunting.

Tumors of the pineal gland. Four different kinds of benign tumors are known to develop in the pineal gland, a tiny structure that is located near the center of the brain, but they are quite rare, accounting for less than one percent of all brain tumors. These rare growths develop in children and young adults causing movement disorders and mental deterioration. Because the pineal gland is very near the nerve center that controls upward movement of the eyes, patients with this disease often are unable to look up. Surgery, although technically difficult because of the tumor's relatively inaccessible location, is now more frequently successful in achieving cure. Although the pineal gland is thought to act as a biological clock and may exert some influence over other glands, its removal has no identifiable effect. Radiation is effective in shrinking these tumors and retarding their growth. Shunting may be necessary.

Tumors of the spinal cord. The spinal cord, which is encased in the vertebral column, may be afflicted by benign, cancerous or metastatic tumors. All create symptoms by compressing the spinal cord or by pressing on nerve roots as they leave the spinal cord.

Pain, loss of sensation, paralysis, and incontinence are characteristic symptoms, which are related to the position of the tumor along the length of the cord. Most spinal cord tumors grow slowly, but rapid progression of symptoms—possibly because of interference in the local blood supply —is a neurosurgical emergency that, unless treated, can lead to permanent loss of function below the tumor within twelve to twenty-four hours.

The diagnostic investigation of cord tumors is straightforward. It includes a history and physical examination, X rays of the spine, and CT scans. Lumbar puncture is useful but should be performed at the time of a myelogram, a contrast study in which an opaque iodine compound is injected into the spinal fluid to outline the tumor on X-ray films.

Surgery and radiation are the only treatment options. About 25 percent of cord tumors are metastatic in origin and both radiation therapy and surgery are very useful in preventing paralysis and incontinence. Advances in surgery, including microsurgery and the use of lasers and electric coagulation, have increased the percentage of patients who achieve satisfactory results, a fact of special importance since about 35 percent of spinal cord tumors are benign and potentially curable.

Radiation therapy is appropriate if time is not of immediate concern and the diagnosis is known. Steroids are administered to reduce the edema and swelling that normally occur around central nervous system tumors.

About 15 percent of spinal cord tumors are meningiomas, affecting the protective covering of the cord. Surgery can achieve excellent results if the more important nerve tracks that are closely amassed within the cord can be preserved. Patients with spinal cord gliomas do poorly while those with metastases from myeloma or lymphoma tend to follow a clinical course that reflects the overall status of their disease. Intense radiation therapy can cause problems eighteen to twenty-four months after its administration, a consideration of importance if long-term survival is expected.

SUMMING UP

Brain tumors carry a number of problems that are not found in most other cancers. Since they affect our center of intelligence and emotions, most patients and their families are understandably reluctant to accept a diagnosis of brain tumors. In many instances a benign tumor can be just as serious as a cancerous one—something that is not true with other types of cancer. Primary brain tumors are relatively rare, but the brain is a common site of metastases of cancers arising elsewhere in the body. Many of the symptoms of early brain tumors are subtle and may go unnoticed until there is a buildup of intracranial fluid and serious encroachment on vital brain structures. While most primary brain cancers are not curable, surgery usually can relieve symptoms and prolong life. Many benign tumors, if detected in an early stage, can be cured by surgical removal without causing major residual damage.

17

Breast Cancer

EDWARD F. SCANLON, M.D.,
AND PHILIP STRAX, M.D.

INTRODUCTION

The breast is the most common site of cancer in American women today, accounting for more than one quarter of all cancer cases in women. With about 115,000 new cases each year, one out of every eleven women will develop breast cancer at some time in her life. In 1985 about 38,000 women died of breast cancer. Although the number of new cases of breast cancer has risen over the last two decades, the mortality rate has not changed markedly in the last fifty years. This does not mean, however, that there have not been considerable advances in the diagnosis and treatment of breast cancer. Regular breast self-examination and periodic mammography have become important tools in the early detection of breast cancer, while it is in its most curable stage. Better understanding of the different types of breast cancer has led to a more individualized approach to treatment, which now may include a combination of therapies.

There is also increased emphasis today on the quality of life following treatment of breast cancer. Only a few years ago, little attention was paid to the emotional aspects of breast cancer; indeed, many women went to great lengths to hide the fact that they had been treated for it. This began to change in the 1970s when a number of prominent women—Betty Ford, Margaretta (Happy) Rockefeller, Marvella Bayh, Betty Rollin, among others—talked publicly about their struggles with breast cancer. Their openness encouraged other women to share their experiences with the disease, and has helped remove much of the stigma so wrongly associated with breast cancer in the past.

As women are becoming better informed about the disease, they are participating more in decisions regarding their treatment. Volunteer organizations, particularly the American Cancer Society's Reach to Recovery program, have taken on new importance in helping women and their loved ones cope with the problems, both emotional and physical, associated with breast cancer. Breast reconstruction has become an increasingly important aspect of overall treatment, an important factor for women who fear the disfigurement of a mastectomy.

The broadened treatment options, the deep-seated emotional and cultural factors surrounding breast surgery, and the increased patient participation in treatment decisions make this one of the most controversial areas of cancer therapy. No longer is there a single "best" approach that applies to all women with breast cancer. Even the experts are not in full agreement as to how breast cancer should be treated. In this chapter, authorities representing different aspects of breast cancer diagnosis and treatment have collaborated to present an objective discussion of current approaches to breast cancer. Not all physicians and patients may agree with their viewpoints, as is to be expected in any area of medicine in which definitive treatment protocols are still being developed.

WHO GETS BREAST CANCER?

The cause of breast cancer remains unknown, and, like other cancers, it is thought to develop in response to a number of interrelated factors. The most common factors that increase the risk of breast cancer include:

• Sex of the person. Breast cancer is overwhelmingly a disease of women; less than one percent of cases develop in men.

• Increasing age. Most breast cancer occurs following menopause; two thirds of all cases develop in women over the age of fifty. The disease is rare in women under the age of thirty; the incidence rises sharply in the early forties, leveling off at about age forty-five and then increasing again after age fifty-five.

• Family history. Women whose first-degree relatives—mothers or sisters—have had breast cancer are two to three times more likely to develop breast cancer; the risk is even greater if these relatives have had cancer in both breasts or developed it before menopause.

• Previous breast cancer. Women who have had cancer in one breast have an increased risk of its developing in the other one. An American Cancer Society analysis has found that 5 to 10 percent of women who have had cancer in one breast will eventually have it in both.

These are the major risk factors associated with breast cancer, but a number of other circumstances have been identified that appear to increase its incidence to varying degrees. These include:

• Diet. A high-fat diet has been linked to an increased risk of breast cancer. Obesity also appears to increase the risk.

• Race or national origin. Breast cancer is more common among women of North American or northern European origin than among women in Asian and African countries. Among Americans, the disease is almost twice as common in women of the higher social and economic classes. Some experts now believe these differences may be related more to diet than to racial background. For example, there is a low incidence of breast cancer in Japan, where the diet is very low in animal fat. However, first-generation Japanese-American women in San Francisco have about twice the breast cancer incidence of their cousins in Japan.

• Menstrual history. A long menstrual history—early onset of menstruation plus late menopause—increases the risk, while early menopause, either natural or artificial, decreases it.

• Pregnancy. The risk of breast cancer is higher among women who have never had a baby or whose first full-term pregnancy occurred after the age of 30.

• Hormonal factors. The relationship of hormones to breast cancer is unclear. Some breast cancers are clearly estrogen-dependent while others are not, but there is no convincing evidence that either birth control pills or estrogen supplements cause breast cancer. The possible link between breast cancer and oral contraceptives has been investigated for years, with widely contradictory results. Some studies have found a higher incidence of breast cancer for long-term pill users (more than two to four years) who also have benign breast disease. Consequently the Food and Drug Administration now requires a notice of this information in each package of oral contraceptives.

Estrogen preparations used for replacement hormone therapy during menopause also carry an FDA-mandated warning regarding breast-cancer risk. As with oral contraceptives, a link between estrogen replacement therapy and breast cancer is suspected by some scientists, but has not been proved.

Another hormonal drug linked to an increased risk of breast cancer is diethylstilbestrol, or DES. This drug was used in the late 1940s and through the 1960s to prevent miscarriage. Some recent studies have found an increased incidence of breast cancer among the women who took it; consequently they are now advised to avoid other estrogen preparations and to take extra care in breast self-examination and checkups.

Many folk beliefs about the origin of breast cancer have no basis in fact. It is not true, for example, that an injury to the breast can cause cancer. Sexual stimulation is unrelated to breast cancer, and breast feeding does not seem to alter the risk. Certain viruses can cause breast cancer in some strains of mice, but there is no evidence of a viral cause for human breast cancer; in any event, it is not contagious.

Aside from avoiding a high-fat diet and obesity, at this time there do not seem to be any lifestyle modifications that markedly reduce the risk of breast cancer. Thus early detection and treatment remains the best approach to the disease.

THE STRUCTURE OF THE BREAST

For a better understanding of all aspects of breast care, women should know the basics of breast anatomy and function (Figure 23). Throughout the ages, the female breast has been linked with sensuality and sexual attractiveness. In almost all cultures, men are sexually attracted by the female breast. From puberty onward, women are deeply concerned about their breasts; their size and shape are often equated with femininity and physical attractiveness. While the breast is not vital to reproduction, and breast size is unrelated to sexual responsiveness, myths regarding both persist. It is little wonder that women fear breast cancer and mastectomy more than other forms of the disease. For example, lung cancer, which now kills more women each year than breast cancer does, is not regarded with the same sense of dread.

The healthy breast of a mature woman is composed mostly of fat and glandular tissue. Its primary function is to produce milk to feed a newborn infant. To envision the internal milk-producing apparatus of a breast, think of a bunch of grapes. The grapes represent the clusters of milk-secreting glands (lobules), while the stems represent the hollow ducts that carry the milk from the glands to the nipple. These lobules and ducts are immersed in fatty tissue, which gives the breast its contour and softness. The breast itself has no muscles, but lies on top of the pectoralis major, a large muscle which stretches from the breastbone and collarbone to an attachment point on the shoulder. The breast is held together by fibrous tissue called Cooper's ligaments.

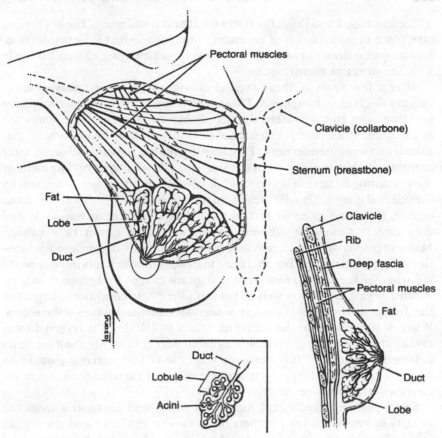

Figure 23 Anatomy of the normal breast.

A network of blood vessels brings nutrients and hormones to the breast tissue. Increased blood flow during the menstrual cycle, pregnancy, and sexual stimulation causes the blood vessels to become engorged. Overall variation in breast size depends on the amount of fat surrounding and protecting the internal structures of the breasts.

The majority of breast cancers are initially detected by the women themselves who discover the presence of a suspicious lump. Although discovering a lump can be alarming—so much so that many women delay seeing a doctor, fearing they will only have their worst suspicions confirmed—the fact is that about four out of five turn out to be benign cysts or other harmless conditions. Each month the breast goes through cyclical changes as it responds to fluctuating hormone levels. Stimulated by estrogen and then progesterone, the breasts become somewhat engorged with extra blood and fluid; the ducts swell and proliferate. These changes take place in anticipation of pregnancy and subsequent milk production. If conception does not take place, the swelling and other changes subside with the onset of menstruation.

After a few years of these cyclical changes, the breasts may develop varying degrees of lumpiness. These lumps are made up of fibrous tissue and tiny cysts and are referred to as fibrocystic changes. The lumps are most prominent in the premenstrual period, and they may produce considerable breast tenderness. Fibrocystic change usually subsides after menopause, but may persist in women who take estrogen replacement or who continue to have relatively high levels of sex hormones produced by the adrenal glands. Usually these benign lumps can be distinguished from cancer; they tend to come and go according to the menstrual cycle and they have a somewhat different feel from a true tumor or a cancer. Mammography and aspiration may be helpful in distinguishing fibrocystic change from cancer. But there are instances in which it is impossible to tell whether the lump is benign or malignant except by a surgical biopsy.

Most breast cancer, as well as benign fibrocystic conditions, begins in the lining of the milk ducts, or sometimes in the lobules themselves. When it is confined to the inside of a duct or lobule, it is referred to as carcinoma *in situ*—a noninvasive stage that may remain dormant for years before spreading. In this dormant stage, it is 100 percent curable by surgical removal. Also, a certain percentage of carcinoma *in situ* never develops into invasive cancer.

Small vessels called lymphatics drain fluids and impurities from the breasts in two ways: lymph ducts between the shoulder and the nipple lead to lymph nodes in the armpits; lymph ducts between the nipples lead to nodes by the breastbone, under the ribs (Figure 24). The lymphatic system is a key component of the body's immune system. The lymphatic fluid contains white blood cells—lymphocytes—which are instrumental in the production of antibodies. All body cells are bathed by lymph fluid, which is transported through the body by the lymphatic vessels. The lymph nodes contain high concentrations of white blood cells, and these nodes function as filters for foreign substances—bacteria, viruses, tumor cells and so forth. This is why the lymph ducts and nodes are a common route for the spread of breast cancer. The cancer also may spread to other parts of the body via the bloodstream.

Breast development is one of the physical changes that signal the onset of puberty. Growth of the breasts and other aspects of sexual maturity are controlled by the hormonal changes that occur during puberty. Development begins with enlargement and darkening of the areola—the tissue surrounding the nipple—followed by enlargement of the breast. Frequently one breast will begin developing before the other, or the size will be uneven. Although this often is a concern to both the girl and her

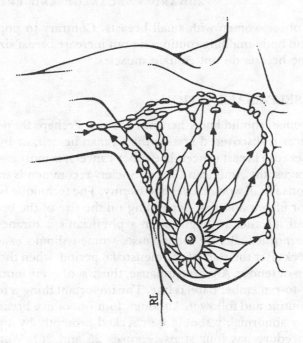

Figure 24 Lymphatic drainage of the breast.

parents, uneven breast development is very common, and unless a breast fails to develop completely it is seldom cause for worry.

Breast appearance varies greatly from woman to woman. Size, shape, and prominence of nipples, areola, and Montgomery glands (the sebaceous glands in the areola that sometimes look like small pimples) all are highly individualistic. Breast appearance changes at different stages of a woman's life. During pregnancy, for example, the areola darkens, the nipples may become more prominent, and the breast enlarges. In the premenstrual phase of the monthly cycle, many women experience an increase in breast "lumpiness" and size; the breasts also may be tender or even painful. During sexual arousal or exposure to cold the nipples may become erect. Nipple size and appearance also vary; in some women the nipples may be flat or even inverted; in others they may be very prominent or have a mulberry shape. All these variations are normal; each woman should become familiar with her own breasts and know how they change at different times in her monthly cycle.

Breasts also change with age. After menopause, breast tissue becomes less dense as the milk glands and ducts shrink, with a resulting reduction in size. Some sagging also may occur. Weight gain or loss can alter breast size, although many thin women are large-breasted and, conversely, there are many obese women with small breasts. Contrary to popular belief, exercise and body-building routines do not increase breast size, primarily because the breasts do not contain muscles.

BREAST SELF-EXAMINATION

Every woman should know her own breasts. Perhaps 90 percent of all breast cancer is discovered first by the woman herself, or by her sexual partner. Because breast cancer, like other cancers, is most easily cured in its early stages, the American Cancer Society recommends monthly self-examinations for all women over age twenty. The technique is simple and takes ten or fifteen minutes, depending on the size of the breasts. Some women find it easier to begin after a physician's assurance that their breasts are normal. Before menopause, women should examine themselves a week after the start of the menstrual period, when the breasts are not swollen or tender. After menopause, the first of every month (or some other easy-to-remember date) is fine. The important thing is to establish a monthly routine and follow it. Although four out of five breast lumps are benign, any abnormality should be checked promptly by a physician.

The procedure has four steps (Figures 25 and 26). Women should begin by examining the surface of their wet skin in the bath or shower, using flat fingers to glide over every part of both breasts, feeling for lumps.

Second, the breasts should be examined in a mirror, both with arms raised overhead and with hands pressed down on hips to flex the chest muscles. Changes in contour, swellings, dimpling or puckering of the skin, or changes in the nipple may be danger signs. Some healthy women have inverted nipples, but nipples that suddenly turn inward may indicate cancer. A lack of symmetry—breasts that don't exactly match—is not important unless it represents a recent change.

Third, the woman should lie on her back with a pillow or folded towel under one shoulder and the arm on that side under her head. With the other hand, she should press the breast gently in circular motions, as if touching the numerals on a clock face, beginning at the outside top of the breast. (Some women find it easier to examine their breasts in vertical strips rather than in a circular manner, a variation that is acceptable.) This procedure should be repeated an inch closer to the nipple, and then another inch closer, and another, until the whole breast has been examined. A ridge of firm tissue in the lower part of the breast is normal. Attention to individual breast structure will make any change more obvious.

The last part of breast examination involves squeezing the nipple gently between thumb and index finger. Any discharge, either clear or bloody, should be checked by a physician. Scaly skin around the nipple may also be a sign of cancer and should be seen by a doctor.

The physician should not only examine the breasts of women patients on a regular basis, but ensure that each woman can do it for herself. Personal instruction seems to provide better motivation than pamphlets or audiovisual methods of teaching alone.

To summarize, although four out of five breast lumps prove to be benign, depending upon the age of the woman, biopsy is the only way to be sure. Other signs that should send a woman to her physician are dimpling and puckering, crusting around the nipple, inversion of the nipple, or nipple discharge.

ROLE OF MAMMOGRAPHY

Although monthly breast self-examination and periodic physical examination by a physician are important, most experts now agree that they are not enough. Mammography—an X-ray examination of the breast—is also an important part of early cancer detection (Figure 26). After a certain age, regular screening by mammography—X-ray examinations of the breast—should be added to the routine. The American Cancer Society now recommends that all women undergo a base-line breast X-ray examination between the ages of thirty-five and forty. Mammography should be repeated every one or two years between the ages of forty and fifty, and every year after fifty.

Some tumors of the breast can be seen on X ray before they become detectable to the fingers of the physician or the woman herself. Recent studies have found that mammography can detect many of these cancers while they are still too small to be felt. Even for women who do not have breast lumps or other suspicious signs, regular mammography is advised after the age of forty to provide a basis of comparison. Mammography can guide the surgeon in performing a biopsy. However, when the physician feels that a biopsy is indicated to rule out the presence of cancer, a normal mammogram should not dissuade him or her from doing the biopsy.

Mammography should be performed by radiological technicians and interpreted by a radiologist skilled in reading mammograms. Usually two sets of pictures are taken of each breast: a view from above with the patient seated, and a side view while she lies on her back. The patient will probably be more comfortable in a two-piece outfit with a top that can be easily removed than in a dress, but no other preparation is needed.

Historic Perspective

Mammography in the detection of breast cancer is not new; indeed, the first record of mammography dates to 1913, when a German pathologist

How to Do Breast Self-Examination

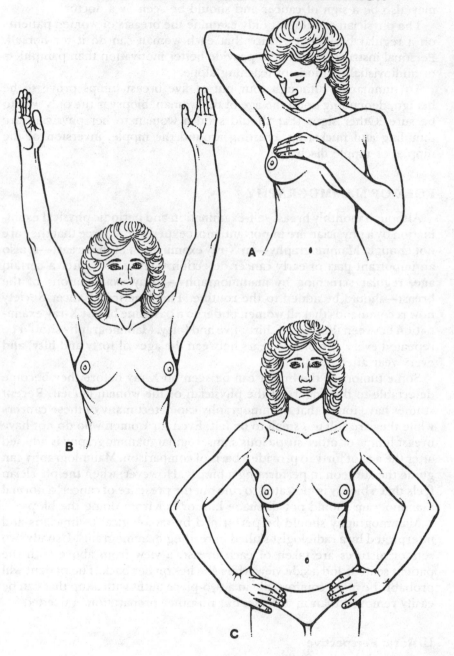

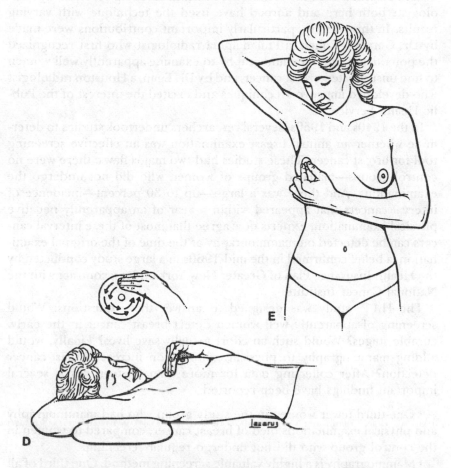

Figure 25 Breast self-examination. All women should examine their breasts each month. For menstruating women, this should be done in midcycle; for others, at a specific time each month. The three-step examination starts in the shower or tub, by carefully feeling each breast for any thickening or lumps (A). Then stand before a mirror, first with arms over head and then lowered, and look for any changes, such as puckering of the skin (B and C). Next lie down and place one arm under your head. Using the other hand, examine the entire breast, moving clockwise and from the outer portion toward the nipple (D). Repeat this procedure on the second breast, placing the opposite arm under your head. Finally, squeeze each nipple to see if there is a discharge (E). Any lump, change, discharge or other unusual finding should be checked by a doctor.

named Salomon used the technique. In the succeeding years, many radiologists both here and abroad have used the technique with varying
results. In this country, particularly important contributions were made
by Dr. Gershon-Cohen, a Philadelphia radiologist who first recognized
the potential of using mammography to examine apparently well women
to find unsuspected breast cancer, and by Dr. Egan, a Houston radiologist
who developed improved techniques and excited the interest of the Public Health Service.

In the 1940s and 1950s, several researchers undertook studies to determine whether an annual breast examination was an effective screening
tool for breast cancer. These studies had two major flaws: there were no
control groups—matched groups of women who did not undergo the
examinations. And there was a large—up to 30 percent—incidence of
interval cancers that appeared within a year of an apparently negative
physical examination. Experts now agree that most of these interval cancers can be detected on mammography at the time of the original examination, a belief confirmed in the mid-1960s in a large study conducted by
the Health Insurance Plan of Greater New York under a contract with the
National Cancer Institute.

The H.I.P. study was designed to answer these questions: Would
screening of apparently well women detect breast cancer in the early,
curable stages? Would such an effort actually save lives? Finally, would
adding mammography to physical examination increase breast-cancer
detection? After collecting data for more than thirteen years, several
important findings have been reported.

• One-third fewer women in the study group who had mammography
and physical examinations died of breast cancer, compared to women in
the control group who did not undergo regular screening.

• Mammography is a highly valuable screening method. One third of all
the cancers found were detected on X ray alone. In the course of eight
years, only three of the forty-four women whose cancers were detected by
mammography alone died.

• The screening program detected cancer in its early stages. Four fifths
of the cancers were still confined to the breast, greatly increasing chances
of long-term survival or cure.

Findings of the H.I.P. study were instrumental in the 1968 establishment
of the Guttman Breast Diagnostic Institute in New York, whose basic
objective has been to develop an approach to breast-cancer screening
that is practical, economical, and effective in detecting early breast cancer. Up to 50,000 women a year have been examined at the institute and
hundreds of early breast cancers have been detected. In addition, improved mammographic techniques have been developed that are being

used by other diagnostic facilities to make mammography safer and more accurate and economical.

The value of annual breast examinations in finding early breast cancer was conclusively shown in the Breast Cancer Detection Demonstration Project, a massive screening program undertaken in 1973 by the American Cancer Society and National Cancer Institute. The study, known as the BCDDP, recruited some 280,000 women from throughout the United States to undergo annual breast examinations for five years, with an additional five-year followup by the twenty-nine participating BCDDP centers.

The women were taught breast self-examination and were encouraged to practice it monthly between their annual checkups, which included a physical examination and mammography. (In the early years of the study, thermography was also used during the annual examination, but was discontinued in 1977 because of high false negative and high false positive rates.)

In all, 4,443 breast cancers were detected among BCDDP participants. Normally, most suspicious breast lumps are discovered by the woman herself, but in the BCDDP, about 90 percent of the cancers were found by mammography, either alone (41.6 percent) or combined with physical examination (47.3 percent), during the annual examinations. A third of these were very small—less than one centimeter in diameter and 80 percent were localized, or confined to the breast, and therefore should have a five-year survival of more than 90 percent. Mammography proved to be one of the more important factors in detecting the very small cancers—a factor that was instrumental in revised recommendations calling for mammography every one or two years for women over forty and annually after the age of fifty.

Even though the value of mammography has been clearly demonstrated by the BCDDP and the H.I.P. study, adoption of the technique as a screening tool has been controversial. In 1975 the National Cancer Institute began to reevaluate the risks of repeated X-ray exposure in mammography compared with the benefits of early detection of breast cancers. This study of the dangers of radiation was complicated by two facts: The carcinogenic results of radiation often take decades to appear and the machines used for mammography vary widely in the dose of radiation (measured in units called rads) per examination (four exposures—two of each breast). Even so, the media reported warnings by individual researchers who felt that mammography itself may increase the risk of breast cancer. Understandably, large numbers of women became concerned by the reports and turned away from mammography as a screening procedure. Marked reduction in radiation exposure has discounted those early reports, and after much public debate and further study the National Cancer Institute issued guidelines stating that X-ray machines used for mammography should deliver no more than 1 rad of radiation per mammogram. The amount necessary for a good picture varies with the machine and with the size and density of the breast. The most modern machines use as little as 0.02 rad to the middle of each breast—considerably less than the amount of radiation delivered in a conventional chest X ray. Women should ask their physicians or radiologists how much radiation they will receive before undergoing mammography. If the answer is over 1 rad per exposure, it is advisable to find another radiologist with more up-to-date equipment.

Minimizing Radiation Exposure

The increased emphasis on mammography has been accompanied by advances in the X-ray equipment and techniques used to reduce radiation exposure. For example, the senograph, developed in France, is a mammography machine with a special X-ray tube and filters. The special combinations of films and screens deliver minute amounts of radiation—a total of .02 to .03 rads to the midbreast for two views.

One special form of mammography is called xeromammography, developed by the Xerox Corporation. It produces a positive image (as opposed to a negative X-ray film) on a Xerox plate, but requires a slightly higher dose of radiation than conventional mammography. Even so, it is an excellent technique that some radiologists feel produces results that are easier to interpret.

The Examination Itself

Mammography is usually done in a radiology laboratory, diagnostic clinic, doctor's office, or hospital outpatient clinic. It takes about a half-hour to complete. Clothing and jewelry above the waist are removed, and women should avoid using talcum powder or skin creams on their breasts just prior to mammography as these may appear as suspicious signs on an X-ray film. During the actual mammographic examination, a woman is positioned so that one breast is resting on a plate above an X-ray cassette (Figure 26). A clear plastic shield may be used as a compression device to somewhat flatten the breast against the plate. Two views are taken of each breast—one from the side and the other giving a top-to-bottom view. While the woman waits, the X-ray films are developed to make sure that they are readable. They will later be interpreted by a radiologist who is experienced in reading mammographic films. In general, cysts show up as clear spots, with well-defined, regular outlines. They may be multiple and may be present in both breasts. In contrast, breast cancer usually appears as irregular, opaque areas with poorly defined edges. It should be emphasized that a mammogram only pinpoints suspicious areas; a definitive diagnosis is reached only by biopsy.

OTHER METHODS OF DETECTION

Mammography equipment and the human hand are the two most widely used tools of breast cancer detection, but neither is 100 percent

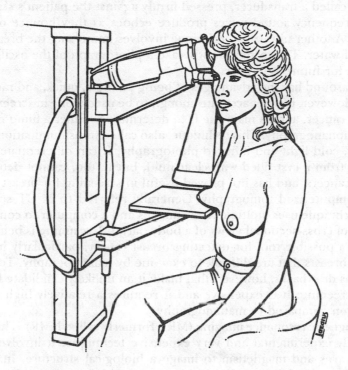

Figure 26 Mammography.

accurate. As noted earlier, very small cancers are difficult or impossible to detect by palpation. Although many of these cancers show up on a mammogram, others do not. In fact, 10 to 15 percent of palpable breast cancers (those detectable on manual examination) are not seen in a mammogram. Thus there is an ongoing search for other techniques that may further improve the chances of early breast cancer detection. These include:

• Thermography. This technique measures minute temperature variations and produces a heat map of the area photographed. Cancers are warmer than normal body tissue, because their rapid growth requires an increased blood supply.

The drawback of thermography is that it misses perhaps 30 percent of cancers, especially the small, early ones not detectable by manual examination. Also, a number of benign conditions also produce "hot" areas. Therefore thermography is not accurate enough to be used in screening.

• Ultrasound. This technique uses sound waves to differentiate solid masses from ones that contain fluid. A technician uses a microphonelike probe called a transducer, pressed firmly against the patient's skin. Very high frequency sound waves produce echoes as they bounce off body tissue. Another ultrasonic technique involves immersing the breasts in a tank of water. The technician will take a photograph of the oscilloscope screen for future reference.

Ultrasound has the advantages of being painless, quick, and radiation-free. However, it is not accurate enough to be used alone in screening for breast cancer, and its main use is to determine whether a lump is a cyst.

• Diaphanography. This technique, also called transillumination, uses a strong, cold light and infrared photography. It can differentiate a solid tumor from a cyst filled with clear fluid, but it, too, cannot detect very small cancers, and has not proved useful in screening for breast cancer.

• Computerized tomography. Generally referred to as CT scanning, this technique uses multiple X-ray images and a computer to construct a series of cross-sectional views of a body part. CT scanning is being studied as a possible tool for detecting breast cancer, particularly in small, dense breasts that are difficult to examine by mammography. Tomography has drawbacks, however, that make it an unlikely candidate for routine screening: It is expensive and it requires a relatively high dose of radiation compared to mammography.

• Magnetic resonance imaging (MRI, formerly called NMR). This is still a highly experimental and very expensive technique. It involves using radiowaves and magnetism to image a biological structure. In experimental studies, MRI has detected large, palpable breast cancers, but it is not yet known whether the technique can be used to tell the difference between cancer and benign growths.

DIAGNOSIS OF BREAST CANCER

A diagnosis of breast cancer can be established only by a biopsy and microscopic examination, although less invasive techniques like mammography and palpation may provide valuable information. Several types of biopsy techniques are used but, increasingly, needle aspiration is being recommended for women whose breasts can be examined this way (Figure 27). The technique entails using a hypodermic needle and syringe to remove a small piece of tissue from the breast mass, which is then examined microscopically. This technique is 96 percent accurate (the errors are almost invariably false negative results in which the needle has missed the tumor). Needle biopsies can be performed in a physician's office or outpatient clinic using only a local anesthetic. This technique has several advantages over a surgical biopsy: It is less costly, does not involve as much discomfort, and has a lower risk of wound infection in the biopsy site. Also, the biopsy incision may interfere with optimal placement of the surgical incision if a later mastectomy is performed.

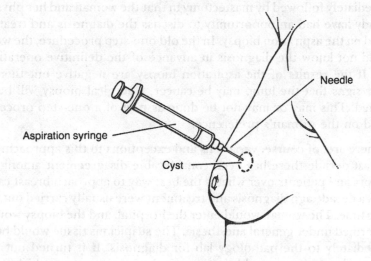

Figure 27 Needle aspiration of breast cyst.

There are, however, situations in which a needle biopsy is not appropriate. Women who have large breasts with a small lump near the chest wall are not good candidates for this procedure. The same applies to women who have a suspicious area that shows up on a mammogram but cannot be felt.

Surgical, or excisional, biopsies involve removing the lump, usually as an outpatient procedure using local anesthesia unless it is being done at the same time as the treatment. Depending upon individual circumstances and preferences, a typical diagnosis/treatment program might be as follows:

1. A lump or other suspicious sign is discovered, either by the woman or her physician.

2. The woman undergoes an examination, which includes mammography.

3. Unless the lesion clearly is not cancer, an aspiration biopsy will be performed or the lump will be surgically removed.

4. If the results are positive, the woman and her physician will discuss the treatment options and decide what the next steps should be. A second opinion may be sought at this time. Although the aspiration biopsy is highly accurate, most surgeons do not do a mastectomy based on it alone. As a general policy, a surgical excisional biopsy will be done and if it too is positive, the definitive treatment will follow at that time. This differs from the previous one-step procedures in which a positive surgical biopsy was immediately followed by mastectomy in that the woman and her physician already have had an opportunity to discuss the diagnosis and treatment based on the aspiration biopsy. In the old one-step procedure, the woman would not know the diagnosis in advance of the definitive operation.

5. If the results of the aspiration biopsy are negative but there are other signs that the lump may be cancer, a surgical biopsy will be performed. This may or may not be done as part of a one-step procedure, based on the woman's preference.

There are, of course, variations and exceptions to this approach. Over the last decade there has been considerable disagreement among both doctors and patients over what is the best way to approach breast cancer. Until a decade ago diagnosis and treatment were usually carried out at the same time. The woman would enter the hospital, and the biopsy would be performed under general anesthesia. The suspicious tissue would be sent immediately to the pathology lab for diagnosis. If it turned out to be cancer, the surgeon would then proceed with treatment, which usually meant a mastectomy. Thus a woman going into an operating room for a biopsy would not know whether she would wake up and find she had undergone a mastectomy. Today, women undergoing treatment for breast cancer almost always have the diagnosis established beforehand. Typically, a needle biopsy will be performed. If it is positive, the woman and her physician will discuss treatment options. An excisional biopsy to confirm the diagnosis will then be incorporated into the treatment. This gives the woman and those close to her time to adjust to the diagnosis before undergoing immediate treatment. Before the advent of outpatient biopsies using local anesthesia, the need to undergo two operative procedures using general anesthesia had been a major argument against the two-stage approach.

Today there are more treatment options, and women are more involved in deciding what is best for them. There are pros and cons for both approaches, and these should be fully discussed by the woman, her physician, and her family members. Arguments for the two-stage approach include:

• Most often, suspicious lumps turn out to be benign, especially in younger women. The two-stage procedure spares these women the risk and cost of general anesthesia and the mental anguish of not knowing whether they will emerge from the operating room minus a breast.

• The pathologic diagnosis in a two-stage procedure involves mounting the tissue on a slide and studying it microscopically. These are called "permanent sections"; the slides may be submitted for a second opinion.

• A two-stage procedure allows time for other tests, such as an estrogen and progesterone receptor test of the cancer, or bone and liver scans to determine whether the disease has spread, before treatment is undertaken.

• A woman can seek a second opinion or discuss treatment options with her doctor following the diagnosis. Plans also can be made for possible breast reconstruction before the mastectomy.

Supporters of the one-step procedure point to the following facts:

• Some women find the time between biopsy and diagnosis, and between diagnosis and treatment extremely stressful.

• Frozen sections are 98 percent as accurate as permanent sections and, as noted above, most errors are false negatives. Instances in which a mastectomy would be performed based on a false positive frozen section would be very rare, contrary to some reports in the popular media.

• The one-step procedure avoids the risk of infection in the biopsy wound.

• In some cases—when the tumor is deep within the breast, or so small that it requires X-ray studies to locate it, or when the breasts are very large or the patient very apprehensive—general anesthesia is necessary for the biopsy. In these cases there may be no need to subject the patient to general anesthesia twice if she is agreeable to a one-step procedure.

The woman in whom breast cancer is suspected should consider all factors carefully before deciding which approach to diagnosis and treatment she wants. A week or two of delay between diagnosis and definitive treatment will probably do no harm. If the patient opts for the two-step procedure, she should take the time to find a physician who will perform it and not fear a short interval between diagnosis and treatment. An extended interval is usually not advised because some types of breast cancer may spread rapidly.

The woman who is having a breast biopsy under local anesthesia as an outpatient in a hospital or doctor's office is usually asked not to eat anything after midnight of the day before. Before the biopsy, she will be given an injection of a local anesthetic into the biopsy area. After the anesthetic takes effect, the surgeon proceeds with the biopsy. The suspicious lump and a small amount of surrounding tissue is usually removed.

The mammograms may be used to help locate the area to be removed. In instances in which a suspicious area shows up on a mammogram but is too small to be felt, an additional procedure may be needed to enable the surgeon to locate the area. This may involve using a preoperative X-ray examination to guide injection of a dye into the area to be removed. Alternatively, a needle may be inserted into the area, again using X rays for guidance. These various procedures help ensure that the suspicious area is accurately located, and only a minimal amount of tissue removed, thus minimizing disfigurement of the breast. Following removal of the lump, the wound will be closed.

For biopsy under general anesthesia, the woman may undergo tests on an outpatient basis before hospital admission for premedication and the biopsy, which is performed in an operating room. If a one-stage procedure has been agreed upon by the woman and her physician, a frozen section examination of the removed tissue will be performed while the patient is still anesthetized. If the biopsy shows no cancer, the incision is closed and the woman can generally return home later the same day or the next day. If the biopsy shows cancer, the surgeon will then proceed to the more extensive operation if this is what both the patient and the surgeon have agreed upon in advance.

TYPES OF BREAST CANCERS

There are several different kinds of invasive breast cancer, as well as tiny noninvasive carcinomas *in situ*, which may or may not progress to an invasive stage. As in other types of cancer, breast cancer is now classified both by the general type and, more specifically, by cell type. Cell classification is important because the different types grow and metastasize at varying rates; therefore the more a doctor knows about the type of cancer, the easier it is to develop an effective treatment regimen. Specific types of breast cancer are:

• *Invasive ductal cancer.* About 70 percent of all breast cancer falls into this category. The cancer cells themself lack specific distinguishing characteristics. The cancers are hard to the touch and, in advanced stages, may cause visible dimpling of the skin or retraction of the nipple. This type of cancer tends to spread rather rapidly to the lymph nodes, even while it is still quite small, and it carries a poorer prognosis than some other types.

• *Medullary carcinoma.* This type of ductal cancer accounts for about 7 percent of breast cancer. It is distinguished by its appearance: it seems to grow in a capsule within the duct and although it may become quite large, it does not metastasize as frequently as the more common invasive ductal cancer and has a better outlook.

• *Comedocarcinomas.* These make up about 5 percent of breast cancer. The tumor begins in the lining of the duct, and grows into the duct itself until it is completely filled. The ducts become dilated to accommodate the larger amount of material in it. When removed and examined in a cut section, the ducts resemble blackheads, hence the name comedocarcinoma. The tumor can grow quite large, but it is not as likely to spread beyond the breast or invade the skin as some other forms of breast cancer; therefore the prognosis is generally good.

• *Mucinous carcinoma.* This is still another form of ductal cancer, so named because its cells produce mucus. It accounts for about 3 percent of breast cancer, and like comedocarcinomas, it may grow quite large without metastasizing.

• *Tubular ductal cancer.* This relatively rare form—it accounts for about 2 percent of all breast cancer—derives its name from the tumor structure. When viewed under the microscope, the tumor shows tube-shaped structures ringed with a single layer of cells. The outlook is better than for invasive ductal cancer.

• *Invasive lobular carcinoma.* These cancers, which account for about 3 percent of breast cancer, start in the breast lobules—the small end ducts that branch off the lobes. The cancer is similar to the invasive ductal type and, like it, has a generally poor outlook.

• *Lobular and ductal carcinomas* in situ. These are tiny cancers that are confined to either the lobules or ducts. They are too small to be felt, but they sometimes appear as tiny areas of calcifications on a mammogram. Often they are discovered during a biopsy for another larger breast lump. A breast will frequently contain several *in situ* cancers; some of these eventually develop into invasive cancers, and it is impossible to tell which lesions will become invasive and which will not. Thus there is disagreement among specialists as to how these *in situ* carcinomas should be treated. It is very rare for carcinomas *in situ* to spread to the lymph nodes; therefore some doctors advocate a wait-and-see approach, with regular mammography and regular breast examinations to detect any change in an early stage. Others advocate a curative mastectomy, especially if there are other risk factors such as a family history of breast cancer early in life.

GROWTH OF BREAST CANCER

Breast cancers grow at widely differing rates (Figure 28 shows the size in centimeters). The fastest can double in size in about thirty days; the slowest doubles in about 200 days; the average time is four months.

In its earliest stages the growth is confined to the membrane lining the lobule or the ducts. At this stage it cannot spread to distant parts of the body. Eventually, however, the cells grow through the wall of the duct or lobule into the fatty tissue that makes up the bulk of the breast. The

318

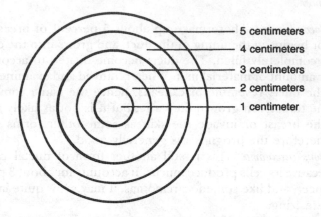

Figure 28 Tumor sizes in centimeters.

tumor must be about one centimeter—less than one-half inch—before a trained person can feel it. (Of course, it is more difficult to feel a growth deep within a large breast.) By this time the cancer may have existed for as long as two years. During this time cancer cells may have escaped from the breast through the veins or the lymph vessels. The spread of cancer through the lymph system is quite common in breast cancer. Cancer cells may collect in axillary lymph nodes, which act as filtration stations in the armpit, just below the collarbone. From there they may spread to other parts of the body. Since these lymph nodes are usually the first way station in the spread of a breast cancer, their study is a most valuable indicator of whether the cancer has metastasized to other parts of the body. The fewer of these underarm lymph nodes that are found to contain cancer cells, the better the prognosis is, with respect to both survival and recurrence.

The most common sites of metastases are the lungs, liver, brain, and bones. If the biopsy does show breast cancer, a number of other tests, including X rays, blood tests, and body scans will be performed to determine whether the cancer has spread. If a mastectomy is to be done immediately after the biopsy in the one-step procedure, these tests should be done before the mastectomy.

Another important test, and one that should be done in all breast cancer biopsies, is the estrogen and progesterone receptor assay. This is performed on a bit of fresh tumor tissue to see whether the cancer's growth is increased by estrogen or progesterone, hormones that vary every month in the bodies of premenopausal women. About 40 percent of breast cancers contain receptors for estrogen. In about two thirds of these cases the tumors will shrink if the body is deprived of estrogen, either by removal of the glands that manufacture this hormone, or by administration of drugs or other hormones to counter it. These receptor tests are important in determining whether hormone manipulation should be undertaken and if so, what kind, or whether chemotherapy should be given when breast cancer recurs.

About 50 percent of all breast cancers develop in the upper outer quadrant of the breast; Figure 29 shows where the others arise. In their early stages, most breast cancers do not produce pain. Still, recurrent or ill-defined breast pain should be investigated by a doctor.

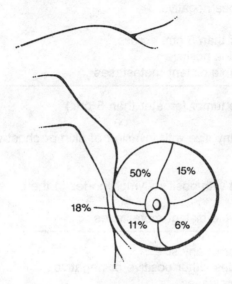

Figure 29 Where cancers arise in the breast.

STAGING

Like other cancers, breast cancers are staged according to a well-defined, elaborate progressive scale. A simplified summary of the scale, developed by the American Joint Committee for the Staging of Breast Cancer in 1982, is presented in Table 16.

Many factors appear to influence the chances of surviving breast cancer. Early detection and treatment are the most important. The overall five-year survival rate is about 75 percent for white women and about 63 percent for black women. This rises to nearly 90 percent for women with Stage I or II cancer that is treated while the cancer is confined to the breast. In recent decades the overall survival rates have gradually improved. According to the National Cancer Institute, 63 percent of white women whose cancer was diagnosed in the early 1960s had a five-year

Table 16
STAGING OF BREAST CANCERS

STAGE I: Small tumor (less than 2 cm. or .78 inches)
Negative lymph nodes
No detectable metastases

STAGE II: Tumor greater than 2 cm. but less than 5 cm.
Lymph nodes negative

OR

Tumor less than 5 cm. across
Lymph nodes positive
No detectable distant metastases

STAGE III: Large tumor (greater than 5 cm.)

OR

Tumor of any size with invasion of skin or chest wall or "grave signs"

OR

Associated with positive lymph nodes in the collarbone area

BUT

No detectable distant metastases

STAGE IV: Tumor of any size
Lymph nodes either positive or negative
Distant metastases

survival. This rose to 68 percent in 1970–73, and to 74 percent in 1973–75. Comparable data for black women were 46, 51, and 63 percent. Most experts agree that the racial difference in survival can be attributed to the stage of cancer at the time of diagnosis. Among white women, about half of the cancers are in Stage I or II; 41 percent have regional spread (Stage III), and 9 percent have distant metastases. In contrast, only 33 percent of black women have their cancers diagnosed while in Stages I or II; 50 percent are diagnosed in Stage III, and 17 percent already have distant metastases.

TREATMENT

Of all the issues discussed in this chapter, none has generated more controversy among physicians and patients than the treatment of breast cancer. New knowledge about the way breast cancer develops has prompted a reevaluation of treatments. For example, some breast cancers spread so quickly that there are distant metastases before the local tumor is detectable by any of our present means.

Surgery remains the most commonly used local treatment and physicians agree that in most cases surgery may offer the best hope for cure, although there are instances in which radiation therapy can produce equally good results. (The different types of operation for breast cancer are illustrated in Figure 30.) Radiation therapy is also a local treatment, intended to kill cancer cells that have not been surgically removed and to halt their spread to other parts of the body. Neither surgery nor radiation therapy will eradicate those cancer cells that have escaped from the breast through the lymph or blood vessels. The body's immune system will, for a time, kill or wall off most of these free-floating cells. But if the primary tumor is not eliminated, the number of transported cells will become too large for the body's natural immune defenses, and metastases will begin to grow. Thus the principle of local treatment, whether by surgery or radiation therapy or both, is to eliminate the primary source of the cancer cells before their dissemination becomes too great. The controversy revolves around how little or how much breast tissue needs to be removed or treated to ensure that the primary cancer has been eliminated.

Surgical Treatment

The evolution of current surgical treatments of breast cancer began shortly before the turn of the century, when the disease was virtually incurable. At that time Dr. William Halsted, a Baltimore surgeon, felt that the poor results stemmed from the fact that the operations then used were inadequate. He devised the operation that still bears his name—the Halsted radical mastectomy, in which the entire breast, underlying muscles, and the axillary lymph nodes all were removed. His operation was based on the idea that the cancer extended widely within the breast and spread initially through the muscles into the axillary lymph nodes. The cancers treated in his early operations were large, but he demonstrated that through extensive surgery, a cure for breast cancer might be possible.

Several concurrent developments led to a modification of the Halsted procedure during the 1930s. As women became more educated about the warning signs of breast cancer, they began seeing their doctors while the disease was in its early stages. Researchers found that breast cancer seldom extended into the underlying chest muscles and that recurrence in this area was unusual. Radiation equipment and therapy improved, adding another dimension to local treatment.

An English surgeon, Dr. P. H. Patey, developed a modified radical mastectomy in which the breast and axillary lymph nodes were removed but the underlying muscle was left intact. This operation is not as disfig-

322

Different Types of Mastectomies

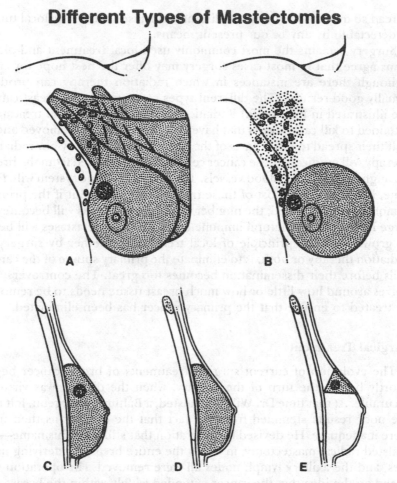

Figure 30 Shaded areas indicate what is removed in each procedure. The cancer is designated by the blackened lump.
A. Radical mastectomy, showing removal of breast, lymph nodes, and surrounding muscle.
B. Modified radical mastectomy, showing removal of breast, lymph nodes, and surrounding tissue but not the underlying muscle.
C. Simple mastectomy, showing removal of breast, nipple, and skin, but not the lymph nodes or muscle.
D. Subcutaneous mastectomy, showing removal of breast but not the nipple and skin. (Since this procedure is usually done prophylactically, no tumor is shown.)
E. Lumpectomy or segmental mastectomy, showing removal of the cancer and surrounding tissue.

uring as the Halsted procedure, which left a depression that extended to the collarbone, and it also preserves much of the range of arm motion. The modified radical mastectomy gradually gained worldwide acceptance as time demonstrated that its cure rate was about the same as for the Halsted operation. In the United States a marked increase in the number of modified radical mastectomies began about 1970, and by 1977 a survey by the American College of Surgeons showed that almost 70 percent of breast cancers were being treated by this operation. It should be noted, however, that cancers deep within the breast that invade the chest wall muscle require the more radical procedure.

Another operation that has increased in popularity in recent decades is the simple mastectomy, in which the entire breast is removed, but not the muscles or axillary lymph nodes. Also referred to as a total or complete mastectomy, this operation is favored by doctors who believe in leaving the lymph nodes to help fight residual cancer cells in the area. A few lymph nodes may be removed to see if they have cancer cells in them. It is used for very early cancers—carcinoma *in situ* and Stages I and II—and for patients who are not well enough to withstand more extensive surgery. It may be followed by radiation therapy, except for *in situ* carcinomas or early Stage I cancers. Simple mastectomy also may be performed in some instances to relieve the discomfort of patients whose breast cancers have ulcerated, even when there are metastases elsewhere in the body.

Over the last fifteen years there has been considerable controversy over whether a simple mastectomy gives a woman as good a chance of survival as the more extensive radical or modified radical procedures. In 1971 the National Surgical Adjuvant Breast Project undertook a major study to try to resolve the question. A total of 1,665 women at thirty-four institutions in the United States and Canada participated in the study. They were randomly assigned to be treated by one of three modalities: radical mastectomy, total or simple mastectomy without removal of the axillary nodes but with irradiation, or total mastectomy without radiation therapy. In the latter group, the axillary nodes were removed only if some were found to contain cancer. These women were then followed for ten years and results of the study were published in early 1985. The researchers found that 57 percent of the women whose cancers were confined to the breast (no spread to the axillary nodes) were alive with no evidence of cancer at the end of ten years, regardless of the method of treatment. Similarly, no difference in survival was noted among the various treatment groups for women whose cancers had spread to the lymph nodes— 38 percent were alive at the end of ten years regardless of the approach to treatment. The researchers concluded that there was no advantage to the more extensive surgery or regional radiation therapy so far as long-term survival was concerned.

Still another operation is the subcutaneous mastectomy, in which the inner breast tissue is removed through an incision under the breast, leaving the breast skin and nipple. Although this procedure may make later breast reconstruction easier and at one time was advocated by some plastic surgeons, a number of other considerations militate against it. Most breast surgeons consider it an inadequate treatment for any type of breast cancer. Since the areola and nipple are connected to the underlying breast tissue, some is inevitably left behind. It is also difficult to remove all of the breast tissue at the edges of the incision and the portion of the breast near the armpit. Subcutaneous as well as simple mastectomies have been used for women who are at high risk of developing breast cancer, either because of a strong family history or a biopsy showing a premalignant lesion. Some women in these situations develop an almost paralyzing fear of breast cancer and find they actually prefer to undergo a prophylactic subcutaneous mastectomy and breast reconstruction rather than live with their fears. Except in very unusual circumstances, most breast surgeons do not recommend these prophylactic mastectomies; instead they advise that the women be followed carefully for any changes that indicate cancer before undergoing treatment. Any woman considering such a prophylactic mastectomy is advised to undergo counseling beforehand.

Perhaps the most controversy has centered on the lumpectomy, also called partial mastectomy, quadrantectomy, tylectomy, or segmental mastectomy, in which only the cancer and surrounding tissue is removed, leaving the rest of the breast intact. At about the same time that Dr. Patey was developing the modified radical mastectomy in England, a group of surgeons working under Dr. Mustakallio in Helsinki, Finland, felt that removal of only the cancer, followed by radiation therapy to the breast and axillary lymph nodes, could produce equally good results. Over a period of many years and a large number of cases, they showed that this combination of lumpectomy and radiation therapy produced about the same results as a radical mastectomy if the tumor was 2 cm. (about three fourths of an inch) or less in diameter.

In 1976 the National Surgical Adjuvant Breast Project undertook a study to compare segmental mastectomy, both with and without irradiation, with simple mastectomy. In all, 1,843 women participated in the study, which was carried out at eighty-nine institutions in the United States and abroad. The women all had Stage I or II breast cancers smaller than 4 centimeters. This study found that segmental mastectomy, followed by breast irradiation in all women and adjuvant chemotherapy in women with positive nodes, provided the best chances of five-year survival. Women participating in the study were randomly assigned to one of three treatments: Total mastectomy, segmental mastectomy alone, or segmental mastectomy followed by breast irradiation. The axillary lymph nodes in all women were examined, and those who had positive nodes also received chemotherapy. More recently, a National Cancer Institute consensus panel has recommended that chemotherapy be used only in premenopausal women.

There are still knowledgeable surgeons who do not feel that there are yet enough data to support concluding that a lumpectomy is as effective as more extensive operations. One of the characteristics of breast cancer is that, generally, the smaller the tumor, the longer the recurrence-free period after treatment. Women with breast tumors less than 2 centimeters have a ten-year survival rate of over 95 percent. Any comparison of the two therapies against small, localized cancers obviously requires a number of years, and some physicians feel that still more time is needed to show any difference in results between the methods.

Another difficulty in evaluating lumpectomy is the problem of microscopic foci—tiny areas of cancer cells outside the observed lump. These have been found in 30 percent of breast cancer patients. Surgeons favoring mastectomy feel that these will later grow into cancers that must be removed. Other experts maintain that microscopic foci will not cause further trouble during the patient's lifetime or that they can be removed when and if they do.

Whichever operation is chosen, the woman usually undergoes a number of tests beforehand, such as bone and liver scans, to search for possible metastases. These are generally done on an outpatient basis and the woman usually checks into the hospital the evening before the actual operation. On the morning of the operation, the patient is sedated before the trip to the operating room.

A simple lumpectomy may take less than half an hour to do, and the patient is sometimes sent home the same day or the next day. More typically, however, axillary lymph nodes are sampled at the time of the lumpectomy; the total procedure may take an hour to do and require three or four days of hospitalization. Mastectomies take two to four hours, and the patient usually can expect to stay in the hospital for four or five days. In some institutions, programs are being developed to teach the woman to care for herself, allowing her to go home even sooner. If breast reconstruction is done at the same time as the mastectomy, the hospital stay may be extended for a few days.

The incision for a mastectomy may be either horizontal or vertical, depending on the technique preferred by the surgeon and the location of the tumor. The patient should feel free to ask what type of incision is planned and whether she may state a preference: many women choose the horizontal incision because it is less likely to show in a swimsuit or a low-cut dress.

Another topic the patient should discuss with her surgeon before mastectomy is breast reconstruction. Although eradication of the cancer is the chief concern of the doctor and patient, there is a trend toward immediate reconstruction at the time of the mastectomy.

After a mastectomy the incision is covered by a dressing and drainage tubes or suction devices are inserted to remove fluids. These stay in place until the amount of drainage is no longer a problem. For some women this may be several days; others may need the drainage tubes for several weeks, in which case the woman will leave the hospital with the tubes in place.

After surgery the chest may feel numb for days and the arm may lose its full range of motion. When the surgeon approves, the patient can begin simple exercises—squeezing a sponge with the hand, raising the arm overhead, walking the fingers up a wall—to restore full function. These exercises may also help prevent the accumulation of fluid in the arm (lymphedema). Several factors should be considered before beginning the exercises, however. For example, women who have undergone breast reconstruction should not stretch the tissues until healing is well under way, usually about seven to ten days after the operation. In any event, a woman should consult her physician for advice about specific exercises.

The stitches may be removed either before or after the patient leaves the hospital. She can usually begin to participate in a full range of activities, without arm or shoulder stiffness or numbness, within a month. Complete rehabilitation may take several months, however.

Psychologic Factors

The loss of any major body part is emotionally traumatic, but for many women the breast is a major source of self-esteem. For years breasts have symbolized femininity and desirability in advertisements, movies, and other media. It is no wonder that many women suffer anger or depression, often severe enough to jeopardize their physical recovery, after mastectomy.

The depression may take many forms: crying spells, feelings of worthlessness, loss of appetite, insomnia, disinterest in sex or other activities. Such reactions are normal for a while, but they should not become permanent conditions. Fears of being shunned by the sexual partner, the family, or others may haunt the patient.

The best therapy is to talk about these feelings. The physician can help by discussing the problems faced by women with breast cancer both before and after treatment. Many hospitals have support programs built around nurses, social service workers, and members of the psychiatry department. In the American Cancer Society's Reach to Recovery program, volunteers—each one a woman who has had breast cancer who has undergone special training—visit the patients. Reach to Recovery now has volunteers who have undergone all types of treatment—mastectomy, lumpectomy, or other surgery, radiation therapy, chemotherapy, and reconstruction. (For more details see the section "Sources of Information," Chapter 11, "Cancer Rehabilitation," and the Directory of Resources in the Appendix.)

Arm Swelling

One of the more common late complications of mastectomy is lymphedema—swelling of the arm on the same side as the surgery. This may occur after the lymph nodes in the armpit are removed or are irradiated, so that fluid in the arm does not drain via the lymph system. Anything that increases the formation of fluid in the arm increases the risk of swelling. Lymphedema is not as common today as in the past when more radical mastectomies were performed.

Currently there are no very effective treatments for lymphedema, although frequent elevation of the affected arm and elastic sleeves, such as the pressure bandages used to treat varicose veins, sometimes help. The best advice is to avoid infections of the hand or arm, which may further hinder the drainage of the lymph fluid in the arm. Excessive exposure to the sun, tight sleeves, rings, and bracelets, and heavy work with the affected arm also may lead to increased fluid formation. Injections, vaccinations, and blood pressure tests should be done on the opposite arm. However, physicians' opinions vary on this subject, so check with your doctor for advice about your individual situation.

Breast Prostheses

Unless a mastectomy patient has undergone immediate breast reconstruction, she usually begins to wear a temporary prosthesis (an artificial breast) before leaving the hospital. This can be a soft Dacron pad brought by the Reach to Recovery volunteer, or a homemade version of tissues, cotton balls, or other types of padding.

After the scar is completely healed (four to six weeks after surgery), the patient can be fitted for a full prosthesis. Available in corset shops, surgical supply stores, and some large department stores, these breast replacements are made of polyester or foam rubber or consist of pockets filled with liquid or silicone gel. The filled kind are more lifelike in consistency, but can leak if punctured by pin or fingernail. Prostheses come in all shapes and sizes, and in both light and dark flesh tones.

Many women mistakenly assume that a mastectomy means an end to wearing sweaters or other figure-revealing clothes. In fact, most women find that they can wear most of their previous clothes without embarrassment or alteration. (A skimpy bikini may not be possible, but there are many fashionable bathing suits that can be worn.) A selection of clothes should be taken to the prosthesis fitting, along with a good friend who can act as an observer and make sure that the prosthesis is lifelike from all angles. Of course, the prosthesis should be comfortable. Mastectomy bras with a pocket to hold the prosthesis or a washable cloth cover for it are also available.

Small-breasted women can make their own prostheses. Instructions are available from the American Cancer Society. But prostheses are very helpful for all mastectomy patients, especially if they are large-breasted. For those women, lack of a properly fitted prosthesis can lead to aches in the back and shoulders and poor posture.

Radiation Therapy

Radiation therapy has a number of applications in the treatment of breast cancer. It prevents cell reproduction; since cancer cells grow and divide more rapidly than normal ones, it acts to check a malignant growth. In breast cancer, radiation therapy is used most often as an adjunct to surgical treatment, especially following a segmental mastectomy. It is rarely the sole treatment for breast cancer, although it may be used alone against inflammatory breast cancer, for breast cancer so advanced that mastectomy would not be effective (Stage IV), or for patients who are too ill to undergo mastectomy or who are absolutely opposed to it. Radiation therapy also may be administered to reduce the size of a large breast tumor to make it easier to remove or to alleviate the pain caused by metastases, especially in the skeletal system.

Contrary to some thinking in the past, radiation therapy is no longer considered necessary to destroy cancer cells after a mastectomy. Instead, it is used most often following a lumpectomy. In recent years a number of radiation therapy specialists have argued that radiation therapy following removal of the breast tumor alone is as effective as the more extensive mastectomy in achieving a cure for cancer. In this approach the surgery may be an excisional biopsy, lumpectomy, or segmental mastectomy, sometimes with removal of some of the lymph nodes for staging purposes. A few days after the tumor is removed, a series of radiation treatments—usually four or five a week over a four-to-six-week period—is administered on an outpatient basis.

A total of about 5,000 rads of radiation will be directed to the breast, chest wall, and remaining lymph nodes. These treatments may be followed by a second phase of radiation therapy, consisting of a concentrated booster dose of radiation to the area where the cancer occurred. The radiation may be administered in one of two ways. In one method, several tubes are implanted into the breast to hold the radioactive iridium seeds. This is usually done under local anesthesia, although some women may request that a general anesthesia be used instead. The implants will remain in place fifty to sixty hours and will deliver about 2,000 rads directly to the surrounding tissue. The woman remains in the hospital while the implants are in place, and will be confined to her room with limited visitors to protect others against the small amounts of radiation that are released by the implants. After they are removed, there is no further exposure to the radiation and the woman usually goes home the same day.

Alternatively, a series of external radiation treatments using a concentrated electron beam may be administered. The procedure is similar to the previous radiation treatments, requiring that the woman come to the radiation therapy department daily for five to ten treatments.

Improved machinery and techniques have reduced the number of adverse effects of radiation therapy. After a few weeks of radiation therapy, most women find that their skin in the treated areas looks and feels sunburned. This redness is gradually replaced by a tanned look. Eventually the skin may become thickened, and some women find it is more sensitive while others experience a decrease in sensitivity. The breast may become smaller and firmer because the radiation stimulates development of fibrous tissue; other women find the breast is larger because of a buildup of fluid.

Since the radiation does not penetrate to the deeper internal organs, there is generally no nausea or vomiting. If these do occur, antinausea drugs can be taken. There may be a slight cough due to minor exposure of the lung to the radiation. Many women also find that the treatments leave them feeling more tired than usual, although most are able to go about their normal routine. (For more information, see Chapter 8, "Radiation Therapy," and Chapter 10, "Coping with Problems Related to Cancer and Cancer Treatment.")

Chemotherapy

Chemotherapy has been a major advance in cancer therapy. It is not used alone as an initial treatment of breast cancer, but is often used with mastectomy or radiation or both. Adjuvant chemotherapy is commonly used in patients whose lymph nodes show signs of cancer, indicating a high risk of distant spread. Treatment, usually administered in brief courses given every three or four weeks, may continue for a year or longer. The length of therapy is not necessarily related to the seriousness of the disease.

Adjuvant chemotherapy for breast cancer usually involves a combination of drugs, sometimes three or four, given intravenously. Among the types of drugs prescribed are alkylating agents, such as L-phenylalanine mustard (L-PAM or melphalan, with the brand name of Alkeran) and cyclophosphamide (Cytoxan). These agents work by interfering with the division process of cancer cells. Other chemotherapy agents include antimetabolites, such as 5-fluorouracil (5-Fu) and methotrexate, which interfere with the formation of metabolic substances that are essential to production of DNA in cells.

Some antibiotics, such as doxorubicin (Adriamycin), are also used, because they interfere with the duplication of DNA needed for cell division. Finally there are mitotic inhibitors, such as vinblastine sulfate (Velban) and vincristine sulfate (Oncovin), derivatives of the periwinkle plant, which interfere with the separation of the cell's essential genetic information into two distinct daughter cells.

The use of adjuvant chemotherapy to treat breast cancer started in 1958 in a study conducted as part of the National Surgical Adjuvant Breast Project. Patients were given low doses of an anticancer drug for two days following surgery. Although the regimen was much more restricted than what is now proposed, premenopausal women with four or more positive lymph nodes who took the drug experienced improvement in both five- and ten-year survival. A recent consensus panel convened by the National Cancer Institute found that adjuvant chemotherapy is of most benefit to younger premenopausal women whose cancer had spread to the lymph nodes. No added benefit has as yet been proved for women with localized cancer and no lymph node involvement.

While chemotherapy does increase the effectiveness of surgery or radiation therapy, it is not without side effects, although most are reversible. Nausea, loss of appetite, temporary hair loss, temporary bone marrow depression (which increases susceptibility to infection and bleeding), anemia and fatigue are common. The drugs can also interfere with menstrual function and produce symptoms of menopause. Adjustments in dosage and method of administration can alleviate many of these side effects. Others, such as nausea, can be prevented or treated. Hair loss, commonly seen with the use of such drugs as doxorubicin (Adriamycin), can be prevented in up to half of all patients with the use of a scalp-cooling device.

Different types of breast cancers respond differently to chemotherapy. Responses of patients to the drugs also vary. For this reason drug therapies must be evaluated periodically to be sure that the medication is effective, or continues to be effective. (For a more detailed discussion, see Chapter 7, "Principles of Cancer Chemotherapy.")

Hormone Therapy

About 40 percent of breast cancers are "hormone-responsive"—that is, their growth rate is altered by the presence or absence of the female hormones, estrogen, and progesterone. The hormone responsiveness of each breast cancer should be determined by estrogen and progesterone receptor tests at the time of the initial biopsy, as described previously. Of patients whose tumors respond to estrogen, two thirds will benefit from hormone therapy, which may involve either the elimination or addition of estrogen. Two key factors in hormone therapy are the menopausal status of the patient and the effect of hormones on the cancer. Some breast cancers are stimulated by hormones; hormonal manipulation often produces a remission in these cancers, especially if they have spread to distant organs.

The first step in hormonal manipulation usually involves eliminating estrogen and other female sex hormones. In the past this usually meant removal of the ovaries in premenopausal women, and sometimes the adrenal glands and pituitary as well. The ovaries may be removed surgically or exposed to radiation, but today a more common approach is to use drugs that either block the action or halt the production of the hormone. (See Chapter 7, "Principles of Cancer Chemotherapy.")

In some instances surgical removal of other hormone-producing glands, specifically the adrenals and the pituitary, still may be recommended in advanced cancer. Removal of the adrenal glands, which rest atop the kidneys, eliminates androstenedione, a male hormone that postmenopausal women convert to estrogen. The adrenal glands can be removed at the same time as the ovaries, or afterward if the cancer progresses. After menopause the removal of the adrenal glands alone— leaving the ovaries—may reduce bodily estrogen enough to slow the growth of estrogen-dependent tumors.

The pituitary gland controls the ovaries and the adrenal glands; it also controls the milk glands in the breast by producing prolactin, a hormone that may also increase the growth of breast cancers. The pituitary is located in the center of the skull, behind the nose, and is usually removed by surgery through the roof of the mouth and nasal passages. The operation is called a hypophysectomy.

After adrenalectomy or hypophysectomy, the patient will need daily doses of cortisone to continue normal bodily functions. In addition, fludrocortisone (Florinef) may be necessary to regulate salt processing; pitressin may be given to conserve water. Women whose pituitary or adrenal glands have been removed should carry medical identification bracelets and information on emergency treatment for their condition at all times.

Additive Therapy

In a curious paradox, women who experience an improvement from treatment to halt estrogen production or action may later benefit from large doses of estrogen and other hormones. About 60 percent of women with positive estrogen receptor tests will benefit from additive therapy, which usually involves giving diethylstilbestrol (DES). Women who are five or more years postmenopausal seem to have the greatest benefit. Side effects include nausea, vomiting, vaginal bleeding, diarrhea, urinary frequency, fluid retention, bone pain in women with metastases to these sites, and changes in skin pigmentation.

Other hormones that may be administered during additive therapy include androgens, progestins, and corticosteroids. Androgens, which are male hormones, may cause growth of facial and body hair and other signs of masculinization. The type of hormone given depends upon age, site of metastases, and responses to previous antihormone therapies.

Considerations in Treatment Selection

With so many treatments now available for breast cancer, it is understandable that many women are confused or at a loss to know what is best for them. As emphasized throughout this chapter, there is no single approach to treatment that is best for all women. The matter is further complicated by the fact that even the experts disagree. In some cases it is tempting for a woman to go from doctor to doctor until she finds one who agrees with her preconceived idea of how she would like to be treated. While seeking a second or even a third opinion is justified and even encouraged, there are real hazards to this kind of doctor-shopping. Also, one must be sure that the second opinion comes from a highly qualified physician.

In recent years the National Institutes of Health has sponsored several Consensus Development Conferences, bringing together panels of physicians, researchers, consumers and others to review the data and recommend specific courses of action. The conclusions reached by these panels are summarized in *The Breast Cancer Digest,* published by the Department of Health and Human Services, as follows:

*Consensus Panel of Treatment of Primary Breast Cancer: Management of Local Disease (1979)**

• Total mastectomy with axillary dissection (also known as modified radical mastectomy), a procedure that preserves the pectoral muscle, should be recognized as the current treatment standard for women with Stage I and some women with Stage II breast cancer.

• In most cases, a diagnostic biopsy should be separated from definitive treatment.

• The question of postoperative radiation therapy remains moot pending further results of adjuvant clinical trials.

• Ongoing clinical trials exploring the roles of lesser surgical proce-

---

* Reprinted from *The Breast Cancer Digest: A Guide to Medical Care, Emotional Support, Educational Programs and Resources,* 2nd Edition, National Cancer Institute, Bethesda, MD, 1984.

dures and primary radiation therapy, because of their exciting preliminary results, warrant support from both patients and physicians.

Consensus Panel on Steroid Receptors in Breast Cancer (1979)*

• Estrogen receptor assays provide valuable information for making clinical decisions on the type of therapy to be employed, when hormonal therapy is under consideration.

• Every primary tumor should be assayed for estrogen receptor content.

• Estrogen receptor status is a useful prognostic indicator for Stage II (and perhaps other) patients.

Consensus Panel on Adjuvant Chemotherapy for Breast Cancer (1985)†

Outside the context of a clinical trial, and based on the research data presented at the 1985 Consensus Development Conference, the following statements can be made:

• For premenopausal women with positive nodes, regardless of hormone receptor status, treatment with established combination chemotherapy should become standard care.

• For premenopausal patients with negative nodes, adjuvant therapy is not generally recommended. For certain high-risk patients in this group, adjuvant chemotherapy should be considered.

• For postmenopausal women with positive nodes and positive hormone receptor levels, tamoxifen (an antiestrogen drug) is the treatment of choice.

• For postmenopausal women with positive nodes and negative hormone receptor levels, chemotherapy may be considered but cannot be recommended as standard practice.

• For postmenopausal women with negative nodes, regardless of hormone receptor levels, there is no indication for routine adjuvant treatment. For certain high-risk patients in this group, adjuvant therapy may be considered.

Treatment options should be discussed fully before a decision is made. The discussions should include the woman and close family members, her primary-care physician, and the specialist(s) who will carry out various aspects of treatment. The physicians should answer all questions in clear, understandable language and make sure the woman knows what is involved at each stage of her treatment. Although the physicians are obligated to recommend what they consider the best course of treatment for a patient, in the final analysis it is the patient who must decide what is

---

* Ibid.

† Reprinted from National Institutes of Health Consensus Development Conference Statement *Adjuvant Chemotherapy for Breast Cancer,* held September 9 to 11, 1985.

best for her. The more information and understanding that go into the decision, the better for all concerned.

Breast Reconstruction

Breast reconstruction has become increasingly popular among mastectomy patients in recent years, including women who have adjusted well to using a breast prosthesis. Although a reconstructed breast does not look exactly like the natural one, improved plastic surgery techniques, using silicone implants and, if needed, muscle, skin, or fatty tissue taken from other parts of the body, can achieve remarkable results. Even an areola and nipple can be made from other body tissue.

Successful breast reconstruction was first used for women whose breasts were damaged by burns or other injuries. The early procedure was a complex and costly series of operations, which involved taking tissue from elsewhere on the body and moving it, step by step to preserve its blood supply, to the mastectomy site. The development of silicone implants greatly simplified the procedure (Figure 31). The consistency is not exactly like that of the other breast, and the old mastectomy scar remains, although it fades considerably with time. However, the reconstructed breast looks like a natural breast under clothes—even low-cut dresses and bathing suits.

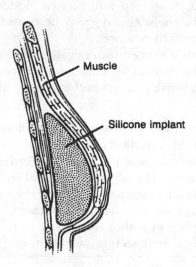

Muscle

Silicone implant

Figure 31 A reconstructed breast, with the implant placed under the muscle.

Almost any woman who has had a mastectomy can have breast reconstruction. This includes women whose skin has been damaged by radiation and those who have had a radical mastectomy, in which the pectoral muscles are removed in addition to the breast. The reconstruction may be more difficult in these instances, but it is not impossible.

Increasingly reconstruction is being done at the same time as the mastectomy, especially if radiation treatments are not being planned. After the breast is removed, a silicone prosthesis is inserted, the incision is closed and drainage tubes inserted. In some women there may be an inadequate amount of skin or too marginal a blood supply to do a complete immediate reconstruction. In these instances a balloonlike device called an expander is inserted instead of the prosthesis. After the incision is healed, a saline solution is injected through the skin to "inflate" the expander. After the tissues have stretched enough to accommodate the silicone prosthesis, the expander is removed and the permanent implant is inserted.

An immediate reconstruction has several advantages: It avoids a second major operation, an additional scar, and increased expense. It also provides the psychological advantage of awakening from surgery and finding a near-normal contour where the natural breast had been. Most patients who can plan a reconstruction with their surgeon and plastic surgeon before a mastectomy do not seem to experience the same sense of loss as women who undergo a mastectomy without such planning.

In most postmastectomy reconstructions, the original mastectomy line is followed and there is no new scar. There may be an additional scar elsewhere on the body if donor tissue is needed from another site, usually the abdomen, side or back. Even the deformity created by a radical mastectomy can be corrected and an almost normal contour restored. Breast reconstruction has been performed as long as ten to twenty years after a mastectomy.

Although women who have undergone a mastectomy but have metastases elsewhere in the body are generally not considered candidates for reconstruction, the option is available to them and should be considered if the patient and her doctor feel it will enhance the quality of her life. Regardless of the stage of her disease, then, any woman who has had a mastectomy is a potential candidate for reconstruction unless her physical or emotional state indicates that she could not tolerate surgery and the recuperative period after surgery.

Reconstruction usually takes about one and a half hours, sometimes longer. It requires the use of an implant or the woman's own tissue. Implants are generally made of plastic filled with silicone gel or saline and come in many shapes and sizes, to match the remaining breast. Often it is necessary to reduce or tighten the other breast if there is great size discrepancy. If a woman's own tissue is used, it will be taken from the lower abdomen (rectus abdominus muscle tissue), leaving a scar just above the pubic hairline, or from the back (latissimus dorsi muscle and tissue), leaving a horizontal incision along the skin lines of the back.

After reconstruction, patients are usually able to get out of bed the next day, if not sooner, and to return to work within a week. Arm mobility begins to return within a few days and should be back to normal in two weeks or so. The two most common complications are loss of the skin over the implant due to an impaired blood supply, and the formation of a capsule—hard, fibrous scar tissue—around it. The latter is less common if the prosthesis is placed under the muscle. Also, regular breast massage can help avoid this problem and keep the breast soft and supple.

A few months after the initial reconstructive surgery, women who choose to do so can have a nipple and areola added to their new breast. This is almost always done in a second operation to allow time for the reconstructed breast to stabilize in shape and position so that the new nipple is symmetrical in location, size, and projection with the remaining one.

The areola is fashioned from pigmented skin found elsewhere on the body. For a woman whose areola is pink, skin from behind the ear is generally used to match the color. If her areola is brown, the graft can be taken from the upper inner thigh. In either case, the scar heals quickly and is barely visible. If the areola of the normal breast is very large and the breast is being lifted or reduced, part of this areola may be used for the reconstruction.

The nipple itself can be created in one of three ways. Unless the remaining nipple is very small, the lower portion of it can be used without any noticeable loss of size. If it is too small to use, a new nipple can be fashioned with skin from the earlobe or upper inner thigh, although this new nipple may not project as much as the original. Finally, a nipple can be formed by gathering up a thick layer of skin in the center of the breast where it is usually removed in preparation for the areola implant and using that as the nipple. If it is too light in color, pigmented skin from elsewhere can be grafted over it.

Whichever method is used, the results are generally satisfactory and provide the finishing touch for many women, making them feel that they now have a breast that is a reasonable facsimile of the one they have lost.

Social and Emotional Factors

In recent years, women have become more knowledgeable about factors that increase their risk of developing breast cancer. For example, in a Gallup survey conducted for the American Cancer Society, 62 percent of the women polled knew that having sisters or a mother with breast cancer increased the likelihood of their having it too. More than half realized that previous breast cancer increased their chances of developing it again.

Although women may be more knowledgeable, they are not necessarily more diligent about things like regular breast examinations. In the Gallup survey for the ACS, 80 percent of the women surveyed said that they examined their breasts for lumps, but only 27 percent said that they had done it twelve or more times during the previous year. When asked why they did not practice breast self-examination, a third said they relied upon their doctors to do this, 17 percent felt there was no need for them to do so, and 16 percent felt they did not know how to do it properly. Three out of four women knew about mammography, but only 41 percent of those over the age of forty had had breast X rays, and 15 percent of the women over the age of fifty who were polled had yearly mammography. Only 45 percent of women over the age of forty had their breasts examined yearly by a physician.

Other surveys have confirmed that women are taking a more active role in treatment decisions, particularly regarding breast cancer. In its National Survey on Breast Cancer, the National Cancer Institute found that only three out of ten women in 1980 said they would let their doctors alone decide whether or not a breast should be removed. In contrast, 70 percent said they wanted to discuss the decision first with a spouse or someone close to them, and 90 percent said they would want a second opinion.

Contrary to popular belief, the NCI survey found that fear of disfigurement was not one of the major concerns. Only 12 percent cited this as a worry; more important were concerns that the surgery would not cure the cancer or that the effects of radiation therapy or chemotherapy would be debilitating.

IMPACT ON LOVED ONES

Although the most serious and immediate effects of breast cancer are experienced by the woman herself, it is important to recognize that this is a disease that affects the entire family. The impact of breast cancer on sexuality is a major concern of both the woman and her partner. Dorothy Rodriguez eloquently summed this up in the book by Jory Graham, *In the Company of Others:* "Men and women do not leave their sexuality at home when they enter a hospital for cancer treatment any more than they leave their emotions at home. If anything, their needs for physical intimacy and human warmth increase."

In the past, we have often tended to dismiss this aspect of cancer treatment as trivial compared to the more immediate concern of saving a life. The increased emphasis on the quality of survival, and not just survival per se, has helped change this. In our society, the breasts are so closely identified with femininity and sexuality that it is understandable that many women having a mastectomy suffer diminished self-esteem and worry about loss of sexual attractiveness. A British survey confirmed this; it found that half of all women who had had a mastectomy had subsequent sexual problems; the figure rose to 70 percent among women who had both a mastectomy and chemotherapy.

Very often the problems are due to a woman's loss of self-esteem and misguided feelings of shame. Fearing that their partner will be repelled by their scar or other disfigurement, they will avoid sexual intimacy. After a while the partner will feel rejected and resentful. Communication breaks down, making the situation worse. Counseling may be needed to restore communication and dispel unnecessary fears.

Of course, cancer therapy may have a temporary debilitating effect on sexual responsiveness. Chemotherapy may cause nausea, vomiting, fatigue, loss of hair including genital hair, and sores in both the mouth and vagina. Radiation therapy may cause fatigue. Hormone therapy may cause vaginal dryness and hot flashes and other symptoms of menopause. Depression is common following any cancer treatment and this, too, can diminish interest in sex.

Yet another factor relates to persistent myths and misconceptions. A man may experience guilt feelings that his fondling of a breast somehow produced the cancer, and therefore will hesitate to touch the remaining one. Although there is no basis for such fears, they need to be faced and discussed. Some men also have the mistaken notion that a breast that has been treated with radiation therapy is somehow dangerous. Of course there is no residual radiation following treatments or removal of radioactive implants; reassurances may help overcome such needless fears.

The overwhelming majority of men—81 percent in a recent survey— maintain that their feelings of love and sexual desire are not altered by a mastectomy. But there are men who, even though they want to support their partners in every way, find it difficult to adjust. They simply cannot control or hide the fact that they are repelled by the scar or altered body image. These feelings also should be recognized and discussed. Professional counseling may be advisable for such couples.

Of course, breast cancer also happens to unmarried women. Fears about establishing future relationships are common and, again, should be recognized and discussed. A doctor, a woman in a similar situation, or a professional therapist may be helpful.

The effects of breast cancer on other family members should not be overlooked. Children are concerned about what effect their mother's illness will have on them and their family structure. They should be told about the nature of the illness and its treatment. Secrets and unanswered questions often provoke more concern than open, frank discussions. Adolescent children may be particularly affected. A daughter may be asked to assume a mother's role just at a time when she is trying to declare her independence of the family. Adolescent girls also may develop an inordinate fear that they, too, will develop breast cancer. Honest and understandable information regarding risks and other facts about breast cancer can help dispel these fears.

The impact of a mother's breast cancer on an adolescent son is often neglected, but studies have found that, as a group, they have the most problems in dealing with the situation. Aloofness, behavior changes including delinquency or alcohol and drug abuse, are common signs of trouble. In such instances frank, open discussions between father and son are advised since most boys are more comfortable talking about intimate topics with males than with their mothers.

SOURCES OF INFORMATION

There are numerous organizations, counseling groups, films, books, hot lines and other sources of help and information for breast cancer patients and their families. Information about services available in your area may be obtained from your local American Cancer Society. The many ACS programs include Reach to Recovery, I Can Cope, and Can-Surmount. Reach to Recovery is widely acclaimed as one of the most helpful programs for women with breast cancer. Reach to Recovery volunteers all are women who have had breast cancer themselves and may have had a variety of treatments. They undergo special training in how to help other women, and are available to visit women in the hospital before and after treatments. The volunteer brings literature, a breast prosthesis when needed, and other items that will be of use to the patient. Perhaps most important, the volunteers provide a positive role model while letting the patient know that her concerns and fears are normal and shared by other women. The volunteer also is available to show the patient how to do the arm exercises, provided her physician thinks she is ready to start them. A hospital visit from a Reach to Recovery volunteer must be requested by the patient's physician. Sometimes physicians neglect to mention this to the patient; if a woman would like a Reach to Recovery visit while she is still in the hospital, she should let her physician know. Reach to Recovery also provides information for husbands and other family members. Local American Cancer Society units can provide more information about Reach to Recovery and other programs in your area.

A personal physician or hospital patient education department are still other sources to learn about local services and programs. The Office of Cancer Communications of the National Cancer Institute also offers a number of booklets and educational materials as well as guidance to local resources. For more information, write the Office of Cancer Communications, National Cancer Institute, Building 31, Room 10A18, Bethesda,

MD 20205 or call 1-800-4-CANCER. Other hot lines and resources are listed in the Directory of Resources in the Appendix.

SUMMING UP

The most frequent site of cancer in American women is the breast (even though lung cancer now kills more women than breast cancer). Although more than two thirds of women with breast cancer are cured today, the five-year survival rate could be increased even more if more cancers were diagnosed at an early stage. Unfortunately, most women do not examine their breasts each month or have their breasts examined annually by a doctor. Mammography remains an under-utilized tool; most women and/or their physicians still do not follow the guidelines calling for a baseline mammogram between the ages of thirty-five and thirty-nine, every year or two between forty and forty-nine and annually after age fifty.

Surgery remains the therapy most likely to ensure a cure of breast cancer. Newer, less drastic surgery, often combined with radiation therapy, may be equally effective against small, localized cancers. Radiation therapy and chemotherapy also promote survival by killing cancer cells that have spread beyond the original tumor.

Many organizations help women through the ordeal of breast cancer and rehabilitation. Emotional support from the sexual partner and family of the patient is essential to recovery. Talking about the aftereffects of breast cancer enables most patients to live productive, fulfilling lives after surgery. Some women choose surgery to reconstruct the removed breast. In short, there is no reason why fear and ignorance should keep women from the early detection that might save lives.

18

Cancer of the Colon and Rectum

Jerome J. DeCosse, M.D., Ph.D.

In the course of a year approximately 138,000 Americans develop cancer of the large bowel—the lowermost portion of the gastrointestinal tract, which is made up of the colon and rectum. Large bowel cancer is a leading cause of cancer death among both sexes, exceeded only by cancer of the lung in men and of the lung and breast in women. At present half of these patients can expect to be cured, a figure that could be greatly improved by more diligent attention to established methods of screening for bowel cancer. This chapter reviews what is known about large bowel cancer, describes how it can be prevented or detected in its early stages, addresses the principles of treatment, and tells how patients may care for themselves following surgery.

ANATOMY OF THE LARGE BOWEL

The large bowel, also referred to as the large intestine, is about three to four feet long, arching across the body from right to left. It begins at the cecum, the point at which the small intestine enters the colon, and ends at the anus. The last four inches are called the rectum; the remainder is the colon, which is divided into five parts: the cecum, ascending colon, transverse colon, descending colon, and sigmoid colon (Figure 32). Most cancers of the large bowel occur on the left (or distal) side in the segment closest to the rectum.

About one of seven large bowel cancers can be reached when the physician performs a rectal examination with a finger inserted into the anus. Therefore a digital rectal examination, along with simple chemical testing of a small stool sample for microscopic (occult) blood, should be part of a periodic or general physical examination. In fact the examination for occult blood is a simple, inexpensive test that can be performed at home by placing a small amount of stool on chemically treated paper and returning it by mail for laboratory analysis. Since most bowel cancers ooze small amounts of blood, the presence of blood in the stool indicates that further examinations should be performed to rule out cancer. It should be noted, however, that other conditions such as hemorrhoids also may result in blood in the stool, therefore a positive occult blood test does not necessarily mean cancer.

CAUSES OF LARGE BOWEL CANCER

Cancer of the large bowel occurs much more frequently in the United States, Western Europe, Australia, and New Zealand than in Japan, Africa, and most of the developing or third world countries. Furthermore, since most types of cancers increase in frequency as we grow older, the fact that the number of older people in the United States is growing would also explain the rise in the incidence of large bowel cancer. The number of deaths, however, has remained constant, indicating that the overall cure rate is improving. This improvement, for reasons that are unknown, seems to be confined to women.

Although the cause of large bowel cancer is not known, most epidemiologists (doctors who study the statistical patterns of disease) associate it with diet—in particular, the low-fiber, high-protein, high-fat content that characterizes the diet of most Americans and people in other urban, industrialized societies. For example, when the Japanese, who have a very low incidence of large bowel cancer in their homeland, move to Hawaii and the continental United States and adopt the typical American diet,

343

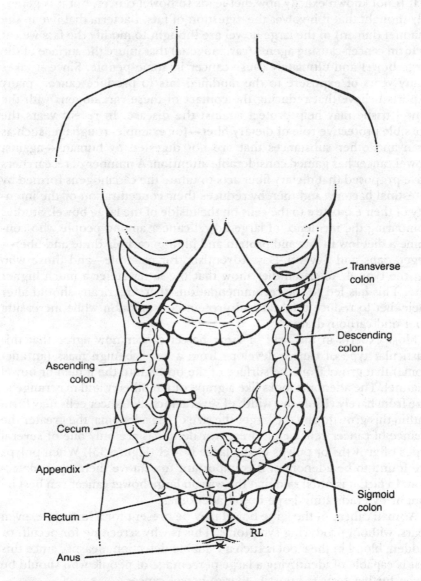

Figure 32 Normal colon and rectum.

Transverse colon

Descending colon

Ascending colon

Cecum

Appendix

Rectum

RL

Anus

Sigmoid colon

their descendants suffer the higher risk of large bowel cancer that is seen in the general American population.

It is not known exactly how diet leads to bowel cancer, but it is generally thought that it involves the digestion of fats. Bacteria that live in the channel (lumen) of the large bowel are thought to modify the fats we eat to form cancer-causing agents (carcinogens) that injure the surface of the large bowel and ultimately cause cancer in some people. Since it takes many years of exposure to the modified fats to produce cancer, many experts believe that reducing the contact of these carcinogens with the bowel tissue may help protect against the disease. In recent years the possible protective role of dietary fiber—for example, roughage, such as bran and other substances that are not digested by humans—against bowel cancer has gained considerable attention. A number of researchers have proposed that dietary fiber acts to dilute the carcinogens formed by intestinal bacteria and thereby reduces their concentration or the intensity of their exposure to the cells on the inside of the large bowel. Studies comparing the incidence of large bowel cancer among people who consume a diet low in fats and protein and high in carbohydrate and fiber—vegetarians and Seventh-Day Adventists, for example—and those who eat the typical American diet show that the latter suffer a much higher rate. This has led to the recommendations that Americans should alter their diet to reduce total fat and protein consumption while increasing fiber and carbohydrate.

Most experts in the field of large bowel cancer now agree that this particular type of cancer develops from a small benign mass (an adenoma) that grows from the surface of the bowel into the lumen or bowel channel. The adenoma looks like a grape or a mulberry and may range in size from barely visible to a width of several inches. Cancer cells may form within this growth, and the larger the size of the adenoma, the greater the chance of cancer cells being present. Adenomas are only one of several types of growths or polyps of the large bowel (Figure 33). When polyps are found to be adenomas, it is important to remove them upon detection. In fact, it is often said that the war on large bowel cancer can best be fought by eradicating large bowel adenomas.

A small cancer of the large bowel may be present for a long time, even years, without producing symptoms. This is why screening for occult, or hidden, blood in the stool is such a valuable detection measure since this test is capable of identifying a large percentage of people who should be given further tests for possible large bowel cancer.

As the cancer grows, the growth patterns and symptoms tend to vary in different areas of the large bowel. On the right side of the colon near the end of the small intestine, the cancers tend to grow into the space within the bowel. Because the colon channel is larger in the cecum and ascending colon, cancer in these locations may become large enough to produce

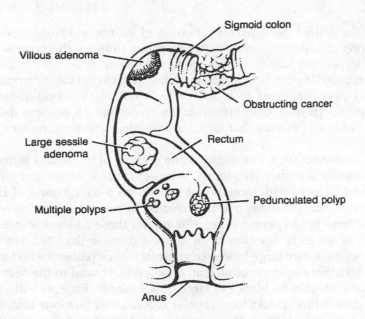

Figure 33 Composite illustration showing various types of colon tumors.

pain on the right side and to be felt upon examining the abdomen with the hand. These cancers also are well known to cause bleeding. Any older patient, particularly a person with an unexplained iron-deficiency anemia —a kind of anemia that is almost always caused by a slow, imperceptible loss of blood—should be examined for possible right-sided colon cancer. A chemical test for hemoglobin—the oxygen-carrying molecule in the blood—as well as a test for occult or hidden blood should be performed on all such patients. If these are positive, further investigations such as colonoscopy should be performed.

The channel on the left side of the colon is narrower than that on the right, and cancer in this area has a tendency to grow around and encircle the bowel wall. For this reason, left-sided colon cancer characteristically narrows or constricts the bowel channel, causing partial blockage of flow through the intestine. The main symptom of partial colon blockage is increasing constipation, often with bloating and gaseous distention of the abdomen. Cancers in the left colon also may cause bleeding, but anemia is less severe than it is in right-sided colon cancer.

The rectum—the lowermost four inches of the colon—has a larger channel (the ampulla) than the rest of the large bowel. Cancer in the rectum commonly produces diarrhea that often contains blood. In part the diarrhea is spurious, or false, because the tumor in the rectal wall gives the patient the constant sensation of incomplete stool evacuation, resulting in repeated, unnecessary attempts to move the bowels.

Of all patients who develop large bowel cancer, about 85 percent have what is called "sporadic" cancer, meaning that, except for the presence of large bowel adenomas in some, there is nothing unusual about their health background. In contrast, in the remaining 15 percent there are identifiable risk factors that signal a possible predisposition to the disease.

Ulcerative colitis, for example, is one of these predisposing factors that may lead to a higher frequency of bowel cancer. About one of every hundred patients with large bowel cancer has a background of chronic ulcerative colitis that has not been treated by removal of the bowel. The risk of large bowel cancer is greatest among those patients whose colitis began at an early age, has been active for more than ten years, and involves the entire large bowel. In contrast, colitis patients who have had only a transient episode of ulcerative proctitis, limited to the rectum, do not have a higher incidence of large bowel cancer. Patients with chronic ulcerative colitis should have regular colonic examinations that include endoscopy, even if there are no symptoms. During endoscopy, a flexible fiberoptic instrument with special lights is inserted into the large bowel, enabling the doctor to examine the entire organ and, if necessary, remove small amounts of tissue for biopsy. This permits doctors to identify those patients who have abnormal cell activity at an early, even precancerous, stage. Surgery at this stage will prevent the later development of cancer.

About one of every hundred patients with large bowel cancer has a family background of polyps (familial polyposis) in the large bowel. Familial polyposis, also known as Gardner's syndrome, is equally common in men and women, and the children of an affected parent have a 50 percent chance of inheriting the disease. A person with this condition can develop hundreds or even thousands of adenomas in the large bowel, usually beginning in adolescence. If the colon is not removed, these patients almost always develop large bowel cancer before the age of forty. Some have other medical problems, including cysts and fatty tumors (lipomas) beneath their skin and in their bones, particularly in their jawbones. If these cysts or lipomas occur in a young person, they should serve as a warning that the large bowel should be examined for the presence of precancerous polyps.

About 10 to 15 percent of all patients with large bowel cancer will not have polyposis themselves, but will have one or more close relatives who have had large bowel cancer. The nature of inheritance in these families is not as well understood as it is in those with familial polyposis. When this kind of family background is present, the characteristics of the large bowel cancer tend to be different: the patient is likely to be younger and the cancer is more likely to arise in several places on the right side of the colon. Additional adenomas are commonly, but not always, present. Still, adult members of such families should be watched closely, even if they do not have symptoms pointing to disease or cancer of the large bowel because of the increased risk of developing the disease.

SCREENING FOR COLON CANCER

As noted earlier, the present cure rate for colon cancer could be greatly improved by earlier detection and treatment of the disease. A wide-ranging study by the American Cancer Society concluded that all persons over the age of forty, including those with no symptoms, should have a digital rectal examination annually. This examination is easily performed and, while it may be embarrassing for the patient, it involves no discomfort. The doctor gently inserts a rubber-gloved finger into the rectum. The doctor can then ascertain the smoothness of the rectal wall surface and, in men, the size and characteristics of the prostate. At the time of a digital rectal examination, a stool sample is taken for chemical testing for occult or hidden blood.

There are many types of tests for stool occult blood. Most use slides impregnated with a chemical that is capable of detecting the presence of blood even in microscopic amounts. Patients taking this test should consume a meatless high-fiber diet free of vitamin C for at least forty-eight hours before preparing for the initial part of the test. The actual test consists of taking two separate stool samples on each of three consecutive days. These samples, which are small amounts of feces, are placed on the slide and must be examined within four days. The slide is treated with a drop of developer that is included in the test kit. If a blue color appears, this indicates that there is blood in the stool. This test is inexpensive, simple to do, and gives immediate results. Increasingly, it is recommended as a screening test that should be done on a regular basis among people over the age of forty, or even younger among those who are at a risk of developing colon or rectal cancer.

Men and women who are at a high risk of developing colon or rectal cancer should receive more frequent and intensive examinations beginning at an early age, perhaps as early as age twenty. This group includes persons with familial polyposis (Gardner's syndrome), ulcerative colitis, a history of adenomas or prior large bowel cancer, or a strong family history of colon or rectal cancer. If any abnormalities are found with these simple examinations, the patient may be asked to undergo colonoscopy or a barium enema, an X-ray examination—or even both. Furthermore, as an added precaution, sigmoidoscopy should be performed every three to five years *after two initial sigmoidoscopies one year apart are negative* (meaning they do not yield any findings of bowel disease).

This examination involves using the sigmoidoscope, a metal or plastic tube 25 centimeters or 10 inches long, with a fiberoptic ring made of plastic light-conducting fibers that enables the doctor to see the tissues exposed at the end of the instrument (Figure 34). Ordinarily the patient has an enema with a phosphosoda solution an hour before the examination. During the actual examination, the patient may be lying in a face-down, kneeling position, or lying on his or her side on the examining table. A digital rectal examination should be performed first. Sigmoidoscopy, while not comfortable, should not be painful to the patient because the instrument is inserted very gently. Sometimes air may be forced into the opening to help expand the bowel walls to make it easier to pass the instrument through the large intestine and to examine the walls. During the examination, the wall of the rectum and lower portion of the sigmoid colon—the S-shaped lower colon—are examined. Any abnormal area should be biopsied; this is easily done since the instrument can be used to collect small amounts of tissue that later will be examined under the microscope. This can be done painlessly and with only brief, negligible bleeding from the biopsy site.

Flexible sigmoidoscopes have become available in the past few years. Longer than the rigid models—35 to 65 centimeters in length—they contain a flexible fiberoptic system that permits bending the instrument from the handle (Figure 35). The flexible sigmoidoscope is basically a recently developed, shortened version of the colonoscope, which can be

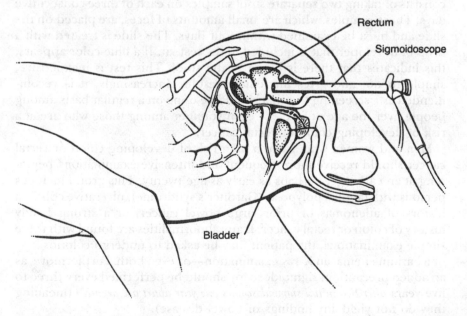

Figure 34 Sigmoidoscopy.

as long as 165 centimeters or nearly five feet. The design and flexibility of these instruments permit the endoscopist, usually a gastroenterologist or surgeon trained in these examinations, to see and examine the entire length of the large bowel. Biopsies of abnormal or suspicious-looking areas can be taken easily through the colonoscope with a special biopsy tool. This examination is ordinarily performed as an outpatient procedure, but preparation is much more extensive than for sigmoidoscopy. Preparation before colonoscopy includes consuming a liquid diet and cleansing the bowel with laxatives and an enema.

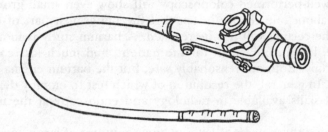

Figure 35 Olympus flexible sigmoidoscope (reproduced with the permission of the Olympus Corporation).

The colonoscope has a number of uses other than visual examination and collection of tissue for biopsy. For example, polyps can be completely removed through the colonoscope, reducing the need for major abdominal surgery. Patients undergoing this procedure may be admitted to the hospital overnight, but the practice varies from doctor to doctor—many will send the patient home after a few hours of observation, since bleeding is the only significant complication and occurs only rarely.

Still another examination is the barium enema X ray. Barium sulfate, a contrast material that shows up on X-ray film, is introduced through the catheter inserted into the rectum. A series of X-ray films are then taken, the barium is withdrawn, and air is introduced into the rectum for a final set of X-ray pictures known as air-contrast studies. The air-contrast aspect of the barium enema study is important because this technique provides excellent X-ray images of the colon, including polyps. However, the barium enema examination with air contrast is not a substitute for rigid or flexible sigmoidoscopy or digital rectal examination, since the rectal channel is large and tumors in the lower rectum may be missed. As in the case with colonoscopy, a more extensive preparation is necessary for the barium enema. Packaged kits for bowel preparation for barium enema and endoscopic examinations are widely available at pharmacies, and the doctor performing the examinations will usually tell the patient what preparations are necessary and how to use them. Neither the barium enema nor the colonic endoscopy is dangerous or painful, although some mild discomfort may be felt with both examinations.

There is an ongoing controversy among scientists and physicians regarding the diagnostic value of the barium enema X-ray examination with air contrast as compared with colonoscopy. All physicians agree on the importance of air-contrast X-ray films as an integral part of the barium enema study. If it is well performed, a barium enema examination with air contrast will show all significant growths larger than one quarter of an inch. A well-performed colonoscopy will show even small growths, but there is about one chance in ten that the uppermost part of the large bowel, the cecum, will not be reached. A barium study is more widely available, less inconvenient for the patient, and much less costly than colonoscopy. Both are reasonably safe, but the barium enema is a little more so. In general, the resolution of which test to employ depends on the local skills available in radiology and endoscopy at the individual hospital.

Screening those persons without any symptoms of large bowel cancer is undoubtedly an effective measure in modern preventive medicine. There is good evidence from several different university research studies that early detection of colon cancer before the onset of signs and symptoms increases the chances for a cure. A Kaiser-Permanente study, for example, strongly suggested that early detection of large bowel cancer through the use of digital and sigmoidoscopic examination reduced the death rate from this disease in the population group studied. These results do not include any additional beneficial effect that the discovery and removal of adenomas may have had. Two other large studies showed excellent long-term survival rates for people with bowel cancer who were screened with sigmoidoscopy. About 90 percent of these patients survived fifteen or more years, a rate so much better than expected among patients who did not undergo such screening that other factors are not likely to have biased the results. These studies provide strong evidence that detection of large bowel cancer before symptoms appear greatly decreases the death rate from this disease, and that the benefits derived outweigh any cost involved. Indeed, they are highly cost-effective, since treating colon cancer—or any cancer, for that matter—in its early, most curable stages costs less, both in terms of money and human suffering, than treating advanced cancer.

WARNING SYMPTOMS

Anyone with persistent symptoms that could be caused by a problem in the large bowel should see a doctor promptly. The most common symptom of a large bowel cancer is a change in bowel habits, usually either diarrhea, which is typical of a rectal cancer, or constipation, which is typical of a cancer in the left colon. If the tumor has extended beyond the wall of the colon and spread elsewhere in the body, symptoms might include enlargement of the liver, abdominal bloating, pain in the lower back, or bladder symptoms. Blood in the stools, as noted earlier, is another common early symptom, but this is not always apparent without a test for occult, or hidden, blood. Any recent change in bowel habits, or rectal bleeding or lower abdominal pain that does not subside promptly is a clear indication that medical attention should be sought.

Of course, the presence of these symptoms does not necessarily mean cancer. Hemorrhoids are a far more common cause of blood in the stool than cancer is. Typically, the bleeding from hemorrhoids appears as bright red blood found on the toilet tissue or present on the surface of the bowel movement or dripping into the toilet bowl. Patients who notice such bleeding should not panic; the blood loss is small, even though it might appear to be heavy. Hemorrhoids also cause anal discomfort and itching. Patients with these symptoms should be reassured that cancer probably is not involved; even so, a thorough examination of the rectum by a doctor is still necessary. This should include a digital examination, sigmoidoscopy, and possible examination with an anoscope, which is a small sigmoidoscope that enables a doctor to see the inside of the rectum.

Patients with potentially more serious problems will undergo a more extensive examination, which should include a full history of past health problems; general physical examination, including a digital rectal examination; test for occult blood; and sigmoidoscopy. In addition, either a barium enema examination with air contrast or colonoscopy is advisable. At the time of sigmoidoscopy or colonoscopy, biopsies should be taken from any suspicious area. Although a cancer of the large bowel may be readily apparent to the naked eye during sigmoidoscopy or colonoscopy, or be equally apparent from X rays taken during a barium enema, biopsies still should be obtained for microscopic confirmation of disease before treatment is started.

Symptoms affecting the lower gastrointestinal tract can be caused by a host of diseases other than cancer. One of the most common is diverticulosis, the formation of small out-pouchings or pockets within the wall of the colon. About 20 percent of all people over the age of sixty will have one or more diverticulae. These out-pouchings sometimes become inflamed, leading to altered bowel habits, usually alternating bouts of diarrhea and constipation; lower abdominal pain, fever, and bleeding in the stool. Most people with diverticulosis, however, usually have no, or only minor, symptoms.

Narrowing of the bowel can result from scarring and thickening of the intestinal muscle, and when this occurs sometimes colonoscopy is necessary to rule out the possibility of cancer. Symptoms also may come from other intestinal inflammatory diseases, such as chronic ulcerative colitis or regional ileitis, also known as Crohn's disease. Since patients with these conditions do, in fact, suffer a higher rate of large bowel cancer, biopsies of the surface of the large bowel may be in order to identify any abnormal precancerous tissue changes (dysplasia) so that the disease can be diagnosed in its earliest stages and appropriate preventive measures undertaken. These may include surgery to remove all or part of the colon, thus eliminating the threat of future cancer.

About one out of twenty people with large bowel cancer may suddenly develop obstruction of the bowel or a perforation—that is, an opening in the large bowel. In cases of obstruction, a complete blockage of the bowel occurs, leading to pain and distension of the abdomen. The patient is unable to have a bowel movement or to expel gas. Surgery is the only treatment. In the case of perforation of the bowel, acute lower abdominal pain, which often spreads to the entire abdominal area, occurs. This condition is known as peritonitis and it calls for emergency surgery and treatment with antibiotics. Antibiotics are needed because the spilling of the bowel contents into the abdominal, or peritoneal, cavity can lead to life-threatening infection.

TREATMENT OF LARGE BOWEL CANCER

If diagnostic studies do confirm the presence of large bowel cancer, the patient ordinarily will be admitted to the hospital for further preparation and treatment. The problem is not really an emergency, and a waiting period of up to a few weeks before admission does no harm unless the intestine is partially obstructed. Since patients with large bowel cancer are usually older, the assessment of other organ systems, such as the heart or lungs, will also be necessary. Modern surgery, however, is so well developed that all but the most seriously ill patients can do well, albeit with a somewhat increased surgical risk, if there are significant heart or lung problems.

If the patient is to have a rectal operation, special studies such as an X-ray study of the kidneys, ureters, and bladder (a pyelogram) may be necessary to determine their positions and whether they too have been invaded by cancer. In addition, other blood and radiologic studies such as brain, liver, and bone scans may be performed to be as sure as possible that the tumor is limited to the large bowel and that the odds for a cure are good. As might be expected, these preoperative studies are not carried out in cases where obstruction or perforation have occurred.

Preparing the large bowel for operation requires thorough cleansing with enemas followed by oral antibiotics, usually one with an erythromycin base and neomycin, on the day before the operation. Safe surgery of the large bowel demands having a clean, dry colon. Therefore both strong laxatives and enemas must be used to ensure that the colon is well prepared for the operation. Patients also are asked to go on a special diet in preparation for the surgery. This entails eating low-residue foods that produce little stool, followed by a full liquid diet and, finally, a clear liquid diet. This part of the preparation can begin before admission to the hospital or the patient may be admitted two or three days before the operation, at which time the dietary preparation will begin. Since some diarrhea will be produced by this regimen, extra fluids are needed to make up for the fluid loss.

The main objective of the operation is to remove the tumor and a wide border of colon both above and below the cancer as well as the lymphatic tissue that drains it. With rare exceptions, such as cases in which there is serious infection or inflammation of the bowel, the continuity of the intestine is restored by rejoining the ends, a procedure known as anastomosis. Thus the colon, even though somewhat shorter than before, will function normally following the surgery. If an anastomosis cannot be performed at the time of the cancer surgery, a temporary colostomy—a surgically created opening between the colon and the outer surface of the body—will be made. After healing has taken place, this will be repaired, restoring normal colon function.

If the cancer is in the rectum, it may be necessary to form a colostomy. Although many people have the mistaken notion that large bowel cancer inevitably means a colostomy, it is now actually the exception rather than the rule. Over the last twenty years, a variety of operative techniques have been developed, and now only about one of seven patients with rectal cancer requires a permanent colostomy. Techniques for restoring the continuity of the bowel include a very low anastomosis, an anastomosis from the floor of the pelvis (the perineum), or in some instances, a local removal of the rectal cancer through the anal canal. Occasionally after a low anastomosis is performed, a temporary colostomy may be needed to protect the area from infection until healing has taken place. In these instances the colostomy will be closed in an operation two or three months after the initial cancer surgery. (The management of both temporary and permanent colostomies is discussed later in this chapter.)

In recent years it has become clear that for some patients, radiation therapy provides additional benefits in treating rectal cancer. In some instances the radiation therapy may take place before the surgery; in others the operation may be performed first, with the course of post-surgery radiation to be determined by the exact nature of the cancer found during the operation. In either instance, proper timing of the radiation in relation to the operation is important to achieve the maximum benefit of both and to ensure proper healing following the surgery. (For a more detailed discussion, see Chapter 8, "Radiation Therapy.")

In some instances drug treatment also may be recommended following surgery for large bowel cancer. These treatments—known as adjuvant, or supplementary, chemotherapy—may add an additional element of protection to those patients with more extensive tumors, or those whose cancers may have spread to other parts of the body. In adjuvant chemotherapy, the anticancer drugs are given orally or intravenously or both, periodically for up to several years after the surgery. These drugs may be given even if there is no evidence of spread beyond the colon, depending upon the extent of the cancer. (See Chapter 7, "Principles of Cancer Chemotherapy.")

After the operation the surgeon will be able to tell the patient and his or her family the visible extent of the tumor. About three to five days later, the pathologist's report on the microscopic nature of the tumor will be submitted. This report ordinarily will classify the tumor specimen by the Dukes staging system, named for a London pathologist, Cuthbert Dukes, who developed the classification system in 1932. Since that time some modifications have been made. In general, a Dukes A tumor has not penetrated through the full thickness of the bowel wall. The cure rate of a Dukes A tumor exceeds 90 percent. In a Dukes B tumor, the cancer has penetrated the full thickness of the bowel wall, but lymph nodes are not involved. The cure rate in these cancers is about 70 percent. If there has been spread to the lymph nodes, the likelihood of cure diminishes and in these circumstances patients may be advised to have additional radiation therapy, chemotherapy, or both.

Immediately following an operation for large bowel cancer, the patient can expect to have a plastic tube placed through the nose and into the stomach to drain secretions. This tube will remain in place for several days, and during that time no food will be given by mouth. Instead, all nourishment will be intravenous. The surgical staff will examine the patient's abdomen regularly, and when normal bowel sounds return, oral feeding gradually can resume. This process normally takes four to seven days.

When patients with a cancer in the sigmoid colon or rectum are operated on, there is often also a temporary paralysis of the bladder as a result of the operation on the rectum, which is close to the nerves that serve the bladder. These patients must have a urinary catheter in place for several days after the operation until the paralysis subsides and normal urination resumes. In many instances patients actually prefer the catheter, because it spares them the discomfort or pain in their wound associated with standing up to urinate or moving around in bed to use the bedpan.

After a major abdominal operation a patient can ordinarily expect pain at the incision, but in decreasing intensity, for about two days. The pain will be effectively blunted by painkilling drugs. For an additional two days the patient can expect pain in the wound or incision when he or she turns, coughs, or moves about. After about four days there is no pain at all.

A patient who has had colon surgery with an anastomosis and restoration of intestinal activity can expect to leave the hospital about eight days following the operation. By that time the patient will be able to eat solid foods, the antibiotics will have been discontinued, and strength regained. A further convalescent period will be required at home, but, in general, regular work can be resumed about six weeks later, although many patients who do paper work will resume part-time activity promptly, often while still in the hospital. Upon stretching, some pain may occur at the site of the scar, but this will go away in a few months.

When it has been necessary to remove the entire rectum, the patient will have two incisions—one on the abdominal wall and one at the perineum, the area between the coccyx (tailbone) and the genitals. Ordinarily the lower wound is closed completely, but on occasion it is necessary to keep it open and pack it with sterile packing material. The pack will be removed about five days after the operation, and the area will then heal. When the rectum must be removed and a colostomy constructed, a longer hospital stay is required, often extending up to fifteen days or more, before the patient is able to return home for continued convalescence.

POTENTIAL COMPLICATIONS

Modern surgery, with all the marvelous progress of the last twenty years, still occasionally produces some unfortunate results in a small number of patients. The most frequent complication to arise in colon surgery is infection. This is understandable because intestinal surgery carries the potential of contamination of the area of operation with bacteria from the colon. There is also the ever-present hazard of infection from the air, skin, and other sources of bacteria. For this reason thorough preparation of the bowel along with administration of antibiotics before, during, and after surgery are important to prevent infection. Postoperative infections, when they occur, can cause serious problems, but most often they only delay discharge from the hospital and healing of the site of the operation until the antibiotics can eradicate the bacteria.

Other kinds of complications are relatively unusual and include such problems as an opening of a presumably healed incision, slow closure of the wound (most often this occurs in incisions made in the perineal area), and slow recovery from the surgery.

In some instances the surgeon will discover that the cancer has spread so extensively that it cannot be totally removed. In these cases the surgeon removes as much as possible to prevent blockage of the colon. Anticancer drugs and radiation may then be administered postopera-

tively to arrest or slow tumor growth. Still, these complications are exceptions; colon surgery is a safe and successful procedure for the vast majority of patients.

COLOSTOMY CARE

The colostomy, when needed, is ordinarily constructed in the lower left
area of the abdominal wall; occasionally it is constructed within the main
incision. Ordinarily the colostomy is constructed at the time of the cancer
operation in the manner in which it will remain—provided, of course, that
a permanent one is needed. It appears as a small, reddish, round opening
of healthy-looking mucosal tissue—the type of tissue that lines the mouth
and throat, for example—on the abdominal wall. A plastic bag called a
colostomy pouch (Figure 36) is placed over the opening, and within a few
days after the operation, as the bowel recovers its normal function, intestinal secretions will begin to exit from the opening, which is called a
stoma.

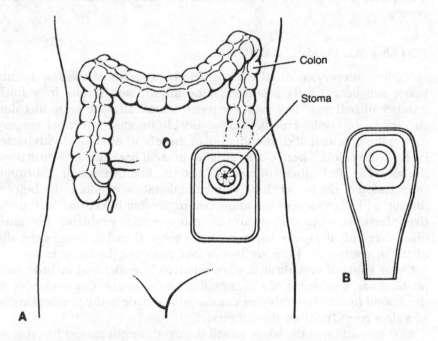

Figure 36A Disposable close-end colostomy pouch over the stoma.
        36B Disposable drainable pouch (pouches shown are Hollister
pouches with karaya and adhesive seals).

Several days after the operation, when the patient is beginning to move around and walk, the surgeon and nursing staff will start teaching the patient how to manage the colostomy. During the next few days in the hospital, the patient will be helped to achieve independence. In many instances the help of a specialized stomal therapist will be valuable. These therapists are well-trained nurses who provide advice on techniques of irrigation or cleansing of the stoma. A number of modern plastic devices have been developed that greatly simplify care and help the patient achieve confidence and security in living with a colostomy. Thousands of active people from all walks of life have colostomies and engage in a full range of professional, social, sexual, and athletic activities without awkwardness, embarrassment, or accident.

As a rule, patients in the United States are taught to irrigate their colostomy. Daily irrigation is not always necessary or desirable, but on the whole, most patients feel more satisfied when they are able to irrigate the colostomy each morning or every other morning and then wear a patch over the colostomy until the next irrigation.

The time each patient requires to adjust to a colostomy varies. If the patient has had regular bowel movements in the past, this pattern will continue after a colostomy. With a set routine of irrigation, the daily bowel movement will, in effect, be eliminated by the irrigation and the patient will be free of "spillage" in between. In the beginning, the irrigation takes much more time until the patient becomes accustomed to the procedure, but eventually it should be accomplished within an hour. In any instance, it is extremely important that the patient manage the colostomy and not let the colostomy manage the patient.

A time should be chosen for irrigation that is most convenient for the patient and family. The patient should be able to take over a bathroom for about an hour without interruption, so that the procedure can be accomplished smoothly and systematically. It may help to have the telephone nearby or else shut off until the irrigation is completed. It is important to be able to relax during the procedure. Most colostomy patients, or "colostomates" as they are called, are expert in self-care before they leave the hospital, although some may require minimal assistance from a family member in the beginning. The sooner the patient accomplishes his or her own care, the faster will be the return to a normal way of life. Should special problems connected with the irrigation or wound care arise, the services of a visiting nurse are available in most communities.

The irrigation technique requires enough water to accomplish a good evacuation of the bowel. One quart of lukewarm water is the average volume needed, and up to two quarts is always sufficient. Each person needs to make his or her own adjustments for volume. A well-lubricated catheter or cone should be inserted into the stoma to a depth of no more than one or two inches to help the water enter the intestine. The cone method, which gently opens the stoma, is gaining in popularity and appears to be safer than the catheter.

The patient should be sure that the irrigation bag is not hung too high; otherwise the water will enter too fast at too high a pressure, resulting in cramps. The bottom of the bag should be at shoulder level. Air should be expelled from the tubing and the water should be lukewarm, neither too cold nor too hot. If cramps do occur, it sometimes helps to sit back against a chair and take several slow, deep breaths or rock back and forth until relief is obtained.

Mucus is normally produced by the colostomy stoma because it is a natural product of the bowel surface, acting as a lubricant. The patient should keep a waterproof dressing over the stoma to prevent undergarments from being stained. Any rubbing or irritation of the stoma may cause a slight abrasion, an additional reason to keep a lubricated gauze dressing over it. Redness or roughening of the skin around the stoma is sometimes seen during bouts of diarrhea or whenever the stool is in contact with the skin longer than normal. The problem is akin to a baby's diaper rash. Meticulous skin care will prevent most skin problems—a shower or tub bath after the irrigation is helpful. Diaparene, stoma barrier cream, or some other soothing medication may be used to heal the skin and prevent further irritation during bouts of diarrhea or intestinal flu. When diarrhea occurs the patient may need to wear a temporary appliance, such as a drainable Hollister karaya bag, for a few days to protect the skin from irritating enzymes until the diarrhea ceases.

AFTER THE SURGERY

A normal appetite should return comparatively quickly following the operation. Unless the patient has a prescribed diet for another medical condition, such as diabetes, a well-balanced, normal diet should be resumed before discharge from the hospital. In the beginning, however, some foods, such as nuts, seeds, coleslaw, celery, and binding foods should be eliminated. The patient also should avoid foods that produce excessive gas, such as beans, cabbage, and onions. Preparations of bismuth subcarbonate or charcoal are effective in controlling gas and odor.

If constipation occurs, the patient should add such foods as cooked fruit, vegetables, juices, and fluids, and avoid those foods that tend to constipate. Colostomy patients should not take a laxative unless it is prescribed by the physician.

If diarrhea occurs, the patient should examine his or her diet to see if foods that produce loose, frequent stools are being eaten. Most people, including colostomy patients, occasionally get intestinal flu, and this possibility should be considered when diarrhea occurs. Commonly, intestinal flu is accompanied by headache, muscle aches, loss of appetite, and fever.

If these symptoms are present, a physician should be consulted. During these occasional intestinal upsets, a temporary appliance with bag should be worn for the sake of cleanliness and skin care until the diarrhea subsides.

A panty-type, two-way-stretch girdle is the best type of undergarment for women with a colostomy, and a wide-belted athletic supporter seems best for men. These garments serve three purposes: they support the recently healed abdominal wound and help keep a dressing in place over the incision as well as cover the stoma. If the posterior, or perineal, incision has been left open, sitz baths will have to be continued until closure is complete. Closure can take several months. During this time, disposable diapers can be worn over the wound dressing under the girdle or supporter to keep undergarments from becoming wet from the wound secretions.

Most patients can wear their usual clothes, but tight dresses and trousers may prove uncomfortable. Pants suits and A-line dresses are usually the most comfortable for women. Nonconstrictive slacks are usually best for men, and some avoid possible discomfort from a belt by switching to suspenders.

As stressed earlier, it is crucial for patients to learn to manage their colostomy rather than become enslaved by it. This means engaging in normal, pleasurable activities. Travel, for example, should not prove a great problem for colostomates; a patient can irrigate the bowel wherever there is a toilet and a sink with running water. The patient should plan ahead by preparing a small kit with all the necessary items, including appliances for irrigation and care of the stoma. A flight bag is good for this purpose. Some string to hang the irrigating bag in bathrooms away from home should be included; a door hinge often makes a good hook in an emergency. When planning a trip abroad or extensive travel, the patient's physician should be consulted, particularly regarding medicine to prevent diarrhea.

Most sports, with the exception of body-contact sports, are recommended and encouraged. These include golfing, swimming, tennis and other non-contact sports.

SEX AND THE COLOSTOMY PATIENT

The affection and love that human beings have for each other is precious and wonderful and not based solely on physical attraction. Nonetheless, the patient with a colostomy may feel reluctant about sexual activities. This hesitation is understandable, but almost always unfounded. The colostomy constructed by modern surgery and cared for by proper irrigation and general cleanliness is not a repellent object or a source of offensive odor, as many people fear. Patients who are sexually active should have no embarrassment in continuing their sexual lives. Older patients who are sexually active should act similarly. The patient and the patient's partner will quickly realize how little the colostomy affects their physical activity and mutual regard. Colostomy surgery, in contrast to major prostate and bladder surgery, does not interrupt or damage the nerve pathways that excite and maintain sexual arousal; thus sexual performance and response should be unaffected by a colostomy, at least physiologically. If problems occur in this aspect of one's life, they should be openly discussed, since they are more likely to be psychological than physical.

FOLLOW UP

After an operation for large bowel cancer, patients will have to see their doctor periodically for follow-up. The main goal of these visits, which will occur every few months for the first few years after treatment, will be to detect any recurrence of the tumor or the development of a new one. Hence it will be necessary to have checks of the intestinal secretions for occult blood, periodic sigmoidoscopic examinations, and, from time to time, a colonoscopy or a barium enema with air contrast, or both. The main reason for these examinations is that the patient who has had cancer of the large bowel has an increased risk of developing another one at a different location within the large bowel. Periodic chest X rays and general examinations are performed at the same time.

Recently, follow-up of patients has been aided by a new test called the carcinoembryonic antigen (CEA) test. This is a blood test that detects a substance produced by the large bowel tumor that may provide an early warning. The test is useful but not perfect, because the CEA may be elevated in persons who smoke or have other conditions.

IF THE TUMOR RECURS

At the present time about half of all patients with large bowel cancer will develop a recurrence. On occasion a simple area of spread detected in the lung or in the liver can be removed and the patient will have another chance for a cure. This is one reason for careful follow-up after the initial treatment.

Recurrence follows one or more of several patterns. Patients who have recurrent rectal cancer often develop pain in or near the perineum, and radiation therapy is particularly effective in controlling a tumor at that site. The cancer may spread through the lymph channels or veins to the liver. Treatment with effective drugs can be administered directly into the liver. If the cancer has spread to the liver or to other areas of the body, chemotherapy administered orally or intravenously can be beneficial.

Cancer specialists regard cancer of the large bowel as a "transitional" tumor, meaning it is beginning to show responsiveness to drug treatments. Although 5-fluorouracil has been the standard anticancer drug used in large bowel cancer, the present trend is to employ other drugs as well. Hence the patient may receive three or four different chemotherapeutic drugs, including 5-fluorouracil. This approach makes possible long-term relief and a high quality of life.

SUMMING UP

Cancer of the colon and rectum are very common in most developed countries, including the United States. At present about half of all patients who develop large bowel cancer will be cured. Wider application of currently available screening methods along with more intensive use of available diagnostic methods are capable of detecting cancers of the colon and rectum in their early, most treatable stages. If these screening and diagnostic techniques are combined with appropriate operative treatment and careful follow-up, many more than the present 50 percent of patients can be cured. In the past, many people have avoided prompt medical attention when they suspected bowel cancer, fearing that the treatment would greatly diminish the quality of life. For example, many people still assume that colon cancer surgery automatically means a colostomy, when, in fact, colostomies are the exception rather than the rule. Even when a colostomy is required, most people learn to care for it before they leave the hospital. In short, large bowel cancer is in the process of coming under control in every sense of the word.

19

Cancer of the Esophagus

ROBERT J. MAYER, M.D.,
AND MARC B. GARNICK, M.D.

Cancer of the esophagus is one of the more difficult malignancies to treat; fortunately, it is relatively rare compared to other cancers of the digestive tract. About 9,400 new cases are diagnosed each year and there are about 8,000 deaths. The disease is much more common in men than in women, and blacks are afflicted three to four times as often as whites. The average age of the patient at the time of diagnosis is sixty-eight to seventy years.

There are marked geographic differences in esophageal cancer. For example, it appears to be increasing in the southeastern United States. In the Hunan province of northern China, it is one of the most common cancers. In some parts of Iran, esophageal cancer accounts for more than half of all malignancies and is twenty times more common than in the United States. It is also quite common in parts of South Africa.

CAUSES OF ESOPHAGEAL CANCER

The cause of cancer of the esophagus has not been definitely identified, but several factors that increase the risk of developing it have been identified. In the United States, the leading risk factors are use of tobacco and alcohol. When used together, as they often are, the carcinogenic effect is multiplied. People who both smoke and drink are thirty times more likely to develop esophageal cancer than are people who neither drink nor smoke.

Chronic irritation of the lower esophagus because of gastric reflux—the backward flow of stomach acid into the esophagus—appears to increase the risk of esophageal cancer, but the correlation is not as great as with smoking and alcohol use. Exposure of the esophagus to lye, as might happen during a suicide attempt or accidental swallowing of the caustic substance by a child, also increases the risk.

DIAGNOSIS

Since the esophagus is the tube through which food passes en route to the stomach (Figure 37), the most common sign of possible esophageal cancer is a difficulty in swallowing. At first the problem occurs mostly with solid foods, but as the cancer grows even liquids and soft foods become difficult to swallow. Unfortunately, by the time this symptom appears and a person seeks medical help, the cancer is likely to be well advanced in the esophagus and to have spread to other parts of the body. Other warning signs include seemingly unexplained choking on a piece of food that would normally be easy to swallow, painful spasms after eating, and frequent bouts of "indigestion" or reflux.

Early diagnosis is critical to the successful treatment of esophageal cancer. At present, metastasis has already occurred in at least half of patients by the time of diagnosis. In parts of China, where esophageal cancer is very common, extensive screening programs have been effective in detecting the cancer early, when a chance of cure is most likely.

The diagnosis of cancer of the esophagus is straightforward. Persistent difficulty in swallowing is a clear indication that the possibility of esophageal cancer should be investigated. Tests include an X-ray examination of the esophagus (an esophagogram). During this examination the patient swallows a chalky solution containing barium. The passage of the barium through the esophagus is followed with a fluoroscope, and X-ray pictures are taken at points during the examination. These X-ray films will usually be able to show whether a tumor is causing the difficulty in swallowing or whether the problem is due to a muscular disorder. The X rays cannot distinguish a malignant tumor from one that is benign.

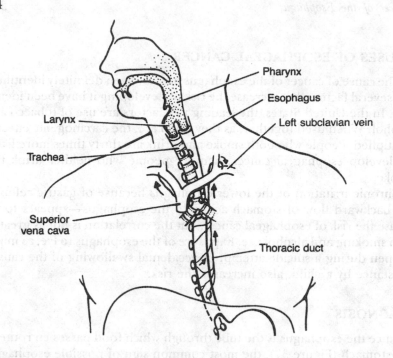

Figure 37 Normal esophagus with lymphatics.

Normal X rays do not entirely rule out the possibility of cancer; therefore, additional studies are needed if esophageal cancer is suspected. These studies include esophagoscopy, a test that entails passing a flexible tube with fiberoptic instruments through the mouth and down the throat into the esophagus. To prevent discomfort and gagging, a mild sedative is given and the throat is sprayed with an anesthetic. The examination takes fifteen to thirty minutes to perform and can be done in a physician's office or outpatient clinic. The fiberoptic devices used enable the examining physician to see the affected area and also to take small tissue samples for later biopsy studies. Esophagoscopy is considered a safe examination with minimal discomfort, although perforation of the esophagus—a potentially serious problem—occurs in a small number of patients.

Other tests that may be performed include chest X rays, CT scanning, and blood tests. These are intended mostly to assess the extent of the cancer and the patient's general health.

Cancer of the esophagus spreads both by local invasion of surrounding tissues and also through the lymph system and bloodstream. The esophagus lacks a serosa, an outer membrane found in most other parts of the body that acts as a protective barrier against the spread of invasive cancer cells. This is one reason for the relatively rapid local spread of esophageal cancer. Metastases to the lung and liver are common as the cancer advances.

TREATMENT

Surgery and radiation therapy are the two methods used to treat cancer of the esophagus. Depending upon the type of cancer and its location, a patient may have either or both treatments.

More than one third of all esophageal cancers occur in the lowermost portion where the esophagus empties into the stomach (the esophago-gastric junction). Most cancers in this area are adenocarcinomas—malignancies made up of abnormal glandular cells. Cancers occurring in the body of the esophagus are usually squamous cell carcinomas—malignancies that arise in the epithelial cells lining the organ. When the cancer is located in the lower esophagus, the usual surgical approach involves removal of the lower part of the esophagus and upper portion of the stomach. To restore the patient's ability to eat normally, the remaining portion of the esophagus and stomach are reconnected, either by extending a portion of the stomach to replace part of the missing esophagus or sometimes by using a portion of the colon or small intestine. Patients with advanced esophageal cancer that cannot be surgically removed still may have their ability to swallow restored by insertion of a special prosthetic tube.

Radiation therapy may be used, either alone or in combination with surgery, usually before the operation, to reduce the size of the tumor. Radiation therapy directed to the esophagus poses several difficulties. If the cancer is in the upper part of the esophagus, the radiation may damage the spinal cord. The lungs also may be damaged by radiation. Thus special care must be taken, both in administering the proper dosage and in directing it to the cancer without damaging the spinal cord and lungs.

In some research centers cancer chemotherapy is being added as an adjunctive treatment, either before or after surgery. The drugs most commonly used are cisplatin, 5-fluorouracil, nitomycin, methotrexate, or bleomycin.

Since progressive difficulty in swallowing is a major problem with esophageal cancer, treatment to restore swallowing is often undertaken even when a cure is unlikely. Liquid diets and nutrition supplements are often needed. Sometimes artificial feeding through a tube inserted into the stomach may be recommended to maintain nutritional status. An opening in the pharynx to divert the flow of saliva from the blocked esophagus also may be recommended for patients who can no longer swallow.

SUMMING UP

Esophageal cancer is a particularly difficult disease to treat and has a high mortality rate. Early diagnosis affords the best chance of a cure. Given the relative poor outcome even with extensive surgery and radiation treatment, increased emphasis on prevention is warranted. Since the majority of esophageal cancers are linked to tobacco and alcohol abuse, prevention should be directed to discouraging people from smoking and encouraging moderation in alcohol use.

20

Cancer of the Eye

FREDERICK A. JAKOBIEC, M.D., D.SC.

INTRODUCTION

Cancer of the eye or its supporting structures is relatively rare, with only 2,500 new cases and 400 deaths a year. Men and women are equally affected. Most eye cancers are curable, especially if they are diagnosed early. Advances in eye surgery, including the use of radiation therapy, cryotherapy (freezing), and lasers, now make it possible to eradicate the cancer and still save the eye in an increasing number of patients.

In general, eye cancer can be divided into three categories, as determined by the site in which the cancer originates (see Figure 38). These locations are the eyeball itself; within the bony orbit (socket) that contains the eye and its surrounding protective soft tissues; and the eyelids and conjunctiva, the latter being the membrane that covers the surface of the eyeball and lines the back side of the lids.

368

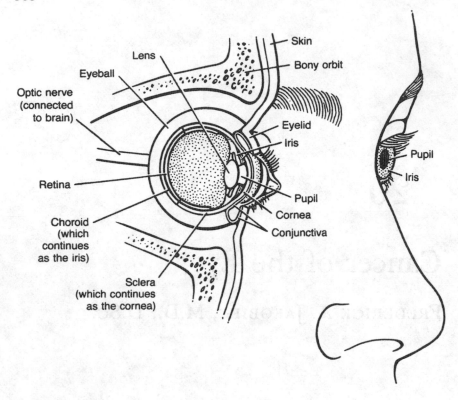

Figure 38 Anatomy of the normal eye.

The cause of most eye cancers is unknown. However, retinoblastoma, a type of eye cancer that occurs during infancy and early childhood, follows a well-recognized hereditary pattern which strongly suggests that a cancer-causing gene may be the instigating factor.

DIAGNOSIS OF EYE CANCER

A rapidly growing eye cancer usually produces symptoms such as double vision, a protrusion of the eyeball, or other obvious changes leading to early diagnosis and treatment. A slow-growing tumor of the retina or optic nerve may cause more subtle changes, which can go unnoticed until the cancer is more advanced. Any changes in vision or other problems such as a protruding eye, squinting, or changes in the eyelid should be seen by an ophthalmologist. Although eye cancer is rare and most eye problems have a benign cause, the possibility of cancer should be ruled out as soon as possible.

A number of different instruments are now available that enable an ophthalmologist to examine most parts of the eye by noninvasive techniques. The degree of protrusion of the eyeball is measured with a special device called an exophthalmometer. The anterior portions of the globe, including the cornea and iris, can be viewed using a slit lamp. The retina and other posterior portions of the globe can be examined with an ophthalmoscope and other instruments designed to enable the ophthalmologist to see into the eye. Fluorescein angiography, a diagnostic test in which dye is injected into a vein in the arm, can be used to help the doctor visualize the blood vessels of the eye and identify a tumor.

CT scanning and ultrasound examinations may be used to locate the tumor and to plan surgical treatment. Radionuclide studies, in which a radioactive material is injected into the circulation and then followed by scanning devices, also may be useful both in diagnostic tests and in follow-up examinations to detect metastases. As in most cancers, however, the final diagnosis is established by a tissue biopsy. Needle biopsies, in which a small amount of tissue is removed by a hollow aspiration needle, are possible for tumors in the back of the eye.

CANCERS OF THE EYEBALL

The two most common kinds of cancer that arise in the globe itself are malignant melanoma and retinoblastoma. The first is a disease of adults and commonly begins in the pigment-forming cells (the melanocytes) of the iris, the ciliary body, or the choroid. The choroid is located between the whitish fibrous tissue of the outside of the eye (the sclera) and the innermost layer of the eye (the retina); it contains blood vessels and pigment. Retinoblastoma arises from the retina and occurs in infants and young children; this type of eye cancer has become much more curable in recent years.

Malignant melanomas of the iris appear to be quite different from melanomas arising elsewhere in the body, including other parts of the eye. Death from melanoma of the iris, a very slow-growing tumor, is practically unknown. In some patients periodic examination may be all that is required until the tumor reaches a certain size or causes deformity of the pupil. More commonly, however, the melanoma will be removed at the time of biopsy.

A melanoma of the choroid is much more serious than that of the iris. About 60 percent of patients with this type of eye cancer are alive five years after diagnosis. Patients often die from metastases to the liver. If the tumor is near the macula, the central part of the retina and the point of maximal visual acuity in the back of the eye, a decline in vision usually prompts a patient to see a doctor. Otherwise, melanoma of the choroid may not produce symptoms during its early stages, although sometimes it may be found during a routine eye examination.

The best treatment for choroidal and ciliary body melanomas is somewhat controversial at this time. Approximately eight years ago a hypothesis was advanced that, in the course of removing an eye containing a melanoma, cancer cells might be squeezed into the bloodstream, so that the removal of the eye itself might therefore promote the spread of tumor cells outside the eye. A corollary of this hypothesis is that removing an eye containing a tumor upsets the body's immunologic defenses against its spread.

Data used to support this hypothesis were the low level of spontaneously occurring metastases away from the eye from choroidal melanomas before enucleation (removal of the eye) is performed, and the high rate of metastases that develop one to two years after the melanoma has been removed. This hypothesis has not been proved, nor has it been totally disproved. Many experts believe that the spread of metastases beyond the eye within the first two years is not unlike the development of metastases from cancers elsewhere in the body, which also have a tendency to appear one to two years after treatment.

This hypothesis, however, has strengthened the argument in many cases for so-called conservative forms of radiation therapy, which may successfully treat the tumor and allow the preservation of vision. Plaques of cobalt-60 or iodine-125 may be sewn on the outside of the eye (to the sclera) so that the requisite amount of radiation therapy can be delivered to the underlying tumor, and then the plaque is removed one to two weeks later. Another form of therapy is external-beam heavy-ion or particle irradiation, but unfortunately, as of this writing, this therapy is available only in Boston and San Francisco. All forms of radiation therapy result in the disappearance or shrinkage of the tumor one to two years after the dose was administered, and the disappearance appears to result from radiation damage to the tumor cells as well as to the blood vessels that supply the tumor.

One of the various forms of radiation therapy is recommended when vision has been well preserved despite the presence of the tumor. The location of the tumor in the eye is a major factor in determining whether there will be radiation side effects to the retina, the lens (leading to cataract formation), or to the optic nerve. The survival rate is quite comparable for patients who have been treated with radiation therapy versus those who have been treated with removal of the eye. For very large tumors that have caused detachment of the retina and a significant disorganization of the eye structures, most authorities still recommend removal of the eye, which is performed very gently to avoid spreading the cancer cells into the bloodstream. It is also possible to deliver 2,000 to 2,500 rads of radiation therapy to the eyeball prior to removing the eye, in the hope of devitalizing cells so that even if small numbers do enter the bloodstream, they are sufficiently weakened to be unable to establish a successful metastasis.

Retinoblastoma is a very malignant childhood eye cancer that is highly curable by radiation therapy if it is diagnosed in an early stage. The most common early signs of retinoblastoma are the development of a squint or the appearance of a white area in the center of the pupil, the part of the eye that normally looks back with a red reflex. Since this disease is most common in babies and children under the age of two, ages when the child is too young to complain about visual problems, it may go unnoticed in its early stages. The disease may arise in several locations within the same eye, and in about a fourth of patients, both eyes will be affected. This is particularly true for the inherited form of the disease, which accounts for 30 to 35 percent of cases.

The treatment of retinoblastoma depends upon the stage of the disease and the state of the other eye. If the cancer is still small, external-beam radiation therapy, localized radiation therapy by means of implanting radioactive plaques, and cryotherapy offer the best chance of a cure while preserving vision. A combination of radiation therapy and chemotherapy may be used if the cancer has started to spread within the eye toward the optic nerve. The entire eyeball may be removed if the disease is more advanced. More extensive surgery, including removal of the muscles and optic nerve, may be necessary if the cancer has spread to the optic nerve and socket tissues. Chemotherapy may be administered after the operation in an effort to eliminate any cancer cells that may have spread to other parts of the body, and radiation therapy and chemotherapy may have to be administered to the brain.

Formerly, retinoblastoma was often fatal. Today the overall cure rate is about 85 percent, but it can exceed 90 percent with a high probability of preserving vision if the disease is diagnosed and treated in an early stage. Following treatment, the child should be examined several times a year for the next four to six years to search for recurrence or development of cancer in the remaining eye.

TUMORS OF THE ORBIT

Tumors arising in the orbit, or eye socket, often cause squinting or a forward bulging (proptosis) of the eye. Diagnosis usually involves X-ray studies of the orbit and skull and CT and ultrasound scanning, followed by biopsy to confirm the diagnosis and determine the type of cancer. Tumors that may involve the orbit include lymphoma, meningioma and glioma of the optic nerve, lacrimal gland tumors, metastatic cancer arising elsewhere in the body, and rhabdomyosarcoma, a cancer of the muscles that control movement of the eyeball.

Not all of the foregoing tumors (such as meningioma and glioma) are cancers in the sense of being able to spread through the bloodstream to distant sites beyond the orbit. These tumors are locally infiltrative and can spread toward the brain and thereby cause death, so that it seems appropriate to give some general information about them.

Treatment depends upon the type of tumor. Meningiomas are treated with surgical removal. Lymphomas of the orbit can usually be treated with local radiation therapy after a biopsy, unless there is evidence of lymphoma elsewhere in the body. The treatment of gliomas of the optic nerve depends upon the location of the tumor. These are slow-growing tumors that occur most often in children and young adults. They are treated with surgery if the tumor does not extend back to the optic chiasm, the point of crossing of the right and left optic nerves on the underside of the brain. Since the optic nerve is really an extension of the brain, surgery involving the area behind the orbit should be performed by a neurosurgeon. Radiation therapy is now the preferred treatment for tumors that extend to the chiasm and beyond. A cure may not be possible, but since the tumor progresses slowly, it may not recur for decades.

The lacrimal gland is located in the upper outer quadrant of the socket, just beneath the bony orbital rim. Fortunately most tumors and swellings of this structure are either noninfectious inflammations or benign tumors; highly malignant epithelial tumors constitute less than 10 percent of the swellings. This type of cancer progresses rapidly and, if untreated, may prove fatal in several years. Symptoms usually include displacement of the eye forward as well as down and in, with pain and double vision as the tumor interferes with the action of the muscles that move the eye. A biopsy through the lid for a suspected malignancy of the lacrimal gland is performed, and after a firm diagnosis of cancer has been made, the lids, the eyeball, the soft tissues of the socket, and the bones surrounding the tumor are removed *en bloc* (exenteration with radical bone excision); skin grafting may be required to repair the defect that is created. Patients who do not have such radical surgery unfortunately have a uniformly fatal course, but 20 to 30 percent may survive if such surgery is performed in time.

Adults may develop two other malignancies of the soft tissues of the socket, namely hemangiopericytoma and fibrous histiocytoma. The first is a tumor that derives from the cells that form part of the blood vessel walls of small capillaries, whereas the second is a tumor that arises from the connective tissue cells of the orbit that envelop the fat and muscles. CT scanning generally shows a moderately large rounded tumor behind the eyeball or beside it in the socket. The best treatment is wide local excision of the tumor, which is performed by exposing the tumor through a window made in the bone on the outside wall of the socket. Radiation therapy has little to offer for these tumors. If they should recur because of difficulty in removing them at first surgery (the surgeon almost always tries to preserve vision and the muscles that move the eye during wide local excision), radical exenteration of all of the orbital soft tissues along with the eyeball is recommended because of the metastatic potential of some of these tumors.

Cancer of the eye muscles (Figure 39), rhabdomyosarcoma, occurs most often in children under the age of ten and can grow quite rapidly, resulting in marked protrusion or bulging of the eye. There also may be swelling of the eyelid and involvement of the adjacent sinuses. Once the diagnosis of rhabdomyosarcoma in a child is suspected, a biopsy through the lid is performed.

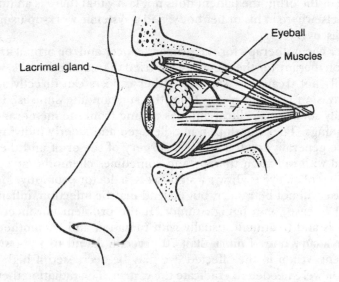

Figure 39 Left eye with muscles and lacrimal gland.

After the diagnosis has been made by a pathologist, a combination of radiation therapy, in doses of 5,000 to 6,000 rads, and multiple chemotherapy is given. In the past, disfiguring orbital exenteration was the only form of therapy available, and it led to cure rates in the range of 30 to 40 percent. With the introduction of combined radiation therapy and chemotherapy, survival is now over 80 percent, and the need for exenteration has been almost totally removed. One of the main problems with radiation therapy is that the eyeball suffers considerable damage, but this appears to be a worthwhile trade-off in view of the improved survival rates from radiation therapy. In the future, it may be possible to treat with only chemotherapy, since much larger cancers of this type elsewhere in the body appear to be successfully treated by unaided chemotherapy.

Metastatic cancers from elsewhere in the body may travel through the bloodstream and establish themselves in either the orbit or in the choroid (the middle vascular layer) of the eyeball. The most common origin for a metastasis to the eye or orbit is from a breast cancer in women and from a lung cancer in men. If the cancer goes to the choroid, visual disturbance will lead to detection of the ocular condition. If the tumor goes to the orbit, either protrusion of the eye or, rarely, a pulling back and retraction of the eye from scar tissue will be encountered; pain, double vision, and drooping of the eyelid are also frequent accompaniments. It has been estimated that in 50 percent of cases where a metastasis has occurred to the eye or the orbit, the patient does not know that there is an underlying cancer elsewhere in his or her body, and a systemic work-up usually leads to its discovery.

Either chemotherapy for the primary cancer and/or orbital and ocular radiation therapy for the metastases is used to treat the tumors, which are generally not treated by surgery. Other cancers can directly spread by local invasion into the socket from the surrounding sinuses. These are generally squamous cell carcinomas arising from the membranes of the sinus linings. They develop in middle-aged and elderly individuals, and they are generally treated by local surgery of the orbit and the sinuses, coupled with radiation therapy and sometimes chemotherapy.

Bulging of an eye is always a sign to see a doctor promptly. Most often the cause will not be cancer, but instead may be infection, inflammation, thyroid disease, or a benign tumor. If the problem is cancer, prompt diagnosis and treatment, usually with radiation and chemotherapy, can achieve a cure rate of more than 70 percent. About two years after the treatment, vision in the affected eye may be decreased if high doses of radiation were needed to eradicate the cancer. The radiation therapy may have to be delivered to the front and side of the eye to avoid the chance of leaving cancer cells behind.

CANCERS OF THE EYELID AND CONJUNCTIVA

Small basal cell cancers arising in the epithelial tissue that covers the eyelids occur mostly among older people. These cancers are closely related to the basal cell carcinomas that develop in other locations on the skin surface. They grow slowly, but can invade the deeper layers of the lids while appearing relatively small on the surface.

Early diagnosis and treatment are advisable because surgery on larger basal cell cancers can result in scarring and deformity of the eyelid. Extensive eyelid surgery also can result in problems with the tear ducts, resulting in either constant tearing or in dry eyes. Both can be very irksome. Radiation therapy also is used to treat basal cell cancers of the eyelid, particularly those that recur following surgery or those located in the inner corner of the eye. During radiation treatments, the globe will be shielded to prevent injury to the lens and retina. Almost all basal cell cancers of the eyelids are curable. Many experts recommend Mohs' chemotherapy for extensive or recurring basal cell carcinomas.

Other types of cancers affecting the eyelids and conjunctiva are quite rare, but are also more lethal when they do occur. For example, there is a rare type of malignant melanoma that arises in the eyelids. This melanoma is highly aggressive and has the ability to spread to distant organs. Advances have been made in freezing these tumors, which in many cases relieves the need for radical surgery. Squamous cell cancers of the eyelids are more serious than basal cell carcinomas and require meticulous treatment by either surgery or radiation therapy, or a combination of the two, to prevent spread. Finally, cancer may arise in the meibomian glands, structures on the eyelid that produce sebum, an oily secretion. Cancers arising in these glands on the upper lid may grow slowly but are potentially very aggressive; with appropriate surgery cures are possible in over 75 percent of cases. Cancers arising in the meibomian glands on the lower lid are more curable, with fewer metastases.

SUMMING UP

Eye cancer is quite rare and frequently diagnosed in its early stages because of changes in vision or appearance. In many instances, the eye cancer can be treated while preserving vision, especially if the disease is detected in an early stage. It should be remembered that eye cancers are generally smaller than cancers hidden in the deeper organs of the body, and their small size and earlier symptoms are responsible for a generally favorable outlook.

21

Leukemia

ROBERT N. TAUB, M.D., PH.D.

INTRODUCTION

Leukemia, or cancer of the blood, was first recognized as a distinct disease around 1830 in Germany. The term "leukemia" comes from the Greek words meaning "white blood" and refers to the whitish or pale pink blood that was first noticed in patients with extremely high numbers of circulating malignant white cells. Leukemia is more accurately described as a cancerous disorder not of the blood itself, but rather of the organs that manufacture the blood cells. These organs, principally the bone marrow and the lymph system (the lymph nodes and spleen), are the places in which normal red cells, white cells, lymph cells, and platelets originate and grow to maturity before entering the bloodstream. The cancerous counterparts of these normal cells go through approximately the same process but with important differences in rate, number, and ability to function.

Although leukemia is the most common of the childhood cancers, it is actually far more common in adults. Approximately 25,000 new cases of leukemia are diagnosed annually in the United States, 22,500 of them in adults and 2,500 in children. Men are affected by leukemia 30 percent more frequently than women. About 17,000 people die from the disease each year. About half of the newly diagnosed cases of leukemia fall into the acute category; the rest are chronic.

Most of the advanced industrial nations have experienced an apparent increase in the incidence of leukemia since the 1930s. Epidemiologists and biostatisticians have not determined whether this is a true increase or whether it can be attributed to improved diagnostic methods and wider access to health care. One important contributing factor is the rising proportion of elderly people in these countries, since cancers of all kinds are more likely to develop in older populations.

TYPES OF BLOOD CANCERS

Although leukemia refers to a malignancy of white cells, red cells also have a cancerous form, called erythroleukemia (literally "red leukemia"). Erythroleukemia appears much less frequently than cancers of the white cells and often involves abnormalities of white cells and platelets, too. Researchers, who have observed that the several different subcategories of white cells can each develop into a particular kind of leukemia, believe that both red and white cells may share a common ancestor in the bone marrow. This common ancestor, the stem cell, may explain why every leukemia, no matter which cell line it affects primarily, generally affects all of the other blood cells to a lesser degree.

The lymph cells give rise to lymphatic leukemias that directly affect the immune system. Granulocytes (or myelocytes), the proper medical name for the white cell group that engulfs bacteria, give rise to granulocytic (or myelocytic) leukemia. Among the subgroups of white cells, the eosinophils that are associated with allergy and the monocytes that defend against such chronic infections as tuberculosis can each develop a corresponding leukemia, although these diseases are much more rare than simple granulocytic leukemia.

The leukemias are also classified according to rate of progression of the disease. Those that progress rapidly are known as acute, while those that are slower in their course are called chronic. This method of classification, although not perfect, is quite useful for diagnosis, treatment, and prognosis. Acute lymphocytic leukemia, for example, is a very different disease from its slower counterpart, chronic lymphocytic leukemia. Each has very different implications for patients, family, and doctor. Patients with acute lymphocytic leukemia, many of them young children, may paradoxically enjoy a much better prognosis than patients with the chronic form. In fact, they now have an excellent chance of being cured of their disease.

On the other hand, many chronic leukemias may cause few if any symptoms and require little or no treatment for many years. At present, about 50 percent of all leukemias are acute, 20 percent are chronic granulocytic, and 30 percent are chronic lymphocytic. Late in its course, a chronic leukemia may transform itself into a more rapidly progressive acute leukemia.

CAUSES OF LEUKEMIA

The basic cause of leukemia is unknown; exposure to radiation, chemicals, and certain drugs appears to increase the risk. Viruses, heredity, and chromosomal abnormalities have also been implicated. A rapidly growing body of research strongly suggests that certain genes called oncogenes may be directly involved in the development of many cancers, including leukemia.

Certain chemicals, such as benzene, have long been known to cause damage to bone marrow cells which form the blood, and it is logical to conclude that they can also cause a cancer in those cells. Many drugs, such as the antibiotic chloramphenicol, also can alter bone marrow function, and may be associated with some cases of leukemia. But chemical and drug exposure accounts for only a very small percentage of the total number of leukemias.

Radiation is the one factor that physicians know for certain can cause leukemia, but the incidence of excessive X-ray exposure is currently very small. The Japanese who survived the atomic bombings at Hiroshima and Nagasaki had an increased incidence of leukemia for twenty years after the event, but the rate has slowed down over the last twenty years, approaching that of normal populations. There is no evidence that routine exposure to X rays at the levels currently used for medical diagnosis increases the risk of cancer, including leukemia.

Cancer researchers now believe that genetics and virology, the study of viruses, hold the greatest promise of finding the cause of leukemia. In both fields, efforts are concentrated on determining how alterations of the genetic material cause cancer. In some cases the cancer-causing genes appear to result from damage arising from hereditary influences or problems that occur during cell division. In other instances, the malignant transformation may be the result of a viral infection in normal genes that control cell growth and reproduction.

Research is also concentrating on oncogenes, cancer-causing genes that are part of many people's normal genetic makeup. These genes can apparently be activated under circumstances that have not yet been identified. Oncogene research is being carried out in many centers with the hope that, by identifying and understanding specific oncogenes, people who are considered at risk can be identified long before a cancer begins. The long-term hope is to find a way to block the action of the oncogene and to prevent or limit the growth of its resultant cancer. Although this is a long way in the future and may never become reality, the concept of the oncogene has given scientists a new and fundamental approach to the study of cancer that many believe will yield fruitful results.

The hereditary causes of leukemia are far from being fully understood. A hereditary predisposition to cancer may imply the inheritance of an oncogene. Close relatives of leukemia patients have an increased risk of developing the disease. The greatest statistical risk is found in the identical twin of a child who has an acute leukemia before age eight. Approximately 20 percent of these individuals will develop the disease within one year of their twin's diagnosis. Genetics obviously plays a strong role here. Brothers and sisters of patients with acute leukemia have five times the risk of the general population. Their increased risk is nevertheless quite small. Children with Down's syndrome and other hereditary or genetic diseases associated with damage or modification of the chromosomes have an increased frequency of leukemia. But whether heredity plays a major role in all leukemia cases is an unanswered question.

Finally, leukemia may be caused by other diseases that damage the bone marrow and by the anticancer drugs used in the treatment of a wide variety of cancers. Diseases that cause severe depression of the marrow, such as aplastic anemia, are associated with a high incidence of leukemia. Patients with myelofibrosis, a disease in which the marrow is replaced by fibrous tissue, may later develop chronic granulocytic leukemia.

More common is the increased incidence of leukemia in patients taking anticancer drugs for the treatment of other malignancies. Most of these patients have received cancer chemotherapy over a relatively long period of time. Typically, acute leukemia develops late in the course of the other disease. Although oncologists do not know the mechanisms by which these drugs induce a leukemia, they believe they understand the underlying processes.

Direct damage to bone marrow and suppression of "immune surveillance"—the protective process that prevents abnormal cells from persisting within the human body—may be responsible. Up to 10 percent of patients with Hodgkin's disease who have been intensively treated with chemotherapeutic drugs or radiation therapy may ultimately display signs of an acute granulocytic leukemia. Specific antileukemia therapy can be used just as effectively in these patients as in previously healthy people. On balance, the benefit from the anticancer therapy in Hodgkin's disease greatly outweighs the risk of later developing a leukemia.

Organ transplant patients who receive drugs designed to suppress the immune system, which would otherwise reject the transplant, also have an increased incidence of cancers, including leukemia. Multiple myeloma, lymphoma, and other cancers of the lymph system also are associated with an increased risk of leukemia, probably because of the reduced immune function that accompanies these disorders. The division between "solid" tumors of the lymph system and the leukemias of the bloodstream is not completely distinct. Experience has shown that some lymphomas can have circulating cells in the bloodstream while the leukemias can sometimes form masses. A basic connection between the lymphomas and the leukemias has long been suspected, but its nature remains unknown.

SYMPTOMS

The early symptoms of leukemia are vague and much like those of many less serious medical problems. Leukemias of all cell types, whether acute or chronic, first make themselves known with remarkably similar characteristics. The common symptoms of the leukemias do not seem to be a direct result of the increase and spread of leukemia cells throughout the patient's body. Instead, the majority arise because the functioning of the remaining normal elements of the blood and bone marrow is impaired. The other organs of the body—the liver, heart, kidney, brain, and digestive system—continue to function quite well, even with a high degree of infiltration and invasion by leukemia cells.

Early detection of leukemia is difficult if not impossible, and usually occurs by accident rather than by design. For example, chronic lymphocytic leukemia is often found in people over sixty-five who are being examined routinely or for other medical problems. Acute leukemia can come on very suddenly, especially in children, and seem like a cold or flu. The symptoms progress rapidly, however, and most people seek medical help quickly. Chronic leukemia, if symptomless, can develop so slowly that the patient may not be able to estimate the date of its onset.

Fever, weight loss, fatigue, and a decline of well-being are the general symptoms of leukemia. Since these are vague symptoms associated with many illnesses, they do not necessarily raise a suspicion of leukemia. Easy bleeding, pallor, and repeated infections are also associated with leukemia and point more directly to the diagnosis.

Fever may be the most common symptom. It is usually caused by an infection of the skin, lung, or urinary tract, but it also may be due directly to the leukemia itself or to the release of compounds by the abnormal white cells. Many cancers are known to cause fever even in the absence of infection, because of the so-called hypermetabolic state that accompanies diseases marked by rapid progression and tissue breakdown. Infections are frequent because the leukemic white cells cannot protect against invasion by bacteria or other organic causes of disease, and too few normal white cells remain to do so. The leukemia produces a general depression of the immune system.

Fungal and viral infections that are rare in healthy people are frequently seen in leukemia patients, as are infections by bacteria that normally are not sufficiently aggressive to cause disease. Chemotherapy exacerbates this susceptibility to infection. Specialists in infectious disease are commonly asked to consult about the diagnosis and proper treatment of infection in the "compromised host," as the debilitated patient with a poorly functioning immune system is called. Infection becomes a more and more difficult problem as the leukemia progresses.

Weight loss, fatigue and paleness, largely caused by anemia, occur in most patients at the same stage of leukemia. These symptoms can be present for some time before a leukemia is identified as the basic problem. The situation was more of an enigma before doctors recognized that the prodrome—the very early symptom complex that can precede the fully developed disease for some months or years—of a leukemia can take this form.

Up to one third of all patients with cancer in the blood have normal or low circulating white blood cell counts. This "aleukemic" condition can occur in any form of leukemia and means that the bone marrow is crowded with extremely high numbers of cancerous white cells that, for some reason, do not migrate out into the bloodstream.

Bleeding problems are not serious early in the course of leukemia, but they can become severe later. Bleeding is usually mild at first, with only small patches of black and blue discoloration under the skin. Later, the suppression of the platelet-forming cells in the bone marrow reduces the number of platelets produced. This, combined with a deficiency of the clotting mechanism, can lead to serious bleeding problems. There may be hemorrhage into the lungs or bleeding into the brain, causing a stroke. Bleeding in the joints is also common. Prior bleeding problems, such as an ulcer or even a hemorrhoid, will be made worse and potentially life-threatening.

Enlargement of the lymph nodes, liver, and spleen is especially prevalent in the chronic leukemias. Pain in the joints and bones sometimes occurs but, overall, pain is not itself a major problem or common direct effect of leukemia.

DIAGNOSIS

All leukemia patients should have a complete initial history, physical examination, and general laboratory investigation, not only to establish a diagnosis, but to provide a base line for treatment and to learn whether other medical problems are present. Although leukemia may be strongly suspected by the physician on the basis of the patient's history and symptoms, the definitive diagnosis must be made by examination of the cells in the bone marrow. Microscopic observation of a sample of the patient's blood can confirm the doctor's clinical impression, but the blood smear may show only mild, indefinite abnormalities that are not in themselves diagnostic of a particular blood disorder. For a bone marrow test, a sample is obtained by either biopsy or aspiration. Both procedures involve insertion of a thin, hollow needle into a marrow-rich cavity within a bone, usually the back of the hip or the breastbone. The procedure takes about fifteen to twenty minutes and can be performed under local anesthesia in an outpatient setting or doctor's office. Complications are unusual and although the test may seem frightening, it involves only minimal discomfort. In fact, many patients say they are more disturbed by the sound and idea than by any feeling of actual pain. A lymph node biopsy may be done, but this procedure is usually not required for diagnosis.

The specimen of bone marrow is smeared on slides, stained with certain dyes, and organized and examined under a microscope, usually by a hematologist, oncologist, and pathologist in consultation. The specimen is always abnormal in acute leukemias, containing a greatly increased number of white cells. The cells may be clearly abnormal or they may closely resemble normal cells that have failed to mature from the more primitive "blast" stage into the later adult stage. Chronic leukemias present a similar bone marrow picture, but the cells are somewhat more mature in appearance.

Other blood tests may be performed to determine levels of uric acid, potassium, or calcium, all of which may be altered by the presence of the cancer and, later, by its treatment. In most cases the patient's immune status will be determined by checking the antibody levels in the blood and by a skin testing procedure similar to that used by allergists.

If leukemia is confirmed, immunologic tissue typing, blood typing, coagulation and transfusion studies will be performed. This information is most valuable if acquired before transfusions have made it difficult to test the properties of the patient's own blood. The success of bone marrow transplantation is heavily dependent on tissue typing, which also should be done on the patient's brothers and sisters if this procedure is to be seriously considered.

In difficult cases, special stains may be necessary to confirm the exact diagnosis, especially if the cell type cannot be definitely ascertained or the resemblance to normal cells is very close. Pathologists use many immunologic, chemical, enzymatic, and structural markers, or signs, to ascertain the diagnosis as precisely as possible. An accurate diagnosis is becoming more important as therapy becomes more and more specific. Highly specific antibodies, monoclonal antibodies (See Chapter 9, "Experimental Treatments and Research"), have enhanced the ability of pathologists to diagnose leukemias.

Chromosomal studies have assumed an important place not only in the diagnosis of leukemia, but also in helping to monitor the course of the disease as well as the effectiveness of therapy. The chromosomal abnormalities are found in the leukemic white cells, not in normal white cells or in the cells of other organs in the body. Elucidation, prevention, and control of this change is what the ultimate cure of cancer rests on.

TREATMENT

Immense progress has been made in the treatment of leukemia over the past several decades. New anticancer drugs, improved methods of radiation therapy, bone marrow transplants, and better management of the complications of both leukemia and its therapy have greatly improved the length and quality of life. Even more gratifying is the actual cure of many of the acute leukemias that had been thought to be always fatal, usually within two to four months.

One of the most promising of the therapeutic methods now being developed involves the use of monoclonal antibodies specifically directed against the leukemic cells. If these antibodies, perhaps joined with a toxin that is released into or near the cancer cell, prove effective and safe, a new hope may exist for leukemia patients. Considerable research remains to be done, but results to date are promising.

Although chemotherapy remains the basic treatment for all the leukemias, radiation, administered either by X ray or by radioactive isotopes (such as phosphorus) injected into the bloodstream to concentrate in the bone marrow, has achieved some temporary success in controlling several leukemias, particularly erythroleukemia. Radiation therapy has proved useful in quickly reducing the size of enlarged lymph nodes or spleen. It is used in preparation for bone marrow transplants and to control disease in places such as the brain where chemotherapeutic drugs cannot penetrate (see Sanctuary Organs, below). However, radiation has little to offer in the way of therapeutic benefit. Nor does surgery have a place in the treatment of leukemia, except for biopsy and the exceedingly unusual instances when removal of the spleen is necessary. Immunotherapy, attempted in the past as a way of stimulating the patient's immune system to attack the cancer cells, showed little results and is no longer used. (This should not be confused with monoclonal antibodies, which represent a very different form of immunotherapy.) Plasma exchange (selective removal of white cells from the blood), dietary change, and other forms of alternative therapy have been of little or no benefit.

CHEMOTHERAPY

The goal of chemotherapy is to give a sufficient amount of drugs to destroy nearly all cells, both normal and abnormal, that are contained in the patient's bone marrow. This may require a combination of two to five drugs, each possibly attacking the cancer cells in a different way. Since leukemia cells are known to divide more slowly than their normal counterparts, then theoretically, if almost all the marrow is destroyed, the healthy cells, which grow and regenerate faster, are more likely to repopulate the marrow.

The schedules of chemotherapeutic drug administration have been worked out over years through a combination of theory and trial and error. They are designed to take maximum advantage of the susceptibilities and regrowth cycles of leukemia cells. The proportion of normal cells will then increase with each cycle of chemotherapy in a successfully treated patient. The goal is to induce a complete remission, the state in which all blood tests, including bone marrow examination, have returned to normal. A complete remission is defined as finding no evidence in laboratory tests that the patient has or has ever had a leukemia. Depending on the particular category of leukemia, 50 to 90 percent or more of patients will achieve a complete remission.

Some remissions are not as successful: the patient feels better; the pattern and number of cells in the blood have returned to normal; but the bone marrow, although improved, remains abnormal. The exact degree of these partial remissions is not easily ascertained, since abnormal leukemia cells can closely resemble their normal but immature counterparts. If a remission is not obtained with the usual drugs, the oncologist will try to induce it with second-line or experimental drugs. Patients who do not enter into a period of complete or partial remission do not have as good a prognosis.

Once a complete or partial remission has been induced, the patient will be placed on maintenance chemotherapy, with the dose, schedule, and duration tailored to the patient's specific diagnosis and ability to tolerate chemotherapy. Depending on the timing and specific strategy chosen, these treatments may be termed consolidation, intensification, or reinforcement. Maintenance therapy may be continued for as long as four years in apparently cured patients, especially children. Since relapse after five years of complete remission is rare, patients whose remission surpasses this may be considered cured. On the other hand, patients who do not obtain a complete remission lasting at least four years will almost undoubtedly have a relapse.

Patients who experience a relapse will receive more chemotherapy, possibly with the same drugs that induced the original remission. Repeated relapses generally signal a progressively poorer response to therapy, with remissions becoming shorter and shorter and an effective strategy and drug regimen more difficult to prescribe. Drug resistance on the part of leukemic cells is the fundamental problem. Although doctors do not know the cause of the resistance, they suspect that the chemotherapeutic agents destroy the sensitive cells and establish an environment that allows the resistant cells to flourish.

The major drugs used to treat leukemia are vincristine, methotrexate, G-mercaptopurine, cytosine arabinoside, busulfar chlorambucil, daunorubicin, l-asparaginase, and prednisone. Most of these drugs have been used for at least ten years and oncologists have become familiar with their actions and side effects. Relatively few successful new agents have been developed during the last five to ten years except for s-azacytidine and M-amsa.

The side effects of chemotherapy necessitate hospitalization for almost all patients during the entire process of chemotherapy, until remission is induced. This stay may last six weeks or longer. The low white count induced by the drugs makes patients susceptible to infection, while the reduction in platelets predisposes to bleeding. Patients must be closely monitored, often with daily blood tests in case transfusions of red cells, white cells, platelets, gamma globulin, and clotting factors are needed.

Infection remains a serious problem, although the situation has vastly improved because of new, more powerful antibiotics. Gram-negative bacteria, especially pseudomonas and E. coli, are among the most common causes of infection. Fungal and viral infections also occur and are more difficult to treat. Antileukemic therapy can be complicated by problems other than infection and bleeding, such as cardiac toxicity (induced by daunorubicin), or nerve toxicity (induced by vincristine). The first problem is not reversible on stopping the drug; the second is.

Some patients with chronic leukemia who require no or only mild chemotherapeutic treatment can, after the initial investigations are completed, be treated on an outpatient basis. Maintenance therapy after remission can usually be administered in the outpatient department of a hospital, in the hematologist-oncologist's office, or during relatively brief intermittent hospital stays.

The physical examination plays a relatively small role in the initial diagnosis and evaluation of a leukemia patient. It is hardly ever crucial to the diagnosis but must not be neglected, and should be performed at appropriate intervals to judge the effect of therapy and the regression or progression of the disease. Particular attention should be paid to the lymph nodes, pharynx, gums, eyes (for bleeding), and possible sites of infection such as the skin, mouth, vagina, and anus. This routine and brief inspection should be performed at almost every visit, especially if chemotherapy is being administered and the risk of infection by bacteria or fungi is increased. Changes in the size of the liver and spleen also should be noted.

Patients undergoing intense chemotherapy experience numerous side effects, since the drugs are highly toxic to both normal and cancerous tissue. Nausea and vomiting are almost universal, as is hair loss. Antinausea drugs and timing of chemotherapy can help counter the nausea and vomiting. The hair loss is temporary, but distressing to most patients. (See Chapter 10, "Coping with Problems Related to Cancer and Cancer Treatment," for a more detailed discussion.)

In most cases the patient will remain under the care of his or her internist or general practitioner while the oncologist concentrates on the anticancer chemotherapy. Continuing treatment can usually be given close to home but induction of remission should almost always be carried out in a major medical center. The potential problems and complications are too great to be managed at small community hospitals that are not equipped or experienced in this field.

SANCTUARY ORGANS

Cancer cells invading the tissues surrounding the brain can cause severe headache, nausea, and vomiting. Moreover, cancer cells in the brain and spinal cord are effectively protected from the action of most chemotherapeutic drugs by a thin membrane called the "blood-brain barrier," which prevents the drugs from diffusing into the spinal fluid. The testicles in men are another "sanctuary" organ.

Since all malignant cells in these sanctuaries must be destroyed to prevent a relapse, radiation is used in place of chemotherapy. Although not all leukemia patients show definite evidence of malignant cells in sanctuary areas, most adults and almost all children with acute leukemia now receive about 2,400 rads of radiation to the brain, as well as repeated doses of methotrexate given by direct injection through the blood-brain barrier to the spinal fluid. Except for occasional acute seizures, the additional early side effects of this therapy are small—mostly drowsiness and nausea. Longer-term, some children who undergo this treatment suffer mild impairment of intellect. As is often the case in serious medical problems, risks and benefits must be weighed. On balance, the benefit from treatment of potential sanctuary areas greatly outweighs the loss.

Controversies exist about how best to treat the testicles when they are a potential sanctuary for leukemia cells. Whatever method is used, it is probably wise to consider banking specimens of sperm before administering the therapy. Diminished fertility is a recognized side effect of many of the treatments used in leukemia, although this is not universal. There have been several studies involving boys and young men who were cured of leukemia and later became fathers.

BONE MARROW TRANSPLANTS

In bone marrow transplantation, all blood-forming cells in the body, both normal and malignant, are totally destroyed and then replaced with bone marrow cells taken from a donor. Experience in bone marrow transplantation technique has grown rapidly over the last several years and is strongly encouraging. In the opinion of some investigators, this drastic treatment may eventually offer the best chance of cure. Transplants are now reserved for patients with disease that is resistant to standard therapy. They are performed at only four or five institutions across the United States, and have in some instances reversed an otherwise hopeless situation.

Much more study is required, however, before transplantation will be regarded as the initial treatment of choice for leukemia patients. There has not yet been a rigorous statistical study comparing the results of transplantation with intensive chemotherapy continued after complete remission. The available data, when compared on a less than rigorous basis, do not show a significant difference between the two treatment paths. In any case, transplantation is a realistic therapeutic option for only about one third of patients, since careful genetic matching with a close relative, such as a brother or sister, is necessary and only patients under forty without other disabling medical problems are considered.

In preparation for a bone marrow transplant, the patient is given ultra-high doses of radiation and chemotherapy to destroy all blood-forming cells. Careful immunological tissue testing is carried out to choose the best donor from among the patient's close relatives. The donor's cells are injected into the recipient's bloodstream to reseed the marrow with healthy cells. The leukemia patient is kept in isolation to diminish the chance of infection and is given transfusions and antibiotics as needed.

Two fundamental problems can occur after injection of the donor marrow. The recipient's (host's) immune system can reject the marrow transplant or, the donor's marrow, in its immunologically foreign environment, can reject the host. The latter, a "graft versus host" reaction, can be very serious. Strong suppression of the immune cells in the donor marrow or in the recipient can often control these problems, but fatalities have been caused by either response. For this reason, the closer the genetic match (HLA correspondence) between donor and host, the better the chance of the transplant's "taking." Ways to reduce the graft versus host reaction—such as using highly specific monoclonal antibodies to remove the cells that mediate immunologic function in the donor marrow before it is given to the recipient—are being explored at several research institutions.

SPECIFIC LEUKEMIAS

The following brief descriptions of the four major types of leukemia are intended to augment the preceding general information, which should be read first and which holds remarkably true when applied to each type.

Acute Lymphocytic Leukemia

Acute lymphocytic leukemia is the most common childhood cancer and the leukemia in which oncologists have achieved their highest rates of remission and cure. The incidence of the disease peaks between the ages of two and nine years, then declines rapidly. A second peak occurs in very old age. Males are affected more frequently than females.

The first symptoms experienced by most patients with acute lymphocytic leukemia are anemia, fever, fatigue, and minor enlargement of the lymph nodes. Laboratory examination shows abnormal cells in the blood and in the bone marrow, as well as elevated levels of uric acid in the blood caused by the increased metabolic activity of the cancer cells. Before effective chemotherapy was available, the average survival was about five or six months, with all patients succumbing within two to three years. Steady advances in therapy from single-drug treatment (in the 1950s) to multidrug treatment (in the 1960s) to prophylactic central nervous system radiation (in the 1970s)—all abetted by enormous improvements in supportive care—have radically altered this picture, especially for children. Bone marrow transplantation has its highest success rate in patients with this leukemia.

More than 95 percent of all children with this malignancy will enter complete remission. One half of them will stay in remission on maintenance therapy for two and a half to three years, after which therapy is discontinued. Of these, about 10 percent will relapse and be candidates for a second attempt at induction of remission, although with a lower chance of success than the first time. Altogether more than half of children with acute lymphocytic leukemia are being cured of their malignancy by currently available methods.

Adults now achieve a 70 percent complete remission rate on approximately the same treatment regimen used in children. The addition of other agents to the usual combination of vincristine, methotrexate, and prednisone appears to induce a complete remission in up to 90 percent of patients. The duration of remission is shorter in adults than in children and the apparent cure rate is about 35 percent. In both adult and childhood disease, patients who stay in remission for over four years rarely relapse, and therapy can be discontinued.

Monoclonal antibodies and genetic studies have enabled researchers to subdivide the category of acute lymphocytic leukemia into several sub-classes. These sophisticated techniques are largely of research interest, but they do offer some prognostic information. The early (but not definite) conclusion of this research is that acute lymphocytic leukemia is not a single disease entity, but rather several closely related pathological entities that appear much alike but are different in important ways. In the future, the subcategories may enable physicians to design more specific, more effective treatment schedules.

Acute Granulocytic Leukemia

Acute granulocytic leukemia—cancer of the white cells that engulf bacteria—closely resembles several other leukemias in behavior, treatment, and prognosis. Because these related disorders—acute myelomonocytic leukemia (leukemia of monocytes) and erythroleukemia (leukemia of red cells)—each constitute only about one percent of all blood cancers, they and acute granulocytic leukemia are often conveniently grouped together under the term "acute nonlymphocytic leukemia."

The prominent symptoms of acute granulocytic leukemia (and all the other acute leukemias of blood cells that are not derived from lymphocytes) are pallor, weakness, fever, and fatigue. The typical patient is thirty to sixty years old, the frequency of the disease increasing with age. The natural course of untreated acute granulocytic leukemia leads to an average survival of only two to five months. Chemotherapy has lengthened survival to as long as five years, but the disease is still serious and basically incurable. Treatment regimens for acute granulocytic leukemia and the other nonlymphocytic leukemias are not the same in all cancer centers, and a wide variety of schedules is used for the induction and maintenance of remission. Complete remission can be achieved in about 75 percent of patients, up from only 33 percent some years ago, but it lasts only for twelve to fifteen months.

Several complications can occur in the course of these leukemias. Leukostasis, the clumping of immature white cells, is a dangerous condition that occurs when the white blood cell count is 300,000 or higher, about thirty to fifty times normal. Since it can cause heart attacks and strokes by blocking the arteries, it is treated by removing large numbers of white cells from the patient's blood and increasing the intensity of the chemotherapy. Masses of white cells, called chloromas or myeloblastomas, can form, resulting in nodules beneath the skin, obstruction of the intestines, and other mechanical problems. Monocytic leukemia, one of the nonlymphatic cancers, can be diagnosed with almost complete certainty on the basis of its characteristic visible invasion and infiltration of the cheeks and gums. Infiltration of the central nervous system, which occurs in about 50 percent of patients with acute lymphocytic leukemia, is rarely found in patients with this group of blood cancers, making specific treatment and prophylaxis for disease involving the brain and spinal column unnecessary. Bone marrow transplantation has not been extensively tried in cases of acute nonlymphatic leukemia, in part because of the older age of the patients in this group.

Abnormalities of the chromosomes occur in over 50 percent of patients with acute granulocytic leukemia and related disorders. Evidence strongly suggests that each patient's individual chromosomal makeup has a strong direct bearing on prognosis. Patients found to have abnormal genes in their leukemic cells (not in their other normal cells) typically have a less favorable prognosis.

Erythroleukemia, while it appears to be a malignancy of red cells, is actually a malignancy of both white and red cell lines. This observation suggests that the origin of this cancer may lie in the stem cell, the common ancestor in the marrow of both white and red cell lines. The clinical picture of erythroleukemia resembles the general description of the leukemias as a group. The disorder is difficult to treat satisfactorily; most patients have severe anemia and require repeated transfusions. Although complete remission is obtainable in 40 to 50 percent of patients, the average survival from the time of diagnosis is six to eight months.

Chronic Granulocytic Leukemia

Chronic granulocytic leukemia represents about 20 percent of all blood cancers and characteristically occurs in people aged forty to sixty. The onset of the disease is slow and insidious, with the patient generally coming to the conclusion that something is truly wrong after about three to six months. Enlargement of the liver, spleen, and lymph nodes occurs in over half of patients. Laboratory studies show a white blood cell count ten to twenty times normal. These white cells and those in the bone marrow are more mature in appearance than they are in the acute leukemias. Anemia and bleeding problems are frequent, as is a curious increase in the level of vitamin B_{12}.

Enzyme and chromosomal studies are important in the diagnosis of chronic granulocytic leukemia. These testing methods are used to follow the progress of the disease and the response to chemotherapy. The so-called "Philadelphia" chromosome, the first abnormal chromosome found in the leukemias, occurs in over 90 percent of patients with this disease. Intensive therapy can reduce the number of white cells that display the Philadelphia chromosome, and successful reduction is closely correlated with the duration and completeness of remission.

Without treatment, chronic granulocytic leukemia pursues a slow course with progressive anemia, bleeding, enlargement of organs, and infection. Treatment is based completely on chemotherapy, involving four drugs—busulfan, cyclophosphamide, L-PAM, and hydroxurea, each used as a single agent. Although these drugs are relatively ineffective in the acute leukemias, they can induce a complete remission in 90 percent of chronic granulocytic patients. They exert their beneficial action without many of the troublesome effects that accompany multidrug therapy. Complete remission usually lasts two to four years, after which the disease accelerates and increases in severity. The white cell count mounts, and more immature-looking cells are found displaying chromosomal abnormalities. Clinical signs cannot predict when the disease will enter the accelerated stage. The patient will initially feel worse, lose weight, and have fever, but not so remarkably as to signal the onset of the new phase clearly. A "blast crisis" may occur, with high numbers of circulating immature white blood cells. More intensive therapy using several anti-cancer drugs in combination can induce a remission for another three to six months, but no treatment is satisfactory for this stage of disease. Irradiation of the bone marrow and surgical removal of the enlarged spleen have not improved results. Bone marrow transplantation has been unsuccessful, except in the rare cases when an identical twin was available as a completely compatible donor. Newer techniques of chemotherapy and possibly monoclonal antibodies could offer an improved prognosis in the future.

Chronic Lymphocytic Leukemia

Chronic lymphocytic leukemia, constituting approximately 30 percent of all leukemias, is the most common form of blood cancer found in industrialized countries, occurring two to three times more frequently in men than in women. The patients it affects are older than patients affected by any of the other leukemias, and the incidence increases steadily with age. In fact, it is unusual to see a patient under age sixty with this disease.

The cause of chronic lymphocytic leukemia is unknown, although strong evidence points to problems of function and control in the immune system. Diagnosis is very often discovered by accident in the course of routine blood testing for other medical reasons, since fully 25 to 30 percent of newly diagnosed patients have no symptoms. As in chronic granulocytic leukemia, for many patients the onset of symptoms is imperceptibly slow.

The course of the disease varies widely, but generally reflects the low degree of aggressiveness displayed by the malignancy. The lymphocytes that accumulate are small, long-lived, and not fully capable of performing their usual protective functions. The white blood count may be low or high, with either condition well tolerated by patients. A high white blood count does not necessarily indicate a poor prognosis. The degree of bone marrow infiltration by small lymphocytes is a much more accurate sign of degree of disease.

Enlargement of the spleen, liver, and lymph nodes is common; anemia and bleeding problems are not prominent in the malignancy, although they can occur. Diminished immune function makes infection a recurrent problem. Antibody levels run about 50 percent lower than normal and slowly decline over the course of the cancer.

Many patients with chronic lymphocytic leukemia continue to show a low-grade, symptomless abnormality of blood and bone marrow for years, leading doctors to question the value of treatment. About half of such patients are given no chemotherapy but are simply monitored at appropriate intervals. For patients with stronger symptoms, treatment with chlorambucil or busulfan is indicated. Either drug is effective in over 65 percent of patients, but the actual induction of a complete remission with a single agent is practically unknown. Complete remission can be achieved with multidrug regimens, but there is no evidence to support that the initial use of these more intensive schedules offers significant benefit. The tendency among oncologists is to reserve multidrug treatment for patients who do not respond to simple drug therapy. Radiation can be used to control local disease and, if needed because of anemia or simple physical problems, to reduce the size of the spleen.

Patients with chronic lymphocytic leukemia are treated for most of their course on an outpatient basis. The average life-span after diagnosis is four years. General debility and infection are the principal clinical problems experienced during the later stage of the disease. About 15 percent of patients with chronic lymphocytic leukemia will, with little or no treatment, live for another ten to fifteen years relatively untroubled by their disease.

SUMMING UP

Tremendous progress has been made over the last thirty years in treating leukemia, with an ever-increasing number of patients, especially children, now being cured of the disease. Although the treatment is complex, lengthy, and itself produces illness, the marked success in achieving total and partial remissions makes it worthwhile for most patients.

22

Liver Cancer

ROBERT J. MAYER, M.D.,
AND MARC B. GARNICK, M.D.

INTRODUCTION

The liver, which weighs up to four pounds in an adult, is the body's largest internal organ and one of its most complex (Figure 40). It performs numerous biochemical functions, including detoxifying alcohol and other potentially harmful chemicals. Bile, cholesterol, digestive enzymes, and complex proteins are among the vital substances manufactured in the liver. It serves as a storehouse for glycogen, which is converted into blood sugar (glucose) to provide fuel for all the body's cells. It is also essential in a number of metabolic processes and serves as a storehouse for vitamins A and D.

Cancer of the liver can be divided into two distinct categories: primary

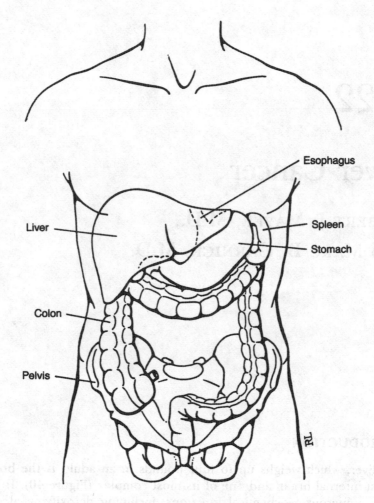

Figure 40 Normal liver and adjacent organs.

or secondary, depending upon the site of origin. Primary liver cancer originates in the liver itself and is relatively rare in the United States, accounting for only 1 to 2 percent of all cancers. About 90 percent of all primary liver cancers in the United States are hepatocellular carcinomas, meaning they arise in the liver cells. About 7 percent start in the liver's bile ducts, and the remaining are angiosarcomas, which are very rare but of growing importance because they are associated with polyvinylchloride (PVCs) and other similar industrial toxins.

Secondary liver cancer is a result of metastases from a cancer elsewhere in the body, frequently the breast, lung, or colon. It is quite common, since many cancers that are not cured by surgical removal or other treatments will spread to the liver.

The pattern of incidence for liver cancer is quite different in other parts of the world, particularly some of the developing countries. In Africa and parts of Asia, primary liver cancer is one of the most common malignancies. In Ethiopia, for example, it accounts for 20 percent of all malignancies, and in some developing countries primary liver cancer may be the leading cause of cancer death.

The age at which the cancer is likely to develop also varies geographically. In the United States, most patients with hepatocellular carcinoma are of late middle age or older. In Africa, the disease is more likely to strike during young adulthood or early middle age, and somewhat later in Asia.

The reasons for these geographic differences are unknown, but a number of factors that increase the risk of liver cancer have been identified. Cirrhosis, either from alcoholism or from other diseases such as viral hepatitis, is a major predisposing factor for liver cancer. In the United States, a person with cirrhosis is forty times more likely to develop primary liver cancer than a person with a normal liver, and 30 to 70 percent of all patients with hepatocellular cancer also have cirrhosis. It should be noted that cirrhosis can develop from several causes other than alcoholism, including viral and (less commonly) parasitic infections, nutritional deficiencies, and hemochromatosis, a disease characterized by excessive iron deposits in the body tissue. Statistically, the cirrhosis of hemochromatosis, followed closely by that caused by viral hepatitis, are the most likely to evolve into cancer. Hemochromatosis is a relatively rare metabolic disorder; in contrast, viral hepatitis is fairly common. In some parts of the world, particularly the developing countries of Africa and Asia, viral hepatitis is endemic and a major precursor of liver cancer. Still, most people who have viral hepatitis recover completely and do not go on to develop liver cancer. In addition, the recent development of a vaccine against viral hepatitis is considered a major step in preventing the primary liver cancer that is associated with this disease.

A number of environmental toxins also have been linked to an increased risk of liver cancer. Since the liver performs so many biochemical functions, including detoxifying potentially harmful chemicals, it is exposed to a large number of environmental carcinogens. Aflatoxin, which is derived from some molds; azo compounds, a family of nitrogen compounds; and Thorotrast, a contrast substance once used in X-ray examinations but which has been discontinued, are among the substances linked to an increased risk of liver cancer. Oral estrogens, particularly those used in birth control pills, have been associated with a number of cases of benign liver tumors that can cause acute bleeding problems and, in some instances, the eventual development of cancer. The number of such cancers is small, however, and the risk appears to be minimal for most women except those with a history of liver disease.

DIAGNOSIS

About 13,000 new cases of primary liver cancer are diagnosed each year and there are about 10,000 deaths annually from the disease. In the United States, men are more likely to develop the disease than women.

In its early stages, liver cancer often produces no obvious symptoms. As the disease progresses, likely symptoms include weight loss, malaise, loss of appetite, abdominal swelling, and pain. Fever is not uncommon; some patients also may develop jaundice. Ascites, a buildup of fluid in the abdominal cavity, is another relatively common development. These symptoms occurring in a person who has had cirrhosis or other liver disease raise a possibility of cancer. In some instances, signs of metastases to other parts of the body, such as bone pain, cough from lung involvement, or gastrointestinal bleeding, are the symptoms that prompt the patient to see a physician.

When the physician examines the patient with liver cancer, an enlarged, painful liver is the most common finding. The tumor may take the form of a single mass or a number of small nodules. At this point it is important to determine whether the problem is a primary or secondary liver cancer or a benign tumor. A number of tests may be performed to arrive at a precise diagnosis and, if it is cancer, to determine the extent of liver damage and whether it has spread to other parts of the body. Initial studies will include liver function tests, which measure the blood levels of bilirubin, the chemical by-product by the breakdown of old red blood cells by the liver, and of enzymes normally present in liver cells but which may enter the bloodstream in increased concentrations if the liver is diseased. Anemia is a common finding, as are a number of other abnormalities that can be detected by blood tests. But none of these tests provides a definite diagnosis. At one time, researchers thought that testing the blood for elevated levels of a substance called alphafetoprotein (AFP) might provide a useful screening examination, especially for high-risk groups such as people with cirrhosis. However, a number of diseases, including cancers of the testes, stomach, pancreas, and lungs, as well as pregnancy, can produce elevated levels of AFP. Also, further studies have found that about 30 percent of Americans with liver cancer will not have an elevated AFP. Nevertheless, a high blood level of AFP in an adult man with other symptoms of liver cancer strongly suggests a positive diagnosis.

Although cancer is the most common cause of a mass in the liver, other possibilities include benign tumors, abscesses, abnormal growths of the bile ducts, and cysts, either fluid-filled or from parasites. A number of examinations are available to help establish a diagnosis of liver masses. Liver scans using a radioactive contrast substance may be performed, but abnormal findings may be difficult to distinguish from those of cirrhosis. In angiography of the liver, a catheter is threaded into the hepatic artery and an opaque substance that makes the blood vessels of the liver visible on X rays is injected through it. This examination, which takes up to three hours to perform and requires overnight hospitalization, is one of the most useful tests in confirming the presence of a liver tumor. Clusters of small new blood vessels that develop in the tumor, or distortions of normal vessels can be seen on the angiograms, the X rays taken during the examination. In addition, angiography can provide highly useful information about the nature of the tumor, indicating whether it is a primary or secondary liver cancer or benign, and whether it can be surgically removed.

Other diagnostic tests that may be performed include bone scans, chest X rays, and CT and ultrasound examinations. A biopsy will provide a definite diagnosis, but potential bleeding problems may rule out taking a tissue sample via a needle inserted through the overlying abdominal wall. Instead, abdominal exploratory surgery is called for, or laparoscopy, an examination in which a flexible tube (a laparoscope) is inserted into the abdominal cavity through a small incision. This allows the examining physician to view the liver and other abdominal organs directly and also to take a small sample of tissue for later microscopic study.

TREATMENT

Primary liver cancer may be treated by either surgery or chemotherapy or a combination of the two. If the patient still has good liver function and has no obvious signs of metastases, exploratory surgery may be performed to determine the extent of the cancer and the feasibility of its removal. Surgical treatment is most likely to succeed in those instances in which there is a solitary tumor, confined to one lobe, that can be entirely removed. Unfortunately, only a minority of primary liver cancers fall into this category; more often the malignancy has spread through the liver, and the entire cancer cannot be removed. In other patients the liver already may be extensively damaged by cirrhosis or other diseases that hinder the organ's ability to regenerate. Normally the liver has an amazing capacity to regenerate, provided enough healthy tissue remains. For example, up to 80 percent of the liver can be removed, and with adequate postoperative support of metabolic and other liver functions, the organ will begin to regenerate within a few days and will completely regrow in two to four months. This experience, however, usually occurs in young patients with benign tumors or accident victims, rather than in cancer patients who are more likely to have extensive liver damage that precludes successful surgical removal of the entire cancer.

Chemotherapy, most often with doxorubicin, 5-fluorouracil, or methotrexate, will sometimes relieve symptoms and prolong survival. Administering the anticancer drugs directly into the liver, via a catheter inserted into the hepatic artery—the vessel that supplies the liver with blood—or threaded nonsurgically from the brachial artery, may decrease the side effects of the chemotherapy. But since the catheters themselves may lead to side effects, the therapeutic advantages of such an approach remain unproved.

Another experimental approach to treatment involves blockage of the arteries (Figure 41) leading to the portion of the liver that is the main site of the cancer. This technique, known as hepatic artery ligation or embolization, is aimed at slowing the cancer's growth by diminishing its blood supply. The arterial ligation is sometimes combined with regional administration of chemotherapy or radiation therapy.

SECONDARY LIVER CANCER

The liver is one of the most common sites of metastatic cancer; it is estimated that 50 to 60 percent of all cancers may eventually spread to the liver. Cancers of the stomach, pancreas, esophagus, lung, colon, and breast and melanoma almost always spread to the liver if they are not cured in their earlier, localized stages.

The probability that cancer has metastasized to the liver can be determined by physical examination and laboratory tests. The presence of an enlarged, hard liver in a patient who has cancer elsewhere in the body, particularly a type that commonly spreads to the liver, is a good indication of metastasis.

Treatment

The treatment and prognosis for patients with metastatic liver cancer depend upon the type of primary cancer and degree of spread to other parts of the body. Some cancers, particularly those of the colon and

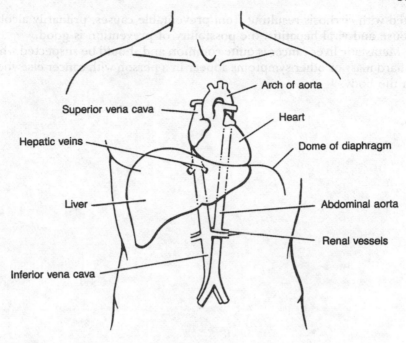

Figure 41 Liver with major vessels.

rectum, as well as carcinoid or other endocrine cancers, often spread to the liver. In such instances surgery may be the best treatment, especially if there is a single liver mass. Up to 25 percent of patients who fall into this category, and are able to undergo surgical removal of the metastatic tumor, are cured.

If there are multiple tumors in the liver, but the cancer does not appear to have metastasized to other parts of the body, regional chemotherapy administered directly into the liver's circulation may be used. A typical regimen might involve giving the anticancer drugs for three to six weeks. By that time a type of drug-induced hepatitis may occur, necessitating that the drugs be stopped for a period, and then resumed when the side effects abate. Thirty to 50 percent of patients treated in this manner have been reported to show improvement. However, substantial damage to the liver and bile ducts can occur with the treatment.

SUMMING UP

Primary liver cancer is relatively rare in the United States, but quite common in developing countries of Africa and Asia. It is a difficult cancer to treat, with very low rate of survival. However, since it is often associated with cirrhosis resulting from preventable causes, primarily alcohol abuse and viral hepatitis, the possibility of prevention is good.

Metastatic liver cancer is quite common and should be suspected when a hard mass or other symptoms appear in a person with cancer elsewhere in the body.

23

Lung Cancer

CLIFTON F. MOUNTAIN, M.D., AND KAY HERMES, B.S.

INTRODUCTION

Lung cancer was first clearly described by doctors about 150 years ago, and at the turn of the century this disease was still considered a rarity. In 1865 Dr. W. T. Cooke, in his book *On Cancer, Its Allies and Counterfeits*, noted, "Specimens of cancer of the lung and of the brain are occasionally exhibited at the pathological society as curiosities which have been discovered at the autopsy . . . the early detection of its nature is rarely effected." The incidence of this disease has changed dramatically since this report; lung cancer is now the leading cause of cancer death for both men and women. The failure to detect lung cancer early, however, remains just as dramatically unchanged and the majority of patients with lung cancer have extensive disease at the time of diagnosis.

Studies in all parts of the world have consistently shown the association between cigarette smoking and lung cancer. In fact, in most reported studies less than 10 percent of lung cancer patients are nonsmokers. The increase in lung cancer deaths has paralleled the increase in tobacco consumption, with the higher incidence in men attributed to the greater prevalence of smoking among men. The recent increase in lung cancer among women parallels the trend of increased smoking by women. Until 1984, breast cancer was the leading cause of cancer death in women; in 1985, however, lung cancer assumed this dubious distinction. The paradox remains, however, that the great majority of smokers do not develop lung cancer and some nonsmokers do develop the disease. The relationship between smoking and cancer is explored more fully in Chapter 3, "Smoking and Cancer."

Industrial exposure to various chemicals and minerals is also considered to increase the risk of developing lung cancer. People employed in mining or processing uranium are also at higher risk because of exposure to inhalation of radon daughter products resulting from disintegration of radioactive atoms in this element. An increased incidence of lung cancer has been reported among survivors of the atomic bombings at Hiroshima and Nagasaki. Individuals exposed to asbestos (with tobacco an important co-factor), nickel, chromates, coal gas, mustard gas, arsenic, beryllium, heavy doses of printing ink, and vinyl chloride have been found to have high lung cancer rates. Because a relatively small number of people are involved in industries that expose them to these risk factors, the impact on the total lung cancer picture is probably small. Nevertheless the products of a technological-industrial society cannot be ignored, nor can the possible cancer-producing role of atmospheric pollutants. For example, there is a somewhat higher incidence of lung cancer in large urban areas where there are more pollutants in the air than in rural areas.

A number of other factors, such as diet, may have an effect on the development of lung cancer. For example, a low vitamin A intake may be associated with increased risk. The possibility that genetic factors predispose some individuals to lung cancer is suggested by the occurrence of "familial clustering," an unusually high incidence of this disease in some families. Some cancer specialists have noted a relationship between lung diseases and inherited abnormalities in blood enzymes. Two examples are chronic obstructive lung disease (emphysema) and alpha-1-antitrypsin (A_1AT) deficiency, and lung cancer and the production of aryl hydrocarbon hydroxylase (AHH), an enzyme involved in the conversion of components of tobacco smoke to carcinogenic forms.

Lung cancer occurs most often in both men and women in the 55 to 65-year age group. Over recent decades, incidence of lung cancer has inceased twofold in the 40 to 44-year age group and tenfold in the 60 to 64-year age group. Part of this increase is attributable to a decrease in competing causes of death, such as infectious diseases, particularly in the early decades of life, and an overall increase in life expectancy. About 144,000 new cases of lung cancer were diagnosed in 1984—94,000 in men and 46,000 in women, with a total of 125,000 deaths.

The complexity of malignant changes in the lung, or any other organ, defies simple answers. Therefore, in terms of present knowledge the problem of lung cancer remains largely one of prevention, early diagnosis, and prompt treatment.

THE RESPIRATORY SYSTEM

The respiratory system consists of those parts of the body involved in breathing—that is, the inhalation of air containing oxygen, needed by all living cells, and exhalation of carbon dioxide, the waste product of the cells' energy production process. Figure 42 shows the position of the lungs in the chest and their relationship to other organs. The right lung has three sections, or lobes, and the left lung has two. The lungs are soft and spongy and, in healthy adults, are a mottled pinkish gray color, but may be blackened due to carbon particles. The lungs and inner walls of the chest (thoracic cavity) are covered with a thin double membrane called the pleura. The two layers are separated by a "potential" space called the pleural cavity, which is not apparent unless air or fluid collects between the two layers or unless the lung collapses. In the normal state the two layers of pleura lie next to each other, separated only by a thin fluid that allows their two touching surfaces to move easily during the breathing process. About 12 percent of lung cancer patients have, at the time of diagnosis, a pleural effusion, meaning that fluid is present in this space, usually as a result of the spread of cancer to the pleural surface.

The breathing "tree" (Figure 43) may be considered a kind of upside-down tree dividing into smaller and smaller branches. The air containing oxygen is inhaled through the nose and proceeds through the nasal cavities, then to the pharynx (back of the throat), the larynx (voice box), the trachea (windpipe), and finally to the mainstem bronchi. The main bronchi branch into lobar bronchi, going to each lobe of the lung, and then into segmental bronchi leading to the next smaller subdivisions. The branching process continues until the smallest bronchi form bronchioles ending in the alveolar ducts which lead into innumerable tiny, thin-walled clusters of sacs called alveoli. The average lung has about 300 million of these sacs, which provide the actual surface for the exchange of oxygen and carbon dioxide.

The arteries and veins of the lungs branch progressively into smaller and smaller vessels, following the structure of the respiratory tree, until

Normal Position of Lungs

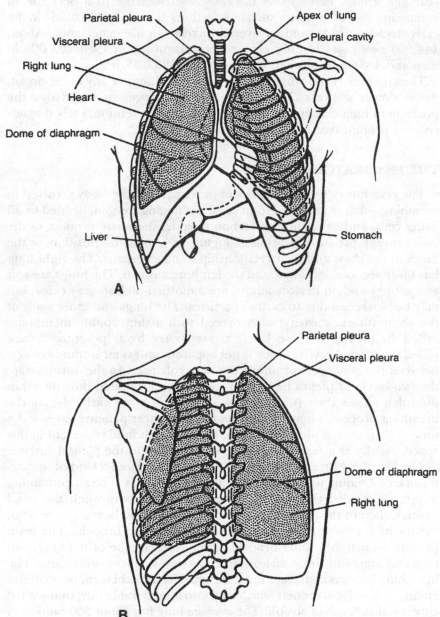

Parietal pleura

Visceral pleura

Right lung

Heart

Dome of diaphragm

Liver

Apex of lung

Pleural cavity

Stomach

A

Parietal pleura

Visceral pleura

Dome of diaphragm

Right lung

B

Figure 42 The lungs and their relationship to other chest organs from front **(A)** and back **(B).**

Normal Respiratory System

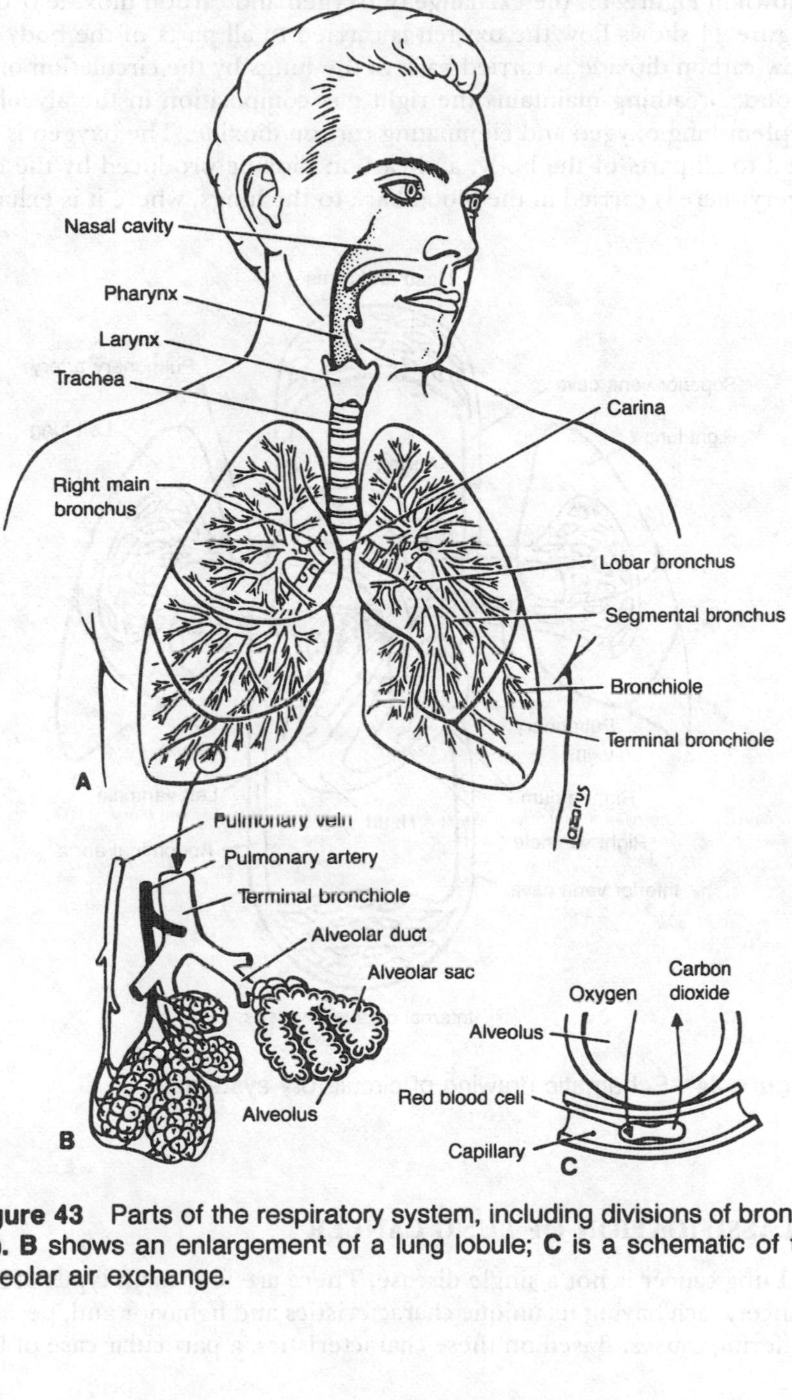

Figure 43 Parts of the respiratory system, including divisions of bronchi (**A**). **B** shows an enlargement of a lung lobule; **C** is a schematic of the alveolar air exchange.

they reach the alveoli where capillaries are formed. In the alveoli, as shown in Figure 43, the exchange of oxygen and carbon dioxide occurs. Figure 44 shows how the oxygen is carried to all parts of the body and how carbon dioxide is carried back to the lungs by the circulation of the blood. Breathing maintains the right gas composition in the alveoli by replenishing oxygen and eliminating carbon dioxide. The oxygen is carried to all parts of the body, and carbon dioxide produced by the cells everywhere is carried in the blood back to the lungs, where it is exhaled.

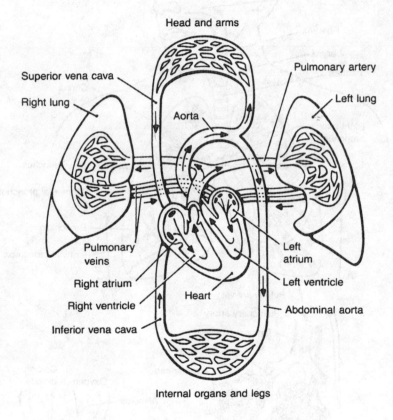

Figure 44 Schematic drawing of circulatory system.

CLASSIFICATION OF LUNG CANCER

Lung cancer is not a single disease. There are four main types of lung cancer, each having its unique characteristics and behavior and, perhaps, differing causes. Based on these characteristics, a particular case of lung cancer can be classified as either a squamous cell carcinoma, adenocarcinoma, undifferentiated small cell (oat cell) carcinoma, or undifferentiated large cell carcinoma. The great majority of tumors are either squamous or adenocarcinoma. Undifferentiated small cell accounts for about 20 percent and large cell for 10 to 15 percent.

The airways are lined with rows of hairlike cells called cilia resting on a layer called the basement membrane. In the bronchial wall there are layers of smooth muscle, mucous glands, connective tissue, as well as cartilage, which provides support. Goblet or mucous cells secrete mucus, which covers the surface of the bronchi and serves to catch foreign particles in the air moving in and out of the lungs. The hairlike cells continually beat this mucus upward toward the throat to keep the lungs clean and free of impurities. A lung cancer begins when one or more of the cells in the bronchial tree or lung begins to divide and grow abnormally. A small area of thickening or piling up of these cells gradually becomes an irregular, warty outgrowth that erodes through the cells lining the bronchial tree. The precise cause of the abnormal growth is unknown, but is thought to be a result of repeated injury to normal cells, probably from multiple sources, such as carcinogens, viral agents, genetic alterations, or even the aging process. Unfortunately, whatever its cause, much of the abnormal growth takes place before the cancer can be seen and diagnosed.

Squamous cell lung cancer is the only type of lung cancer that goes through recognized phases. The precancerous phase may last several years, during which abnormal, but not cancerous, cells are found in the sputum, but no tumor can be seen on chest X rays. The origin of these cells can, however, usually be found by careful examination of the bronchial tree with a flexible instrument called the fiberoptic bronchoscope. In later stages the lung cancer can be seen on the chest X ray or it grows large enough to cause symptoms, such as pneumonia or the collapse of a lung segment.

Squamous cell cancers commonly arise in the larger lobar and segmental bronchi of the central part of the lung. Patients with this type of cancer respond better to treatments with surgery and radiation therapy than do those with other types of lung cancer. Squamous cell cancers apparently tend to remain confined to the chest longer than the other types, providing an improved chance of complete eradication and cure.

Adenocarcinoma is a type of lung cancer in which the tumor cells form recognizable glandular structures. It arises in much smaller bronchi than those in which squamous cell cancer occurs, and thus is the most frequently diagnosed peripheral cancer. It is often associated with scarring of the lungs and may be seen as a subpleural mass that invades the overlying pleura. The prognosis for adenocarcinoma, except for patients with early (Stage I) tumors, is poorer than for squamous cell carcinoma. It is the most commonly diagnosed lung cancer in women. A subtype of adenocarcinoma called bronchioloalveolar, or alveolar cell lung cancer arises from the terminal bronchioles or alveolar walls. It is not associated with smoking and, according to some reports, has a better prognosis than other adenocarcinomas.

Undifferentiated small cell or "oat cell" carcinoma cells are generally small and round, or oval, or shaped like oat grains. It is the most aggressive of all the lung cancers, and many patients have distant metastases at the time of diagnosis even if the primary tumor is apparently small. Undifferentiated small cell cancer generally is not treated surgically, but the use of multidrug chemotherapy has recently produced encouraging results. A decade ago only half of all patients with small cell carcinoma were expected to live more than two months from the time their disease was diagnosed. But now, for patients who respond to chemotherapy the expected median survival time has been extended to two years. Long-term cure remains an elusive goal, but a number of patients with small cell lung cancer live five years or more.

Large cell lung carcinomas occur less frequently than the other cell types. There is some controversy over whether this is a unique cell type or merely a category of atypical or uncharacteristic squamous cell carcinomas and adenocarcinomas that are not recognized as such. Large cell carcinomas generally behave like adenocarcinomas.

Anatomic Classification

Accurate assessment of the primary tumor, the regional lymph nodes, and the presence or absence of distant spread is vitally important in planning treatment and estimating the prognosis for lung cancer patients. The disease is classified according to the extent of the primary tumor (T), the status of regional lymph nodes (N) and distant spread or metastasis (M). The extent of the cancer in each of these important areas is then described by means of a simple code in which numerical suffixes designate the absence of tumor or increasing levels of disease; for example, T_1, T_2, T_3, T_4; N_0, N_1, N_2, or N_3; and M_0 or M_1. The TNM subsets are combined into a small number of stages of diseases in which patients in each stage group have a similar life expectancy, with that for Stage I being the longest.

DETECTION OF LUNG CANCER, SCREENING, AND TUMOR MARKERS

The timing of diagnosis and treatment in the natural history of a lung cancer is critical to the subsequent course of the disease. Great effort has been made to develop screening techniques or to find "marker" substances that will detect lung cancer when it is still potentially curable. The National Cancer Institute Cooperative Early Lung Cancer Group has conducted investigational screening programs for several years to determine whether the use of periodic chest X rays and sputum cell examinations are effective in diagnosing lung cancer in high risk individuals. These high risk groups include men over forty-five years of age who are long-term heavy cigarette smokers.

Interim reports from all three participating centers (the Mayo Clinic, Johns Hopkins University, and Memorial Sloan-Kettering Cancer Center) clearly show that these screening procedures do identify a higher proportion of curable lung cancers than are found in the general public. The tumors detected by microscopic examination (Pap smears) of sputum are largely squamous cell cancers of the major bronchi, while those detected by X ray are peripheral, with two thirds of them being adenocarcinomas. These screening programs have not been successful in detecting early small cell lung cancer, nor have they made significant differences in overall death rates from lung cancer.

The stage of disease at the time of diagnosis and treatment in patients whose lung cancer is of the non-small cell type is a proxy of survival, since curative treatment is seldom possible in patients with advanced disease. In patients with small undifferentiated cell lung cancer, a larger proportion of "complete responders" to the drugs are seen in the early stage groups.

Although mass screening programs are not likely to be cost-effective for the general population, the high risk individual can make rational use of regular monitoring—e.g., with sputum cytology and chest X-ray examinations for early lung cancer. Anyone over forty with a history of heavy cigarette smoking or exposure to other known carcinogenic agents, or with a chronic cough, especially one that gets worse and produces phlegm, or with a history of bloody sputum (hemoptysis), or recurrent bouts of pneumonia should be particularly concerned about the possibility of lung cancer.

Markers

Curious hormonal syndromes have been observed for many years in association with lung cancers, but only recently with the development of sensitive biochemical tests (e.g., bioassays and immunoassays) have physicians been able to describe the biochemistry of these effects. Lung cancer cells can produce many biochemical substances that are not produced, or are produced in much smaller amounts, by normal cells. A large number of these substances, including both endocrine and nonendocrine hormones and antibodies (immunological markers), have been studied in the hope that lung cancer might one day be diagnosed early by means of a blood test. Although none of these studies have found such a substance yet, recent research offers some hope for a test useful for cancer detection. For example, monitoring the level of carcinoembryonic antigen (CEA)—a substance found in fetal cells—in the blood of lung cancer patients following therapy has been useful in detecting recurrent or metastatic disease. A higher than normal CEA level is often observed before symptoms of metastases appear. Patients with undifferentiated small cell cancer have an especially high incidence of hormonal abnormalities, such as elevated levels of calcitonin or ACTH hormone.

Symptoms and History

Lung cancer has no specific symptoms and often mimics benign respiratory ailments. In fact, in the earliest stages of disease there are usually no symptoms. Only 10 percent of all lung cancer patients have been diagnosed from routine chest X rays as a part of a physical examination or during the investigation of another complaint.

Symptoms associated with lung cancer include a chronic cough, a change in pulmonary function, blood in the sputum, wheezing unrelated to asthma, repeated episodes of pneumonia, fever, weakness, weight loss, and chest pain. Hoarseness, shortness of breath, enlargement of lymph nodes in the neck, shoulder and arm pain, difficulty swallowing, and drooping of the upper eyelids are signs of more advanced disease. More than half of all lung cancer patients have had bronchitis for years, and very often the symptom that brings the patient to the doctor is a worsening of "smoker's cough."

A common nonpulmonary symptom associated with lung cancer is "clubbing" or broadening of the fingernails, which is seen in 10 to 12 percent of patients. Enlargement of the breast in males is almost as common and frequently accompanies a group of bone and joint disorders called hypertrophic pulmonary osteoarthropathy. It is not uncommon for a patient with lung cancer to have symptoms of distant metastasis as the first evidence of the tumor. Bone pain and abnormalities related to the central nervous system such as headaches, blurred vision, and dizziness are the most frequent early symptoms of widespread disease. The course of the disease depends upon five factors: the general health of the patient at the time of diagnosis, specific cancer cell type, stage of disease, type of treatment, and, lastly, the poorly understood relationship between the tumor and the environment in which it grows—the patient.

Infection is the most common complication of lung cancer. Collapse of a segment, lobe, or all of the lung (atelectasis), or obstructive pneumonitis (inflammation caused by the tumor obstructing a bronchus) occurs in 60 percent of all patients. About 12 percent of patients have pleural effusion or fluid in the lungs at the time of diagnosis. Spread of lung cancer to other structures in the chest, such as lymph nodes, is common and may cause paralysis of the nerves affecting the voice and the movement of the diaphragm.

Chest X Rays

A chest X ray is the single most useful examination to detect lung cancer. Although routine chest X rays are no longer recommended for healthy, low risk people, many experts recommend that people who fall into a high risk group should undergo periodic X-ray examination. Comparing present X rays with earlier films is invaluable in finding abnormalities in the early stages of their development. Lung cancer most often appears on the chest X ray as a centrally located mass 1½ to 2 inches in diameter. In addition to the standard X rays, a number of special techniques may be used to determine the characteristics of lung cancer. Tomograms are films that show lengthwise thin slices through an organ and may reveal tumors that are obscured in the chest X ray. CT (computerized tomography) scans are used to show the relationship of the lung cancer to other structures of the chest, such as the degree of invasion of the chest wall or encroachment of tumor on major blood vessels.

Diagnosis

To diagnose lung cancer—or any other cancer—the abnormal cells must be studied under a microscope. Increasingly, lung cancer is being diagnosed via pulmonary cytology—the microscopic examination of samples of sputum containing cells obtained from the bronchial passages or the pleural fluid. These cytology studies can now provide a definitive diagnosis in 80 to 90 percent of patients, including patients with microscopic or occult cancer who have normal X-ray studies.

Needle Biopsy

When other sampling techniques fail to provide a diagnosis, a needle biopsy may be performed. This technique, in which the doctor, guided by a fluoroscope, inserts a long, thin needle into a suspected tumor and withdraws a small tissue sample, is particularly useful for patients who are not candidates for surgery and for whom a definitive diagnosis is needed to plan other treatment.

The main complication of needle biopsy is development of a pneumothorax, the leaking of air into the pleural space which causes the lung to collapse. Pneumothorax, which may occur in 5 to 20 percent of needle-biopsy patients, usually resolves spontaneously but sometimes further treatment is needed to reinflate the lung. Needle biopsy is usually performed in patients with Pancoast's, or superior sulcus, tumors—those located in the apex or groove along the top edge of the lung—since a tissue diagnosis is essential before the usual treatment plan of radiation followed by surgery can be initiated.

Bronchoscopy

Bronchoscopy is also an essential procedure in the diagnosis and treatment of lung disease. Since the majority of lung cancers originate in the lining of the bronchus (the bronchial epithelium), visual inspection of the bronchi is of great value in diagnosis and in determining the extent of the lung disease. Bronchoscopy is usually performed with a bronchofiberscope (Figure 45)—a flexible tube with lighting and magnifying devices which is inserted through a nostril and then advanced slowly down the throat and into the trachea, the main bronchus, lobar bronchi, and into the segmental bronchi in the periphery of the lung. The physician is able to see the illuminated surface of nearly the whole tracheobronchial tree and to obtain samples of tumor cells by "washing" an area with a small amount of liquid, or by using minute nylon brushes to obtain cells over a larger area. Biopsies of abnormal areas can also be taken using a small cutting instrument, the biopsy forceps. The precise location of the tumor and any extension can be determined. From this information, the physician can tell if the cancer is completely removable and, if so, how much lung tissue would have to be removed to rid the lung of all of the cancer.

Fiberoptic bronchoscopy is performed under either local or general anesthesia, depending on the extent of the examination required and the sequence of further procedures or surgery. Patients need not worry that they will not be able to breathe, since oxygen is supplied to the lungs during the procedure either through a mask or a special channel in the bronchoscope. A local anesthetic and moderate sedation are used to reduce any discomfort and control the gag reflex or possible bronchial spasm. Fiberoptic bronchoscopy is a remarkably safe procedure, with less than one percent of patients experiencing any complications. If small specimens have been taken for biopsy, patients may cough up a small amount of blood, but this is no cause for alarm.

Although flexible fiberoptic bronchoscopy is now used 95 percent of the time, a limited examination of the upper tracheobronchial tree can be accomplished with an instrument called the rigid bronchoscope. This instrument is inserted through the mouth over the base of the tongue and gently passed into the trachea, down the mainstem bronchi as far as the lower-lobe bronchi. Rigid bronchoscopy is usually performed under local anesthetic, but in some instances general anesthetic may be used. Patients have no trouble breathing during the procedure, since the instrument does not obstruct the flow of air in and out of the bronchial tubes.

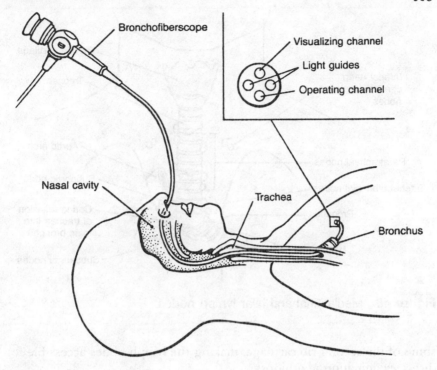

Figure 45 Bronchofiberscope examination. Inset shows detail of scope endpiece.

The spread of lung cancer to the lymph nodes in the mediastinum, the chest space between the lungs (Figure 46), is common. In some patients the spread of cancer to the mediastinal lymph nodes is suggested by the findings from chest X rays, tomograms, or CTs. Mediastinal lymph nodes can also be examined and biopsied by mediastinoscopy and mediastinotomy. These procedures are performed under general anesthesia and, like bronchoscopy, have a remarkably low complication rate. Mediastinoscopy is performed by inserting an instrument, the mediastinoscope, through a small V-shaped incision at the center of the base of the neck and passing it behind the breastbone (sternum) to lie directly in front of the trachea. The physician can then see and biopsy the lymph nodes on either side of the trachea and its first branch point.

In patients who have centrally located tumors in the left upper lobe of the lung, mediastinotomy may be indicated, since the lymph nodes most likely to be involved—those under the aorta—are not accessible by mediastinoscopy. This procedure involves a small incision and removal of

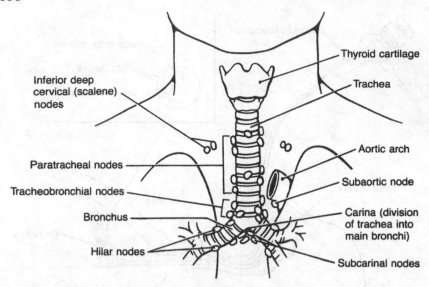

Figure 46 Mediastinal and hilar lymph nodes.

some of the second rib cartilage, making the lymph nodes accessible for direct examination and biopsy.

These two procedures are used only in patients who have been evaluated by other less invasive methods, and for whom the results of bronchoscopy and sputum studies are available. In some patients the lymph node examination provides the only microscopic evidence of a cancer that has been shown on X rays but not specifically diagnosed by cytology or other biopsies.

When lung cancer has spread to the lymph nodes in the mediastinum there are fewer opportunities for applying surgical treatment; however, in some patients removal of all of the disease can be accomplished. Surgical treatment may be selected for patients with non-small cell lung cancer with the lymph node metastasis limited to those nodes nearest the lung lobe containing the cancer—that is, the lower paratracheal or subcarinal lymph nodes. If the results of mediastinoscopy or mediastinotomy show that the lymph nodes on the opposite side of the trachea or high in the trachea near the neck are involved with metastatic lung cancer, surgical treatment is not recommended. If small cell lung cancer is diagnosed from mediastinal lymph node biopsies, or if involvement of the heart or major vessels is discovered, surgical treatment is not planned.

Mediastinoscopy and mediastinotomy are not usually performed in patients who have superior sulcus or small peripheral tumors with no indication on the chest X rays or other films of spread to the mediastinum. Also, these procedures are seldom indicated for patients whose cancer is known to be inoperable on the basis of other tests.

Pleuroscopy

Although infrequently used, pleuroscopy is valuable for patients who have undiagnosed fluid in the chest or whose cancer may have spread to the pleura. The procedure involves insertion of a thoracoscope or fiberoptic bronchoscope into the pleural space. All of the pleural space can then be examined visually and fluid and biopsy samples can be withdrawn. Pleuroscopy can cause moderate chest wall discomfort, but no other complications occur.

Thoracentesis

The removal of fluid from the chest, or thoracentesis, involves inserting a needle in the space between the lung and the chest wall and using gentle suction to withdraw the fluid into a syringe or other container. The fluid is then examined for the presence of cancer cells. Thoracentesis may be undertaken to relieve symptoms such as shortness of breath or pain caused by the collection of large amounts of fluid in the pleural space. No anesthetic is necessary other than that applied locally to the skin where the needle is inserted.

Diagnostic Thoracotomy

In a small number of lung cancer patients, all diagnostic procedures may fail to establish a diagnosis; if suspicion of cancer persists, an exploratory operation may be undertaken. This procedure, thoracotomy, involves surgical opening of the chest and removal of a part of the lung containing a solitary nodule or other undiagnosed mass. A thoracotomy is seldom performed if there are doubts as to whether a tumor is removable. Instead, the operation is usually reserved for those cases in which the surgeon thinks he or she can proceed immediately to complete removal of the tumor if cancer is diagnosed. There are, however, instances in which it is impossible to judge this before the full operation.

Other Diagnostic Tests

Lymph Node Biopsy. Lymph nodes in the neck may be biopsied if they are enlarged or show other abnormalities. Since clinical judgment regarding these lymph nodes is remarkably accurate, a routine biopsy of them in search of possible metastasis is usually not done.

Radionuclide Scans. A small amount of sterile radioactive material is injected into the patient's arm vein. The radioactive isotopes may be taken up by cancerous tissues; these areas will then show up on the scan. The examination is not painful and complications are very rare.

Radionuclide scans are performed most often in patients with small cell lung cancer, which has frequently spread to distant organs at the time of diagnosis. In such instances, scans and bone marrow biopsy are usually performed as part of the diagnostic workup. In contrast, radionuclide scans of the brain, liver, bone, and adrenal glands in patients with squamous cell, adenocarcinoma, or large cell cancer will seldom if ever detect distant metastases unless accompanying symptoms or laboratory results suggest their presence.

The diagnostic tests for the investigation and treatment of lung cancer are undertaken in a logical manner, beginning with those that have the least risk and cost. The evaluation must provide two essential answers: the definitive microscopic diagnosis of the cancer-cell type and an accurate determination of the extent of the disease.

PREOPERATIVE EVALUATION

Most lung cancer patients have some degree of coexisting heart and lung problems that are common in heavy smokers or that accompany the aging process. In a number of patients these diseases prohibit consideration of thoracotomy and lung surgery. Thus the status of each patient's cardiac and pulmonary systems is carefully evaluated before an operation is planned. Spirometry—a test that measures the breathing efficiency of the lungs—is widely used. In some clinics the contribution of each part of the lung to overall respiration is assessed by using radioactive xenon-133 gas. From the results of these and other simple tests, such as measuring the patient's respiratory rate before and after exercise, the physician can determine how much lung tissue can be safely removed and still permit the patient to have relatively normal activities and maintain a good quality of life.

Cardiac evaluation includes a careful history with details of treatment for hypertension and any abnormal heart rhythms. In patients with coronary artery disease—for example, people who suffer from angina pectoris or who have abnormal electrocardiographic findings—additional tests are performed. In some patients with coronary artery disease, a combined approach of simultaneous coronary bypass surgery and lung operation is feasible.

TREATMENT

The primary methods of treatment for lung cancer are surgery, radiation therapy, and chemotherapy. The treatment plan depends on the individual patient's general health, the cell type of cancer, and the stage or extent of the disease.

Surgery

Surgical resection (removal) is the first choice of treatment for all patients with non-small cell lung cancer whose disease is completely confined to the lung (Stages I and II) and who can tolerate the operation necessary to remove all of the known cancer. Certain carefully selected patients with lung cancer that has extended into the mediastinum or the chest wall or who have limited involvement of the mediastinal lymph nodes (Stage III) also may undergo surgical treatment, if all of the cancer can be safely removed. Patients with any spread to distant organs or to the lymph nodes in the opposite side of the trachea or neck, or who have disease in the opposite lung, do not have surgery as their primary treatment.

Patients with cancer in the apex of the lung (Pancoast's or superior sulcus tumor) that is considered removable are usually treated with radiation therapy first. Preoperative radiation treatment is not used, however, for tumors in other locations, since this has not proved beneficial in patients undergoing surgery for lung cancer in other parts of the lung tissue. Patients with metastases to lymph nodes in the mediastinum for whom complete removal is deemed advisable usually are assigned to receive postoperative radiation therapy.

Non-small cell lung cancer, particularly in patients with Stage I disease, can often be cured. Patients with squamous cell carcinoma have the best overall outcome, but those with Stage I adenocarcinoma have an equally good prognosis. Patients with Stage II and III adenocarcinoma have a better outcome following complete removal of the primary tumor than can be offered with any other kind of treatment, but the prospect of long-term cure is poorer than for patients with squamous cell tumors.

Surgical Procedures

The risk of pulmonary surgery depends primarily on the patient's age, general physical condition, and the extent of the operation. As with all major operations, a small number of patients will succumb to complications despite proper care before, during, and after surgery. Nevertheless, chest surgery is now widely practiced and the large majority of patients do well.

Thoracotomy performed under general anesthesia is the general term used for the surgical opening of the chest. The usual thoracotomy incision follows the ribs around from the back just below the shoulder blade to the front of the chest. The ribs are then spread apart and after examination of the mediastinum and lung, the appropriate operation is performed. After the physician has made the incision and is able to examine the disease in the chest, samples of the mediastinal lymph nodes are taken for immediate examination by the pathologist by frozen section, and the presence or absence of cancer cells is reported to the surgeon. The goal is to remove all of the cancer while saving the greatest amount of lung tissue. Removal of a wedge or segment of lung tissue may be indicated for small tumors that have no lymph node metastases. A lobectomy (removal of one lobe), a bilobectomy (removal of more than one lobe) and pneumonectomy (removal of the whole right or left lung) are other procedures.

In patients with peripheral lung cancers extending to the ribs or chest wall, the tumor may be removed by wedge resection or lobectomy, with complete resection of the involved ribs and chest wall. If the resulting wound is too large to allow closing the skin, the chest wall is repaired using a meshlike substance called Marlex, or a combined muscle and skin graft. Although this is an extensive procedure, it is very worthwhile, since lung cancers of this kind seldom have metastasized and the result in a large number of patients is satisfactory.

Palliative Surgery

There are few situations in which surgery for lung cancer is undertaken if a cure is unlikely. If the tumor is causing serious bleeding or if infection with abscess formation is present, a whole lung may be removed to relieve these distressing conditions, or even as an emergency procedure in patients known to have further disease.

When a part of the lung is removed, the surgical margins also are checked for cancer cells by the pathologist. If cancer cells are present at the surgical margins, further surgery is necessary to remove all of the remaining disease. Some patients, however, may not be able to lose any further lung tissue and still be able to breathe satisfactorily. In these patients, the operation will be limited to what has already been removed and will be considered palliative. The sites containing cancer cells will be marked with silver clips so that postoperative radiation treatment can be directed to them. If only a small amount of cancer is left behind, the radiation treatment may eradicate it, producing a cure.

In a small number of patients, the possibility of total removal of the cancer cannot be determined by preoperative tests. Depending on the risk of surgery in an individual patient, thoracotomy may be undertaken to give the patient the benefit of a chance of total surgical removal. If all of the lung cancer is not completely removable, partial resection is seldom performed, since no benefit from this procedure can be shown. Rather, radiation therapy or chemotherapy or both are recommended.

Recovery from Surgery

For a short time following pulmonary surgery, all patients receive breathing assistance with a mechanical ventilator. This assistance, which is seldom needed for more than two or three days, maintains and stabilizes oxygen consumption until the patient has recovered from the anesthesia and can breathe alone. Patients undergoing surgery for lung cancer usually are discharged from the hospital seven to ten days following the operation, although full recovery may take several weeks longer. Patients are usually asked to return to the doctor or clinic in four to six weeks for a checkup. As with any major surgical procedure, it may be several months before an individual regains normal energy, but this depends on many factors, such as general physical condition before the operation, age, and any accompanying disease, as well as the extent of the surgery. After removal of part or all of a lung, most patients must limit their physical activities to some degree depending on the amount of lung tissue removed and the condition of the remaining lung. Most patients regain a satisfactory quality of life following pulmonary surgery, since their ability to do so is carefully evaluated before the operation.

Regular checkups for patients following surgical treatment are usually scheduled every three months for two years, then twice a year for the next five years, and every year thereafter. A chest X ray, sputum tests, and blood analyses are routinely done at these visits to detect any recurrence or metastases of the cancer as soon as possible. Patients undergoing successful treatment for lung cancer are at high risk to develop a second primary tumor (particularly if they continue to smoke), a problem that can often be treated by additional surgery.

Radiation Therapy

Radiation from an ionizing source, such as X rays or a cobalt-60 unit, destroys cancer cells by injuring their capacity to divide. The term to "sterilize the tumor" means there are no cells remaining in the treated area that can produce more cancer cells. Although some technical factors may be responsible, failure of radiation therapy to eradicate the local tumor is due primarily to the presence of more cancer cells than can be destroyed by a safe dose of radiation. There is, however, ample evidence that some lung cancer patients can be cured with radiation therapy. The success rate depends on the amount of lung cancer and the dose of radiation.

The total amount of radiation, measured in a unit called a rad, is given in a series of treatments spread over several days or weeks. Both normal and cancerous cells are injured by the treatment. The interval before the next treatment provides time for the cells to repair these injuries. Normal tissues have a greater ability to repair themselves, thus the number of tumor cells surviving each treatment becomes progressively smaller than the number of normal cells, and the tumor shrinks. Finally, if enough radiation can be given, all of the cancer cells will be destroyed and the patient will be cured. Although normal cells have been injured, enough remain to repair the damage. The amount of radiation that can be given, therefore, is limited primarily to this tolerance or ability of the normal cells to repair themselves.

Selection of Patients for Radiation Therapy

A great many lung cancer patients are treated with radiation therapy and derive significant benefit and, in some cases, even cure from it. Patients with squamous cell carcinoma, adenocarcinoma, and large cell carcinoma whose lung cancer cannot be completely removed by surgical treatment, and who have no evidence of metastases to distant organs, may undergo radiation treatment for possible cure. Surgery is without question the first choice of treatment for patients with operable lung cancer. However, some patients with this level of disease may not be able to tolerate surgery for a variety of reasons and instead, a cure with radiation therapy will be attempted. High-dose radiation is not usually recommended for patients whose general condition is very poor or if the tumor-free lung is very inadequate.

Planning Radiation Therapy

The usual treatment plan for cure (as opposed to merely relieving symptoms) includes a radiation dose of 5,000 to 6,000 rads delivered in daily treatments over a period of several weeks. Some patients undergo a treatment plan that includes two weeks (five days) of treatment followed by two weeks' rest and two more weeks of treatment. Others receive daily radiation until the total planned dose has been delivered. Although there are advantages to both schemes, neither has been proved superior to the other in terms of survival rates.

A team of highly specialized persons is involved in giving radiation treatment. The plan for each patient is carefully worked out under direction of the radiation therapist or radiation oncologist, and also involves physicists and other technical and nurse specialties. Computerized tomography is used, and has proved of great value in determining the regions of the chest that will need to be treated and the areas to which the beam of radiation must be directed. The goal of this planning is to spare as much normal tissue as possible while delivering the most lethal blow to the lung cancer. Using X-ray pictures of the patient's chest as a guide, an outline of the area to be treated is drawn with long-lasting dye on the patient's chest and back (Figure 47) and is not removed until treatment is completed so that the radiation can be directed to exactly the same place each day. Usually the patient receives alternate treatments to the front and back of the chest so that the cancer gets the proper dose of radiation while the skin and underlying tissues receive minimal radiation effects. The adjacent normal tissues are protected as much as possible from the radiation beam by lead shielding constructed individually for each patient. Each treatment only lasts about two minutes, but medical personnel cannot remain in the room since they would be exposed to a small amount of radiation each time a patient was treated. Adjacent to the treatment room is a control room with a closed-circuit television and intercom system to monitor and communicate with the patient during the short treatment session (Figure 48). Although the procedure may seem frightening, the patient has no discomfort or pain during the treatment and is aware only of a slight whirring sound of the equipment. The radiation therapist controls the treatment from a nearby room and the patient can talk to the doctor or therapist at any time.

Effects of Radiation Therapy

Most patients experience fatigue within a few hours of radiation treatment, a feeling that continues throughout the course of therapy. It does not indicate that the patient's condition is worsening. Patients are advised to get additional rest, and not to plan to get much done while they are undergoing treatment. The tiredness usually wears off within a week after the completion of therapy. Radiation treatment usually does not cause nausea, but if it does occur, antinausea medications can be given.

A dry or sore throat and a sense of difficulty in swallowing (dysphagia) are minor, temporary complications of radiation therapy. This problem may be noticed shortly after the treatment ends but only lasts a week or two and does not indicate that the lung cancer is worse or has spread. A soft or liquid diet may be recommended until the discomfort subsides.

All patients who undergo high-dose radiation to the lungs eventually have permanent changes in the lung tissues called radiation fibrosis. Fibrosis, a process similar to scarring, entails the formation of fibrous connective tissue as a repair or reactive process in an organ that normally does not have fibrous tissue. It becomes apparent on chest X-ray films nine to ten months following treatment, and may be accompanied by the escape of fluid from the tissues (effusion), although usually no symptoms occur. The nonirradiated, healthy lung tissue that remains takes over supplying the body's need for oxygen. Depending on the amount of lung function that is damaged, patients usually must accept some modification of their physical activities, but life-threatening consequences are rare.

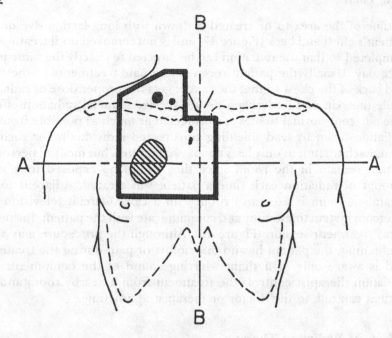

Figure 47 The heavy black line in this portal drawing represents the line that is drawn on the chest to mark the area to which radiation therapy will be directed. Lines A and B relate to the technical aspects of the radiation therapy. The lung tumor is the area marked by parallel lines; the dark areas in the upper chest are lymph nodes.

(From Lee, R. E., "Radiotherapy for Lung Cancer," in Straus, M. (ed): *Lung Cancer, Clinical Diagnosis and Treatment,* 2d ed., New York: Grune & Stratton, 1983, p. 223 [used with permission].)

Many lung cancer patients also suffer from emphysema, a condition in which the alveoli lose their elasticity, resulting in breathlessness. Smoking is the usual cause. Radiation treatments can make the emphysema worse, since the formation of scar tissue further reduces lung function.

About a year after radiation for lung cancer, some patients have a slight hardening of the shoulder and chest muscles that causes muscular aching and stiffness. To prevent this, patients having lung radiation should begin to exercise while they are receiving the treatments.

The skin is usually only mildly affected by the radiation treatments. Reactions include loss of hair (only in the treated area), which grows back after about three months; shedding of the outer layer of the skin; and tanning, or increase of pigment. The skin does not get "burned" from radiation treatment, a problem that occurred years ago before refinements in the present equipment were made. Most patients are advised not

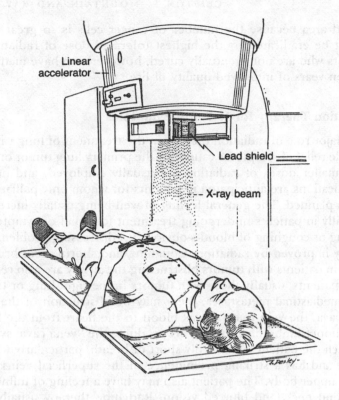

Figure 48 Patient receiving treatment under a linear accelerator.
(From "Living with Lung Cancer" by Cox, B.S.; Carr, D.T.; Lee, R.E.: Rochester, Minn., Mayo Foundation, 1977. Illustration by J. N. Desley. Used with permission.)

to get a suntan, apply a heating pad, or irritate the treated area with ointments or medicines. A mild lotion or ointment will usually be recommended by the radiation therapist.

Results of High-dose Radiation Therapy

The goal of radiation therapy in patients selected for high-dose treatment is to eradicate the local cancer and, it is hoped, cure the patient. The extent to which this can be accomplished depends on the size and extent of the lung cancer, the cell type, and the dose of radiation that can be given safely. In 30 to 40 percent of patients with non-small cell lung cancer, radiation will sterilize the local disease; 3 to 25 percent may live for five years or more. Distant metastases that can take place even during the treatment are responsible for failure in patients whose local disease has been controlled. In some patients, the lung cancer recurs in the treated area because the number of cancer cells is so great that they cannot be eradicated by the highest tolerated dose of radiation. Even patients who are not eventually cured, however, can have many months or even years of improved quality of life.

Radiation Therapy for Relief of Symptoms

A major role of radiation therapy in the treatment of lung cancer is to provide relief of symptoms caused by the primary lung tumor or metastases. Smaller doses of radiation are usually employed, and no serious complications are anticipated in patients for whom only palliative radiation is planned. The general feeling of well-being usually increases dramatically in patients undergoing treatment for relief of symptoms. The spitting or coughing of blood—obviously a distressing problem—can be greatly improved by radiation. Coughing and shortness of breath (dyspnea) in patients with tumors obstructing the airway are also relieved. In some patients, usually those with tumors in the right lung or those who have mediastinal metastases, there may be obstruction of the superior vena cava, the vein that returns blood to the heart from the head and neck, upper limbs, and chest. This produces the "vena caval syndrome" in which the patient is markedly short of breath, particularly when lying down, and has a striking prominence of the superficial veins over the entire upper body. The patient also may have a feeling of fullness in the head and neck, and blurred vision. Radiation therapy usually relieves these symptoms. Occasionally the problem recurs, but the treatment can be repeated, usually with good results.

Chest pain and pain in the arm and shoulder, caused by the invasion of cancer from Pancoast's or superior sulcus tumors into the bony structures of the chest wall, spine, and nerves, are alleviated by radiation treatment. These patients, who also may have Horner's syndrome—drooping eyelid or numbness of the arm—need a higher dose of radiation, and the area treated includes the vertebral structures.

Bone pain, caused by metastases of the lung cancer to the bones, is another common symptom. Radiation therapy effectively relieves this pain by shrinking the tumor deposit.

In small cell lung cancer, adenocarcinoma, and large cell carcinoma, the brain is a common site of distant metastasis. Patients with small cell tumors may have brain metastases as a part of generalized spread of the disease, but in those patients with adenocarcinoma or large cell tumors, brain metastasis often occurs as a single site. Metastasis to the brain causes symptoms similar to those of a primary brain tumor—for example, headache, vision disturbance, confusion, loss of muscle function, and convulsions. The great majority of patients with brain metastases treated with radiation to the brain obtain relief of these symptoms.

Radiation therapy to the brain as a prophylactic or preventive measure for patients with adenocarcinoma and large cell carcinoma is being investigated in several centers, but is not in general use at this time. Prophylactic brain radiation, however, is widely used in combined treatment programs for patients with small cell lung cancer.

Radiation treatment is the most effective palliative treatment for lung cancer, preventing some complications of the disease and alleviating others. In some patients, complete local eradication of the tumor results in long-term survival, while in others cure cannot be achieved because of metastases. The potential for success in controlling or curing lung cancer with radiation treatments is contingent upon the size and extent of the disease, the cell type, and the radiation dose that can be tolerated.

Chemotherapy

Chemotherapy has proved very useful in the treatment of patients with undifferentiated small cell lung cancer and is the treatment of choice for this disease. Multiple-drug chemotherapy regimens have prolonged the life of patients with small cell lung cancer, and long-term survival has been achieved for some. In patients with squamous cell carcinoma, adenocarcinoma, and large cell carcinoma, chemotherapy is reserved for those patients who have disease that cannot be managed by surgery and radiation therapy. This includes patients who have progressive disease following these treatments and those who have distant metastases when they are seen initially.

Chemotherapy for Non-small Cell Lung Cancer

Chemotherapy for non-small cell cancer is recommended only for patients not confined to bed and in fairly good general health—that is, those who are strong enough to care for themselves. They should have no medical contraindications, such as heart or kidney disease or significant weight loss (ten percent of their normal weight or greater). Although complete cure is rare, life expectancy may be prolonged in 30 to 40 percent of patients. In some medical centers chemotherapy may be given in conjunction with radiation therapy or surgery as an adjuvant treatment. This is done in an attempt to treat microscopic metastatic or residual disease that is not otherwise apparent. Protocols involving various schedules for combining chemotherapy and radiation therapy or, in some cases, immunotherapy for inoperable patients are under investigation.

Since drugs or combined regimens have not yet proved to be effective for non-small cell lung cancer, chemotherapy is not recommended as standard treatment for patients with widespread disease. Most anticancer drugs have serious side effects, and the potential for benefit in a given patient must be evaluated on an individual basis. A trial of chemotherapy consisting of two or three cycles of drugs known to have antitumor activity in large numbers of patients may be given to stronger patients. For those patients whose disease responds to the drugs, as shown by tumor regression or shrinkage, treatment is continued.

In a few patients a complete clinical remission is achieved and maintenance treatments will be continued for a year. Chemotherapy is not continued in patients whose disease does not remain stable or who fail to improve.

Chemotherapy for Undifferentiated Small Cell Cancer

Combination chemotherapy using three or four drugs is a standard treatment for patients with small cell lung cancer. The goal of such treatment is to achieve a complete remission, meaning that no cancer remaining after treatment can be found by X ray or other testing methods. The patient's general health and the stage of disease, generally referred to as "limited" (meaning no distant metastases except to lymph nodes in the neck), or "extensive" (meaning spread of the disease to distant organs such as the opposite lung, liver, brain, or bones), are the primary factors determining treatment response and long-term outcome. A number of combination drug regimens and schedules are effective, but regardless of the regimen, 80 percent of patients with extensive disease will have an objective response: the tumor shrinks measurably but is still evident. A few of these patients achieve the complete remission necessary for long-term survival—in this disease, defined as three or more years.

Complete remission rates of 75 to 100 percent have been reported for patients with limited small cell cancer. The duration of remission varies, but 9 to 32 percent are now reported to live for more than thirty months, a remarkable degree of progress considering that just a decade ago, less than 1 percent of all patients lived for that long.

Combined and Adjuvant Therapy for Lung Cancer

The curability of lung cancer by the primary treatment methods—surgery, radiation therapy, and chemotherapy—is limited by the extent of the tumor that is present at the time treatment is started. In order for lung cancer to be cured, all of the cancer cells must be either removed or rendered incapable of reproducing themselves. To accomplish this, treatment plans may be structured to use the cell-kill potential of one type of treatment to enhance the effectiveness of another kind of treatment. This approach has been, and still is, the major thrust of experimental treatment programs.

Radiation treatment has been used as adjuvant therapy both before and after surgical treatment. Several years ago a multiuniversity cooperative study involving a large number of patients showed that radiation treatment given before surgery did not provide significant benefit for patients undergoing subsequent removal of the lung tumor. This study was done prior to present knowledge of the importance of staging and histologic classification or refinements in staging procedures, such as imaging and mediastinoscopy. Since that time, preoperative radiation for patients with Pancoast's or superior sulcus tumors has been widely used, and there has been some limited investigation of preoperative radiation in operable patients with mediastinal lymph node metastases.

For many years postoperative radiation treatment has been used almost universally in patients who during surgery were found to have mediastinal lymph node metastases, large tumors or other signs of advanced disease. However, the failure to cure lung cancer by surgical treatment is, in the great majority of patients, due to distant metastases. Thus even if the radiation therapy were 100 percent effective in controlling local disease, it might have only a small impact on the overall cure rate. This does not diminish the value of postoperative radiation treatment, since complete control of the primary disease is essential. Rather, it points out that improved cure rates from surgical treatment will have to come from the use of systemic treatment that can effectively eradicate distant metastases, or from the ability to diagnose patients before metastases have occurred.

Many experimental programs have evaluated the use of chemotherapy and immunotherapy (which involves agents to stimulate or restore the body's own disease-fighting mechanisms) as adjuvants to surgery, but no agents or combinations have been found that improved the survival rates significantly over those achieved with surgery alone. It is not unreasonable to hope, however, that the results of present investigations eventually will contribute to improved cure rates for patients undergoing surgical treatment.

Investigations of radiation combined with chemotherapy for patients with limited non-small cell lung cancer have not shown conclusively that the combination is superior to high-dose radiation alone. Some studies using newer chemotherapy agents, although not yet confirmed in other clinical trials, have reported an improved outcome for patients treated with the combined regimen.

SUMMING UP

In terms of our present knowledge, the problem of lung cancer is largely one of prevention and earlier diagnosis. The treatments available are most effective when the cancer is small and the individual is still healthy. The quality and length of life for patients with lung cancer have been improved by increased understanding of the biology of the disease and the valuable information, even in the form of negative results, obtained from experimental treatment programs. The promise of an improved outcome for patients with lung cancer rests with such efforts.

Patients faced with a diagnosis of lung cancer often have great fear that nothing can be done for them. In this chapter we have attempted to show that a number of treatments are available. Physicians experienced in treating lung cancer can provide a plan for each patient that will offer the maximum possibility for control of the cancer and maintenance of the quality of life.

Anxiety and fear usually go hand in hand with serious medical problems. The best remedy for this is to get answers and thorough explanations to all medical questions from the physician who is responsible for the patient's care.

24

Hodgkin's Disease and Other Lymphomas

MORTIMER J. LACHER, M.D.

INTRODUCTION

The lymphomas, cancers of the lymph system, include a wide range of malignant disease that is generally divided into two large families: Hodgkin's disease and the non-Hodgkin's lymphomas. About thirty thousand Americans are diagnosed as having lymphoma each year. About 40 percent, or twelve thousand, have Hodgkin's disease, the remaining 60 percent of patients have non-Hodgkin's lymphoma and are divided among a wide number of types, varying with the classification system used.

In 1982, a consensus among leading pathologists resulted in a system of classification that defines ten distinct subtypes of non-Hodgkin's lym-

430

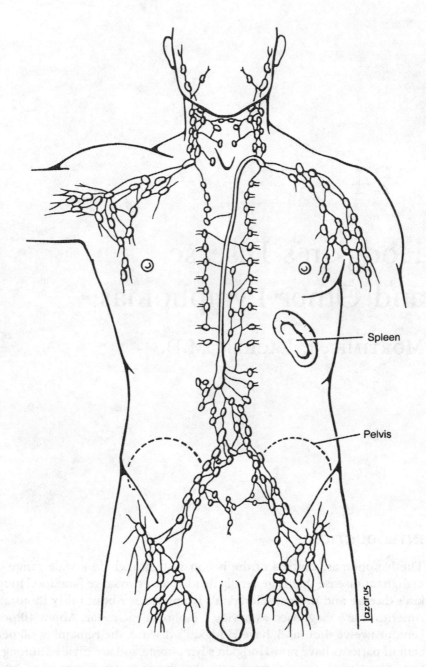

Spleen

Pelvis

Figure 49 Normal lymphatic system.

phoma. The Working Formulation of the Non-Hodgkin's Lymphomas for Clinical Usage emerged from a meeting sponsored by the National Cancer Institute, which attempted to unify six major classification systems of non-Hodgkin's lymphoma that were already in existence. These included the Rappaport classification, initially proposed in 1966, which emphasized the relationship between histology (microscopic cell structure) and prognosis, and the Lukes and Collins classification, proposed in 1974, that was based on the immunologic characteristics of lymphoid cells (recognizing malignant lymphomas of B-cell and T-cell origin). The three classification systems are summarized in Table 17. It is anticipated that the Working Formulation Classification will now be used in preference to all previous systems.

However, the existence of multiple, competing classification systems for the non-Hodgkin's lymphomas merely attests to their imperfect nature. Better understanding of the functions of the underlying lymphoid tissue will eventually reduce this confusion, or, as has been the case in Hodgkin's disease, as the treatment improves even without a full understanding of the exact nature of the tissues, subclassification may become less important.

Almost all Hodgkin's disease and most non-Hodgkin's lymphoma arise in the lymph nodes; the remainder start in collections of lymph tissues elsewhere in the body. The principal cells within the lymphatic system, lymphocytes, plasma cells, and macrophages are collectively organized in lymphoid tissue. The lymph nodes and spleen are examples of highly developed lymphoid tissues. Other lymphoid tissue is found distributed along the gastrointestinal tract, in the tonsils, adenoids, and the Peyer's patches in the small intestine. Practically speaking, however, lymphoid tissue is found throughout the body because circulating blood lymphocytes are distributed to all tissues. In addition, a system of tiny, transparent vessels called lymphatics carry lymphocytic cells in the lymphatic fluid to all parts of the body.

Lymphocytes, a type of white blood cell, are produced in the lymph nodes, and are essential to fighting infection. In addition, they play a prime role in a group of immunologic disorders that include the connective tissue disorders rheumatoid arthritis and systemic lupus erythematosus.

It is the job of the lymphocytes to synthesize immunoglobulins that help protect against bacterial, viral, and other forms of infection. In addition, the system of lymphocytes, now recognized to be made up of two interacting families of cells known as B and T lymphocytes, participate in the body's defenses against cancer cells as well. The complexity of this extraordinary role of the lymphatic system is just beginning to be unveiled.

The cause of lymphomas is unknown. Attempts have been made to establish a correlation between infectious mononucleosis and Hodgkin's disease, but this has proved to be an uncertain relationship. Epidemiologic studies have failed to indicate that an infectious agent, such as the Epstein-Barr virus, the presumed cause of mononucleosis, may be a factor. High levels of antibodies against Epstein-Barr virus have been found in patients with Hodgkin's disease as well as in those with Burkitt's lymphoma, a cancer of the lymph system that is common in parts of Africa, but the pattern is too inconsistent to permit any firm conclusions. Some studies also suggest that there may be a genetic factor; for example, some families have a higher-than-normal incidence of lymphomas, but absolute proof of this possible relationship is not yet available.

HODGKIN'S DISEASE

Hodgkin's disease can occur at any age, but in the United States it is most commonly seen in young adults aged fifteen to thirty-five years, with a second peak in frequency during the years from fifty to sixty. In Japan, the first peak does not occur, and Hodgkin's disease among children under the age of ten is seen more frequently in underdeveloped countries. (Childhood Hodgkin's and other lymphomas are discussed in Chapter 34, "Wilms' Tumor, Lymphomas, and Other Solid Tumors Occurring in the Young.") About 60 percent of all Hodgkin's patients are men; the reasons for this are unknown.

Onset and Diagnosis

An enlarged lymph node, often in the neck, armpit, or groin, is the major symptom that prompts a person with Hodgkin's disease to see a doctor. Other symptoms that may occur include a persistent but remittent, unexplained fever or intermittent cyclic episodes of fever (called Pel-Epstein fever), unexplained weight loss, general malaise, drenching night sweats, and uncontrollable itching that frequently leads to self-inflicted scratches of the skin. The itching is usually more intense at night, while the fever is typically highest in the late afternoon. Sometimes the disease is discovered after a chest X ray shows enlarged lymph nodes around the aorta. In some instances, immediately after consumption of alcohol the patient experiences pain in areas where there are Hodgkin's nodes.

A biopsy is necessary to diagnose all lymphomas. In Hodgkin's disease, the biopsy specimen is often a lymph node removed from the neck. Since most instances of an enlarged lymph node are due to infection or other self-limited cause, it is often advisable to wait for several weeks, or even months, before doing a biopsy, unless there are other symptoms that suggest Hodgkin's of some other lymphoma. Sometimes, a short course of a broad-spectrum antibiotic, such as tetracycline or erythromycin, may be prescribed on the theory that an underlying infection is causing the enlarged node.

If the lymph node does not return to its normal size, or if it continues to grow, or if there are several enlarged nodes in an area, a biopsy should be performed. This is usually done in a hospital surgical outpatient facility or while hospitalized, depending on the type of surgery and anesthesia that may be necessary to obtain an adequate specimen. This initial biopsy is almost never done by a cancer specialist; instead, a family physician, general surgeon, or specialist in head and neck operations is most commonly called upon to perform the initial biopsy.

The finding of a particular kind of malignant cell, called the Reed-Sternberg cell, is the major factor that distinguishes Hodgkin's disease from other lymphomas. This cell is present in almost all patients with Hodgkin's and confirms the diagnosis. In addition to finding the Reed-Sternberg cell, which is a giant cell with several nuclei, the Hodgkin's tumor has a characteristic abnormal structural appearance. These two factors usually establish a diagnosis of Hodgkin's disease; in some rare instances, a diagnosis is based on histologic and clinical findings, even when the Reed-Sternberg cell cannot be found.

In the current commonly used classification system, four different cellular types of Hodgkin's disease have been identified, depending upon the degree of architectural disorder within the node and the kinds of cells that predominate. (These are known as lymphocyte predominant, nodular sclerosis, mixed cellularity, and lymphocyte depleted, depending upon the degree of architectural disorder within the node and the kinds of cells that predominate.) Although the particular type of Hodgkin's disease affects to some extent the patient's prognosis, it is the stage of the disease that is the most important factor, both in the choice of treatment and in its success.

After Hodgkin's disease has been diagnosed, a series of investigations is performed to determine the extent (stage) of the disease and, thereby, the course of therapy. Although one popular view holds that Hodgkin's generally begins in one group of lymph nodes and then spreads via the lymphatic vessels directly to the adjacent nodes, this clearly does not account for the finding that Hodgkin's disease is usually generalized, meaning it is found both above and below the diaphragm, at the time of diagnosis. Nor does that theory explain the typical finding that only one node in a group of nodes may be positive for Hodgkin's disease, while all the others are normal. In fact, the realization that Hodgkin's disease is more widespread at the onset than meets the eye of even the most meticulous investigators led to the more intense, very extensive wide-field radiation treatment (with or without chemotherapy) that has led to the long survival that many patients now achieve.

On the basis of the extent of the tumor discovered at the time of diagnosis, a classification known as the Ann Arbor modification of the Rye staging system for Hodgkin's disease (as well as other lymphomas) has been devised. The stages are:

Stage I, the designation for cancer involving a single node or region of nodes;

Stage II, indicating involvement of two regions of lymph nodes, restricted either above or below the diaphragm;

Stage III, indicating the presence of Hodgkin's both above and below the diaphragm;

Stage IV, indicating involvement of organs outside the lymph nodes, such as the lungs, liver, or bones.

Each stage may be further characterized by whether there are other symptoms, referred to as B-symptoms, such as weight loss, fever, or night sweats. Generally, the presence of these symptoms indicates somewhat more serious disease than the simple enlargement of the lymph nodes without other symptoms. Severe itching, which is disturbing and unpleasant, is not usually considered among the B-symptoms, nor is there a clear correlation with prognosis.

On the average, half of all patients will have Stage I or II Hodgkin's at the time of diagnosis, and about 30 percent of all patients will have symptoms such as fever, weight loss, or general malaise, although most Stage I patients do not. It is generally presumed, however, that more disease is present or potentially present than is designated by the stage determined by the various diagnostic methods at our disposal and therefore all currently recommended treatment covers more extensive areas than are determined by staging.

Patient Evaluation

The clinical evaluation of a patient with Hodgkin's disease is relatively complex. It begins with a complete medical history and physical examination, in which special attention is paid to the spleen, liver, and all lymph nodes, even though they may have to be examined by special means. For example, the nodes at the back of the throat may require that a throat specialist view them using special mirrored instruments.

In the early stages of Hodgkin's disease, many laboratory tests may be normal, although there is usually an abnormal erythrocyte sedimentation rate (the time it takes red blood cells to settle to the bottom of a special test tube) and there may be mild anemia and an elevated white blood cell count. More specific testing will often find a diminished ability of the immune system to respond to various antigenic substances injected within the skin. Patients with Hodgkin's disease commonly develop anergy (the inability to react normally) to substances like tubercilin, various fungal antigens, or to a specific chemical called DNCB (dinitrochlorobenzene). Abnormal levels of blood immunoglobulins have been discovered in the blood of patients with Hodgkin's disease, as well as members of their families.

The evaluation of a patient with Hodgkin's includes chest X rays, sometimes with additional computerized tomography (CT) scans. Bilateral pedal lymphangiography, a test in which an iodized substance is injected into the lymphatic passages of the legs and then followed via X rays as it moves upward into the lymphatics in the retroperitoneal space in the abdomen, should be performed to detect enlarged nodes. Occasionally, a distorted pattern of lymphatic flow is observed. As the technical quality of abdominal CT scans improves, as well as the ability to interpret them correctly, the CT scan may eventually replace the lymphangiogram for patients with Hodgkin's disease. At the present time, however, it is recommended that both tests be done. As of this writing, the general use of Magnetic Resonance Imaging (MRI) is still in its early phase of development and evaluation. It is currently used only as a supplement to the CT scan in patients specifically selected by their physicians in instances where it may prove especially useful.

Other possible tests include bone marrow biopsy, bone X rays or scans, ultrasonic or radioactive nuclide examinations of specific organs, and kidney X rays (pyelograms). Until recently, exploratory abdominal surgery was commonly done, primarily to remove the spleen and multiple lymph nodes and to biopsy the liver. There is a movement away from this operation and it is now recommended only if it is expected to alter the course of treatment.

Treatment

The outlook for patients with Hodgkin's disease has improved dramatically in the last three decades, and it is now one of the most encouraging areas of cancer therapy. Thirty years ago, the average survival was thirty months from onset of symptoms until death, with only about 15 percent of patients surviving five or more years. Advances in chemotherapy and radiation therapy have resulted in the current five-year survival rate of nearly 90 percent and an estimated ten-year survival of almost 70 percent.

Hodgkin's disease is treated with radiation therapy and chemotherapy, either alone or in combination. Patients with Stage I or II disease are treated with radiation therapy, directed not only to the parts of the body in which the disease has been identified, but also to almost all adjacent and even nonadjacent areas in which Hodgkin's disease could be present at the outset or could develop at a later time. For example, even a patient whose tumor can only be identified in the left neck area typically receives radiation to all the nodes in the upper half of the body and, in addition, is treated in potential areas of tumor development below the diaphragm, down to the level of the fourth lumbar vertebra (which corresponds to the level of the navel). It was the institution of this extensive radiation therapy that accounted for the first marked improvements in survival with Hodgkin's disease.

The radiation is delivered via a high-powered megavolt linear accelerator, with attempts to shield the parts of the body that do not require treatment and which are sensitive to radiation, such as the lungs, thyroid, ovaries, and testes. The usual total dose varies between 3,600 and 4,000 rads, with the areas of obvious tumor involvement sometimes "boosted" to 4,400 rads. The radiation is usually administered on an outpatient basis over a twelve-week period. (See Chapter 8, "Radiation Therapy," and Chapter 10, "Coping with Problems Related to Cancer and Cancer Treatment.")

Radiation therapy for Hodgkin's disease is complex and is continually being refined. It must be administered by a radiation oncologist who is experienced in treating this type of lymphoma.

The role of radiation therapy for patients with Stage III and IV Hodgkin's has not been clearly defined. Patients with Stage III disease who do not have systemic symptoms may be treated with either radiation or chemotherapy, or both.

Primary treatment with chemotherapy is usually administered to patients with Stage IV Hodgkin's. Some studies have indicated that combined radiation and chemotherapy also should be used to enhance the response and survival of patients with Stage III Hodgkin's who are symptomatic. Even patients with Stage I or Stage II are now being treated with initial radiation therapy followed by a combination of chemotherapeutic drugs, or initial combination chemotherapy followed by radiation. A regimen of combined radiation and chemotherapy for all stages is now the general rule for children with Hodgkin's. In these patients, every effort is made to limit the size of the radiation field and the dose of radiation because it is especially damaging to the child's bone-growth centers. Multidrug chemotherapy may be administered simultaneously. In this way, many of the permanently disabling side effects of treatment have been avoided in children while enhancing their survival rates. The same effects of initially combined radiation and chemotherapy may be true for adult patients. More evidence shows a longer disease-free remission and extended total survival as more patients surpass the ten-year mark.

Patients with Stage III or IV Hodgkin's are treated with various chemotherapy combinations, with the MOPP combination the best known. MOPP stands for Mustargen (nitrogen mustard), Oncovin (vincristine), procarbazine, and prednisone. Some physicians prefer to eliminate the prednisone, especially when chemotherapy is used with radiation therapy. Many other drug combinations are equal to the MOPP regimen in terms of response rates and remission, but some are believed to be less toxic, resulting in fewer side effects, both immediate and long-term.

Other regimens that use alternative agents instead of the nitrogen mustard are sometimes better tolerated. In particular, when thiotepa is substituted for nitrogen mustard, there is minimal or no nausea and vomiting at the time of treatment and the effect on male and female fertility is minimal, when used in a combination (TVPP) with vinblastine (Velban), vincristine (Oncovin), prednisone, and procarbazine (Matulane).

The combination of doxorubicin (Adriamycin), bleomycin (Blenoxane), vinblastine (Velban), and dacarbazine (DTIC-Dome), known as ABVD, has also been used very effectively with less toxic effect on subsequent fertility. This combination, however, is associated with severe nausea and vomiting, marked (albeit temporary) hair loss, and potential cardiac problems. Other combinations utilize cyclophosphamide (Cytoxan) in combination with vincristine, prednisone, and procarbazine (CVPP, or sometimes known as C-MOPP) or substitute chlorambucil for nitrogen mustard in another effective four-drug combination (chlorambucil, vincristine, prednisone, and procarbazine). Another useful combination substitutes vinblastine for vincristine as MVPP (nitrogen mustard, vinblastine, prednisone, and procarbazine).

The chemotherapy is usually administered on an outpatient basis, and overnight hospital stays are rarely used for intravenous administration of any of the drug combinations. The usual course of therapy involves six four-week cycles of the drugs. Among the most common side effects are nausea and vomiting, which may be made more tolerable by antinausea drugs. (See Chapter 7, "Principles of Cancer Chemotherapy," and Chapter 10, "Coping with Problems Related to Cancer and Cancer Treatment.") The most effective way to avoid nausea and vomiting is to employ effective therapies that do not have the most unpleasant side effects.

It is now common to continue therapy for nine months to a year or more, depending on the initial extent of the disease and the patient's response to the first six months of therapy. Other protocols call for the immediate use of at least two different combinations of chemotherapeutic drugs, applied in alternating cycles. For example, an eight-drug combination of alternating MOPP with ABVD may be given.

Patients who do not achieve a complete remission or who relapse after an initial remission require repeated therapy with alternative combinations of chemotherapy and radiation. Unfortunately, the low ten-year survival among these patients attests to the fact that success is still limited in this area.

Patients who achieve a complete remission on either multidrug chemotherapy or radiation therapy need to be closely monitored with regular checkups for signs of recurrence and for signs or symptoms related to delayed complications from the primary treatment. For example, radiation therapy, when administered in the most commonly used and recommended "mantle" field to the nodes in the chest, always affects the heart, thyroid gland, and the lungs. Suppression of the thyroid gland function (hypothyroidism) caused by the primary radiation therapy treatment is now known to affect about 60 percent of the patients. Fortunately, this effect can readily be diagnosed and treated. Some of the chemotherapeutic protocols are particularly suppressive of fertility and these effects may be irreversible. The primary need to save a life must for now take precedence over these late effects.

NON-HODGKIN'S LYMPHOMAS

The non-Hodgkin's lymphomas encompass a broad and disparate group of cancers affecting the lymphoid tissue. These lymphomas most commonly occur among people forty-five and older. Non-Hodgkin's lymphomas vary widely in aggressiveness, cell type, complications, and responsiveness to treatment, and, in general, the prognosis is not as good as for Hodgkin's disease.

As with Hodgkin's disease, the cause of these various lymphomas is unknown, although certain circumstances appear to increase their incidence. Immunologic disorders, either naturally occurring or those resulting from suppression of the immune system in organ transplant patients, for example, increase the risk of non-Hodgkin's lymphoma. Burkitt's lymphoma, a relatively curable form of non-Hodgkin's lymphoma commonly found in Africa and occasionally in the United States, is often associated with the Epstein-Barr virus and a chromosomal abnormality.

Symptoms and Diagnosis

Early symptoms of non-Hodgkin's lymphoma often involve enlarged lymph nodes. Fever, weight loss, intestinal disturbances, bleeding, infection, and the buildup of fluid in the membranes lining the chest or abdominal cavities are other possible symptoms.

Non-Hodgkin's lymphomas also are associated with several distinct disorders, including a skin disorder called mycosis fungoides, which, except for its name, has nothing to do with any fungal infection. Its cause, like that of the other lymphomas, is unknown. Although patients with mycosis fungoides initially experience only generalized itching and reddened skin, which may never progress to the more serious forms of the disease, most patients are ultimately plagued with ulcerating skin tumors. The lymph nodes undergo malignant change and appear as lymphomas.

In some patients, blood changes also occur, resulting in a disorder known as Sezary syndrome. Treatment of mycosis fungoides uses combinations of radiation and chemotherapy similar to those employed in the non-Hodgkin's lymphomas. In the early stages, when the disease is more confined to the skin, the radiation techniques and some of the chemotherapy are specifically designed to treat only the skin.

Patients with non-Hodgkin's lymphomas should undergo a thorough examination that includes evaluation of the liver and kidneys, assessment of the immune system, careful examination of the lymph nodes, and a variety of laboratory tests. These include a complete blood count, bone marrow study, chest X rays, and perhaps lymphangiography.

Table 17
PATHOLOGIC CLASSIFICATION OF NON-HODGKIN'S LYMPHOMAS

RAPPAPORT CLASSIFICATION	WORKING FORMULATION OF THE NON-HODGKIN'S LYMPHOMAS FOR CLINICAL USAGE	LUKES AND COLLINS
Low Grade		
Diffuse lymphocytic, well differentiated	ML,* small lymphocytic	Small lymphocytic and plasmacytoid lymphocytic
Nodular, poorly differentiated lymphocytic	ML, follicular, predominantly small cleaved cell	Small cleaved FCC,** follicular only or follicular and diffuse
Nodular, mixed lymphocytic-histiocytic	ML, follicular, mixed small cleaved and large cell	Small cleaved FCC, follicular; large cleaved FCC, follicular
Intermediate Grade		
Nodular histiocytic	ML, follicular, predominantly large cell	Large cleaved and/or noncleaved FCC, follicular
Diffuse lymphocytic, poorly differentiated	ML, diffuse small cleaved cell	Small cleaved FCC, diffuse
Diffuse mixed lymphocytic-histiocytic	ML, diffuse, mixed small and large cell	Small cleaved, large cleaved or large noncleaved FCC, diffuse

PATHOLOGIC CLASSIFICATION OF NON-HODGKIN'S LYMPHOMAS

RAPPAPORT CLASSIFICATION	WORKING FORMULATION OF THE NON-HODGKIN'S LYMPHOMAS FOR CLINICAL USAGE	LUKES AND COLLINS
Diffuse histiocytic	ML, diffuse large cell	Large cleaved or non-cleaved FCC, diffuse
High Grade		
Diffuse histiocytic	ML, large cell immu-noblastic	Immunoblastic sar-coma, T-cell or B-cell type
Lymphoblastic convo-luted/noncon-voluted	ML, lymphoblastic	Convoluted T-cell
Undifferentiated, Burkitt's and non-Burkitt's	ML, small noncleaved cell	Small noncleaved FCC
	Miscellaneous Composite Mycosis fungoides Histiocytic Extramedullary plasmacytoma Unclassifiable	

* ML = malignant lymphoma   ** FCC = follicular center cell
Modified from the National Cancer Institute-sponsored study of the classifications of non-Hodgkin's lymphomas.

Source: John E. Ultmann and Renée H. Jacobs, "The Non-Hodgkin's Lymphomas," *Ca: A Cancer Journal for Clinicians*, Vol. 35, No. 2, 1985.

Lymphangiography is much less useful in the non-Hodgkin's lympho-mas than in Hodgkin's disease since this technique fails to visualize the mesenteric nodes so commonly involved in the non-Hodgkin's lympho-mas. On the other hand, the use of abdominal/pelvic CT scan has become indispensable for determining the presence of lymph tumors below the diaphragm in the non-Hodgkin's lymphomas. Bilateral pedal lymphangi-ography, so useful in Hodgkin's disease, now has limited use in patients with non-Hodgkin's lymphoma and it may be dispensed with in favor of CT scanning.

The development of Magnetic Resonance Imaging (MRI) is adding another extremely useful diagnostic tool to the evaluation of the presence of disease in the lymphomas. Since the use of the MRI is so relatively new, it remains to be seen which of the methods (CT or MRI) will prove to be the most useful. It may turn out that both methods have to be used to achieve a full dimensional view of the extent of the tumor.

Prognosis and Treatment

The prognosis of patients with non-Hodgkin's lymphomas varies according to the areas affected and whether the disease is confined to the lymph nodes or has spread to other organs, such as the lungs, central nervous system, digestive tract, or bones. But the microscopic appearance of the lymphoma cells is currently considered the most critical factor in determining the prognosis and approach to treatment. In general, it is more important than the stage or extent of the disease. The new Working Formulation attempts to address this issue by its classifying the tumors as "low grade," "intermediate grade," and "high grade" malignant lymphomas. The implication is that the low grade tumors have the best prognosis and the high grade tumors have the worst. However, as treatment methods improve, some of the "high grade" tumors that appeared to be the most lethal with the worst prognosis despite the lowest incidence of bone marrow invasion (10 percent) may soon become the most amenable to chemotherapy, with a high rate of complete remission and even cure. (For example, Rappaport's diffuse histiocytic lymphoma is comparable to the Working Formulation tumor designated as the diffuse large cell type.)

The non-Hodgkin's lymphomas currently considered to have the best prognosis and designated as the nodular, poorly differentiated, lymphocytic type (NPDL, Rappaport) or follicular, predominantly small cleaved cell (as designated in the Working Formulation among the low grade tumors) have the highest incidence of bone marrow involvement (about 70 percent). Despite the staging classification that puts these tumors into the Stage IV category, these nodular or follicular tumors are considered to be relatively indolent, with a median survival of more than seven years. However, no outstanding therapy known to us at this time seems to be able to effect a consistent permanent cure and the current treatment approaches are considered by some to be just palliative.

The treatment of non-Hodgkin's lymphoma is undergoing continuous reevaluation. Patients with Stage I and II disease, as well as those whose disease is confined to the skin, have a relatively good prognosis. Some patients, particularly those with lymphocytic lymphoma or skin lymphoma, may require minimal treatment, such as simple removal of the lesions or local radiation therapy; some may simply be carefully monitored until progression of the disease demands that therapy be started.

Although Stage I or II lymphomas that appear to be restricted to lymph nodes may be treated with local radiation, which achieves a high degree of local control, the disease is likely to recur elsewhere in the body. Nevertheless, there is a possibility of long-term remission or cure. Some patients with low grade lymphoma (nodular poorly differentiated lymphoma, or NPDL), which accounts for about 70 percent of low grade lymphomas, may be treated at first by deferring any specific radiation or chemotherapy while carefully monitoring until progression of the disease demands that therapy be started.

The complexity of the treatment of the non-Hodgkin's lymphomas is exaggerated by both the diverse range of tumor types and the wide range of treatment options. The choices may range all the way from nothing but careful monitoring, to minimal therapy (using single agents such as chlorambucil or cyclophosphamide, or using alternating doses of prednisone and chlorambucil or cyclophosphamide), to aggressive therapy lasting at least six months, or continuing for at least two cycles past the achievement of complete remission (which may then extend the treatment for years) with as many as nine complex agents used in alternating cycles. Such aggressive treatment may involve drugs that are sometimes difficult to administer and are associated with high levels of unpleasant side effects.

Current chemotherapeutic protocols for diffuse large cell lymphoma (DHL under the Rappaport system), for instance, involve some of the most complex combinations of drugs and delivery cycles, including the following:

CHOP: cyclophosphamide (Cytoxan), doxorubicin (Adriamycin), vincristine (Oncovin), prednisone;

COP-BLAM: cyclophosphamide (Cytoxan), vincristine (Oncovin), prednisone, bleomycin (Blenoxane), doxorubicin (Adriamycin), procarbazine (Matulane);

M-BACOD: methotrexate (with leucovorin rescue), bleomycin (Blenoxane), doxorubicin (Adriamycin), cyclophosphamide (Cytoxan), vincristine (Oncovin), dexamethasone (Decadron);

ProMACE-MOPP: prednisone, methotrexate (with leucovorin rescue), doxorubicin (Adriamycin), cyclophosphamide (Cytoxan), epipodophyllotoxin VP-16, and mechlorethamine—also known as nitrogen mustard (Mustargen), vincristine (Oncovin), procarbazine (Matulane), and prednisone.

The most complex therapy is not necessarily the best treatment. Every effort is being made to simplify treatments, reduce the toxicity, and find new agents or combinations of known agents that will have a more specific effect with fewer complications.

Chemotherapy is used eventually in almost all patients with non-Hodgkin's lymphoma, except those who achieve a cure from localized radiation therapy. Current regimens now extend treatment beyond the traditional six-month period, or until the patient appears to be truly in complete remission. Flexibility of the protocols is now emphasized, rather than rigid adherence to a set cycle and definite end point.

The rates for cure and survival in non-Hodgkin's lymphomas vary widely and, on the whole, are not as good as those for Hodgkin's disease. Overall, the rate of complete remission ranges from 40 to 70 percent, depending on the cellular type of the disease, its extent of spread, and the drugs used. It is anticipated that many patients currently being treated for large cell lymphoma (DHL) may be cured. Lymphoblastic lymphoma—which occurs predominantly in young males and is characterized by cells with surface markers of an immature T-cell identical to the malignant cell of acute lymphocytic leukemia—is now being treated more aggressively, sometimes using bone marrow transplants, or acute leukemia type drugs and radiation therapy combinations. Patients with this lymphoma may now achieve complete remissions and survival of more than five years; previously these patients usually died within less than one year of diagnosis.

SUMMING UP

The outlook for patients with lymphoma, particularly Hodgkin's disease, has improved markedly in recent decades. The prognosis is best for those patients whose Hodgkin's disease is limited and who do not have systemic symptoms. In the non-Hodgkin's lymphoma group, the cellular structure is a more important guide to treatment and prognosis; for example, patients who have the "nodular" type of lymphoma have a favorable prognosis, even if there is bone marrow involvement (Stage IV).

In addition, many more patients with diffuse histiocytic lymphoma (DHL, or diffuse large cell lymphoma), once considered to be among the more aggressive and difficult to control lymphomas, now appear to be able to achieve a much higher rate of complete remission and long survival using current chemotherapeutic regimens.

Patients suspected of having lymphoma should undergo a thorough evaluation and should be cared for by physicians experienced in the most up-to-date approaches to the particular form of the disease. There is much to be discovered and applied before all patients can be cured and complications of therapy are reduced to a minimal level. It is evident, however, that we are on the right track.

25

Cancers of the Mouth, Pharynx, and Larynx

Harvey W. Baker, M.D.

INTRODUCTION

Cancers of the mouth, pharynx, and larynx—the upper air and food passages—account for about 6 percent of all human cancer. About 40,000 new cases are diagnosed each year, with cancer of the larynx (11,500 cases) being the most common, followed by cancer of the mouth (10,400), pharynx (8,800), tongue (5,200), and lip (4,500). These tumors occur in a clearly identified population group, share common causal factors, are predictable in their behavior, and are generally easily diagnosed. More than almost any other cancer, they require a multidisciplinary team approach for effective management. When diagnosed early, these cancers are highly curable; even the more advanced are being controlled with improved treatment methods, if they are identified before the disease has spread to distant sites.

CAUSE AND NATURAL HISTORY

Cancers of the mouth, pharynx, and larynx occur predominantly in males over the age of forty-five, and almost all use or have in the past used tobacco in one form or another—cigarettes, pipes, cigars, chewing tobacco, or snuff. Excessive drinking of alcohol also plays a role in causing these cancers. While it is unusual to find heavy drinkers who are not also smokers, the history of alcoholism is so predominant in some of these cancers, particularly those of the pharynx, that it is evident that alcohol is at least a co-carcinogen. Other causal agents include excessive exposure to sunlight, which may result in cancer of the lips; untreated late syphilis which is associated with cancer of the tongue; and rare cases of iron deficiency anemia associated with cancer of the hypopharynx. A great number of these cancers occur in Southeast Asia where chewing betel nuts is a common practice.

Chemically, the cancers arise in the lining of the upper air and food passages known as the mucosa or mucous membranes. When examined under a microscope, the great majority are identified as similar in structure to squamous cell or epidermoid carcinomas, cancers of the skin. The grade or differentiation of a given squamous cell carcinoma is important in predicting its behavior. For example, a "low-grade" or well-differentiated cancer shows a microscopic resemblance to normal skin or mucosa, has a sluggish growth rate, and is therefore slow to spread. A "high-grade" or poorly differentiated tumor is more primitive in its appearance and behaves in a much more aggressive fashion.

When exposed to a carcinogen such as tobacco, extensive areas of the mucosal lining of the upper airways and digestive tract become prone to developing cancer. Biopsies, taken of normal-appearing mucosa at a distance from a tumor frequently reveal premalignant changes or even malignancy that is not yet invasive (carcinoma *in situ*). This phenomenon, called "field cancerization" is responsible for the high incidence of multiple cancers which appear in this area. Studies have indicated that almost one out of three patients who are cured of one cancer in this region will develop another, particularly if they continue using tobacco or alcohol.

The cancers begin as small areas of mucosal change which can be recognized by a trained observer. Shallow superficial ulceration ensues, gradually spreading to involve more of the surface mucosa. Later, there is invasion of deeper tissues and even adjacent bone. The rate of invasion varies widely and is closely related to the grade or degree of differentiation of the cancer when viewed under a microscope. The spread of these squamous cell carcinomas is predominantly via lymphatic channels to lymph nodes in the neck. Lymph node involvement usually occurs in a predictable fashion, beginning just beneath the jaw or high in the neck and progressing to the lower neck just above the clavicle. Early spread of cancers via the bloodstream is rare, and most tumors remain confined to their site of origin or to lymph nodes in the neck for relatively long periods of time. Therefore, aggressive attempts at treatment are often successful. As tumors become more advanced, however, spread does occur, usually to the lungs or bone, and about 50 percent of patients who die of these cancers have distant metastases.

DIAGNOSTIC METHODS AND STAGING

Many squamous cell carcinomas of the upper air and food passages are accessible and relatively easy to recognize. However, some cancers of the pharynx or larynx can only be seen by mirrors or fiberoptic telescopes. When direct examination of these areas is necessary, topical spray anesthesia or general anesthesia may be required while using either a laryngoscope or nasopharyngoscope, both special instruments for viewing the upper airway. If a suspicious mucosal change is identified, a biopsy must be taken to definitively diagnose the disease. This is accomplished by removing a sample of the abnormal tissue, under local or general anesthesia. The tissue is examined under a microscope by a trained pathologist who can identify the type of cancer and determine the grade or degree of differentiation of the cancer cells.

When a diagnosis of cancer is reached, the next step that should be undertaken is staging, a process that enables the treating physician to estimate the extent of the cancer. Staging involves visualizing, palpating (examining by touch) and, when possible, measuring the primary cancer and noting any growth into nearby tissue or impairment in mobility of the affected areas. The neck is carefully palpated in search of any enlarged or abnormal lymph nodes. At times, a variety of radiographic techniques are used to determine the extent of disease. These include conventional X rays, studies with radiopaque media such as barium or iodized oil. Computerized tomography studies—CT scans—are also useful. MRI scans (magnetic resonance imaging) are also proving useful in evaluating the extent of many tumors. The possibility of distant spread of cancer to the lungs is always evaluated by studying chest X rays.

CANCER OF THE MOUTH

The mouth or oral cavity includes the lips, the buccal mucosa or lining of the cheeks, the gums or gingivae, the hard palate and the floor of the mouth (Figure 50). The mobile portion of the tongue, known as the oral tongue, is easily seen and is also considered part of the oral cavity, while the base of the tongue, located farther back and not readily visible, is considered part of the pharynx. Malignant tumors may arise anywhere on the mucosal lining of the mouth. They are predominantly squamous cell carcinomas and are generally graded as well-differentiated or moderately well-differentiated tumors, depending on how closely the cancer cells resemble the cells of the site of origin.

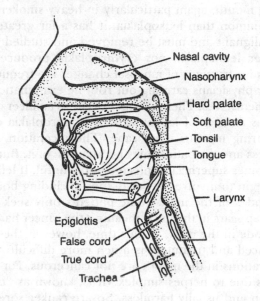

Nasal cavity
Nasopharynx
Hard palate
Soft palate
Tonsil
Tongue
Larynx
Epiglottis
False cord
True cord
Trachea

Figure 50 Anatomy of normal mouth and larynx.

Symptoms and Diagnosis

A variety of benign tumors and tumor-like conditions occur in the mouth. These can usually be recognized by experienced physicians and dentists. Some tumors are simply removed, others are biopsied to rule out cancer, and still others require local treatment or merely periodic examination. There are two changes in the normal mucous membrane of the mouth which are recognized as being potentially dangerous: one is leukoplakia and the other is erythroplakia.

Leukoplakia is a whitish patch which may appear anywhere in the mouth. It varies from a diffuse, filmy mucosal change to a thickened white plaque marked with cracks or crevices. Leukoplakia usually results from chronic irritation of the mucosal lining of the mouth caused by tobacco, ill-fitting dentures, poor dental hygiene, or even minute electric currents generated by dissimilar metals in dental fillings. But not all changes diagnosed as leukoplakia are premalignant. In some cases in which the disease is at an early stage of development, the source of the chronic irritation can be identified and eliminated and no further treatment is required. Thickened or elevated patches of leukoplakia, however, are more serious and require biopsy or simple surgical removal.

Erythroplakia is a name given to a reddened, velvety patch which may appear in the mouth, again particularly in heavy smokers and drinkers. While less common than leukoplakia, it has a far greater potential for becoming malignant and must be removed and studied under a microscope. Neither leukoplakia nor erythroplakia produces any warning symptoms, and early signs of mucosal changes are frequently picked up by dentists or physicians carrying out routine examinations or noted by the patients themselves. These changes occur as an ulcer or "sore" which may appear as an area of leukoplakia or erythroplakia or in otherwise normal-appearing mucous membrane. The ulceration, when small, is usually painless and the patient may be unaware of it. But, as it enlarges, the ulcer becomes superficially infected and painful. If left untreated, the cancer will begin to involve deeper tissues, including bone, and eventually lymph nodes of the neck. Some patients only seek medical advice when a lump appears in the neck, meaning the cancer has already spread to a lymph node in the neck. By this time, however, the cancer is much farther advanced and treatment is much more difficult.

Many ulcerations in the mouth are not cancerous. For example, small painful ulcers due to herpes simplex virus, known as "cold sores," are quite common and usually harmless. So are canker sores. Other ulcerations may be due to poorly fitting dentures or other specific infections. Still, any ulcer in the mouth that persists more than two weeks is potentially dangerous and should be evaluated by a physician. Many physicians and dentists are capable of performing a biopsy of a suspicious mucosal lesion in the mouth. At times, however, the patient will be referred to a specialist for both biopsy and definitive treatment.

Treatment

Evaluation and management of the patient with mouth cancer frequently involves participation of a team of specialists. The pathologist confirms the diagnosis through biopsy and determines the grade or differentiation of the tumor. A radiologist is often helpful in studying the extent of the cancer. Dentists may be called to do dental extractions and work to improve dental hygiene, which is particularly important when radiation therapy is used. Because of their smoking habits, many patients with oral cancer have chronic lung disease and require evaluation and treatment by a lung specialist or other medical specialists if surgery is planned. Since chronic alcoholism often produces peptic ulcers or liver disease, evaluation by a gastroenterologist may be required. Definitive treatment of the cancer may require the combined efforts of surgeons, radiation oncologists, and medical oncologists. A new and entirely different team may be called upon for rehabilitation of the patient following treatment.

The treatment of an oral cancer depends to a large extent upon its stage. Early localized cancers which have not spread to lymph nodes in the neck (Stages I and II) are very often controlled with either surgery or radiation therapy. The two treatment approaches are seldom competitive and both have distinct advantages as well as limitations.

During surgery, wide removal of the cancer occasionally involves adjacent or underlying bone. The surgeon immediately examines the tissue under a microscope to make sure that the cancer is being adequately removed. If only a small growth is removed, there is little post-surgery disability, whereas more extensive surgical procedures for larger cancers may require post-surgical reconstruction with skin grafts taken from other areas of the body. When radiation therapy is called for, it may be accomplished with external beam radiation, usually given over a five-to-six-week period, or interstitial radiation, which involves the insertion of radioactive needles into the tumor and surrounding tissues. Often, both external and interstitial radiation are used for a given tumor. (For further discussions of what is involved in radiation treatment, see Chapter 8, "Radiation Therapy," and Chapter 10, "Coping with Problems Related to Cancer and Cancer Treatment.")

Although these early stage cancers do not show evidence of spread to lymph nodes in the neck, "prophylactic" or elective treatment of the neck nodes is often included in the primary treatment when there is a high probability of microscopic spread to these nodes (for example, many cancers of the tongue). Surgical removal of lymph nodes in the neck by a procedure known as radical neck dissection, and radiation therapy to the entire neck can be equally effective when there is microscopic spread of cancer to neck nodes.

While surgery and radiation therapy are both effective for most early stages of cancers, neither treatment alone is highly effective for more advanced cancers. In such cases, there is a trend to combine the two forms of treatment and the end results have shown improvement. Extensive cancers of the mouth are often treated first with radiation therapy, followed by surgery to remove any residual cancer. At times, however, radiation therapy is used after surgery, particularly if the pathology studies of the removed tissue suggest a possibility that some cancerous tissue was left behind, as might be the case when only a small amount of tissue surrounding the cancer can be removed. Statistically, the results are the same whether radiation therapy precedes or follows surgery.

Since even the results of combined radiation and surgery for more advanced stages of oral cancer are far from satisfactory, a number of clinical trials in recent years have been undertaken in which these courses of treatment have been combined with one or more courses of chemotherapy. Drugs used in these studies include cisplatin, bleomycin, and methotrexate, and are given under the close supervision of a medical oncologist. While the early results of the combination of chemotherapy with conventional radiation therapy and surgery have been encouraging, too little is known as yet about long-term cure to warrant general adoption.

CANCER OF THE PHARYNX

The pharynx is made up of three general areas: the nasopharynx, which is situated behind the nasal cavity and above the soft palate; the oropharynx, which includes the soft palate, the tonsils, the base of the tongue and the back or posterior wall of the throat; and the hypopharynx, which is that part of the throat adjacent to the larynx and joining the esophagus (Figure 51). The squamous cell carcinomas that arise in the mucous membrane of the pharynx are less well-differentiated and more hazardous than those seen in the mouth. They have a tendency to spread more rapidly to lymph nodes in the neck and to move to distant sites.

Symptoms and Diagnosis

The symptoms of pharynx cancer are similar to those of upper respiratory infections. Lesions of the nasopharynx may result in obstruction of one nasal passage or slight bleeding from either the nose or the throat. The eustachian tube, which connects the nasopharynx with the middle ear, may also become blocked by cancer, causing one ear to become "stopped up," a sensation similar to that often experienced by passengers in an aircraft making a sudden ascent or descent. Advanced cancers of the nasopharynx may produce pain behind an eye or in the temple and occasionally weaken the eye muscles, resulting in double vision.

Cancers of the oropharynx may cause a "sore throat" which is usually mild, but noticeable when swallowing food. Since some sensory nerves in the pharynx also supply sensation to the ear canal, the discomfort in the throat may involve the ear on that side as well. Slight bleeding from the throat may also be an early symptom. Cancers of the hypopharynx cause soreness or discomfort in the throat and ear similar to lesions of the oropharynx. As they become more extensive, these tumors interfere with swallowing and may cause hoarseness as well.

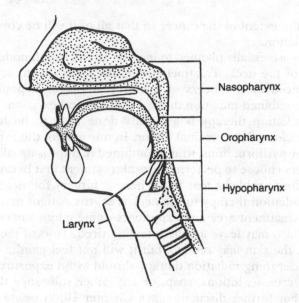

Figure 51 Anatomy of normal pharynx.

These symptoms may occur in almost anyone at one time or another. When they persist for more than two weeks, however, they are potentially serious and require a physician's complete examination of the pharynx to rule out the possibility of cancer. Patients who gag easily may not be able to tolerate this kind of examination without use of a topical spray anesthesia.

Some cancers of the pharynx cause few or even no local symptoms and their first sign may be spread to a lymph node in the neck. Any adult, particularly a heavy smoker or drinker, who develops a firm lump in the neck should undergo a careful examination for possible cancer. Certainly the appearance of a firm enlarged lymph node in the neck is a warning sign to see a physician promptly.

When the physician observes an abnormality in the pharynx, a biopsy is indicated. This is usually performed by a surgeon specializing in head and neck cancer using local or general anesthesia. When a diagnosis of cancer has been confirmed, careful staging is determined on the basis of physical examination and often a variety of X-ray studies.

Treatment

Radiation therapy is the treatment of choice for cancer of the pharynx. Before beginning treatments, the radiation therapist will do studies to determine the extent of the cancer so that all of it will be covered in the field of radiation.

The fields are usually planned to include all the lymph nodes in one or both sides of the neck. Treatment generally takes five to seven weeks. More advanced local cancers of the oropharynx or hypopharynx are treated by combined radiation therapy and surgical excision. In the oropharynx, radiation therapy is generally done first, to be followed by surgical excision of any residual tumor. In one area of the hypopharynx, known as the pyriform sinus, where combined therapy is usually required, many doctors choose to perform surgical treatment first because difficult wound-healing problems may occur here if surgery follows radiation.

During radiation therapy to the neck area, the patient may lose some hair in the treatment area and experience some minor hoarseness. The treatments also may leave a patient feeling tired. Toward the end of the treatments, the skin may redden, but it will not feel painful or burned. Patients undergoing radiation therapy should avoid exposure to the sun and use of creams, lotions, soap, or any other substance that may be irritating. (For further discussion, see Chapter 10, "Coping with Problems Related to Cancer and Cancer Treatment.") But most people tolerate the treatments well without excessive discomfort or disruption of day-to-day activities.

The use of chemotherapy prior to radiation or surgery is being studied for advanced stage cancers of the pharynx in trials similar to those for cancers of the oral cavity. Again, while early results are encouraging, the effects on long-term survival and cure are not fully known.

CANCER OF THE LARYNX

The larynx is a complex anatomic structure located between the hypopharynx above and the trachea or windpipe below (Figure 52A and 52B). It includes three distinct and important areas: the glottis, consisting of the "true" vocal cords, two narrow bands which move toward or away from one another and vibrate to produce sound; the supraglottis, a larger area above the vocal cords consisting of several prominences and folds of tissue, the ventricular bands—or "false" cords, the aryepiglottic folds, the epiglottis and arytenoids; and the subglottis, a narrow rounded space below the vocal cords communicating with the trachea.

While cancers arising from the mucous membrane lining the larynx are practically all squamous cell carcinomas, they differ widely in their behavior depending on their site of origin. Cancers of the glottis or true vocal cords are low-grade, well-differentiated tumors which progress very slowly, taking a long time to spread to lymph nodes in the neck. On the other hand, cancers of the supraglottic region are high-grade, poorly differentiated lesions which are aggressive in their behavior with rapid

Anatomy of the Larynx

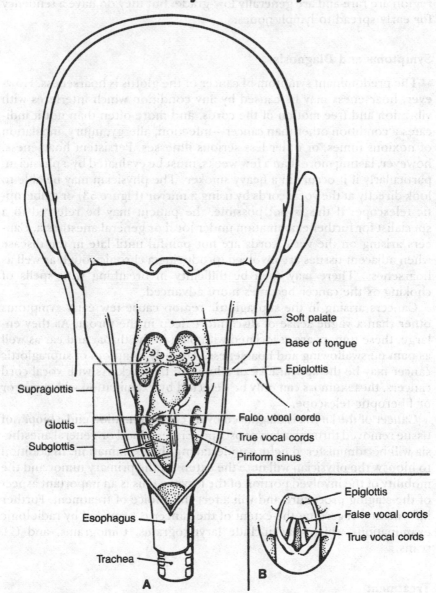

Soft palate

Base of tongue

Epiglottis

Supraglottis

False vocal cords

Glottis

True vocal cords

Subglottis

Piriform sinus

Esophagus

Trachea

A

Epiglottis

False vocal cords

True vocal cords

B

Figure 52A The larynx as it appears from behind.
52B Larynx from behind and above.

growth and early spread to the lymph nodes. Cancers of the subglottic region are rare and are generally low-grade, but they do have a tendency for early spread to lymph nodes.

Symptoms and Diagnosis

The predominant symptom of cancer of the glottis is hoarseness. However, hoarseness may be caused by any condition which interferes with vibration and free motion of the cords, and more often than not it indicates a condition other than cancer—infection, allergy, injury, inhalation of noxious fumes, or other less serious illnesses. Persistent hoarseness, however, lasting more than a few weeks, must be evaluated by a physician, particularly if it occurs in a heavy smoker. The physician may be able to look directly at the vocal cords by using a mirror (Figure 53) or a fiberoptic telescope. If this is not possible, the patient may be referred to a specialist for further examination under local or general anesthesia. Cancers arising on the vocal cords are not painful until late in the disease when adjacent tissues are involved, producing a chronic cough as well as hoarseness. There may even be difficulty in breathing with spells of choking as the cancer becomes more advanced.

Cancers arising in the supraglottic region cause few early symptoms other than a vague sense of discomfort deep in the throat. As they enlarge, these tumors are associated with pain in the throat and ear as well as pain on swallowing and hoarseness. An early symptom of supraglottic cancer may be the appearance of a lump in the neck. As with vocal cord cancers, these tumors can only be detected by examination with a mirror or fiberoptic telescope.

Cancer of the larynx is diagnosed by direct examination and a biopsy of tissue removed through a laryngoscope. Either a local or general anesthesia will be administered before undertaking the examination. In addition to biopsy, the physician will note the extent of the primary tumor and the mobility of the involved portion of the larynx. This is an important aspect of the staging procedure and will affect the choice of treatment. Further information regarding the extent of the cancer is provided by radiologic examinations which may include laryngograms, tomograms, and CT scans.

Treatment

Early cancer confined to the vocal cords is highly curable. Well over 85 percent of such tumors can be permanently controlled with radiation therapy alone. Certain selected early tumors can also be treated by limited surgical procedures, including partial removal of the larynx or destruction of the tumor using laser surgery—a painless treatment that

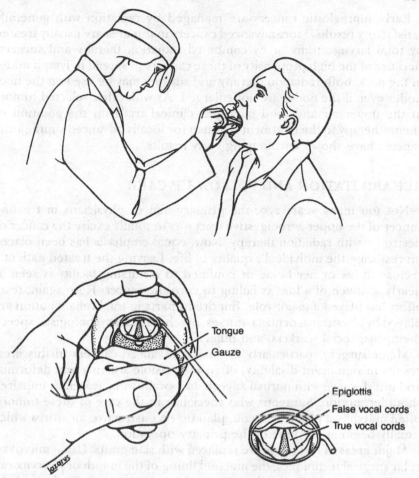

Figure 53 Examination of larynx using a mirror.

involves using intense light beams to vaporize the cancerous lesions. Laser surgery is becoming increasingly common; most major medical centers now have physicians who are trained in using this technique. Both limited surgery and laser treatments preserve the voice, although the resultant speech is usually not as good as that following radiation therapy. When cancer of the glottis is more advanced with deep invasion and fixation of a vocal cord, or when it persists following radiation therapy, it is generally treated by total removal of the larynx. While total laryngectomy is generally curative, it results in loss of the normal voice and intensive training is required to enable the patient to speak and be understood. (See Chapter 11, "Rehabilitation of the Cancer Patient.")

Early supraglottic cancers are managed by radiation with generally satisfactory results. More advanced cancers in this area are usually treated by total laryngectomy or by combined radiation therapy and surgery. Because of the high propensity of these cancers to spread to lymph nodes in the neck, both radiation therapy and surgery may be used on the neck nodes even if the nodes are not enlarged. As with other selected tumors in the upper air and food passages, clinical trials on the addition of chemotherapy to the treatment regimen for locally advanced supraglottic cancers have shown encouraging early results.

REHABILITATION AND FOLLOW-UP CARE

Not too many years ago, the primary aim of physicians in treating cancer of the upper aerodigestive tract was to totally excise the cancer or destroy it with radiation therapy. Now, equal emphasis has been placed on restoring the individual's quality of life. Leaving the treated patient a recluse in his or her home or confined to a nursing facility is seen as nearly as much of a loss as failing to cure the cancer. Here again, team effort has played a major role. Important parts in total rehabilitation are played by physicians, dentists, nurses, psychiatrists, psychologists, speech therapists, social workers, and others.

Major surgery, particularly for more advanced cancers in this area, results in significant disability, often with visible scarring and deformity and interference with normal speech and swallowing as well as impaired shoulder motion. Surgeons who specialize in the care of these tumors, often aided by a plastic surgeon, plan on reconstructive measures which usually begin at the time of the primary operation.

Major areas of lost tissue are replaced with skin grafts. Using microvascular surgical techniques, the mucosal lining of the mouth or pharynx can even be replaced by transplanted segments of intestine. Portions of the removed lower jaw may be replaced by bone grafts or by implanted metal struts. (See Figure 54.) The prosthodontist aids in the recovery of normal chewing and swallowing by improving the alignment of the jaws and replacing teeth. Loss of the palate or the upper jaw is usually better corrected by specially designed dental plates than by other reconstructive measures. Physiatrists and specially trained paramedical personnel help the patient improve shoulder motion and recover normal speech and swallowing. Teams of visiting nurses and social workers ease the patient's return from the hospital to the community, always with the aim of restoring him or her psychologically and functionally to the point where former activities can again be undertaken and enjoyed.

Approximately half of the patients who have a total laryngectomy can regain a serviceable voice known as esophageal speech (Figure 55A, B, C). They are taught by skilled speech therapists, some of whom have had

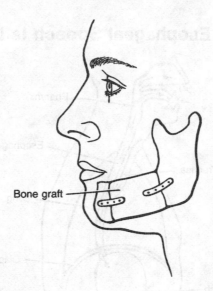

Bone graft

Figure 54 Reconstructive surgery of lower jaw.

laryngectomies themselves. Speech improvement can be assisted by participation in the activities of local chapters of the International Association of Laryngectomees, an organization supported by the American Cancer Society for many years. For patients who have great difficulty in regaining speech, a variety of electronic and vibrating aids are also available.

It has long been known that the most difficult part of learning to speak after a laryngectomy is mastering the ability to trap air in the throat or esophagus. Once that has been accomplished, the tongue, lips, and cheeks can then form sounds and words as the air is expelled. A number of surgical techniques have been devised to allow air to be forced from the trachea into the throat through artificial passages. These procedures have been tremendously improved in recent years by the use of plastic valves which effectively prevent the inhaling of saliva or liquids when the patient swallows. Ingenious techniques for total reconstruction of the larynx are currently being studied in laboratories and represent a hope for the future.

A final component of total care of the patient with cancer of the upper air and food passages is regular follow-up examinations by a physician. This is essential for two reasons: First, recurrences of these cancers, perhaps more than any other cancers, can be successfully re-treated when detected early. The patient is at greatest risk of recurrence during the first eighteen months after treatment, and during this period should be seen

How Esophageal Speech Is Done

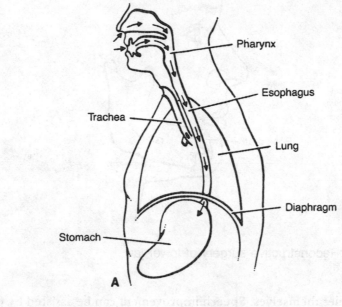

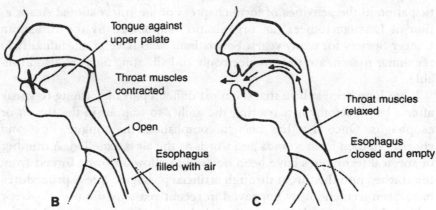

Figure 55A To do esophageal speech, first take in air through mouth and nose.

    55B Trap air by closing mouth. Press tongue against hard palate, swallow air and trap it in upper part of esophagus using the tongue and throat muscles.

    55C Expel air while causing pulsation with throat muscles (instead of vocal cords) and form sounds with lips. The tongue aids in release of air *or injecting* it into the esophagus to help make sounds.

and reexamined at frequent intervals. Second, and equally important, is the detection of new areas of premalignant or malignant change in the mucosa of the upper aerodigestive tract. These changes are frequent and when noted at an early time are controllable, often by simple measures. A difficult task for the physician is to convince the patient of the high risk of continuing his smoking and drinking habits. Heavy smoking in particular is known to increase the incidence of new cancers in this area and the patient must be given all possible support in efforts to abstain.

PROGNOSIS

Staging is used both in designing a treatment regimen and also in determining the likely prognosis. Although many things are taken into consideration in determining the stage of cancer, a simplified version is as follows:

Stage I. Cancers are small and localized, without any evidence of spread to adjacent tissue or lymph nodes. Patients with Stage I cancers of the upper aerodigestive tract have a 90 percent cure rate, defined as being alive without evidence of cancer five years after treatment.

Stage II. Cancers are somewhat larger than Stage I, but still confined to their site or origin without evidence of lymph-node involvement or metastases. The survival rate for Stage II cancers is 50 to 70 percent.

Stage III. Cancers are locally advanced, with spread to adjacent tissue and possibly to the lymph nodes. The survival rate for Stage III is 25 to 35 percent.

Stage IV. Extensive local cancer with spread to the lymph nodes and perhaps metastases to distant organs. Prognosis is poor, although modern treatment can prolong life and improve its quality.

SUMMING UP

Cancers of the mouth, pharynx, and larynx are fairly common, especially among long-term users of tobacco and/or large amounts of alcohol. If detected in their early stages, these cancers are highly curable. Improved methods of treatment and reconstructive surgery, as well as increased emphasis on rehabilitation, make these cancers less devastating than in the past. Today, most patients undergoing treatment for these cancers can expect to resume a normal, productive life. Even if extensive facial or neck surgery is required, modern reconstructive surgery can reduce the degree of disfigurement that made these cancers so fearful to past generations.

26

Multiple Myeloma

ELLIOTT F. OSSERMAN, M.D.

INTRODUCTION

Multiple myeloma is a type of cancer that affects chiefly the skeleton and blood. It is one of a group of diseases called "plasma cell dyscrasias," all of which are characterized by an imbalanced proliferation of plasma cells. Some plasma cell dyscrasias are benign, with an unpredictable course. Some appear to be a transient hypersensitive response, for example, to a drug or a virus. Others may be chronic and associated with an inflammatory or infectious process, such as rheumatoid arthritis or osteomyelitis. Sometimes people with "benign" plasma cell dyscrasias go for twenty or more years without having the condition progress. In others, however, it may evolve into myeloma or other symptomatic disorders, many of which are quite rare.

Multiple myeloma can develop at any age from young adulthood to advanced age, with the peak incidence among people in their mid-fifties. It occurs about equally in men and women, although some studies have found a slight preponderance among men. An increased number of multiple myeloma cases has been reported in recent years and, in large medical centers, it is now more common than Hodgkin's disease. Some of this rise has been attributed to improved diagnostic techniques, meaning that previously undetected cases are now being diagnosed. But it appears there is also a higher actual incidence of the disease. The reasons for this increase are unknown, although exposure to certain environmental toxins—for example, chemicals used in the manufacture of paper pulp or plastics—is thought to be a possible cause.

Even though the cause of multiple myeloma remains unknown, a good deal has been learned in recent years about both the development and the treatment of the disease. Only twenty years ago, the outlook for most myeloma patients was poor, generally with a relentless progression of the disease and death within a few months. By employing modern treatments, the mean survival is now more than four years, with most patients able to continue living productive lives without the severe pain, paralysis, and other disabilities that were once hallmarks of myeloma.

The immune system is composed of several specialized cells (Figure 56), the principal ones being T (thymus) and B (bone marrow) lymphocytes. Plasma cells are derived from the maturation of B cells (Figure 57) and normally do not multiply. In myeloma and other plasma cell dyscrasias, something goes awry with the immune system and plasma cells proliferate independently. This results in the overproduction of specific protein products called immunoglobulins, which are also called antibodies.

Normally, the immune system incorporates a vast number of different antibodies (Figure 58) in order to provide protection against a wide variety of infectious bacteria and viruses. By contrast, in plasma cell dyscrasias, only one clone or family of cells is involved and this results in the production of a single type of protein, called monoclonal immunoglobulin. These monoclonal proteins are easily detected in the serum or urine of patients with multiple myeloma and they are a hallmark of diagnosis.

SYMPTOMS AND DIAGNOSIS

In most instances, skeletal pain is the first symptom of myeloma. The pain is caused by infiltration of the plasma cells into the marrow, and consequent destruction of the bone. Initially, the skeletal pain may be mild and transient; in other instances, it may develop suddenly as a severe pain in the back, rib, leg, or arm, often the result of an abrupt movement or effort that has caused a spontaneous bone fracture. As the disease progresses, more and more areas of bone destruction develop, frequently resulting in skeletal deformities, particularly of the ribs, sternum (breast-bone), and a shortening of the spine. The latter may cause a loss of five or more inches in stature. Skeletal deformities were quite common in the past, but because of improved general management of the disease and chemotherapy, these are now much less common.

The symptomatic stage of myeloma is usually, if not always, preceded by an asymptomatic period in which there is an abnormal production of

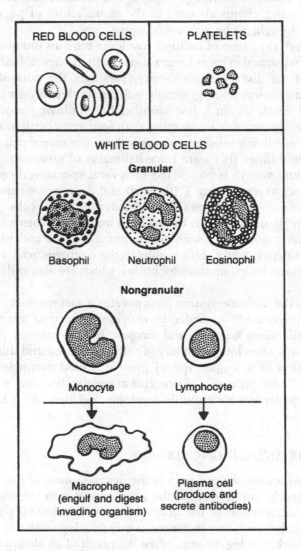

RED BLOOD CELLS   PLATELETS

WHITE BLOOD CELLS

Granular

Basophil   Neutrophil   Eosinophil

Nongranular

Monocyte   Lymphocyte

Macrophage
(engulf and digest
invading organism)

Plasma cell
(produce and
secrete antibodies)

Figure 56 Components of blood.

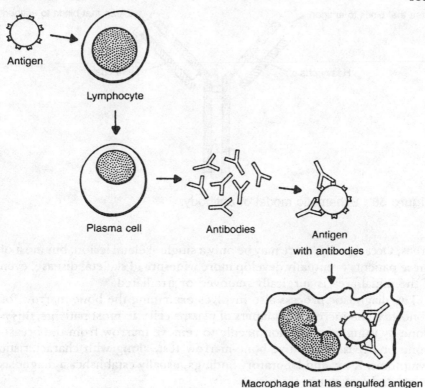

Antigen

Lymphocyte

Plasma cell

Antibodies

Antigen
with antibodies

Macrophage that has engulfed antigen

Figure 57 Natural active immunity. Antigen (invading organism) encounters lymphocyte, which in turn produces plasma cells. Plasma cells manufacture specific antibodies which attach to the antigen. Eventually, the covered antigen is ingested by the macrophage.

monoclonal proteins. This may show up as unexplained protein in the urine (proteinuria) or an elevated erythrocyte sedimentation rate—a test that measures the distance red blood cells settle in a test tube in an hour. Even if there are no other symptoms, all instances of unexplained proteinuria should be subjected to further analysis for a particular type of protein, called Bence Jones protein. If this protein is present, intravenous pyelography, a kidney examination that involves injection of a dye into a vein to make kidney structures visible on an X ray, should be avoided because it can cause irreversible renal failure.

In most patients, X rays will show a number of osteolytic areas, in which the bones have a "punched-out" appearance. There are, however, many instances in which the initial X rays appear normal or may show diffuse osteoporosis—a thinning of the bones—without the discrete osteolytic

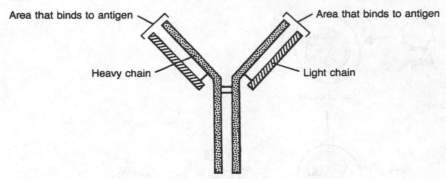

Figure 58 Schematic model of antibody.

areas. Occasionally, there may be only a single skeletal lesion, but most of these patients eventually develop more widespread skeletal disease, even if the initial area is surgically removed or irradiated.

The diagnostic process also involves examining the bone marrow for abnormal and increased numbers of plasma cells. In most patients, this is done by using an aspiration needle to remove marrow from the breastbone or pelvis. A positive bone-marrow test, along with characteristic symptoms, X ray and laboratory findings, usually establishes a diagnosis of multiple myeloma.

OTHER ABNORMALITIES

Almost all patients with myeloma also have anemia, either at the time of diagnosis or as the disease progresses. The severity of the anemia varies from person to person; in many it remains moderate and is well tolerated, while in others it may become a major problem requiring repeated blood transfusions. The anemia associated with myeloma results from a combination of factors, including destruction of the bone marrow, accelerated destruction of red cells, blood loss, kidney problems, the effects of chemotherapy or radiation therapy, infections, or nutritional factors. The anemia usually does not respond to iron, vitamin B_{12}, folic acid, or liver therapy.

Increased susceptibility to bacterial infections, particularly pneumococcal pneumonia, is also relatively common and is a result of the impaired antibody production. Fortunately, most patients with bacterial infections are readily treated with antibiotics. There is also an increased susceptibility to herpes zoster (shingles), but apparently not to other viruses.

As noted earlier, myeloma patients have monoclonal or M-type proteins in their serum and/or urine. Each of these proteins is unique to the particular patient and remains unchanged throughout the course of the disease. Interestingly, there is increasing evidence that many, if not all, of these monoclonal proteins are antibodies directed against specific antigens, often substances occurring naturally within the body. Further study along these lines may help elucidate the cause of myeloma and also may make diagnosis easier.

The specific protein abnormalities also are instrumental in certain complications associated with myeloma. For example, particular monoclonal proteins may be correlated with clotting problems. Others may be related to excessive response to cold, leading to Raynaud's phenomenon, a circulatory disorder in which inadequate blood reaches the fingers and toes and which may cause gangrene. Circulatory problems affecting the central nervous system and retina are related to certain types of monoclonal globulins.

Kidney problems, including renal failure, have long been associated with myeloma. Some kidney impairment may be caused by Bence Jones protein in the urine, but several other factors also contribute to potential renal failure. The bone destruction that occurs in myeloma leads to hypercalcemia—excessive calcium circulating in the blood. To rid the body of the excess calcium, the kidneys increase their output of urine, which can lead to serious dehydration if there is an inadequate intake of fluids. The dehydration may be compounded by vomiting, which makes it impossible to replace the lost fluid by drinking extra fluids. Patients who experience symptoms of hypercalcemia—increased urination, loss of appetite, and vomiting—should seek immediate medical care, since this can be life-threatening. Myeloma patients also may have excessive uric acid in their urine (hyperuricosuria), which also contributes to kidney impairment.

In unusual instances, the myeloma resembles plasma cell leukemia, with an enlarged liver and spleen, and an excessive number of circulating plasma cells. Patients with this type of myeloma will have symptoms similar to other types of leukemia: weakness, anemia, and bleeding.

Previously, neurological complications developed in a significant percentage of patients with myeloma. These neurological manifestations were caused by direct pressure on the spinal cord, nerve roots, cranial or peripheral nerves, or by a fracture of a vertebra. Compression of the spinal cord can lead to paralysis and paraplegia, obviously a very serious complication. Although paraplegia still develops occasionally in untreated patients, it almost never occurs among patients who are receiving proper chemotherapy and management of the disease.

About 10 percent of patients with myeloma experience amyloidosis, deposits of insoluble fragments of a monoclonal protein. The most frequent sites of amyloid deposits are the tongue, heart, gastrointestinal tract, nerves, muscles, and ligaments, especially the carpal tunnel area of the hand. This can lead to carpal tunnel syndrome—pain, numbness, or tingling in the hand and fingers.

TREATMENT

Notable advances have been made over the last twenty years in the treatment of multiple myeloma. Not only has the median survival time been increased three- to sevenfold, the quality of life among people with the disease has been improved dramatically. These improvements are due both to more effective chemotherapeutic agents and to increased attention to keeping physically active. Indeed, keeping mobile is a cardinal factor in the successful management of myeloma. Regular and programmed walking, swimming, and mild sports are strongly encouraged. The only physical activities to be avoided are those that involve excessive straining and heavy lifting.

To overcome the skeletal pain that discourages physical activity, pain medication such as aspirin, with or without codeine, should be taken. If painkillers are inadequate, radiation therapy to the most painful areas may be recommended. The radiation doses needed for pain relief are small—about 1,800 to 2,400 rads, or even less in some instances. The radiation dosage should not induce or aggravate bone marrow failure, which may hinder the simultaneous administration of chemotherapy.

Maintaining adequate body fluids also is essential in the overall management of myeloma. Adequate hydration is necessary to avoid kidney problems associated with excessive circulating calcium. Many myeloma patients also have high levels of uric acid, which also contributes to kidney complications. This usually requires drinking about two quarts of water a day. In addition to a high intake of fluids, prednisone, a derivative of the adrenal hormone cortisone, and allopurinol (Zyloprim), a drug to control uric acid, may be prescribed to lower the calcium and uric acid levels and improve kidney function.

Chemotherapy usually cannot be started until renal function is restored because the drugs may increase the urate load on the kidneys. The most commonly used drugs are the alkylating agents—anticancer drugs that act directly to damage the cell's molecular structure, interfering with its growth and reproduction.

The two drugs that are the most effective in the long-term treatment of myeloma are melphalan (Alkeran, L-PAM) or cyclophosphamide (Cytoxan). Both can be taken by mouth and are generally well tolerated. Initially, a relatively high loading dose of the chosen drug is given for seven to ten days to achieve a maximum response. The dosage is then lowered to the long-term maintenance level, which should be high enough to suppress the abnormal proliferation of plasma cells without seriously impairing normal blood production. If the myeloma becomes resistant to one drug, the patient may be switched to the other.

An improvement in symptoms usually occurs in two to four weeks. Blood counts should be checked twice weekly during the first month of chemotherapy, weekly for the second month, and at progressively longer intervals once the maintenance therapy is well established. Repeated bone marrow studies are sometimes useful in evaluating the efficacy of the treatment, but in most cases they are not needed. Instead, an adequate assessment usually can be made from blood counts, protein studies, and observation of symptoms.

Other drugs may be added to the regimen as needed. Prednisone is highly effective in controlling excessive blood calcium; antibiotics may be prescribed to overcome bacterial infections; analgesics should be taken as needed to control pain.

By following the regimen outlined above, most patients can achieve a remission in their myeloma. As yet, there is no cure for the disease. Each patient should be examined by his or her doctor at regular intervals. Since the disease and its treatment are complex, it is important that the treating physician be experienced in managing myeloma. To keep track of a patient's progress, it is useful to maintain an ongoing graph showing results of the periodic laboratory and physical findings. These graphs not only help the physician evaluate the patient's progress, but also are useful in letting the patient see the effects of treatment—an important factor since the day-to-day management of myeloma is the patient's responsibility.

SUMMING UP

Great strides have been made in the understanding and treatment of multiple myeloma over the last twenty years. In the early 1960s, the outlook for a person with myeloma was discouraging, with death usually occurring within a few months of diagnosis. Today, more than 80 percent of patients can expect a remission of one to five years or even more, during which they can continue to lead productive and reasonably comfortable lives. Much of the current success in treating myeloma depends upon the patient's daily adherence to a regimen that includes physical activity, adequate fluid intake, and low maintenance doses of chemotherapeutic drugs to suppress the overproliferation of plasma cells.

27

Cancer of the Gallbladder, Bile Ducts, and Pancreas

WALTER LAWRENCE, JR., M.D.

INTRODUCTION

Cancers of the pancreas, gallbladder, and bile ducts are part of the large family of cancers that we refer to as gastrointestinal cancer. These anatomic structures are attached to the intestine as part of the system of organs that provide additional digestive juices.

Almost everyone finds organs such as the lung, rectum, and breast easy to identify as specific locations in the body where cancer may develop, but the anatomy of the pancreas and the biliary tree is often less well understood. The gallbladder, bile ducts, and the pancreas are all located closely together in the upper abdomen, but the cancers that arise from these structures have some major differences in terms of their rate of growth and severity. However, these three sites are in such close proximity to each other in the body that they may produce similar symptoms despite the individual differences in the subsequent course of patients with each type of cancer.

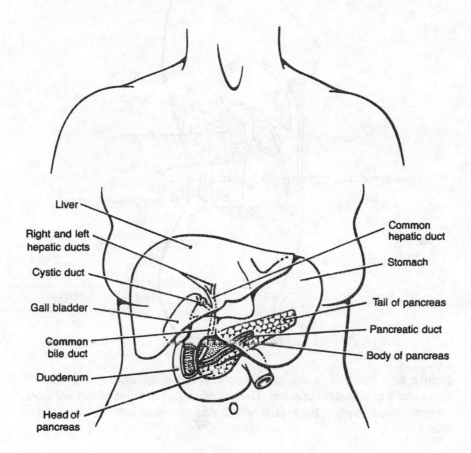

Figure 59 Normal gallbladder, bile ducts, pancreas and adjacent organs.

The relationship of these anatomic structures to surrounding abdominal organs, and to each other, is shown in Figures 59 and 60. The gallbladder is an appendage or pouch of the bile duct, a tube that acts as a bile conduit from the liver to the intestine where the bile normally plays an important role in the digestive process. Under normal circumstances, the gallbladder acts as a storage unit for bile until there is a need for it.

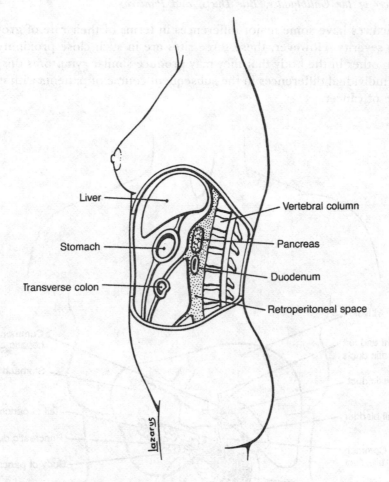

Figure 60 Position of the pancreas in relation to other abdominal organs and the vertebral column. This location just in front of the vertebral column helps explain back pain which can develop from cancer at this site.

The gallbladder is capable of emptying its contents when needed, and this occurs as a response to the appearance of food in the intestine. The human gallbladder is a frequent site for the development of stones, the most common reason for its removal, and the body can function satisfactorily without the luxury of the gallbladder if there is a legitimate need for removing it. The biliary duct system, of which the gallbladder is an "offshoot," is the only channel for the transport of bile from the liver to the upper small intestine, the duodenum. Partial or complete blockage of this tube by a stone that has traveled out of the gallbladder, or by a tumor, will produce jaundice, characterized by a yellow discoloration of the skin due to a backup of the bile pigments into the circulating blood.

The pancreas is still another gland contributing digestive juices. Many people are familiar with the pancreas of beef cattle, which are known as "sweetbreads." In humans, the pancreas is near the back of the upper portion of the abdominal cavity, lying behind the stomach and in front of the kidneys. Specialized cells within the pancreas produce insulin, a hormone essential for the metabolism of carbohydrates and other nutrients. The pancreas also produces enzymes that contribute to digestion. These enzymes enter the duodenum at the same site that the bile duct drains the bile from the liver into this same structure. The lower end of the bile duct actually travels through a short part of the head of the pancreas on its way to the intestine, an anatomic explanation of the blockage of the bile duct (and jaundice) that occurs in many patients with cancer arising from the pancreas itself. Although there are differing growth and behavior features of the cancers arising from the gallbladder, bile duct, and pancreas, their anatomic proximity is the major reason why the symptoms from each may be similar to those from the others. It also explains why cancers of these sites are described in the same chapter.

INCIDENCE AND CAUSES

Cancer of the Gallbladder

Gallbladder cancer is the most common cancer of the bile-duct system, although it occurs less frequently than cancer arising in the pancreas itself. Gallbladder cancer tends to occur in women three times as often as in men and it develops among elderly people more frequently than other gastrointestinal cancer. Although there have been some claims of weak environmental or industrial associations with this cancer, the major disease association that may be a causative factor is the presence of gallstones. It is estimated that 80 to 90 percent of patients with gallbladder cancer also have gallstones. This observation is intriguing because gallstones are so common among Americans, but it does not prove that gallstones actually cause cancer. Nevertheless, either the stones or the irritation, infection, or metabolic changes that they produce is an important factor in the development of this form of cancer. At the same time, it should be stressed that the incidence of gallstones in our population is much higher than the frequency of gallbladder cancer and it is quite clear that the overwhelming majority of people who have gallstones will never develop this form of cancer. This should be reassuring to people who know they have gallstones but have not been advised to have their gallbladders removed.

Cancer of the Bile Ducts

The tube system that drains the bile from the liver to the intestine, to which the gallbladder is physically attached, is a relatively rare site for cancer to develop; certainly, cancer of these structures is much less common than of either the pancreas or the gallbladder. The cause of bile duct cancer is unknown, but there has been an association noted between patients who have ulcerative colitis—a poorly understood chronic inflammatory disease of the colon and rectum—and bile duct cancer. The mechanisms that may link these two diseases in different and separate organ systems are unknown. Another association noted in the Orient, but not in the United States, is with a parasitic infestation that rarely occurs outside Asia. It is also of interest that the association noted between gallstones and gallbladder cancer is a more frequent occurrence than the presence of gallstones in patients who develop bile duct cancer.

Cancer of the Pancreas

Of the three sites discussed in this chapter, the pancreas has the highest incidence of cancer, and the outlook for the usual form of pancreatic cancer also is the poorest. Pancreatic cancer is the fifth most common cause of death from cancer in the United States (after lung, colorectal, breast, and prostate gland cancers). It usually develops among people fifty to seventy years old and is responsible for approximately twenty-three thousand deaths a year. It is more common among men than women and, in the United States, more frequent in blacks than whites. In the past thirty years, there has been a slow, steady increase in incidence of this disease, which raises questions regarding possible causal factors.

The specific cause of pancreatic cancer is unknown and epidemiologic studies have yielded confusing results. Diabetic patients may be more prone to pancreatic cancer than others, but this is difficult to establish with certainty. Chronic alcoholism and inflammation of the pancreas, or pancreatitis, have been suggested as causative factors by some, but not all, studies. In men, there appears to be a small increase in risk of pancreatic cancer for those employed in the dry-cleaning business or in occupations involving close exposure to gasoline for ten or more years. Cigarette smoking appears to increase the risk of pancreatic cancer in women, but evidence supporting this is not striking. Decaffeinated coffee was considered a dietary factor in increasing the risk of pancreatic cancer among women in one study, while another claimed an association between coffee consumption and pancreatic cancer in both sexes. It should be noted that a number of experts have questioned the conclusions of these "case control" studies that seem to implicate coffee as a cause of pancreatic cancer. Still, another dietary factor revealed by some epidemiologic studies is the association between diets high in meat and fat consumed in the Western world, when contrasted with diets of the Japanese, where pancreatic cancer is less common. It is fair to say that the cause of pancreatic cancer is probably a combination of multiple dietary and environmental factors and no single one, such as cigarette use, coffee or alcohol consumption, can be implicated with confidence.

DIAGNOSIS

As noted earlier, cancers arising in these sites often produce similar symptoms, even though they are different diseases. For cancers of the bile ducts or the head of the pancreas, the usual warning is jaundice, a yellowing of the skin that results from blockage of the bile duct system. At the beginning, the yellow discoloration may be subtle and it may be more apparent to friends and relatives than to the person affected. The white portion of the eyes may be the only place where this abnormal coloration is noted; this is particularly true if the person is black.

With time, there is a progressive deepening of the discoloration and there will be other clues that the bile is not getting through to the intestine in normal fashion. For example, itching of the skin may develop due to deposits there of some of the increased levels of the bile products in the circulating blood. The "backup" of the bile in the blood leads also to an increased excretion of this pigment in the urine, turning it a dark red or "wine" color. The stools, which are normally brown as a result of bile in the intestinal content, will gradually become light and clay colored. All of these symptoms are the result of mechanical blockage of the normal system for bile drainage from the liver to the intestine.

Gallbladder cancers may grow outside the gallbladder itself and produce a similar blockage of the adjacent bile duct system (and jaundice) but this is less frequent with this specific site of cancer until the disease has grown to the point where it mechanically affects adjacent anatomical structures, including the bile duct.

Of course, the development of jaundice does not establish a diagnosis of cancer—a number of other disorders, particularly hepatitis, also produce jaundice. Ultrasonic examinations, CT scans, and other X-ray tests may be performed to confirm whether an obstruction of the bile duct system is the cause of the jaundice, as well as the actual site of any such obstruction. Some tests provide leads as to the cause of such a blockage; however, there are many instances in which bile ducts are obstructed by something other than cancer. A gallstone that has left the gallbladder and subsequently blocked the main bile duct is the most common cause of obstruction. Tests prior to the initiation of definitive treatment establish the diagnosis and actually may show signs of spread of the cancer, which will affect the treatment plan. But final clarification of the situation may require an abdominal operation since these various diseases often tend to mimic each other.

A major problem with this group of cancers is that most other symptoms noted for any of these three types are actually caused by the spread of cancer to other organs and tissues, both near or far from the original cancer itself. This may be manifested by back pain, abdominal swelling from an abnormal buildup of fluid, or other symptoms resulting from continued growth and spread of the cancer to other areas. These circumstances usually prevail when a cancer has progressed without blocking the bile duct system. By observing the positions of these abdominal organs, as shown in Figure 59, it can be noted that cancers arising in the gallbladder or the body (not the head) of the pancreas might extend in this way without producing jaundice. In these instances, symptoms usually develop too late to allow effective treatment.

TREATMENT

The way in which cancer of these organs signals its presence affects the treatment plan considerably. If the first warning sign is jaundice, due to a mechanical blockage of the bile duct system, some relief of this obstruction is required to prevent progressive deterioration of liver function. The liver performs vital metabolic functions for the body, and these are seriously hampered by blockage of normal bile flow into the intestine. Thus, the jaundice from obstruction must be corrected to prevent premature death from liver failure. The treatment solution for this problem is a mechanical one, either surgical relief of the obstruction by removing the cancer, or a bypass of the obstruction, which may be achieved by operative or nonoperative means.

If the first manifestation of the cancer is a symptom caused by spread of the disease to other structures, such as the liver, abdominal cavity, or other sites, or if there is X-ray evidence of such spread, removal of the cancer is rarely feasible. In these instances, some biopsy procedure to establish conclusively the diagnosis is mandatory, and this must be designed to fit the specific situation. It may even require abdominal surgery, but it is preferable to establish the diagnosis by some form of X-ray-guided needle biopsy, if feasible, to avoid an abdominal operation that has no potential for complete removal of the cancer itself. Other therapeutic approaches that may prove beneficial in these frustrating circumstances include those involving radiation therapy and/or chemotherapy, but these are never curative for this group of cancers.

Based on these general treatment principles, it is probably best to describe the treatments that are employed for each of the three individual types of cancer. Whether treatment is directed to a possible cure or only to attempts to relieve symptoms usually depends upon the extent of the cancer at the time of diagnosis. The short-term benefits usually prove to be the focus of treatment since the long-term results obtained with this group of cancers are discouraging at the present time. However, an understanding of individual treatment strategies is best understood if one has some idea of the possible outcome of available treatments. Approaches to treatment and likely outcomes for each cancer site are summarized in the following sections.

Cancer of the Gallbladder

If the cancer is unsuspected and found at the time of an operation for gallstones, or during some other surgical procedure, it usually has not penetrated the gallbladder wall or spread to surrounding structures. Over 90 percent of these patients with unsuspected gallbladder cancer that is discovered in this fashion will enjoy a normal life expectancy after simple removal of the gallbladder itself.

If the cancer has produced symptoms, the outlook is much less optimistic. Only about 5 percent of such patients will enjoy normal life expectancy despite the fact that the treatment may temporarily relieve the symptoms. This poor outlook can be explained by the fact that the symptoms usually indicate that the cancer has spread from the gallbladder to other structures and that simple gallbladder removal is not sufficient to solve the problem. In such instances, the treatment strategy is directed to relieving the symptoms. For example, if there is bile duct obstruction and jaundice, the symptom can be relieved by insertion of a special tube through the obstructed site, either surgically or by an X-ray-guided procedure in which the tube is introduced through the lower chest wall and passed into the liver and down to the bile duct system. This may relieve the obstruction and the jaundice, but it does not affect the cancer itself. Localized radiation therapy can be applied to the cancerous area in some patients; this will retard the cancer grown in the region of the portals through which the treatment is administered. Chemotherapy programs also are employed for patients with gallbladder cancer that cannot be removed, but these have limited long-term value.

What is the future of treatment of gallbladder cancer? Clearly, new diagnostic methods are needed to identify early, asymptomatic gallbladder cancers at a stage in which removal can produce a successful cure. Although removal of gallbladders containing gallstones will yield only a few cancers, the potential for curing those that are present should encourage this approach, particularly in those patients requiring abdominal surgery for some unrelated indication.

Cancer of the Bile Ducts

The overall figures for long-term, essentially normal survival after treatment of bile duct cancers range from 5 to 10 percent, but those patients whose cancers can be removed have a 20 to 35 percent chance of a normal life span. The specific location of the cancer in the duct system plays some role in this outcome; the distal tumors near the intestine may have better long-term outlook due to the greater feasibility of their removal.

Since bile duct cancers block bile flow, the treatment strategy must include relief of this obstruction, even though it may not be possible to remove the cancer completely. When the cancer is in the superior portion of the bile duct system near the liver itself (see Figure 59), it is often difficult to remove the entire cancer since the normal bile duct in this location is immediately adjacent to many other structures (including blood vessels) that cannot be removed. If the cancer has spread to surrounding tissues, partial removal of the cancer and the obstructed duct can be accomplished and a tube inserted to facilitate bile flow into the intestine, allowing at least temporary relief of the problem. Radiation treatments to this area following the operation may provide additional benefits by curtailing the growth of residual cancerous tissue that cannot be removed. Chemotherapy also may help. Although this treatment approach is not curative, it may result in significant benefit to the patient because many of the cancers at this site are slow-growing.

In the less common situation in which the cancer is small and confined to the bile duct near the liver, the duct may be removed and the duct openings at the base of the liver can then be attached to a segment of intestine, thereby reestablishing normal bile flow. The process of "plugging in" the bile channel to the intestine is accomplished by sewing the structures together, often around a supporting plastic tube. In this situation, the operation itself may be curative.

When the cancer is in the bile duct adjacent to the pancreas and the intestine—the part most distant from the liver—the preferable operative treatment is total removal of the cancer. This operation entails removal of the surrounding tissues (a portion of the pancreas and a part of the small intestine) and is quite similar to the operation for cancer of the pancreas, which is described in the following section. Almost a third of patients with bile duct cancer who undergo this operation will enjoy a long-term survival or a cure.

Unfortunately, the situation is different if the cancer has spread to other areas. In these instances, a bypass operation to achieve bile flow into the intestine may be performed. Postoperative chemotherapy programs may curtail the growth of the cancer and prolong survival.

Cancer of the Pancreas

The outlook for patients with pancreatic cancer is poor at the present time, with only about 1 to 2 percent achieving a cure. Patients whose cancers can be surgically removed have a slightly better outlook (3 to 7 percent), but subsequent recurrence of cancer growth is all too common. As might be expected, the best long-term results are obtained if the cancers are detected in an early stage when they are still very small. The actual operation includes removal of the major portion of the pancreas, the section of intestine attached to the pancreas, and the attachment of the bile duct in this area. Reconstruction is then accomplished by attaching the bile duct, the remaining pancreas, and the stomach to the intestine. This allows reasonably normal digestive function after recovery from the operation.

There are some more favorable, albeit atypical, types of pancreatic cancer, such as those that produce abnormal quantities of hormones or have fluid-filled cystic components, but these make up a small minority of the total. The remaining patients, particularly those with larger cancers, have a life expectancy of approximately six months if the cancer is not removed and often only fifteen to eighteen months when removal is accomplished.

Frequently, by the time pancreatic cancer is detected, it has spread to other abdominal tissues, explaining why surgical treatment is so discouraging. There are a minority of patients with pancreatic cancer who are found to have localized tumors that can be removed, but even these patients frequently have a recurrence of the disease. Despite this generally poor outlook after surgery for pancreatic cancer, removal of the cancer is carried out for the patients who have localized tumors. This does prolong survival for most patients and it temporarily relieves symptoms. And, in a few patients, a cure is achieved. More often, however, the cancer cannot be removed entirely because, during the operation, it is found that it has spread to other vital structures. In this instance, an operation to bypass the bile duct obstruction is employed, similar to that described for cancers arising in the bile duct system itself. The nonoperative approach to bypassing the obstruction (described earlier) may be employed if preoperative assessment shows spread that makes removal of the cancer impossible.

Various means of applying radiation therapy can be added to these operative treatments, as well as chemotherapy, but overall benefit and survival time are limited in most instances. Sadly, pancreatic cancer remains one of our most difficult treatment problems and progress in improving both early diagnosis and treatment is sorely needed.

Outlook for the Future

Most experts agree that prevention or means for very early diagnosis are the only real hopes for improving our approach to this serious trio of cancers. Various tumor markers in the blood serum are being studied in cancer research centers, and other screening and diagnostic methods are under investigation. It is unlikely that there will be significant further advances in the surgical or radiation therapy aspects of treatment, but either might be more effective if the cancers could be detected in an earlier stage. Lastly, current chemotherapy programs have a limited effect, but progress overall in this field may lead to more effective application of drug treatments for these cancers. Certainly, more progress is needed on all fronts for this group of cancers that have proved so difficult.

28

Cancer of the Female Reproductive Tract

S. B. GUSBERG, M.D., D.Sc.

One out of every twenty women will, at some point, develop cancer of the reproductive organs. An estimated 76,400 new cases of gynecological cancer are diagnosed each year, causing about 22,700 deaths. Although this is still a high figure, it is much lower than a few decades ago. The outlook for gynecological cancer has improved dramatically in recent years, due in large part to extensive screening programs aimed at early detection and advances in treatment. The death toll from uterine cancer, for example, has dropped more than 70 percent since the 1930s. Cervical cancer, if detected in its earliest stages, is now almost 100 percent curable. And even more lives could be saved through more extensive efforts for early diagnosis.

PREDISPOSING FACTORS AND SYMPTOMS

The female reproductive tract is an elegant complex of organs designed specifically for the creation of new human life (Figures 61 and 62). Any of these organs may develop cancer, but the incidence varies greatly from one to another. The cervix and endometrium (the lining of the uterus) are the most common sites of gynecological cancer, followed by cancer of the ovaries. The vulva and vagina are less frequent cancer sites, while cancer of the fallopian tubes is very rare.

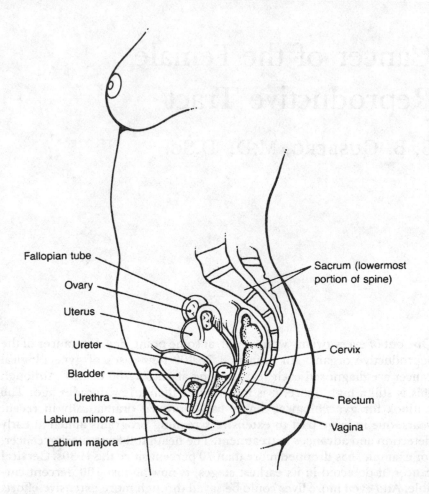

Figure 61 Normal female reproductive system.

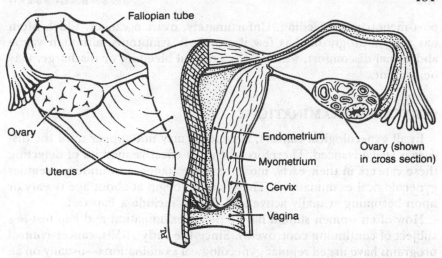

Fallopian tube

Ovary

Uterus

Endometrium

Myometrium

Cervix

Vagina

Ovary (shown in cross section)

Figure 62 View of female reproductive organs from back.

Most gynecological cancers occur after the menopause, although some are seen in younger women. A number of risk factors have been identified that appear to increase a woman's chance of certain gynecological cancers. For example, an increased risk of cervical cancer has been associated with sexual activity at an early age and multiple sexual partners. Genital herpes and other genital viral infections, such as genital warts, may increase the risk of cancer of the cervix. The incidence of endometrial cancer is increased among women who are obese, have never been pregnant, began menopause late, or who have had long-term estrogen replacement following menopause. A history of ovarian problems, such as menstrual irregularities or bleeding between periods, seems to increase the risk of cancer of the ovaries. A rare form of vaginal cancer in adolescent girls has been linked to their mothers' use of diethylstilbestrol, or DES, an artificial hormone that was sometimes given to women in the 1950s and 1960s to prevent miscarriage. (It should be noted, however, that even among DES daughters, this cancer is very rare; other reproductive problems, such as infertility, appear to be more common than cancer among these women.)

Unusual bleeding often is the first obvious symptom of gynecological cancer. Cervical cancer causes bleeding in up to two thirds of patients. Unlike menstruation, this bleeding is unpredictable as to frequency, duration, amount, or other characteristics. In some instances, a watery discharge may accompany or replace the bleeding. Cervical cancer may also cause pain in the lower pelvic area but this is a late symptom. Cancer of the endometrium, a disease affecting mostly older women, usually causes post-menopausal bleeding. Unfortunately, ovarian cancer, which often has a poor prognosis, has few if any early symptoms, although vague abdominal discomfort, without any unusual bleeding or discharge, may be present.

SCREENING EXAMINATIONS

In all gynecological cancers, symptoms may not appear until the disease is well advanced. Therefore, the most effective method of detecting these cancers in their early, most treatable stages is to undergo regular gynecological examinations. These should begin at about age twenty or upon becoming sexually active and should include a Pap test.

How often women should have a pelvic examination and Pap test is a subject of continuing controversy. Since the early 1950s, cancer-control programs have urged regular gynecological examinations—usually on an annual basis—for all women. Recently, however, the necessity and cost-effectiveness of yearly examinations have been questioned. Since most gynecological cancers are slow-growing, often taking years to develop, critics of yearly screening contend that for women who have normal Pap smears and no other risk factors, an annual examination is unnecessary before the age of forty. In keeping with this, the American Cancer Society now recommends an annual pelvic examination and Pap smear for the first two years after age twenty or commencement of sexual intercourse, and every three years thereafter until age sixty-five, provided no abnormalities are found. In contrast, the American College of Obstetrics and Gynecology still recommends yearly pelvic examinations and Pap smears. This organization, while conceding that invasive cancer takes several years to develop, points out that early precancerous cellular changes are detected in annual Pap tests. It also notes that cancer detection is not the sole purpose of a gynecological examination; signs of infection, polyps and other growths, rectal abnormalities, ovarian cysts, and other such disorders are detected by pelvic examinations. Both groups advise yearly or even more frequent examinations for high-risk women: those over the age of forty, diabetics, women whose mothers took DES while pregnant with them, women with a strong family history of gynecological cancer, or women taking estrogens, and of course those with abnormal Pap smears.

The gynecologic examination should take place in a comfortable, well-lighted room. It should include examination of the breast. For the pelvic examination, the woman lies on her back with her knees and feet drawn up close to the body. The feet may be placed at the edge of the examining table or in stirrups attached to it. During the examination, the doctor uses a speculum—an instrument shaped like a duck's beak—to open the vagina so that it and the cervical area can be viewed. A cotton swab or an aspirator (a vacuum device like a bulb baster) is used to pick up a few cells that have been shed from the cervix surface (Figure 63). These are mounted on a slide, stained, and examined under a microscope—a test commonly referred to as a Pap smear. The doctor uses gloved fingers to feel for growths in the vaginal and cervical areas and the rectum. He or she will, at the same time, press on the abdomen to feel for any uterine growths or ovarian or any other abnormalities.

Special speculums are available for young girls, virgins, and women whose vaginas have atrophied through age or abnormalities. The speculum may feel cold, but the examination should not hurt. However, there is sometimes a slight discharge afterward; therefore, the woman may want to bring a thin sanitary napkin or a tampon to the examination room. It is also important for the bowel to be emptied in the morning before coming for the examination.

When viewing the cervix, the doctor looks for red or eroded areas, ulcerations, masses or growths, whitish patches (leukoplakia), or any combination of these. When feeling a growth during the manual examination, the doctor will try to determine its size, shape, surface texture, consistency (in comparison with normal tissue), fragility (for example, whether it breaks apart easily), and the firmness of its attachment to nearby structures.

THE PAP SMEAR

The Pap smear is our most important test for early detection of cervical cancer and its precancerous stages. It is inexpensive, painless, quick, and 90 percent accurate. The technique, named after the late Dr. George N. Papanicolaou, a Greek American medical scientist, is used to examine epithelial cells, which are normally shed from the cervix or other internal body surfaces, such as the inside of the cheek or bronchial tubes. Normal cells are uniform in size, and their nuclei appear as small, dark dots when the cells are mounted on a slide and stained. In contrast, abnormal cells vary greatly in size and shape, and their nuclei are large and irregular.

The Pap smear is usually interpreted by a laboratory, which grades it from I to V:

Class I. All cells are normal.

Class II. Some cells are abnormal, but none indicate cancer. In these cases, the physician will ask the patient to return for a repeat test in three to six months.

Class III. More abnormal cells are present than in Class II, but there is no definite evidence of cancer. A repeat Pap smear may be performed, but in any case, a biopsy is needed to rule out the presence of cancer or a precancerous lesion. Some patients with noncancerous overgrowth of the

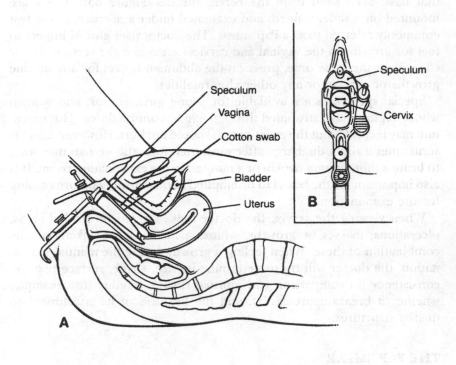

Speculum

Vagina

Cotton swab

Bladder

Uterus

Speculum

Cervix

A

B

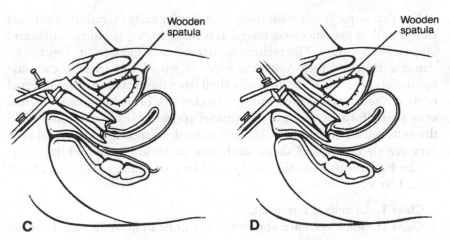

Wooden
spatula

Wooden
spatula

C

D

Figure 63 Steps in doing a Pap smear. **A.** Cotton swab technique for cervical smear. **B.** Cervix seen through speculum. **C.** Cervical scraping smear. **D.** Vaginal smear.

cervix—such as that commonly seen in DES daughters—often will have subsequent Pap smears that are normal without any treatment.

Class IV. Some of the cells are definitely cancerous. In these cases, the doctor will order a biopsy, and other cancer tests.

Class V. Many cells show signs of cancer. The cells are more disorganized and less mature than in Class IV. Again, the doctor will advise a biopsy and other tests to determine the extent and nature of the cancer.

Before undergoing a Pap test, a woman should allow the cells of the cervix to accumulate undisturbed for a few days before seeing the doctor. This includes the avoidance of tampons, birth-control foams or jellies, or douches. By following these guidelines, she can help ensure the accuracy of the test.

Although the primary objective of the Pap test is to study cells shed from the cervix, it also may reveal other cancers from nearby reproductive organs, such as the vagina or endometrium (the lining of the uterine cavity). However, the test is not as accurate in detecting cancer of these other organs. It is 90 percent accurate for vaginal cancer and only 50 percent accurate for endometrial cancer, compared to 90 to 95 percent accuracy for cervical cancer. The Pap test may also reveal certain infections, such as yeast or fungal infections of the vagina, and genital herpes.

OTHER DIAGNOSTIC TESTS

A number of tests, in addition to the Pap smear, are used in the diagnosis of gynecological cancer. These include colposcopy, in which a speculum is inserted into the vagina and the area is viewed with a magnifying instrument called a colposcope (Figure 64). After the speculum is inserted, the doctor may swab the area with a brown solution—a procedure called a Schiller test. Any abnormal areas will then appear white or yellow. During colposcopy, a doctor may also remove tissue samples with a special punch instrument for a biopsy. No anesthesia is needed for a colposcopy, which can be performed in ten or fifteen minutes in a doctor's office—a great advance over the surgery formerly necessary to get a close view of these areas. If tissue for a biopsy is removed during colposcopy, an uncomfortable sensation somewhat like menstrual cramps may occur. There also may be a brown vaginal discharge for a couple of days due to the application of a solution to prevent bleeding. But there are no adverse long-term effects.

If colposcopy and biopsy do not provide a definite diagnosis, a more extensive cone biopsy, or conization, may be needed. This involves removing a larger, cone-shaped section of tissue. The procedure usually requires general anesthesia and a brief hospitalization. In diagnosing cervical cancer or precancerous lesions, conization usually entails remov-

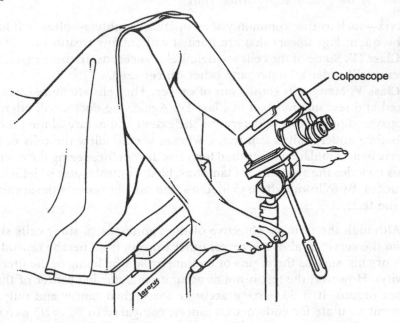

Colposcope

Figure 64 Colposcope examination.

ing tissue from the center of the cervix. This should not cause later fertility problems (Figure 65).

Because cancers of the reproductive organs often spread to adjoining organs, such as the ureters, bladder, rectum or colon, other tests of these organs may be ordered before treatment begins. These tests may include an intravenous pyelogram of the kidneys and a cystogram of the bladder. In these examinations, a dye or some other contrast medium is injected into the organs to make their structures visible on X-ray films. A barium enema, in which a solution containing barium is infused into the colon followed by X-ray studies, may be performed to study the lower intestinal tract. The colon and rectum also may be examined directly via colonoscopy, a procedure in which a long, hollow tube with fiberoptic viewing devices is inserted into the anus and threaded into the large bowel. If the cancer seems advanced, body scans of the bones and liver, as well as studies of the lymph glands, may be needed to detect any spread or metastases to distant organs.

CANCER OF THE CERVIX

Cervical cancer is one of the most common cancers, occurring in 2 percent of all women by the age of eighty. About 61,000 cases are diag-

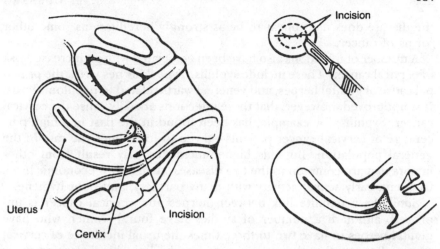

Figure 65 Cone biopsy of cervix.

nosed each year; 45,000 of these are in the earliest stages when the disease is almost totally curable. Even so, only half of the women with invasive cervical cancer are cured, largely because of delay in diagnosis and treatment.

Who Gets Cervical Cancer?

The average age for diagnosis of preinvasive cervical cancer is thirty-eight, and most cases of invasive cancer occur in women forty-five to fifty-five years old, with the incidence dropping for older women. Although the causes of cervical cancer are unknown, several risk factors have been identified that appear to increase the likelihood of getting it. Most of these involve sexual or marital history. For example, cervical cancer occurs significantly more often in women who become sexually active at an early age and who have multiple sex partners. This has been substantiated by studies that have found that prostitutes have four times the expected rate of cervical cancer, while nuns have a very low incidence.

The risk of cervical cancer also appears to be related to economic class and ethnic background. Women at the lowest end of the economic scale have almost five times more cervical cancer than upper-income women. Black women have twice the incidence of whites. Jewish women have a very low rate, but experts are divided on whether this stems from heredity, personal hygiene, fidelity, or the circumcision of Jewish men. A family history of cervical cancer indicates a slightly higher-than-usual risk, but the disease does not appear to be as strongly hereditary as some other forms of cancer.

A number of infections also have been associated with an increased risk of cervical cancer. These include syphilis, Type 2 herpes virus, the principal cause of genital herpes, and venereal warts related to papilloma virus. It is not proved, however, that these infections actually cause the cervical cancer. Syphilis, for example, has been found in the past in a high percentage of cervical cancer patients—three to four times the rate in the general population. But this higher incidence may result from other factors that are common to the two diseases, such as low economic level, frequent, early sexual activity with many partners, and poor hygiene.

Similarly, a definite link between herpes and cervical cancer is unproved, although a number of studies have found women who have genital herpes to have two to three times the usual incidence of cervical cancer. Reports that the two diseases may be linked has alarmed many women and health officials in recent years because of the rapid increase in genital herpes, particularly among young women. Although a number of possible associations have been found, most of these are largely circumstantial. For example, an unusually large number of women with cervical cancer have antibodies to herpes, showing that they were exposed to the virus at some time. But data from antibody tests may be inconclusive because it is hard to tell the antibodies for Type 2 herpes virus from those of Type 1, the herpes virus that causes cold sores. Also, women whose risk of cervical cancer is increased by early, frequent sexual intercourse with multiple partners also are more likely to acquire genital herpes. Finally, many women with herpes never get cervical cancer, and conversely, many women with cervical cancer have never had genital herpes. Studies with laboratory animals have found that cancer can be produced by injecting the animals with herpes-infected cells. More research is needed, however, before we will know if this applies to humans. In the meantime, doctors recommend that women with genital herpes be particularly diligent about having regular pelvic examinations and Pap tests. At present, a papilloma virus, responsible for genital warts, has been implicated as a factor in cervical cancer.

Many other factors have been studied without finding any link to cervical cancer. These include menstrual history, number of pregnancies, and the use of birth control devices such as diaphragms or IUDs. Coal tar derivatives in douches, various vaginal creams, and similar products also have been studied; while these may irritate the cervix, they have not been clearly linked to cervical cancer.

The use of oral contraceptives also has been extensively studied to learn whether there is a possible association with cervical cancer. So far, the results indicate that birth control pills do not increase the risk of cervical cancer, although this is a subject of continued controversy and speculation. Again, a number of other factors must be considered in assessing any risk. Women whose frequent sexual activity with numerous partners places them at increased risk tend to prefer oral contraception. And women who do not use oral contraceptives tend to use barrier methods, such as diaphragms or condoms, which may actually protect against cervical cancer. Women with mild or moderate dysplasia who want to use birth control pills should have a pelvic examination and a Pap test at least once a year.

Patterns of Growth

Cervical cancer usually grows very slowly, and before the cervix shows definite signs of malignancy, it goes through a number of precancerous stages. The earliest is called dysplasia, which is a change in some of the cells that make up the surface of the cervix. In some women, this cell layer increases its activity, and as the cells proliferate, they lose their usual structural organization. This stage is not cancerous, and the cells often return to normal without treatment.

When the entire surface of the cervix has undergone these early changes, the growths may enter a phase in which the cells fail to mature normally—a characteristic of cancer cells. At this stage, these undifferentiated cells do not spread to or invade neighboring tissue. The growths are therefore referred to as "carcinoma *in situ*," which means "in its original position." At this preinvasive stage, the cancer is almost always without symptoms. It may remain localized for eight to ten years before it begins invading surrounding tissue. Preinvasive cervical cancer can be detected by a Pap smear 97 percent of the time and prompt treatment can bring a total cure. Once the cancer invades the surrounding tissue, it may still be highly curable, but more extensive treatment may be required.

Although dysplasia and carcinoma *in situ* are easily detected by a Pap smear, a biopsy is needed to confirm a diagnosis of cancer. A biopsy that requires only a small tissue sample may be done on an outpatient basis; a more extensive biopsy requires hospitalization (usually only overnight) and general anesthesia. Curettage (scraping of the lining of the uterus) may be performed at the same time to determine whether the cancer has spread to the body of the uterus.

Cervical cancer spreads in "tongues" of malignant cells that invade the surrounding tissue, extending to lymph channels and blood vessels, and thence to lymph nodes and to distant organs. The earliest stage—carcinoma *in situ*—is almost always located at the external end of the cervix. From here, it usually extends upward, into the cervical canal. When it becomes invasive, the growth may proceed sideways or backward, toward the pelvic wall. Less often, it spreads downward, beneath the surface of the vagina, or into the large bowel and bladder. The growth is classified into five stages:

Stage 0. Preinvasive carcinoma *in situ* (100 percent five-year survival).

Stage I. Cancer confined to the cervix (85 percent five-year survival).

Stage II. Cancer extends to the upper third of the vagina or the tissue around the uterus (the parametrium), but not the pelvic wall (50 to 60 percent five-year survival).

Stage III. Cancer involves the lower third of the vagina and/or the pelvic side wall, and possibly the kidneys (30 percent five-year survival).

Stage IV. Cancer extends beyond the pelvic organs, involving the bladder or rectum, a metastases to distant organs, most often the lung, liver, and sometimes the bone (10 percent five-year survival).

In Stages III and IV, the cancer also involves the lymph nodes in 50 percent or more of the patients, increasing the chance of distant spread. As noted earlier, extensive cancer may be present before there is any pain or bleeding. In some cases, the cancer is quite extensive before intersecting a blood vessel to cause any bleeding.

Treatment of Cervical Cancer

The method of treating cervical cancer depends largely upon the stage of the disease. Preinvasive cervical cancer, which is virtually 100 percent curable, often can be treated without extensive surgery, and in many cases, women can even bear children after the treatment. More extensive invasive cancer usually requires a hysterectomy—removal of the uterus and cervix—or irradiation, either of which end a woman's ability to have children.

The treatments most often used for preinvasive cervical cancer are conization, cryosurgery, or hysterectomy. Conization involves the removal of cancerous tissue in a cone-shaped wedge. This operation requires general anesthesia and a short hospital stay. It is used most often in women who still want to have children. Careful follow-up to ensure against recurrence is a must; most doctors urge a semiannual pelvic examination and Pap test following conization.

Cryosurgery uses carbon dioxide to kill the cancerous cells by freezing. It is used to treat severe dysplasia and preinvasive cancer, and may be performed in a doctor's office since it requires no anesthesia. It may cause minor discomfort, similar to that of mild menstrual cramps, which can be controlled by pain medication. Cryosurgery may be followed by an irritating vaginal discharge lasting two to four weeks. If this occurs, sanitary napkins, not tampons, should be used. To protect the cervix, sexual intercourse should be avoided for ten days. Complications such as fever, chills, heavy bleeding, or pain should be reported promptly to the doctor.

Stage I through Stage IV cancers are usually treated with surgery, radiation, or a combination of the two. The general state of health, the stage of the cancer, and response to radiation determines the treatment that is best suited to an individual patient. In general, however, Stage I cancers are usually treated by radical hysterectomy alone; the other stages may be treated by either surgery or radiation, or, in some cases, a combination of the two. Chemotherapy is used infrequently to treat patients whose cancers have spread to other organs or for those whose cancers have recurred or in whom other therapies have not been effective.

Hysterectomy

Although hysterectomy literally means "removal of the uterus," in hysterectomy for cancer of the cervix other structures and tissues that may be affected by cancer also are removed. In Stage I or II cancers, the uterus, the upper vagina, the ligaments supporting the uterus and adjacent lymph nodes are usually removed. This may occasionally be followed by radiation therapy. In any case, treatment gives a 65 to 85 percent survival rate. Whether or not the ovaries also are removed depends upon a number of factors, including the woman's age and general health. Some surgeons advocate removing the ovaries, especially in women who are approaching menopause or who have already stopped menstruating, on the grounds that this is a sure preventive of subsequent ovarian cancer. Other doctors believe that the ovaries should be left intact in young women, to prevent an abrupt, artificial menopause. These alternatives and the pros and cons of each should be discussed by the woman and her doctor before the operation (Figure 66).

In more advanced cancer, radiation therapy is usually chosen. Infrequently, if the bowel or bladder is involved the surgeon may perform an exenteration. In this operation, the lower colon, rectum, or bladder—or any combination of these depending upon the extent of the cancer—will be removed, as well as the affected sex organs. If the rectum and/or bladder are removed, artificial openings (ostomies) to provide for the exit of body wastes will be needed. (For more on this type of surgery, see Chapter 18, "Cancer of the Colon and Rectum," and Chapter 33, "Urinary Tract Cancer.")

Radical hysterectomy and exenteration are usually performed through a four-to-eight-inch incision below the navel. The incision may be either horizontal or vertical. A vaginal hysterectomy—removal of the uterus through the vagina—does not leave a scar, but it prevents the surgeon from seeing the full extent of the cancer. For this reason, a vaginal hysterectomy, which is useful in treating noncancerous conditions, usually is not recommended for cervical or uterine cancer.

The average hysterectomy takes forty-five to ninety minutes, but radi-

Different Types of Hysterectomies

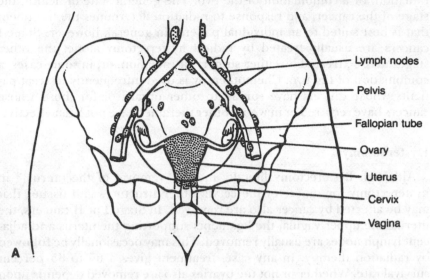

- Lymph nodes
- Pelvis
- Fallopian tube
- Ovary
- Uterus
- Cervix
- Vagina

A

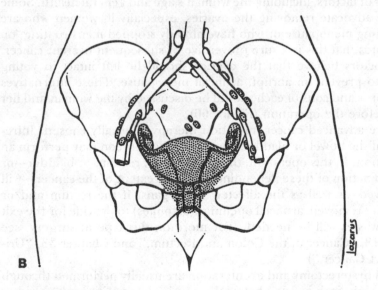

B

Figure 66A Hysterectomy for noncancerous conditions (shading shows what is removed).

66B Radical hysterectomy (uterus, uterine ligaments, top third of vagina, ovaries, fallopian tubes, and lower lymph nodes are removed, others are sampled).

cal hysterectomy may last for several hours. The woman usually is given a general anesthetic, but spinal anesthesia is sometimes used. Most abdominal surgery is followed by temporary difficulty in urination and defecation, and hysterectomy may exacerbate this because of the need to shift the bladder to obtain access to the cervix. Therefore, a urinary catheter may be used for the first few days following surgery. Bladder and bowel function may not return to normal for a week or more; the average hospital stay for a radical hysterectomy is ten to fourteen days. A further recuperation period of four weeks at home may be advised; but, in general, most women can resume normal activities in six to eight weeks.

Radical hysterectomy is generally considered a safe operation in expert hands, with a very low mortality rate. The most common complication is a ureterovaginal fistula—a small opening between the ureters (the tubes that carry urine from the kidney to the bladder) and the vagina, but this is uncommon. Any unusual bleeding, pain, fever, chills, or other complications should be reported promptly to the doctor.

Most women have a vaginal discharge or some light bleeding after a hysterectomy. This usually subsides in a week. Sexual intercourse should be avoided for six weeks, but after that a woman should expect to resume normal sexual relations. Many women fear that a hysterectomy in some way alters sexual pleasure or response. In most cases, there is no physical cause of diminished sexual pleasure or desire. Women are fully capable of orgasm after a hysterectomy because the key structures—the clitoris and lower vagina—remain intact. In unusual cases, there may be scarring or a shortening of the vagina, resulting in painful intercourse, but these complications are the exception rather than the rule. Sexual problems following a hysterectomy are more likely to be of psychological than physical origin, and they should be discussed with the doctor and sexual partner. Indeed, many women find that they take even more pleasure in sex following a hysterectomy because they are freed of any worries over becoming pregnant.

Radiation Therapy

In women whose cancers respond to radiation therapy, this treatment provides a cure rate comparable to that of surgery. In fact, radiation is the preferred therapy for women in whom surgery may pose an added risk; for example, the elderly, diabetics, or patients weakened by other diseases.

However, not all cervical cancers respond to radiation therapy. To test radiation sensitivity, the physician can use a small dose of radiation—either as an implant or in the form of X rays—followed a week later by a biopsy to gauge its effectiveness. The biopsy is examined to determine if the cancer cells show any changes, such as death or dissolution. If the radiation does not appear to be working, then surgery is the treatment of choice.

Radiation therapy can be administered in a variety of ways. Radium, radon, and radioactive cobalt or cesium are the radiation sources used most often to treat gynecological cancers. X rays may be beamed through the skin or radioactive implants may be placed in the uterus or the vagina, or both. Radioactive implants usually are inserted into the uterus and/or vagina under general anesthesia, and remain in place for two to four days (Figure 67). Although a variety of devices are used to keep the implant in the proper position, the woman generally must remain hospitalized and move about as little as possible to avoid radiation damage to adjacent organs. A bladder catheter is used to take care of urination, and a special low-residue diet is used to avoid the necessity for bowel movements. Any discomfort from the implants may be treated with sedation or pain medication. Nausea, another common complication of radiation therapy, usually can be controlled with antinausea drugs. (For more information, see Chapter 8, "Radiation Therapy.")

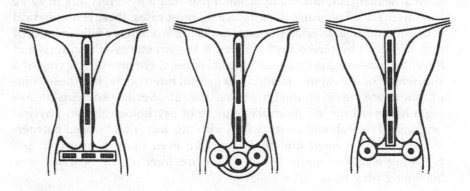

Figure 67 Different types of radioactive implants.

While the radiation implant is in place, the woman will stay in a private room, with strict limitations on how long nurses and visitors may remain in the room. Visitors should be limited to people over the age of eighteen who are not pregnant or likely to become pregnant soon. They are advised not to come too close to the patient's bed. Nurses may wear lead aprons to protect themselves from unnecessary radiation exposure.

The implant usually is removed in the hospital room, with a mild sedative given beforehand. After the implant is removed, the woman can return to a normal life, with these exceptions: for the first ten days to two weeks, she should not take a tub bath, have sexual intercourse, use tampons, or douche.

X-ray therapy also is used in conjunction with the radioactive implants. The best results are obtained with low-intensity therapy administered over a period of time, usually every day for four to six weeks. Both implants and X rays may be combined with surgery in unusual circumstances.

Follow-up after Treatment

After therapy for cervical cancer is complete, the woman should return for follow-up visits at least once every two months during the first year, once every four months during the second year, every six months in third and fourth years, and once a year thereafter. Pap tests are used to evaluate the success of surgical treatment. Women treated with radiation, however, must undergo biopsies because Pap smears in these patients may be misleading. Radiation causes changes in cells similar to those that indicate possible cancer. Biopsies should be negative three months after the ulcers and other effects of radiation have healed.

Preventive Hysterectomy

One out of every three American women over the age of fifty has undergone a hysterectomy. Most of these operations are performed for noncancerous conditions, such as fibroids or hyperplasia. In recent years, a good deal of controversy has surrounded the need for many of these operations. As early as 1953, published reports maintained that up to one third of all hysterectomies probably were unnecessary. Such reports have raised an outcry from consumer groups as well as segments of the medical community. In some cases, the necessity for the surgery can be determined only after laboratory analysis of the uterus. An example might be heavy and prolonged menstrual bleeding, which is often seen in women approaching menopause.

A prophylactic, or preventive, hysterectomy may be recommended for a woman who has severe hyperplasia, especially if her family is complete. Sometimes the uterus is removed during surgery to remove adjacent organs, such as the ovaries. This is considered a good practice in postmenopausal women who are otherwise healthy. The likelihood of developing cervical cancer drops after age sixty-five, so prophylaxis becomes less important in older women. Hysterectomy is not recommended for young women with cervical abnormalities related to DES exposure before birth, since these changes are almost always benign. (These women should be carefully followed, however, and should have an annual Pap test.)

Women in any doubt over whether a hysterectomy is needed should not hesitate to seek a second opinion. Insurance companies, county and state medical societies, and teaching hospitals or university medical centers all are good sources of doctors qualified to give an impartial second opinion.

CANCER OF THE UTERUS AND ENDOMETRIUM

Most uterine cancer begins in the lining, or the endometrium. This type of cancer has increased considerably since the late nineteen-forties. At one time, it was only one sixth as common as cervical cancer; now it is more common, with about 39,000 cases diagnosed each year, resulting in approximately 6,000 deaths. Several reasons have been cited for this increase. Women are living longer, and thus have more opportunity to develop uterine cancer. The increased use of estrogens following menopause also has been linked to a rise in endometrial cancer. Finally, improved diagnostic techniques are enabling doctors to detect these cancers in earlier, more treatable stages.

Most uterine cancer occurs in women between the ages of fifty and sixty-five, with a mean age of sixty-one. About a fourth of the patients are under the age of fifty, but only 4 percent are younger than forty years of age. Heredity appears to be important: 12 to 28 percent of the patients have a family history of this type of cancer. Women with uterine cancer seem to be of a higher social and economic status than patients with cervical cancer. Some have never married or had children, and an unusual number are overweight. Many have diabetes and high blood pressure—both conditions that may be attributed to weight and age. Obesity is a clear cofactor in causing uterine cancer.

Menstrual problems also tend to be more common in women with uterine cancer. Many women who develop the disease before menopause have histories of excessive menstrual flow at puberty or later, unusually frequent periods, or times when menstruation stopped for a while. Women whose cancer develops after menopause frequently have continued menstruating after the age of fifty, or have had excessive or prolonged bleeding at menopause.

The Role of Estrogen

The role of estrogen in endometrial cancer is a subject of continuing research and debate. Though this relationship was discovered more than thirty years ago, in the mid-nineteen-seventies a number of studies confirmed that women taking estrogen for postmenopausal symptoms had more than four times the risk of endometrial cancer, compared to other women their age who were not on hormone therapy. Also, many of the disorders associated with a higher rate of uterine cancer—menstrual problems or failure to ovulate, for example—may be linked to hormonal disorders in which excessive estrogen may be present. The increased incidence of uterine cancer in obese women also may be linked to excessive estrogen. Most estrogen is produced in the ovaries until menopause, when the amount in the body decreases slowly. However, a certain amount of estrogen also is manufactured in the fat cells and overweight women have higher levels of this hormone than their normal-weight counterparts. Although evidence that estrogen alone causes cancer may be incomplete, the incidence of endometrial cancer seems to rise with the dosage and duration of estrogen therapy. In addition, the hormone has been shown to cause endometrial cancer in laboratory animals and precancerous adenomatous hyperplasia in women.

Estrogen therapy is very effective in controlling the hot flashes and sweats caused by the diminishing supply of natural estrogen during the menopause. There is also evidence to suggest that estrogen therapy as well as diet and exercise may prevent or reduce the thinning of bones in older women—a condition that can lead to fractures.

Most experts now recommend a conservative approach to estrogen therapy in older women. Many urge that if estrogen is used, it be given in the lowest dose needed to control symptoms, and that it be continued for no more than one year. Many doctors also now recommend that the estrogen be discontinued every few weeks, and that another female hormone, progesterone, be given for ten to thirteen days each month. This leads to a shedding of the endometrium, similar to that which occurs during menstruation. Thus women on this combination therapy will have periods, even though they are no longer ovulating. By preventing a buildup of the endometrium, which occurs when estrogen alone is given, doctors expect that this will minimize the risk of endometrial cancer during estrogen therapy. In any event, the dosage should be reassessed after six months, and women on estrogen therapy should have a pelvic examination and endometrial tissue sample every year or two. Estrogen should not be prescribed for depression or nervous disorders or other menopausal symptoms unrelated to hormones. And no woman with cancer of the breast or uterus or with undiagnosed vaginal bleeding should take estrogen. While estrogen is a potent hormone with several beneficial qualities, it should not be prescribed casually or without control. Under controlled circumstances, however, its benefits will be greater than its risks.

Symptoms and Diagnosis

Bleeding is the first sign of 90 percent of uterine cancers. In 10 percent, a watery discharge occurs before bleeding. If uterine cancer is suspected, tests to examine cells from the endometrium will be performed. A Pap test is less than 60 percent accurate in detecting endometrial cancer. To

increase the chances of obtaining cells from the uterine lining, the doctor
will try to obtain the tissue samples from as high in the cervical canal as
possible by using an aspirator. Diagnosis is confirmed by a dilation and
curettage—an examination, commonly referred to as a D&C, in which the
cervix is widened or dilated and the uterus lining is scraped with an
instrument called a curette—or by an aspiration curettage. This entails
using a long, thin disposable tube connected to a syringe or vacuum
pump to withdraw a small tissue sample (Figure 68). This method requires no anesthesia and can be done in a doctor's office. A D&C involves
using a light anesthesia and is usually performed in a hospital, although it
does not necessarily involve an overnight stay. To avoid unnecessary
D&Cs in premenopausal women, most experts recommend that a Pap test
and colposcopy be performed first. This will exclude the possibility of
cervical cancer as the cause of the symptoms. Then a month's wait will
determine whether the menstrual cycle will return to normal. If bleeding
continues after the next period, a D&C, or aspiration curettage, should
then be performed to determine the source.

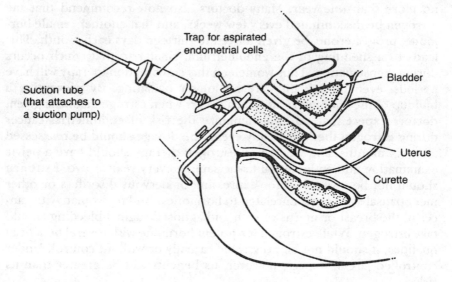

Figure 68   Uterine suction curettage.

Abnormal bleeding is difficult to determine during the menopause. In
the large majority of women, menstruation gradually tapers off. Periods
will be skipped irregularly, but with increasing frequency. It is sometimes
hard to tell if the bleeding is abnormal, and not just another irregular

period. Remember, however, that the bleeding due to cancer is "lawless"; it follows no rules in frequency, duration, amount, or character.

After the menopause, it is easier to document the onset of abnormal bleeding. Any bleeding that occurs more than a year after the last menstrual period should be investigated, even though only a third of such cases will be due to cancer. The bleeding is usually scant to moderate at the beginning, but follows no pattern.

In many cases of abnormal or heavy bleeding during menopause, an overgrowth of the uterine lining—a condition called endometrial hyperplasia—will be found. A variant of this overgrowth, adenomatous hyperplasia, has been shown to precede endometrial cancer. Progesterone, a hormone that stimulates menstruation, may be given for ten to thirteen days in several cycles to help the uterus shed the extra layer of endometrial cells. The doctor may then decide to wait to see if the condition subsides after the menopause is complete. If the overgrowth persists and intensifies, a hysterectomy may be recommended.

Classification and Treatment

Early diagnosis and treatment of uterine cancer is important because it can spread to other organs. The most common patterns of spread are from the lining of the uterus along the inside walls and into the cervical canal or fallopian tubes, or into the muscle of the uterus, and through the lymph ducts to the ovaries. It also may spread through the circulatory system to distant organs, such as the lungs and bones.

Traditionally, uterine cancer is classified according to degree of involvement. We also classify the cancer according to the size of the tumor. Using these classification systems, the various stages are as follows:

Stage 0. Overgrowth, or adenomatous hyperplasia, of the endometrium. This is a precancerous condition that may initially be treated by hormone therapy or a D&C. If the hyperplasia persists, hysterectomy may be recommended, especially in women near menopause or whose families are complete. Five-year survival is 100 percent.

Stage I. Cancer is confined to the body of the uterus and the uterus is of normal size. Hysterectomy with removal of tubes and ovaries is the preferred treatment, and may be the only therapy needed, particularly if the cancer is small and well differentiated. The five-year survival is more than 90 percent in such instances.

Stage II. The cancer involves the cervix as well as the uterus. A combination of radiation therapy plus removal of the uterus and ovaries and sometimes lymph nodes, cervix, and part of the vagina may be advised. The radiation therapy may include both a radium implant before surgery and X-ray treatments either before or after surgery. The five-year survival is about 60 to 70 percent.

Stage III and Stage IV. The cancer has spread beyond the reproductive organs to other pelvic structures or to the bladder or rectum or to distant organs. Treatment is individualized according to the organs involved. Radiation therapy will be administered before and/or after surgery. Depending upon the other organs involved, chemotherapy also may be administered. Survival depends upon the degree of spread and involvement of other organs.

In virulent tumors of any stage, the pelvic and higher abdominal lymph nodes are biopsied to determine the need for adjunctive radiotherapy or chemotherapy. By far the most commonly encountered tumor is the Stage I and an excellent cure rate can be expected.

CANCER OF THE OVARIES

Ovarian cancer is the third most common gynecological cancer. There are about 18,000 new cases each year, and about 11,400 deaths. The relatively poor survival rate (about 41 to 43 percent) can be attributed to the fact that ovarian cancer seldom produces any symptoms until it has reached an advanced stage.

Ovarian cancer is rare in women under the age of thirty-five, and is most often diagnosed before the age of sixty-three. When it occurs in premenopausal women, it is more curable than when it strikes after menopause. Women with ovarian cancer tend to have had few children, and may have a history of menstrual problems. A history of breast cancer or cancers of the intestine or rectum increases the risk of ovarian cancer. However, none of these factors is common enough to define a high risk group.

Diagnosis of Ovarian Cancer

As yet, there is no simple screening test for ovarian cancer. Pap smears and colposcopy are not helpful in detecting cancer of the ovaries. Occasionally a biopsy of the endometrium will suggest a cancer farther up the reproductive tract, or X rays of the pelvic area will detect a dermoid cyst, a type of tumor that may infrequently become malignant.

When symptoms occur, they are often mistaken for a gastrointestinal problem. Abdominal discomfort, swelling, nausea, vomiting, constipation, flatulence, or urinary urgency, pain, or retention are the most common symptoms. These are caused by the tumor pressing against the bowel or bladder. But the cancer may grow as large as a grapefruit without producing any symptoms. Vaginal bleeding occurs in only one out of four cases.

When ovarian cancer is suspected or an ovarian tumor is felt during a pelvic examination, a biopsy should be performed. Four fifths of all ovarian growths are benign, but to determine this, biopsy samples must be obtained. This may involve an exploratory laparotomy, in which an incision is made below the navel, and an instrument called a laparoscope is inserted into the pelvic cavity (Figure 69). The laparoscope enables the doctor to look at the ovaries and other pelvic organs, and also to obtain tissue samples. In some cases, more extensive exploratory surgery may be required, but this is not as common today as in the past due to refined laparoscopic techniques.

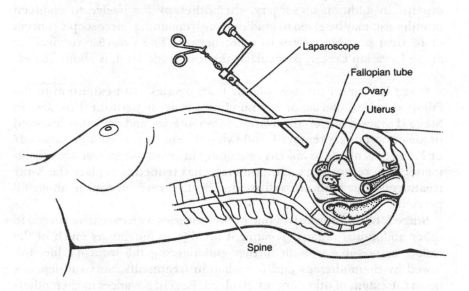

Figure 69 Exploratory laparotomy.

Classifications of Ovarian Cancer

Ovarian cancers are classified according to stage, cell type, and grade. About 85 percent of all ovarian cancers are epithelial tumors, meaning they arise in the tissue covering the ovary (epithelial tissue lines the various cavities or covers the organs). The grade refers to the nature of the tumor cells; for example, whether they are mature, well-differentiated, and low-grade cells as opposed to immature, undifferentiated, and high-grade cells. Low-grade tumors are often referred to as "borderline," with a low level of malignancy, and therefore have a better outlook than high-grade cancers. The stages of ovarian cancer are as follows:

Stage I. Cancer is limited to one or both ovaries, with little or no accumulation of fluid (ascites). Most ovarian cancers in this stage are treated by removal of the ovaries, tubes, and uterus. The fold of fatty tissue that is suspended from the adjacent bowel (the omentum) also may be removed. In some cases, in which the cancer is of a low grade and limited to one ovary, the second ovary and uterus may be spared if the woman is young. Before such a decision is made, biopsies from the second ovary and various other pelvic and abdominal organs should be examined and show no sign of cancer, and even then, most doctors would advise against this conservative treatment because of the high risk of missing a microscopic cancer in the other ovary or other reproductive organs. In addition to surgery, chemotherapy for twelve to eighteen months also may be given to eradicate any remaining microscopic cancers or to treat possible spread to other organs. The five-year survival for Stage I ovarian cancer, particularly the low-grade kind, is about 78 percent.

Stage II. Cancer involves one or both ovaries, with extension to the fallopian tubes, uterus, or surrounding pelvic or peritoneal tissues. In Stage II ovarian cancer, the ovaries, tubes, uterus, and any other involved tissue or organs are removed. Following the surgery, chemotherapy and/or X-ray treatments to kill any remaining microscopic cancer are recommended. In recent years, chemotherapy has tended to replace the X-ray treatments, but both are still used. The five-year survival is about 68 percent.

Stage III. Cancer involves one or both ovaries with extensive spread to other abdominal organs. Treatment involves removing as much of the cancer as possible without further endangering the woman's life, followed by chemotherapy and/or radiation treatments. Survival depends upon the extent of other organs involved. Recent advances in chemotherapy have improved the cure rate and offered hope for even more advances.

Stage IV. Cancer involves one or both ovaries, with distant spread outside the abdominal cavity, for example, to the lungs or bones. Treatment is the same as for Stage III.

Where to Go for Treatment

Ovarian cancer requires the skill of an adept surgeon who is experienced in treating this disease. Some medical centers have better survival rates than others, although it is not clear whether this is due to the type of cases (for example, low-grade vs. high-grade) treated or the skill and experience of the staff. Before undergoing treatment, it is important to determine that the surgeon and other members of the team are experienced in treating ovarian cancer, and are up-to-date on the newest advances in both chemotherapy and radiation treatments. Since most ovarian cancers are detected in Stages III and IV, experience in handling potentially complicated cases is important. Before undergoing treatment, the woman should determine that the surgeon and other members of the treatment team have this kind of experience. Names of qualified physicians may be obtained from Comprehensive Cancer Centers, major medical centers, and teaching hospitals, or from the National Cancer Institute. (See "Directory of Resources.")

Follow-up

Women who have undergone treatment for ovarian cancer should be followed closely for at least several years. This follow-up includes frequent pelvic examinations, breast examinations, and prompt investigation of any symptoms, such as abdominal swelling, pain, weight loss, constipation, nausea, or vomiting. Sometimes, usually following completion of the radiation treatments or chemotherapy, a second laparotomy may be performed. This "second look" operation has several purposes: It can determine whether the radiation or chemotherapy has reduced a previously inoperable cancer to one that can now be removed or whether there has been any recurrence. Or if a patient is still on chemotherapy, this follow-up laparotomy can determine if the patient has progressed to the point where the drugs can be discontinued.

Artificial Menopause

Premenopausal women who have their ovaries removed will experience an abrupt artificial menopause, with the symptoms associated with this stage of a woman's life. Obviously, menstruation will cease, as will the ability to bear children. There may be hot flushes and sweats, and a thinning of the vaginal tissue. Not all women will experience these symptoms, and in most they are not severe enough to require treatment. Severe symptoms can be controlled with hormone therapy, if this is not contraindicated by the cancer. In some patients, hormone replacement therapy is valuable even if the woman is free of symptoms.

Many misconceptions persist about the menopause. It does not signal the end of sexual activity or its enjoyment; indeed, many women find they are more sexually responsive because they are freed from the fear of pregnancy. If vaginal thinning and dryness makes intercourse uncomfortable, a lubricating cream or estrogen preparation should be used. Some women may have an increased tendency to gain weight, especially around their abdomens. Our nutritional requirements are lower as we grow older; to maintain ideal weight, it is important to decrease food consumption and, at the same time, increase exercise. To prevent a "middle-aged spread," abdominal muscles should be kept in tone by doing exercises designed to strengthen them. Exercise and adequate calcium intake are important to maintain the bones of postmenopausal women.

CANCER OF THE VAGINA

Vaginal cancer is rare, accounting for less than 2 percent of gynecological cancers. Most occur in older women; the incidence rises after the age of fifty, with most patients in their sixties. In rare instances, however, vaginal cancer also may occur in young women and adolescents. Many of these cases involve young women whose mothers took DES to prevent a threatened miscarriage. This practice was halted in the 1970s after it was discovered that the hormone caused reproductive-tract problems in the offspring.

Symptoms and Diagnosis

The most common symptoms of vaginal cancer are abnormal bleeding, staining, or a watery discharge. The symptoms may occur after intercourse, which may be painful. Difficult or painful urination or pain in the pelvic area may be signs of more advanced cancer.

Vaginal cancer may be detected by a Pap smear or during a pelvic examination. The presence of whitish, raised patches on the surface of the vagina may be precancerous lesions and indicate the need for a biopsy to establish the diagnosis.

Treatment

Vaginal cancers are treated by radiation, surgery, or a combination of the two. External radiation treatments are often combined with radium implants inside the vagina. This method is most effective for early cancer, especially when it involves only the upper third of the vaginal wall. The five-year survival rate is 55 percent. However, if the cancer has spread to the tissue surrounding the vagina, the survival rate is 31 percent or less.

Surgical treatment involves removal of the cancerous portion of the vagina as well as a hysterectomy. Since the vagina is elastic, the patient can usually have normal intercourse after healing. If more extensive surgery is necessary, plastic surgery may be used to create an artificial vagina.

DES Daughters

DES (diethylstilbestrol) was sometimes administered to pregnant women between 1945 and 1970 to prevent miscarriage. In 1971, medical studies began to show that daughters of women who took the hormone before the eighteenth week of pregnancy often had certain abnormalities of the reproductive tract. Most of these abnormalities turned out to be harmless, but in a very small number of young women, the abnormality involved a rare type of vaginal cancer called clear-cell adenocarcinoma. So far, approximately 350 cases of adenocarcinoma have been discovered among DES daughters in the United States. Because it is not known how many women took DES during pregnancy, it is impossible to compute the risk for their daughters, but the disease seems to be very rare.

The added danger of radiation in young patients makes hysterectomy the preferred treatment for adenocarcinoma. Since this type of cancer often metastasizes to the lung, yearly chest X rays are recommended. Semiannual gynecologic checkups, including Pap smears, also are advised.

Most DES abnormalities involve an overgrowth of the cervix or vagina. The area is covered by moist, red tissue of the type normally found only in the uterus. This tissue is harmless, although it may cause heavy menstrual periods. One out of five DES daughters has an extra rim of tissue around the cervix. Depending on the shape, it may be called a cockscomb, hood, collar, or pseudopolyp. These growths do not interfere with sexual activity, pregnancy, or childbirth.

Other DES abnormalities that have been reported include smaller-than-normal uteri and, among some, a difficulty in conceiving or carrying a fetus to term. So far, the majority of women exposed to DES before birth have not encountered serious problems. However, these DES daughters are still relatively young. Annual or, in some cases, semiannual gynecologic examinations, beginning with puberty, are recommended to detect any problems in early, treatable stages. The examination will be less stressful for a young girl if she knows exactly what the doctor will do: breast examination, pelvic examination, Pap smear, and perhaps colposcopy. Some girls like to have their mothers present during a gynecologic examination; in any event, the girl's feelings and fears should be discussed with the doctor beforehand.

When DES-related abnormalities were first discovered, some physicians recommended preventive hysterectomy for DES daughters, especially those with overgrowths of the cervix. Since the increased risk of cancer now seems to be very small, most experts today believe that preventive surgery is unnecessary. However, DES daughters should use birth control pills, "morning after" pills (one of the few remaining uses for DES in humans), or other estrogen products only under a physician's supervision.

CANCER OF THE VULVA

Vulvar cancer also is quite rare, making up only 3 to 4 percent of gynecologic cancers. Although the vulva—the fatty folds of flesh surrounding the vaginal opening—is the most accessible of the female reproductive organs, vulvar cancer has had a low cure rate of only 40 percent. Many more patients are now cured since the disease is diagnosed earlier, when the survival rate is 75 percent; unfortunately diagnosis is often delayed. The patient may be reluctant to consult a physician about the most common early symptoms—itching—or the physician may not recognize it as cancer, wasting months with inappropriate treatments.

Symptoms and Diagnosis

Women in their fifties and sixties are the most common victims of vulvar cancer. Its incidence shows no relationship to family history, marital or sexual factors, race, or religion. Although itching is often the only early symptom, some women may experience burning, bleeding, or a discharge. Later, a painful lump or sore may form. Leukoplakia—white patches on the surface of the vulva—occur in 40 percent of cases, and often precedes the malignancy. In fact, many experts consider these white patches precancerous and advocate their removal.

Since the outer part of the vulva is covered with skin, it is also subject to skin cancers, such as basal cell carcinomas, melanomas, and Bowen's disease. (See Chapter 30, "Skin Cancer.") Any suspicious sores or other lesions should be promptly investigated.

Treatment

Cancer of the vulva is usually treated by surgical removal of the vulva, the clitoris, and the lymph nodes in the groin and thigh. If the cancer is confined to the outer layer of skin, a simple vulvectomy, which does not involve removal of the lymph nodes, may suffice.

The opening left by the surgery is usually closed by joining the remaining skin flaps, so that skin grafts are infrequently needed. However, the removal of lymph nodes may cause fluid to collect under the skin flaps; therefore, a suction catheter may be inserted to drain away this fluid, at least for the first three days or so after the operation.

Swelling of the legs due to accumulation of fluid is the most common complication of a vulvar cancer surgery. To minimize this, antibiotics are usually given before and after surgery, and sterile saline solutions, sitz baths, and heat lamps may be used to help promote healing. Hospitalization after surgery generally lasts two weeks; most women can expect to return to work or their normal routines in six to eight weeks.

Chemotherapy, in the form of 5-fluorouracil ointment, may be used to treat very early vulvar cancer (carcinoma *in situ*). Chemotherapy also may be used for patients who cannot undergo surgery or in cases in which the cancer already has metastasized.

SEX AFTER GYNECOLOGIC CANCER

Most women—an estimated 95 percent—who undergo treatment for gynecologic cancer eventually regain their former sexual patterns. This includes sexual desire and orgasm. Counseling before and after surgery for both the woman and her sexual partner is an important element in regaining sexual function. In most cases, the only factor that can make sex impossible is the conviction that it is so.

All patients—and their sexual partners—should understand the nature of the disease, of their therapy, and of the physical, psychological, and sexual effects of that therapy. A conference with physician, surgeon, and other treating physicians is recommended following the diagnosis and before the start of therapy. Whatever her age, marital status, or level of sexual activity, the patient must know in heart and brain that most malignancies can be arrested, that she can regain her sexual function, and that no form of cancer can be transmitted to a sexual partner.

After vulvectomy or other vaginal surgery, the patient should wait until her physician recommends resuming intercourse. She and her partner should begin slowly and gently. Lubricating jelly in generous amounts is helpful. The couple may try a variety of positions before finding the most comfortable one.

If the patient finds intercourse painful despite these measures, corrective plastic surgery may help by removing scar tissue. Some physicians use a graduated set of glass tubes to teach patients that the vaginal opening is large enough for intercourse. This technique may eliminate fears contributing to the difficulty.

If vaginal intercourse remains painful, the physician or a sex therapist may teach the patient and her partner alternative means of attaining sexual pleasure. The most important factor is the willingness of the couple to work at sexual satisfaction.

Although the age of most vulvar cancer patients makes it unlikely, pregnancy is still possible after vulvectomy. Delivery may require a cesarean section.

SUMMING UP

The reproductive tract is the third most common site of cancer in American women today. This is a great improvement over former times, when the uterus was the leading site of fatal cancer in women, as it still is in some parts of the world. The great increase in cures is due to accurate, simple diagnostic techniques such as the Pap test of cervical cancer, the discovery of precancerous lesions, and modern treatment. However, broader application of these tools could make invasive cervical cancer a disease of the past, increasing the current 55 percent survival rate to 100 percent. More frequent checkups would also improve detection of uterine cancers, raising the current 70 percent survival rate.

Many women delay seeking a diagnosis through fear: fear of cancer itself, fear of loss of pelvic organs, fear of surgery or of anesthesia, fear of loss of childbearing or of sexual ability, fear of invalidism or of aging brought about by loss of the sexual organs. Many of these fears are groundless, based on inaccurate or outmoded information. For example, early diagnosis, before the development of symptoms, permits treatment without loss of sexual function, pelvic organs, or "femininity." In short, most forms of gynecologic cancer are highly curable. Regular checkups, prompt, appropriate therapy, and careful follow-up would permit the majority of patients to be cured.

29

Cancer of the Male Reproductive System

GERALD P. MURPHY, M.D., D.SC.,
K. MICHAEL CUMMINGS, PH.D.,
AND CURTIS J. METTLIN, PH.D.

INTRODUCTION

The most common sites of cancer of the male reproductive system are the prostate, testes, and penis (Figure 70). Each of these cancers has a different pattern of occurrence, and altogether they affect men from early adulthood to the last decades of life, although much more frequently after age fifty. While prostate cancer is among the most common cancers in men, penis cancer occurs very rarely in the United States. And while most cancers of the reproductive system strike late in life, testicular cancer is most common among men between the ages of fifteen and thirty-four. The possibilities of prevention, detection, and successful treatment vary according to the type of cancer but have improved enormously in all types over the past thirty years. This chapter examines these three cancers in order of the frequency of their occurrence.

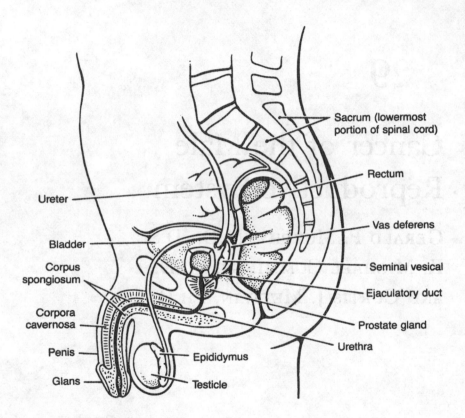

Ureter

Bladder

Corpus spongiosum

Corpora cavernosa

Penis

Glans

Epididymus

Testicle

Sacrum (lowermost portion of spinal cord)

Rectum

Vas deferens

Seminal vesical

Ejaculatory duct

Prostate gland

Urethra

Figure 70 Male genitourinary system.

PROSTATE CANCER

Cancer commonly originates in the prostate gland, which is located in the male pelvis just beneath the bladder (Figure 71). Normally about the size of a walnut, the prostate encircles the top of the urethra—the tube through which urine and the male ejaculate leave the body. One main function of the prostate gland is to provide the milky white seminal fluid that makes up the male ejaculate by mixing with sperm just before ejaculation. The other function is to act as a valve so that sperm and urine flow in the correct direction.

Before 1900, prostate cancer was considered a rare disorder. Today it is second only to lung cancer as the most frequent cancer among Ameri-

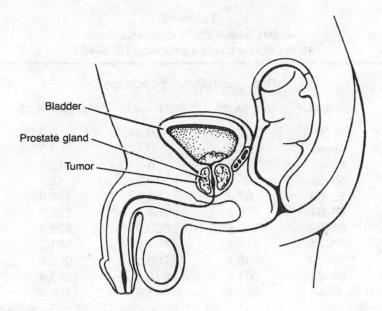

Figure 71 Prostatic cancer.

can men, accounting for 18 percent of all male cancer cases. In 1985, there were about 86,000 new cases of prostate cancer in the United States, resulting in 25,500 deaths. The reasons for the increase are not known, but the fact that an increasing number of men are living longer than at the turn of the century is a factor. Prostate cancer occurs most frequently among older men; only 2 percent of cases occur in men under age fifty. The current average age of prostate cancer patients at the time of diagnosis is about seventy-three years.

Data from three national cancer surveys conducted in the United States by the National Cancer Institute (NCI) provide a basis for examining changes in cancer incidence over time. Between 1937 and 1971, the incidence of prostate cancer increased 53.3 percent among white males and 151.6 percent among nonwhite males. Rates for black males are greater than those for whites in every age group. In the age group fifty-five to fifty-nine years, for example, the rate for blacks is 138 percent higher than for whites (Tables 18 and 19). For both whites and blacks, the

greatest increase in new cases occurred in older age groups. In fact,
prostate cancer increases in incidence with age more rapidly than any
other cancer.

Complete mortality statistics have been collected nationwide in the

Table 18
ANNUAL AGE-SPECIFIC INCIDENCE RATES
OF PROSTATIC CANCER BY RACE, 1973–1977

Rate per 100,000 population

AGE GROUP	ALL RACES	WHITE MALES	BLACK MALES
< 40	0.04	0.04	0.08
40–44	1.0	0.7	3.5
45–49	4.8	4.1	12.4
50–54	20.8	19.3	42.7
55–59	67.8	61.6	146.8
60–64	165.7	154.4	326.5
65–69	318.5	303.0	538.4
70–74	514.1	487.6	851.7
75–79	735.1	705.6	1020.9
80–84	961.2	949.5	1293.4
85+	1060.7	1043.9	1258.5

Source: Young, J. L., Jr., Percy, C. L., Asire, A. J. (eds.): "Surveillance, Epidemiology, and
End Results: Incidence and Mortality Data, 1973–1977." National Cancer Institute Monograph 57, DHHS Pub. No. (NIH) 81-2330, 1981.

United States since 1930. Deaths from prostate cancer for both white and
nonwhite men increased by about 150 percent between 1930 and 1974
(Figure 72). Until 1945, the death rate among whites was higher than
among nonwhites. Today, however, the death rate is about 87 percent

Table 19
AVERAGE ANNUAL PROSTATE CANCER INCIDENCE
RATE PER 100,000 POPULATION BY RACE, 1937–1971

YEAR	WHITE	NONWHITE
1937–1939	30	31
1947–1948	35	50
1969–1971	46	78

Rates are age-adjusted to 1950 United States population.

higher among blacks than whites. The average age of death from prostate cancer is 77 years for whites and 72.4 years for blacks.

By comparing mortality statistics of prostate cancer in different countries, researchers have tried to find clues as to the cause of the recent increases in both incidence and mortality. The highest death rates are found in Northern European countries as well as New Zealand, Australia, the United States, and Canada. The lowest death rates are found among South and Southeast Asian countries. Intermediate rates occur in Eastern European and Latin American countries.

Comparison of prostate cancer mortality rates of Japanese immigrants to the United States against those in Japan shows substantially higher mortality among Japanese-Americans. A similar observation has been documented for Polish immigrants. Such changes in risk suggest that external rather than hereditary factors may play the major role in causing this disease.

Causes

Although the actual cause of prostate cancer is unknown, the leading hypotheses suggest that the major contributing factors may include genetic or hormonal predisposition, viral, sexual, environmental, and dietary factors. Hard facts are elusive, however, because in situations where members of the same family have been afflicted, it may reflect merely their similar environmental and ethnic makeup rather than a definitive genetic cause.

Because many prostate cancers respond favorably to treatment with hormones, some experts believe that the disease may be due to hormonal factors. As evidence, researchers point to the fact that the male hormone androgen is needed for normal prostatic development and the disease has rarely, if ever, been detected in men who have been castrated, and thus have no androgen in the body. Hormonal differences have been reported in patients with prostate cancer, but it is not clear whether they preceded the cancer or occurred as a result of it. Evidence in favor of a viral cause comes from studies that have identified certain viruses occurring more frequently in prostate cancer patients than in patients with cancers in other organ systems. Other limited studies have found an association between previous gonorrheal infection and prostate cancer, but this association may reflect the effects of therapeutic procedures to control the gonorrhea infection.

Sexual factors in the origin of prostatic cancer have been suggested by the finding that the risk of prostate cancer varies with marital status, sexual experience, and a history of venereal disease. Prostate cancer patients are more likely to have been married, to have had more marital partners, to have had more premarital and extramarital sexual partners,

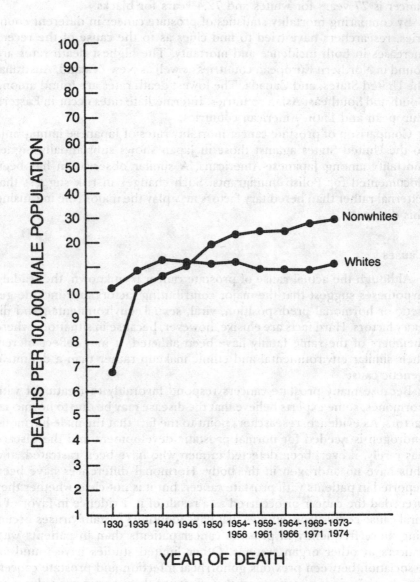

Figure 72 Age-adjusted mortality rates for prostatic cancer per 100,000 males, 1930–73, by race.

and to report greater coital frequency in the ten years preceding hospitalization than patients with no genitourinary cancer. Researchers at Roswell Park Memorial Institute in Buffalo, New York, found a lower mortality rate due to prostatic cancer among Catholic priests compared with the general population of white males of comparable ages. Other studies, however, have failed to find any association between sexual factors and the disease. It may be that sexual activity itself is not a cause of the disease but rather that sexual activity could be related to another more directly linked factor such as hormonal or viral influences.

Interest in the role of dietary factors in causing cancer has increased over the past several years. A correlation was found between prostatic cancer mortality and per capita consumption of dietary fat in forty countries. In the United States, an analysis of mortality rates from 1950 to 1969 revealed that more deaths from prostate cancer occurred in areas with high consumption of beef and dairy products. Other support for a dietary hypothesis comes from the findings of lower rates of prostate cancer among certain ethnic and religious groups which traditionally consume less fatty foods. In Japan, an increase in the consumption of milk, meat, and eggs has paralleled the recent increased rate of prostate cancer. The lower rate of prostate cancer among Seventh-Day Adventists may be related to their ovolacto vegetarian diet that is free of meat, poultry, and fish.

In attempting to isolate environmental causes of prostate cancer, researchers have discovered a link between the disease and workplace exposure to rubber and cadmium. Two studies also found an association between air pollution and prostate cancer mortality. Cigarette smoking and alcohol consumption have not been found to be associated directly with the disease, although some studies have reported a lower rate of prostate cancer in patients with cirrhosis of the liver.

Benign prostatic hypertrophy, a noncancerous enlargement of the prostate gland, has been suggested as a possible precursor to cancer of the prostate because of its high prevalence in older men. Nearly half of all men over age fifty have some degree of prostatic enlargement, most of which is not cancer. However, 80 percent of prostate cancer patients have some degree of prostatic hypertrophy. Studies attempting to evaluate the relationship between benign prostatic hypertrophy and prostate cancer, however, have produced no uniformity of opinion.

Symptoms and Diagnosis

Cancer of the prostate may enlarge and harden the gland and be felt during a digital rectal examination (Figure 73). This examination should be performed every year on all men over the age of forty. Because the prostate encircles the uppermost part of the urethra, the flow of urine from the bladder can become obstructed. The first symptoms of prostate cancer usually include urinary difficulties such as weak or interrupted flow of urine, inability to urinate, difficulty in starting urination, the need to urinate frequently, blood in the urine, urine flow which is not easily stopped, and painful or burning sensation when urinating. Back pain is also a common symptom. Although the onset of obstructive urinary symptoms may be a sign of cancer, in most men these symptoms are due to benign conditions.

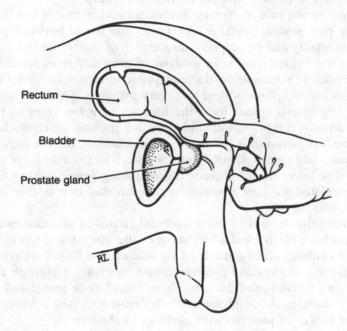

Figure 73 Rectal digital examination of the prostate gland.

The majority of men with prostate cancer, however, have no symptoms at all, which is why routine rectal digital examination by a physician is an important screening test. About 50 percent of prostatic nodules detected by digital rectal examination are ultimately found to be cancer. The American Cancer Society recommends that all men over the age of forty have an annual digital rectal examination. Although this procedure cannot always ensure early detection of the disease, it remains the most effective test.

If a nodule in the prostate is suspected of being cancer, a biopsy is usually performed to determine the diagnosis. The biopsy is performed by inserting a needle through the rectum or through the perineum (the skin between the anus and the scrotum) to obtain a small sample of the suspicious tissue for microscopic examination. If the diagnosis is confirmed, a complete workup is performed to determine the extent of the disease, and thus decide on treatment.

Stages of the Disease

Prostate cancer is divided into four stages according to how far the cancer has spread (Figure 74). Subclassifications of these stages may be used as well. In stage A, the cancer is confined within the prostate gland and is not felt on rectal examination. Cancer found in this stage of the disease may be detected during laboratory examination of prostate tissue when a patient has benign prostatic hypertrophy indicated by obstructive urinary symptoms.

Stage A tumors are usually subdivided into stage A1 and stage A2. In stage A1, the cancer is confined to one or two histologic (microscopic) areas of the gland, and the cancer cells are easily differentiated, meaning they are similar to the original prostatic cells. In stage A2, the cancer is spread throughout the gland, and the cancer cells are not necessarily differentiated; the cells may bear very little resemblance to normal ones. Patients with stage A1 cancer have very good chances of surviving to normal life expectancy even when no treatment is administered. Those with stage A2 cancer have a somewhat poorer prognosis, and treatment is usually required.

In stage B, the cancer is still confined to the prostate gland but is palpable on rectal examination. Stage B may be further divided into stage B1, characterized by a single small nodule (less than 1.5 cm in size) or stage B2, characterized by either a large nodule (greater than 1.5 cm) or multiple nodules. Studies indicate that approximately 50 percent of stage B2 cancers advance beyond the prostate gland, while 16 percent of B1 tumors spread. For all stage B cancers, surgical removal of the gland is usually considered necessary, although there may be exceptions to this.

In stage C, the cancer has spread throughout most of the prostate gland and has begun to invade the seminal vesicle or bladder neck. It is during stage C that many patients begin to experience urinary difficulties. Stage C may be further subdivided into stage C1, characterized by a small tumor with no involvement of the seminal vesicles, and stage C2, characterized by a larger tumor (greater than 70 grams) with invasion of the seminal vesicles. Studies have shown that patients with clinical stage C2 cancer have higher incidence of spread to the pelvic lymph nodes than do patients with stage C1 cancer.

Once the cancer has reached stage D, it has spread beyond the prostate gland into the surrounding lymph nodes or bone. Stage D cancers are usually subdivided into D1, in which the cancer is confined to the prostate

STAGE CHARACTERISTICS

A1 Focal, Incidental Finding

A2 Diffuse, Incidental Finding

B1 Small, Discrete Nodule,
Confined to Prostate

B2 Large or Multiple Nodules or Areas,
Confined to Prostate

C1 No Involvement of Seminal Vesicles,
Localized to Periprostatic Area

C2 Involvement of Seminal Vesicles,
Localized to Periprostatic Area

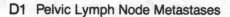

D1 Pelvic Lymph Node Metastases

D2 Bone, Distant Lymph Node,
Organ, or Soft Tissue Metastases

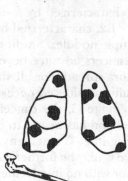

Figure 74 Stages of prostatic cancer.

and pelvic lymph nodes, and D2 which involves the lymph nodes beyond the pelvis and possibly the soft tissues and bones. Patients with stage D frequently suffer from urinary difficulty, blood in the urine, back pain, and weight loss. There are many patients with widespread metastases who have absolutely no symptoms. Patients with advanced cancer or those who progress to stage D have a five-year survival rate of 23 percent. Death usually results from renal failure because of urethral obstruction or from spread of the disease to the lung or central nervous system.

The course of the disease does not always follow the ABCD pattern from one stage to the next. For example, a stage A lesion could progress to advanced metastatic disease, skipping the intermediate stages. Research has demonstrated that the aggressiveness of a tumor can depend on its size and the degree of cell differentiation. In other words, the larger the tumor and the less one is able to differentiate cancer cells from one another, the greater the tendency for the cancer to spread beyond the prostate gland.

A complete workup of any prostate cancer is necessary to rule out the presence of more widespread disease. The workup usually includes laboratory studies of acid phosphatase, and alkaline phosphatase in the blood, X rays of the skeletal system, bone marrow aspiration, and radionuclear bone scan. Lymphography, an injection technique which makes pelvic and abdominal lymph nodes visible on X rays, is sometimes used to assess the stage of the disease, but it cannot always detect early microscopic invasion of the cancer. Lymph node involvement in prostate cancer is an important factor influencing the results of treatment. Before making a decision about treatment many physicians may recommend a surgical exploration of pelvic lymph nodes to see if they are free of cancer.

Treatment

Physicians differ in their choices of treatment for prostatic cancer, especially in the early stages of the disease. Therapy must be adjusted to each patient's needs, taking into consideration general health status, family situation, and occupation.

In stage A1, there is a wide range of treatments. Some studies have found that even without treatment, survival is not markedly affected. But others advocate radical prostatectomy in which the entire gland, with its capsule and seminal vesicles, is surgically removed. This type of surgery usually causes impotency because of the severance of the pelvic sympathetic nerves and, in 10 to 15 percent of cases, may also result in urinary incontinence. An alternative to surgery is radiation therapy for both the prostate and lymph nodes in the pelvis or, in certain cases, insertion of radioactive needles directly into the prostate through an incision in the abdominal wall. Impotence follows radiation therapy in 30 to 40 percent of cases. Potency often can be restored, however, with penile implants or prostheses.

In stages A2, B1, and B2, the treatment choices are largely the same as for stage A1. Studies evaluating different treatments for prostate cancer in stages A and B of the disease all show good results.

Successful treatment of patients with stage C disease is hard to achieve. Recurrence after radical prostatectomy is reported in 20 to 60 percent of those in stage C. External radiation therapy with and without hormone therapy has been associated with five-year survival rates ranging from 61 to 77 percent. The most difficult factor in treating patients in the later stages of the disease is that nearly 50 percent of the patients who are initially thought to have stage C clinical tumors may, upon surgical exploration, turn out to have cancer spread into the pelvic nodes. In an additional 10 percent, the cancer may have spread to the bone marrow.

Although cure is possible in advanced stages of the disease, the primary objective of therapy is the relief of pain and urethral obstruction. Therapy for patients with stage D disease will often involve the use of hormones. It has been known for some time that the growth and function of the prostate gland is influenced by the male hormone testosterone. In 1941, it was first demonstrated that surgical removal of the testes or injection of female hormones to suppress the manufacture of male hormones may cause prostatic atrophy. Clinical treatment with female hormones may cause impotence, swelling of the breasts, fluid retention, and progressive hardening of the arteries. While hormonal therapy may relieve symptoms, it will not actually cure the disease.

In recent years, nonhormonal chemotherapy has been used experimentally as a successful treatment for patients with advanced prostate cancer. Such a study conducted by the National Prostatic Cancer Project shows that several chemotherapy agents are effective in decreasing pain, slowing tumor growth, and increasing survival in patients with advanced disease. The same organization is currently testing other anticancer drugs and evaluating the usefulness of chemotherapy in earlier stages of the disease, both alone and as an adjuvant to other therapies. As with most anticancer drugs, some patients may experience nausea and vomiting, hair loss, anemia, increased susceptibility to infections, and reduced blood-clotting ability. Increasingly, many of these adverse reactions can be controlled or minimized. There are a number of drugs that may be given to counter nausea and vomiting. Antibiotics may be administered to prevent infections. Also, dosages of the anticancer drugs may be reduced or combined with other drugs to minimize reactions.

Survival Rates

Survival is largely dependent on the clinical stage of the disease at the time of diagnosis. The overall five-year survival rate for patients with clinical stage A is 78 percent. For those with stages B, C, and D, the overall five-year survival rates are 68, 58, and 23 percent respectively.

This represents a substantial degree of improvement in patient survival since 1950 (Figure 75). Survival rates increased substantially for both white and black men. Blacks experienced the biggest gain.

Accompanying the increase in survival rates between 1950 and 1973 was an increase in the percentage of prostate cancer cases diagnosed early in the curable localized stage. For white patients, the percentage of clinically localized tumors detected increased from 48 percent in 1950–51 to 61 percent in 1970–73; for black patients, the percentage increase was from 41 percent in 1950–54 to 54 percent in 1970–73. One explanation for the poorer survival rate among black males is the relatively later stages of disease at which diagnosis and treatment take place.

CANCER OF THE TESTICLE

Cancer of the testicle occurs usually in one of the two testicles contained within the scrotal sac, located behind the penis. After puberty, the testicles are responsible for production of the male hormone testosterone as well as the sperm necessary for reproduction. Testicular cancer accounts for only 1 to 2 percent of all cancers in men but is the most common cancer occurring in men between the ages of fifteen and thirty-four years, accounting for 19 percent of all cancer cases in this age group. It is also one of the most easily cured cancers if detected in the early stages of the disease.

The incidence and mortality rates of testicular cancer have two peak periods; there is a prominent peak in the age group twenty-five to thirty-four years, and a lesser one beginning after age seventy-five. The incidence of testicular cancer is four times greater in whites than in blacks and mortality is 2.5 times higher among whites (Table 20).

The overall mortality rate from testicular cancer in the United States has changed little during the past forty years, although, for reasons that are not entirely clear, its incidence nearly doubled in white men during this period. Among countries reporting cancer incidence statistics, the highest rates of this cancer were reported from Denmark, North America (among whites), the United Kingdom, and Northern European countries. The lowest rates were reported among North American and African blacks.

The vast majority of testicular tumors—nearly 95 percent—arise from the cells that produce sperm. These germ cell tumors are divided into two groups—seminomas and nonseminomas—depending on the microscopic characteristics of the affected cells. Seminomas occur primarily in men between the ages of twenty-five and forty-five years, with decreasing frequency after that age. Seminomatous tumors account for 30 to 40 percent of all testicular tumors. When first diagnosed, nearly 75 percent of seminomas are confined to the testes and 25 percent have already spread, usually to the lymph nodes of the abdomen and pelvis.

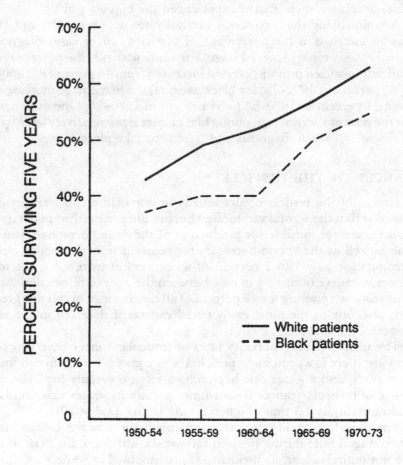

Source: DHEW Publication No. (NIH) 77-992
Cancer Patient Survival Report No. 5

Figure 75 Five-year survival rates for prostatic cancer, 1950–73, by race.

Table 20
AVERAGE ANNUAL INCIDENCE AND MORTALITY RATES
PER 100,000 UNITED STATES MALE POPULATION FOR TESTICULAR CANCER
BY RACE, 1973–1977

AGE (YEARS)	White Males		Black Males	
	INCIDENCE	MORTALITY	INCIDENCE	MORTALITY
0–14	0.22	0.06	0.31	
15–24	4.74	1.40	0.41	0.20
25–34	9.32	1.50	2.16	0.43
35–44	6.60	1.33	1.31	0.65
45–54	4.17	0.95	0.65	0.43
55–64	2.32	0.54	0.63	0.63
65–74	1.12	0.76		
75+	1.78	1.29	2.66	
Overall*	3.60	0.80	0.80	0.30

*Age-adjusted to 1970 U.S. population

Source: Young, J. L., Jr., Percy, C. L., Asire, A. J. (eds.): "Surveillance, Epidemiology, and End Results: Incidence and Mortality Data, 1973–1977." National Cancer Institute Monograph 57, DHHS Pub. No. (NIH) 81-2330, 1981.

Embryonal cell carcinomas, teratomas, teratocarcinomas, and choriocarcinomas are the nonseminomatous types of germinal tumors. These account for 20 to 25 percent, 5 to 10 percent, 20 to 25 percent, and 1 to 3 percent, respectively, of all testicular tumors. Embryonal cell carcinomas and teratocarcinomas occur primarily in young adults from age fifteen to thirty-four. Generally, the nonseminomatous tumors are more aggressive than the seminomatous type; 60 to 70 percent of patients with nonseminomatous tumors are found to already have lymph node metastases at the time of diagnosis. In the remaining 10 to 15 percent of cases, there is a mixture of types of tumors.

Causes

No single cause has been identified in cancer of the testicle. The cell types that arise in testicular cancers suggest that there are multiple factors involved. A major known risk factor is undescended testicles, or cryptorchidism.

The risk of developing a malignant tumor, usually a seminoma, is about five times greater in those with undescended testes than in those with normal testes. This may be due to a congenital imperfection of the testes rather than the fact that they are in an abnormal position. The risk of testicular cancer is reduced to the normal statistical level if the undescended testicle is surgically placed in the scrotum before six years of age.

The frequency of undescended testes in white males is considered to be increasing. It has been suggested that the increases in incidence of both undescended testes and testicular cancers may be a consequence of the mother's use of female hormones during pregnancy. Estrogens, such as diethylstilbestrol (DES), were commonly used between 1940 and 1960 in women who were in danger of having a miscarriage. Some researchers now think that this practice may be a factor in both undescended testes and testicular cancers in male offspring. In laboratory experiments, DES has produced undescended testes in rats. In certain strains of mice, estrogen administration has directly induced testicular cancer in laboratory research. In addition, undescended testes are twice as frequent among infants whose mothers had taken oral contraceptives within one month of conception. Several studies have reported an increased risk of testicular cancer following inflammation of the testes due to mumps and among those with a history of physical injury to the testes. The importance of trauma as a causal factor is difficult to assess since the trauma may simply call attention to the presence of a tumor, or the presence of a tumor may predispose the individual to testicular trauma.

Socioeconomic status may also be related to testicular cancer. Professional men and skilled workers have a higher risk of testicular cancer than do other groups. Exposure to a variety of potentially noxious compounds such as zinc and cadmium have been suspected as possible causal factors as well, although no conclusions can yet be drawn on the basis of available evidence. Clearly, there is much speculation but few hard facts in the study of the cause of this cancer.

Symptoms and Diagnosis

The usual symptoms of testicular cancer include a lump in the testicle, painless swelling, or an altered consistency. The affected individual may feel a dull ache or heavy dragging sensation in the lower abdomen, groin, or scrotum. Acute pain is uncommon unless the patient is also suffering from epididymitis—inflammation of the epididymis, the cordlike structure along the back of the testicle. In many patients, the testicular tumor is discovered incidentally during the course of a routine medical examination. The mildness of the typical early symptoms combined with ignorance or fear of cancer often leads patients to delay seeking medical attention until the disease has spread to other parts of the body. If, however, the disease is detected in the early stages and treatment begins immediately, cancer of the testes is one of the most easily curable cancers.

The individual can help in the early detection of testicular cancer by performing a simple self-examination procedure to check for any small lumps or changes in size of the testicles. Palpation of the testicle is best performed with two hands (Figure 76). Each testicle is gently held with the fingers of both hands and is palpated by rolling between the thumbs and fingers. The examination should be done once a month, preferably after a warm bath or shower when the scrotal skin is most relaxed.

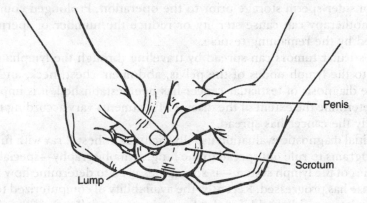

Figure 76 Testicular self-examination: Gently roll each testicle between the thumb and fingers of both hands. If any hard lumps are found, see your doctor as soon as possible. (Do not confuse the epididymis at the back of the testicles with a tumor.) Examination should be performed after a bath or shower when the scrotal skin is most relaxed.

The typical testicular tumor is a painless lump, about the size of a pea, often located on the front part of the testicle. The epididymis, which hugs the back border of each testicle, should not be confused with an abnormal lump. If a lump is discovered, a physician should be seen immediately (Figure 77).

New diagnostic techniques are often helpful in differentiating a testicular cancer from benign scrotal conditions. Ultrasound tests will often differentiate between epididymitis and testicular cancer. Radionuclide scanning of the scrotum may indicate "cold spots" indicative of a tumor. Suspicion of the presence of a tumor may require surgical exploration through an incision above the groin to verify the diagnosis by biopsy. If a mass within the testicle is discovered, the entire testicle is usually removed.

Removal of a testicle produces no serious side effects and, contrary to popular belief, does not leave the patient impotent. Once such a cancer is cured, the patient may have an active sex life. Even when both testicles are removed, the patient does not lose the ability to initiate and maintain erection of the penis. For cosmetic purposes, some patients have the surgeon place a prosthetic device resembling a testicle in the scrotum. When the lymph nodes in the abdomen are removed, however, the surgeon must sever or damage the nerves responsible for ejaculation. As a result, the sperm produced in the remaining testicle can no longer emerge from the penis. Those undergoing this type of surgery may want to consider sperm storage prior to the operation. Prolonged courses of chemotherapy can cause sterility or reduce the number of sperm produced by the remaining testicle.

Testicular tumors can spread by traveling through the lymphatic vessels to the lymph nodes of the pelvis, abdomen, chest, neck, and lung. Once diagnosis of testicular cancer has been established, it is important to determine the extent of the disease. Treatments vary according to how widely the cancer has spread.

Initial diagnostic evaluation usually includes a chest X ray with full lung tomograms to rule out spread to the lung. Lymphography—special X-ray studies of the lymph system—is sometimes used to determine how far the disease has progressed. Recently, the availability of computerized tomography has provided additional information, especially when the disease may have spread to the abdomen. In patients with nonseminomatous tumors, staging is usually done by means of surgical removal of a lymph node in the abdomen.

Certain blood tests also are important in staging and planning treatment of testicular cancer. Blood levels of alphafetoprotein (AFP), a primitive cellular protein, and human chorionic gonadotropin (HCG), a sex hormone, must be obtained on all patients with suspected testicular cancer. Approximately 90 percent of patients with nonseminomatous testicular cancer will have an elevated level of one or both of these substances.

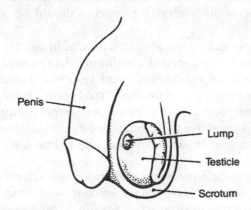

Figure 77 Tumor of the testicle.

Assessment of AFP and HCG levels increases the accuracy of diagnosis, and staging allows the doctor to closely monitor the patient's response to treatment and to detect early recurrence following treatment.

Stages of the Disease

Testicular tumors are divided into five stages according to how extensively the cancer has spread. In stage A, the tumor is confined to the testicle and there is no evidence of spread beyond that organ. In stage B1, there is evidence of minimal spread to lymph nodes in the abdomen or pelvis (less than six positive nodes with no nodes greater than 2 cm. in diameter). In stage B2, there is evidence of moderate lymph node metastases in the abdomen and pelvis (more than six positive nodes or some nodes larger than 2 cm. in diameter). In stage B3, there is massive lymph node involvement in the abdomen and pelvis but no evidence that the cancer has spread above the diaphragm or to other solid organs. In stage C, there is evidence that the cancer has spread above the diaphragm to other organs, the brain, or bone.

Treatment

Testicular cancer can be highly curable if detected early. Improvements in diagnostic and staging procedures, intensive chemotherapy regimens, and development of multitreatment regimens combining chemotherapy and surgery have all contributed to the improved survival rates for this disease.

Surgical removal of the testicle and all adjoining tissue—this is called radical orchiectomy—is the first step in the treatment of testicular cancer. This initial procedure provides a basis for additional diagnosis, controls the primary tumor effectively, and may eliminate the possibility of further spread of the cancer. Subsequent treatment depends on the type of tumor and the stage of disease as well as several other factors not yet identified.

Since seminoma is a tumor highly sensitive to irradiation, radiation therapy is considered the frequent treatment of choice for patients. Radiation is directed to the nodes in the abdomen and pelvic area, and sometimes to nodes in the chest and neck area. Cure rates for patients receiving radiation therapy alone range from 75 to 93 percent for stages B and A respectively. The results of radiation therapy for patients with advanced cancer, either stage B3 or C, show that nearly 40 percent of patients can expect tumor-free survival. There has been a recent trend to treat patients with advanced disease with chemotherapy, particularly with vincristine and vinblastine, and the combination of cisplatin, vinblastine, and bleomycin. Nonseminomatous tumors are usually treated by surgical removal of the lymph nodes in the abdomen (lymphadenectomy). In patients with stage A disease, the tumor-free survival rate is reported to be nearly 100 percent. Patients with stage B1 or B2 disease are treated with follow-up surgery alone (lymphadenectomy) or by surgery followed immediately by chemotherapy. These patients can expect a survival rate of approximately 90 to 95 percent. Patients with advanced disease (either stage B3 or C) initially receive chemotherapy followed by surgical removal of residual disease. These patients can expect a 50 to 70 percent tumor-free survival rate.

Prognosis

Patients with seminomas have the best prognosis, while those with choriocarcinomas have the poorest outlook. The stage of the disease at the time of detection and treatment is an important predictor of prognosis. Data from Roswell Park Memorial Institute indicate that the three-year survival rate of patients with localized seminomas is 98 percent, whereas for those with regional and distant spread of the disease it is 63 and 28 percent, respectively. For embryonal carcinoma, the three-year survival rate is 55 percent for localized and 35 and 5 percent for regional and distant spread, respectively.

If testicular cancer is treated before it has spread to the lymph nodes, the rate of cure is greater than 90 percent. This high degree of successful treatment demonstrates the importance of early detection practices such as testicular self-examination. Even among patients with advanced disease, improvement in treatment during the past decade has substantially increased survival rates.

CANCER OF THE PENIS

The penis consists of two parallel cylindrical bodies called the corpora cavernosa, and beneath them the corpus spongiosum, through which the urethra passes. The cap-shaped extension at the end of the penis is called the glans and the skin covering the glans is called the prepuce or foreskin.

Incidence

Cancer of the penis is a rare disease in the United States accounting for 0.2 percent of all cancers in males. The disease is more common in elderly men and blacks, and incidence rates increase steadily after age fifty-five.

While the disease is rare in this country, penile cancer is relatively common in other parts of the world. In Uganda, for example, cancer of the penis accounts for 7 percent of all cases of cancer and is one of the most common cancers among men. A similar high incidence is reported for Ceylon, Thailand, Vietnam, India, Mexico, and Puerto Rico. The onset of penis cancer at a relatively younger age has been noted in Asia, Paraguay, and Uganda.

Causes

In cultures where circumcision of all or part of the foreskin is routine in male infants, there appears to be a very low incidence of penis cancer. Personal hygiene practices have been suggested as possible factors in the disease as well. Comparison of rates in noncircumcising African tribes with different standards of personal cleanliness tend to support this theory. Phimosis, a condition caused by improper hygiene which leads to tightening of the foreskin so that it cannot be drawn over the glans of the penis, has been mentioned in the case histories of 53 percent of Danish men with penis cancer. In this study, 9.4 percent of penis cancer patients had a history of venereal disease compared with only 3.6 percent of control cases, a highly significant observation. A greater frequency of venereal disease in patients with penis cancer may, however, be another indication of improper sexual hygiene rather than the direct cause of the cancer.

Penis cancer is most common among men in the lower socioeconomic groups. The association of penis cancer with social class, the fact that the disease is more common in nonwhites, and geographic variation may relate to possible dietary factors. Variations in diet have been found by class, race, and region, and the relationship between diet and other types of cancer may point to a possible association between diet and penis cancer. Studies have found greater than expected rates of cervical cancer among spouses of patients with penis cancer, suggesting some common factor for the two diseases.

Symptoms and Diagnosis

The first symptom of cancer of the penis is typically a painless, small nodule, warty growth, or ulcer. Pain or bleeding appears later and may be present in 25 percent of patients. The site of origin of the tumor is often the glans of the penis or the inner surface of the foreskin. A foul-smelling discharge and infection may be associated with an ulcerating lesion. The cancer spreads through the lymphatic vessels to the lymph nodes in the groin and the iliac nodes in the abdomen. About 30 percent of patients already have metastases to the lymph nodes in the groin at the time of diagnosis. Distant metastases to the abdominal nodes, liver, and lungs are rare, occurring only in about 10 percent of cases.

The diagnosis of cancer of the penis presents little difficulty because of its location and exposure. However, the determination of lymph node involvement is more difficult. Surgical node dissection or needle biopsy of lymph nodes to obtain samples of tissue for microscopic examination is sometimes performed to evaluate the extent of the spread of the cancer. Lymphography is sometimes used to diagnose deep-seated metastases. As with other cancers, the treatment for patients with penis cancer depends on the location and spread of the disease.

Stages of the Disease

Cancer of the penis is most commonly classified into four stages. In Stage I, the cancer is limited to the glans of the penis or foreskin without evidence of metastases. In Stage II, the cancer extends through the shaft of the penis without evidence of metastases to lymph nodes in the groin or hip area. In Stage III, the cancer has spread to the lymph nodes in the groin, but is still operable. In Stage IV, the cancer has spread beyond the shaft of the penis, with inoperable lymph node involvement or distant metastases to other organs such as the lung.

Treatment

Surgical removal of the tumor is the primary treatment. Surgery involves either partial or total removal of the penis (penectomy). Partial removal of the penis must include at least two centimeters from any visible tumor. Small tumors which are limited to the foreskin can be treated by circumcision. Superficial tumors have also been cured by radiation therapy alone.

The lymphatics of the penis drain not only to the nodes in the groin area, but also to the deep iliac nodes in the abdomen and may involve both sides of the body at the root of the penis. About 40 to 50 percent of patients with lymph node involvement can be cured by node dissection. Extension of the cancer beyond the pelvis precludes cure by surgery. Chemotherapy or radiation therapy may be of value in patients with distant metastases.

Prognosis

The prognosis of patients with cancer of the penis is most favorable when the tumor is confined to the penis. The five-year survival rate for patients with Stage I disease is well above 80 percent. Survival for Stage II is about 50 percent and for Stage III, approximately 30 to 40 percent. Patients with distant metastases have a poor prognosis.

SUMMARY

The most important factor associated with survival in all male reproductive cancers is the extent of the disease at the time of diagnosis. Improvement in the survival rates for these cancers over the past thirty years is due in large part to improved methods of diagnosis, which can detect the disease at an early, more curable stage. The patient himself can contribute most effectively to early detection through self-examination and regular doctor checkups. Greater awareness of these cancers and improvements in treatment may further reduce the mortality rates for cancer of the male reproductive system.

30

Skin Cancer

Thomas B. Fitzpatrick, M.D.

INTRODUCTION

Skin cancer is the most common of all human cancers. Indeed, more skin cancers are diagnosed, treated, and cured each year than all other cancers combined. During the past ten years, there has been a growing interest and inquiry into this form of cancer, due largely to its alarming increase among Americans. Consequently, more has been learned about skin cancer in the past decade than in the previous fifty years.

The most common skin cancer is basal cell carcinoma, followed by squamous cell carcinoma. Altogether, at least 400,000 Americans develop these cancers each year. Of these, the vast majority are quickly cured once the disease is correctly diagnosed. The most serious type of skin cancer is malignant melanoma. It is also the most rare, with about 22,000 new cases per year and 7,400 deaths (compared to 1,900 deaths from all other types of skin cancer). However, there also has been a sixfold increase in this type of cancer in recent decades, and in some areas the rise has been even greater. In Connecticut, for example, the number of cases per year has risen seven and a half times, from 12 per million in 1939 to 90 cases per million in 1980.

Most skin cancers are relatively slow-growing, spreading very little. In addition, they are easy to see and diagnose, and are readily cured. Even melanoma now has a strikingly better outlook than a few years ago, as a result of earlier diagnosis, heightened awareness of the disease on the part of both physicians and patients, and improved treatment methods.

THE SKIN AS AN ORGAN

Although the skin functions as the body's protective covering and is readily recognized, many people do not think of it as a vital organ. But actually, the skin is the body's largest organ, playing a number of important roles. In addition to protecting the inner organs from the outside environment, the skin retains body moisture and helps regulate temperature. Through the skin's sensitive nerve endings, we make contact with the world through the sense of touch, which perceives pain, temperature (hot and cold), and textures, among other things. The skin also contains hair follicles, sweat glands, and several different kinds of cells within its layers (Figure 78).

Human skin differs according to its location on the body. The skin of the lips and eyelids is very sensitive and delicate, while that of the feet is generally the toughest and the skin on the back is the least sensitive.

SKIN TYPES

Four skin types have been identified by dermatologists, based on the tendency to tan or burn upon thirty minutes' exposure to noontime summer sun (Table 21). People would be wise to adjust the amount of time spent in the sun according to their skin type. Those with Types I and II should be careful to limit their sun exposure (or use effective sun-protective preparations) since all three of the most common types of human skin cancer are markedly increased in people with these skin types.

Those with Types III and IV are far less susceptible to sun-induced cancers, and can freely enjoy the sun and the out-of-doors. However, even those with darker skin must be aware that overexposure to sunlight will result in an increased probability of skin cancer.

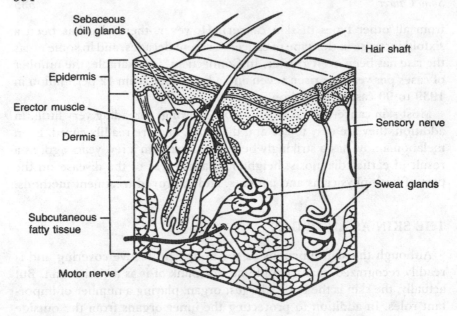

Figure 78 Cross section of normal skin.

SUSCEPTIBILITY

Skin cancer, except for malignant melanoma, develops most typically in older white people, especially farmers, sailors, construction workers, and gardeners—those who have worked out-of-doors most of their lives. Malignant melanoma develops in younger persons and in professional, indoor workers who obtain intermittent sun exposure, for example weekend sun bathers. It seems to be a general rule that sun exposure, while certainly not the only cause of malignant changes in the skin, greatly increases the chances for their development. Skin cancers are definitely more common in hot, sunny climates. In the United States, the South and Southwest report more than twice as many cases as the North. Some recent studies also suggest that fluorescent light may play a limited role in the development of skin cancer.

The great majority of skin tumors arise on the parts of the body most exposed to the sun. The face, tops of the ears (mostly in men), and backs of the hands are particularly vulnerable, as are the scalps of bald men. But all parts of the skin can develop cancer, and some patients even develop the disease in areas that are hardly exposed at all.

Most skin cancers originate in three specific cell types present in the epidermis, the outer layer of the skin (Figure 79). Basal cell carcinomas develop from the bottom, or basal layer of cells that make up the border

Table 21
SKIN TYPE AS DETERMINED BY REACTION
TO THIRTY MINUTES OF NOONDAY SUMMER SUN

SKIN TYPE	REACTION	SUSCEPTIBILITY TO CANCER
I	Always burns, never tans	Highest
II	Always burns or tans less than average	High
III	Mild burn, tans about average	Average
IV	No burn, tans more than average	Low

between the epidermis and the dermis, which lies just beneath. Squamous cell carcinomas arise from the squamous cells that constitute the upper layers of skin in contact with the outer environment. Melanomas arise in melanocytes, or pigment cells. These cells manufacture and secrete the pigment which causes us to "tan" in response to sun exposure. Tanning protects the skin naturally from burning. Blacks very rarely get skin cancer because their dark skin protects them from the harmful effects of the sun's rays. Some tumors arise from sweat glands or hair follicle cells, but these are rather rare.

WHEN TO SEE A DERMATOLOGIST

Informed patients can do a great deal to help prevent serious skin cancer since they are the most aware of changes in the appearance of their own skins. Occasional self-inspection of skin areas and the reporting of any suspicious changes to a dermatologist is the best method of early detection and successful treatment of skin cancer.

Although it is not difficult to identify skin abnormalities, a dermatologist is probably the best choice of physician if skin cancer is suspected. While most doctors can deal quite effectively with common rashes, spots, and many other superficial skin disorders, the expertise of a skin specialist is called for to make the prompt and accurate diagnosis which is needed to deal with persistent sores or other abnormalities that suggest skin cancer.

The following six signs should alert the patient to the need for medical attention:

536

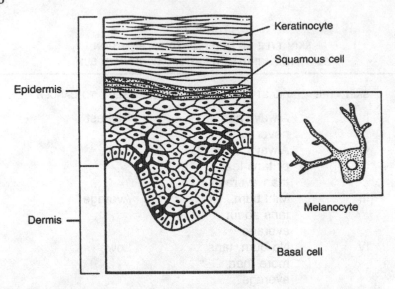

Figure 79 Various types of cells in which skin cancer arises.

1. Any ulcer of the skin that does not heal in six weeks
2. Any lump or growth that bleeds persistently
3. Any lump or growth that enlarges, especially those that are hard or firm to the touch
4. Any pigmented "mole" that is splotchy, brown, black, or has irregular indented borders like a maple leaf
5. Any growth or mole that is changing in size or shape
6. Any mole that itches or is tender

Patients who heed these warning signs of potentially malignant lesions and seek immediate medical attention will vastly improve their prospects for cure. Early diagnosis is especially important in cases of malignant melanoma.

IN THE DERMATOLOGIST'S OFFICE

The experienced dermatologist can immediately recognize, or at least strongly suspect, most types of skin cancer. To help confirm the diagnosis, the doctor will ask questions about the rate of development, the presence of itch, pain, or bleeding, and whether the problem area has been previously injured or X-rayed. The patient's occupation, home location, degree of sun exposure, other illnesses, medications, and family history will also be taken into account in the diagnostic process.

The dermatologist will observe and record the size, shape, color, irregularities, presence of ulcer and bleeding tendency of the skin lesion, and will also note whether it is raised, hard, tender to the touch, has smooth, regular, or irregular borders. The dermatologist will look for lesions elsewhere on the body. He or she will also check to see if adjacent lymph nodes are enlarged—usually a sign that the cancer may have already spread.

The next step in the diagnostic process will depend on the size of the lesion and on the tentative diagnosis. In many cases, the removal of a small piece of skin, or biopsy, will be required. If the growth is less than one centimeter in diameter, it will probably be removed in its entirety during the biopsy procedure. This is called an excisional biopsy (Figure 80). If the lesion is very large, then only a piece of it will be removed to be studied under a microscope.

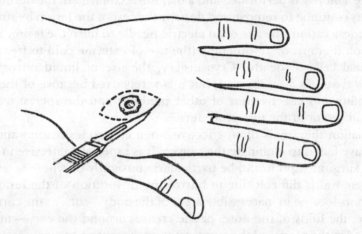

Figure 80 Excisional biopsy of growth on the hand.

Excisional biopsy serves as both diagnosis and treatment. This is especially true if the outside edges of the biopsy tissue, when examined under a microscope in a pathology laboratory, are found to be "clean" of cancer cells. This is proof that the cancer has been completely removed from the skin. If, however, the margins show cancer cells, the dermatologist or surgeon must go back and remove more surrounding tissue until the pathologist returns a satisfactory report.

Most skin biopsies for dermatologic purposes are simple, quick procedures performed under local anesthesia in the doctor's office. After injecting the anesthesia under the skin, the suspicious area and surrounding tissue are removed for later examination under a microscope. If the excised area is small, no stitches are required; larger excisions may, however, require stitches. If melanoma is suspected, the patient will be referred to either a general or plastic surgeon, who will perform a wider, deeper biopsy and remove more of the surrounding tissue. Other procedures may follow if the material tested is positively identified as malignant melanoma.

Most growths are easily assessed by clinical examination, but a biopsy must *always* be performed if there is any chance that the skin lesion is malignant. It is not always easy to define the total extent of the cancer or to be sure of its precise nature. For example, some skin cancers may burrow in different directions at different skin levels. In this case, biopsy margins must be examined carefully and their original orientation in the body marked so that the dermatologist will know in which direction to continue to search for abnormal cells.

Once a biopsy is performed and a diagnosis confirmed, the dermatologist may continue to remove and destroy the rest of the lesion by surgery, electrodesiccation (the use of an electric needle to burn the lesion away), radiation therapy, or cryotherapy (the use of extreme cold to freeze the abnormal cells to death). Cryosurgery, the use of liquid nitrogen to destroy tissue, is also effective, but it is rarely used because of the wide availability and effectiveness of other methods and the special training and skill required for this procedure.

Radiation therapy is often effective when electrodesiccation and surgery have failed to eliminate the cancer. It is especially effective in areas where surgical scars would be particularly unsightly or where access for total removal is difficult due to burrowing or location of the lesion.

Tumors located in inaccessible areas of the body—such as the corner of the eye, the folds of the nose, or the creases around the ears—must be removed in the course of the first treatment, because a recurrence may be very difficult to cure. If surgery is used in such cases, the procedure indicated will probably be the Mohs technique. In the Mohs technique, the tissue is removed layer by layer and examined by a pathologist until a cancer-free layer is reached. This step-by-step excision permits a definitive cure, usually in the course of one surgical session.

When there is local recurrence of skin cancer, the standard practice is to employ a treatment method other than the one first used. Radiation is very effective, but it is generally reserved for older patients because a thin white area of scar tissue may appear. Chemotherapy is not used for skin cancers, but it is widely used by local application for some precancerous conditions, such as solar (actinic) keratoses. Laser therapy has not been used for skin cancer, although it has been used in the treatment of some benign skin disorders.

BASAL CELL CARCINOMA

Basal cell carcinoma is by far the most common form of cancer, constituting about 65 percent of the 400,000 nonmelanoma skin cancer cases diagnosed each year in the United States. Basal cell cancer occurs most frequently in middle-aged and older people; almost all patients are forty-five years of age or more. It is, however, being seen in increasing numbers of young people, because of the popularity of suntanning.

This type of cancer in its moderately advanced stage often produces "rodent" ulcers, characterized by a central depressed area with an open ulcer or sore. Basal cell tumors are found more often in men than women, possibly because a greater number of men work in outdoor occupations where they are exposed to sunlight. This cancer is very rare among blacks and those with darkly pigmented skin.

Those most susceptible to basal cell cancer are people with skin types I and II who regularly experience prolonged sun exposure, live in regions near the equator, and have a family history of skin cancer. Another rather rare risk factor is exposure to arsenic, which was used in tonics and cough medicines for many years. This substance is accumulated in the body to some degree, and dermatologists are seeing a high incidence of basal cell cancers in elderly people who took arsenic preparations many years ago. Skin that has been damaged by burns or X rays is also more susceptible to basal cell cancer.

Basal cell cancers are very slow-growing, taking months or even years to achieve a size that would suggest an abnormality. They are generally painless and have no symptoms unless ulcers form and a small amount of bleeding occurs. The tumors are usually, unless long neglected, small and single, with a round or oval shape. They may be pink or red and scaly, although they are usually white, waxlike or pearly, and hard, rather than simply firm. During examination, the dermatologist will often draw the nearby skin tight to bring out the characteristic shiny translucent appearance. Some patients with an apparent genetic tendency to grow basal cell cancers will have multiple growths in different body locations and a high degree of recurrence. Basal cell carcinomas rarely, if ever, spread to other parts of the body. They do, however, spread locally and, although they are not very aggressive, they can invade and slowly destroy nearby bone and cartilage if not treated properly. If properly attended to on the first attempt, however, basal cell carcinoma is totally cured in about 96 percent of patients.

Before treatment begins, a biopsy must be taken to confirm the true nature of the lesion. An easily curable basal cell cancer, darkened in color by melanin (a dark brown skin pigment), can resemble a dangerous melanoma, and vice versa. The prognosis and treatment course for each of these is different and only a biopsy can supply the necessary information for correct treatment to begin. X-ray therapy, cryosurgery, and electrodesiccation are all effective methods of therapy with very high rates of cure. These cancers must be destroyed well beyond their visible borders because they often extend beneath the skin and are larger than they may appear.

The vast majority of basal cell carcinomas are small and easily removed, but if local recurrence develops, even years later, it is customary to use a different treatment on the second attempt. Recurrent basal cell cancers are more serious than initial cases. Therefore, the first treatment should be aggressive and patients should be reexamined regularly—every six months immediately following treatment and then once a year to ensure early detection of a recurrence.

SQUAMOUS CELL CARCINOMA

Squamous cell carcinoma, the second most common type of skin cancer, usually arises from cells called keratinocytes, which constitute the uppermost layer of the skin. It tends to affect the same group as basal cell carcinoma—older white people with skin types I and II whose skin is frequently exposed to the sun. It is rarely seen in those under age fifty-five or sixty. Burns, chronic ulcers, constant friction, and prolonged contact with certain industrial chemicals also appear to be contributing influences.

Squamous cell cancers are more variable in appearance than basal cell cancers and tend to grow more rapidly. They can develop sores in their centers that do not heal (Figure 81). These lesions are small, rough, crusty, and reddish but their best identifying feature is their hardness. They are more invasive than basal cell cancers and may be attached to body structures beneath the skin. They occur in approximate order of declining frequency on the cheek, ear, neck, temple, forehead, and hand. Biopsy is required for a definitive diagnosis. A warning patch of whitish tissue, called leukoplakia, may develop on the lips before the actual cancer, and is potentially reversible at the earliest stage.

Unlike basal cell cancers, squamous cell cancers sometimes spread to other parts of the body. Even so, only about 2 percent of these cancers spread. Lesions arising in burn scars or X-ray scars have a much higher incidence of metastases, or spreading—about 20 percent. In general, local invasion is the principal problem with this type of cancer; thus, initial therapy should be aggressive to decrease the chances of recurrence. Surgery to remove the cancerous growth and surrounding tissue, sometimes followed by radiation therapy, is commonly used in treating squamous cell cancers, resulting in a five-year cure rate of about 90

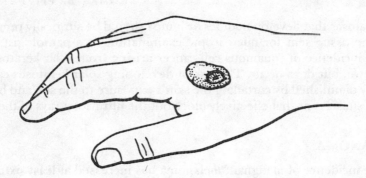

Figure 81 Squamous cell carcinoma.

percent. Electrodesiccation and curettage (scraping) can be used to treat some lesions in the early stages.

In treating more advanced lesions, the best practice, wherever possible, is to have a multispecialty team of dermatologist, surgeon, and radiation therapist. Once the cancer has spread, the prognosis is significantly poorer. Surgical removal of the lesion, combined with chemotherapy is usually the best method of achieving complete elimination of the cancer.

SOLAR KERATOSES

Solar keratoses, also called actinic keratoses, are sun-induced skin lesions that appear in middle-aged individuals, mainly those with skin types I, II, and III. They occur rarely in blacks, Indians, and dark-skinned whites. These are slow-growing pre-cancers and generally asymptomatic, although they may be accompanied by an itch or tenderness. Lesions appear flat, rough, scaly, and usually round, about a half inch across. They may be pink, yellow, or brown and tend to appear on the scalp of bald men, on the face, tip of the ear, side of the neck, back of the hands, tops of the shoulders, and shins. They may be single but are commonly multiple and scattered, and are found more frequently in men than in women. Although at first barely noticeable, these lesions can change into squamous cell carcinomas if not removed.

Treatment of solar keratoses is very effective and easily performed, usually with topical chemotherapy or occasionally with liquid nitrogen, electrodesiccation, curettage, or dermabrasion. The tumor is biopsied only if the presence of malignant growth is suspected. Topical application of the anticancer drug 5-FU in the form of cream or liquid twice daily for about three weeks is generally effective and does not affect adjacent normal skin. All the affected skin will react to the drug by producing a bright red color that disappears when the keratoses have been removed.

Keratoses that develop nodules or lumps should be surgically removed and the tissue sent for microscopic examination by a pathologist. The actual incidence of squamous cell cancer arising from solar keratoses is unknown, but does occur. The risk of developing solar keratoses can be greatly diminished by curtailing the skin's exposure to the sun and by the use of sunscreens that effectively block out the ultraviolet rays of the sun.

MELANOMA

The incidence of malignant melanoma has increased at least sixfold in the United States since 1945. In 1985, an estimated 22,000 new cases were reported. It is the single most deadly of all skin diseases and an estimated 5,500 Americans now die of the disease yearly. Melanomas start in the melanocytes, the pigment-forming cells that secrete melanin. Melanomas generally occur in whites over the age of forty-five who have skin types I and II. Men and women are equally affected. Few blacks, Orientals, and others with dark skin are affected, and heredity seems to play a role in susceptibility.

Exposure to the sun is believed to be a major factor in the transformation of a normal pigment cell into a malignant melanoma. The relationship between the mortality rate from this disease and geographic latitude is striking. White people living near the equator and in Australia have a much higher mortality than those who live in more temperate climates. In the United States, the disease is more common in the Southeast and Southwest.

Most melanomas start in areas exposed to the sun. In women, the susceptible areas include the back, the face, and the lower legs. In men, the torso is most often affected. Rarer sites in whites are the palms, soles, and under the nails; these sites are commonest in black people. Any pigmented growth in these locations should be regarded with suspicion and checked by a doctor.

Moles

Malignant melanomas can arise in any skin area that contains melanocytes, but body moles, also called pigmented nevi, are particularly vulnerable (Figure 82). Although some moles, especially those on the face and torso, originate in pigment cells, they sometimes contain little pigment and are light in color. All moles are initially benign tumors of varying shape, but it is significant to note that about 20 to 30 percent of all melanomas begin in the pigment cells of moles.

For many years, dermatologists have believed that some types of moles were more likely to develop malignant changes than others. Although this has not yet been proved, there are certain rules to remember in keeping

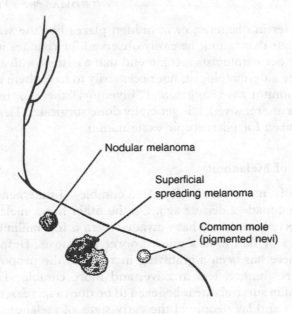

Nodular melanoma

Superficial
spreading melanoma

Common mole
(pigmented nevi)

Figure 82 Two types of melanoma and a common mole.

close watch on potentially malignant moles. Most nonpigmented moles are completely harmless and should be brought to a doctor's attention only for cosmetic reasons or if they develop questionable and rather obvious signs such as bleeding, change in size, ulcer formation, or darkening in color. Any new mole that appears after age thirty, that itches or is tender, should be promptly looked at by a dermatologist.

Often these are dysplastic nevi, or acquired pigmented skin lesions that differ from ordinary moles in several respects. Dysplastic nevi contain variable mixtures of tan, brown, black or red/pink in a single mole. They usually have irregular borders, with pigment fading into the surrounding skin. They always have a flat portion that is level with the skin, often at the edge of the nevus. They are often larger than ordinary moles and many people have large numbers of them—sometimes a hundred or more scattered over the body. Dysplastic nevi occur most often on parts of the skin exposed to the sun, especially the back, but they also may be found on the scalp, breasts, and buttocks. Some people inherit the tendency to develop dysplastic nevi, but in others, the growths occur sporadically, usually beginning in adolescence and continuing throughout life. People with dysplastic nevi have a higher risk of developing melanoma—about 5 to 10 percent compared to 0.7 percent for the general population.

Researchers recommend the removal of all moles that meet any of the following criteria: present at birth, no matter what the size; larger than one centimeter in diameter; or in hidden places like the scalp, mouth, vagina, or anus that cannot be easily observed for changes in color and shape. Some dermatologists recommend that a patient with any moles at all should see a dermatologist, not necessarily to have them all removed but just to monitor any changes, and "inventory" them for future check-ups. If moles are removed, it is generally done surgically. Tissue samples are always taken for microscopic examination.

Early Signs of Melanoma

Caught early, melanoma is very often curable—a statement that could not have been made a decade ago. On the other hand, melanomas that are not detected until they have invaded even a few millimeters of the deeper layers of skin have a much poorer prognosis. Despite a rising mortality, there has been a gratifying increase in the proportion of tu-mors that are thinner, less invasive, and more curable. This striking improvement in survival rate is believed to be due to increased awareness by physicians and lay people of the early signs of melanoma.

The unique aspect of primary melanoma of the skin among all the potentially fatal cancers (breast, stomach, uterus, lung, colon) is its easy access, not only for visual examination, but also for histologic study—a biopsy is easily obtained and decisive. This easy accessibility is especially important in primary melanoma because curability is directly related to the size and depth of invasion of the tumor—a growth that in the most common type, the superficial spreading melanoma, fortunately proceeds relatively slowly over a period of a few years. This provides a grace period in which early tumors can be detected.

In the vast majority of cases, early melanoma can easily be recognized by three physical characteristics—coloration, contour, and size—of the lesion. Although the same characteristics are sometimes present in other types of lesions, the likelihood of a false-positive diagnosis is minimized once the physician becomes familiar with the typical features of primary melanoma of the skin. However, since biopsy should be considered man-datory for all suspected lesions, the risks of making a false-positive diag-nosis are negligible when compared with the potential consequences of a false-negative or a missed diagnosis of melanoma.

Treatment

Melanomas are treated by surgical removal of the entire lesion and should never be removed by electrodesiccation. A wide border of normal tissue surrounding the lesion is usually removed as a precautionary mea-sure. As of 1985, the overall five-year survival rate for all melanomas was over 80 percent—in contrast to the 1960 figure of 60 percent. This improvement is the result of early detection and increased awareness.

The usual surgical approach to melanoma is not to biopsy it in part, but to remove it totally, leaving the site to heal itself. If microscopic examination of the removed tissue shows that the melanoma has penetrated more deeply into the skin, additional tissue will be removed in subsequent surgery. If the melanoma has already spread to nearby lymph nodes, the five-year survival rate drops dramatically.

Once a melanoma has spread, treatment depends on the individual case. Chemotherapy and radiation therapy have not proved effective. Immunotherapy—stimulation of the body's immune and antibody system in an effort to make it attack the malignant cells—has had some limited success when used with chemotherapy.

Prevention of Melanoma

In preventing melanoma from occurring and spreading, the same rules apply as with all skin cancers. Avoid overexposure to the sun and follow the basic rules for early detection of any suspicious lesions. All patients with a family or personal history of melanoma should see a dermatologist regularly, as should those who have had a mole removed that was reported to have precancerous cells.

CANCERS METASTASIZING TO THE SKIN

Cancers that begin elsewhere in the body sometimes spread to the skin. These cancers appear as firm nodules, possibly with a surrounding red area of inflammation, and may first be detected on the scalp. They are relatively rare; lung and colon cancers in men and breast and colon cancers in women are among the most frequent to spread to the skin. Treatment of the skin lesion is generally by surgery or by high doses of local radiation therapy; chemotherapy may be administered to treat the metastases.

BENIGN SKIN LESIONS

There are many skin problems which, because of their lumpy, nodular, or dark appearance, may frighten patients into thinking of cancer. Seborrheic keratosis, for example, is a brown or black plaque-like wart commonly found on the back, chest, and forehead of older people. Although harmless, these lesions can sometimes be mistaken for cancer. They can easily be removed with electrodesiccation or liquid nitrogen. In general, however, it is best to have a suspicious skin lesion checked by a dermatologist on the chance that it may be malignant. Better to discover that it is benign (in which case you may want to remove it for cosmetic reasons) than to wait until it has spread, reducing your chances of a painless and complete cure.

THE SUN AND THE PREVENTION OF SKIN CANCER

Since exposure to the sun is so clearly a principal factor in the development of skin cancer, a commonsense program of prevention should be observed. Individuals with skin types I and II should avoid the sun as much as possible. For some people, this means total avoidance, which may be an extreme measure but is certainly the wisest course for those with light-sensitive skin.

Although sunburn heals readily and leaves no immediate damage, sun-induced skin damage is cumulative and irreversible and often equated with acute sunburn. Repetitive short exposures, even with no visible sunburn, can also lead to long-term skin damage. Tanning parlors, which use strong ultraviolet lamps, also damage the skin and are believed to increase the risk of skin cancer. The harmful portion of the sun's rays lies in the ultraviolet range. These rays are most intense between the hours of 10 A.M. and 2 P.M. The intensity of ultraviolet rays in the shade is often as much as 50 percent of that in bright sun. Even on cloudy, hazy days, 70 to 80 percent of the sun's ultraviolet rays reach the ground. A sandy beach increases ultraviolet intensity by 25 percent, and snow by 100 percent.

The use of effective sunscreen preparations on all exposed parts of the body is very important. In fact, since some clothing (specifically loose-knit fabrics, regardless of color) transmits more than 20 percent of the sun's ultraviolet rays, susceptible individuals may need to apply sunscreens to their upper bodies even when dressed. There are two types of effective sun-blocking products: sun-blocking agents which are completely opaque, usually thick and white, and often containing zinc oxide; and sunscreens which are usually liquid or lotion. The box in which they come explains the sunscreen ratings of the different sun products.

SUMMING UP

Skin cancer, although the most common cancer seen in the United States, is also the most curable. Early diagnosis and treatment sufficient to completely remove the cancer results in the highest cure rates. Disfigurement can be minimized by treatment at an early stage, before the cancer has spread to the underlying tissue.

The majority of skin cancer can be prevented by avoiding the sun. Conversely, the marked increase in skin cancer, including malignant melanoma, can be attributed largely to the popularity of suntanning.

It is important to have all moles checked by a dermatologist if they appear "ugly," have splotchy pigmentation, or irregular borders. All persons with a family history of melanoma should be examined by a dermatologist.

31

Cancer of the Stomach and Small Intestine

ROBERT J. MAYER, M.D.,
AND MARC B. GARNICK, M.D.

INTRODUCTION

Stomach cancer, once one of the most common malignancies in the United States, is now relatively rare, accounting for less than 3 percent of all cancers. In 1985, about 24,700 Americans developed stomach cancer, which caused 14,300 deaths. The disease is more common in men than women; in 1985, the disease was diagnosed in 15,000 men compared to 9,700 women.

Reasons for the dramatic drop in stomach cancer over the last five decades are unknown. In the 1930s, stomach cancer was by far the leading cause of cancer death in American men and ranked behind only uterine and breast cancers in women. Now it occurs only about one quarter as often as fifty years ago. The decline is worldwide, but it is much more pronounced in some areas than others. While marked declines in stomach cancer have occurred in the United States, Canada, New Zealand, and many tropical countries, the rate has remained fairly steady in others. In Great Britain, for example, it is still the third leading cause of cancer death and the disease is still relatively common in Japan, China, Chile, and Iceland.

CAUSES OF STOMACH CANCER

The cause of stomach cancer is unknown, but several predisposing conditions and related factors have been identified. It occurs most often among people from the lower social and economic classes, indicating that a poor diet may be a factor because the economically disadvantaged sometimes lack adequate refrigeration and often subsist on tainted or decaying food. In countries with a high incidence of stomach cancer, the disease is uncommon among the more affluent. When people from a country with a high rate of stomach cancer, such as Japan, move to the United States or other areas with a low incidence, their personal risk of developing the disease is unchanged. Succeeding generations, however, have a risk comparable to that of their adopted country. This has led researchers to postulate that diet or other environmental factors encountered early in life, rather than hereditary or genetic factors, predispose a person to develop stomach cancer.

The possible relationship between diet and stomach cancer has been studied both in Japan and among Japanese who have emigrated to Hawaii. The method of food preparation rather than particular foods appear to be associated with an increased incidence of stomach cancer. For example, consumption of foods like uncooked pickled vegetables, salty sauces, and dried salted fish correlated with an increase in stomach cancer, but unprocessed raw vegetables and raw fish did not.

The question of whether nitrates, chemicals that are widely used as food preservatives, cause stomach cancer is unresolved. Enzymes from bacteria that normally inhabit the intestinal tract can convert nitrates into nitrites; animal studies have implicated nitrites as potential carcinogens. Some population groups with a high intake of nitrates have higher rates of stomach cancer. There are many sources of nitrates; in some areas, well water contains high levels of the substance.

Conditions that reduce the production of acid by the stomach also seem to increase the cancer risk. These include pernicious anemia, the inability of the bone marrow to produce normal red blood cells due to insufficient absorption of vitamin B_{12}, and a type of gastritis marked by widespread atrophy of the tissues that produce gastric acid. Previous stomach surgery, such as removal of part of the organ because of benign ulcers or other disorders, seems to increase the risk of cancer fifteen or twenty years later. Chronic reflux of bile into the stomach is still another circumstance linked to a higher incidence of stomach cancer. At present, the mechanism by which these various circumstances may promote stomach cancer is unknown. Benign polyps and stomach ulcers have sometimes been linked to an increased cancer risk, but there is no firm evidence for this.

DIAGNOSIS

Early diagnosis of stomach cancer is essential if treatment is to be successful. In some countries where stomach cancer is relatively common, such as Japan, screening examinations for the disease are recommended. As a result, a larger percentage of stomach cancers are detected in an early, superficial stage and may account for the somewhat higher survival rate in Japan, compared to the United States.

In its early stages, stomach cancer may not cause any noticeable symptoms. Abdominal pain and discomfort, similar to those of a benign ulcer, are usually the first problems experienced by most patients with stomach cancer. Complaints of vague, persistent indigestion, a full feeling, or gas are common. Frequently, the patient will attempt to treat these early symptoms with antacids or home remedies; on the average, symptoms have been present for more than six months before the patient seeks medical attention. But weight loss, lack of appetite, and progressive upper abdominal pain over a period of several months typically prompt most patients to see a doctor. Even so, stomach cancer may not be suspected since these are symptoms that accompany many disorders. Sometimes a tumor, or mass, may be felt by the doctor during the physical examination, raising a suspicion of stomach cancer. A tumor large enough to be felt usually, but not always, indicates regional spread of the cancer.

There are no laboratory tests that specifically detect stomach cancer. However, a blood test showing iron deficiency anemia in men or occult (microscopic or hidden) blood in the stool should indicate that further tests are in order to determine if there is a gastrointestinal lesion accounting for the blood loss.

X-ray studies of the upper gastrointestinal tract will show whether there is a suspicious growth. Stomach cancer develops most often in the lower portion closest to the beginning of the small intestine (Figure 83). About 30 percent develop in the cardia, the area near the opening from the esophagus; 20 percent arise in the lesser curvature; 3 to 5 percent in the greater curvature and up to 10 percent involve sites throughout the organ.

Gastric ulcers (ulcers that develop in the stomach) deserve special attention, not because the ulcer may progress to a cancer, but because the

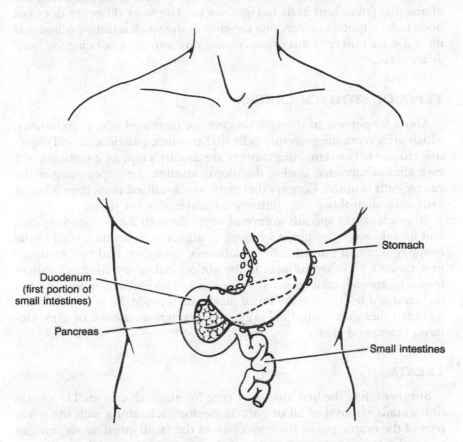

Figure 83 The stomach with adjacent organs and lymph nodes.

ulcer may actually be a cancer that has an eroded surface, making it appear like an ordinary ulcer. The ulcerating type of stomach cancer has the greatest potential for a cure, provided it is detected before it spreads to surrounding tissues. All gastric ulcers, especially recurring ones, should be carefully examined via gastroscopy—a test that involves passing an endoscope, a flexible hollow tube with fiberoptic viewing devices, through the throat into the stomach. To minimize any discomfort and gagging, the patient first gargles with a topical anesthetic or has it sprayed on the throat. A mild sedative, such as diazepam (Valium), also will be given. The endoscope is then passed down the throat and through the esophagus into the stomach. Small biopsy samples of tissue can be collected during the examination for later study by a pathologist. All gastric ulcers should be followed carefully, with repeat gastroscopy and biopsies of any that fail to heal in six to eight weeks. The same diligence does not need to be applied to ulcers that develop in the small intestine (duodenal ulcers) since cancer of this organ is quite rare and does not disguise itself as an ulcer.

TYPES OF STOMACH CANCER

About 90 percent of stomach cancers are ulcerated adenocarcinomas, which arise from the secretory cells that produce gastric acid and digestive enzymes. The remaining cancers are usually a type of lymphoma or a rare kind of sarcoma. During the biopsy studies, the appearance of the cancer cells is noted. Cancers that grow as a localized mass have a better prognosis than those that diffusely infiltrate adjacent tissue.

Stomach cancer spreads in several ways: through the lymphatic system and blood vessels; by direct invasion to adjacent structures, such as the esophagus, small intestine, liver, pancreas, or colon; and by "seeding" new cancers on other surfaces in the abdominal cavity. Stomach cancer tends to spread early in its development; quite often, it already has metastasized by the time the initial diagnosis is made. Sites of metastases include other gastrointestinal organs, lungs, bones, uterus, ovaries, kidneys, brain, and skin.

TREATMENT

Surgery offers the best chance of cure for stomach cancer. The operation entails removal of all or part of the stomach, along with the lower part of the esophagus or the upper part of the small intestine, depending upon the location of the cancer. If the cancer has spread to adjacent organs, such as the liver, spleen, pancreas, or colon, the affected parts of these organs also may be removed, provided there are no distant metastases. In situations where a cure is unlikely, surgery to remove the primary cancer may improve symptoms.

About 75 percent of patients whose cancers are confined to the stomach lining without spread to the deeper layers or other organs are potentially curable with surgical treatment. The five-year cure rate falls to 10 percent among patients with more advanced cancer, which, unfortunately, is most often the case. Overall, the five-year cure rate for stomach cancer is about 10 percent, a statistic that has not changed in the last twenty years.

Chemotherapy may be of significant, albeit temporary, benefit to patients with stomach cancer. The use of single anticancer drugs has produced a reduction in the size of the tumor in about a quarter of patients in whom this approach has been tried. A combination of drugs, principally FAM (5-FU, doxorubicin [Adriamycin], and mitomycin C) or FAMe (5-FU, doxorubicin, and methylCCNU), increases the response rate to 40 to 45 percent, but the average survival is still less than one year.

The use of adjuvant chemotherapy for patients whose cancer is potentially curable with surgery is being studied at several research centers. Since metastases will eventually develop in more than two thirds of patients undergoing surgery to remove their primary stomach cancer, there is a logical place for adjuvant chemotherapy as a preventive measure. Preliminary studies indicate that patients given 5-FU and methylCCNU following surgery may have a longer disease-free survival than patients treated with operation alone. But further study is needed before adjuvant chemotherapy can be recommended for all patients.

Radiation therapy alone, except for the local treatment of intestinal obstruction or metastases to the bones, is of little value in treating stomach cancer. The amount of radiation needed to eradicate the stomach cancer is greater than a patient can tolerate. The use of moderate amounts of radiation therapy following surgery, either alone or in combination with chemotherapy, has not significantly improved survival.

FOLLOWING TREATMENT

After removal of the stomach, many patients are surprised to learn that they can still eat their favorite foods, but meal patterns usually have to be changed. Patients who have had part or most of their stomachs removed can no longer handle a large meal without experiencing such symptoms as indigestion, cramps, gas, diarrhea, nausea, or dizziness—a condition referred to as "dumping syndrome." To overcome this, the patient should eat six or eight small meals during the day. Some foods may have to be pureed or well cooked to make them easier to digest. Of course, foods that prove irritating should be avoided. Before leaving the hospital, the patient and the person who prepares the meals should consult with a nutritionist or dietetic counselor for specific dietary guidelines.

CANCER OF THE SMALL INTESTINE

Cancer of the small intestine is quite rare; only about 2,200 new cases are diagnosed each year, and there are about 800 deaths. Men and women are equally affected.

The major predisposing factor for cancer of the small intestine appears to be long-standing disease, particularly Crohn's disease (regional enteritis). People with this chronic inflammatory bowel disease should be particularly alert to signs of possible intestinal cancer.

The rarity of small-intestine cancer and the vague or nonspecific symptoms they produce make diagnosis difficult. Chronic intestinal bleeding, intermittent obstruction of the bowel, and recurring abdominal pain are the warning signs. The presence of a tumor can be established with X-ray studies; an endoscopy with biopsy will confirm the diagnosis.

Three types of cancer may arise in the small intestine: adenocarcinoma, lymphoma, or carcinoid tumors. Treatment depends upon the type of cancer. Adenocarcinomas are treated by surgical removal of the cancer. At the time of surgery, however, metastases has occurred in about half of the patients. Lymphomas are treated with both surgery and combination chemotherapy and are associated with a far more favorable outcome than that observed for adenocarcinomas.

Patients with carcinoid tumors—slowly growing cancers that secrete hormones that can cause circulatory and digestive problems—may occasionally live for ten or fifteen years with their disease, even in the presence of metastases. Drugs can be given to counteract many of the distressing effects produced by the tumor hormones. Some patients may benefit from surgical reduction of large tumors and chemotherapy also can produce improvement.

SUMMING UP

The steady decline in stomach cancer in the United States over the last few decades has markedly lowered the death toll from this disease. It remains one of the less curable cancers, however, largely because it usually has reached an advanced stage by the time of diagnosis. Improvement in the death rate rests with a better understanding of the cause of stomach cancer as well as improved means of diagnosis and treatment.

32

Cancer of the Thyroid Gland

C. STRATTON HILL, JR., M.D.

INTRODUCTION

The thyroid gland is an important part of the human endocrine system that comprises a number of hormone glands throughout the body. The endocrine system is so named because the glands that make up this system secrete their hormones into the bloodstream rather than into a duct or directly into the interior of an organ like the stomach. A hormone (derived from the Greek word for messenger) is a chemical substance which produces an effect on a part of the body distant from the gland that originally secreted the hormone, although the ultimate effect may be on the entire body. Like nerves, the hormone-secreting glands are a controlling system in the body, but, unlike nerves, they do not have to be directly "connected" from one organ to another.

LOCATION OF THE THYROID GLAND

The thyroid gland is located in the front of the neck directly over the thyroid cartilage, or Adam's Apple (Figure 84). It is attached by support- ive tissue and moves upward with the cartilage during swallowing to help close the windpipe, thus preventing food and liquids from entering the lungs. This upward movement permits the physician to examine the gland better by feeling it under the skin. The close attachment of the gland to the larynx further aids examination of the gland by allowing the physician to feel a large portion of the rear part of the gland by gently pushing the trachea to one side or the other (Figure 85).

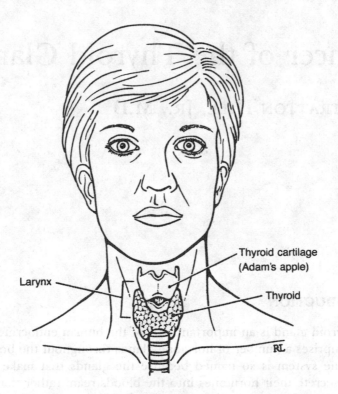

Figure 84 Location of thyroid gland and relationship to larynx.

Although located in the front of the neck in the fully developed adult, the thyroid gland does not start out there during fetal development. In fact, it originates on the floor of the embryo's pharynx and migrates toward the front of the neck during development. Failure of this normal

Steps in a Thyroid Examination

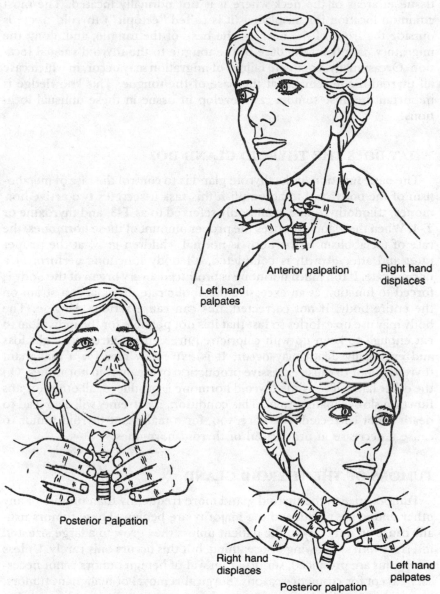

Anterior palpation

Right hand displaces

Left hand palpates

Posterior Palpation

Right hand displaces

Left hand palpates

Posterior palpation

Figure 85 Examination of thyroid gland from front and back.

migration process can account for the not-so-rare finding of thyroid tissue in areas of the neck where it is not normally located. The most common location for misplaced (it is called "ectopic") thyroid tissue is outside the front of the neck, at the base of the tongue, and along the migratory path from the base of the tongue to the thyroid's usual location. Occasionally, complete failure of migration may occur, in which case all thyroid tissue remains at the base of the tongue. This knowledge is important because tumors can develop in tissue in these unusual locations.

WHAT DOES THE THYROID GLAND DO?

The basic function of the thyroid gland is to control the rate of metabolism of the body, and to accomplish this task it secretes two active hormones, triiodothyronine, commonly referred to as T-3, and thyroxine or T-4. When the gland produces the proper amount of these hormones, the rate of metabolism in the body is normal, children grow at the proper rate, and after growth is completed, all body functions perform at a normal rate. If too much hormone is produced, every organ of the body is forced to function at an excessive metabolic rate that places a strain on the entire body. If not corrected, this can cause serious damage. The body may use up calories so fast that it is not possible for the individual to eat enough to keep up with caloric requirements. Extreme weight loss and eventually death may occur. It is extremely rare for a malignant thyroid tumor to cause excessive production of the thyroid hormones. On the other hand, if too little thyroid hormone is produced, all other organs function slower than normal. This condition, if extreme, will also lead to death if not corrected. It is rare, too, for a malignant thyroid tumor to cause a decrease in production of thyroid hormones.

TUMORS OF THE THYROID GLAND

Tumors arise in the thyroid gland more frequently than tumors of any other endocrine gland, and the majority are benign. These tumors usually cause no difficulty to the patient unless they grow to a large size and interfere with swallowing or breathing, but this occurs only rarely. Unless symptoms are produced, surgical removal of benign tumors is not necessary except for cosmetic reasons. Surgical removal of malignant tumors, however, is usually the most appropriate treatment. Since malignant thyroid tumors are in the minority and the removal of all thyroid masses would result in the vast majority of patients undergoing unnecessary operations, it is important to distinguish between benign and malignant tumors before surgery. This is possible in the case of a rare kind of thyroid cancer, medullary carcinoma, but for the more common types of thyroid tumors, a definite preoperative diagnosis is difficult to obtain. Great strides toward improving the chances of a definitive preoperative diagnosis have been made in the past decade, largely due to technological developments and to the increasing skill of pathologists in interpreting tissue specimens removed from the gland by simple needle biopsy.

Diagnosis

Most thyroid tumors are discovered by the patient while looking in a mirror shaving or applying makeup, or by friends or relatives who notice a bulge in the front of the neck just below or to one side of the Adam's Apple. These tumors occur five times more frequently in women than in men, and are especially common in women of childbearing age. Consequently, many thyroid tumors are discovered incidentally by obstetricians during prenatal examination, a point that emphasizes the fact that thyroid tumors usually do not produce symptoms. When symptoms are present, they are related to either the enlargement in the neck, e.g., discomfort on swallowing, or to disturbance in thyroid function.

There are a number of ways to treat a thyroid tumor. In general, if the tumor is benign, as evidenced by a scan, biopsy, and clinical impression, and is producing no symptoms or cosmetic concern, surgery is not necessary. If the tumor is malignant, the consensus at present is that it should be surgically removed.

Past History of Radiation Exposure

An important indicator of the likelihood of a malignant thyroid tumor is whether the patient has been exposed to X-ray treatments to the head and neck area during infancy or before puberty. Before antibiotics were available for control of infectious diseases of the head and neck, such as tonsillitis, adenoiditis, and mastoiditis, it was popular to treat these conditions with moderate doses of X-ray radiation. The medical profession at that time did not know that these treatments could expose the thyroid gland to significant amounts of radiation and they were not aware of the consequences of this exposure. Clinical studies done on several large groups of patients who underwent this treatment have established that the likelihood of a thyroid tumor being malignant as a result of this exposure is significantly increased. Similar results were obtained in studies of natives of the Marshall Islands who were accidentally exposed to radiation from the atomic bomb that was detonated on Bikini Atoll in 1954. Inhabitants of some of the islands were exposed through drinking water contaminated by radioactive iodine from the fall-out.

Another outdated and inappropriate medical practice, the treatment by X ray of newborn infants who had breathing difficulty, accounted for exposure to radiation of the thyroid in a significant number of patients. It was erroneously believed that infants whose thymus gland appeared too large on chest X rays had difficulty breathing because their upper respiratory tract was obstructed by the thymus. The X-ray treatments, needlessly administered to shrink the thymus, also exposed the thyroid gland, which is located in the same general area. The physician needs to carefully question the patient with a thyroid tumor about exposure to any source of radiation received before puberty because this increases the probability of a malignant tumor.

Laboratory Tests and Procedures

Blood Tests

The blood test that is now used to diagnose thyroid cancer can only detect the presence of a certain type of thyroid cancer, not the absence of it or of any other kind of cancer. Thus, blood tests for thyroid cancer are not useful at present, except for detecting the rare medullary carcinoma variety. Patients should therefore question a diagnosis that thyroid cancer is not present when that assessment is based on a blood test. Blood tests are available, however, that give a reasonably accurate indication of the recurrence or metastasis of certain types of thyroid cancer in patients who have been previously treated for the disease.

Imaging Techniques

Radioactive iodine, or other isotopes, can produce an image of the thyroid gland in graphic form which provides useful information. Since thyroid hormones are made by combining naturally occurring iodine with proteins in the thyroid gland, this gland is the body's chief user of iodine. This very fortunate phenomenon can be used to produce a "picture" of the thyroid gland which is useful in diagnosing abnormal conditions. If radioactive iodine is used in place of normal or stable iodine, energy particles are emitted that can be received by a device which can then translate the pattern and intensity of these particles into an image, and a picture, called a thyroid scan, is created. If every part of the gland uses iodine uniformly, a normal picture of the gland results. If some parts of the gland do not use or take up iodine in a normal way, the distribution of iodine is not uniform and an abnormal picture is created. Malignant tissue characteristically does not use iodine in a normal way and therefore an abnormal picture is more likely to be created when there is a malignant tumor in the thyroid gland than when there is a benign one. Unfortunately, this test is not as precise as it sounds because normal tissue can overlie a malignant tumor, creating a falsely reassuring image. Other factors may also influence the thyroid scan, so that it is not always accurate, but in general it gives a good indication of whether or not a tumor of the thyroid gland is malignant.

In scientific jargon, radioactive substances are called "hot," and this usage has been adopted by the clinician to describe areas of increased and decreased concentrations of radioactivity as "hot" or "cold," respectively. Sometimes an area with only a small decrease in concentration is referred to as a "cool" area, but this description is not particularly useful. Malignant tissue is not the only condition that will produce an area of decreased concentration of an isotope; a benign cyst filled with fluid will also fail to metabolize iodine and produce a "cold" spot. "Hot" areas, that is, areas concentrating more iodine than the surrounding tissue, are only rarely malignant.

The technique of imaging internal body structures by ultrasound has greatly improved in recent years and one of its new major uses is to distinguish hollow cystic structures from solid ones. Ultrasound may be used as the next logical step if the thyroid scan revealed a "cold" tumor, or it may be used as the initial evaluation technique after physical examination of the nodule. If the tumor proves to be cystic, fluid can be removed easily by suction with a small needle (aspiration) and the cells it contains studied for malignancy. If the cells are normal and the cyst does not recur, no additional treatment is necessary. Frequently the cyst reaccumulates fluid and must be repeatedly aspirated. If the cells contained in the fluid appear malignant or suspicious, the cyst should be removed.

Needle Biopsy

Needle biopsy of the thyroid gland has been used for many years in a few medical centers but now there is more widespread interest in the technique. The major limitation to needle biopsy in the past was the lack of trained pathologists to interpret the rather scanty amounts of tissue which needle biopsy provides. Another problem is the bleeding that occasionally follows it. The recent growth in interest in the technique centers on the use of small needles for aspiration (suction) biopsies. Biopsies obtained in this way provide unconnected cells rather than a small slice of tissue for study. The advantage of small needles is the low probability of hemorrhaging as a complication. More and more pathologists have been trained in interpreting the aspirated material, and several centers throughout the country can perform this examination with a high degree of accuracy. The patient to whom this procedure is proposed should inquire about the experience of the physician doing the biopsy and the pathologist interpreting the specimen.

In the hands of experienced surgeons and pathologists, needle aspiration can provide a definitive answer about the nature of a thyroid tumor, solid or cystic, in the shortest possible time and with the least cost. Unfortunately there are certain cell types in the thyroid that are difficult to interpret, particularly lymphocytes, whether normal or abnormal, and some specimens will produce equivocal results. Surgical biopsy may be necessary to resolve any uncertainty because lymphoma, a serious malignant disease, may occur in the thyroid.

MALIGNANT TUMORS OF THE THYROID
Types

Three principal tumors develop in the thyroid gland and are distinguished on the basis of their cell of origin, the appearance of their cell structure under the microscope (morphology), and their clinical course. The thyroid gland has two principal tissue cell types which perform hormonal functions. The cell which performs the characteristic function of the thyroid (secreting thyroid hormone) is called a "follicular" cell, composes the bulk of the gland, and is arranged in thousands of microscopic sac-like structures called "follicles." Tumors of this cell type can take several forms, and the names applied, such as papillary or Hürthle cell, basically describe their form as it appears under the microscope. Since the cells of these tumors maintain a reasonably close resemblance to the normal follicular cell, they are grouped together into the category "differentiated carcinoma of the thyroid." A tumor composed of these cells which has lost all resemblance to the normal follicular cell is called "anaplastic" carcinoma and placed in the category "undifferentiated carcinoma" (Table 22).

The second cell of the thyroid is derived from a structure far removed from the thyroid gland. During the embryological period, certain cells migrate from the primitive central nervous structure and are eventually spread throughout both lobes of the thyroid gland. These cells maintain their separate function, producing calcitonin, a hormone that regulates calcium and bone metabolism. A tumor of these cells is extremely rare, but when it occurs it is called medullary or "C-cell" carcinoma of the thyroid.

Cells of the supporting and connective tissue which form a framework for the tissue cells are also present in the thyroid, as are cells which make up the walls of blood vessels. Lymphocytes, too, have a great affinity for the thyroid gland. All of these cell types have been known to form malignant tumors in any portion of the body in which they are found, including the thyroid, but they are not primarily thyroid tumors, so they will not be discussed in this chapter. If a lymphoma (see Chapter 24, "Hodgkin's Disease and Other Lymphomas") initially appears in the thyroid, the patient should be examined for manifestations of this disease in other parts of the body, because lymphoma is basically a systemic disease.

Table 22
TYPES OF THYROID CANCER

TUMORS OF FOLLICULAR CELL ORIGIN
Differentiated carcinoma
Papillary carcinoma
Follicular carcinoma
Mixed papillary and follicular carcinoma
Hürthle cell carcinoma
Undifferentiated carcinoma
Spindle and giant cell carcinoma
TUMORS OF NONFOLLICULAR CELL ORIGIN
Medullary carcinoma
OTHER MALIGNANT TUMORS FOUND
IN THE THYROID GLAND
Epidermoid carcinoma
Lymphoma (all types)
Fibrosarcoma
Hemangiosarcoma
Osteogenic sarcoma
Osteochondrosarcoma

DIFFERENTIATED THYROID CANCER

The types of cancer in this category are called follicular, papillary, mixed follicular and papillary, and Hürthle cell. Differentiated thyroid cancer is clearly the most common thyroid cancer, accounting for approximately 85 percent of all thyroid cancers, and is four times as common in women as in men. It occurs most often among people twenty to fifty years old and is recognized as the thyroid cancer induced by exposure to moderate doses of radiation therapy, usually requiring many years after exposure for the tumor to develop. In fact, cases have been reported up to twenty-eight years after exposure. Fortunately the practice of treating benign conditions of the head and neck with radiation therapy has been abandoned, so that the number of these cases should greatly diminish in the years ahead.

The tumor itself is usually discovered accidentally by the patient, a friend or relative. A significant number are discovered during routine prenatal examinations by obstetricians. In men, the size of the neck may insidiously increase until the shirt collar becomes tight, yet there is no obvious tumor.

The most common finding during a physical examination is a single tumor about one quarter to one half inch in diameter in one of the thyroid lobes. Occasionally it may grow to a relatively large size before the patient or the family notices it and the patient seeks medical attention. The second most common finding is enlarged lymph nodes in the front of the neck on the same side as the tumor. It is to this chain of lymph nodes that the tumor is likely to spread first (Figure 86).

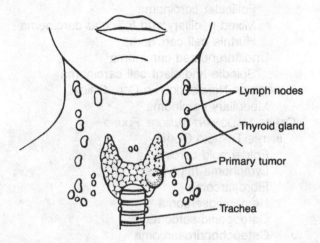

Figure 86 Primary tumor and most common metastatic site to deep cervical nodes (internal jugular chain).

Those who study disease often make references to the natural history of a disease or tumor, that is, the effect the disease or tumor would have on the patient if it were allowed to go untreated. The natural history of a disease can either subside or progress until it eventually overwhelms the patient and causes chronic disease and death. The natural history of a tumor can take one of several paths. The tumor can spontaneously disappear, although this is rare. It can, after it has attained a certain size, either cease to grow and not spread to other parts of the body, or cease to grow but spread to other parts of the body, or continue to grow and spread to other parts of the body. A tumor which grows rapidly and spreads to other parts of the body is considered an "aggressive" tumor, while one that grows slowly and spreads slowly is referred to as indolent.

Differentiated thyroid cancer is, in most cases, best described as an indolent malignant tumor. In fact, some patients have had enlarged lymph nodes in their neck for decades, which they have ignored, but which when biopsied were found to have differentiated thyroid cancer which had already metastasized (spread to other parts of the body). The thyroid gland is then removed and a primary tumor is found. In addition, many patients with biopsy-proved primary tumors and even with ones which have metastasized have refused treatment and have survived for long periods of time. Although it would seem that the need for early diagnosis and treatment does not apply to this tumor, it should be realized that not all differentiated thyroid cancers are indolent, and investigators have been unable to determine which factors cause one tumor to be more aggressive than another. It is therefore prudent to treat all differentiated thyroid cancers as soon as practicable.

Most doctors agree that primary differentiated thyroid carcinoma should be treated by surgical removal of the tumor and that all tumor tissue should be removed if possible. If both thyroid lobes have tumors, they should both be removed. If the lymph nodes of the neck are involved and the tumor has invaded the muscles and other structures of the neck, it may be necessary to remove some of them. There is disagreement among doctors, however, about the extent of surgery required when the tumor is confined to one lobe of the gland and only occupies a small part of it. This situation occurs more frequently than involvement of both lobes. Some doctors advocate removal of only the lobe containing the tumor along with the isthmus (connection between the lobes), others advocate removing the entire gland. There would probably be no objection to the latter procedure if the risk of complications (damage to the recurrent laryngeal nerve, resulting in vocal cord paralysis, and damage to the parathyroid glands, resulting in blood calcium disturbance) were less. Of the two complications, parathyroid damage is the more serious medically, but to the patient a change in the voice may be devastating.

An attempt to remove the thyroid completely places the patient at risk of losing all the parathyroid glands, four small structures in the lower neck which together control the calcium level in the body (Figure 87). This is not necessarily a bad reflection on the capability of the surgeon performing the operation because, although the parathyroid glands may be identified, the blood supply is extremely fragile. If it is interrupted, the result may be death to the glands, and consequently, hypoparathyroidism, in spite of the most meticulous operation by the surgeon. Hypoparathyroidism can be very difficult to treat and may produce serious consequences for the patient. Since it has not been conclusively shown that patients who have the entire thyroid gland removed survive longer than those who do not, placing the patient at risk of developing hypoparathyroidism is often unjustified.

The ideal solution to the controversy of whether the thyroid should be entirely or only partially removed would be to conduct a scientifically controlled study with two comparable patient groups. One group would be treated by removal of the entire thyroid gland and the other by removal of one lobe and isthmus, the section bridging the left and right lobes. The course of the two groups would be followed over sufficient

566

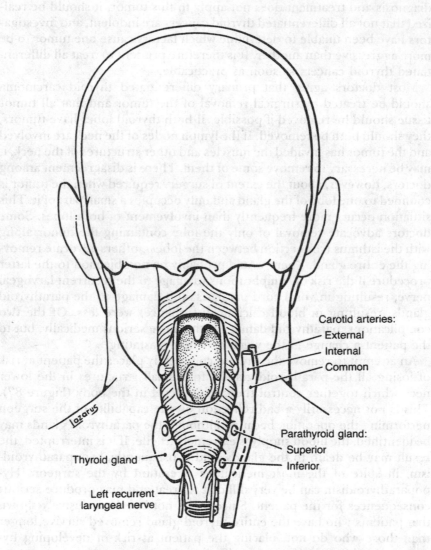

Figure 87 View of pharynx from the back, showing parathyroid glands and recurrent laryngeal nerve.

time to determine which group had a better quality of life, fewer complications from treatment, and a longer survival. Unfortunately the indolent growth of this tumor and its low incidence makes this approach difficult.

At the present time, the consensus is to compromise. Most large medical centers recommend a "near total" thyroidectomy for disease found to be confined to one lobe. In this procedure the lobe containing the tumor is completely removed, along with the isthmus and most of the opposite lobe. A small rim of the back portion of the lobe is left in order to spare at least one of the four parathyroid glands. One gland is sufficient to maintain parathyroid function which, along with calcitonin, regulates calcium and bone metabolism.

At the time of surgery it is wise for the surgeon to sample nodes in the anterior part of the neck to determine if the disease has spread beyond the confines of the gland. The anterior part of the neck is the area in front of the windpipe between the two carotid arteries at either side. Nodes in this area are removed and given to the pathologist for immediate study during the surgery. If positive nodes are found, a "compartmental dissection" should be done, removing all the nodes in this area (see Figure 88). Sometimes the surgeon will discover lymph nodes outside the anterior compartment and behind the neck muscles that were not detected during the physical examination before surgery. In these cases, neck dissection may be necessary, but rarely is radical neck dissection (which can be considerably disfiguring) necessary, because most experienced surgeons can successfully remove the malignant tumor in its entirety without it. It should be remembered, however, that radical neck dissections can be necessary in rare situations for the treatment of thyroid cancers.

Radioactive Iodine

The rationale for using radioactive iodine in the treatment of differentiated thyroid carcinoma stems from the fact that thyroid follicular cells accumulate and concentrate iodine in a greater quantity than any other cells of the body. Radioactive iodine is metabolized in the same way stable iodine is, and one of the early steps in the metabolic process is to "trap" iodine inside the thyroid cell in a concentration far greater than the surrounding blood or other body tissues. Unlike stable iodine, radioactive iodine disrupts the cell function and, if intense enough, will destroy the cell. Malignant cells do not carry out this metabolic process with the same efficiency as normal cells, so the effectiveness of this treatment method varies from tumor to tumor. Also, the tumor may initially metabolize radioactive iodine fairly efficiently, but with later treatments this ability may diminish or be lost altogether.

Radioactive iodine is administered by mouth, in either liquid or capsule form. Absorption takes place in the usual manner, through the intestines,

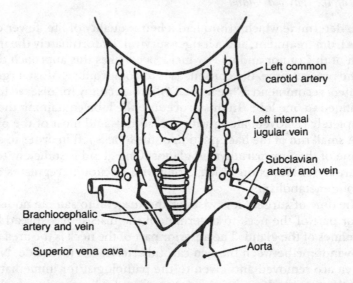

Figure 88 Front compartment between two carotid arteries; lymphatic drainage system shown on patient's right.

and the radioactive iodine then circulates in the bloodstream to all parts of the body. The individual who is treated with radioactive iodine not only exposes the thyroid cells to the effects of radiation, but exposes the entire body as well, so the treating physician must weigh the potential benefits of treatment with radioactive iodine against the potential harm of whole-body radiation. If an adequate pretreatment test dose of radioactive iodine indicates that the malignant tissue, either in the neck or elsewhere, does not concentrate the isotope, there will then be no benefit from this type of treatment and the radiation exposure to the whole body would not be justified. The situation may not be all-or-none, and in that case the physician must use his best judgment to decide whether the balance favors treatment with radioactive iodine.

Radioactive iodine is used in the treatment of well-differentiated thyroid carcinoma when surgery is not possible, when the benefits of surgery do not justify the risks, or when the disease has spread. Doctors disagree about the role of radioactive iodine as part of the initial treatment of differentiated thyroid cancer, a controversy which is an outgrowth of the disagreement about the extent of surgery required. Physicians who feel that removal of the affected lobe and the isthmus is sufficient for initial surgical therapy do not feel that radioactive iodine has any place in the initial therapy. Those physicians who feel that all tissue must be either removed or destroyed are also divided in their opinion, but experience has shown that it is almost impossible for a surgeon to completely remove all tissue that concentrates radioactive iodine. Since the greatest amount of radiation comes from the beta particle of the isotope, which has the energy for penetrating one or two millimeters, it is best to destroy all thyroid tissue, malignant or not, as early as possible, when it is small and can be done effectively. In cases where some thyroid tissue has been intentionally left behind to protect the parathyroid glands, destruction of the remaining tissue by radioactive iodine is a planned part of the initial treatment.

Other physicians, however, view all such tissue remaining in a normal location (in the "bed" of the removed thyroid), whether intentionally left or not, as nonmalignant tissue which should not be destroyed with radioactive iodine. If, on the other hand, tissue is found in abnormal locations, such as the lymph nodes in the jugular chain in the front of the neck, it clearly is malignant and a stronger case can be made for radioactive iodine. But even in this situation, no unanimity of opinion exists. Advocates of hormonal therapy feel that the administration of thyroid hormones is sufficient to prevent tumor growth, and radioactive iodine is not needed.

Hormonal Therapy

Hormonal therapy of differentiated thyroid cancer is performed by administering thyroid hormone by mouth, regularly and for a long time. The use is based on the premise that, for the thyroid tumor to grow, there must be an adequate amount of the thyroid-stimulating hormone TSH (produced by the pituitary gland) circulating in the bloodstream. If the tumor is deprived of this hormone, it will not grow and, indeed, may even disappear. The thyroid hormone is able to suppress TSH production by "negative feedback," a mechanism which controls many hormonal functions. The concentrating of thyroid hormone circulating in the bloodstream determines how much TSH the pituitary will secrete. As the thyroid hormone concentration increases, the TSH concentration decreases and, if a sufficient amount of thyroid hormone is given (see Figure 89), the TSH can be completely shut off. Some physicians feel so strongly about the dependence of thyroid tumors on TSH that they recommend thyroid hormone therapy alone when it is known that the disease has spread. In rare instances, because of the indolence of most thyroid cancer, some physicians recommend hormonal therapy as the treatment for the primary tumor. While it is clear that most thyroid cancers depend on TSH, it is not certain that all do.

Thyroid hormones are given not only for suppression of the pituitary gland and consequent suppression of the thyroid tumor, but also to prevent hypothyroidism and its ill effects. Suppressive doses are somewhat higher than simple replacement doses.

Hormonal Feedback System

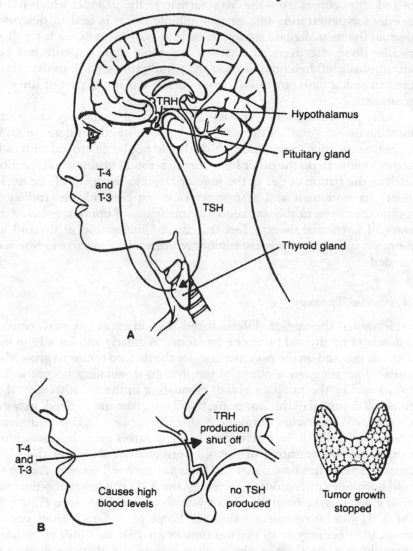

Figure 89A Normal relationship between TRH and TSH and the blood levels of T-4 and T-3.

    89B Negative feedback approach to stop thyroid cancer growth by taking high doses of T-4 and T-3 orally. This decreases or totally shuts off TRH production and in turn TSH production stops. Theoretically, if tumor is deprived of this hormone (TSH), it will stop growing and may even disappear.

It is difficult to assess the effectiveness of thyroid hormone therapy because of the indolent nature of this well-differentiated thyroid cancer. Certainly it is not prudent to continue this type of therapy alone in the face of a tumor that continues to grow. If such large amounts of thyroid hormone are needed to suppress TSH (which is easily measurable in the laboratory) that the result is hyperthyroidism, then this form of therapy alone is also clearly inadequate.

External Beam X-ray Therapy

This type of therapy is rarely used to treat well-differentiated thyroid cancer. Occasionally during surgery, disease is encountered that invades the wall of the trachea, the thyroid cartilage, and the cricoid cartilage underneath the surrounding soft tissue, which cannot be removed without producing serious scarring or a serious functional defect, such as a permanent tracheostomy or laryngectomy. Such cases, as well as those in which the tumor does not concentrate radioactive iodine, should be treated with "sterilizing" doses of external beam X-ray therapy administered to the tissues that cannot be surgically removed. The surgeon can help the radiation therapist by implanting metal clips at the edges of these tissues left behind in order to identify the boundaries of the treatment field for the X-ray treatments which will take place later.

Treatment—Recurrent or Metastatic Disease

Surgery is the appropriate treatment for not only initial disease, but also recurrent or spreading tumors, providing it is accessible and does not substantially decrease the patient's ability to function. Because of the slow-growing nature of this tumor, extensive surgical procedures which would be inappropriate in the treatment of many other cancers, such as removing solitary tumors in the lung, are often appropriate. When recurrent and metastatic tumors (those that have spread) cannot be surgically treated, radioactive iodine is the recommended treatment. For those tumors that do not concentrate radioactive iodine, or lose this ability after several treatments, external beam X-ray treatment or chemotherapy may prove beneficial.

Many patients have, however, lived for long periods of time with known metastatic disease and little or no further treatment. In most instances these patients are taking thyroid hormone and are presumed to be controlled because of the suppression of TSH secretion from the pituitary.

ANAPLASTIC CANCER OF THE THYROID

This is a very different disease from well-differentiated thyroid cancer. Rather than being slow-growing, it is unfortunately characterized by rapid progression often ending in death within several months of diagnosis.

Anaplastic thyroid cancer starts in a variety of ways. Some patients who have been diagnosed and treated for differentiated thyroid cancer suddenly experience an acceleration of tumor growth, with the tumor spreading throughout the body. It is not known why this change occurs, but it may be that anaplastic cancer evolves from differentiated thyroid cancer, although the cellular pattern for anaplastic cancer under the microscope bears no resemblance to the characteristic follicular cell of the other. There are, however, areas of differentiated cancer intimately associated with the anaplastic, and areas which appear to be transitional in appearance from one type to the other, further supporting the idea that this tumor can originate in the differentiated variety.

Sometimes anaplastic thyroid cancer is found in association with a goiter, that is, an enlargement of the thyroid gland that is usually benign. Goiters are not uncommon and seem to run in families, especially among women. Many people ignore them and never seek medical advice; some carry their goiter to their grave without its ever causing any problem. Others, however, notice a sudden acceleration of growth, with the goiter rapidly impinging upon their windpipe and causing difficulty breathing, but no other symptoms. In some such cases, differentiated carcinoma is found to be associated with the anaplastic cancer, and the goiter is presumed to have been a slow-growing differentiated cancer which has been transformed into the anaplastic variety.

Although it is wise to seek medical advice if a goiter changes in any way, not all goiters which enlarge suddenly mean cancer. For example, bleeding may occur in the goiter and produce sudden enlargement.

Anaplastic cancer may arise in a person with known previous thyroid disease and progress in much the same way as it does in patients with previous cancer or goiter: the tumor appears suddenly in the neck and grows rapidly. The fast growth may interfere with the blood supply to the skin overlying the tumor, causing ulceration of the skin.

Treatment

There is no reliable treatment to alter the course of this disease. It is presumed to have already spread by the time it is diagnosed, even if it appears to the surgeon that there was complete removal of the tumor at the time of the operation. In the majority of cases, the tumor grows quite large and invades surrounding structures in the neck, clearly making complete surgical removal impossible. In an attempt to control the tumor locally and to prevent it from obstructing the patient's breathing, as much tissue as possible will be surgically removed, and the remaining tissue treated by radiation therapy. These two treatment methods complement each other and result in a greater reduction in tumor size than would be possible by either alone.

Since the tumor is presumed to have spread by the time of diagnosis, immediate systemic therapy is necessary but, unfortunately, there is no consistently effective chemotherapy drug. Dactinomycin and doxorubicin are two agents that have shown the greatest success rate, but even they are not very effective. Fortunately this tumor is rare, accounting for approximately 5 percent of all thyroid cancers. The rarity of the disease, and therefore the scarcity of patients to study, hampers research into new drugs which might effect control of the disease.

MEDULLARY CARCINOMA OF THE THYROID

Medullary carcinoma of the thyroid accounts for approximately 10 percent of all thyroid cancers. This tumor is derived from cells which migrate from the primitive nervous system in the embryo and ultimately end up in the thyroid gland. These cells produce a hormone called calcitonin which acts on calcium and bone metabolism. For these reasons, medullary thyroid carcinoma probably should not be called a "true" thyroid cancer. Because the cells produce calcitonin, the term "C-cell carcinoma" has been proposed.

Medullary thyroid cancer may occur sporadically or may be hereditary. In the familial form, it is transmitted as a dominant trait, meaning that it occurs in every generation and can occur in both men and women. The two forms cannot be distinguished, even under a microscope, but do differ in two significant ways: the sporadic type seems to have a slightly better prognosis and the familial type is often associated with a syndrome involving two other endocrine tumors.

Sporadic Medullary Cancer

Sporadic medullary carcinoma of the thyroid is likely to occur in only one lobe, and when it spreads to other parts of the body, it tends to spread to lymph nodes in the neck early in the course of the disease. When examined under a microscope, these tumors exhibit a protein called amyloid, which contains the hormone calcitonin. The cells of this tumor occur in closely packed "sheets," and do not form follicles, as differentiated carcinoma does.

Medullary cancer is the only thyroid cancer that can be diagnosed with certainty prior to the removal of tissue by biopsy or surgery. This can be done by measuring the amount of calcitonin in the blood of the patient, because the tumor produces excess amounts of this hormone. Following removal of the tumor, the calcitonin level usually drops, but may not return to normal. Over the years the level of hormone usually increases, whether or not recurrent or metastatic disease can be demonstrated.

Approximately one fourth of patients with advanced medullary thyroid cancer develop severe unexplained watery diarrhea, and some patients have been known to have up to thirty stools a day. The urge to defecate may occur suddenly and it may be difficult or impossible for the patient to control.

Familial Medullary Cancer

Familial medullary carcinoma almost always involves both lobes of the gland. Its microscopic appearance and the way in which it spreads to other portions of the body are identical to the sporadic variety, and it also produces excess calcitonin. The main distinguishing feature of familial medullary thyroid cancer is a family history of the disease. Theoretically, 50 percent of the patient's brothers and sisters may have it. Parathyroid tumors and a tumor of the adrenal medulla may occur simultaneously with, before, or after the discovery of this kind of thyroid cancer. The parathyroid tumor produces excess parathyroid hormone, causing elevated calcium concentration in the blood, and the adrenal medullary tumor may produce an excess of adrenaline-like substances in the blood which elevate the blood pressure. The adrenal tumor commonly arises in both right and left adrenal glands and may be multiple on one or both sides. Some patients may have small tumors composed of nerve tissue on the eyelids, lips, tongue, and inside of the mouth, and on the nerve endings in the gastrointestinal tract.

Surgical removal of the tumor is the most appropriate treatment for the sporadic variety, and a total thyroidectomy is generally performed for two reasons. First, although there may be no family history of this cancer, it is possible that there has been a gene mutation and the patient represents a new familial variety, in which case the tumor is likely to be present on the other side too. Second, to reduce the blood calcitonin as much as possible, it is desirable to remove the calcitonin-producing cells in the lobe opposite the side of the known tumor. Although the calcitonin level cannot be completely relied upon as an indicator of recurrent disease, a continuing low level is some reassurance that the tumor has not recurred or spread.

Surgical removal of the tumor is also the most common treatment for the familial variety. However, if the other tumors associated with medullary thyroid cancer are present, it is desirable to remove the tumor of the adrenal medulla before either the thyroid or parathyroid tumor is removed. Although without stress the adrenal medullary tumor may not produce symptoms, surgery, trauma, or other types of stress may cause excessive secretion of substances which cause a very high blood pressure that can be extremely hazardous. Patients who have the adrenal tumor can be conditioned for surgery with medication that will protect them from blood pressure changes. The treatment for recurrent and spreading tumors is surgical removal if possible. If this is not possible, radiation therapy and chemotherapy, although less effective than surgery, are appropriate.

FOLLOW-UP FOR THYROID CANCER

After initial therapy, patients with differentiated carcinoma should see their doctor every three months the first year, every six months during the second year, and at yearly intervals after that, if no recurrence or metastasis has been found. If recurrence or spreading occurs, the follow-up interval should revert to three months and then progress to longer intervals. Patients with medullary cancer should probably see their doctor every three months for five to eight years, and then every six months. Patients with anaplastic thyroid cancer should be followed closely and the treatment should be tailored to fit their individual needs.

Radioactive iodine scanning follow-up is used to detect differentiated carcinoma when the doctor cannot feel the presence of a tumor during a physical exam. Physicians are not in agreement about the frequency of scanning follow-up, but one typical schedule is to repeat the scan within a year following the total dose of radioactive iodine. If this scan shows no concentration of the isotope in any part of the body, no further scanning should be done for five years. If the five-year scan is also normal, further scanning is usually not necessary unless distinct clinical signs appear.

Thyroglobulin

Thyroglobulin is the protein in which the thyroid hormone is stored. Patients who have had all of their thyroid tissue removed will have low levels or none of this substance in their bloodstream. Since differentiated carcinoma is capable of producing great amounts of this material, its presence is a sign of recurrent or metastatic disease of this type. Periodic measurements of this substance can be useful in the follow-up of patients with differentiated carcinoma. But since even a rising level of thyroglobulin is not always an indication of the presence of differentiated carcinoma, treatment is not justified and, for this reason, some physicians avoid using the test.

SURVEILLANCE PROCEDURES
FOR PATIENTS WITH EARLY X-RAY EXPOSURE

A special committee appointed by the National Cancer Institute has made recommendations for follow-up procedures for people with a history of exposure to X ray of the head and neck in infancy and childhood. The recommendations suggest that, on the basis of initial physical examination, patients should be divided into three categories. In Category I are patients with no abnormalities apparent to eye or touch. For these people, a careful reexamination of the thyroid gland is recommended at least every two years, but a thyroid scan is not necessary. In Category II are those patients with a discrete nodule or nodules that can be felt by the physician. These patients should have surgical removal of the gland, regardless of findings on a scan. Category III comprises those patients with diffuse enlargement of gland but without a palpable nodule. Patients in this category should be very carefully studied to determine the exact nature of the enlargement.

Appropriate studies for Category III patients include determination of TSH, thyroid hormone, and antithyroid antibody levels in the blood and possibly a needle biopsy to differentiate among the various forms of benign enlargement and among the thyroid diseases, other than cancer, that can result in an enlarged gland. A thyroid scan should be performed and, if no areas of abnormal concentration are found, the patient should be placed on hormone therapy to shrink the enlarged thyroid tissues, since they may conceal a silent "cold" nodule buried deep in the gland. The patient should then be reexamined in six months and, if a nodule is present, undergo exploratory surgery. If no nodule is felt, the patient may continue on thyroid therapy indefinitely and be reexamined annually. If the scan shows a definite cold area but no nodule is felt, the patient should be placed on thyroid hormone and reexamined in six months. Exploratory surgery is not necessary in this case unless a nodule is felt.

SUMMING UP

Tumors of the thyroid gland occur more frequently than those of any other endocrine gland, excluding male and female gonadal tumors. Most of these tumors are benign and seldom produce symptoms. Ionizing irradiation is known to induce benign thyroid tumors and one type of thyroid cancer. Persons who were exposed to moderate doses of ionizing radiation during infancy and childhood have an increased risk of developing thyroid cancer.

There are several types of thyroid cancer, the most common being the differentiated variety. This type is slow-growing and patients who undergo treatment generally enjoy a long survival. The outlook is not as good for patients with anaplastic carcinoma. Medullary carcinoma falls between the differentiated and anaplastic varieties. In any event, surgical removal of the tumor is the treatment of choice for all cancers arising in this organ.

33

Urinary Tract Cancer

GEORGE W. JONES, M.D.

Urinary tract cancers, originating mostly in the bladder and kidney, account for 9 percent of all cancer in men and 4 percent of all cancer in women. These cancers tend to afflict whites more frequently than blacks and generally strike those over the age of fifty. While the direct cause of urinary tract cancers is unknown, research suggests a relationship with certain industrial chemicals and dyes and tobacco, and associations have been reported with certain analgesics such as aspirin and phenacetin, as well as with saccharin and cyclamates, chronic urinary tract infections, and hormones. Heredity does not seem to play a significant role except in a few rare instances.

In understanding cancer of the urinary tract, a basic knowledge of this vital biological system is helpful. The kidney, ureter, bladder, and urethra are its basic component parts (Figures 90, 91). The outer portion of the kidney, the parenchyma, receives blood through the renal artery, extracts water, chemicals, and nutrients needed by the body, and produces waste fluid for excretion. This waste is transported through the pelvis and ureter to the bladder where it collects until excreted through the urethra. In men, the urethra runs from the bladder through the prostate located just below, and out through the penis. In women, there is no prostate, and urine is excreted directly from the body through the shorter urethra.

Most of the urinary system is lined with the same type of cells, all of which are susceptible to the same type of cancer—transitional cell carcinoma. Bladder cancer, which is the most common type of transitional cell cancer, is also the most common urinary tract cancer, accounting for 6 percent of all tumors in men. The kidney is the site of about 4 percent of cancer in men.

WARNING SIGNS

Blood seen in the urine (hematuria) is by far the major warning sign of urinary tract tumors, even when it is visible only through microscopic or chemical tests. When blood has been detected in the urine, there are several ways to determine its exact source. Obtaining urine directly from the bladder by use of a catheter can give the physician more information, as can a study of what point during urination the blood appears (if it is visible).

In men, blood occurring in the beginning of urination implies a problem in either the prostate gland or the urethra. In women, the same symptom generally indicates urethral bleeding, although bleeding is overlooked more often in women than in men. Blood seen at the end of urination suggests a tumor in the prostatic urethra, the bladder neck, or the lower portion of the bladder. In women, this symptom, usually recognized as blood on the toilet tissue or in the last drops in the bowl, indicates an abnormality of the bladder neck. Total hematuria, when blood occurs throughout the entire urination process, may represent an abnormality of the prostate in men or in any portion of the upper urinary tract, ureter or kidney, or bladder in both sexes. Fortunately, most hematuria results from nonmalignant problems, such as infections, but tests should be sought to be certain that cancer is not the cause.

Pain experienced during urination (dysuria) usually indicates a problem in the lower urinary tract. In the case of cancer of the kidney or ureter, abdominal or localized back pain may be caused by a passage of blood clots from the upper urinary tract. Pain may spread into the lower abdomen, groin, or genitals. Pain caused by tumors in the upper urinary tract may be constant in the back, side, or abdomen and can develop into a nagging discomfort that is not precisely located. Bladder cancer causes

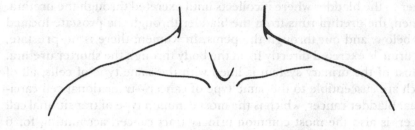

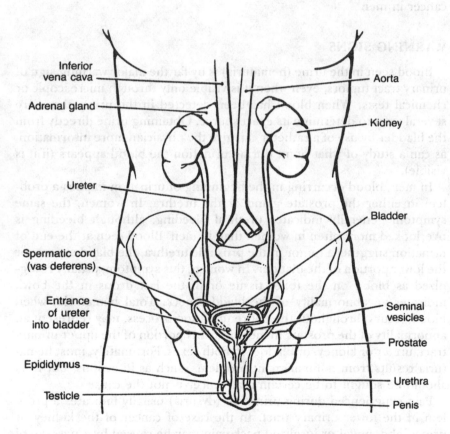

Figure 90 Male genitourinary system.

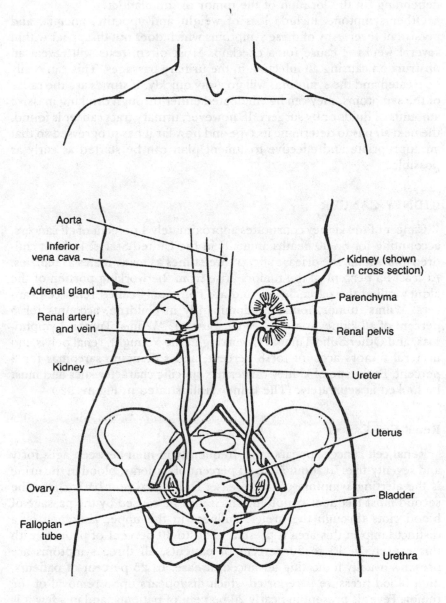

Figure 91 Female genitourinary system.

bleeding with or without pain and total, terminal, or initial hematuria, depending on the location of the tumor in the bladder.

Other symptoms include loss of weight and appetite, anemia, and persistent fever. Any of these symptoms which does not disappear within several weeks is cause for a checkup. Most often, tests will reveal an obstruction causing an infection in the urinary passages. This can easily be treated and the symptoms will go away quickly. If stones are the cause of the symptoms, they can be eliminated either through drinking massive amounts of fluids or by surgery. If, however, urinary tract cancer is found, the next step is to determine its type and how far it has progressed so that an appropriate and effective treatment plan can be started as early as possible.

KIDNEY CANCER

Cancer of the kidney constitutes approximately 4 percent of all cancers, accounting for 8,900 deaths annually in the United States. In both children and adults, the disease affects three times as many males as females. At least 85 percent of the tumors arise from the working portion of the kidney called the parenchyma, and are commonly called renal cell cancers. Wilms' tumor, found predominantly in children, accounts for 5 percent of all kidney tumors (see Chapter 34, "Wilms' Tumor, Lymphomas, and Other Solid Tumors Occurring in the Young"), renal pelvis and ureteral tumors account for 8 percent, and soft tissue sarcomas for 2 percent. Each type of kidney cancer has specific characteristics and must be looked at separately. (The kidney is illustrated in Figure 92.)

Renal Cell Cancer

Renal cell cancer appears most frequently in men between ages forty and seventy-five. In about 50 to 65 percent of patients, blood in the urine is the alerting symptom of the disease. Dull, persistent backache is the second most frequent symptom, which may be caused by the passage of blood clots through the ureter. Fullness in the upper abdomen or a distinct lump in this area is present in 20 to 30 percent of patients with this cancer. In 15 to 20 percent of patients, all three symptoms are present, usually indicating advanced disease. In 25 percent of patients, high blood pressure is reported which disappears upon removal of the tumor. Fever is present in nearly 20 percent of patients, and in a few it is the only symptom. Loss of appetite with or without nausea and vomiting, constipation, weakness, and fatigue are also seen occasionally.

Diagnosis is usually sought after a patient has reported any of the above symptoms or laboratory tests have revealed anemia, kidney or liver failure, or X rays have detected chest lesions, unexplained broken bones,

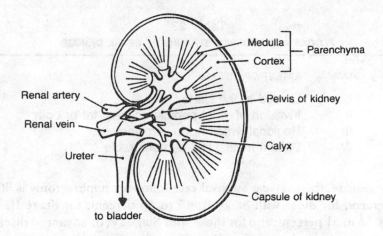

Figure 92 Cross section of normal kidney.

vague muscle disorder, or an unusual type of heart failure. Nearly one third of patients will have metastases (spread of the disease from the kidney to other organs and areas) at the time of diagnosis.

As in all cancers, the specific management or treatment of renal cell cancer is based on both the extent and the type of disease present. Various types of kidney X rays, which include intravenous pyelogram (IVP), are used to assess the suspected kidneys. To do an IVP, a dye is injected intravenously while the patient lies on his back. Several X rays are taken during the next thirty minutes; the patient then urinates and another X ray is taken. Confirmation of the diagnosis is usually made by studying the blood supply to the suspected tumor by means of a renal arteriogram. This test involves the injection of a dye into the renal artery and thus into the tumor. X rays record the movement of the dye and can be analyzed to determine what variety of disorder is present. A CT scan and chest X ray allow the physician to determine the approximate extent of the cancer. Ultimate confirmation depends on biopsy—the surgical exploration, removal, and pathological study of the area involved.

The staging system most commonly used is shown in Tables 23 and 24. Survival appears to depend mainly on the extent to which the cancer has invaded local tissue and on whether there is distant metastasis. Once metastasis develops, survival depends primarily on the extent of the disease and the interval between treatment and the appearance of the metastasis. In one study of eighty-six patients with metastatic renal cell cancer, 42 percent were alive at the end of one year, 21 percent after two years, and 10 percent after five years.

Treatment for renal cell cancer is usually radical nephrectomy—complete removal of the cancerous kidney. In patients with the earliest stage

Table 23
FLOCKS AND KADESKY STAGING OF RENAL CANCER

STAGE	EXTENT OF DISEASE
I	Limited to the kidney
II	Invasion of renal pedicle or renal fat or both
III	Regional lymph node involvement
IV	Distant metastasis demonstrable

of the disease, the five-year survival rate following nephrectomy is 60 to 78 percent; for those with Stage II, 45 to 65 percent; for Stage III patients, 35 to 51 percent; and for those with Stage IV, or advanced disease, the five-year survival rate is 8 to 10 percent. Since most cases of renal cell cancer involve only one kidney, patients are usually left with the other kidney intact and functioning normally. In some cases of advanced disease, distant metastases in soft tissue and bone have been surgically removed, decreasing the discomfort of the patient. Removal of the kidney in the face of widespread disease (palliative nephrectomy) is reserved for patients with severe bleeding or pain.

Radiation therapy, hormonal therapy, chemotherapy, and, very recently, immunotherapy have also been used in certain patients, with good results. More research is needed, however, to define the role of these treatment methods. Follow-up evaluation is a necessary component of complete treatment in all cases.

Table 24
STAGING OF RENAL CANCER

ROBSON ET AL.	TNM SYSTEM	EXTENT OF DISEASE
I	T 1	Confined to kidney (small)
	T 2	Confined to kidney (large)
II	T 3a	Perinephric spread, confined to Gerota's fascia
III A	T 3b	Renal vein or vena caval disease
III B	N1–N3	Regional nodal spread
III C	T 3b	Focal vascular and lymphatic in-
	N1–N3	volvement
IV A	T 4	Adjacent organ invasion other than adrenal
IV B	M 1	Distant metastasis
	N 4	Juxtaregional lymph nodes

Renal Pelvis Tumors

Transitional cell carcinoma of the upper urinary tract affects the kidney's collecting system. Renal pelvis cancers are the most common of this system, constituting nearly 8 percent of all cancers of the kidney and amounting to about 1,500 cases a year. These tumors are found more frequently in men than in women and, as in bladder cancer, this probably reflects the fact that men are generally more frequently exposed to tobacco and industrial dyes and chemicals than are women. However, Scandinavia and the Balkan countries of Yugoslavia, Bulgaria, Romania, and Greece report a higher incidence of renal pelvis cancer in women than in men.

Because of the slow-growing nature of this type of cancer, 50 percent of patients show that the cancer has invaded the underlying muscle when first diagnosed. About 3 to 4 percent of patients have cancer in both kidneys and approximately 30 to 50 percent will also have cancer of the ureter or bladder. Renal pelvis cancer most often afflicts people sixty to eighty years of age and the most common sign is blood throughout the entire urination process. Backache may also be present from either obstruction of the upper urinary tract or the passage of blood clots. Symptoms such as weight loss, loss of appetite, and weakness are not usually present early in the course of the disease but occur during the later stages.

Diagnosis is indicated through IVP and/or retrograde pyelography, another X-ray test in which dye is injected into the ureter. The outlines of the renal collection system can be seen on the X-ray film to aid in the diagnosis of a tumor. Ultrasound, or sonography, is sometimes used in confirmation as well. Urinary cytology, the microscopic study of the cells in the urine, although of variable reliability for the upper urinary tract, is an essential part of the investigation of a patient suspected of having tumors of the renal pelvis. CT scanning of the abdomen is often used in an effort to establish the extent of involvement or displacement of the lymph nodes, ureters, and other structures in the immediate vicinity of the kidney. Direct endoscopic examination of the pelvis and a biopsy may confirm the diagnosis. Endoscopy of the ureter and bladder is necessary to determine whether there is an associated lesion, a distinct possibility in cancers of the collecting system.

Once the diagnosis of cancer has been confirmed and the stage of the disease determined, treatment begins with surgical exploration of the involved kidney. The surgery most often includes removal of the kidney, its ureter, and a portion of the bladder in the most extreme cases. In other instances, just the kidney and ureter are removed or just that portion of the renal pelvis from which the cancer arises, leaving the kidney in place.

The extent of surgery depends upon the grade and stage of the cancer, the position of the tumor, and the condition of the other kidney, located on the opposite side of the body. Periodic follow-up of the patient after surgery is necessary due to the high rate of recurrence of tumors in the bladder and the remaining urinary tract.

Cure rates depend largely upon whether the muscle has been invaded. Estimates of five-year survival range up to 33 percent for patients with widespread cancer, and from 50 to 91 percent for those with lesser involvement. Above all, survival rates reflect the time lag between the onset of symptoms and the diagnosis and treatment. As in all cancers, the earlier the diagnosis, the better the chance for survival.

URETERAL CANCER

Tumors of the ureter have a peak incidence between sixty and seventy years of age and are three and a half to four times more likely to occur in men than in women. The relatively infrequent incidence of these cancers makes it impossible to determine risk factors, but they may be the same as those for cancer of the bladder. Most patients with cancer of the ureter are smokers. Blood in the urine occurs in 75 to 80 percent of patients, representing the most common symptom of ureteral cancer. Although most of these tumors appear in the lower ureter, a considerable number of patients will also have flank or back pain or cramps which may indicate an obstruction in the upper urinary tract. Frequent and painful urination occur less often but may be present in half of the patients with ureteral cancer.

After urinalysis has shown abnormalities, the IVP is the basic screening test for ureteral cancer. Cystoscopy and ureteroscopy, an examination of the internal bladder and ureter with a "periscope," are necessary to study the urinary tract. These studies are needed to observe the opening of the ureter into the bladder where a significant number of these tumors occur, sometimes blocking the passageway. Collection of the urine directly from the ureter through a catheter and examination of the cells therein is also instrumental in diagnosing ureteral cancer before surgical biopsy.

Treatment consists of removal of the kidney, ureter, and a portion of the bladder when the tumors of the upper ureter are highly malignant, more advanced, or multiple. For low-grade, low-stage tumors in the lower ureter, the treatment of choice is surgical removal of the lower ureter and a portion of the bladder and reconnecting the remaining ureter to the remaining bladder. If, however, the opposite kidney functions well, and there is poor function of the kidney on the side of the cancer, removal of the kidney bearing the cancer and the ureter is the usual treatment. Following any of these surgical procedures, the patient will continue to urinate normally.

Neither radiation therapy nor chemotherapy has played a significant role in the treatment of cancer of the ureter. In cases of large tumors that cannot be completely removed by surgery, radiation therapy may be of palliative value only, treating the symptoms without curing the disease. There have been a few instances reported of a good response using combination therapy, which includes taking the anticancer drug cisplatin.

The stage and grade of the cancer influence the five-year survival rate more than the type of treatment used. Two thirds of patients with superficial disease and 25 percent with invasive disease will survive five years. About 40 to 45 percent five-year survival rate occurs for all patients regardless of the stage and grade.

Regular follow-up examinations to survey the urinary tract and likely areas of metastasis are necessary for all patients who have had urinary tract cancers. These examinations will be at shorter intervals in the months just after surgery and then will become less frequent.

BLADDER CANCER

The most frequent cancer of the urinary tract, bladder cancer afflicted some 40,000 Americans in 1985—29,000 men and 11,000 women. An estimated 10,800 deaths occurred during that year—7,300 men and 3,500 women. Although the exact cause of bladder cancer is unknown, the following risk factors seem to increase one's chances of contracting the disease:

1. Occupational hazards, including dyes, rubber, cable, leather, paint, auramine, benzidine, alpha-napthylamine, magenta, 4-aminodiphenyl, and 4-nitradiphenyl.

2. Tobacco use. The risk of bladder cancer in smokers is more than twice that of nonsmokers.

3. Chronic bladder infections. Changes occur in the bladder as a result of repeated or persistent infection.

4. Schistosomiasis, a disease occurring mostly in the Middle East, particularly Egypt, has been associated with bladder cancer. The parasitic worm called *Schistosoma haematobium*, which lodges in the bladder, has been found in 97 percent of Egyptian patients with bladder cancer.

Carcinogenic agents are often transformed into even more dangerous forms by the body's metabolic processes (such as the conversion of nitrates into nitrites) and excreted in the urine. Because the urine is collected and stored for hours in the urinary bladder, this area has the greatest exposure to carcinogens than any other part of the urinary tract.

The first and most common symptom of bladder cancer may be persistent or intermittent visible blood in the urine. It occurs abruptly and usually without pain. Characteristically, the urine may appear clear for days or weeks only to have the blood reappear. The bleeding may be visible only through microscopic examination of the urine. The color of the urine can range from smoky to rusty to bright or deep red. Although most instances of blood in the urine are due to conditions other than cancer, investigation is wise so that early diagnosis and treatment can be instituted if cancer is present.

Symptoms of bladder irritability, frequency, urgency, and pain are found in about one third of patients with bladder cancer. These are also symptoms of possible urinary tract infection. If they persist, they should be checked by a physician. In older patients with these symptoms, urological evaluation is most important, since bladder cancers more often affect older people. Patients with persistent, recurrent lower urinary tract infections should have urologic investigation to determine the cause. Infections can be an early warning sign of bladder cancer. The symptoms of advanced bladder cancer include weight loss, loss of appetite, weakness, and general discomfort.

Screening tests used to detect bladder cancer include urinalysis, in which chemical or microscopic assessment of the urine may reveal small amounts of blood. A CT scan, including an IVP, is usually performed. Cystoscopy and an endoscopic surgical biopsy will usually confirm the diagnosis.

Once diagnosed, the cancer will be staged (Figure 93). Superficial or low-grade tumors involve only the lining of the bladder, while high-grade tumors extend down through the muscle in the wall of the bladder as well as to the more distant areas outside the bladder. Low-grade tumors (Grades I and II) are less malignant in microscopic appearance and have a better prognosis than Grade III. Approximately 65 percent of patients have cancers which are low stage and low grade at the time of diagnosis, and the average time between the onset of symptoms and the first visit to the doctor is about nine months.

Treatment

Superficial bladder tumors are generally treated by transurethral resection and fulguration. This involves the use of an instrument that is passed through the urethra (a technique similar to cystoscopy), which permits electrical cutting and burning of the cancer, a technique known as encoscopic resection and fulguration. This treatment can be repeated as often as necessary and may be used to control persistent or recurrent growths as long as they remain superficial and accessible. Periodic follow-up every two to three months for the first couple of years and every three to four months thereafter is advisable.

Chemotherapeutic agents such as thiotepa, mitomycin, and others are sometimes introduced into the bladder in varying concentrations at regu-

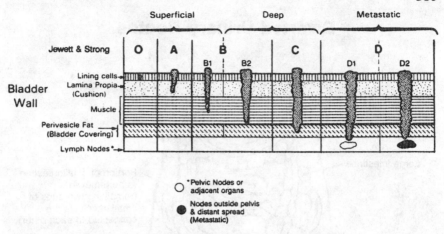

Figure 93 Staging of bladder cancer according to Jewett and Strong.

lar weekly intervals usually for a total of about six weeks. Transurethral surgery (TUR) and intravesical (within the bladder) chemotherapy are used even for deep, more aggressive tumors. Sometimes TUR is used to relieve the symptoms of high-stage and high-grade tumors of the bladder in those patients who are poor risks for surgery. More recently, lasers are being used to treat superficial bladder tumors.

If the cancer is deeply invasive or high grade, removal of the bladder (cystectomy) and urinary diversion (changing the route of the urine to a new reservoir) may be attempted (Figure 94). This is usually done after radiation therapy has been applied to the pelvic area and only if the cancer is still confined to the bladder wall. In poor-risk patients (those with severe cardiac problems, for example), irradiation of the bladder is done to relieve symptoms and discomfort. Often these tumors can be effectively controlled in this manner. Radiation therapy is very effective in the treatment of some bladder cancers.

Urinary diversion is generally performed at the time of cystectomy or possibly before. One technique involves attaching the ureters to a segment of bowel, usually the small intestine, that has been isolated to make a pouch which will collect the urine. One end of the pouch, the conduit, is closed and the open end is brought through a small opening in the abdominal wall and attached to the wall and its surface. This opening is called a stoma, and urine passes through it into an external bag which holds the urine until it is emptied manually. This type of urinary diversion is called a Bricker's pouch, named after the surgeon who developed the technique.

In some cases, another type of urinary diversion is done, using the

Diverted Urinary Routes

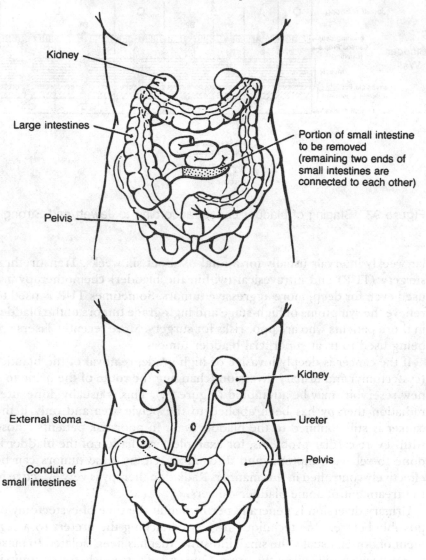

Figure 94 Diverted route of urine after removal of bladder. Ureters are attached to an isolated portion of small intestines that is closed at one end and open at the other to form a stoma.

lower portion of the large bowel (sigmoid colon) and no segment is isolated. This is called a ureterosigmoidostomy and has the advantage of having no outside stoma (Figure 95). The disadvantage with this type of diversion, however, is an increased likelihood of complications such as kidney infection and biochemical blood changes, although these complications can be controlled fairly well if it is necessary to use this form of diversion. As in all surgical procedures, the possible complications must be weighed against the potential benefits.

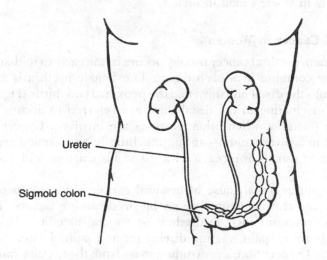

Ureter

Sigmoid colon

Figure 95 Ureterosigmoidostomy.

Cystectomy, radiation therapy, chemotherapy, or a combination of these are all used in the management of deep or metastatic carcinoma of the bladder, depending on the extent of the disease. When only a small portion of the bladder is affected by cancer, radiation therapy followed by removal of only that segment is sometimes effective and does not require urinary diversion.

Until recently, there have been no anticancer agents of value in the treatment of bladder cancer. Cisplatin and cytoxan have shown varying degrees of effectiveness in patients with metastatic bladder cancer. Continuing research in this area is under way and may lead to a larger number of effective agents.

Survival rates for bladder cancer patients are steadily improving as better means of detecting and controlling the disease are developed. Patients with low-grade superficial cancer have a five-year survival rate of 70 percent following TUR. Those with more invasive disease have a significantly lower life expectancy, although those with Stage B-2 and C cancers have a 40 to 50 percent five-year survival rate with or without preoperative radiation and surgical removal of the bladder.

URETHRAL CANCER

In both men and women, primary cancers of the urethra are rare. Since first reported in 1800, only about 1,000 cases in women and 500 in men have been recorded. It is the only urinary tract cancer that occurs more commonly in women than in men.

Urethral Cancer in Women

In women, urethral cancer usually occurs in the early to mid-sixties and it is more common in white women. The female urethra is arbitrarily divided into the distal one third and the proximal two thirds (Figure 96A). Cancers originating in the distal third are referred to as anterior, and entire or posterior when other portions are involved. Cancer also has occurred in a diverticulum—an outpouching in a weakened segment of the urethra, usually the result of a distal obstruction and subsequent infection.

Although the actual cause of urethral cancer in women is unknown, infection and chronic irritation may be predisposing factors. The most common symptoms include urethral or vaginal bleeding. Urinary frequency, burning, pain, vaginal discharge, and painful intercourse also may occur. On occasion, a protruding mass from the urethra can be seen. There may be difficulty in urinating; less commonly, there may be a complete blockage, making urination impossible.

Urethral cancers in women are staged O through D (Table 25). In general, distal cancers are of a lower stage than proximal ones.

Treatment and prognosis are more related to the site of the cancer and stage than to the type of cancer. Treatment of distal O, A, or B cancers include surgery and radiation implants. Stage C or proximal tumors require preoperative radiation therapy to reduce the mass followed by removal of the bladder, urethra, anterior vaginal wall and, if present, the reproductive organs. Sometimes complete removal of the vagina and vulva also may be necessary if the cancer is extensive. The five-year survival for the more superficial distal cancers is 50 percent, and about 25 percent for the more extensive or deeper cancers.

Urethral Cancer in Men

Although very rare, this cancer has been reported in teenage males as well as in men over eighty years of age. The median age, however, is between fifty-five and sixty years.

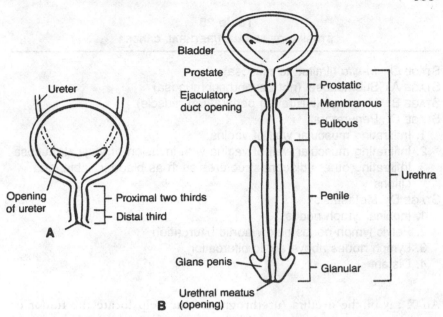

Figure 96A Female urethra. B Male urethra.

The male urethra is about 21 cm (4.8 inches) and traverses the prostate and penis, extending from the bladder neck to the urethral meatus in the glans penis (Figure 96B). Its lining varies according to location along the tract; therefore, various types of cancer may occur along it. The most common are squamous cell, accounting for 75 to 80 percent, followed by transitional cell (14 to 16 percent) and adenocarcinoma (5 to 7 percent). The tumors occur most commonly in the bulbous urethra (50 percent) and penile urethra (36 percent), and least often in the prostatic urethra (6 percent).

The frequency of inflammatory conditions of the urethra may mask the underlying cancer in its early stages. The usual lapse of time between onset of symptoms and diagnosis ranges from two or three months to up to four years.

As in women, the cause of urethral cancer in men is unknown, although a history of chronic infection, irritation, and obstruction of the urethra are common. Venereal disease or frequent urethral dilations also may be significant. Symptoms vary and may include urethral bleeding, a bloody or foul-smelling discharge, difficulty in urination, and pain in the groin. Profuse bleeding following urethral dilation should arouse suspicion of a tumor.

A urethral mass often can be felt, but a biopsy is needed for diagnosis.

594

Table 25
STAGING OF FEMALE URETHRAL CANCER

STAGE O *In-situ* (limited to mucosa)
STAGE A Submucosal (not beyond submucosa)
STAGE B Muscular (infiltrating periurethral muscle)
STAGE C Periurethral
  1. Infiltrating muscular wall of vagina
  2. Infiltrating muscular wall of vagina with invasion of vaginal mucosa
  3. Infiltrating other adjacent structures such as bladder, labia, and clitoris
STAGE D Metastasis
  1. Inguinal lymph nodes
  2. Pelvic lymph nodes below aortic bifurcation
  3. Lymph nodes above aortic bifurcation
  4. Distant

An X ray of the urethra (urethrogram) may help locate the tumor or suspicious area. Cells collected during a washing of the urethra are useful in diagnosis, but endoscopy is needed for the biopsy and also to look at the area. Further assessment of the urinary tract, pelvis, and groin by CT scan and endoscopy of the bladder are needed to evaluate the stage of the cancer (Table 26).

If the cancer is in the distal part of the penis, part of the penis may have to be removed. Five-year survival following this treatment may exceed 60 percent. If the cancer is located higher, complete removal of the penis is necessary. Transurethral resection and cauterization of the area or radiation therapy have been effective in some instances. If the lymph nodes in the groin are involved, they also should be removed.

Table 26
STAGING OF MALE URETHRAL CANCER

STAGE O   *In situ* (confined to urothelium)
STAGE A   Into but not beyond the lamina propria
STAGE B   Into but not beyond substance of corpus spongiosa
           Into but not beyond prostate
STAGE C   Direct extension into tissues beyond corpus spongiosum
           (corpora cavernosa muscle, fat, fascia, skin, direct skeletal
           involvement or beyond prostatic capsule)
STAGE D-1 Regional metastasis groin and/or pelvic LN
STAGE D-2 Distant metastasis

More extensive bulbomembranous cancer requires removal of the bladder and testicles in most cases, with a generally poor outcome. Recently, a combination of chemotherapy, preoperative radiation therapy and removal of the bladder and urethra has been attempted with a goal of restoring potency with an artificial erectile implant. More study is needed to determine the effectiveness of this approach.

Prostatic urethral cancer is very rare. In half of the patients, transurethral resection may be performed. Removal of the bladder and urethra followed by radiation therapy is the recommended course.

URINARY STOMAS

An understanding of the need for urinary diversion by a stoma, or ostomy, is necessary for its acceptance by the patient. Once this understanding is achieved, the surgeon can determine the proper location for the stoma. The surgeon and an enterostomal therapist will select a site that can comfortably support the appliance that will be used to collect the urine. The patient must become very familiar with the type of appliance to be used. Proper stomal care and resolving problems will allay fears and build confidence. Children adjust readily to the care of the appliance and find out soon that it is not an obstacle to their lifestyles or normal activities. If problems do occur, stomal therapists are available to help. Further guidance can be obtained from the Ostomy Association (see "Directory of Resources").

Postoperative monitoring of the patient should be done regularly by the physician or therapist. Support and a positive attitude regarding the ostomy from family, friends, and the medical team are vital to acceptance by the patient.

Positive reinforcement will also be needed to help the male patient recover from the loss of sexual function as a result of radical surgery or radiation. Inability to have an erection can lead to emotional problems, especially in the early post-operative stages. There are means of rehabilitation, usually implantation of a penile prosthesis, which can restore nearly full sexual function, short of procreation. Recent experience suggests that, in spite of extensive radiation therapy, sexual function is generally preserved and erection may be recovered with sexual activity.

In women, vaginal reconstruction with the use of segments of intestine restore ability to have sexual intercourse. For both sexes, increased attention to restoring or maintaining sexual function has helped improve the quality of life following cancer treatment. (For further discussion, see Chapter 10, "Coping with Problems Related to Cancer and Cancer Treatment.")

SUMMING UP

Considerable gains have been made in recent years in the diagnosis and treatment of urinary tract cancers, but there is still much to be done. A more concerted effort by both the public and medical professionals is needed to recognize and, hopefully, diagnose these cancers earlier. The identification of more carcinogens and the control of exposure to them, precisely determined standard techniques for surgery, and improved chemotherapeutic agents should further improve survival and quality of life.

34

Wilms' Tumor, Lymphomas, and Other Solid Tumors Occurring in the Young

R. BEVERLY RANEY, JR., M.D.

The diagnosis of cancer in a child or young adult always comes as a shock. We tend to think of cancer as a disease of aging, and, indeed, most cancer patients are older adults. Still, cancer does strike the young, and, when it does, parents often feel helpless and even guilty. Thus at the very beginning, when cancer is first diagnosed in a child, it is important for parents to realize that the disease was not caused by anything they did or failed to do. It is also natural for parents to feel that they have no control; that everything is out of their hands. This, of course, is not the case. Parents should be involved, as much as possible, in making treatment decisions and, when appropriate, in the treatment itself.

In dealing with childhood cancer, the psychological toll on parents, the ill child, and other family members can be devastating; it is therefore important to establish lines of communication not only with the physicians and others who are treating the child, but also with other parents who have experienced the tragedy of childhood cancer. Communication and understanding within the family are also extremely important. It is natural to want to shield the child and his or her siblings from the knowledge of cancer, but very often this places a double burden on all concerned. When this happens, each is left to cope with fears and uncertainty without the benefit of sharing these emotions. Coping with childhood cancer is never easy, but, more than ever before, many children are being treated successfully and most can experience lengthy disease-free periods. Knowing about the specific type of cancer, its treatment and usual course all are valuable in coming to terms with the disease. In this chapter, the more common forms of solid tumors seen in children will be discussed; leukemia, brain cancer, and other childhood cancers are dealt with in the sections covering these specific diseases.

PATTERNS OF CHILDHOOD CANCER

There are several differences between the types of cancer occurring in children and those seen mostly in adults. For example, the most common adult cancers are tumors of the lung and colon in both sexes, breast cancer in women and prostate cancer in men. In contrast, leukemia is the most common form of cancer in children (see Chapter 21, "Leukemia"). Among the types of solid tumors occurring in childhood, those arising in the brain, lymph nodes, kidney, adrenal gland, soft tissues, and bone are the most prevalent.

The most common warning sign of a solid cancer is a mass or lump that is unrelated to any recent injury. The discovery of a mass or lump anywhere in a child's body is a warning sign that should be investigated by a physician. This advice is as important in adults as it is in children. Indeed, bringing a suspicious mass or lump to the attention of a physician is often the first step in reaching a correct diagnosis, regardless of age. At this initial stage, it may not be necessary to consult a cancer specialist; taking the child to the family physician or pediatrician may suffice. To diagnose cancer, other possible causes for the presence of the mass must first be ruled out. The possibility of an infection or abscess probably will be investigated, for example. To do this, the physician will determine whether there is a fever or local tenderness, and tests, such as bacterial cultures, blood counts, and possibly X-ray studies, will be performed.

If these tests rule out infection or other nonmalignant causes, the next step would be to perform a biopsy, which is a microscopic examination of a sample of tissue taken from the mass to determine whether cancer is present. To perform the biopsy, the primary physician will enlist the aid of a surgeon, possibly a pediatric surgeon, to judge whether all or just a sample of the mass should be removed. These surgical procedures, even if relatively minor, are usually best performed in a hospital with the child under general anesthesia.

If the mass is diagnosed as cancer—a judgment that is made by a pathologist—further studies will be needed to determine the extent of the disease. If the cancer has spread to other parts of the body—for example, the lungs, brain, liver, bones, bone marrow, kidneys, etc.—the treatment program is based on the extent of the disease and the ultimate outlook for a cure is lessened. Tests to determine whether the tumor has spread include physical examination, blood counts, and other laboratory studies, and possibly examinations of the bone marrow and spinal fluid. In the course of a typical investigation, the tests may include X-ray films; ultrasound studies, which use high-frequency sound waves to map internal structures; computerized tomography (CT) scans, and nuclear scans using radioactive substances to pinpoint internal structures. It is important to determine the stage or extent of the cancer to plan the most effective treatment.

Treatments needed for cure are often prolonged and rigorous, and may require extensive surgery, chemotherapy, and radiation therapy. It is fortunate that children are so resilient, both physically and emotionally. Despite the discomfort and problems caused by these treatments, children generally do very well. They can often tolerate chemotherapy better than adults and are less likely to have severe and persistent vomiting, especially if they are treated before the teenage years. Also, an older person may have many other serious medical problems in addition to cancer, whereas children tend to be quite healthy. Since children have a potentially long life ahead of them, physicians usually make every effort to reduce the possible complications of treatment, particularly those that may occur in later years, even after the cancer is cured. Such problems include retarded growth, or damage to the lungs, reproductive organs, or brain. By carefully selecting the surgery, radiation therapy, chemotherapy, or any combination of treatment, the least physical damage can be achieved without hindering the chance of a cure. It is known, for example, that the growing portions of a child's bones are sensitive to radiation therapy; therefore, the dosage and area treated must be considered carefully for each patient to minimize retarded growth. This concern with lack of bone growth is not a factor in adults with cancer.

There are many varieties of childhood solid tumors; each has differing patterns of spread and varying degrees of responsiveness to surgery, chemotherapy, and radiation therapy. But because these cancers are relatively rare, especially in contrast to the leukemias, it has been only in recent decades that the best approaches to successful treatment have been defined. About twenty-five years ago, several pediatric cancer centers joined in a cooperative study to learn more about childhood cancers and to develop more successful treatment programs. The benefits of these efforts have been considerable, even though much remains to be done. The field of pediatric oncology is still expanding, and it can be said with confidence that research now under way will lead to even more effective treatment and better survival rates.

LYMPHOMA

Lymphomas, cancers of the lymph nodes (Figure 97), are, after leukemia and brain tumors, the most common cancers encountered in children and young adults under the age of twenty-one. The two broad categories of lymphoma include Hodgkin's disease and the family of lymph-cell cancers collectively called non-Hodgkin's lymphoma. Both disorders are two to three times more common in boys than in girls, especially in children under the age of thirteen.

Hodgkin's disease usually begins as a slowly enlarging lymph node in the neck area, either under the jaw or occasionally just above the collarbone. Often the child has no other symptoms. The enlarged nodes are usually relatively firm and not tender. If physical examination and the results of various laboratory and X-ray studies fail to detect tuberculosis, infectious mononucleosis, or some other viral or bacterial infection, then a biopsy should be performed. Sometimes the physician may choose to wait a few weeks or simply give a broad spectrum antibiotic to see if the node will return to its normal state, but if it does not, a biopsy is definitely indicated. The diagnosis is then established, although occasionally a repeat biopsy is necessary to be certain that the structure of the lymph node is abnormal and that unusual cells, known as Reed-Sternberg cells, required for a diagnosis of Hodgkin's disease, are, indeed, present.

Once a diagnosis of Hodgkin's disease has been confirmed, the next step is to determine whether the disease is elsewhere in the body. This is done by looking for enlargement of the lymphatic structures in the throat, chest, spleen, and abdomen. Hodgkin's disease spreads in a systematic, downward fashion, nearly always moving from the neck to lymphatic tissue in the chest and then to the spleen and lymph nodes lying along the major blood vessels in the abdomen and their branches in the pelvis. If the spleen is involved, as is the case in approximately a third of the patients, then the liver may also contain tumor. Involvement of the lungs, bones, or bone marrow are less frequent in children than in adults; if Hodgkin's disease is found in any of these sites, it means that the disease is widespread.

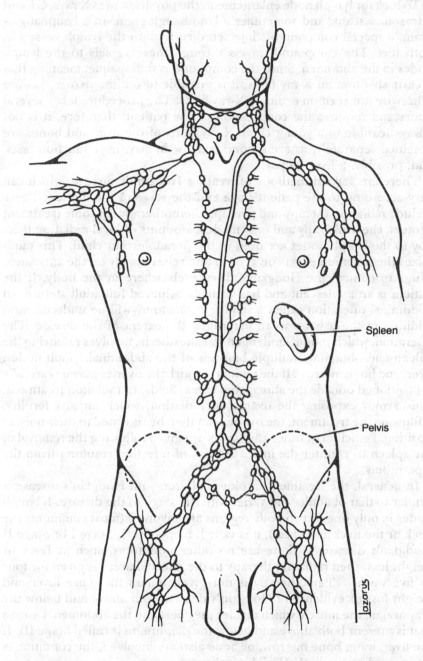

Figure 97 How lymph nodes are distributed throughout the body.

To look for lymph node enlargement, the physician uses X rays, CT and ultrasound scans, and sometimes a lymphangiogram. In a lymphangiogram, a special compound is injected directly into the lymph vessels in both feet. The compound travels through these vessels to the lymph nodes in the abdomen. Since the compound is radiopaque, meaning that it casts shadows on X-ray films, it is possible to outline tissues that are otherwise not seen on ordinary X-ray films. The procedure takes several hours and requires the cooperation of the patient; therefore, it is not always feasible in a young child. X-ray films of the liver and bones are obtained separately, as are a bone marrow biopsy, liver function tests, and, possibly, a liver biopsy.

There are several methods of treating Hodgkin's disease, which can vary according to the patient's age and the stage of the disease. These include radiation therapy and perhaps chemotherapy. In some treatment centers, chemotherapy and only modest amounts of local radiation therapy to the lymph nodes are used in the preadolescent child. This minimizes the radiation effects on growth and relies mostly on the anticancer drugs to control the Hodgkin's disease elsewhere in the body. If the patient is an adolescent and has virtually achieved full adult stature, an abdominal operation called a staging laparotomy will be undertaken in addition to the usual tests to determine the extent of the disease. The operation, which is done under general anesthesia, involves removing the spleen and obtaining multiple biopsies of the abdominal lymph nodes, liver, and bone marrow. If the patient is a girl, the ovaries may be carefully repositioned outside the anticipated areas (fields) of radiation treatment. This avoids exposing the ovaries to radiation, which impairs fertility. Following the treatment, the ovaries can then be returned to their normal position. Penicillin or other antibiotics are given following the removal of the spleen to counter the increased risk of infection resulting from the laparotomy.

In general, the treatment of older children with Hodgkin's disease is similar to that of adults and varies with the stage of the disease. If lymph nodes in only one or two body regions are involved (most commonly the neck or the neck and chest), it is called, respectively, Stage I or Stage II Hodgkin's disease. If there are no other symptoms, such as fever or weight loss, then radiation therapy to the affected areas is given for four to five weeks. Chemotherapy is not given unless there are fever and weight loss or evidence of Hodgkin's disease both above and below the diaphragm, the muscle which divides the chest and the abdomen. Disease that is present both above and below the diaphragm is called Stage III. If the liver, lung, bone marrow, or bone also are involved, the condition is designated as Stage IV Hodgkin's disease.

The outlook depends not only on the extent of the disease but also on how responsive the tumor is to treatment, a factor that often can be determined by the microscopic appearance of the cancer cells. Great progress has been made in treating Hodgkin's disease in recent years. At one time, it was almost always fatal, but today up to 90 percent or more of all of the children and young adults with Stage I and II Hodgkin's are surviving for five or more years. If the disease is more advanced, the outlook for a cure is somewhat diminished; about 80 percent of those with Stage III Hodgkin's can expect a cure, while the cure rate may be only 50 percent for Stage IV disease. Long-term studies of the late effects of successful treatment on such factors as growth and fertility are now under way, and these indicate that most youngsters who are cured of their Hodgkin's can expect to live normal lives.

Non-Hodgkin's Lymphoma

Non-Hodgkin's lymphoma covers a group of similar diseases that tend to evolve much more quickly than Hodgkin's disease. The lymph glands are affected by rapidly dividing cells of the lymphatic system, which have often spread to involve the bone marrow and occasionally the brain and other parts of the central nervous system. The initial symptoms may be somewhat different from those of Hodgkin's. The child often has a cough or difficulty in breathing because of enlargement of the thymus gland in the upper chest. Alternatively, there may be an abdominal mass with swelling and pain. Sometimes persistent vomiting indicates that the bowel is obstructed by tumor, a condition that requires prompt surgery.

There are several types of non-Hodgkin's lymphomas. These can be differentiated by studying the appearance of the cancer cells under a microscope and also by their responsiveness to treatment. For example, one type is called Burkitt's lymphoma; children with this form of the disease usually have several large tumors that fill the abdomen and grow rapidly, causing kidney damage in the process. Before and during the initial treatment of Burkitt's lymphoma, it is important to determine the child's fluid status, which includes monitoring such factors as diet, amount of urination, weight, and kidney function. Samples of the bone marrow and spinal fluid are examined before beginning chemotherapy and radiation therapy, because this type of cancer often spreads to these areas. While treatment can help many children with Burkitt's lymphoma, unfortunately more than half will die of the disease, usually within a year from the time of diagnosis.

While the precise cause of Burkitt's lymphoma is unknown, the disease is now thought to be related in some patients to a viral infection. The Epstein-Barr virus is often found in association with Burkitt's lymphoma, although the disease is not contagious from person to person. Fortunately, it is a relatively uncommon disease.

Other types of non-Hodgkin's lymphoma include diseases known as lymphoblastic (formerly called lymphosarcoma), histiocytic, and pleomorphic lymphomas. These can occur in the chest, abdomen, pelvis, or neck. The diagnosis is made by biopsy, and treatment consists of multiple-drug chemotherapy plus low-dose radiation therapy to the affected area. Staging of these cancers is not as important as in Hodgkin's disease, because all children with non-Hodgkin's lymphoma will need chemotherapy. Still, children with localized non-Hodgkin's disease have a better outlook than do those whose cancer is widespread in the abdomen, chest cavity, or bone marrow.

Before the development of effective chemotherapy, over half the children with non-Hodgkin's lymphoma fared poorly. Now, the cure rate, defined as being alive and free of disease after five years, for early non-Hodgkin's lymphoma is close to 75 percent, since the treatment prevents the spread of the tumor into the bone marrow, a serious problem similar to that of leukemia. The anticancer drugs are now given for eighteen months, but this may be shortened in the future as ongoing research studies are completed. Although the outlook for children with this group of diseases is generally not as favorable as in Hodgkin's, the prospects are far better now than only fifteen years ago, and they are continually improving.

EMBRYONAL TUMORS

Embryonal tumors occur mostly in very young children and are rarely seen after the age of sixteen years. They are called embryonal tumors because they are similar to structures present in the developing fetus. There are three forms of embryonal cancers: Wilms' tumor, which affects the kidney; neuroblastoma, which usually arises in the abdomen; and rhabdomyosarcoma, a cancer of the muscle that can occur anywhere in the body.

Wilms' Tumor

Wilms' tumor is rare—only about five hundred new cases are diagnosed each year in the United States. Still, it is the most common type of kidney cancer in children, and it has become a model for the study of many aspects of childhood cancer. Three national studies of children with Wilms' tumor have been organized to explore a variety of questions related to cancer treatment and, also, to increase our understanding of this particular type of cancer (Figure 98).

Wilms' tumor is nearly always discovered as a hard mass in the abdomen or flank of an otherwise healthy preschool child. The average age of these patients is three years. The tumor is diagnosed by a test called an intravenous pyelogram, in which X-ray films are taken before and after a

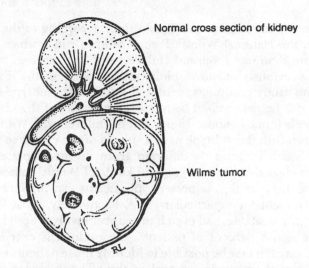

Figure 98 Kidney with Wilms' tumor.

radiopaque solution is injected into the bloodstream. The radiopaque solution travels through the bloodstream to the kidneys and makes them visible on the X-ray films. Other tests include an ultrasonic examination of the kidneys and adjacent blood vessels, along with a chest X ray.

The extent and types of treatments depend upon the stage of the tumor. In Stage I Wilms' tumor (defined as a localized cancer) surgical removal of the kidney, followed by chemotherapy, is now the preferred approach to treatment. Less than fifteen years ago, doctors thought that radiation therapy also was needed following the surgery, but studies have found that this is not necessary in Stage I Wilms' tumor. In Stage II, the cancer has penetrated the kidney surface. Again, the kidney is removed and followed by chemotherapy. Whether additional radiation therapy is beneficial is still under study. In any event, more than 90 percent of all children with Stage I and II Wilms' tumors are now being cured, and it is possible that, in ongoing studies, we will be able to reduce even further the amount and duration of chemotherapy without lessening the cure rate.

Stage III Wilms' tumor is that in which the cancer has spread to adjacent tissue, while Stage IV is that in which the cancer has spread to the lungs. About 80 percent of the children with Stage III Wilms' can be cured by a combination of surgical removal of the diseased kidney followed by radiation therapy and chemotherapy. The cure rate for Stage IV disease is about 60 percent. These figures are considerably higher than the overall survival of only 40 percent for all stages of Wilms' tumor thirty years ago.

In addition to the staging of Wilms' tumor according to the extent of the disease, the National Wilms' Tumor Study Group, which collected data on more than one thousand children with the disease, brought to light other previously unknown biologic factors about the disease. For example, this study group has identified a particular subtype of Wilms' tumor that can be determined by microscopic study of the cancer cells. This subtype is found in about 15 percent of children with Wilms' tumor. Many children with this subtype have a spread of the cancer to the bones and brain, which is distinctly different from the usual pattern of the disease. It is clear that there are several kinds of Wilms' tumors, and by determining the type that is present, physicians can provide the most effective treatment for a particular child. Fortunately, most Wilms' tumors are highly treatable, and even if the cancer involves both kidneys, as it does in about 5 percent of patients, the outlook is excellent. With ongoing research, it may be possible to identify those patients who can be effectively treated with only removal of the affected kidney, as well as those whose regimen should include chemotherapy and radiation treatments.

Neuroblastoma

Neuroblastoma is a tumor that can arise anywhere in the sympathetic nervous system, which consists of the adrenal glands, located one on top of each kidney, and the ganglia, collections of nerve cells that lie on both sides of the spine from the neck to the pelvis and along the abdominal great artery (the aorta) (Figure 99). Most neuroblastomas occur in the abdomen and are often quite large. The tumor has already spread to the bones and bone marrow in about 70 percent of the cases at the time of diagnosis, indicating its aggressiveness.

Most children with neuroblastoma show signs of chronic illness, such as slow growth, weight loss, lack of interest, irritability, intermittent diarrhea, fever, and abdominal pain. The average age of children with neuroblastoma is two years. Like Wilms' tumor, diagnostic tests usually include an intravenous pyelogram, ultrasonic examination, and X-ray studies of the chest and entire skeleton. In addition, samples of urine are tested for the presence of certain chemicals that are manufactured by the tumor cells and then excreted in the urine. These chemicals are called VMA for vanillylmandelic acid, HVA for homovanillic acid, and dopamine. Samples of bone marrow also are usually obtained for biopsy, since neuroblastomas frequently spread to the bones and marrow.

After the diagnostic studies are completed and the extent of the disease is determined, a decision is made as to whether an operation should be performed. The use of surgery depends upon the size of the tumor and the general condition of the child. If the tumor is only on one side of the

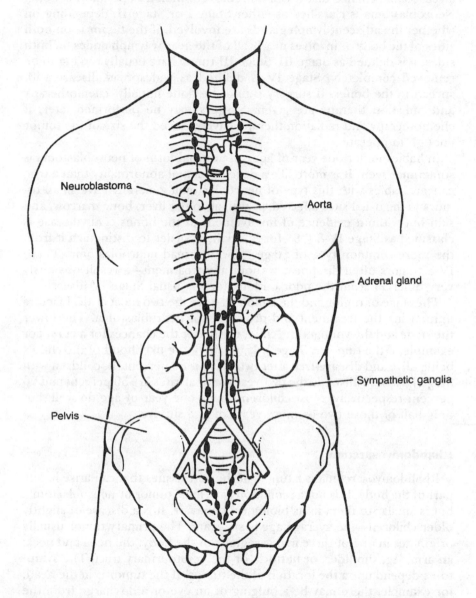

Figure 99 Distribution of sympathetic ganglia along spine and abdominal aorta.

body and has not spread to the bones or other distant parts, and if there is a reasonable chance that it can be removed, then an operation is done. Neuroblastoma is classified as either Stage I or Stage II, depending on whether the adjacent lymph glands are involved. If the tumor is on both sides of the body or involves nearly all of the nearby lymph nodes on both sides, it is defined as Stage III. Stage III tumors are usually too big to be removed completely. Stage IV is defined as widespread disease with spread to the bones. If surgery cannot be done initially, chemotherapy and radiation therapy are given. Surgery may be performed later, if chemotherapy and radiation therapy have reduced the size of the tumor enough to operate.

In babies under one year of age, an unusual form of neuroblastoma is sometimes seen. It is more like a developmental abnormality than a true cancer. Babies with this type of neuroblastoma generally have small tumors in the usual sites affected, as well as in the liver, bone marrow, and skin but without evidence of involvement of the bones. This disease is classified as Stage IV-S ("S" for Special), in order to distinguish it from the more common type of Stage IV widespread neuroblastoma. These IV-S tumors often disappear without any treatment—a result obviously very different from the poor outlook for the usual Stage IV disease.

The stage of tumor and the child's age are the two most critical factors influencing the treatment and prognosis of neuroblastoma. The lower the stage and the younger the child, the better the chances for a cure. For example, if the tumor is Stage I, II, or IV-S, the likelihood of the child's being alive and disease-free after two years is 80 percent. In children with Stage III and IV disease, the two-year survival rates are 50 percent and 20 percent respectively. Most children under one year of age do well, but only half of those two or more years of age survive.

Rhabdomyosarcoma

Rhabdomyosarcoma is a tumor of the soft tissues that can arise in any part of the body. It is not as common as Wilms' tumor or neuroblastoma, but is similar to them in its biological behavior. It is a disease of slightly older children—the average age is six years. The primary tumor usually originates in one of three major regions of the body: the head and neck; an arm, leg, shoulder, or buttock; or the genitourinary tract. The symptoms depend upon the location of the tumor. If the tumor is in the head, for example, there may be a bulging of an eye or a discharge from the nose or ear. If an extremity is involved, there may be a lump that can be seen or felt. Tumors starting in the genitourinary tract may produce difficulty in urinating, bleeding, constipation, and pain.

Rhabdomyosarcoma, like those of Wilms' tumor and neuroblastomas, spreads through the bloodstream and lymph nodes. Distant spread most often goes to the lungs, although the bone marrow, bones, and other soft tissues may also be affected.

Treatment and outlook, as might be expected, are directly related to the site of origin and the extent of the disease. Several national studies have indicated that all patients with rhabdomyosarcoma should receive multiple-drug chemotherapy to stop distant metastases. Children whose tumors are completely removed (Stage I disease) usually do not need radiation therapy. Their two-year survival rate is about 85 percent. Radiation therapy is recommended, however, for children who have tumor cells remaining after surgery (Stages II and III), to reduce the likelihood of regrowth. Two-year survival rates for Stage II and III disease are 70 percent and 50 percent respectively. In Stage IV, there is spread to distant organs and the two-year survival drops to 20 percent.

The benefit of surgery in children with rhabdomyosarcoma is closely related to the site of the tumor. It is usually impossible to remove all tumor that arises in the head and neck because it is so close to vital organs. However, the prospects of complete removal and cure are excellent if the tumor is limited to the eyelid. Children with tumors of the urinary tract or sex organs often can benefit from limited surgery, combined with other treatments. Prospects for curing tumors in the testicular region are excellent.

THE DYING CHILD

While the outlook for children with cancer has improved greatly, there still are instances in which the cancer recurs and spreads, eventually leading to death. When this tragic outcome seems inevitable, it is important that the child be surrounded by friends and family. The dying child should be made as comfortable as possible, and it is important to realize that heroic resuscitation measures are of no value when the cancer has become uncontrollable.

Grief over the loss of a child is one of life's most difficult trials. Families should not try to cope with this alone; the doctors, nurses, other family members, close friends, and support groups all are resources that can help lessen the burden. A deep sense of loss and grief is experienced by siblings; even very young children grieve over the loss of a brother or sister. Very often, the surviving child will experience profound feelings of guilt following the death of a brother or sister, especially after a long illness. The surviving child may have resented the extra attention given to the dying sibling, and may even have wished that the brother or sister was dead. Understandably, this can lead to guilt feelings when death occurs. These and other expressions of grief should be identified—even when they are not expressed as sadness or other expected behavior—and dealt with in an open and understanding manner.

Many parents find that sharing their experiences with other parents who have had a child with cancer can be invaluable in coming to terms with the impact of the disease on all family members. One of the most active groups in this area is The Candlelighters Foundation, an international organization based in Washington, D.C. It was formed in 1970, and has grown from 35 families to more than 160 groups worldwide. The name comes from the ancient Chinese proverb, "It is better to light one candle than to curse the darkness." The organization has been affiliated with the American Cancer Society since 1980 and it also has many affiliated groups. More information about Candlelighters can be obtained from local offices of the American Cancer Society or by contacting the national headquarters (The Candlelighters Foundation, Suite 1011, 2025 I Street, NW Washington, D.C. 20006; phone (202) 659-5136).

SUMMING UP

The cancers discussed in this chapter are relatively rare. The outlook for children with Hodgkin's disease and other soft-tissue tumors has improved dramatically in recent decades, and further gains can be expected as the result of ongoing research. In the treatment of these cancers, it is important to seek out experienced physicians and medical centers, since skill, judgment, and clinical knowledge are paramount in obtaining the best treatment. Ideally, the treatment should be coordinated through a pediatric cancer center, since the physicians and other staff of these specialized hospitals are the most familiar with the special aspects of treating these uncommon tumors.

Coping with childhood cancer is always difficult for the entire family. Parents should make every effort to establish honest and open communication with the treatment team, and to participate in treatment decisions. Support groups (see "Directory of Resources") that include parents who have had similar experiences are particularly helpful.

Fortunately, improvements in pediatric cancer management have led to a remarkable increase in survival rates for most childhood cancer. In view of the great strides that have been made in the last two decades and the accelerating accumulation of knowledge about cancer, it is reasonable to expect further gains for the future. Ongoing research is constantly enabling us to produce more effective treatments with less adverse side effects—all of which improve both the rate and the quality of survival.

Directory of Resources

National Headquarters
90 Park Avenue
New York, NY 10016
The ACS provides information on all
sites of cancer and offers patient
education and information about
community services and rehabilitation
programs. The ACS has 58 divisions
and 3,000 local units throughout the
country. (See list of Chartered
Divisions below.)

Chartered Divisions
Alabama Division, Inc.
402 Office Park Drive
Suite 300
Birmingham, AL 35223

Alaska Division, Inc.
1343 "G" Street
Anchorage, AK 99501

Arizona Division, Inc.
634 West Indian School Road
P.O. Box 33187
Phoenix, AZ 85067

Arkansas Division, Inc.
5520 West Markham Street
P.O. Box 3822
Little Rock, AR 72203

California Division, Inc.
1710 Webster Street
P.O. Box 2061
Oakland, CA 94604

Colorado Division, Inc.
2255 South Oneida
P.O. Box 24669
Denver, CO 80224

Connecticut Division, Inc.
Barnes Park South
14 Village Lane
P.O. Box 410
Wallingford, CT 06492

Delaware Division, Inc.
1708 Lovering Avenue, Suite 202
Wilmington, DE 19806

District of Columbia Division, Inc.
Universal Building, South
1825 Connecticut Avenue N.W.
Washington, DC 20009

Florida Division, Inc.
1001 South MacDill Avenue
Tampa, FL 33609

Georgia Division, Inc.
1422 W. Peachtree Street, N.W.
Atlanta, GA 30309

Hawaii Pacific Division, Inc.
Community Services Center
Building
200 North Vineyard Boulevard
Honolulu, HI 96817

Idaho Division, Inc.
1609 Abbs Street
P.O. Box 5386
Boise, ID 83705

Illinois Division, Inc.
37 South Wabash Avenue
Chicago, IL 60603

Indiana Division, Inc.
9575 N. Valparaiso
Indianapolis, IN 46268

Iowa Division, Inc.
Highway #18 West
P.O. Box 980
Mason City, IA 50401

Kansas Division, Inc.
3003 Van Buren Street
Topeka, KS 66611

Kentucky Division, Inc.
Medical Arts Building
1169 Eastern Parkway
Louisville, KY 40217

Louisiana Division, Inc.
Masonic Temple Building, 7th Floor
333 St. Charles Avenue
New Orleans, LA 70130

Maine Division, Inc.
Federal and Green Streets
Brunswick, ME 04011

Maryland Division, Inc.
1840 York Road, Suite K-M
P.O. Box 544
Timonium, MD 21093

Massachusetts Division, Inc.
247 Commonwealth Avenue
Boston, MA 02116

Michigan Division, Inc.
1205 East Saginaw Street
Lansing, MI 48906

Minnesota Division, Inc.
3316 West 66th Street
Minneapolis, MN 55435

Mississippi Division, Inc.
345 North Mart Plaza
Jackson, MS 39206

Missouri Division, Inc.
3322 American Avenue
P.O. Box 1066
Jefferson City, MO 65102

Montana Division, Inc.
2820 First Avenue South
Billings, MT 59101

Nebraska Division, Inc.
8502 West Center Road
Omaha, NE 68124

Nevada Division, Inc.
1325 East Harmon
Las Vegas, NV 89109

New Hampshire Division, Inc.
686 Mast Road
Manchester, NH 03102

New Jersey Division, Inc.
2600 Route 1
CN2201
North Brunswick, NJ 08902

New Mexico Division, Inc.
5800 Lomas Blvd., N.E.
Albuquerque, NM 87110

New York State Division, Inc.
6725 Lyons Street
P.O. Box 7
East Syracuse, NY 13057

New York City Division, Inc.
19 West 56th Street
New York, NY 10019

Long Island Division, Inc.
535 Broad Hollow Road
(Route 110)
Melville, NY 11747

Queens Division, Inc.
112-25 Queens Boulevard
Forest Hills, NY 11375

Westchester Division, Inc.
901 North Broadway
White Plains, NY 10603

North Carolina Division, Inc.
222 North Person Street
P.O. Box 27624
Raleigh, NC 27611

North Dakota Division, Inc.
P.O. Box 426
Hotel Graver, Annex Building
115 Roberts Street
Fargo, ND 58102

Ohio Division, Inc.
1375 Euclid Avenue
Suite 312
Cleveland, OH 44115

Oklahoma Division, Inc.
3800 North Cromwell
Oklahoma City, OK 73112

Oregon Division, Inc.
0330 S.W. Curry
Portland, OR 97201

Pennsylvania Division, Inc.
Rt. 422 & Sipe Avenue
P.O. Box 416
Hershey, PA 17033

Philadelphia Division, Inc.
1422 Chestnut Street, 2nd Fl.
Philadelphia, PA 19102

Puerto Rico Division, Inc.
(Avenue Domenech 273
Hato Rey, P.R.)
GPO Box 6004
San Juan, PR 00936

Rhode Island Division, Inc.
345 Blackstone Boulevard
Providence, RI 02906

South Carolina Division, Inc.
2442 Devine Street
Columbia, SC 29205

South Dakota Division, Inc.
1025 North Minnesota Avenue
Hillcrest Plaza
Sioux Falls, SD 57104

Tennessee Division, Inc.
713 Melpark Drive
Nashville, TN 37204

Texas Division, Inc.
3834 Spicewood Springs Road
P.O. Box 9863
Austin, TX 78766

Utah Division, Inc.
610 East South Temple
Salt Lake City, UT 84102

Vermont Division, Inc.
Drawer C
13 Loomis Street
Montpelier, VT 05602

Virginia Division, Inc.
4240 Park Place Court
P.O. Box 1547
Glen Allen, VA 23060

Washington Division, Inc.
2120 First Avenue North
Seattle, WA 98109

West Virginia Division, Inc.
Suite 100
240 Capitol Street
Charleston, WV 25301

Wisconsin Division, Inc.
615 North Sherman Avenue
P.O. Box 8370
Madison, WI 53708

Milwaukee Division, Inc.
11401 West Watertown Plank Road
P.O. Box 26555
Wauwatosa, WI 53226

Wyoming Division, Inc.
Indian Hills Center
506 Shoshoni
Cheyenne, WY 82009

COMPREHENSIVE CANCER CENTERS

The following institutions have been designated Comprehensive Cancer Centers by the National Cancer Institute. To earn this designation, the institution must meet certain criteria, including support of a strong research program in the prevention, diagnosis, and treatment of cancer; an ability to participate in integrated, nationwide clinical trials; and the capacity to perform advanced diagnostic techniques and treatment modalities.

Alabama
Comprehensive Cancer Center,
    University of Alabama in
    Birmingham
University Station
Birmingham, AL 35294
(205) 934-6612

California
UCLA Jonsson Comprehensive
    Cancer Center, UCLA Center for
    Health Sciences
10833 Leconte Avenue
Los Angeles, CA 90024
(213) 206-6017 (public)

University of Southern California
Comprehensive Cancer Center
2025 Zonal Avenue
Los Angeles, CA 90033
(213) 224-6600

Connecticut
Yale University Comprehensive
Cancer Center
333 Cedar Street
New Haven, CT 06510
(203) 436-3779

District of Columbia
Howard University Cancer Center
2041 Georgia Avenue NW
Washington, DC 20060
(202) 636-7697
Vincent T. Lombardi Cancer Research
Center, Georgetown University
Medical Center
3800 Reservoir Road NW
Washington, DC 20007
(202) 625-7066

Florida
Comprehensive Cancer Center for the
State of Florida, University of Miami
School of Medicine
PO Box 016960-D8-4
Miami, FL 33103
(305) 547-7707 ext 203

Illinois
Northwestern University Cancer
Center, Health Sciences Building
303 East Chicago Avenue
Chicago, IL 60611
(312) 266-5250
Illinois Cancer Council
36 South Wabash Avenue Suite 700
Chicago, IL 60603
(312) 346-9813, I-800-4-CANCER

Rush–Presbyterian–St. Luke's Medical
Center
1753 West Congress Parkway
Chicago, IL 60612
(312) 942-6642
Cancer Research Center, University
of Chicago
5841 South Maryland Avenue
Chicago, IL 60637
(312) 962-6180
University of Illinois
PO Box 6998
Chicago, IL 60608
(312) 996-8843 or 996-6666

Maryland
The Johns Hopkins Oncology Center
600 North Wolfe Street
Baltimore, MD 21205
(301) 955-3636

Massachusetts
Dana-Farber Cancer Institute
44 Binney Street
Boston, MA 02115
(617) 732-3150 or 732-3000

Michigan
Comprehensive Cancer Center of
Metropolitan Detroit
110 East Warren Avenue
Detroit, MI 48201
(313) 833-0710 ext 356 or 393

Minnesota
Mayo Comprehensive Cancer Center
200 First Street SW
Rochester, MN 55901
(507) 284-8285

New York
Roswell Park Memorial Institute
666 Elm Street
Buffalo, NY 14263
(716) 845-2300

Columbia University Comprehensive
Cancer Center, College of
Physicians & Surgeons
701 West 168th Street
New York, NY 10032
(212) 694-6900
Memorial Sloan-Kettering Cancer
Center
1275 York Avenue
New York, NY 10021
(212) 794-7984

North Carolina
Duke Comprehensive Cancer Center
PO Box 3814
Duke University Medical Center
Durham, NC 27710
(919) 684-2282

Ohio
The Ohio State University
Comprehensive Cancer Center
Suite 302, 410 West 12th Avenue
Columbus, OH 43210
(614) 422-5022

Pennsylvania
Fox Chase/University of Pennsylvania
Comprehensive Cancer Center
7701 Burholme Avenue
Philadelphia, PA 19111
(215) 728-2717

Texas
The University of Texas Health
System Cancer Center, M.D.
Anderson Hospital and Tumor
Institute
Box 90, 6723 Bertner Avenue
Houston, TX 77030
(713) 792-3030

Washington
Fred Hutchinson Cancer Research
Center
1124 Columbia Street
Seattle, WA 98104
(206) 292-6301

Wisconsin
The University of Wisconsin Clinical
Cancer Center
600 Highland Avenue
Madison, WI 53706
(608) 263-8600

CHILDREN'S CANCERS

Ronald McDonald Houses
c/o Golin Harris Communications,
Inc.
500 North Michigan Avenue
Chicago, IL
(312) 836-7129

Run in coordination with local
children's hospitals and McDonald's
Corporation, these houses provide
a place for children and/or their
parents to stay during treatment.
There are more than 85 houses
throughout the United States and
Canada. To locate one near you,
call or write A. L. Bud Jones,
International Coordinator, at the
address above.

The Candlelighters Childhood Cancer Foundation
2025 I Street NW, Suite 1011
Washington, DC 20006
(202) 659-5136

Supported by grants from the American Cancer Society and other donations, this is an international organization of self-help groups of parents of children and adolescents with cancer. There are 225 Candlelighters groups throughout the world. To locate a group near you, call or write the national office.

DES

DES Action
Long Island Jewish Medical Center
New Hyde Park, NY 11040
(516) 775-3450

HOME HEALTH CARE

Foundation for Hospice and Homecare
519 C Street NE
Washington, DC 20002
(202) 547-6586
A nonprofit organization devoted to research and public awareness of hospice and home care issues.

National Association for Home Care
519 C Street NE
Stanton Park
Washington, DC 20002
(202) 547-7424
The largest association representing providers of home health care services throughout the United States.

National Homecaring Council
235 Park Avenue South
New York, NY 10003
(212) 674-4990

Local agencies approved/accredited by the Council provide homemaker-home health aide services. Contact the Council for references.

National League for Nursing
10 Columbus Circle
New York, NY 10019
(212) 582-1022
Major regional agencies associated with the National League for Nursing follow:
Visiting Nurse Association of Los Angeles
2530 West 8th Street
Los Angeles, CA 90057
Visiting Nurse Association of New Haven
1 State Street
New Haven, CT 06511
Visiting Nurse Association of Chicago
310 South Michigan Avenue, 13th Floor
Chicago, IL 60604

Community Health Services of
Portland
P.O. Box 8250
98 Chestnut Street
Portland, ME 04104

Visiting Nurse Association of
Baltimore
5 East Read Street
Baltimore, MD 21202

Visiting Nurse Association of Boston
100 Boylston Street
Boston, MA 02116

Visiting Nurse Association of
Metropolitan Detroit
7700 Second Avenue
Detroit, MI 48202

Visiting Nurse Association of Omaha
1201 South 42nd Street
Omaha, NE 68105

Visiting Nurse Service of New York
107 East 70th Street
New York, NY 10021

Community Home Health Services of
Philadelphia
21 South 12th Street
Philadelphia, PA 19107

Visiting Nurse Association of Dallas
4606 Greenville Avenue
Dallas, TX 75206

HOSPICES

**Foundation for Hospice and
Homecare**
(See entry under Home Health
Care)

Hospice Association of America
210 7th Street SE
Suite 301
Washington, DC 20003
(202) 547-5273
Formed with the support of the
National Association for Home Care
and the Association of Community

Cancer Care Centers, this
organization represents the
interests of the broad range of
hospice providers throughout the
country.

National Hospice Organization
1910 N. Fort Myer Drive, Suite 902
Arlington, VA 22209
(703) 243-5900
This organization will provide the
names of local hospices throughout
the country.

INDUSTRIAL AND OCCUPATIONAL HAZARDS

**Office of Information and
Consumer Affairs, Occupational
Safety and Health Administration,
Department of Labor**

Room N3637
200 Constitution Avenue NW
Washington, DC 20210
(202) 523-8151

LEUKEMIA

Leukemia Society of America
National Headquarters
733 Third Avenue
New York, NY 10017
(212) 573-8484

There are 57 chapters in 30 states and the District of Columbia. For a location near you, contact the National Headquarters.

PATIENT EDUCATION

American Cancer Society, "I Can Cope"
A hospital-based support and education program for patients with all types of cancer. Various members of the treatment team provide information to patients and their families and counsel them about coping with the physical and emotional effects of cancer. Contact your ACS division to determine whether a hospital in your area has this program.

PUBLIC INFORMATION

American Cancer Society local units can provide information and materials on cancer, or will refer callers to resources in the community. In addition, a toll-free answering service, the Cancer Response System, has been set up in fourteen states and will be expanding nationwide in the coming years. (800) ACS-2345.

Cancer Information Service
(800) 4-CANCER; in Alaska: (800) 638-6070; in Washington, DC and suburbs in Maryland and Virginia: 636-5700; on Oahu: 524-1234 (call collect from neighboring islands). The Cancer Information Service is a nationwide toll-free telephone program sponsored by the National Cancer Institute. Trained information specialists are available to answer questions about cancer from the public, cancer patients and their families, and health professionals. Spanish-speaking staff members are available in some areas during daytime hours.

Office of Cancer Communications, National Cancer Institute
Building 31, Room 10A18
Bethesda, MD 20205
(301) 496-5583
An office of the federal government that publishes and makes available free pamphlets about all aspects of cancer and its treatment.

Consumer Products Safety Commission
5401 Westbard Avenue
Washington, DC 20207
(800) 638-2772

For information on specific products suspected of causing cancer.

Food and Drug Administration
Office for Consumer Communications
5600 Fishers Lane, Room 15B-32
Rockville, MD 20857
(301) 443-3170
For information on specific food additives and substances that are suspected of causing cancer.

REHABILITATION

American Cancer Society, CanSurmount
A short-term visitor program to help patients and their families cope with all types of cancer. Trained volunteer cancer patients counsel fellow patients and family members in the hospital or at home on a one-to-one basis. See list of ACS divisions to locate one near you.

Breast Cancer

Reach to Recovery
American Cancer Society rehabilitation program in which trained volunteers who have had breast cancer help patients cope with their physical, emotional, and cosmetic needs. Contact your local chapter for details.

Encore
YWCA program of exercise and discussion for women who have undergone breast surgery. Open to the public. Contact your local YWCA or call the National Board of the YWCA at (212) 614-2827.

Patient Referral Service, American Society of Plastic and Reconstructive Surgeons
233 North Michigan Avenue, Suite 1900
Chicago, IL 60601
(312) 856-1834
This society will provide names of three local surgeons who perform breast reconstruction surgery.

Laryngectomy

American Cancer Society, Laryngectomy Patient Rehabilitation
In association with the International Association of Laryngectomees (IAL), laryngectomee volunteers provide pre- and/or post-operative support. Contact your ACS division for nearest group.

Ostomy

United Ostomy Association, Inc. (U.O.A.)
2001 West Beverly Boulevard
Los Angeles, CA 90057
(213) 413-5510
Volunteers, most of whom are ostomates, visit patients with ostomies in hospitals and their homes upon the request and with the consent of the patient's physician. Local U.O.A. chapters also run monthly information meetings.

SMOKING

American Cancer Society, "Fresh Start" program
Quit smoking clinics offered by ACS. Most are free but some ask for donations to cover costs. See list of ACS offices to locate one near you.

American Institute for Preventive Medicine
1911 West Ten Mile Road
Suite 101
Southfield, MI 48075
(313) 352-7666/Dr. Don Powell
Network of over 110 hospitals nationwide who sponsor the "Smokeless" program to quit smoking. Call for the hospital in your area.

American Lung Association
"Kick the Habit" program is offered in 150 locations throughout the United States. Six sessions over four weeks costs $40, with free maintenance program included. Look up your local chapter or call the national office at (212) 315-8700.

Schick Laboratories
1901 Avenue of the Stars
Suite 1530
Los Angeles, CA 90067
(213) 553-9771
Offered in California, Oregon, Washington, and Texas, this course costs $495 for five days followed by a weekly session for four weeks. Contact: Gary Smith.

Seventh Day Adventist
Intensive five-day stop-smoking programs available free or at a nominal cost. For the nearest location, call your local Seventh-Day Adventist Church.

Smokenders
An international organization with offices in nearly every state. The program costs $295. To locate one near you, call (800) 243-5614. In Connecticut or west of the Mississippi River, call (800) 828-4357.

SUPPORT SERVICES

Concern for Dying
250 West 57th Street
New York, NY 10019
(212) 246-6962
Physicians, lawyers, educators,
ministers, and others interested in
education toward the "prevention of
the futile prolongation of the dying
process and the assurance of
patient autonomy in regard to
treatment during terminal illness."

Society for the Right to Die
250 West 57th Street
New York, NY 10019
(212) 246-6973
The society is engaged in
educational, judicial, and legislative
activity. It provides "living will"
documents and appropriate terminal
care documents in states with right-
to-die laws.

TRANSPORTATION SERVICES

Corporate Angel Network
This program provides free air
transportation to and from
treatment centers for cancer
patients and an accompanying
family member on private corporate
airplanes. (For patients capable of
walking without assistance only.
Subject to availability.) Call
Westchester County Airport, (914)
328-1313. (Nationwide.)

American Cancer Society, Road to Recovery
A program in which volunteers
transport patients to and from
medical facilities for treatment,
rehabilitation and other care.

Glossary

ADENINE. A purine base, one of the four biochemical building blocks of DNA, the hereditary material found in all cells.

ADENOSINE MONOPHOSPHATE. A component of this base with the sugar ribose and with phosphoric acid; important in metabolism.

ADENOMATOUS. Pertaining to multiple glandular growth.

ADENOSINE TRIPHOSPHATE. A nucleotide consisting of adenine, ribose, and three molecules of phosphoric acid linked together. It is the main "energy currency" of the cell since chemical energy is liberated when one or two of the phosphoric acid groups come off.

ADJURANT. A substance that assists or enhances another; in immunology, a substance that intensifies the immune response to an antigen.

ADRIAMYCIN. An anticancer drug derived from natural sources. It interferes with cell division.

AGAR. A dried adhesive substance derived from seaweed dissolved in salt solutions. It is used as a nutrient medium for culturing bacteria.

ALLOSTERIC CHANGE. Usually referring to a biologically active protein, such as an enzyme: the change of shape, and therefore function, caused by interaction with another molecule.

ALPHAFETOPROTEIN. A class of proteins found normally in embryonic tissues which, although absent in the adult organism, may reappear to signal the onset of certain kinds of cancer.

AMINO ACIDS. The chief chemical components, or "building blocks," of proteins.

ANGIOSARCOMA. A malignant tumor originating in a blood vessel.

ANTIBIOTIC. An antibacterial or antifungal substance produced by a living organism, such as fungus, and used to treat infectious diseases.

ANTIBODY. Protein (immunoglobulin) formed by the body's immune system to react with foreign proteins or other large molecules.

ANTICARCINOGEN. An agent that counteracts the effects of a cancer-causing agent.

ANTIGEN. A substance foreign to an animal's system that stimulates the production of antibodies.

ANTIGEN/ANTIBODY COMPLEX. The association of molecules formed by the reaction of an antigen with an antibody.

ANTIGENICITY. Potency to act as an antigen.

ANTIMETABOLITE. A chemical close in structure to a normal metabolite. Antimetabolites substitute for a normal metabolite and thus block crucial metabolic steps. Sometimes more toxic to tumor cells than to normal cells (because of tumor cells' more rapid metabolism) and useful as antitumor agents.

ANTISERUM. A serum that contains antibody or antibodies.

AROMATIC AMINES. A class of chemical compounds, some of which have been shown to produce cancer.

ATTENUATED ("tamed"). A form of bacteria or viruses, grown in culture, that is no longer virulent (no longer causes serious disease) but still causes the body to make antibody effective against the virulent form.

AUTOGRAFT. Transplantation of tissue from one site to another within the same individual.

AUTOIMMUNE DISEASE. Disease in which an individual's immune system attacks his own tissue. Arthritis, other rheumatic diseases, and systemic lupus erythematosus (SLE) are probable examples of autoimmune disease.

BCG (Bacillus Calmette-Guérin). A bacillus related to the tubercle bacillus. A preparation from it serves for immunization against tuberculosis. It enhances the function of normal immune defense mechanisms, and has been used experimentally in the prevention and treatment of certain neoplasms.

BCNU. An antitumor drug belonging to the family of compounds known as nitrosoureas. It interferes with cell division.

BIOASSAY. Determination of the active power of a sample of a drug by comparing its effect on biological systems to the effect of a standard preparation.

BLEOMYCIN. An antibiotic derived from soil and commonly used in cancer chemotherapy.

BIOHAZARD. A biological agent or technique which is a potential or actual source of danger to a laboratory experiment, worker, or the outside environment.

BIOPSY. The removal and microscopic examination of tissue from the living body for purposes of diagnosis.

B-LYMPHOCYTES (B-cells). A type of lymphocyte originating in the bone marrow and found in many parts of the lymphoid tissue. They are the precursors of plasma cells, which form humoral antibodies.

B-TYPE PARTICLES. Extracellular viral particles or incomplete particles in the process of release from cells infected with mouse mammary tumor virus. Distinguished from C-type particles by their dense, eccentric core.

BLOOD COUNT. The number of red cells, white cells, and platelets in a sample of blood.

BRONCHOGENIC. Originating in a bronchus, one of the largest air passages within the lungs.

BURKITT'S LYMPHOMA. A cancer usually affecting the facial area. It is found most frequently in African children.

C-TYPE PARTICLES. The electron-dense particles that appear in the electron micrographs of the RNA-containing leukoviruses.

CANCER. Uncontrolled cell proliferation which, when untreated, is fatal. Usually associated with formation of secondary tumors tending to infiltrate the surrounding tissues and give rise to metastasis.

CAPILLARY. Minute blood vessel.

CARCINOGEN. A cancer-causing agent.

CARCINOGENESIS. A production of cancer.

CARCINOMA. A malignant tumor originating from epithelial tissues, such as skin, mucous membranes in glands, lungs, urinary bladder, nerves, etc. Eighty to ninety percent of all malignant tumors are carcinomas.

CCNU. An antitumor drug related to BCNU (see BCNU).

CEA. Carcinoembryonic antigen, a protein material isolated originally from colon cancer cells. It may be present in other forms of cancer as well. Appears useful for diagnosis and assessment of treatment.

CELL CYCLE. See MITOTIC CYCLE.

CELL DIFFERENTIATION. The process of acquiring completely specialized characters, such as occurs in the progressive diversification of cells and tissues of the embryo.

CELL LINE. The progeny of a piece of tissue explanted and grown in tissue culture.

CELL-MEDIATED IMMUNITY. The type of immunity that protects the host from fungus infections, tuberculosis, and tumors, and that comes from cells rather than soluble antibodies. (Also see HUMORAL IMMUNITY.)

CHEMOTHERAPY. Treatment by chemicals; drug treatment.

CHORIOCARCINOMA. A cancer occurring in a part of the placenta.

CHROMATOGRAPHY. A method of separation of chemical substances from each other, based on the different speed with which they move through a porous solid support in a stream of liquid or gas.

CLINICAL TRIAL. The systematic investigation of materials or methods, according to a formal study plan, as a means of determining effect or relative effectiveness, generally in a human population with a particular disease or class of diseases. In cancer research, a clinical trial generally refers to the use of therapeutic materials or techniques, although methods for prevention, detection, or diagnosis may be the subject of such studies.

CLONE. The progeny of a single cell or organism by asexual reproduction.

COBALT-60. A radioactive isotope of the element cobalt; an important source of gamma radiation used widely in radiation therapy for cancer patients.

CO-CARCINOGEN. An environmental agent that acts with another chemical or a physical or biological factor to cause cancer.

COLON. The middle and longest section of the large intestine, joining the rectum and the cecum; also used to refer to the entire large intestine.

COLONOSCOPE. An appliance for examining the lower part of the large intestine.

COLOSTOMY. The surgical creation of a new opening from the colon to the surface of the body for exit of body wastes normally passed through the anus.

COMBINATION THERAPY. Different treatments such as chemotherapy, surgery, etc., applied in some combination.

COMPLEMENT. A group of proteins occurring in blood which attach to antigen-antibody complexes. If the antigen is part of a cell, the reaction with antibody and complement may destroy the cell. An important part of the immune defense system.

COOPERATIVE PROGRAMS. Collaborative arrangements among investigators from several institutions for the purpose of answering specific research questions or accomplishing particular research goals. Such programs are generally conducted according to specific research plans which permit precise statistical evaluation of results. (See CLINICAL TRIALS.)

CORDOTOMY. Division of the spinal cord for the relief of pain; also removal of a vocal cord.

COMPUTERIZED TOMOGRAPHY SCAN (also CT Scan or computed tomography, formerly computerized axial tomography, or CAT, scan). A scanning procedure combining X rays and computer processing to detect abnormalities of body organs. An X-ray beam is rotated around the part of the body, resulting in a series of X-ray pictures. The information in these pictures is put together by a computer to produce a complete picture of a thin slice of the organ.

CONIZATION. Surgical removal of a cone-shaped piece of the uterine cervix for microscopic examination, useful in determining whether cancer has invaded other parts of the cervix.

CROSS-REACTION. Reaction of an antibody with an antigen other than the antigen originally used to stimulate the production of the antibody. Usually indicates chemical relatedness between the two antigens.

CT SCAN. See COMPUTERIZED TOMOGRAPHY SCAN.

CURE. Generally refers to elimination of all evidence of cancer for a period of at least five years, although this definition is sometimes expanded to include restoration of life expectancy to equal that of comparable persons without cancer.

CYCLIC ADENOSINE MONOPHOSPHATE. A biochemical compound used by the cell to process information across the cellular membrane from external stimuli such as hormones.

CYCLOTRON. An accelerator in which atomic particles are propelled by an alternating electric field in a constant magnetic field.

CYTOLOGY. Scientific study of cells, their origin, structure, and functions.

CYTOPLASM. The liquid (nonparticulate) material in the cell.

CYTOTOXICITY. Toxic to cells. Often used to indicate unwanted side effects on healthy cells of drugs used in the treatment of cancer or other diseases.

DENSITY GRADIENT SEPARATION. A laboratory technique for separating different cells, cell components, or large molecules according to the speed with which they move through solutions of salts, sugars, etc.

DEOXYRIBONUCLEIC ACID. See DNA.

DES (diethylstilbestrol). A synthetic female sex hormone, which when administered to pregnant females may cause cancer in their offspring.

DIAGNOSIS. The art of distinguishing one disease from another; the determination of the nature of a cause of disease.

DIETHYLSTILBESTROL. See DES.

DIGESTIVE TRACT. System responsible for the body's breakdown and use of food; it is composed of the mouth, pharynx, esophagus, stomach, small intestine, large intestine (including the colon and rectum), and accessory glands.

DIPLOID. Relating to the number of chromosome pairs in the somatic cells. The diploid number of chromosomes is characteristic of each species; it is twice the haploid number. In humans the haploid number is 23 and the diploid number 46, or 2×23.

DNA (deoxyribonucleic acid). One of the two nucleic acids found in all cells. The other is RNA (ribonucleic acid). These exert primary control over life processes in all organisms.

ELECTRON. Negatively charged subatomic particle.

ELECTRON MICROSCOPE. An optical instrument using a beam of electrons to produce an enlarged image of an object (up to 300,000 magnifications) on a fluorescent screen or photographic plate.

ELECTROPHORESIS. The separation of substances according to the direction and speed of their movement in an electric field.

ENDONUCLEASES. Enzymes that split nucleic acids (DNA or RNA) anywhere along their chains.

ENDOPLASMIC RETICULUM. An intracellular membrane system to which ribosomes attach. The site of many metabolic reactions including protein synthesis.

ENDOSCOPE. An instrument for the examination of the interior of a hollow organ, such as the urinary bladder.

ENZYME. A catalytic protein intimately associated with all chemical processes occurring in the cell, such as muscle contraction, nerve conduction.

ESTROGEN/PROGESTERONE RECEPTOR ASSAY. Tests to determine whether the growth of a breast cancer depends on female sex hormones. Best done at the time of biopsy.

ETIOLOGIC AGENT. Causative factor.

EUPLOID. Having the "correct" number of chromosomes characteristic of the cells of a particular species—for example, 46 in the case of human cells.

EWING'S SARCOMA. A malignant tumor of the bone which always arises in medullary tissue (marrow), occurring more often in cylindrical bones, with pain, fever, and leukocytosis as prominent symptoms.

EXCISION. An act of cutting away or taking out.

EXFOLIATIVE CYTOLOGY. Microscopic examination of cells flaked off from interior body surfaces—for example, the Pap test.

EXONUCLEASES. Enzymes that break down nucleic acids (DNA or RNA), starting at the end of the chains.

EXPERIMENTAL MODELS. Generally, biological systems used to anticipate the results of experiments in humans. Often used in reference to animal species whose reactions to manipulations or materials such as drugs serve as a basis for predicting effects in humans.

FIBROBLASTS. Cells in connective tissue.

FLUORINE-18. A short-lived radioisotope of fluorine used as a tracer.

FROZEN SECTION. Technique in which a biopsy sample is frozen, using dry ice, and then thinly sliced for microscopic examination.

GAMMA RAYS. Electromagnetic radiation of extremely short wavelength, even shorter than X rays, and emitted by many radioisotopes—e.g., cobalt-60 and radium.

GENE. A unit of heredity: a segment of a cell's or virus DNA that specifies the synthesis of a specific protein. Synthesis of the final product is called expression; if the product is not made, the gene is called repressed.

GENETIC. Of or pertaining to the genes, the biologic units of heredity located in the small rod-shaped bodies in the nucleus of a cell.

GENETIC CODE. The code by which the sequence (spatial arrangement) of nucleotide bases in "messenger RNA" specifies the sequence of amino acids in a protein.

GENETIC DOGMA. The theory (by Crick and Watson) which postulates that genetic information is always transferred from DNA to RNA and from there to protein. The recent discovery of reverse transcriptase indicates that there are exceptions.

GENOME. The entire body of genetic information carried by a cell.

GERM CELLS. Sperm cells and ova.

GIANT CELL SARCOMA. A tumor of bone characterized by large numbers of giant multinucleated cells on a background matrix of smaller, single-nuclei cells.

GLIOMA. A tumor composed of tissues which represents the supporting structure of nervous-tissue glial cells in any one of its stages of development.

HAPLOID. Refers to the number of chromosomes in the germ cells (gametes) of a species. It is half the number of chromosomes in the body (somatic) cells, which is called the diploid number. The haploid and diploid numbers are characteristic of each species (in humans the haploid number is 23).

HeLa. An "established" cell line in tissue culture, originally derived over twenty years ago from a cervical carcinoma and since then grown for hundreds of cell generations in many laboratories. A favorite test system of many researchers.

HEPATOMA. A liver tumor.

HETEROGRAFT. A transplant of tissue from an individual of one species to an individual of another species.

HETEROPLOID. Having an "incorrect" number of chromosomes for the cells of its species. Frequent in cell lines that have been grown in tissue culture for a long time—e.g., HeLa cells.

HISTONES. A class of basic proteins occurring in the nucleus of nearly all higher organisms, associated with DNA.

HODGKIN'S DISEASE. A form of cancer affecting the lymphatic and other tissues that play a part in the individual's ability to fight infection.

HOMOGRAFT. Transplantation of tissue from a member of one species to another member of the same species not genetically identical.

HORIZONTAL TRANSMISSION (of tumors). Transmission from individual to individual. (See VERTICAL TRANSMISSION.)

HORMONE. A chemical product of the endocrine glands of the body which, when secreted into body fluids, has a specific effect on other organs.

HOST. An animal or plant that harbors or nourishes another organism (parasite).

HUMORAL IMMUNITY. Immunity carried by soluble, circulating antibodies (immunoglobulins) in serum and other body fluids. An important defense mechanism against certain microbes.

HYPOPHYSECTOMY. Surgical removal of the pituitary gland.

HYPOPHYSIS. Pituitary gland.

HYPOTHESIS. A supposition assumed as a basis of reasoning.

IMMUNE SURVEILLANCE. A mechanism for the elimination of spontaneously arising neoplasms resulting from the immune response to the new antigen(s) of the neoplasm.

IMMUNOASSAY. Test to determine whether certain body fluids such as blood and urine contain specific antibodies, antigens, and other biologic substances.

IMMUNOFLUORESCENCE. A technique for making stained cells fluoresce under a microscope to aid in seeing and/or counting them.

IMMUNOTHERAPY. Treating a patient by using his body's own capacity to respond immunologically.

INCIDENCE. The rate at which a certain event occurs, such as the number of new cases of a specific disease occurring during a certain period.

INTERFERON. A substance produced in cell culture or human tissue in response to viral infection.

ISLET. A cluster of cells or isolated tissue.

ISOGENIC. Relating to individuals or strains genetically alike with respect to specified genes (e.g., for transplantation antigens), such as identical twins or highly inbred animals.

ISOGRAFT. Transplantation from one member to another isogenic member of the same species, such as an identical twin.

ISOTOPE SCAN. Test in which a radioactive isotope is injected into a vein (or given by mouth in some circumstances) and then followed with a special camera.

KARYOTYPE. The chromosome characteristics of an individual or a cell line, usually presented in a systematized form. Important in the diagnosis of certain hereditary diseases.

LASER (from *l*ight *a*mplification by *s*timulated *e*mission of *r*adiation). A device that produces an extremely intense, small, and nearly nondivergent beam of radiation in the visible region with all the waves in phase. It is capable of mobilizing immense heat and power when focused at close range, and may be used as a tool in surgical proceedings.

LEUKEMIA. Cancer of the organs that form the blood, such as the lymph glands and bone marrow, causing an overproduction of white cells. Acute lymphocytic leukemia is the severe, rapidly advancing type of leukemia most common in childhood. Chronic lymphocytic is a type of leukemia, generally more indolent than acute leukemia, occurring primarily in adults.

LEUKOCYTES. White blood cells important for the body's defense against infection. Two main groups exist: polymorphonuclear and monomorphonuclear leukocytes; the latter are divided into many types, including monocytes, lymphocytes, plasma cells, macrophages, etc.

LIVER. The body's largest internal organ, lying near the stomach. Among other functions, it plays an important part in the body's conversion of foods to energy.

LYMPH. A nearly colorless liquid composed of excess tissue fluid and proteins and found in the lymphatic vessels of the body.

LYMPHATIC SYSTEM. Circulatory network of vessels carrying lymph, together with the lymph organs, such as lymph nodes, spleen, and thymus, that produce and store cells of importance in the body's defense mechanisms.

LYMPHOMA. Any neoplastic disorder of the lymphoid tissue.

LYMPHOCYTE. A white blood cell in the body that is responsible for protecting the individual from slow-growing pathogenic bacteria (such as tuberculosis), fungus (such as thrush), and tumors. See CELL-MEDIATED IMMUNITY.

LYMPHOSARCOMA. A malignant neoplastic disorder of lymph tissue.

LYSOSOMES. A class of subcellular particles containing enzymes that break down macromolecular compounds. Important in phagocytosis and in the breakdown and removal of the body's own dead cells.

MACROPHAGE. A type of white blood cell whose primary function is phagocytosis, which is followed by degradation of the ingested material.

MAMMOGRAPHY. X-ray examination of the breast used for detection and diagnosis of disease.

MARKER. A detectable chemical substance in the body signaling the presence of cancer or other biologic activity.

MASTECTOMY. Excision of the breast.

MELANOMA. A malignant tumor originating from cells containing dark pigment.

MESON (also mesion). A subatomic particle.

METABOLISM. The sum of all the physical and chemical processes by which living organized substance is produced and maintained, and also the transformation by which energy is made available for the uses of the organism.

METABOLIC PATHWAY. The sum of the reactions involved in the synthesis or degradation of a particular chemical compound. Any substance produced by metabolism or by a metabolic process.

METAPHASE. The stage in cell division during which the dividing chromosomes can be made visible.

METASTASIS (plural, metastases). The transfer of disease from one part of the body to another. In cancer, the new growths are characteristic of the original tumor.

METASTASIZE. Spread by metastasis.

MITOCHONDRION. A subcellular particle in which many of the energy-yielding metabolic processes of the cell occur. It is a relatively large, highly organized particle containing a large number of enzymes in an organized spatial arrangement.

MITOSIS. The process of cell reproduction.

MITOTIC CYCLE. The stages in which cells in culture (and presumably in growing time in the body) divide. A "resting" or "gap" phase (G_1) during which the cell carries out its own metabolic functions is followed by the "synthetic" (S) phase during which the DNA in the nucleus is duplicated. After a second "gap" phase (G_2) the "mitotic" (M) phase occurs, during which the nucleus disappears and the "mitotic spindle" forms. The two new sets of chromosomes separate at opposite ends of the cell, two new nuclei form, and the cell finally divides into two daughter cells that repeat the cycle. Antitumor agents interfere mainly with events during the S and M phase, during which the processes necessary for cell division occur.

MITOTIC INDEX. The percentage of cells in any cell population actually undergoing mitosis at the time of observation; an indicator of the growth activity of a tissue.

MOLECULE. A very small mass of matter; an aggregation of atoms, specifically a combination of two or more atoms that form a specific chemical substance.

MOPP. A combination of four antitumor drugs used for the treatment of Hodgkin's disease.

MUCOPROTEIN. Any one of a series of proteins containing chemically bound sugar.

MULTIPLE MYELOMA. A malignant tumor arising in the bone marrow and leading to a proliferation of plasma cells making proteins closely related to immunoglobulins (Bence-Jones proteins).

MUTAGEN. A chemical that causes mutations in a cell population. Most mutagens are also carcinogens, and vice versa.

MUTATION. A change in the genome that is apparent either as a physical change in chromosome structure or as a change of gene expression. A mutation can occur either in somatic cells (somatic mutation) or in germ cells, but only a change in germ cells will be transmitted to the offspring of sexual reproduction.

MYCOSES. Diseases caused by fungi.

MYELOMA. A malignant tumor of the bone marrow.

NEURAMINIDASE. An enzyme that affects the outer membranes of cells.

NEUROBLASTOMA. A malignant tumor of the nervous system, composed of immature nerve cells.

NEUTRON. A subatomic particle.

N-NITROSO COMPOUNDS. A class of compounds that include nitrosoureas and nitrosamines. They may have both antitumor and cancer-producing properties.

NITROSOUREA. A subclass of urea compounds shown to have both antitumor and cancer-producing properties.

NODE. A swelling or protuberance.

NODULE. A small node that is solid and can be detected by touch.

NUCLEIC ACID. See RNA and DNA.

NUCLEOLUS. A dense body inside the cell nucleus that is apparently responsible for the synthesis of ribosomal RNA. Different strains of a species may have different numbers of nucleoli in their cells, and the number of nucleoli may thus serve as a genetic marker.

NUCLEOSIDE. A compound of a pyrimidine or purine base with a sugar, usually ribose or deoxyribose. The sugar in the nucleoside is ribose in the case of RNA and deoxyribose in the case of DNA.

NUCLEOTIDE. A compound of a nucleoside with one, two, or three molecules of phosphoric acid. The compounds with one phosphatic acid group (monophosphates) are the building blocks of the nucleic acids.

NUCLEUS. One major component of the cell. A rounded body containing the gene-bearing chromosomes. Some cells, most notably red blood cells, do not contain a nucleus.

NUTRIENT. A substance that provides nourishment.

OCCULT BLOOD TEST. Examination of a small sample of stool to see whether it contains otherwise unapparent traces of blood. Used in screening for cancers of the colon and rectum.

ONCOLOGY. The study of tumors.

ONCOGENIC. Tumor-causing.

OVARY. Reproductive organ in which the ova, or eggs, are formed.

OSTEOGENIC SARCOMA. A highly malignant tumor of bone that usually affects individuals in their twenties or thirties.

PALLIATIVE. Affording relief of some symptoms, but not cure; an alleviating treatment.

PALPATION. Technique in which a doctor uses his or her fingers and hands to examine the body surface and underlying organs.

PANCREAS. A large, elongated gland behind the stomach. The secretion or juice of the pancreas is involved in digestion, and contains a variety of digestive enzymes. The islets of Langerhans in the pancreas are the site of insulin production.

PAP TEST. An exfoliative cytology technique, developed chiefly by the late Dr. George N. Papanicolaou, that involves the microscopic examination of cells shed from organs such as the cervix or bronchi to detect cancer and precancerous conditions.

PATHOGENIC. Capable of causing disease.

PHAGOCYTOSIS. Ingestion of solid particles by cells, an important defense mechanism often carried out by macrophages.

PHARYNX. Tubular passage that is part of the respiratory and digestive system; it connects with the nose, mouth, larynx, and esophagus.

PI-MESON. A subatomic particle. Of possible use in therapy of some tumors.

PINOCYTOSIS. The absorption of liquid by cells.

PLASMA (in biology). Fluid part of blood after removal of the cells but still containing the clottable protein (fibrinogen).

PLASMA CELL. A type of leukocyte that synthesizes circulating antibodies (immunoglobulins).

PLASMA MEMBRANE. The outer membrane around a cell.

PLATELETS. Small, disk-shaped particles in the blood which play a role in coagulation.

PLEURAL EFFUSION. The presence of fluid in the space formed by the membrane covering the lung and lining the chest cavity.

POLYMERASE. An enzyme involved in the synthesis of large molecules within the cell for the transfer of genetic information.

POLYNUCLEAR HYDROCARBONS. A class of complex molecules that may be cancer-causing.

PRECANCEROUS LESIONS OR CHANGES. Changes in tissue not yet malignant but definitely abnormal and potentially capable of further, possibly malignant transformation.

PROGNOSIS. A forecast as to the probable course and outcome of disease; the prospect as to recovery from a disease as indicated by the nature and symptoms of the case.

PROSTATE. Gland in the male reproductive system that lies just below the bladder and surrounds part of the canal that empties the bladder.

PROSTHESIS. Replacement for any part of the body, such as an artificial limb.

PROTEIN. Any one of a group of complex organic compounds, widely distributed in plants and animals and forming the principal constituents of the cell protoplasm; essentially a combination of amino acids strung together like beads on a chain.

PURINE BASES. A class of organic compounds forming, with sugars (ribose or deoxyribose) and phosphoric acid, the building blocks of nucleic acids. Most important are adenine and guanine. See NUCLEOTIDE and NUCLEOSIDE.

PYRIMIDINE BASES. A class of organic compounds forming, with sugars (ribose or deoxyribose) and phosphoric acid, the building blocks of nucleic acids. Most important are cytosine (RNA and DNA) and uridine (occurring in RNA) and thymine (in DNA).

P-450 ENZYMES. A class of enzymes involved in the detoxification, by oxidation, of aromatic hydrocarbons and other toxic compounds. Paradoxically, some of the compounds formed by this oxidation are more highly carcinogenic, though less acutely toxic, than the original compounds.

RADIATION THERAPY (also radiotherapy). The treatment of disease by X rays or other radiant energy.

RADIOIMMUNOASSAY. A highly sensitive method for the quantitative estimation of certain biological substances, combining antigen-antibody formation and radioactive techniques.

RADIOISOTOPES. Isotopes whose atoms are unstable and emit radiation while disintegrating. (Isotopes are forms of a single element with slightly different atomic weights.)

RADIUM. An intensely radioactive metallic element found in minute quantities in pitchblende and other uranium minerals. The radioactivity of radium is a result of disintegration of the atom.

RATE. A fixed ratio between two conditions. For example, in terms of any given disease, the mortality rate is the ratio between persons who die and those who survive.

REGISTRY. Organized collections of clinical, laboratory, X-ray, and other kinds of medical data and information.

REMISSION. The decrease or disappearance of evidence of a disease; also the period during which this occurs.

RETICULOENDOTHELIAL SYSTEM (RES). A network of macrophages and other white cells in the spleen, blood, liver, lymph nodes, bone marrow, and connective tissue. Involved in the phagocytosis of tissue debris and bacteria and the metabolism of iron and blood pigments such as hemoglobin.

RETICULUM. A network, especially a protoplasmic network, in cells.

RETINOBLASTOMA. A cancer of the eye.

REVERSE TRANSCRIPTASE. An enzyme responsible for the synthesis of hereditary material from a specific class of molecular intermediaries.

RHABDOMYOSARCOMA. A rare malignant cancer of skeletal muscle.

RIBONUCLEIC ACID. See RNA.

RIBOSOMES. Granules containing RNA found in the cytoplasm of a cell. Visible only in the electron microscope. They are the site of protein synthesis by the cell.

RNA (ribonucleic acid). One of the two nucleic acids found in all cells. The other is DNA (deoxyribonucleic acid). These exert primary control over life processes in all organisms.

RUBELLA. German measles, epidemic roseola.

S. or SVEDBERG UNIT. A unit for measuring the sedimentation constant, the velocity with which a molecule or particle moves in a gravitational field in the ultracentrifuge. Allows conclusions as to the size and/or shape of the particle.

SARCOMA. A tumor made up of substance like the embryonic connective tissue; tissue composed of closely packed cells embedded in a fibrillar or homogeneous substance. Sarcomas are often highly malignant.

SERUM. The clear portion of any body fluid separated from its more solid elements. Usually refers to the liquid remaining after both the cells and the fibrinogen (clottable protein) have been removed from blood.

SOMATIC CELL. Any cell other than a germ (egg or sperm) cell.

SPECIFICITY. In immunology, pertaining to the special affinity of antigen for the corresponding antibody.

STOMA. An opening established in the abdominal wall for the elimination of bodily wastes, especially in cancer surgery.

STREPTOZOTOCIN. An antibiotic used as an antitumor drug.

THALIDOMIDE. A chemical used commonly in Europe as a sedative and hypnotic in the early 1960s. Discovered to be the cause of serious congenital anomalies in the fetus, notably dysmelia (malformation of limbs) when taken by a woman during early pregnancy.

THERMOGRAPHY. Technique for determining heat patterns of body tissue. Sometimes used to detect "hot spots" produced by cancer, inflammatory diseases, and other disorders.

TISSUE CULTURE. The laboratory cultivation of tissue cells within a flask or other vessel.

TOMOGRAPHY (also laminagraphy or body section roentgenography). Diagnostic procedure using X-ray source and detector to produce a series of pictures of thin cross sections or "slices" of the body. New type uses a computerized image. (See COMPUTERIZED TOMOGRAPHY SCAN.)

TRANSCRIPTION. The transfer of genetic information from DNA to RNA.

TRANSFER FACTOR. A substance extracted from the white cells of an immune individual that can be used to transfer cell-mediated immunity to a nonimmune person.

TRANSFORMATION. Change in the appearance and growth behavior of cells, often involving (in tissue culture) loss of contact inhibition.

ULTRACENTRIFUGE. A laboratory instrument in which samples, through rapid rotation of a container (rotor), can be subjected to gravitational forces several hundred thousand times higher than the earth's gravitation. Used for separation of large molecules or other small particles according to size and/or shape.

ULTRASOUND. Mechanical radiant energy with a frequency greater than 20,000 cycles per second.

ULTRAVIOLET. Referring to invisible rays or radiations beyond the violet end of the electromagnetic spectrum.

UTERINE CERVIX. Neck, or lower part, of the uterus.

UTERINE CORPUS. Body of the uterus.

VACCINE. A suspension of attenuated or killed microorganisms administered for the prevention, amelioration, or treatment of infectious diseases.

VERTICAL TRANSMISSION. Transmission from generation to generation, from parent to offspring.

VIRUS. A member of a group of submicroscopic agents infecting plants and animals that is unable to multiply outside the host tissues.

WILMS' TUMOR. A rare cancer of the kidney usually occurring early in childhood.

X RAYS. Electromagnetic radiations of a wavelength shorter than that of ultraviolet light.

XERORADIOGRAPHY (also xcromammography). Alternative to film mammography in which breast X rays are produced on a special photographic paper instead of film. The images can be viewed without an illuminated box or special lighting.

Index

Italicized page numbers refer to figures and tables.